Varieties of Present-Day English

VARIETIES
OF
PRESENT-DAY
ENGLISH

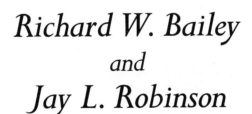

Richard W. Bailey
and
Jay L. Robinson

The University of Michigan

THE MACMILLAN COMPANY, NEW YORK
COLLIER-MACMILLAN PUBLISHERS, LONDON

ACKNOWLEDGMENTS

Charles-James N. Bailey. For "The Patterning of Language Variation." Copyright © 1972 by Charles-James N. Bailey.

Barnes & Noble Inc., American distributors. For "The Language of the Master?" from *The West Indian Novel and Its Background* (Faber and Faber Ltd., publishers) by Kenneth Ramchand. Copyright © 1970 by Kenneth Ramchand.

Cambridge University Press. For "Some Historical Cases of Language Imposition" by L. F. Brosnahan from *Language in Africa*, ed. John Spencer. Copyright © 1963 by the Cambridge University Press.

Cornell University Press. For selections from Robert A. Hall, Jr., *Pidgin and Creole Languages*. Copyright © 1966 by Cornell University. Used by permission of the author and Cornell University Press.

J. L. Dillard. For "Standard Average Foreign in Puerto Rico," an earlier version of which appeared in *Studies in Language, Literature, and Culture of the Middle Ages and Later*, eds. E. Bagby Atwood and Archibald A. Hill (Austin: English and Linguistics Department, The University of Texas, 1969).

Dodd, Mead & Company, Inc. For "Little Brown Baby" from *The Complete Poems of Paul Lawrence Dunbar*. Copyright © 1922 by Dodd, Mead & Company.

East Africa Publishing House. For "Language and National Identification" by Milton Obote from *East Africa Journal* (April 1967).

Faber & Faber Ltd., publishers. For "The Language of the Master?" from *The West Indian Novel and Its Background*, by Kenneth Ramchand. Distributed in America by Barnes & Noble, Inc. Copyright © 1970 by Kenneth Ramchand.

W. H. Freeman and Company. For "Pidgin Languages" by Robert A. Hall, Jr. Copyright © 1959 by Scientific American, Inc. All rights reserved.

Georgetown University, School of Languages and Linguistics. For "The Logic of Nonstandard English" by William Labov from *Report of the Twentieth Annual Round Table Meeting on Linguistics and Language Studies*, ed. James E. Alatis. Copyright © 1970 by Georgetown University Press.

Gloria Glissmeyer. For "Some Characteristics of English in Hawaii."

Indiana University Press. For "The Users and Uses of Language" from *The Linguistic*

iv

Sciences and Language Teaching by M. A. K. Halliday, Angus McIntosh, and Peter Strevens. Copyright © 1964 by M. A. K. Halliday, Angus McIntosh, and Peter Strevens.

Jacaranda Press Pty. Ltd. For "We Are Going" from *My People* by Kath Walker. Copyright 1970 by the Jacaranda Press.

William Labov. For "General Attitudes Towards the Speech of New York City" from *The Social Stratification of English in New York City*. Copyright © 1966 by William Labov.

Longman. For "The Users and Uses of Language" from *The Linguistic Sciences and Language Teaching* by M. A. K. Halliday, Angus McIntosh, and Peter Strevens. Copyright © 1964 by M. A. K. Halliday, Angus McIntosh, and Peter Strevens.

Raven I. McDavid, Jr. For "Go Slow in Ethnic Attributions: Geographic Mobility and Dialect Prejudices."

Ali A. Mazrui. For "The English Language and the Origins of African Nationalism" from *Mawazo* (1967). Copyright © 1967 by Ali A. Mazrui.

National Council of Teachers of English. For portions of "Some Sources of Reading Problems for Negro Speakers of Nonstandard English" by William Labov from *New Directions in Elementary English*. Copyright © 1967 by the National Council of Teachers of English. Reprinted by permission of the publisher and William Labov. For "Doublespeak: Dialectology in the Service of Big Brother," *College English* 33(1972):439–56. Copyright © 1972 by the National Council of Teachers of English. Reprinted by permission of the publisher and James Sledd.

Oxford University Press (Nigeria). For the selection from *Aikin Mata: The Lysistrata of Aristophanes*, translated by T. W. Harrison and James Simmons. Copyright © 1966 by Oxford University Press.

Samuel Selvon. For "When Greek Meets Greek" by Samuel Selvon. Copyright © 1964 by Samuel Selvon.

Roger W. Shuy. For "Language and Success: Who Are the Judges?"

Southern Illinois University Press. For the map from *Vocabulary Change: A Study of Variations in Regional Words in Eight of the Southern States* by Gordon R. Wood. Copyright © 1971 by the Southern Illinois University Press.

The University of Alabama Press. For "Social Aspects of Bilingualism in San Antonio, Texas" from *Publications of the American Dialect Society* 41(1964):7–15. Copyright © 1964 by the American Dialect Society.

The University of California Press. For the map from *A Word Geography of California and Nevada* by Elizabeth S. Bright. Copyright © 1971 by The Regents of the University of California. Reprinted by permission of The Regents of the University of California.

The University of Michigan Press. For the selection from Aristophanes' *Lysistrata*, translated by Douglass Parker. Copyright © 1963 by William Arrowsmith.

The University of North Carolina Press. For "White and Negro Listeners' Reactions to Various American-English Dialects" by G. Richard Tucker and Wallace E. Lambert from *Social Forces* 47(1969):463–68. Copyright © 1969 by the University of North Carolina Press.

The University Press of Hawaii. For the student essay quoted in *Language and Dialect in Hawaii: A Sociolinguistic Essay to 1935* by John E. Reinecke and edited by Stanley M. Tsuzaki. Copyright © 1969 by the University Press of Hawaii.

For Margaret and Machree

Preface

Variety in English is the subject of the readings contained in this book; among questions addressed in separate essays are these: What has caused this variety? Why does variety persist in spite of standardizing forces in society? How widely do national, local, and social varieties of English differ from one another? How should variety be confronted by the teacher of language use who must formulate teaching strategies and make daily decisions on how to implement them?

For answers to such questions, we have turned mainly to the work of sociolinguists—scholars who have turned from too narrow a concern with abstract theorizing about language structure to a close examination of real talk by real talkers, to an attempt to show how language structure is related to the purposes for which talk is used, to the social settings in which talk occurs, to the dynamics of people using language to interact with other people. It is no accident that linguists have begun to concern themselves with language as a pattern of human activity closely related to other patterns of activity. Other scientists, natural, physical, and social—all impelled in part by challenges to human survival in a threatened world—have become impatient with the consideration of things in isolation, preferring instead ecological studies, those that view phenomena as interrelated, mutually dependent systems of cause and effect. And if need has called forth ecological studies by natural scientists hurrying to cleanse man's air and water before he poisons himself, or to find new sources of food before he starves, so a similar necessity and urgency impel the work of sociolinguists, the ecologists of language. Language is a powerful mechanism to bind and to divide. In a world made small, Babel is as frightening an image as Plague and Famine; in a nation torn by class and racial division, by serious conflicts over national values and aims, linguistic differences may be symptoms and causes of fatal disease. Talk may be cheap, as the old adage says: but to misunderstand how it is used, how it varies in the mouths of human beings, and what that variety signifies about attitudes and loyalties may be very costly indeed.

Although this book is intended for use mainly by American readers and has greatest pertinence for those who teach or plan to teach, it is not restricted to a consideration of dialectal diversity in the United States. The book begins with English in the world, because English is not just a national language. Whether they like it or not, educated Americans are world citizens, and if they are responsible for teaching other Americans they must be able to draw parallels between the motives and mechanisms that spread English as an imposed language over much of the globe and the motives and mechanisms leading to the dominance of standard American English over other domestic dialects. Furthermore, when considering dialectal variety in the United States and its possible effects on education and communication, it is instructive to measure the extent of difference to be found against the many forms assumed by English in other national settings.

When the focus of the collection shifts in the middle group of essays to English in the United States, it centers on social dialects—those varieties that reveal a speaker's educational attainment, financial standing, racial or ethnic background: measures by which Americans determine status. This emphasis is in no way intended to demean the valuable and interesting work of an earlier generation of scholars whose interests were in the geographical distributions of dialect differences and their historical origins. Rather, the emphasis derives from an agreement with the many critics and commentators who have announced a crisis in American classrooms—one precipitated by our inability as teachers and as citizens to understand or to deal effectively with individual, social, and racial difference. This crisis demands teachers educated to adopt a point of view different from the ethnocentrism of the past: teachers more aware of how people can and do differ from one another, more objective about cultural diversity and less quick to form judgments about cultures different from their own, more sympathetic to the inevitable multiplicity in human perception as it is shaped by experience and more ready to listen to variety in the language people use to express their perceptions. How a man speaks tells us who he is and what and who he means to be; how we hear him and the consequent judgments we make tell us much about ourselves. Both speaker and hearer may be plagued by stereotypes created out of attitudes rarely examined, attitudes that are strangely persistent in social relations and often savagely pernicious in effects. Several essays in this collection deal with such language attitudes, some with their effects. And, because English teachers must lead the way if beneficial changes in language attitudes are to come about in American classrooms, the final essays address the teacher directly.

Among the essays collected below, several were written especially for this collection or revised for inclusion in it: "Standard Average Foreign in Puerto Rico" by J. L. Dillard; "The Patterning of Language Variation" by Charles-James N. Bailey; "Some Characteristics of English in Hawaii" by Gloria Glissmeyer; "Go Slow in Ethnic Attributions: Geographic Mobility and Dialect Prejudices" by Raven I. McDavid, Jr.; "Write Off vs. Write On: Dialects and the Teaching of Composition" by Richard W. Bailey; "The Wall of Babel; or, Up Against the Language Barrier" by Jay L. Robinson.

To make the collection more useful, we have provided a variety of editorial additions. Introductions to each section and prefaces to each essay direct the reader's attention to specific factors and draw connections between the readings. Study questions further underline important points and raise issues, sometimes asking the student to make further connections or applications of the ideas contained in a selection. Some readers may find it helpful to scan the study questions before reading the essay they follow. A bibliographical supplement of related readings is included for the diligent, some explanatory notes for the puzzled. Finally, in our desire to emphasize real talk by real talkers, we have illustrated many of the essays *about* with examples *of*—of particular dialects talked about, of attitudes discussed, of positions deplored or praised. The book will have served its function if it dispels for its readers a notion encouraged by the existence of the printed word: that there is one invariable and semidivine form of the human word rarely attainable by mere human beings.

We owe thanks to the authors of the essays we include—particularly to those who wrote and rewrote at our behest; to our publishers for patience and help in many things; to Jane Fingland and Susan Goldwater whose dialects reminded us of the diversity of English as they gave unselfishly of their time; and particularly to the Directors of the Institute for Advanced Studies in the Humanities, The University of Edinburgh, who gave us a pleasant place to think about the questions discussed in this collection.

R. W. B.
J. L. R.

Contents

I. ENGLISH IN THE MODERN WORLD

Introduction   1

The Users and Uses of Language   9
  M. A. K. HALLIDAY, ANGUS MCINTOSH, and PETER STREVENS
  Study Questions   37
    Selections from G. Knowles-Williams, "English in South
    Africa, 1960"; The Editor, *The Crisis*; Carl Bereiter,
    Siegfried Engelmann, *et al.*, "An Academically Oriented
    Pre-School for Culturally Deprived Children."

Some Historical Cases of Language Imposition   40
  L. F. BROSNAHAN
  Study Questions   54

The English Language and the Origins of African Nationalism   56
  ALI A. MAZRUI
  Study Questions   70
    Selections from Malcolm Guthrie, "Multilingualism and
    Cultural Factors"; Wallace E. Lambert, "A Social Psychol-
    ogy of Bilingualism"; R. F. Amonoo, "Problems of
    Ghanaian *Lingue Franche*"; R. K. Bansal, *The Intelligibility
    of Indian English*; Ayọ Bamgboṣe, "The English Language
    in Nigeria"; Milton Obote, "Language and National
    Identification."

Standard Average Foreign in Puerto Rico   77
  J. L. DILLARD
  Study Questions   88
    Sample texts from William Labov, "The Notion of 'System'
    in Creole Studies"; Joshua A. Fishman, *Bilingualism
    in the Barrio*.

Pidgin Languages   91
Sample Texts: English-Based Pidgins and Creoles   104
  ROBERT A. HALL, Jr.

Study Questions 109

Sample texts from Ogali A. Ogali, *Veronica, My Daughter*; *Aikin Mata: The Lysistrata of Aristophanes* (tr. T. W. Harrison and James Simmons); *Lysistrata* (tr. Douglass Parker); *The Lysistrata of Aristophanes* (tr. Benjamin Bickley Rogers).

The Language of the Master? 115
KENNETH RAMCHAND
Study Questions 146

Selection from Gerald Moore, *The Chosen Tongue*. Sample text: Samuel Selvon, "When Greek Meets Greek."

II. ENGLISH IN AMERICA

Introduction 151

*The Patterning of Language Variation 156
CHARLES-JAMES N. BAILEY
Study Questions 187

Examples from Oliver Farrar Emerson, *The Ithaca Dialect*; Arthur J. Bronstein, *The Pronunciation of American English*; Walter A. Wolfram, *A Sociolinguistic Description of Detroit Negro Speech*.

*Some Characteristics of English in Hawaii 190
GLORIA GLISSMEYER
Study Questions 222

Selection from C. F. and F. M. Voegelin, "Hawaiian Pidgin and Mother Tongue." Sample texts from John E. Reinecke, *Language and Dialect in Hawaii*; unpublished deposition of Philip Kemp.

Social Aspects of Bilingualism in San Antonio, Texas 226
JANET B. SAWYER
Study Questions 233

Selections from *Hearings Before the Special Subcommittee on Bilingual Education, United States Senate*; Wallace E. Lambert, "A Social Psychology of Bilingualism"; Rafael Jesús González, "*Pachuco:* The Birth of a Creole Language."

Some Features of the English of Black Americans 236
WILLIAM LABOV
Study Questions 255

Selections from Roger D. Abrahams, "Black Talk and Black Education"; Stephen S. Baratz and Joan C. Baratz,

* Essays marked with an asterisk are published here for the first time.

"Negro Ghetto Children and Urban Education." Sample text from *The Complete Poems of Paul Laurence Dunbar*.

*Go Slow in Ethnic Attributions: Geographic Mobility and Dialect Prejudices   258
RAVEN I. McDAVID, Jr.
   Study Questions   270
     Sample texts from Stephen Lesher, "Who Knows What Frustrations Lurk in the Hearts of X Million Americans? George Wallace Knows"; Todd Gitlin and Nanci Hollander, *Uptown: Poor Whites in Chicago*; Arne Zettersten, *The English of Tristan da Cunha*.

General Attitudes Towards the Speech of New York City   274
WILLIAM LABOV
   Study Questions   292
     Selection from Charles C. Fries, *American English Grammar*.

White and Negro Listeners' Reactions to Various American-English Dialects   293
G. RICHARD TUCKER and WALLACE E. LAMBERT
   Study Questions   301
     Selection from Thomas D. Horn, ed., *Reading for the Disadvantaged*.

*Language and Success: Who Are the Judges?   303
ROGER W. SHUY
   Study Questions   316
     Selections from "Student Protests State Test," *Detroit Free Press*; Alfred S. Hayes and Orlando L. Taylor, "A Summary of the Center's 'BALA' Project"; Douglas Barnes, "Language in the Secondary Classroom."

The Logic of Nonstandard English   319
WILLIAM LABOV
   Study Questions   354

III. ENGLISH IN THE CLASSROOM

Introduction   357
Doublespeak: Dialectology in the Service of Big Brother   360
JAMES SLEDD
   Study Questions   381
     Selection from Melvin J. Hoffman, "Bidialectalism Is Not the Linguistics of White Supremacy."

*Write Off vs. Write On: Dialects and the Teaching of Composition   384

RICHARD W. BAILEY
Study Questions   409
   Sample texts from Pauline Kael, "Trash, Art, and the
   Movies"; Harold Rosenberg, *The Tradition of the New*;
   student essays: "Childhood Memories" and "Altruism."

*The Wall of Babel; or, Up Against the Language Barrier   413
JAY L. ROBINSON
Study Questions   448
   Student essay, "What Is Soul?"

Suggested Readings   451

Index   459

Part I

English in the Modern World

"I have been given this language and I intend to use it."

CHINUA ACHEBE

Fixed in print, and used as it is in the United States as the massively dominant and seemingly sole language, English appears uniform, invariable, and unchanging. This impression is strengthened by the use of one register for official purposes, by the canonizing of one dialect—standard English—in dictionaries and grammars, and by generations of pedagogical practice based on the teaching of that one dialect. The forces of standardization in a modern technological state are as powerful as they are various. But "language is not realized in the abstract," note the authors of the first essay in this collection; "it is realized as an activity of people." And because the forces of standardization have not yet completely leveled the individuality resulting from genetic make-up and rearing, removed the human impulse to gather in manageably small groups, or erased the cultural differences that distinguish group from group or nation from nation, language must be as various as the groups who use it and the activities they engage in. English is a world language; and as such it has national varieties. It is the language of large nations with long histories; and as such each of its varieties subsumes dialects. The purposes of this anthology are to exhibit some of the dimensions and details of variety in present-day English and to treat some of the causes and implications of that variety.

No one needs to be reminded that England early planted colonies that were

1

to grow into great modern nations: the United States, Canada, Australia, and New Zealand. In these colonies, settlers dominated the indigenous populations— whose languages either disappeared or were restricted with their users to reservations or wildernesses unattractive to the grasping white men—leaving English the dominant tongue. The pattern of language imposition differed somewhat in the British West Indies, India, Southeast Asia, and Africa. White intrusion in these areas was essentially military and exploitative (although colonies were established, for example in South Africa); and British administrations "presided over communities which throughout remained overwhelmingly non-English in ethnic stock, social habits and language." [a] *In the British West Indies, English eventually established itself as the sole language—although it is spoken in many dialects as well as in creolized form; and West Indians are numbered among the more than 300 million world citizens who use English as their native tongue.*

In India, Malaysia, Pakistan, Ceylon, and in East, Central, West and South Africa, English is considerably more than a borrowed and alien language. In West Africa, for example,

> Newspapers are produced in English, journals in English grow in number year by year, parliamentary debates are for the most part held in English. West Africans are contributing, often through the medium of an impeccable English, to scientific thought and historical investigation; and the new poetry, drama, and fiction in English which is now emerging from West Africa is catching the imagination and commanding the admiration of the English-reading world.[b]

In the independent West African nations of Nigeria, Ghana, Liberia, Sierra Leone (other nations from East and Central Africa could also be listed), English is the official language of government and commerce; it is introduced in the first years of school and quickly becomes the medium of instruction. [c] *In South Asia, although all nations have "decided to administer their countries in their local languages, if not immediately, then in the long run,"* [d] *English persists, if not officially as in India, then by playing an important role in intra- and inter-national communication as well as in education. It is little wonder, then, that English ranks as one of the world's most popular second languages (estimates run between 25 and 50 million speakers) and threatens*

[a] Gerald Moore, *The Chosen Tongue: English Writing in the Tropical World* (London: Longmans, 1969), pp. x–xi.

[b] John Spencer, "West Africa and the English Language," in *The English Language in West Africa*, ed. John Spencer (London: Longmans, 1971), p. 2.

[c] See B. W. Tiffin, "Language and Education in Commonwealth Africa," in *Language in Education: The Problem in Commonwealth Africa and the Indo-Pakistan Sub-continent*, eds. Julian Dakin, B. W. Tiffin, and H. G. Widdowson (London: Oxford University Press, 1968), pp. 63–113.

[d] S. J. Tambiah, "The Politics of Language in India and Ceylon," *Modern Asian Studies* 1:3(1967):224.

to become a genuine international medium—an intellectual and diplomatic lingua franca.

The forces that sustain the use of English, however, rarely resemble altruistic internationalism. Although attitudes are important in the choice of a second language to be learned, more so are practical necessities. The newly formed nations of Asia and Africa are multi-ethnic and multilingual almost beyond the powers of a Westerner to imagine. Had all immigrant groups in America retained their native tongues, the United States could still not match the linguistic complexity of India or of Africa. The Linguistic Survey of India records 179 languages and 544 dialects in use in that nation; Indians perceive themselves as using far more, for in the Census of 1961, in which every individual was asked to supply the name of his mother tongue, 1,652 different names were returned. If anything, the linguistic situation in Africa is even more complex—more than 400 languages in Nigeria alone, for example—and the total number for the continent remains to be counted (estimates run near 1,000). Such a degree of multilingualism, particularly when the number of speakers for each language is small, makes pan-African communication in an indigenous language impossible. Although in India there is a language spoken by many millions which has served as a vehicle of communication for one of the world's great cultures, educated Indians from the North must often communicate with their countrymen from the South in English, their only common language. Such facts explain why, as at the Bandung Conference of 1955—gathering representatives of twenty-nine African and Asian nations—English was the common language of the delegates. Practical value accrues as well to developing nations who use English to retain contact with the Western world. That language makes available technical and scientific knowledge vital to economic and social advancement and provides access to the self-interested beneficence of Western English-speaking governments who dispense pounds and dollars in return for influence in the Third World.

But education in English exacts its own costs, as Asians and Africans are fully aware. One is the development, always risky, of an elite minority cut off from the general population by language and by the Westernized culture inevitably learned with the language. Another is social injustice, rarely avoidable when higher levels of education and employment are open only to speakers of English and when courts and regulatory institutions conduct their business in the alien and minority language. S. J. Tambiah reports that the division between English-educated and non-English-educated groups is "synonymous in Asian politics with others more familiar in the West: the rich and the poor, the privileged and the under-privileged, the elite and the masses." [e] Recognizing such implications for language choice explains to the otherwise puzzled Westerner why bloody riots have occurred in India and Bangladesh over the question of the retention of English as an official language. Finally, there is the personal and psychic cost to the individual who must earn

[e] *Ibid.*

his education in someone else's language, usually the language of his former colonial master; and who must seem to have to acceed to the lower status accorded his native tongue. Gandhi, who campaigned for linguistic as well as political freedom for India, wrote:

The greatest service we can render society is to free ourselves and it from the superstitious regard we have learnt to pay to the learning of the English language. It is the medium of instruction in our schools and colleges. It is becoming the lingua franca of the country. Our best thoughts are expressed in it. Lord Chelmsford hopes that it will soon take the place of the mother tongue in high families. This belief in the necessity of English training has enslaved us. It has unfitted us for true national service. Were it not for force of habit, we could not fail to see that, by reason of English being the medium of instruction, our intellect has been segregated, we have become isolated from the masses, the best mind of the nation has become gagged and the masses have not received the benefit of the new ideas we have received.[f]

Attitudes will, without doubt, ultimately matter in the future of world English. Those in the West who hope for the retention of English in the Third World may hear hopeful notes in some of the many voices discussing the question. To some Africans and Asians, English is no longer "The King-Emperor's English"—the language of the master—but something adopted, and adapted, to their own use. Rather than signifying subservience, English is seen as a medium for achieving and announcing independence and maturity; and notice of preemption is confidently served on the former owners: "The problem is to make the people of England realize," urged a delegate to a conference on African literature, "and in France for that matter, that their languages are no longer their sole property, because they have almost defeated themselves by their own success in propagating their languages."[g]

This feeling on the part of the former colonial subject, that "The King-Emperor's English is now mine," is tied to the political nationalism pushing Africans and Asians to strive for independence. As such, it has interesting parallels to the history of language attitudes in another of the King's rebellious colonies—the large one in North America that tends to forget her revolutionary past. Writing in the afterglow of the War of Independence, Noah Webster gladly accepted the task of helping to forge a new American language, warmed to it by patriotic fervor:

This country must, in some future time, be as distinguished by the superiority of her literary improvements as she is already by the liberality

[f] *The Collected Works of Mahatma Gandhi* (Delhi: Ministry of Information and Broadcasting, 1965), Vol. 14, p. 122.

[g] Gerald Moore in *African Literature and the Universities*, ed. Gerald Moore (Ibadan: Ibadan University Press, 1965), p. 86.

of her civil and ecclesiastical constitutions. Europe is grown old in folly, corruption and tyranny—in that country laws are perverted, manners are licentious, literature is declining and human nature debased. For America in her infancy to adopt the present maxims of the old world, would be to stamp the wrinkles of decrepid age upon the bloom of youth and to plant the seeds of decay in a vigorous constitution.[h]

Old World sounds were as pernicious as Old World maxims, and the King's English had to be forced to give way to that of the American yeomanry. Webster urged (in Dissertations, *1789) the interest of Americans in opposing the introduction of any plan of uniformity with the British language, foreseeing a time, as did Jefferson, when America would have a language "as different from the future language of England, as the modern Dutch, Danish and Swedish are from the German, or from one another."[1] Such division has not, of course, come about—partly because ties between the United States and England have remained close, partly because of conservative and standardizing tendencies in American education enforced by mass literacy, and partly because of the modern development of mass media.*

But the English language used in America was inevitably changed, as it had to meet the demands of a new environment and new governing institutions. Moreover the feeling that America should *have her own national linguistic norms met a practical need for them, forging that complex of beliefs and attitudes, linguistic and sociological fact that we call Standard American English. A new nation, seeking unity, needs a voice to express its unity—a new reference point to convince itself that it is one. Linguistic change, the life of language, inevitably provides the material, in new vocabulary, changed pronunciations, and new usages, from which badges of singularity may be fashioned. A complex of such changes—linguistic, conceptual, perceptual, attitudinal— define the uniqueness of the national variety, American English, just as others define different national norms: Canadian English, Australian English, West Indian English.*

In Asia and in Africa as well, new national and perhaps areal varieties appear to be emerging. Indian English, because of its relatively long history and its extensive use as a literary medium, has enough of a separate identity to serve as a norm for Indian users different from the norm for British English.[j] Some common features have been identified in the English of India, Pakistan, and

[h] Noah Webster, *A Grammatical Institute of the English Language* (Hartford: Hudson and Goodwin [1783]), Pt. 1, p. 14.

[1] Noah Webster, *Dissertations on the English Language* (Boston: Isaiah Thomas, 1789), pp. 22–23.

[j] See Braj B. Kachru, "Indian English: A Study in Contextualization," in *In Memory of J. R. Firth*, eds. C. E. Bazell, *et al.* (London: Longmans, 1966), and "The Indianness of Indian English," *Word*, **21**(1965):391–410; G. Subba Rao, *Indian Words in English: A Study in Indo-British Cultural Relations* (Oxford: Clarendon Press, 1954).

Ceylon, suggesting the existence of a broader variety—South Asian English.[k]
*Similar trends have been noticed for such areas as West Africa, and for West
African nations such as Ghana and Nigeria, where the use of English is extensive,
important, and supported by education and mass media.*[1] *The forces producing
these new varieties are familiar in part from similar cases of the transplantation
of English in North America and Australia: linguistic change introduced by
geographical separation and the influences of new environments, contacts,
and institutions. But other forces are peculiar to those situations where English
is a second rather than a native language: manner and degree of success in
learning English; different uses to which English is put; interference and
transfer from the native language of the English user; and continued and
persistent contact with indigenous languages.*

*The result of the new forces is an extremely varied English in such nations
as Sierra Leone, Ghana, and Nigeria; in fact, it might be more accurate to
speak of many Englishes. The Africanist Jack Berry identifies five types of
English in use in Sierra Leone:*

> (1) Standard English, spoken chiefly by expatriates, (2) a regional dialect,
> closely approximating West African English [that is, sharing features
> with dialects used in other West African nations], (3) Krio, an English-
> based creole spoken as a mother tongue, (4) West African pidgin
> English, and (5) marginal languages, such as those spoken between
> expatriates and their servants. [m]

*Nor does this exhaust the variety. It is said that a keen observer can distinguish
in the English of a West African that speaker's native language, and that the
English of a speaker of Hausa differs from the English of a speaker of Yoruba
in pronunciation and in grammar. If from such variety a standardized West
African English is to emerge, it will do so from one of two sources (or, perhaps,
from an amalgam of both): from an educated variety "as spoken for example
by news-readers on the Nigerian or Ghanaian radio—clear, easy to understand
and a desirable standard for West Africans as a whole to attempt to attain,"
this variety assiduously cultivated for its utility in ever-expanding education; or
from "an uneducated form of West Indian English, which is not quite Pidgin,
but which is spreading rapidly as the result of the great increase in the number
of ex-primary school pupils who will have no further education."* [n] *Should the
latter force prevail, it will not be the first time in history that a demotic
koine has established itself, started through a tenuous hold on the parent
language, naturally enriched by the importation of native materials, self-
consciously used and cultivated, and then dignified by publishers and gram-*

[k] Braj B. Kachru, "English in South Asia," in *Current Trends in Linguistics*, ed. Thomas
A. Sebeok (The Hague: Mouton, 1969), Vol. 5, pp. 627–78.

[1] See Tiffin *loc. cit.*, and Spencer, *loc. cit.*

[m] Tiffin, *op. cit.*, p. 101, paraphrasing Jack Berry, "Pidgins and Creoles in Africa," in
Symposium on Multilingualism (London: Commission for Technical Cooperation in
Africa, Publication No. 87, 1962), p. 221.

[n] Tiffin, in Dakin, Tiffin, and Widdowson, *op. cit.*, p. 101.

marians. *Whatever the future, past history instructs us that the people, not the language planners, will decide. Language must be useful in order to be used, and it must be acceptable to its users.*

The writing of literature in English will doubtless play some role in the development of new national varieties. Writers self-consciously adopt the form of language that will enable them to express their sense of individuality and of place. And because they seek a private vision they inevitably invest a borrowed tongue with perceptions first formed in their native one. The Indian novelist Mulk Raj Anand says that his work in English "has always been mainly a translation from my mother tongue, Punjabi, or Hindustani, into English." He surmises that all Indian writers using English "more or less, translate from their mother tongue into English, and that the intrusion of the idiom and metaphor of the Indian languages makes their writing different from the various styles of English writing in Britain and America."[o] The novelist R. K. Narayan is equally sure that, whatever Indian writers are doing with the language, "We are not attempting to write Anglo-Saxon English. The English language . . . is now undergoing a process of Indianization in the same manner as it adopted U.S. citizenship over a century ago, with the difference that it is the major language there but here one of the fifteen listed in the Indian constitution."[p]

The West African novelist Chinua Achebe sees English as "a new voice coming out of Africa, speaking of African experience in a world language." English, he feels, is "able to carry the weight of my African experience. But it will have to be a new English, still in full communion with its ancestral home but altered to suit its African surroundings."[q] The precise tones of this new voice are at present richly various, from the pidgins or near pidgins of the uneducated to an essentially international English in which only the characters and the experiences are African. From Amos Tutuola there are translations of Yoruba oral traditions into highly idiosyncratic if not nonstandard English. From Gabriel Okara we have "direct substitution of the syntax of his native Ijaw for normal English syntax."[r] And from Joseph Abruquah we have an English that has been praised by a critic for its lack of "striving towards a hybrid of the English language that will pass for African—a language which, almost alas! is becoming a tiresome feature of so much West African fiction in English."[s] Not surprisingly, the voices of all three novelists have been separately heard as heralding the future of West African literary English.

[o] *The King-Emperor's English, or the Role of the English Language in the Free India* (Bombay: Hind Kitabs, 1948), pp. 17–18.

[p] "English in India," in *Commonwealth Literature: Unity and Diversity in a Common Culture*, ed. John Press (London: Heinemann, 1965), p. 123.

[q] Chinua Achebe, "English and the African Writer," *Transition* 18 (1965); quoted by Peter Young, "The Language of West African Literature in English," in Spencer, *op. cit.*, p. 167.

[r] Young, *loc. cit.*, p. 180.

[s] Joe de Graft, cited in L. A. Boadi, "Education and the Role of English in Ghana," in Spencer, *op. cit.*, p. 64.

Citizens of the West must *hear these new voices coming out of the Third World and speaking a variety of our English. For to apprehend that English is not just ours but the world's affords an important perspective from which to view language, particularly for Americans and more particularly for Americans who teach or plan to teach, caught up as we all are in a national mythology that perpetuates the image of a single, right, and invariant form. Several forces combine to make Americans linguistic chauvinists, among them the dominance of the printed word in a culture that worships universal and standardized education; mass literacy and massier media; the power and influence of the United States in world politics and world trade (which make our statesmen and our traders monoglots); and our lack of any real or consistent contact internally with other languages. But chauvinism, in any form, is dangerous in a world transformed to a global village. It is dangerous, too, within a nation as large as ours that still exhibits ethnic and regional diversity.*

To appreciate that English is not just our tongue is an antidote to chauvinism and a corrective to mythology and misconception. When we see the degree of diversity that exists in the national varieties of English without hindering intelligibility for the speakers of those varieties, we will see that variation in American English is relatively slight. To watch movements toward standardized national varieties in Asia and Africa offers us an opportunity to re-view scenes from the natural history of standard English in the United States—to comprehend better the forces that made it, its utility, and the limits on its utility, and the costs of attempting to impose it on everyone. To hear arguments over language choice makes us more aware of the roles played by attitudes, preconceptions, and prejudices in language planning, laying open the difficult-to-appreciate fact that much of the character and value of standard English lies in the eye, the heart, and the viscera of the beholder. The prospective teacher with an eye open to the future might do well to ponder the transformations that would take place in curricula and in the preparation for teaching them if Departments of English Literature were changed to Departments of Literature in English. Similar changes in our view of language use and the form of language to be used will be necessary if we are to appreciate the many functions our language serves in the modern world.

THE USERS AND USES OF LANGUAGE
M. A. K. Halliday, Angus McIntosh, and Peter Strevens

Descriptive study has dominated American linguistics for the past forty years, particularly the study of languages as formal and abstract systems. In recent years, many linguists have come to feel that we cannot understand the nature of human language until we view it in the context of its actual use by human beings in real situations, taking into account the functions it serves and how it varies to fulfill those functions. John Spencer, in calling for a comprehensive approach to the study of English in Africa, comments on the limits placed about contemporary work:

In our research we are still working as Linnaeans; describing, analyzing, classifying, gradually extending our taxonomy of language, increasing the number of well-described specimens and developing our comparative classification. No one doubts the importance of this. But vital also is the post-Linnaean approach, which displays a concern with the ecology of language. I believe we need many more case studies of what modern communications, external influences, mass media and expanded educational opportunities are doing to languages in Africa; how languages, and this includes English and French, are being influenced by their new and constantly changing environment in Africa.[a]

Unlike their American counterparts, British linguists have long emphasized what might be called ecological studies of language. It is fitting, then, to begin our examination of varieties of present-day English with the following sketch by three distinguished British linguists of a definition of what they call institutional linguistics—*the study of language communities, their contacts with one another, variations within single communities according to who uses the language and for what purposes, the interactions between the abstract forms that a language takes and the feelings members of a community share about their language—their senses of linguistic unity or division, their prejudices about what they see as misuse, and their admiration for language institutionalized in literature.*

Reprinted from *The Linguistic Sciences and Language Teaching* by permission of the authors and publishers, Longmans, Green and Co., Ltd., and Indiana University Press. © 1964 by M. A. K. Halliday, A. McIntosh, and P. D. Strevens.

[a] "Language and Independence," in *Language in Africa: Papers of the Leverhulme Conference on Universities and the Language Problems of Tropical Africa, Held at University College, Ibadan,* ed. John Spencer (Cambridge: Cambridge University Press, 1963), p. 38.

In this section we are concerned with the branch of linguistics which deals, to put it in the most general terms, with the relation between a language and the people who use it. This includes the study of language communities, singly and in contact, of varieties of language and of attitudes to language. The various special subjects involved here are grouped together under the name of "institutional linguistics."

There is no clear line dividing institutional from descriptive linguistics; the two, though distinct enough as a whole, merge into one another. The study of context leads on to the analysis of situation types and of the uses of language. The descriptive distinction into spoken and written language naturally involves us in a consideration of the different varieties of language they represent. In institutional linguistics we are looking at the same data, language events, but from a different standpoint. The attention is now on the users of language, and the uses they make of it.

There are many ways of finding patterns among people. Some patterns are obvious: everyone is either male or female, with a fairly clear line between the two. Some, equally obvious, are less clearly demarcated: people are either children or adults, but we may not be sure of the assignment of a particular individual. Humorously, we may recognize all sorts of *ad hoc* patterns, like W. S. Gilbert's classification of babies into "little liberals" and "little conservatives." The human sciences all introduce their own patterning: people are introverts or extroverts; negriform, mongoliform, caucasiform, of australiform; employed, self-employed, nonemployed or unemployed. No clear boundaries here, though the categories, statistically defined and, sometimes, arbitrarily delimited, are useful enough. Other patterns, such as national citizenship, are thrust upon us, often with conflicting criteria: each state tends to have its own definition of its citizens.

In linguistics, people are grouped according to the language or languages they use. This dimension of patterning is sometimes applied outside linguistics: a nation, in one view, is defined by language as well as by other factors. On the other hand, the category of "nation" defined politically has sometimes been used in linguistics to give an institutional definition of "a language": in this view "a language" is a continuum of dialects spoken within the borders of one state. On such a criterion, British English and American English are two languages, though mutually intelligible; Chinese is one language, though Pekingese and Cantonese are not mutually intelligible; and Flemish, Dutch, German, Austrian German, and Swiss German are five languages, though the pairing of mutually intelligible and mutually unintelligible dialects does not by any means follow the various national boundaries.

This is not the only way of defining "a language"; there are as many definitions as there are possible criteria. Even within institutional linguistics various criteria are involved, each yielding a definition that is useful for some specific purpose. The concept of "a language" is too important just to be taken for granted; nor is it made any less powerful by the existence of multiple criteria for defining it. But we have to be careful to specify the nature of this category when we use it.

In institutional linguistics it is useful to start with the notion of a LANGUAGE COMMUNITY, and then to ask certain questions about it. The language community is a group of people who regard themselves as using the same language. In this sense there is a language community "the Chinese," since they consider themselves as speaking "Chinese," and not Pekingese, Cantonese, and so on. There is no language community "the Scandinavians"; Norwegians speak Norwegian, Danes Danish, and Swedes Swedish, and these are not regarded as "dialects of the Scandinavian language," even though they are by and large all mutually intelligible. The British, Americans, Canadians, Australians, and others all call their language "English"; they form a single language community.

This method of recognizing a language community has the advantage that it reflects the speakers' attitude toward their language, and thus the way they use it. All speakers of English, for example, agree more or less on the way it should be written. At the same time, like all institutional linguistic categories and most of the basic categories of the human sciences, it is not clear-cut, because people do not fall into clear-cut patterns. There is a minor tendency for Americans to regard themselves as using a different language from the British, and this is again reflected in minor variations in orthography. But it is a mistake to exaggerate this distinction, or to conclude therefrom that there is no unified English-speaking language community.

Some of the questions that can be asked about a language community and its language are these. First, what happens when it impinges on other language communities? Second, what varieties of its language are there? Under the second question come these subdivisions: varieties according to users (that is, varieties in the sense that each speaker uses one variety and uses it all the time) and varieties according to use (that is, in the sense that each speaker has a range of varieties and chooses between them at different times). The variety according to user is a *dialect;* the variety according to use is a *register.* Third, what attitudes do the speakers display toward their language and any or all of its varieties?

1

Situations in which one language community impinges on another have been called language contact situations. Such situations are characterized by varying degrees of bilingualism. Bilingualism is recognized wherever a native speaker of one language makes use of a second language, however partially or imperfectly. It is thus a cline, ranging, in terms of the individual speaker, from the completely monolingual person at one end, who never uses anything but his own native language, or L1, through bilingual speakers, who make use in varying degree of a second language, or L2, to the endpoint where a speaker has complete mastery of two languages and makes use of both in all uses to which he puts either. Such a speaker is an "ambilingual."

True ambilingual speakers are rare. Most people whom we think of as bilingual restrict at least one of their languages to certain uses: and in any given use, one or the other language tends to predominate. There are probably millions of L2 English speakers throughout the world with a high degree of bilingualism, but who could neither make love or do the washing up in English nor discuss medicine or space travel in their L1. Even those who have learnt two languages from birth rarely perform all language activities in both; more often than not a certain amount of specialization takes place.

This distinction, between an L1 and an L2, a native and a non-native or learnt language, is of course not clear-cut. Moreover it cuts across the degree of bilingualism. Some bilingual speakers, including some who are ambilingual, can be said to have two (occasionally more) native languages. There is no exact criterion for this; but one could say arbitrarily that any language learnt by the child before the age of instruction, from parents, from others, such as a nurse, looking after it, or from other children, is an L1. It is clear, however, that only a small proportion of those who learn two or more languages in this way become ambilingual speakers; and conversely, not all ambilinguals have two L1s.

A point that has often been observed about native bilingual, including ambilingual, speakers is that they are unable to translate between their L1s. This does not mean of course that they cannot learn to translate between them. But translation has to be learnt by them as a distinct operation; it does not follow automatically from the possession of two sets of native language habits. This has been linked with the fact that those with two L1s are usually not true ambilinguals: that they have usually specialized their two or more native languages into different uses. But this cannot be the only reason, since even those who approach or attain true ambilingualism are still usually unable to translate without instruction. It appears that it is a characteristic of an L1, defined in the way suggested above, to operate as a distinct set of self-sufficient patterns in those situations in which language activity is involved. However ambilingual the speaker is, in the sense that there is no recognizable class of situation in which he could not use either of his languages, there is always some difference between the actual situations in which he uses the one and those in which he uses the other, namely that each of the two is associated with a different group of participants.

This raises the question: how unique is or are the native language or languages in the life of the speaker? No sure answer can yet be given to this question. It is clear that for the great majority of bilingual speakers the L2 never replaces the L1 as a way of living; nor is it intended to do so. We may want to attain a high degree of competence in one or more foreign languages, but we usually do not expect thereby to disturb the part played in our lives by the native one. On the other hand those who move permanently to a new language community may, if they move as individuals and not as whole families, abandon at least the active use of their native language and replace it throughout by an L2.

This in itself is not enough to guarantee a particular degree of attainment in the L2. Some speakers are more easily content: they may, for example, not try to adopt the phonetic patterns of the L2 beyond the point where they become comprehensible to its native speakers. Others may simply fail to achieve the standard of performance that they themselves regard as desirable. In this way they cut down the role played by language in their lives. On the other hand there is clearly no upper limit to attainment in an L2. The L2 speaker may live a normal, full life in his adopted language community, absorb its literature and even use the language for his own creative writing, as Conrad and Nabokov have done so successfully with English. Whether the learnt language will ever be so "infinitely docile," in Nabokov's words, as the native language, it is hard to say. Certainly the user of an L2 may learn to exploit its resources as widely as do its native speakers; and though he is more conscious of these resources than the majority of native speakers, in this he merely resembles that minority who have learnt to be conscious of how their native language works: principally the creative writers, literary analysts, and linguists. But while one can set no limit to the possible degree of mastery of an L2, it remains true that such a level of attainment is rarely aimed at and still more rarely achieved.

The individual speaker, in contact with a new language community, may react by developing any degree and kind of bilingualism within this very wide range. Over language communities as a whole, in contact-situations certain patterns tend to emerge. Sometimes the solution adopted, at least in the long term, is not one of bilingualism. What happens in these instances is either that one language community abandons its own language and adopts that of the other—here there will be a transitional period of bilingualism, but it may be very short; or that a mixed language develops which incorporates some features of both.

Such mixed languages have usually had either English or French as one of their components; less frequently Dutch or Portuguese. Those that remain restricted to certain uses, as many have done, without ever attaining the full resources of a language, are called PIDGINS. Some mixtures, however, have developed into full languages; these are known as CREOLES. In some areas, for example in language communities in Sierra Leone, Haiti, Mauritius, and Melanesia, creoles are acquired by children as their L1. Here they have full status as community languages, and there is not necessarily any bilingualism at all. The fact that in most of these areas children are expected to acquire a second language as L2 at school reflects the social status of the mixed languages, but is entirely without prejudice to their linguistic status as full community languages.

In other instances the long term solution has been one of as it were institutionalized bilingualism. This frequently takes the form of a LINGUA

FRANCA. One language comes to be adopted as the medium of some activity or activities which the different language communities perform in common. It may be a common language for commerce, learning, administration, religion or any or all of a variety of purposes: the use determines which members of each language community are the ones who learn it.

Latin was such a lingua franca for a long period in the history of Europe; in certain countries it retains this status to the present day, though to a much restricted extent, as the lingua franca of religion. Among other languages which have been linguae francae at certain times, over certain areas and for certain uses, are Arabic, Malay, Hausa, Classical and Mandarin (Pekingese) Chinese, Swahili, Sanskrit, French, Russian, and English. Since the lingua franca normally operates for certain specific purposes, it is often a more or less clearly definable part of the language that is learnt as L2. There may even develop a special variety for use as a lingua franca, as with Hindustani and "bazaar Malay." These are distinct in practice from the mixed pidgins and creoles, in that each has clearly remained a variety of its original language; but it is difficult to draw an exact theoretical distinction.

Languages such as English and Russian, which are widely learnt as second languages in the world today, are a type of lingua franca. They are a special case only in the sense that they are being learnt by unprecedentedly large numbers of people and for a very wide range of purposes, some of which are new. In any serious study of the problems and methods of teaching English as a second language it is important to find out what these purposes are, and how they differ in different areas and according to the needs of different individuals. Possibly the major aim that is common to all areas where English is taught as L2 is that of its use in the study of science and technology. But there are numerous other aims, educational, administrative, legal, commercial and so on, variously weighted and pursued in different countries.

The task of becoming a bilingual with English as L2 is not the same in all these different circumstances; and it is unfair to those who are struggling with the language, whether struggling to learn it or to teach it, to pretend that it is. English is "a language" in the sense that it is not Russian or Hindi; any two events in English are events in "the same" language. But if we want to teach what we call a language, whether English or any other, as a second or indeed also as a first language, we must look a little more closely at the nature of the varieties within it.

2

In one dimension, which variety of a language you use is determined by who you are. Each speaker has learnt, as his L1, a particular variety of the language of his language community, and this variety may differ at any or all levels from other varieties of the same language learnt by other speakers as their L1. Such a variety, identified along this dimension is called a dialect.

In general, "who you are" for this purpose means "where you come from." In most language communities in the world it is the region of origin which determines which dialectal variety of the language a speaker uses. In China, you speak Cantonese if you come from Canton, Pekingese if you come from Peking, and Yunnanese if you come from Yunnan.

Regional dialects are usually grouped by the community into major dialect areas; there may, of course, be considerable differentiation within each area. The dialects spoken in Canton, Toishan, Chungshan, and Seiyap, all in Kwangtung province, are clearly distinct from one another; but they are all grouped together under the general name of "Cantonese."

Within Cantonese, the local varieties form a continuum: each will resemble its neighbors on either side more closely than it resembles those further away. Among major dialect areas, there is usually also a continuum. There may be a more or less clear dialect boundary, where the occurrence of a bundle of ISOGLOSSES (lines separating a region displaying one grammatical, lexical, phonological, or phonetic feature from a region having a different feature at the same place in the language) shows that there are a number of features in which the dialects on either side differ from each other: but the continuum is not entirely broken. Thus there is a fairly clear distinction between Cantonese and Mandarin in the area where the two meet in Kwangsi, and there is indeed a strip of country where the two coexist, many villages having some families speaking Cantonese and some speaking Mandarin. Nevertheless the variety of Cantonese spoken in this dialect border region is closer to Mandarin than are other varieties of Cantonese, and the Mandarin is closer to Cantonese than are other varieties of Mandarin.

This situation represents a kind of median between two extremes: an unbroken continuum on the one hand, as between Mandarin and the "Wu," or lower Yangtsze dialect region, and a sharp break on the other, as between Cantonese and Hakka in Kwangtung. In this case the reason for the break is that the Hakka speakers arrived by migration from the north roughly a thousand years after the original settlement of Kwangtung by the ancestors of the modern Cantonese speakers.

This general dialect pattern turns up in one form or another all over the world. An instance of wide dialectal variety in modern Europe is provided by German. Here we have to recognize three, and possibly four, different language communities. The Flemings, in Belgium, speak Flemish, though this is now officially regarded as a variety of Dutch; the Dutch speak Dutch; Germanic speakers in Switzerland regard themselves, in general, as speaking a distinct "Swiss-German." The Germans and the Austrians, and the Swiss in certain circumstances, regard themselves as speaking German. But over the whole of this area there is one unbroken dialect continuum, with very few instances of a clear dialect boundary; ranging from the High German of Switzerland, Austria, and Bavaria to the Low German of Northwest Germany, Holland, and Belgium.

The normal condition of language is to change, and at times and in places where there is little mobility between dialect communities there is nothing to cause the various dialects of a language to change in the same direction. Under these conditions dialects tend to diverge from each other at all levels, perhaps most of all in phonology and phonetics. It may happen that mutual intelligibility is lost; that the language community is as it were broken up into dialect regions such that there are many pairs of regions whose speakers cannot understand one another. This happened in China. There are six major dialects in modern China: Mandarin, Cantonese, Wu, North Min, South Min, and Hakka; each of which is mutually unintelligible with all the others.

This situation tends to be resolved by the emergence of one dialect as a lingua franca. In China, the spoken lingua franca has traditionally been the Pekingese form of the Mandarin dialect. But under the empire very few people from outside the Mandarin-speaking area ever learnt Mandarin unless they were government officials. Mandarin was the language of administration and some literature; but classical Chinese remained the lingua franca for most written purposes, being supplemented as an educational medium, since it could no longer function as a spoken language, by the regional dialects. In nationalist China some progress was made toward introducing Mandarin as a "second language" in schools, and the process has continued in communist China, where with the expansion of educational facilities, Mandarin is now regularly taught at some state in the school career. It is in fact becoming a "standard" or "national" language.

A similar process took place in Germany. "Standard German" of course is "standard" only for the language community that considers itself as speaking German (not, however, limited to Germany itself). The concept of a standard is defined in relation to the language community: to a Dutchman "standard" could only mean standard Dutch, not standard German.

In Germany, and similarly in China, there is no suggestion that the dialect chosen as the standard language is any better than any other dialect. A modern state needs a lingua franca for its citizens, and there are historical reasons leading to the choice of one dialect rather than another. It may have been the one first written down, or the language of the capital; or it may, as in Germany, include a somewhat artificial mixture of features from different dialects. Nor is there any suggestion that those who learn the standard language should speak it exactly alike. The aim is intelligibility for all purposes of communication, and if a Cantonese speaks Mandarin, as most do, with a Cantonese accent, provided this does not affect his intelligibility nobody will try to stop him or suggest that his performance is inferior or that he himself is a less worthy person.

In the history of the English language, dialects followed the familiar pattern. In the fifteenth century England was a continuum of regional dialects with, almost certainly, some mutual unintelligibility. With the rise of urbanism and the modern state, a standard language emerged; this was basically the London form of the Southeast Midland dialect, but with some features from neighbouring areas, especially from the South-central Midlands. The orthography, which in Middle English had varied region by region, became more and more standardized according to the conventions associated with this dialect. As in other countries, for ease of communication, the notion of a "correct" orthography grew up: by the late seventeenth century educated people were expected to spell alike, although in earlier times individuality had been tolerated in spelling just as it had been (and still was) in pronunciation.

The emergence of a standard language gives rise to the phenomenon of "accent," which is quite distinct from "dialect." When we learn a foreign language, we normally transfer patterns from our native language on to the language we are learning. These may be patterns at any level. Those of form, however, and most of those of phonology and orthography, tend to be progressively eliminated. This is because they may seriously impair intelligibility; they are less directly interrelated, thus reinforcing each other less; and they are easier to correct once observed, because they are not patterns of muscular activity. With phonetic patterns, on the other hand, there is greater intelligibility tolerance, more reinforcement, and much greater difficulty in correction even when they are observed. Transference of phonetic habits, in other words, is easier to tolerate and harder to avoid than transference at other levels. So we usually speak with a "foreign accent," even when our grammar and lexis are in general conformity with the native patterns of the learnt language.

So also when a speaker learns a second dialect. He generally speaks it with "an accent": that is, with phonetic features of his native dialect. The learning of a standard language is simply the learning of a second dialect, the dialect that happens to have been "standardized." Most speakers, learning the standard language of their community, continue to speak with the phonetics of their native dialect, and there is usually no loss in intelligibility.

It is quite normal for members of a language community which has a standard language to continue to use both the native and the learnt (standard) dialect in different situations throughout their lives. This happens regularly in China and even in Germany. But while in a rural community, where there is less movement of people, the native dialect is appropriate to most situations, in an urban community the relative demands on native and standard dialect are reversed. The population is probably made up of speakers of various different dialects, so that the standard language becomes a lingua franca amongst them; in addition there is greater mobility within and between towns.

As a consequence, many speakers drop their native dialect altogether, having very few situations in which to use it, and replace it with the standard language. In so doing, they transfer to the standard language the phonetics of the native dialect, speaking it with a regional "accent." In time, this form of the standard language with regional accent comes to be regarded itself as a dialect. Today, for example, people use the term "Yorkshire dialect" equally to refer both to the speech of Leeds, which is standard English with generalized West Riding phonetics, and to the speech of Upper Wharfedale, which is an "original" West Riding dialect. Since urban speech forms expand outward at the expense of rural ones, the longer established dialects of England are disappearing and being replaced by the standard language spoken with the various regional accents.

This process is liable to happen anywhere where there is a high degree of industrialization and consequent growth of cities. What is peculiar to England, however, is the extent to which, concurrently with this process, a new dimension of dialect differentiation has come into operation. In most countries, even those highly industrialized like Germany, the way a person speaks is determined by the place he comes from: he speaks either the regional dialect or the standard language with regional accent. In England, however, and to a lesser extent in France, Scotland, Australia, and the United States, a person's speech is determined not only by the region he comes from but also by the class he comes from, or the class he is trying to move into. Our dialects and accents are no longer simply regional: they are regional and social, or "socioregional." Nowhere else in the world is this feature found in the extreme form it has reached in England. It is a feature of English life which constantly amazes the Germans and others into whose national mythology the facts, or some version of them, have penetrated.

The dialect structure of England today can be represented by a pyramid. The vertical plane represents class, the horizontal one region. At the base, there is wide regional differentiation, widest among the agricultural workers and the lower-paid industrial workers. As one moves along the socioeconomic scale, dialectal variety according to region diminishes. Finally at the apex there is no regional differentiation at all, except perhaps for the delicate shades which separate Cambridge and Oxford from each other and from the rest.

This regionally neutral variety of English, often known as "RP," standing for "received (that is, generally accepted) pronunciation," carries prestige and may be acquired at any stage in life. It tends to be taught by example rather than by instruction. Certain institutions, notably the preparatory and public schools, create, as part of their function, conditions in which it can be learnt. The speaker of this form of English has, as is well known, many social and economic advantages. There are, for example, many posts for which he will automatically be preferred over a candidate who does not speak it. If there are any posts for which the opposite is true, as is sometimes claimed, these are posts which are not likely to arouse serious competition.

When a speaker states what language he regards himself as speaking, he is defining a language community. By implication a language community may be delimited regionally, although national frontiers may enter into the definition of the region. When he states what dialect he speaks, he is defining a dialect community. Here again the delimitation that is implied is normally regional; but there are some countries, notably England, in which it is socioregional. If the community has a standard language, there may be not only dialects but also accents: in other words "new dialects," varieties of the standard language with regional or socioregional phonetic patterns. The line dividing dialect and accent is often not clear-cut, and the speaker may well conflate the two. All his observations, but especially those on dialect and accent, may be colored by value-judgments; but the discussion of these we leave to the final section of this chapter.

3

A dialect is a variety of a language distinguished according to the user: different groups of people within the language community speak different dialects. It is possible also to recognize varieties of a language along another dimension, distinguished according to use. Language varies as its function varies; it differs in different situations. The name given to a variety of a language distinguished according to use is "register."

The category of register is needed when we want to account for what people do with their language. When we observe language activity in the various contexts in which it takes place, we find differences in the type of language selected as appropriate to different types of situation. There is no need to labor the point that a sports commentary, a church service, and a school lesson are linguistically quite distinct. One sentence from any of these and many more such situation types would enable us to identify it correctly. We know, for example, where "an early announcement is expected" comes from and "apologies for absence were received"; these are not simply free variants of "we ought to hear soon" and "was sorry he couldn't make it."

It is not the event or state of affairs being talked about that determines the choice, but the convention that a certain kind of language is appropriate to a certain use. We should be surprised, for example, if it was announced on the carton of our toothpaste that the product was "just right for cleaning false teeth" instead of "ideal for cleansing artificial dentures." We can often guess the source of a piece of English from familiarity with its use: "mix well" probably comes from a recipe, although the action of mixing is by no means limited to cookery—and "mixes well" is more likely to be found in a testimonial.

The choice of items from the wrong register, and the mixing of items from different registers, are among the most frequent mistakes made by non-native speakers of a language. If an L2 English speaker uses, in conversation, a dependent clause with modal "should," such as "should you like another pint of beer . . . ," where a native speaker would use a dependent clause with "if," he is selecting from the wrong register. Transference of this kind is not limited to foreigners; the native schoolboy may transfer in the opposite direction, writing in his Shakespeare essay "it was all up with Lear, who couldn't take any more of it."

Linguistic humor often depends on the inappropriate choice and the mixing of registers: P. G. Wodehouse exploits this device very effectively. Fifty years ago the late George Robey used to recite a version of "The house that Jack built" which ended as follows: ". . . that disturbed the equanimity of the domesticated feline mammal that exterminated the noxious rodent that masticated the farinaceous produce deposited in the domiciliary edifice erected by Master John."

Dialects tend to differ primarily, and always to some extent, in substance. Registers, on the other hand, differ primarily in form. Some registers, it is true, have distinctive features at other levels, such as the voice quality associated with the register of church services. But the crucial criteria of any given register are to be found in its grammar and its lexis. Probably lexical features are the most obvious. Some lexical items suffice almost by themselves to identify a certain register: "cleanse" puts us in the language of advertising, "probe" of newspapers, especially headlines, "tablespoonful" of recipes or prescriptions, "neckline" of fashion reporting or dress-making instructions. The clearest signals of a particular register are scientific technical terms, except those that belong to more than one science, like morphology in biology and linguistics.

Often it is not the lexical item alone but the collocation of two or more lexical items that is specific to one register. "Kick" is presumably neutral, but "free kick" is from the language of football. Compare the disc jockey's "top twenty"; "thinned right down" at the hairdresser's (but "thinned out" in the garden); and the collocation of "heart" and "bid" by contrast with "heart" and "beat."

Purely grammatical distinctions between the different registers are less striking, yet there can be considerable variation in grammar also. Extreme cases are newspaper headlines and church services; but many other registers, such as sports commentaries and popular songs, exhibit specific grammatical characteristics. Sometimes, for example, in the language of advertising, it is the combination of grammatical and lexical features that is distinctive. "Pioneers in self-drive car hire" is an instance of a fairly restricted grammatical structure. The collocation of the last four lexical items is normal enough in other structures, as in "why don't you hire a car and drive yourself?"; but their occurrence in this structure, and in collocation with an item like "pioneer" or "specialist," is readily identifiable as an advertising slogan.

Registers are not marginal or special varieties of language. Between them they cover the total range of our language activity. It is only by reference to the various situations, and situation types, in which language is used that we can understand its functioning and its effectiveness. Language is not realized in the abstract: it is realized as the activity of people in situations, as linguistic events which are manifested in a particular dialect and register.

No one suggests, of course, that the various registers characteristic of different types of situation have nothing in common. On the contrary, a great deal of grammatical and lexical material is common to many of the registers of a given language, and some perhaps to all. If this was not so we could not speak of "a language" in this sense at all, just as we should not be able to speak of "a language" in the sense of a dialect continuum if there was not a great deal in common among the different dialects.

But there tends to be more difference between events in different registers than between different events in one register. If we failed to note these differences of register, we should be ignoring an important aspect of the nature and functioning of language. Our descriptions of languages would be inaccurate and our attempts to teach them to foreigners made vastly more difficult.

It is by their formal properties that registers are defined. If two samples of language activity from what, on nonlinguistic grounds, could be considered different situation types show no differences in grammar or lexis, they are assigned to one and the same register: for the purposes of the description of the language there is only one situation type here, not two. For this reason a large amount of linguistic analysis is required before registers can be identified and described. It is one thing to make a general description of English accounting, to a given degree of delicacy, for all the features found in some or other variety of the language. Most native speakers will agree on what is and what is not possible, and the areas of disagreement are marginal. It is quite another thing to find out the special characteristics of a given register: to describe for example the language of consultations between doctor and patient in the surgery.

For such a purpose very large samples of textual material are needed. Moreover much of the language activity that needs to be studied takes place in situations where it is practically impossible to make tape recordings. It is not surprising, therefore, that up to now we know very little about the various registers of spoken English. Even studies of the written language have only recently begun to be made from this point of view. For this reason we are not yet in a position to talk accurately about registers; there is much work to be done before the concept is capable of detailed application.

While we still lack a detailed description of the registers of a language on the basis of their formal properties, it is nevertheless useful to refer to this type of language variety from the point of view of institutional linguistics. There is enough evidence for us to be able to recognize the major situation types to which formally distinct registers correspond; others can be predicted and defined from outside language. A number of different lines of demarcation have been suggested for this purpose. It seems most useful to introduce a classification along three dimensions, each representing an aspect of the situations in which language operates and the part played by language in them. Registers, in this view, may be distinguished according to field of discourse, mode of discourse, and style of discourse.

"Field of discourse" refers to what is going on: to the area of operation of the language activity. Under this heading, registers are classified according to the nature of the whole event of which the language activity forms a part. In the type of situation in which the language activity accounts for practically the whole of the relevant activity, such as an essay, a discussion, or an academic seminar, the field of discourse is the subject matter. On this dimension of classification, we can recognize registers such as politics and personal relations, and technical registers like biology and mathematics.

There are on the other hand situations in which the language activity rarely plays more than a minor part; here the field of discourse refers to the whole event. In this sense there is, for example, a register of domestic chores: "hoovering the carpets" may involve language activity which, though marginal, is contributory to the total event. At the same time the language activity in a situation may be unrelated to the other activities. It may even delay rather than advance them, if two people discuss politics while doing the washing up. Here the language activity does not form part of the washing up event, and the field of discourse is that of politics.

Registers classified according to field of discourse thus include both the technical and the nontechnical: shopping and games playing as well as medicine and linguistics. Neither is confined to one type of situation. It may be that the more technical registers lend themselves especially to language activity of the discussion type, where there are few, if any, related nonlanguage events; and the nontechnical registers to functional or operational language activity, in which we can observe language in use as a means of achievement. But in the last resort there is no field of activity which cannot be discussed; and equally there is none in which language cannot play some part in getting things done. Perhaps our most purely operational language activity is "phatic communion," the language of the establishment and maintenance of social relations. This includes utterances like "How do you do!" and "See you!" and is certainly nontechnical, except perhaps in British English where it overlaps with the register of meteorology. But the language activity of the instructor in the dance studio, of the electrician and his assistant, of the patient consulting the doctor in the surgery, or of research scientists in the performance of a laboratory experiment, however technical it may be, is very clearly functioning as a means of operation and control.

This leads to "mode of discourse," since this refers to the medium or mode of the language activity, and it is this that determines, or rather correlates with, the role played by the language activity in the situation. The primary distinction on this dimension is that into spoken and written language, the two having, by and large, different situational roles. In this connection, reading aloud is a special case of written rather than of spoken language.

The extent of formal differentiation between spoken and written language has varied very greatly among different language communities and at different periods. It reached its widest when, as in medieval Europe, the normal written medium of a community was a classical language which was unintelligible unless learnt by instruction. Latin, Classical Arabic, Sanskrit, and Classical Chinese have all been used in this way. By comparison, spoken and written varieties of most modern languages are extremely close. The two varieties of French probably differ more than those of English; even popular fiction in French uses the simple past (preterite) tense in narrative. But spoken and written English are by no means formally identical. They differ both in grammar and in lexis, as anyone by recording and transcribing conversation can find out.

Within these primary modes, and cutting across them to a certain extent, we can recognize further registers such as the language of newspapers, of advertising, of conversation, and of sports commentary. Like other dimensions of classification in linguistics, both descriptive and institutional, the classification of modes of discourse is variable in delicacy. We may first identify "the language of literature" as a single register; but at the next step we would separate the various genres, such as prose fiction and light verse, as distinct registers within it. What is first recognized as the register of journalism is then subclassified into reportage, editorial comment, feature writing, and so on.

Some modes of discourse are such that the language activity tends to be self-sufficient, in the sense that it accounts for most or all of the activity relevant to the situation. This is particularly true of the various forms of the written mode, but applies also to radio talks, academic discussions, and sermons. In literature particularly the language activity is as it were self-sufficient. On the other hand, in the various spoken modes, and in some of the written, the utterances often integrate with other nonlanguage activity into a single event. Clear instances of this are instructions and sets of commands. The grammatical and lexical distinctions between the various modes of discourse can often be related to the variable situational role assigned to language by the medium.

Third and last of the dimensions of register classification is "style of discourse," which refers to the relations among the participants. To the extent that these affect and determine features of the language, they suggest a primary distinction into colloquial and polite ("formal," which is sometimes used for the latter, is here avoided because of its technical sense in description). This dimension is unlikely ever to yield clearly defined, discrete registers. It is best treated as a cline, and various more delicate cuts have been suggested, with categories such as "casual," "intimate," and "deferential." But until we know more about how the formal properties of language vary with style, such categories are arbitrary and provisional.

The participant relations that determine the style of discourse range through varying degrees of permanence. Most temporary are those which are a feature of the immediate situations, as when the participants are at a party or have met on the train. At the opposite extreme are relations such as that between parents and children. Various socially defined relations, as between teacher and pupil or labor and management, lie somewhere intermediately. Some such registers may show more specific formal properties than others:

it is probably easier to identify on linguistic evidence a situation in which one participant is serving the others in a shop than one involving lecturer and students in a university classroom.

Which participant relations are linguistically relevant, and how far these are distinctively reflected in the grammar and lexis, depends on the language concerned. Japanese, for example, tends to vary along this dimension very much more than English or Chinese. There is even some formal difference in Japanese between the speech of men and the speech of women, nor is this merely a difference in the probabilities of occurrence. In most languages, some lexical items tend to be used more by one sex than the other; but in Japanese there are grammatical features which are restricted to the speech of one sex only.

It is as the product of these three dimensions of classification that we can best define and identify register. The criteria are not absolute or independent; they are all variable in delicacy, and the more delicate the classification the more the three overlap. The formal properties of any given language event will be those associated with the intersection of the appropriate field, mode, and style. A lecture on biology in a technical college, for example, will be in the scientific field, lecturing mode and polite style; more delicately, in the biological field, academic lecturing mode and teacher to student style.

The same lecturer, five minutes later in the staff common room, may switch to the field of cinema, conversational mode, in the style of a man among colleagues. As each situation is replaced by another, so the speaker readily shifts from one register to the next. The linguistic differences may be slight; but they may be considerable, if the *use* of language in the new situation differs sharply from that in the old. We cannot list the total range of uses. Institutional categories, unlike descriptive ones, do not resolve into closed systems of discrete terms. Every speaker has at his disposal a continuous scale of patterns and items, from which he selects for each situation type the appropriate stock of available harmonies in the appropriate key. He speaks, in other words, in many registers.

He does not, normally, speak in many dialects, since the dialect represents the total range of patterns used by his section of the language community. But he may, as a citizen of a nation, learn a second dialect for certain uses, and even a third and a fourth. In Britain, choice of dialect is bound up with choice of register in a way that is unique among the language communities of the world: it is a linguistic error to give a radio commentary on cricket in cockney or sing popular songs in the Queen's English. Many of the languages of older nations show some such mutual dependence between dialect and register.

In the newer nations, this is less apparent; instead there is often a tendency for the register to determine, not the choice of dialect, but the choice of language. Machine translation will in time make it possible for each community to use its own language for all purposes. Meanwhile, in many parts of the world, it is necessary to learn a second language in order to be equipped with a full range of registers; and foreign language teaching has become one of the world's major industries. By the time when it is no longer necessary for anyone to learn a foreign language in order to be a full citizen of his own community, it may well be recognized as desirable for everyone to do so in order to be a citizen of the world.

4

It is the individual who speaks and writes; and in his language activity dialect and register combine. In the dialect range, the finer the distinctions that are recognized, the smaller, in terms of number of speakers, the unit which we postulate as the dialect community becomes. Eventually we reach the individual. The individual is, so to speak, the smallest dialect unit: each speaker has his own *idiolect*.

Even the homogeneity of the idiolect is a fiction, tenable only so long as we continue to treat language SYNCHRONICALLY, in abstraction from time. As soon as we consider DIACHRONIC varieties of language, taking in the dimension of persistence and change in time, we have to recognize that changes take place not only in the transmission of language from one generation to the next but also in the speech habits of the individual in the course of his life.

Literacy retards linguistic change. But even in a community with a high literacy rate we can usually observe some differences in speech between successive generations. The individual member of the dialect community may retain his own idiolect unchanged; or he may adopt some features of the dialect of the next generation, even consciously adjusting his language performance to incorporate the neologisms of the young. At the least these will enter into his receptive use of language. In this sense the smallest dialectal unit is not the individual but the individual at a certain period in his life. Here we are approaching the theoretical limit of delicacy on the dialect dimension.

In the register range, the countless situations in which language activity takes place can be grouped into situation types, to which correspond the various uses of language. A corpus of language text in a given use is marked off by its formal properties as a register. Registers, like dialects, can be more and more finely differentiated; here again we can approach a theoretical limit of delicacy, at least in imagination, by progressive subclassification of features of field, mode, and style.

Ultimately, register and dialect meet in the single speech event. Here we have reached the *utterance*, the smallest institutional unit of language activity. In arriving through dialect and register at the "piece of activity," we complete the circuit which led from this in the first place, via the description of substance and form, through context, to language in use. Viewed descriptively, the speech event was the occurrence of a formal item "expounded" in substance. Viewed institutionally, it is an utterance in a situation, identifiable by dialect and register.

In the last resort, since each speaker and each situation is unique, each single utterance is also itself unique. But, as we saw at the beginning, the uniqueness of events is irrelevant to their scientific description, which can only begin when different events are seen to be partially alike. We become interested in one piece of language activity when we can show that it has something in common with another.

It is possible to group together a limited number of utterances according to what they have in common in dialect and register. One way of so delimiting a language variety is to retrace our steps a little up these two scales, to where we meet the individual as a participant in numerous situations. We can then define a set of language events as the language activity of one individual in one register. This intersection of idiolect and register provides an institutional definition of individual style.

Some registers are extremely restricted in purpose. They thus employ only a limited number of formal items and patterns, with the result that the language activity in these registers can accommodate little idiolectal or even dialectal variety. Such registers are known as RESTRICTED LANGUAGES. This is by no means a clearly defined category: some restricted languages are more restricted than others. Extreme examples are the "International Language of the Air," the permitted set of wartime cable messages for those on active service, and the bidding code of contract bridge. Less restricted are the various registers of legal and official documents and regulations, weather forecasts, popular song lyrics, and verses on greeting cards. All these can still be regarded as restricted languages.

The individual may still sometimes be recognizable even under the impersonal uniformity of a restricted language. This is often due to PARA-LINGUISTIC features: these are features, such as voice quality and handwriting, which do not carry formal contrasts. (In languages in which voice quality does carry formal contrasts it is not paralinguistic but linguistic.) Such features, like the phonetic and phonological characteristics by which an individual is sometimes marked out, will appear in a restricted language just as in an unrestricted register. Occasionally we even come across individual formal patterns in a restricted language: there is the bridge player who expects her partner, but not her opponent, to interpret correctly her private structural distinction between "one club" and "a club."

Except in restricted languages, it is normally assumed that individuals will differ in their language performance. In spoken registers the individual may stand out within his own dialect community through idiosyncratic phonetic habits. That he would of course stand out in a dialect community other than his own is trivial, since it is no more relevant to his linguistic individuality than the fact that an Englishman would stand out in France by speaking English. Even phonology gives some scope to individual variety: the present authors pronounce "transparent plastic" in three phonologically different ways. Graphological practice is more uniform: we no longer tolerate individual spelling, though punctuation is allowed to vary somewhat.

Nevertheless, even in written registers the individual stands out. His language is distinctive at the level of form. A person's idiolect may be identified, through the lens of the various registers, by its grammatical and lexical characteristics. This is how we recognize the individual qualities of a particular writer. All linguistic form is either grammar or lexis, and in the first instance it is the grammatical and lexical features of the individual writer's language, together with a few features of punctuation, that constitute his "style."

Individual style, however, is linked to register. It is the writer's idiolect, especially the grammar and lexis of the idiolect, in a given register. In so far as style implies literary style, register here means literary, including poetic, genre and medium. Style is thus linguistic form in interrelation with literary form.

If we refer to "the style of Pope" we presumably imply that there is something in common to the language of the *Essays*, the *Satires* and other works: that they constitute in some sense a single idiolect. In fact, style, like other, related concepts, must be recognized to be variable in delicacy: each genre, and each individual work, has its style. If it is assumed from the start that two texts are alike, the differences between them may be missed or distorted. It is a sound principle of descriptive linguistics to postulate heterogeneity until homogeneity is proved, and the study of literary texts is no exception. By treating the *Satires* and the *Essays* as different registers we can display the similarities as well as the dissimilarities between them.

Literature forms only a small part of written language, but it is the part in which we are most aware of the individual and most interested in the originality of the individual's language. At the same time it is of the essence of creative writing that it calls attention to its own form, in the sense that unlike other language activity, written or spoken, it is meaningful as activity in itself and not merely as part of a larger situation: again, of course, without a clear line of demarcation. This remains true whether or not the writer is consciously aiming at creating an individual variety. Thus the linguistic uniqueness of a work of literature is of much greater significance than the individuality of a variety of language in any other use.

The language activity of one user in one use: this concept will serve as the fundamental variety of a language. Such an individual variety is a product of both dialect and register, and both are involved in its study.

Dialectology is a long-established branch of linguistic studies. In Britain, which has lagged notably behind other European countries and the United States, large-scale dialect survey work did not begin until after the Second World War; but the three national surveys now being conducted at the universities of Leeds, Edinburgh, and Wales have amassed a large amount of material and the first results are now in the course of publication.

Serious work on registers is even more recent in origin. Very large samples of texts have to be subjected to detailed formal analysis if we wish to show which grammatical and lexical features are common to all uses of the language and which are restricted to, or more frequent in, one or more particular register. Such samples are now being collected and studied at University College London, in the Survey of English Usage under the direction of Professor Randolph Quirk; and related work is in progress at the universities of Edinburgh and Leeds. The study of registers is crucial both to our understanding of how language works and in application to literary analysis, machine translation, and native and foreign language teaching.

5

Languages in contact, dialects, and registers are three of the major topics of institutional linguistics. The fourth and last to be considered is the observation of the attitudes of members of a language community toward their language and its varieties. Here we mention briefly some of the attitudes that are relevant to the present discussion, with commentary where necessary.

Most communities show some reverence for the magical powers of language. In some societies, however, this respect is mingled with, and may be eclipsed by, a newer set of attitudes much more disdainful of the language, or of a part of it. The value judgments that underlie these attitudes may be moral or aesthetic, or they may rest on a pragmatic appeal to efficiency. The degree of social sanction they carry varies according to the language community; but whether the judgments and attitudes are social or individual, the individual expounding them frequently claims objectivity for his opinions. A typical formulation is, "Obviously it is better (or: "Everybody agrees that it is better") to say, or write, this than that, because" either "it's clearer," or "it sounds better," or "it's more correct". Less common, and more sophisticated. are "because the best people do it" and "because I prefer it".

The most far-reaching among such value judgments are those passed on whole languages. Those who argue that it is necessary for English to remain the language of government, law, education, or technology in former colonies sometimes claim, in support of their view, that the national languages are not suitable for these purposes. This reason is even put forward by the native speakers of the languages concerned.

The arguments for and against the use of English in such situations are complex; but this particular factor is irrelevant, because it is not true. This misapprehension, that some languages are intrinsically better than others, cannot just be dismissed as ignorance or prejudice; it is a view held by people who are both intelligent and serious, and can bring forward evidence to support it. Nevertheless it is wholly false and can do a great deal of harm.

Essentially, any language is as good as any other language, in the sense that every language is equally well adapted to the uses to which the community puts it. There is no such thing as a "primitive" language. About the origins of language, nothing is known; there is merely a tangle of conflicting speculation, none of it falling within linguistics. But there is evidence that speech in some form goes back at least a hundred thousand years, and quite certainly no society found in the world today, or known to us in history, represents anything but a stage long after language had become a fully developed form of social activity. If historians or anthropologists use "primitive" as a technical term, to designate a certain stage of social development, then the term may be transferred to the language used by a community that is in that stage; but this is *not* a linguistic classification and tells us nothing whatever about the nature of the language concerned.

Among the languages in the world today, there is no recognizable dimension of *linguistic* progress. No language can be identified as representing a more highly developed state of language than any other. Worora, in Western Australia, is as well adapted to the needs of the community which developed it as English is to our own. Neither language could be transferred to the other society without some changes, because the needs and activities are different; in both cases new lexical items would have to be added. But only the lexis would be affected, and only a portion of that. There would be no need for any changes in the grammar. At most there might be a statistical tendency for certain grammatical changes to take place over a very long period; but no simple change would be predictable in any given instance, none would be bound to occur, and certainly none would be necessary to the continued efficiency of the language.

In other words, the changes that would be necessary in Worora, for it to operate as a full language in the modern world, would be those that were also necessary to English as it was before the modern period. Middle English, even Elizabethan English, was not adapted to the needs of a modern state either. One could no more describe an electronic computer in Middle English than in Worora. Different languages have different ways of expanding their lexis, determined by their own internal structure: Chinese, for example, coins scientific terminology in a very different way from Japanese, being a language of a very different type. But all languages are capable of incorporating the lexical additions they require.

Whether or not it is economically feasible for the language of a very small community to be used as a medium for all the purposes of the modern world is of course an entirely different question, which each community has the right to decide for itself. It is worth pointing out that in the next generation machine translation will probably have become efficient enough, and cheap enough, to overcome the problem of translating all the material such a community would need to have translated from other languages. Whatever considerations may affect the choice of a language for science or administration in a newly independent nation, this at least can be made clear:

all languages are equally capable of being developed for all purposes, and no language is any less qualified to be the vehicle of modern science and technology than were English and Russian some centuries ago.

A type of language that particularly attracts adverse value judgments is the mixed language. As long as this remains a pidgin, it can be nobody's L1 and has not the status of a language; it exists only in certain restricted varieties. But in those communities which have developed a mixed language as their L1, the new language has thereby gained full stature and become a completely effective medium of language activity.

In any case a creole is only an extreme result of a normal phenomenon in the development of language: linguistic borrowing. There is no reason why a language with such a history should be less effective than any other. They are languages in the defined sense of the word; some of them are already used as literary media, and they would be fully viable as media of education and science. At present they tend to be more discriminated against than languages with a more conventional history. But there is no justification for discriminating against any language whatever. In most parts of the world today, including Britain, there has to be some measure of linguistic policy and planning; decisions may have to be taken, for example, to establish certain languages as the national languages of a new nation. What matters is that the real issues and problems should not be allowed to become clouded by false notions that one language may be objectively inferior to another.

Many speakers from communities whose language is in some or other respect denied full status, while they would not maintain that their own L1 was in any way inferior, and might vigorously reject such a suggestion, nevertheless in their language activity, as speakers, accept and thereby help to perpetuate its diminished status. In countries where English, or some other L2, is the mark of education and social standing, conversation in the government office or college staff common room normally takes place in English. Alternatively, if the L1 is allowed into these surroundings, no sentence in it is complete without at least one item from English.

This is sometimes explained on the grounds that the speakers do not share a common L1, as indeed they may not. It often is in countries which face a really difficult national language problem that a foreign language flourishes as a lingua franca. As is well known, many speakers from minority communities, whose language is not a strong candidate for national status, so firmly oppose the claims of any other language from within the country that they prefer to assign this status to a foreign language, which at least has the merit of being neutral. Probably this is at best a temporary solution; moreover there is reason to suggest that shelving the problem makes it more difficult to solve in the future.

But the lacing of L1 utterances with L2 items is not confined to multi-lingual societies. It is likely to happen wherever a foreign language is a mark of social distinction and the sole medium of language activity in certain registers. English probably occupies this position more than any other language. There are of course no grounds on which the linguist, who observes and describes this phenomenon, could object to it as a use of language: it works. But he may also reasonably point out that the use of English in situations for which the L1 is adequately developed, and of English items in L1 utterances where L1 items are available, tends to inhibit the progress of the L1 toward regaining its full status in the community.

6

Within our own language community, value judgments on English as a whole are relatively rare. Occasionally one hears it compared unfavorably with French, by those who subscribe to the myth sedulously kept alive by the French themselves, that French is a "more logical" language. What are extremely common, however, are value judgments on varieties of English: sometimes referring to registers but principally to dialects. The English language community, especially the British section of it, is almost certainly unique in the extent to which its members pass judgment on varieties of their language. One of the few other communities that at all resembles us in this respect is the French. The English attitudes are of course bound up with the socioregional character of our dialects; as such, they are class attitudes rather than individual attitudes. Nearly all the widely accepted value judgments can be traced to this origin, though some reflect it more directly than others.

It is at the new urban dialects, the varieties of the standard language with regional accent, that the most severe criticisms are leveled. The "original" dialects, now confined to the rural areas, have become quaint. They are tolerated; sometimes they may be praised, as "soft," "pleasant," or even "musical." And, somewhat inconsistently, though it is the rural dialects which provide the only instances of pairs of mutually unintelligible varieties remaining in England, it is often on grounds of incomprehensibility that criticism is directed at the urban dialects.

Perhaps the most frequent complaint is that formulated in various terms implying some sort of linguistic decay. The urban dialects are said to be "slovenly," "careless," or "degenerate." Similar terms were used about English and French in the nineteenth century, by those who regarded all recent linguistic change as a process of degeneration and decay. It is implied, and sometimes stated explicitly, that in the urban dialects there has been some loss of the communicative power of language.

This is simply nonsense. All the dialects, including all forms of standard English, are subject to change, both through the normal tendency of language to change and as a result of external factors such as movement of populations. Rate of change in language varies considerably, between different languages, between dialects, and at different times and places; even at different levels within the same variety of a language. English has altered rather strikingly over the last thousand years; the dialect now functioning as standard English is one of those that has changed the most, though it is difficult to measure comparative rates of change very accurately.

To the way of thinking that these attitudes represent, probably the slovenliest people in the world would be the French and the north Chinese: Parisian and Pekingese are the result of a high rate of change over long periods. There is no difference between the type of change undergone by these two languages and that which has affected the dialectal varieties of English, including the dialect that has become standardized and its modern regional derivatives.

There is actually no such thing as a slovenly dialect or accent. That the dialect of Sheffield or Birmingham had evolved in a different direction from one's own is hardly a matter for reproach, and anyone who labels it debased is committing two errors. First, he is assuming that one type of standard English preserves an earlier variety of the language from which others have deviated; this is not true. Second, he is claiming that there is merit in this imagined conservation; if there was, such merit might appropriately be claimed by the Italians, the Cantonese, and the Germans in reproach to their slovenly neighbors the French, the Pekingese, and the English.

Traditionally, this charge of debasement rested on straightforward moral grounds: it was wrong and irresponsible to let the language fall into decay. More recently the same imputed shortcoming has come to be criticized from another point of view, that of loss of efficiency. Since the fault is imaginary, the grounds on which it is censured might seem unimportant. But one comment at least is called for. Many people, including for a time some linguists, have been taken in by the spurious rigor of some pseudoscientific "measurements" of the "efficiency" of language. There is no evidence whatever that one language, or one variety of a language, can be more efficient than another. Nor is there, either in our intuitive judgment or yet in mathematics or linguistics, any means of measuring whatever such efficiency might be. Information theory, which has a place in the quantitative description of a language, implies nothing about the relative efficiency of languages or the effectiveness of language activity.

A second accusation has been brought against the urban dialects that is somewhat different from that of slovenliness, in either its moral or its utilitarian form. This is an aesthetic criticism. The dialects are labeled "harsh," "grating," "guttural"—this probably refers to the higher frequency, in some varieties, of glottal closure unaccompanied by oral stops—or simply "ugly."

Here the person judging is on safer ground, if he means that he personally does not like the sound of certain varieties of English: no one can dispute that. The formulation may be a general one, but there is a broad human tendency to generalize one's prejudices, and we probably all know people who would not distinguish between "I dislike the sound of Cardiff English" and "Cardiff English is ugly."

It is true that there is often a wide range of agreement in these aesthetic judgments. What is not realized, however, is that they are usually learnt. An Indian brought up in the Indian musical tradition will not agree with European judgments on European music, and a European who does not know the Chinese language and Chinese cultural values does not appreciate— that is, agree with Chinese judgments of—the sounds of Chinese poetry. Whether or not the adult ever does produce an unconditioned aesthetic response, in general what we like is as much a result of what we have learnt to like socially as of what we have grown to like individually. In language, we know already that people from different language communities respond quite differently to the aesthetic qualities of the dialects of a given language: a Persian or a Japanese not knowing English would be as likely to prefer Birmingham to RP as the other way round. The chief factor in one's evaluation of varieties of a language is social conditioning: there is no universal scale of aesthetic judgment. Those who dislike the Birmingham accent often do so because they know that their children will stand a better chance in life if they do not acquire it.

It is thus the socioregional pattern of English dialect distribution that gives rise to both the aesthetic and the moral or pragmatic value judgments on the urban and rural dialects, in so far as these judgments are held in common by a large section of our language community. In many countries such judgments either are not passed at all or, if they are, are regarded both by those who pass them and by those who listen to them as subjective expressions of personal taste. Foreign students in Britain listen in polite wonder while their teatime hosts in Leeds or Manchester explain how important it is that they should not copy the speech of their landladies: "everybody agrees," they are told, that this is an ugly, distorted form of English.

Not everybody does agree, in fact: such views seem to be most general among speakers of mildly regional varieties of standard English. But when these attitudes are shared by those who themselves speak the dialect, and no other, they become rather harmful. A speaker who is made ashamed of his own language habits suffers a basic injury as a human being: to make anyone, especially a child, feel so ashamed is as indefensible as to make him feel ashamed of the color of his skin.

Various courses of instruction are available in spoken English, under headings such as "Speech and Drama," "Elocution," and "Normal Voice and Speech." In general three different kinds of instruction take place. The first is concerned with techniques of speaking on the stage and in public; this is a form of applied phonetics, and is often very successful. The second is concerned with personal attainments such as voice quality and clarity in speech, and is often linked to aspects of social behavior under the general heading of "developing the personality"; these aspects lie outside the scope of application of linguistics or phonetics.

In the third type of instruction, which is again applied phonetics, the individual is taught to use some accent of English other than the one he has acquired naturally. This may be for particular professional purposes, as in the schools where dance-band leaders and pop singers can acquire the pronunciation considered appropriate to their calling, and the courses in which actors, for the purpose of character parts, may learn reasonable imitations of regional accents or at least a conventional Mummerset. It may, on the other hand, be for general social purposes; classes are held where those who speak with a regional accent can learn a pronunciation which they have found carries greater social prestige and better prospects of employment. Here the teaching is catering for social attitudes to language; but they are still recognized as social attitudes.

In the extreme forms of such accent teaching, however, the particular accent taught is extolled by those who teach it as "more beautiful" and "better" than any other. This accent is generally a variety of RP with a number of special vowel qualities and lip postures. Sometimes the speech of a particular individual is held up as a model for imitation; but more often an absolute aesthetic merit is claimed for the way of speaking that is taught. Some of the teachers have themselves been taught that there is a scale of values on which vowels may be judged, ranging from "bad and ugly" to "good and beautiful." The teacher is thus attempting to alter the speech of her pupils for reasons which seem to her sensible and obvious, but which are inexplicable to most of the pupils. The view that some sounds are inherently higher or lower than others on an absolute scale of aesthetic values has no evidence to support it, though it is of interest to phoneticians to know how widely it is held.

Perhaps the most uncomfortable of all the conflicts of approach between linguists and phoneticians on the one hand and teachers of "speech" (who may invoke the authority of these disciplines) on the other, are those centering on the subject commonly known as "Normal Voice and Speech." This subject is included within the curriculum for speech therapists, in which phonetics also plays a prominent part. "Normal" here is used prescriptively; the assumption is that one particular accent of English is in some way "normal," all others being "abnormal", and that the "normal" accent is RP. Such judgments, as we have seen, reflect no property of the accent itself, but merely the social standing of those who have acquired it.

If all the patients treated by speech therapists belonged to this group, the confusion would do no actual harm. But those with speech defects are a representative cross section of the whole population, the majority of whom do not speak RP, so that the background provided by "Normal Voice and Speech" is both culturally loaded and, for many, therapeutically irrelevant. Many phoneticians continue to provide courses for students of speech therapy because they hope to give an objective training which will counterbalance the prescriptive nature of "Normal Voice and Speech"; but the harnessing of two such differently conceived subjects in a single course can only be likened to an attempt to combine astronomy with domestic science, or perhaps rather chemistry with alchemy.

7

The English tendency to linguistic intolerance is not confined to strictures on the sounds of language. Value judgments also flourish in grammar. In grammar, however, the features subjected to those judgments are on the whole not dialectal. Many dialectal grammatical patterns pass unnoticed in speech provided the speaker is using the phonetics of RP: even such a markedly regional clause structure as that exemplified by "they've never been to see us haven't the Joneses" is tolerated in spoken English if the accent is an acceptable one. It would not on the other hand be tolerated in writing.

In grammar we have a set of arbitrary prescriptions and proscriptions relating to particular patterns and items. Some are applied to written English only, others to both spoken and written. Neither the prescribed nor the proscribed forms correspond to any particular regional varieties. As with the dialectal prescriptions, there are various ways of giving a bad name to the proscribed forms: they are called "slipshod" and "crude," sometimes simply "wrong." "Incorrect", taken from a different register, is sometimes used as if it was an explanation of "wrong."

In this context "slipshod" and "crude" are meaningless, and a native speaker of English who happened not to know which of a pair of forms was approved and which censured would have no evidence whatsoever for deciding. As effective language activity, there is nothing to choose between "do it as I do" and "do it like I do," just as soup has the same food value however it is eaten (or whether it is "eaten" or "drunk"). "Wrong" is a social judgment: what is meant is "the best people use this form and not that form." These are in effect social conventions about language, and their function is that of social conventions: meaningless in themselves, they exert cohesive force within one society, or one section of a society, by marking it off from another.

As we have seen, all languages have formally distinct varieties. What is unusual about the language situation in Britain is the extent to which rules are consciously formulated for what is regarded as appropriate grammatical behavior. Other communities have sometimes attempted to impose patterns of linguistic form, generally without much success; at the most, what is prescribed is the distinction between the spoken and the written language, some forms being rejected as inappropriate to the latter. Conventions in the spoken language are normally confined to lexical taboos: certain items are not to be used before children, strangers, or members of the opposite sex. In Britain, rules are made for speech as well as for writing, and the speaker's grammar contributes, alongside his phonetics and phonology, to his identification on the social scale.

Since "incorrect" linguistic behavior whether dialectal or otherwise may be counted against one in many situations, the solution chosen by many speakers, in face of the prevalent attitudes, is to acquire a second idiolect. Indeed so strong is the feeling that there are correct and incorrect forms of linguistic behavior that if one asks, as the present writers have asked many groups of university students, "What is the purpose of the teaching of English in English schools?" a frequent answer is, "To teach the children to speak and write correct English." The old observation that parents in the new dialect regions send their children to school so that they can be taught to "talk proper" is by no means out of date. If children have to learn new speech habits, it is the social attitude to their dialect, and no fault of the dialect itself, that is forcing them to do this: at least they need not be taught that their own speech is in some way inferior or taboo.

Some voices are raised against the prevailing attitudes, and some of the rules are occasionally called into question. Priestley once wrote, in *English Journey* (London, Heinemann in association with Gollancz, 1934, p. 290), "Standard English is like standard anything else—poor tasteless stuff." Hugh Sykes-Davies, in *Grammar Without Tears* (London, The Bodley Head, 1951, pp. 131–132), suggested reversing the polarity of prescription and proscription: "the use of the indirect cases of *who* should be avoided wherever possible by putting the preposition at the end of the sentence, and making *that* the relative, or omitting the pronoun altogether. It is better to say 'the man I found the hat of' than 'the man whose hat I found." But here the speaker is still being told how to behave; there is still a right and a wrong in language.

Serious interest in dialectal varieties of the language is fostered by such bodies as the Yorkshire Dialect Society, which publishes both literary work in, and academic studies of, the Yorkshire dialects, urban as well as rural. Detailed surveys of the dialects of England, Wales, and Scotland are, as has been mentioned, now well advanced. The Linguistic Survey of Scotland takes account of urban varieties of Scots; and although the English Dialect Survey has not yet turned its attention to the new dialects in England this is because the original, now rural, dialects are fast disappearing and must be recorded first. And teachers and university students seem to be becoming increasingly aware of the artificial and arbitrary nature of the conventional notions of "good English" and "bad English."

Interwoven with the highly prescriptive attitudes toward the linguistic behavior of individuals is a strong protective feeling for the language as a whole. Unlike the selective judgments, which are rare among language communities, the defensive "leave our language alone" attitude is very commonly found. Perhaps the most striking instance of this in Britain is the fierce resistance to any suggestions for spelling reform. So strong is the feeling against it that it seems unlikely at present that any orthographic revision of English will be undertaken for a long time.

Here again China provides an interesting example for comparison. Because of the complexity of the Chinese script, and the fact that it acts as a barrier to linguistic unification, at various times during the last fifty years suggestions have been made for its replacement by a phonological script; a number of versions have been devised, some using the roman alphabet and others not. In 1956, one romanized version was officially adopted as an auxiliary script for limited purposes, and its use has been very gradually extending; whether it will ever generally replace Chinese characters remains to be seen.

It has been argued that if the English expect their language to operate as an international medium they should consider reforming the script in the interests of foreign learners. On the other hand any project for doing so would face enormous difficulties. The linguist, as a linguist, does not take sides in this issue, though as a private citizen he may; but he is qualified to act as a consultant, and to make suggestions as to how best to revise the orthography if it is once decided to do so. Apart from this, the role of linguistics at this stage is to help clear the air for rational discussion of the problem, as of all the other problems that are raised by the complex and deep-rooted attitudes of the members of a language community toward their language.

STUDY QUESTIONS

1. Define the following terms used in the essay:

descriptive linguistics	dialect
institutional linguistics	pidgin
synchronic	creole
diachronic	lingua franca
register	restricted language
idiolect	paralinguistic features

2. What role do *field*, *mode*, and *style* play in the definition of a register? Give examples.
3. The difference between *dialect* and *register* is not always clear-cut. What dialects are typically associated with the following registers: the technical language of cowpunching? popularized folk singing? tough-guy talk in American films?
4. Give examples of language used for "phatic communion." Do you use different forms for different audiences—for people much older or much younger than yourself? Are any forms restricted to or more frequent in telephone conversations?
5. The use of [n] for [ŋ] in words like *talking*, *working*, and *learning* is sometimes a distinctive contrast between the English used by men and that used by women. In the Detroit Dialect Survey, for example, Shuy and his associates found that middle class women used [n] for [ŋ] in 15.3 per cent of the possible occurrences, whereas men from the same class made the substitution in 63.8 per cent. Similar contrasts between men and women were found for other social classes.[a]

[a] Roger W. Shuy, Walter A. Wolfram, and William K. Riley, *Linguistic Correlates of Social Stratification in Detroit Speech* (East Lansing, Mich.: mimeographed, 1967), p. 73.

Mention other such distinguishing features, including vocabulary differences, that define male and female styles of English. Can you think why profanity is fairly common in the oratory of women's liberation movements?

6. The authors notice "a minor tendency for Americans to regard themselves as using a different language from the British" (p. 11). What linguistic features in the essay itself identify the writers as British? Make a brief list of other differences you may have noticed between British and American English.

7. The authors suggest that "urban speech forms expand outward at the expense of rural ones" (p. 18). Why should this be so?

8. What legitimate functions are served by standardized or national languages? Are such functions the same for all linguistic communities? For example, would a standard language have the same status and functions in a multi-dialectal community as in a multilingual community?

9. In practical terms, how does *dialect* differ from *accent*, as the authors use these terms? How is the phenomenon of accent related to the emergence of a standard language? Would it be accurate to talk about accent in the United States? An Eastern commentator was reported to have said of President Johnson's speech: "I can't stand to hear foreign policy discussed in a corn pone accent." What did the commentator mean by accent? Did President Johnson *not* speak standard English?

10. The authors say of dialects in England: "Our dialects and accents are no longer simply regional: they are regional and social, or 'socioregional'" (p. 18). What does the defining term mean? Are the dialects of the United States also socioregional? Is standard English in the United States a socio-regional dialect?

11. Value judgments about varieties of English reflect the social attitudes of those who make them. Comment on the attitudes embodied in the following:

a. Slovenly speech habits are not peculiar to South Africa. They are partly the results of universal laziness which takes the line of least resistance, slurs vowel sounds and fails to pronounce consonants clearly. Partly, they are a kind of inverted snobbery—the fear that young people, especially, have of appearing to "put on side," to exhibit differences in their manner of speech from the companions with whom it is so important to them that they should be identified. Careful pronunciation has come to be confounded with affectation and an "Oxford accent."[b]

b. There is a wide variety of imperfect English being spoken by various groups in America. We Negroes have long objected to projection of this stereotype of our speech. Lately, Italo-Americans have rightly become vocal in their protest against the use of "Italian" English in the news media. Chinese Americans reject the "no tickee, no laundry" stereotype. And American Indians insist that their English vocabulary consists of more than the single word, "how!" And yet black folk, who pioneered in action against such distortions, are now being called upon to accept "black" English as a separate distinct language, as their "mother" tongue. By what linguistic legerdemain has this transmutation been achieved?

[b] G. Knowles-Williams, "English in South Africa, 1960," *English Studies in Africa* (1960):65.

I've long been aware of the search for survivals of Africanisms in the speech of Southern Americans of both races. Dr. Lorenzo D. Turner, a pioneer in this study, was a teacher of mine. As I now recall, he found such survivals minimal, except for Gullah. Melville J. Herskovits, another pioneer in this field, and some others have claimed a more extensive incorporation of Africanisms in American speech. But as far as I know the attempt to isolate the speech of the American Negroes as a separate language, has been a development of relatively recent years, certainly since World War II.

Any genuine effort to improve the speech of black folk, a longtime handicap, is vital. But such an effort is impaired by implication that an imperfect speech pattern is adequate. It simply is not. For those children whose parents have been denied adequate education, corrective instruction should, I believe, begin at the earliest stage of formal education—at nursery school and kindergarten levels and, certainly, not later than the first grade. But first it must be recognized that "black" English is a serious handicap, a relic of slavery and not a cherished African heritage like the famed Benin bronzes, the precious Congo wood carvings, the architectural stone structures of Zimbabwe, or the American Negro spirituals.[c]

c. When the children first arrived [at a preschool for economically disadvantaged children], they had, as expected, a minute repertoire of labels to attach to the objects they used or saw every day. All buildings were called "houses," most people were called "you." Although Urbana is in the midst of a rural area, not one child could identify any farm animals. As obvious as their lack of vocabulary was their primitive notion of the structure of language. Their communications were by gesture (we later discovered that one boy could answer some questions by shaking his head, but that he did not realize that a positive shake of the head meant yes), by single words (Teacher: "What do you want?" Child: "Doll."), or a series of badly connected words or phrases. ("They mine." "Me got juice.")

The pronunciation of several of the children was so substandard that, when they did talk, the teachers had no notion of what they were saying. . . . Although most of the children could follow simple directions like, "Give me the book," they could not give such directions themselves, not even repeat them. Without exaggerating, we may say that these four-year-olds could make no statements of any kind. They could not ask questions. Their ability to answer questions was hampered by the lack of such fundamental requirements as knowing enough to look at the book in order to answer the question, "Is the book on the table?"[d]

---

[c] The Editor, *The Crisis* (official organ of the NAACP), **78.6**(August 1971):174–75.

[d] Carl Bereiter, Siegfried Engelmann, *et al.*, "An Academically Oriented Pre-School for Culturally Deprived Children," in *Pre-School Education Today*, ed. Fred M. Hechinger (Garden City, N.Y.: Doubleday, 1966), pp. 113–15.

SOME HISTORICAL CASES OF LANGUAGE IMPOSITION

L. F. Brosnahan

No language is intrinsically more difficult to learn than any other language and children all over the world develop fluency in their mother tongues at about the same rate. But second language learning varies considerably in difficulty, partly because of the structural differences between the first and the second languages and, perhaps more important, because of the varying roles that the second language may play in community life. In multilingual countries such as Switzerland, every citizen in certain villages may speak two or more languages every day. These languages are likely to have varying functions, one perhaps being spoken at home or to adherents of the same religious faith and another being spoken at work or at school. This functional differentiation parallels the situation in monolingual countries where different dialects or speech styles may likewise vary according to a speaker's relations with his hearers.

Certain changes in social patterns may radically alter the role that different styles, dialects, or languages play in community life. Military and cultural conquest may lead to the introduction of a wholly new language, whereas more subtle shifts in the social structure may affect community beliefs about the nature of language appropriate to formal and informal communication in the culture. In the essay that follows, L. F. Brosnahan discusses some of the influences that result in major realignments in languages over a wide territory. Linguists and other social scientists do not yet fully understand why some communities resist these changes while others seem to welcome them. Albanian and Basque speakers, for example, resisted the spread of Latin over most of Europe during the Roman Empire, whereas Rumania and Spain underwent a linguistic revolution. By examining the social roles that languages play in both ancient and modern times, we can begin to understand the factors that enhance or inhibit the spread of linguistic uniformity in all cultures. Such investigations help explain the spread of English as an official language in Asia and Africa and the encroachment of a standardized national language on socioregional dialects. Professor Brosnahan begins and ends his essay by referring to the problem of national languages in the developing nations of Africa.

Reprinted from *Language in Africa: Papers of the Leverhulme Conference on Universities and the Language Problems of Tropical Africa, Held at University College, Ibadan*, ed. John Spencer. © Cambridge University Press 1963. Used by permission of the author and Cambridge University Press.

The situation of English and French, and to a lesser extent Arabic, in those areas of Africa that are the special concern of this Conference is not one which, in its general features, is unique. On the contrary, the imposition of an official or administrative language on the homelands of other languages is a phenomenon which has occurred on numerous occasions in human history. Yet, strangely enough, it does not seem to be one which has been much investigated. Linguists, so far as they touch on the topic, are almost always concerned more narrowly with the reciprocal influencing of the superstratum and substratum languages in sound, grammar or vocabulary, while historians tend to be primarily interested in the factors, political, administrative, etc., involved in the imposition and subsequently, and usually regard the linguistic situation as hardly worthy of comment.

It seemed worthwhile, therefore, by way of introduction to survey what seemed the salient features of a few of the better known occurrences of the phenomenon, in so far, of course, as they could be inferred.[1]

THE SPREAD OF LATIN

In some ways the most interesting and indeed also the best-known instance of the spread and development of a language in earlier history is that of Latin. It is the story of how, in the last few centuries before our era, the language spoken by an originally minor and insignificant group of people, living in an undistinguished area in the central part of the Italian peninsula, was carried over wide stretches of the then-known world at the heels of their conquering legions.

After an obscure beginning, Rome comes into history as it extends its control over the central area of Italy and to the outlying islands of Sicily, Sardinia, and Corsica. Northward, after several centuries of undecisive contacts with the Celts, Roman authority was extended to the foothills of the Alps with the establishment, and partial colonization, of Gallia Cisalpina toward the end of the third century B.C. Further afield, by 200 B.C. footholds were secured on the Dalmatian coast, and, after the Second Punic War, in Spain.

During the next century the land route from Italy to Spain was opened and secured by the conquest and removal of the Ligurians, the absorption of the Greek-founded colonies of Massilia, Antibes, etc., and by the pacification of the Allabroges and the Arverni. From the Provincia, Gallia Narbonensis, thus established, Roman arms in the last century B.C. carried imperial

[1] For this venture I have relied mainly on the standard histories and reference books. I have also received much help from my colleagues, and I am especially under obligation for bibliographical references, guidance, and advice to Dr. B. G. Martin of the Department of Arabic and Islamic Studies, and Mr. H. Guite of the Department of Classics, University College, Ibadan.

authority northward over the rest of Gaul and eventually across to a couple of obscure islands on the edge of the known world.

In an eastern direction, Rome early became embroiled in the internal warfare of the Greek states, and eventually annexed the Greek homeland. After two centuries of turbulence, Roman authority was firmly established in Illyricum. During the first century A.D., unrest and the growing threat of tribal unions against the empire led to Roman expeditions across the Danube and the subsequent establishment of the Province of Dacia with a number of garrison towns and colonies.

At its greatest extent, the Empire to the north and west reached from the Atlantic coast to the lower stretches of the Danube. Over all this area the pattern of Roman imperialism was similar. Military conquest and pacification was the first step—though often disturbed, *pax romana* was a general reality and an essential condition for all development. The establishment of strong points and garrison towns, connected by a network of excellent roads, was the second. A civil administration and the distribution of offices and plots of land to civil servants, settlers, and retiring legionaries followed. Commerce was facilitated and encouraged. An urban civilization rapidly developed, trades and crafts flourished, and wealth accumulated. Roman culture and Roman education were sought after, and successfully acquired, and some of the better-known figures of the intellectual and political life of the later empire, Seneca, Martial, and Quintilian, Trajan and Diocletian, to name only a few, were of provincial origin.

It was in these circumstances that Latin rapidly became the general language of the towns and of trade, and gradually extended its dominion along the roads between the towns and out into the countryside. This was a process which took several centuries, but it was, linguistically, highly successful. Fifteen centuries after the collapse of the Empire whose tongue it was, Latin survives over a large proportion of the former imperial area as the thriving languages of a number of peoples from the Atlantic Ocean to the Black Sea. Even in Dacia, the latest established of the Provinces, the first to be overwhelmed by the barbarian invasions and thus the shortest-lived, Latin, within two centuries, had so effectively displaced the original vernaculars of the region and become so firmly rooted itself that it survived the successive invasions of the Goths, the Huns and Avars, and the Slavs, to survive as the speech of Rumania and Moldavia down to the present day.

The story of Latin is different in the East. Roman power was extended over Greece itself by the middle of the second century B.C., and, subsequently, with the defeat of the last of the Seleucids in 63 B.C., to Syria. In the next two centuries the Roman Empire was pushed out to the banks of the Euphrates and down to the ruins of Babylon.

This was an area dotted with what are now merely romantic, but at that time were important, cities—Heliopolis, Palmyra, Tarsus, Seleucia—and provided with good roads and communications. Roman administration moved in, colonies were established, and legionaries settled in many regions of Asia Minor and the Middle East. But here Latin came up against another language, and one at least its equal, Greek; and, to put it simply, made no progress. On the contrary: the Hellenic culture of the Empire of the East and its Greek-speaking peoples swallowed Latin completely. Instead of the inhabitants of these new domains eagerly seeking the culture and speech of imperial Rome, it was the incoming administrators, settlers, and legionaries who sought to acquire the Greek language, and indeed prided themselves on their accomplishment. Over this wide area, which later, with the establishment of Constantinople, was even further extended, there survives no linguistic trace of *Imperium Romanum.*

THE CASE OF GREEK

At the dawn of history, as revealed in the Homeric poems, the Greeks seem to be a loose confederation of tribes established around the coasts and on the islands of the Aegean Sea, frequently quarrelling among themselves but united by a common language and culture, and able in stress to make common cause.

During the succeeding centuries the city-states and civilization, the culture, and the literature characteristic of Greece developed. But the Greek-speaking area was not at first significantly extended, and up to the second half of the fourth century B.C., save for a few colonies along the western Mediterranean, it was limited to southern Italy, the Greek peninsula, Macedonia, Thrace, the coast of Asia Minor, and the islands of the Aegean. In the fourth century B.C., however, Greece burst out from these limits and, under the brief but flashing leadership of Alexander, the bounds of the empire were pushed rapidly eastward. The Persian empire collapsed, and Alexander crossed the Euphrates and the Tigris, pressing on through Parthia and Bactria to the borders of India. Greek control of this empire was momentary, and ended in welter and confusion with Alexander's death; but under the empires subsequently emerging, particularly those of the Seleucids in Asia Minor and the Ptolemies in Egypt, Greek cultural influence spread.

The able Seleucid emperors, and to a lesser extent the Ptolemies, seem to have encouraged a policy of deliberate Hellenization. They were, of course, in the first generations, descendants of generals of Philip of Macedon and Alexander, and themselves Greek in education, culture, and outlook. But the basis of their policy was more pragmatic than sentimental: a body of Greek citizens to provide stability in the state and recruitment for the army. To this end, they did what they could to encourage Greek soldiers and Greek settlers to emigrate to Asia and Egypt; to the military colony with its land and its obligations to serve, or to the town, new or established, to form a leavening in the population and a cadre of administrators.

Though constant struggle, internal and external, made a mockery of this stability and exhausted the armies, the policy of Hellenization was remarkably successful. The Greek language, the Koine, as a lingua franca, and Greek culture made steady progress around the Mediterranean world. Greek teachers established themselves in the towns, Greek schools developed and Greek writers emerged—as Goad put it,

> To be civilized was to be Greek-minded, although not necessarily of Hellenic race. Every aspirant to honour vaunted his Greek culture, his knowledge of Greek literature and custom, with the clear sense that Hellenism stood for the higher intellectual life in contrast to the darkness and anarchy of barbarism. Hellas, by which was now meant the community of all Greek-minded men, had begun to realize that she had a mission—to civilize, or Hellenize, the world.[2]

The advancing influence of Rome in Asia Minor—by 63 B.C. as far as the Euphrates, and by A.D. 116, after Trajan's Parthian expedition, past Babylon to the mouth of the Tigris—did nothing to hinder the development of Greek. On the contrary, over the whole area, or at any rate over the territory as far as the Euphrates, Roman military authority provided the stability lacking in the previous period, a unifying force, which had the effect of facilitating the process of Hellenization. The result was, to quote Atkinson, that

> at the time of the foundation of Constantinople, in the 4th century A.D., Greek was practically the only language of the near and middle east with the exception of isolated pockets in remote regions. Thus it came about that on the separation of the eastern empire from the west, the Byzantines were Greeks in language and by tradition and the Greek language remained the language of that strange outlying bastion of the ancient world, which almost survived the middle ages and did not succumb till the middle of the 15th century.[3]

THE SPREAD OF ARABIC

A third example of a highly successful extension of a language is that of Arabic. Arabic is a Semitic language, related to Akkadian, Hebrew, Aramaic, and numerous other languages and dialects which have developed since earliest times in the cradle of human civilization. Our first traces of it seem to be Arabic-sounding names which have survived in works of Herodotus and other Greek writers. From just before the beginnings of our era, however, inscriptions begin, usually in Aramaic, with occasional, apparently Arabic words; but it is not until the third century that inscriptions in the language we have come to know as Arabic really begin.

Over the next few centuries various dialects of this language are discernible, but gradually, as is often the case in such circumstances, one of these dialects begins to emerge as a more generally used literary medium. The real

[2] H. Goad, *Language in History* (London, 1958), p. 33.
[3] *Chambers's Encyclopedia*, *vide* Greek Language.

flourishing of this dialect, however, was due to the most important event in the whole history of Arabic, namely its use by Mohammed and in the scriptures, the Koran. Carried by the wave of Islam, Arabic burst out of its homeland, and in an almost unbelievably short time flowed far and wide in Asia, Europe, and Africa.

Within the first decades of the Caliphate, Arab armies and religious fervor had conquered the whole of Syria, Iraq, northern Mesopotamia and Egypt. Successful excursions were made along the coast of North Africa as far as Tripoli. Persia was also added to the Islamic Empire, and the victorious armies pressed northward to the borders of Armenia and to the Oxus river. Under the Omayyads the process of expansion continued, Bukhara and Samarkand were taken, and an Islamic state established in Turkestan. To the east, Arab armies reached the Indus; to the west, almost all the coast of North Africa came under their control, and at the beginning of the eighth century the invasion of Spain began. By the middle of this century a unified Islamic Empire was at its greatest extent. It was, however, short-lived—to the features of internal dissension and political intrigue which seem to be inseparable from Oriental empires, there were added the schisms and disputes of Shi'is and Sunnīs—and over the next few centuries the Islamic Empire broke up into a series of independent Moslem states.

These states proved subsequently quite unable to offer any successful resistance to the Seljuk invasion from Asia, but the Arabic language was more successful. It is true that at the original edges of the Empire, in Asia, in Persia, and in Spain, Arabic gave way again to the vernaculars over which it had been imposed, but in the central regions the story is different. It absorbed all the other Semitic dialects of Arabia; save in the territories remaining to the Byzantine Empire, it displaced the Greek which had been the general *lingua franca* of the Levant for half a millennium; it dispossessed Coptic in Egypt, and it pushed back into the desert the Berber language of North Africa. It became, over the period from the eleventh to the sixteenth centuries, the general language of all the peoples from Aleppo to Aden and from Oman to Morocco.

It is still today the main, and in most places the only, language of this whole area. In addition, as the language of the Koran and of a rich literary inheritance, as the language of learning and of the law, it is the classical language of the religious and the educated through the whole Islamic world which stretches far beyond these boundaries. It is without question one of the great languages of the world.

TURKISH

One case which seems to me quite instructive for the general understanding of language imposition is that of Turkish. Turkish-speaking people from central Asia have invaded the Near East and Eastern Europe on several

occasions over a long period of time. The first major penetration in the
historical period was that of the Seljuks who emerged from Turkmenistan
in the tenth century, adopted Islam as their religion, and in the eleventh
century established an empire with its capital at Baghdad. Very rapidly
their authority was carried over Armenia, Georgia, much of Asia Minor,
and Syria. The original unity of this empire disintegrated in the twelfth
century, but was, in the subsequent invasions of Genghis Khan and the
Osmanli Turks, largely restored and under the latter, considerably extended.
By 1453, Constantinople was in Turkish hands, together with Bulgaria and
Serbia and much of the Balkan peninsula. Under Suleiman the Magnificent,
Hungary, Transylvania, and Moldavia were added in the west, and to the
east the boundaries of control were extended across Arabia and Persia. By
1517, Cairo and Egypt were also brought in, and parts of the North African
coast as far as Algiers. At its height, in the seventeenth century, before
disintegration set in, the Ottoman Empire, one of the great universal states
of modern times, stretched from the very gates of Vienna—the siege of which
was raised by the opportune arrival of John Sobieski, King of Poland—to
the Indian Ocean, and from Tunis to the Caucasus.

The decay of this extensive empire was by no means rapid. Its political
and military organization was at its best close-knit and stable, and nearly
three centuries of internal intrigue, external conflict—from the Russo-
Turkish wars of the eighteenth century through the various minor wars of
independence in the Balkans during the nineteenth century to the Arab
Revolt in the desert in the twentieth century—and economic exploitation,
especially in the nineteenth century, were necessary to bring the Ottoman
Empire to a collapse in 1918.

With the Turks came their language. Under the Seljuks it seems that
Turkish became the generally spoken language in Anatolia, gradually
replacing the Greek and any odd remnants of earlier languages. It must also
have been used more widely through the Middle East as an official and
military language in the various petty principalities which formed the
successors to the Seljuk Empire. Later, under the developing Ottoman
Empire, Turkish spread, as the official language, well into Europe and over
most of the Arabic-speaking peoples of the Near and Middle East.

Thus, as Lewis points out, from the tenth century to 1918, that is, for a
thousand years, Turkish was the official language of administration and
authority in the Near and Middle East. Indeed, there can be no doubt
about its authority:

So deep-rooted was the feeling that only the Turks were equipped by nature to
govern that in the fourteenth century we find a Mamluke secretary of Syrian birth
addressing the Arabs in Turkish through an interpreter rather than in his mother
tongue, for fear lest he should lose face by speaking the despised language of the
subject people. As late as the beginning of the nineteenth century Napoleon, when
he invaded Egypt, tried unsuccessfully to appoint Arabic-speaking Egyptians to

positions of authority and was forced to resort to Turks who alone could command obedience.[4]

Yet, as the Ottoman Empire crumbled, so did the domain of Turkish. As the Turks retreated to Anatolia, their language went with them. In no other part of that extended Empire, even after a very long period of implantation and sheltering, has Turkish taken root.

This must be reckoned a most unsuccessful case of an imposed language.

GENERAL FEATURES OF THESE CASES

We have now considered four cases of the subsequent history of a language imposed over an area of some considerable extent by military authority. In three of these cases the language so imposed has taken root, developed, and flourished and has become the general or only speech of much of its area, replacing previously used languages as the speech of the population. In the fourth case, no such development occurred.

What are the factors involved in this difference of history? Why are some languages successful, in the sense that they survive and spread, and others not? This is clearly a difficult and complex problem, but in the cases surveyed there are some features which may well be significant either in themselves or perhaps as pointers to the decisive factors.

There is assuredly no need for me to labor the point, in speaking to linguists, that nothing in the study of language, so far as I am aware, suggests that any internal features of the language concerned, features of phonology or grammar, or of vocabulary, are likely to be very influential in determining the outer history of that language. Important though these features are in some respects, the influence they can exert on the use of a language is certainly negligible in comparison with that exerted by the interplay of social, political, and military forces.

Several features are common to the four cases discussed. One is that each language was originally imposed on its area by military authority, and a second that, once imposed, it was maintained for at least several centuries by similar authority. These are likely to be basic factors. A language does not in ordinary circumstances spread over a large area of its own accord and even if, without its accord, so to speak, it is spread over a new area, it is unlikely to have any possibility of lasting influence on that area unless it is given a period of time of the order of a good many decades—at least sufficient time, we might surmise, for a minimum of two or three generations of the population of that area. The language of Attila and his Huns, for example, though imposed and widespread, was not maintained, and disappeared without trace in Europe.

The next point tends to differentiate those discussed above from numerous

[4] Bernard Lewis, *The Arabs in History* (London, 1950), pp. 158–59.

other cases of imposition of a language in a new area. This is that the area concerned is itself multilingual. Most of the occurrences of language imposition in Europe seem not to have this characteristic—Norse and High German in northern France, French in England, Polish and Russian in Lithuania, and so on. Few have been successful; Swedish in Finland is perhaps an example. The expansions of Latin, Greek, and Arabic, however, were primarily over areas in which a number of differing languages were spoken. This was only partly true of Turkish—it was true in the European sections of the Ottoman Empire, but not in most of the Asian or African sections, in which there was a linguistic unity conferred by the use of Arabic.

The significance of this factor of the multilingual nature of the area derives from the following considerations. By the very nature of the case, a military authority imposing a language is, seemingly always, simultaneously imposing some sort of political unity on the area concerned. Such political unity will tend to lead to increased contact of commercial, political, economic, or cultural nature among different sections of the united area; but such contact will take place, and in most cases will only be able to take place, through the medium of the imposed, superstratum language. The growth of trade within an empire, for instance, or the dissemination of a religious cult, will be facilitated by a common language, and the only one available is likely to be that provided by the invading empire.

If circumstances are favorable, the imposed language, as it percolates down to more and more of the population, may well be influential in the development of an awareness of belonging to something, a nation or an empire, which is much greater than the village or town of the immediate horizon. In this way such a language may play a considerable role in developing a national consciousness and unity among previously separate and perhaps even warring groups.

Conversely, it is probable that one of the major factors in the practically complete disappearance of Turkish from the Asian and African regions of the Ottoman Empire is simply that these regions were already provided with a widespread common language of communication in Arabic. In these regions Turkish was competing, so to speak, with a language which was already spoken over practically the whole area, was the common vehicle of literature, culture, trade, and of a unifying religion and law. This latter point is particularly stressed by Nallino.[5] Both the Arabs and the Turks were Moslems and, as such, subject in the field of private law to the universal Koranic law. Both the sources and the major works of interpretation and commentary of this law were in Arabic, and in this field it was Turkish which was the subordinate language, and the borrower. In the Arabic-speaking territories of the Ottoman Empire, in general, it was only at the higher levels of public and imperial administration that Turkish functioned as the official language of government.

[5] *Raccolta di scritti editi ed inediti III* (Rome, 1941), pp. 190–91.

It is true, on the other hand, that in the European areas of the Ottoman Empire no such common language existed, and yet Turkish has disappeared almost as completely. I am insufficiently acquainted with the turbulent and involved history of southeast Europe to be able to hazard more than a guess at the factors involved here, but on the surface it appears that there was relatively little coordination of resistance to the Turkish authority between different countries. The Greek War of Independence (1821–7), the Balkan risings of 1875–7, the Russo-Turkish wars, etc., all seem to have been largely separate and separated events generated by individual ethnic and unilingual groups.

A fourth feature in the success of an imposed language seems to be one of a more material nature. Knowledge of the imposed language by inhabitants of the area must confer advantages or benefits which are widely recognized in those societies to be advantages or benefits. In discussing this factor, we must be on our guard, I believe, against thinking of cultural advantages in a somewhat abstract and impractical way. The cultural advantages of a good education in Latin in the first century B.C. included, no doubt, for a citizen of Gaul, the intellectual pleasure of an understanding of rhetorical techniques and considerable practical skill, of an acquaintance with the epic poetry of Virgil, and so on; but these are not, in our imperfect world, the type of cultural advantage which is likely to stimulate the acquisition of a language very widely.

To the citizen of Gaul, no doubt, there were other considerations. Latin was the language of the Empire, of administration, and of trade, and a knowledge of it was a prerequisite to any sort of municipal employment—possibly, though information is scarce, even to recruitment in the Roman legions—and to most if not all other avenues of personal advantage in a concrete and material way. It will also, at any rate in the earlier stages of the Empire, have facilitated the acquisition of Roman citizenship, the rights and privileges of which were, again in the early period, quite substantial.

The Hellenization of Asia Minor was, we may be quite certain, stimulated by similar factors. We know that Greek settlers were encouraged by offers of land and of employment, and by the opportunities in trades, in education and so on, in the newly founded or revitalized cities. In general, I am inclined to suspect that much of what has been seen as the cultural advantages and superiority of a language, and particularly of the classical languages, is a somewhat rose-tinted interpretation, from what might be termed a dysvantage point several centuries later, of the opportunities of lucrative employment for those individuals who spoke them.

At first consideration it would seem that the spread of Arabic was relatively independent of any such substantial benefits to the speakers. Arabic flowed over the Near and Middle East with the banners of Islam; it was carried by people unified and driven by ideals of a religious faith; and a faith which was developed by a desert-living people, and in many ways reflected the simplicity of desert life. Indeed, there is telling testimony of the scorn in which worldly substance was held, in the story of the arrival of the Caliph Omar, the Prophet's brother-in-law, at Jerusalem, to receive the surrender of the city. He rode the five hundred miles across the desert from Medina with a single attendant, and carrying a bag of dates, some barley flour and a goatskin of water. He was met outside the city by his conquering generals dressed in the silks and spoils of victory, and in his fury at their betrayal of the desert life pelted them with dirt, stones, and abuse.

But this was in the first fresh vigor of Islam. In no other religion, perhaps, came the decay of simplicity so rapidly among those in the position to enjoy the material world. Omar's successor, Othman, the third Caliph, has his appointment characterized by Lewis as "a victory of the Old Meccan oligarchic ruling class which, though it had accepted the profits of the new religion far more readily than it had ever accepted its Prophet, still despised the former social outcasts who had hitherto dominated in Medina...".[6] If we allow a century and a half for the several generations which seem necessary for the establishment of a language in a new area, we are brought into the period of Harūn al Rashīd whose court, we infer from the *Arabian Nights' Entertainment*, was no less affected by luxury and indulgence than his empire by greed, plunder, and worldliness. It was as much in this milieu as in the field of religion and learning that Arabic became the common language of the Caliphate.

In this respect it seems likely that Turkish was deficient. On its introduction into the Middle East, Turkish was the language of a central Asian people with a well-organized and capable military system, but with no writing and with no material or intellectual culture to compare with the peoples of the areas invaded. In more than one way it was the Turks themselves who acted as the borrowers and acquired the benefits of an already existing culture. They were, however, rapid learners and, by the period of the great expansions of the Ottoman Empire, had developed a bureaucratic system capable of administering the conquered regions. But in the working of the administration, a sharp division was maintained between the rulers and the ruled, and this is likely to have been a factor of considerable importance in limiting the opportunities for outstanding individuals of non-Turkish origin. In this respect, the Ottoman Empire contrasts sharply with the other cases discussed, especially with the Roman Empire in which the peoples of the Provinces were gradually integrated, through citizenship, into the Empire and given equal opportunities; and with the Islamic Empire in which, again, a policy of conversion—by persuasion and fiscal pressure rather than by compulsion—was adopted toward subject peoples. The division in the Ottoman Empire is also reflected in the language situation: in the Arabic-speaking areas most of the administration seems, save at the gubernatorial level of the Pashas and the Beys, to have been conducted in Arabic. Religion and law were

---

[6] Lewis, p. 59.

also primarily based on this language, and, except in the Turkish-speaking provinces, trade, commerce, and finance were largely conducted in Arabic and Greek. To the generality of the Sultan's non-Turkish subjects, accordingly, a knowledge of Turkish was not a *sine qua non* of personal acquisition and advancement.

If we now refer to the four cases in which we are interested, those of Latin, Greek, Arabic, and Turkish, we may note that though in all four cases there are the features of military imposition in the first place and subsequent maintenance for a period of several decades, it is only in the former three that there is clear evidence of the multilingual nature of the area concerned and of the obvious advantages of a knowledge of the imposed language to the peoples of the area concerned. Over a large proportion of the Ottoman Empire there already existed a widespread and important language, and over the same Empire there seems to have been relatively limited opportunity for rising to the higher ranks of the administration. (It is a little ironical that the practice of conscripting boys from subject provinces to serve in the army and in administration, the *devshirme* system, resulted in political opportunity for the Christian or pagan slaves but not for the Moslem subjects of the Sultan.) And it is in the former three cases that the peoples over whom the languages had been imposed came to acquire them and use them in place of their own original tongues.

This, of course, is the crucial point—that the subject peoples should acquire the language imposed on them. We can easily imagine a case in which a language is imposed on a multilingual area, maintained while the area is unified politically and economically if not culturally, with a knowledge of it personally advantageous to the individual, and yet in which it is not acquired by the population. But whether such a case could occur in practice is, in my opinion, more doubtful. No doubt emotional factors play a role in accelerating or delaying the acquisition of an imposed language, but the instances in which such are most evident—those in which a single people are nationally oppressed and their cultural institutions forcibly repressed, with the result that their language tends to become a rallying point of fervent national opposition—are not really analogous, save perhaps for the Ottoman subjugation of the Balkan states and Armenia, to the cases we have surveyed. It is difficult to maintain an attitude of opposition to an imperial language over several generations when this offers solid material advantages and opens the gates to wider experience and development.

THE RISE OF AN ELITE

In the process by which an imposed language comes to be used by the general population, one feature is very obvious. This is that the development of the use of such language is a relatively gradual one: each member of the population does not come into contact with the new language to a similar extent and at the same time as all other members. Especially is this the case when the military imposition is against an actively hostile population and must proceed from an area or a number of centers secured and controlled. Though details may differ from case to case, it seems inevitable that during the process some part, or section, or class of the population will come to acquire the imposed language more rapidly than the rest.

The result of this process is the appearance of a particular social class, an *elite* or an *intelligentsia*. Particularly where this elite does not consist solely of the old ruling class or classes of the invaded area, the sociological consequences of its development may be extensive and far-reaching, since the class as a whole tends to function, in the first stages of the military invasion and pacification, as the interpreters and minor officials of the new authority; and subsequently and more generally as the medium through which the new language and any new culture is transmitted to the generality of the population.

In the instances discussed above, the gradual nature of the process of successful language expansion can be traced. In most of the Latin-speaking area, the Latin language conquered the towns first and spread only slowly out into the countryside where, in the more remote areas, the substratum languages were a long time a-dying. The indications are that the expansion of Greek in Asia Minor and Syria began with the Hellenized population of some at any rate of the important towns. In both of these areas an intelligentsia and administrative class developed. The evidence for it in the Latin-speaking area is mainly in the gradual extension of Roman citizenship over the inhabitants of the provinces, and in the surprising number of important figures in the later Empire, and in the center of this Empire too, who were drawn from areas outside Italy itself. In the Greek-speaking areas of Asia and Africa the existence and the vigorous intellectual life of the new class is testified to by writings on a variety of topics—literature, history, grammar, geography, etc.—which emanated from these territories in increasing amount from the third century B.C.

In the Arabic expansion also, the development of an intermediary class of "prophets and interpreters of the new" is clearly demonstrated in Egypt. The immediate reaction of the Arabs after their conquest of this country in A.D. 642 was to take over the Byzantine administration more or less intact and simply enjoy the revenues. But this did not last very long and within a century a new Arabic-speaking administrative class was developing. It was from this class that emerged the important and influential intelligentsia of succeeding centuries, the commentators on the law, the historians, the *littérateurs*, and so on.

Information about the language situation in administration in the Ottoman Empire is difficult to obtain. It is remarkable how little attention has been paid to language and its influence on the internal affairs of countries by historians—even in the very detailed analysis and description of the government of the provinces of the Ottoman Empire which is given by Gibb and

Bowen[7] language is not mentioned at any point. We can only surmise, from our knowledge of the political structure of the Ottoman Empire and from the course of subsequent events, that, though there must have been some Turkish-speaking officials between the governors and military commanders and the Arabic-speaking administration at the lower levels, no Turkish-speaking middle class as such developed.

THE POSITION OF ENGLISH IN NIGERIA

I cannot forbear to take a rapid look at English in Nigeria in the light of the preceding study.[8] In Nigeria, as in Gambia, Sierra Leone, and Ghana, English is the administrative language. Its history and development are generally similar in all these countries, and analysis reveals several of the features observed in the preceding survey.

In Nigeria, English gradually replaced Negro-Portuguese as the trade language of the coast during the eighteenth century, but remained very much limited to the coast until the second half of the nineteenth century. This was a period of missionary and commercial penetration, which ended with the British taking over control and setting up an administrative system with English as its language over the whole country. The period of the maintenance of English is thus not very long, about a century in the colonies of the south, but only half this in the north.

The area is multilingual. The number of languages spoken in Nigeria is not even approximately known, but seems unlikely to be less than 150.

The British authority in Nigeria implemented the usual policy of temporally extended empires on arrays of subject peoples, namely, that after pacification it organized an over-all administration and control, it promoted and developed internal trade and communication, and it welded peoples of differing language, religion, and background into a unity; and indeed, particularly in the case of Nigeria, apparently a more effective and stable unity than many outside observers were ready to allow a few years ago. In the process many factors have been involved, but language has been one of them. Ironically enough, the spread of the ideas of independence and nationalism through Nigeria, as through the other colonial territories in West Africa, and the successful organization of resistance to European imperialism, was only possible by means of the common languages imposed on these territories by the European powers.

The next feature, that the language must provide opportunity and

[7] H. A. R. Gibb and H. Bowen, *Islamic Society and the West I* (Oxford, 1957), pp. 137–73.

[8] With the picture sketched here it would be interesting to compare the results of the policy adopted by France in her West African territories, a policy which, in essentials, recalls that of Imperial Rome: deliberate encouragement of the French language by its exclusive use in administration, education, and in the army; and, subsequently, gradual extension of citizenship in metropolitan France.

advantage, is strikingly the case of English in Nigeria. English is the language of commerce and the law, of politics and the administration, of education and of culture at all levels above the local. An adequate knowledge of English is an indispensable requirement for anyone to rise above or to live in any wider context than the village.

And there is no question but that English is widely used. Two points may be noted. First, its use is primarily an urban phenomenon. Its strongholds are the bigger towns, especially those like Port Harcourt, Lagos, Ibadan, and Kano which, because of their commercial and industrial importance, are the centers of the urban drift. We are reminded of the role of the towns and cities in the establishment of Latin in Europe and of Greek in the Levant.

The second point is the rapid development of an English-speaking *elite*. Missionary policy since the very beginnings about the middle of the last century, and Government policy from 1880, has been to foster education in English. This has resulted in the growth of a small but important group of professional men and clerical workers, and it is from this group that the present governing class has largely been recruited. But the tremendous expansion of education since 1940, and especially since 1950, has opened entry to this class to a very wide range of the population—about, or a little more than, half the estimated number of children of school age in the country are enrolled in schools—and thus in a position to acquire some knowledge of English.

It would appear, accordingly, that all the features characteristic of successful implantation and expansion of a language in a new area are present. English has been implanted, has taken firm root, and is expanding. This is realized and its significance understood by responsible opinion. After a rather futile debate on national language in the Federal House of Representatives, the following appeared in the Nigerian *Daily Express* of 23 November 1961 (a newspaper by no means noted for its favoring of England or of things English):

Parliament should be more careful about involving itself in the language tangle into which it is now being drawn. English is the accepted official language, the one outward expression of all that unites the various peoples in this country . . . to seek to replace English with some vernacular at a particular date-line is asking for more than the greatest nationalist of them all can handle. The difficulties are not all of translating text books and scientific formulae or even of cash. What happened in India and more recently still in Ceylon should make the protagonists of this motion have second thoughts.

STUDY QUESTIONS

1. Brosnahan notes on p. 43 that the Greek-speaking people in the eastern part of the Roman Empire did not use Latin for cultural and governmental functions, whereas others in the Empire were enthusiastically adopting it. Why do you suppose this linguistic resistance took place?

2. The Lingua Franca was a contact language—literally "the language of the Franks"—that during medieval times spread from the shores of the Mediterranean in France and Italy to the eastern trading areas in Greece, Turkey, and along the coast to Egypt. By means of this language of sea-going traders, many words of Greek, Turkish, and Arabic origin entered the Romance languages. Today, linguists use the term *lingua franca* as Brosnahan does (p. 44) for any language used as a form of communication between peoples of different linguistic backgrounds. What factors stimulated the growth of Latin, Greek, and Arabic as lingua francas? Why did Turkish not follow the same development in the Ottoman Empire?

3. Brosnahan claims that imposed languages are more rapidly adopted in multilingual areas than in monolingual ones. This suggestion is borne out in modern Brazil where German immigrant communities adopt Portuguese more rapidly in regions where several languages are in regular use than in those where only Portuguese is used. Imagine yourself in the position of a German-speaking immigrant and suggest why this should be so.

4. The rise of a new elite is an important factor in language imposition as the cases described by Brosnahan show. What effect is a high rate of social mobility in a culture likely to have on the prestige language, dialect, or style?

5. Which of the factors described by Brosnahan is likely to encourage the preservation of languages other than English in America? Consider such cases as those of Yiddish, Pennsylvania Dutch, Puerto Rican Spanish in New York City, Norwegian in the Upper Midwest, Cantonese in San Francisco.

6. English gained footing and status in India as one result of Empire. Its use continues to the present day, after independence, as a supplementary official language, although the Indian constitution called for its replacement by Hindi in 1965. What factors might account for its continued use?

7. Historically, standard languages spread at the expense of regional and socioregional dialects. Are the forces that favor such spread similar or different from those that encourage the adoption and spread of an imposed language?

8. Brosnahan notes that some concrete advantage must accrue to individuals in order for them to be motivated to learn and use an imposed language. Might the same generalization apply to learning a prestige dialect? It is often reported, and usually with some amazement, that ghetto-dwelling blacks in the United States retain nonstandard dialects even while admitting the greater prestige of standard English. Can you explain why this might happen?

THE ENGLISH LANGUAGE AND THE ORIGINS OF AFRICAN NATIONALISM

Ali A. Mazrui

The extent of a speaker's skill in mastering a variety of styles, dialects, and languages is directly related to his perception of their importance in his life. Children who emigrate to a region where the language of their parents is not spoken will quickly transfer their linguistic allegiance and typically cease to expand the resources of their native language beyond the styles appropriate to home life. Adults will learn enough of the new language to suit their immediate needs; if a "thick" foreign accent is acceptable in their new surroundings, their progress in the new language will stop once that level of acceptability is reached. If, on the other hand, a more adequate mastery of the new language is required, that level of acceptability can often be reached. Hence it is no accident that German-born psychiatrists often retain many traces of their linguistic origins; in America, at least, such an accent may enhance their professional status. German-born rocket designers, perhaps aware of American misgivings about their work in Hitler's Reich, are much more likely to develop near native-speaker proficiency in English.

Adopting a new style, dialect, or language as one's own carries with it important consequences. As Mazrui shows in the following essay, English came to be considered an appropriate vehicle for nationalistic aspirations in Africa rather than being regarded as the sole property of the white colonists. Conflicting attitudes about English, however, are not difficult to find. To Gandhi, the English language symbolized subservience, and he wrote in 1938 "Surely it is a self-demonstrated proposition that the youth of a nation cannot keep or establish a living contact with the masses unless their knowledge is received or assimilated through a medium understood by the people. Who can calculate the immeasurable loss sustained by the nation owing to thousands of its young men having been obliged to waste years in mastering a foreign language and its idiom, of which in their daily life they have the least use and in learning which they had to neglect their own mother tongue and their own literature? There never was a greater superstition than that a particular language can be incapable of expansion or of expressing abstruse or scientific ideas. A language is an exact reflection of the character and growth of its speakers." [a]

Feelings like Gandhi's have led to the expansion, in India, of education in

Reprinted from *Mawazo*, Vol. 1, No. 1, by permission of the author. Copyright Ali A. Mazrui 1967.

[a] From *Young India*, as quoted in S. J. Tambiah, "The Politics of Language in India and Ceylon," *South Asian Studies*, **1**.3(1967):225.

the student's mother tongue and the relegation of English to a supplementary rather than a dominant role. But the supplementary role is not without importance; Gandhi's activities in quest of independence were aided by his eloquence in English, and later figures important in India's political and intellectual life have appreciated the utility of a "window on the world" opened through use of a world tongue. Mulk Raj Anand agrees with Gandhi that vernacular education is necessary, and he smarts from Indians' use of "the King-Emperor's English"—a utilitarian English learned haltingly from the tongue of the master. Yet he sees a place for English in India:

> But that the English language which inspired us with the ideals of freedom, which opened up splendid vistas of democracy, which influenced and enriched the techniques of our literatures, which gave us a new and vital branch of writing—the Indo-Anglian school of literature —and which served as a gateway to the heart and mind of Europe and America—that this English language should be thrown aside in a fit of sentimental chauvinism! That would, indeed, be suicidal for us, because that would be not only to deprive ourselves of a life-giving influence but also to cut one of "our major lines of communication with the outside world." This English we prize so much, as against the King-Emperor's English, was never the language of our conquerors, for it is not they who cherished it or brought it into our lives: no, it was the language we ourselves took from the heart of England, not as an act of submission, but through a genuine love of its graces. And, even after the last Englishman has left the shores of India, our affection for it will remain undimmed.[b]

Many of the things which one can say about the significance of English for the development of African ideas one can also say about the French language. But there are certain areas of thought where one of these languages has been more important than the other. Among the areas where English has been particularly significant is in the development of certain notions of self-determination.

But ideas of self-determination have their roots in ideas of "freedom" at large. The minimal sense of freedom is the condition of *not being a slave*. The story of African liberation therefore first takes the form of liberation from slave traders and slave owners before it takes the form of opposition to colonial rule.

What is the place of the English language in either form of liberation?

A background factor to be borne in mind is that the Anglo-Saxons[*] were

---

[b] *The King-Emperor's English, or The Role of the English Language in the Free India* (Bombay: Hind Kitabs, 1948), pp. 46–47.

[*] The term *Anglo-Saxon* is here definable by combining a linguistic criterion with a criterion of color. In other words, "Anglo-Saxons" in this article are white people who

preeminent both in the acquisition of slaves and in building empires. It later became a matter of direct political significance not only that England had had the biggest single share of Africa in the "scramble" as a whole, but also that the largest group of Negroes in the New World were English speakers.

What might also be remembered is that these same Anglo-Saxons who took the lead in enslaving Negroes were later to produce from their ranks the foremost champions of abolition. In England they produced William Wilberforce. In the New World they produced John Brown and Abraham Lincoln.

But what was to be done with the Negroes once they were freed from slavery? The term *colonization* came into the vocabulary of Negro politics. Today the word itself connotes Africa's loss of freedom on the advent of imperial rule. But in much of the nineteenth century the term *colonization* was more closely associated with the *liberation* of the Negro outside Africa— and his repatriation back to Africa. Here again the English-speaking world stands out as exceptional. There were Negro slaves in Portuguese Brazil, in Spanish Cuba, and in the Arabian peninsula. But the most enduring "Back to Africa" projects were in the English-speaking world. Why did this happen?[1]

Two factors help to form part of the explanation. On the credit side is Anglo-Saxon liberalism. The same human impulses which demanded freedom for the Negro slave went a step further—and demanded that he be taken back "home" from where he had been uprooted. There was a humanitarian logic in the naiveté of taking the Negro back to his ancestral soil.

But there was also a less favorable side to Anglo-Saxon impulses. To a greater extent than either the Portuguese of Brazil, the Spaniards of Cuba, or the Arabs of Saudi Arabia, the Anglo-Saxons were unhappy about racial integration. No people managed to combine more effectively such a high degree of humanitarian sensitivity with such a highly developed sense of racial exclusiveness. Both the humanitarianism and the racial exclusiveness contributed to the idea of repatriating Negroes back to Africa. The same Lincoln who felt so passionately about emancipating slaves subscribed to the idea of encouraging Negroes to return to their ancestral land. Nnamdi

---

speak English as a first language. Please refer also to my companion piece, "The English Language and Political Consciousness in British Colonial Africa," *Journal of Modern African Studies*, 4, iii (1966). I am indebted to my wife for guidance on some aspects of language, with special reference to French. [For a further discussion of this subject, see this writer's "Some Sociopolitical Functions of English Literature in Africa," in *Language Problems of Developing Nations*, eds. Joshua A. Fishman, *et al.* (New York, 1968), pp. 183–97. *Eds.*]

[1] For a brief discussion of the Afro-Brazil story see Jose Honorio Rodrigues, "The Influence of Africa on Brazil and of Brazil on Africa, "*Journal of African History*, Vol. III, No. 1, pp. 49–67. See also James C. Brewer, "Brazil and Africa," *Africa Report*, Vol. 10, No. 5, May 1965.

Azikiwe of Nigeria reminded us of this latter side of Lincoln in a book he wrote in the early 1930s. Azikiwe recalled that on meeting a deputation of American Negroes on August 14, 1862, Lincoln said:

You and we [Caucasians] are different races. We have between us a broader difference than exists between almost any other two races. . . . There is an unwillingness on the part of our people, harsh as it may be, for you free colored people to remain with us. . . . I suppose one of the principal difficulties in the way of colonization is that the free colored man cannot see that his comfort would be advanced by it. . . . For the sake of your race you should sacrifice something of your present comfort for the purpose of being as grand in this respect as the white people . . . General Washington himself endured greater physical hardships than if he had remained a British Subject.[2]

Such sentiments concerning Negro repatriation had by then already started to affect the African continent. British humanitarianism was giving birth to Sierra Leone: American philanthropy was helping the creation of Liberia. Both countries came to assume symbolic significance for African nationalism later on. And both have their place in the history of the English language in the continent.

A glance at the significance of Sierra Leone might form a useful starting point. Edward W. Blyden, the nineteenth-century Negro intellectual and precursor of Negritude had this to say about Sierra Leone:

It is a very interesting fact that on the spot where Englishmen first began the work of African demoralization, Englishmen should begin the work of African amelioration and restoration. England produced Sir John Hawkins, known to Sierra Leone by his fire and sword policy. Two hundred years later, England produced Granville Sharp, known by his policy of peace, of freedom, and of religion. The land of Pharaoh was also the land of Moses. Alone, amid the darkness of those days stood Sierra Leone—the only point at which the slave trade could not be openly prosecuted—the solitary refuge of the hunted slave.[3]

But, as we have already intimated, Sierra Leone is a part not only of the history of freedom in Africa, but also of the spread of the English language in West Africa. In his book on the origins and future of Pan-Africanism, George

[2] Cited by Azikiwe in *Nigeria in World Politics* (London: Arthur H. Stockwell, 1934), pp. 234–35. For the quotation from Lincoln, Zik refers to Nicolay and Hay, *Abraham Lincoln, Complete Works* (New York, 1894), Vol. 1, 222–25.

[3] Edward W. Blyden, *Christianity, Islam and the Negro Race* (London: W. B. Whittingham, 1888), p. 223. Born on a West Indian Island in 1832, Blyden went to New York at the age of fifteen seeking higher education. The Colonization Society of New York offered him a free passage to Liberia where he landed in January 1850. There he got an education in classics and languages. He later became professor and President of Liberia College, Secretary of State for the Interior and served twice as Liberian Ambassador to the Court of St. James. For Blyden's contribution to the concept of an "African Personality" see Robert W. July, "Nineteenth Century Negritude: Edward W. Blyden," *Journal of African History*, Vol. V, No. 1, pp. 73–86.

Padmore tells us about the role of English among the freed slaves in Sierra Leone in those early days. Padmore says:

The Creoles of the Colony rapidly became the first Westernized community in Africa. Drawn as they were from the heterogeneous elements, cut adrift from their ancestral cultures, traditions and customs, the repatriates intermarried and adopted the English way of life. The Queen's language became their normal medium of communication.[4]

But the Queen's language came to be radically Africanized in Sierra Leone. English gradually became *Krio*, the lingua franca between the Creoles and the indigenous tribes in and around Freetown. Blyden described Krio as a "convenient bridge" between African dialects and the English language.[5]

But the impact of Sierra Leone on West Africa as a whole was perhaps more in the spread of the English language itself than of Krio. There did arise people like Bishop James Johnson who championed the adoption of Krio as the national language of Sierra Leone and as the medium of instruction in schools. But the weight of opinion in Sierra Leone, among both Europeans and Creoles themselves, was against such a move. Indeed, it was almost part of the educational policy of the country to try and eradicate Krio.[6]

A more concrete contribution which Sierra Leone made to the spread of English in West Africa came to be centered on Fourah Bay College, established in 1827 as virtually the first modern institution of higher learning in sub-Saharan Africa. Year after year the College sent out Africans to propagate the Gospel and to spread liberal education in the English language in different parts of Western Africa.

Partly out of the stimulus of the Gospel, and of Western liberal education, a new Negro ambition came into being. In discussing this ambition we might start with a remark made by a great user of the English language, George Bernard Shaw. In April 1933, Shaw said something which, in an important way, touched the deepest ambition of the nascent African nationalism at the time. Shaw said: "Civilizations grow up and disappear, to be replaced by other and stronger civilizations. For all I know, the next great civilization may come from the Negro race."[7]

It is possible that the reason why Shaw illustrated with the Negro race was because in his time that race was regarded as the least likely source of a great civilization. And perhaps precisely because of that prejudice, this socialistic

---

[4] *Pan-Africanism or Communism? The Coming Struggle for Africa* (London: Dennis Dobson, 1956), p. 38.

[5] *Christianity, Islam and the Negro Race, op. cit.,* p. 245.

[6] See letter from the Reverend James Johnson, the African Bishop, in *Sierra Leone Weekly News,* 22 February, 1908. The letter is partially reproduced in Christopher Fyfe's *Sierra Leone Inheritance* (London: Oxford University Press, 1964), pp. 221–22. See also Fyfe, *A History of Sierra Leone* (London: Oxford University Press, 1962), pp. 468–69; and Hollis R. Lynch. "The Native Pastorate Controversy and Cultural Ethno-Centrism in Sierra Leone, 1871–1874." *Journal of African History,* Vol. V, No. 3, 1964, pp. 395–413.

[7] *The New York Times,* April 13, 1933.

Irishman wanted to make sure that the Negro was credited with the same human potential as anyone else.

Whatever the real motives of Shaw's line of speculation, however, it was a line which evoked a response from Nnamdi Azikiwe. For a member of the most humiliated race in recent history the vision of Africa as possibly the next great source of human regeneration was both frustrating and inspiring. It was frustrating because it was so hypothetical and long-term. It was inspiring because such an eventuality would be the ultimate vindication of the Negro's potential. It might well have been considerations such as these which made Azikiwe embrace Bernard Shaw's line of speculation. And yet at that time the only country in Azikiwe's part of Africa which was already independent was not Sierra Leone, but Liberia. To George Padmore, Sierra Leone might indeed have been "the greatest living monument to the memory of the Abolitionists."[8] But to Azikiwe the greatest symbol of the coming Africa was Liberia, given that it was the only sovereign country at the time. Azikiwe saw Liberia as "*the nucleus of black hegemony . . .* the soil where the seed of an African civilization is destined to germinate."[9]

Nor was Azikiwe unusual in his romanticism about Liberia. The country retained this special place in the imagination of West African nationalists well into the 1940s. In 1945, when voices were saying that it was time that the next Pan-African conference was held in Africa, the influential West African Students Union in London wrote to W. E. B. Du Bois urging that "the fifth Pan-African Congress" should be held in Liberia.[10] In his autobiography Nkrumah, too, confesses to having once been inspired by Liberia as a symbol of African sovereignty. "I judged Liberia not from the heights it had reached, but from the depths whence it had come."[11]

In the context of the history of the English language in Africa, Liberia, too, holds a significant position. It is essentially the only country in Africa which owes its English to the New World rather than directly to British rule in the continent. And today Liberia is the only black African country in which English is a native language—at any rate English is the first language of the country's black elite.

Historically, Blyden had seen broad linguistic and cultural implications in the very territorial contiguity between Liberia and Sierra Leone. In the 1880s Blyden had made the following observations:

For 200 years, the Portuguese language was spoken along this coast. Villauit says when he landed here, at Cape Mount and at Cape Mesurado in 1666, "all

---

[8] *Pan-Africanism or Communism? Op. cit.,* p. 23.

[9] Azikiwe, *Liberia in World Politics* (London: Arthur H. Stockwell, 1934), p. 395. The italics are original.

[10] See George Padmore (ed.) *History of the Pan-African Congress* (first published 1947) (London: Hammersmith Bookshop). Second edition 1963.

[11] *Ghana, the Autobiography of Kwame Nkrumah* (Edinburgh: Thomas Nelson and Sons, 1957), p. 184.

the Negroes who came to trade spoke the Portuguese language." But the English language has everywhere driven it out. . . . We have a continuous English-speaking Negro state from the Sierra Leone River to the San Pedro River. . . ."

Blyden went on to philosophize about the suitability of the English language for Africa as compared with either Portuguese or French. He saw English as a mongrel language—a product of the mating of diverse cultures. It was less of a stickler for purity than its Latin neighbors tended to be. The English language was preeminently a language of accommodation and pragmatic synthesis. It was therefore the more suitable as a lingua franca in multilingual situations. In Blyden's words:

English is, undoubtedly, the most suitable of the European languages for bridging over the numerous gulfs between the tribes caused by the great diversity of languages or dialects among them. It is a composite language, not the product of any one people. It is made up of contributions by Celts, Danes, Normans, Saxons, Greeks, and Romans, gathering to itself elements . . . from the Ganges to the Atlantic.[12]

This function of English as a vehicle of communication between Africans of different tribes was later to take a continental dimension. The language was to play a succession of important roles in the movement which came to be known as Pan-Africanism.

But in discussing the origins of movements for unity in Africa one ought to draw a distinction between Pan-Africanism and *Pan-Negroism*. Pan-Negroism is that movement, ideology, or collection of attitudes which are primarily concerned with the dignity of the black people wherever they may be. The banner of Negroism therefore brought sub-Saharan Africans and Afro-Americans together. Pan-Africanism, on the other hand, gradually became an essentially continental movement within Africa itself. And from the point of view of Pan-Africanism the Arabs of North Africa are today more important than the Negroes of the United States. In fact, Tom Mboya of Kenya has even suggested that the proof that Pan-Africanism was not a racial movement was the fact that the Organization of African Unity included Arab as well as black states.[13]

Historically, Pan-Africanism was born out of Pan-Negroism. But while the loyalties of Pan-Negroism were, as Azikiwe put it, "ethnocentric," those of Pan-Africanism became essentially intracontinental.[14]

---

[12] "Sierra Leone and Liberia," *Christianity, Islam and the Negro Race, op. cit.*, pp. 243–44.

[13] *Freedom and After* (London: Andre Deutsch, 1963), p. 231.

[14] See Azikiwe "The Future of Pan-Africanism, *Présence Africaine*, Vol. 12, No. 40, First Quarter, 1962, pp. 7–12. For a historian's view of the influence of American Negroes on African thought see George Shepperson "Notes on Negro American influences on the emergence of African nationalism," *Journal of African History*, Vol. 1, No. 2, 1960, pp. 299–312. See also Shepperson's article, "Abolitionism and African Political Thought," *Transition* (Kampala), Vol. 3, No. 12, January/February 1964, pp. 22–26.

Among the towering founding fathers of Pan-Negroism must be included American Negroes like W. E. B. Du Bois and West Indians like George Padmore and, indirectly, Marcus Garvey. But racial affinity alone could not have converted these feelings of distant fellowship between Africans and Afro-Americans into an international movement. Race alone could not have brought those black fighters together in those early Pan-African conferences. After all, there has been little political intercourse between the Negroes of Brazil and nationalists in English-speaking or French-speaking Africa. Given the limitations of those early years, it was indeed a matter of direct significance for African nationalism that American Negroes were English speakers.

Admittedly, Martinique has made an important contribution to African cultural revivalism, especially through the poetry of Aimé Césaire. And more lately there has been the ideological influence in Africa of the late revolutionary Frantz Fanon.[15] Even Haiti has sometimes attracted symbolic salutation as the first Negro republic outside the African continent.

But English-speaking Negroes in the Americas by far out-numbered French speakers. And this helps to account for the basic Anglo-American orientation of those Pan-African conferences in the early part of this century. Nkrumah's first trip to continental Europe in the 1940s was in an attempt to get French-speaking Africans more actively involved in Pan-Africanism. As Secretary of the West African National Secretariat in London he went to Paris to see the African members of the French National Assembly— Sourous Apithy, Léopold Senghor, Lamine Gueye, Houphouet-Boigny and others. As a result of Nkrumah's visit, Senghor and Apithy went to London to attend the West African Conference which Nkrumah and his colleagues had been organizing. What is significant about this story is not that French Africa was represented at the conference in London, but that special acts of encouragement had to be initiated by the English speakers to get Francophone Africans involved.[16]

This West African get-together was preceded by a broader venture—the historic fifth Pan-African Congress held in Manchester in 1945. The towering figures of that conference too were overwhelmingly English speakers. Two of the most famous came to be Presidents of their countries— Nkrumah himself and Jomo Kenyatta. Virtually the only representation that French-speaking Africa had was in the person of Dr. Raphael Armattoe from Togoland. Armattoe was not really committed to the cause. He was very much a detached guest among African militants. As a measure of his aloofness we might perhaps recall the story that Nkrumah, as Secretary of the Organizing Committee of the Conference, has to tell about him:

---

[15] In the English language see especially Fanon's *The Wretched of the Earth* (trans. by Constance Farrington) (New York: Grove Press, 1963). Fanon was born in Martinique, later joined the ranks of the FLN and fought for Algeria's independence, and wrote psychoanalytical studies on racism and the purifying potential of violence.

[16] Nkrumah's account of this is at once friendly and detached. See his *Autobiography*, *op. cit.*, pp. 54–58.

I remember one evening Makonnen came to see me behind the scenes in a state of great agitation. Could I possibly see a Dr. Raphael Armattoe, he said. Dr. Armattoe, a native of Togoland, who had been invited to speak at the conference, came in and declared that he had lost his portmanteau in which he had several things of value. He felt that since we had been responsible for his attendance at the conference, we should make good the loss he had sustained. He proceeded there and then to list the items and assess their value and presented me with the account. The Congress was already very much in debt but I decided it was better to pay the man and get over it the best way we could.[17]

But while this fifth Pan-African Congress was still more a conference of English-speaking Negroes than of Africans regardless of language, it was nevertheless more Pan-African than any of its predecessors. Here again Nkrumah, as a participant, gives us a useful insight into the significance of the Congress.

He argues that, like Garveyism, the preceding four "Pan-African" conferences were not born of indigenous African consciousness. "Garvey's ideology was concerned with *black* nationalism as opposed to *African* nationalism. And it was this Fifth Pan-African Congress that provided the outlet for African nationalism and brought about the awakening of African political consciousness."[18]

But why did Pan-Africanism in this intracontinental sense now gain an ascendancy over Pan-Negroism? When did the leaders of black Africa become more conscious of the African continent itself and relatively less interested in fellow black people in the New World? One possible answer is that the change took place when anticolonialism replaced Negro dignity as a slogan for the African sector of the black movement as a whole. For as long as the dominant battlecry was Negro dignity, this encompassed both Africans and Afro-Americans. But when *independence* became the paramount fighting slogan of the African sector, the links with the noncolonized Negroes of the New World were weakened. Apart from movements like that of the Black Muslims—which in any case came later—Negro independence was not a meaningful ambition for Afro-Americans in the United States. And this factor diluted the sense of fellowship in diversity between them and African nationalists.

But just as the English language had once helped to make Pan-Negroism possible, it now indirectly helped to weaken Pan-Negroism. It had this latter effect when it facilitated the growth of anticolonialism in the African continent itself.

But how did it facilitate that growth?

In trying to answer that question we might usefully start with a quotation. In her first Reith Lecture in 1961, Margery Perham made a claim which is perhaps all too familiar. She said: "The ideal of democratic freedom . . .

---

[17] *Ibid.*, p. 54.
[18] *Ibid.*, pp. 53–54.

[has] been learned very largely from Britain herself."[19] Her observation was itself part of the imperial tradition—the oral tradition that the ideas which were turned against the Empire were themselves imported by the Empire.

This is an exaggeration which has tended to cloud many people's thinking. And one of the factors which have led to this confusion is that the later African demands for freedom were expressed in *words* which were indeed "imported." And so, many an observer failed to distinguish between new ideas and a new way of expressing old ideas. In English-speaking West Africa this distinction was made more obscure to observers by the use of actual English slogans. The central slogan had to be something which expressed the desire for liberation. In East Africa the word came to be the local Swahili word *Uhuru*, but in West Africa it was the actual English word *Free-Dom*, partly Africanized, which was the more common platform song.

Wilfred Whiteley has been known to reflect on the "irony" that the word *Uhuru*—the rallying point of East African liberation movements—was a loan word from Arabic. It was borrowed from, to quote Whiteley, "Those by whom so many were formerly enslaved."[20] To that extent, both the West African slogan of "Free-Dom," and its African equivalent *Uhuru*, were terms inherited from those who had, at least for a while, denied many an African the very thing which the words denoted. But on the evidence that the word *Uhuru* is derived from Arabic it would be rash to conclude that East Africans learned about the virtues of liberty by listening to the wisdom of the Arabs. Yet many a Westerner has tended to regard the use of words like "Free-Dom" or "self-determination" by Africans as conclusive proof that it was colonialism which tutored Africans into a love for liberty.

We know that there were pockets of resistance to European intrusion among different tribal communities from the outset. Groups like the Ashanti and the Matabele provided adequate evidence of their opposition to being ruled by foreigners from distant lands. It would therefore seem that the love of freedom in this sense among such people owed nothing to European influence. On the contrary, the European intrusion seems to have violated that love. We might then ask in what sense it could still be true that these people learned about self-determination from colonial tutelage. This is where the English language comes into relevance. Resistance to foreign rule in Africa does indeed antedate the coming of the English language, but that resistance did not become *nationalistic* until its leaders became English speakers. When the Ashanti, the Masai, or the Kikuyu harassed intruders with spears three or four generations ago they were "hostile natives." But when they came to attack colonial rule in "sophisticated" language they became "nationalists." In a variety of ways the English language was an important causal factor in the growth of African national consciousness.

[19] *The Colonial Reckoning* (New York: Knopf, 1962).

[20] "Political Concepts and Connotations, "*St. Anthony's Papers No. 10*, African Affairs Number One (London: Chatto and Windus, 1961), p. 18.

Indeed, learning English was a detribalizing process. If one found an African who had mastered the English language, that African had, almost by definition, ceased to be a full tribesman. To an extent which was later to be exaggerated, there was indeed a "Westernizing" process implicit in the very act of learning English.

But why should the learning of a language have this effect? The reason lies in the relationship between language and the culture from which it springs. Language is the most important point of entry into the habits of thought of a people. It embodies within itself cumulative associations derived from the total experience of its people. The English language as a partial embodiment of Anglo-Saxon habits of thought must therefore carry with it seeds of intellectual acculturation for the Africans who learn it. That is why learning English was, to a non-Westerner, a process of Westernization. And to the extent that an English-speaking African was thus partly "Westernized" he was indeed partly detribalized.

Yet to be detribalized was not the same thing as to have national consciousness. Partial detribalization was a necessary condition of feeling nationalistic but not a sufficient condition. By learning a Western language an African might indeed move from tribalism to nontribalism. But it would be pertinent to ask what *kind* of nontribalism. After all, the quality of being detribalized could, in one case, take the form of neo-universalism, a sentiment of African identification with the metropolitan power. But it could, in another case, take the form of nationalistic self-consciousness as an African. On balance detribalization in English-speaking Africa took a more decisive turn into nationalism than it did in French-speaking Africa. Togoland's Dr. Armattoe said something appertaining to this at that fifth Pan-African Congress. He started first with an assurance. He said: "It is sometimes questioned whether French West Africans have any feeling of national consciousness, but I can say that French West Africans would be happier if they were governing themselves." Nevertheless, Armattoe went on to add that French West Africans "sometimes envy the British Africans their intense national feeling."[21]

That was in 1945. In September 1958, it was still possible for French-speaking Africa to vote, in a popular referendum, for a *continuation* of French imperial rule. What was remarkable about the De Gaulle referendum of 1958 was not that Guinea had voted in favor of independence, but that she was the only one. Had a similar referendum been held in English-speaking Africa, the results would probably have been very different. Both French and English had indeed helped to detribalize the leaders of Africa—but on balance it was more English than French which produced practicing nationalists.[22]

[21] See Padmore (ed.), *History of the Pan-African Congress, op. cit.*, p. 36.

[22] Paul-Marc Henry, former head of the Division of Sub-Saharan Africa in the French Ministry of Foreign Affairs said in 1959 that "between 1946 and 1958 one does not find any trace of activity by any French-speaking politician in the various stages of the Pan-

But was this because the English language lent itself more to nationalism? On the contrary, it was French more than English which commanded the militant love of those who spoke it. When this love is evoked in the French people themselves, the result is linguistic nationalism. For French is, after all, their *own national* language. But when a passionate love for French is aroused in those to whom French is only an adopted language, the result is a kind of linguistic universalism. To put it in another way, a Frenchman passionately in love with the French language is a nationalist; but an African passionately in love with French is, at best, a cultural cosmopolitan. Among French-speaking Africans Leopold Senghor is perhaps exceptional not in his love for French, but in the frankness with which he expresses it. He tells us: ". . . . If we had a choice we would have chosen French." He then goes on to rationalize this affection by saying:

First, it is a language which has enjoyed a far reaching influence and which still enjoys it in great measure. In the eighteenth century French was proposed and accepted as the universal language of culture. I know that today it comes after English, Chinese, and Russian in the number of people who speak it, and it is a language of fewer countries than English. But if quantity is lacking there is *quality*.

Senghor then goes on to assure us:

I am not claiming that French is superior to these other languages, either in beauty or in richness, but I do say that it is the supreme language of *communication:* "a language of politeness and honesty," a language of beauty and clarity . . .[23]

In part it is this militant linguistic cosmopolitanism among French-speaking African leaders which arrested the growth of real nationalism in their part of the continent. The English language, by the very fact of being emotionally more neutral than French, was less of a hindrance to the emergence of national consciousness in British Africa.

But there were other factors, too, about English to be taken into account. Among these is the simple but persistent fact once again that the United States was English-speaking. This provided an alternative country of higher education for African leaders from British Africa. Education in Britain or France was indeed quite capable of producing nationalism in its own right. But the fact that these were the imperial countries themselves could sometimes create an ambivalence in an African's attitude towards the country of his education. An African educated in England could indeed hate England but he might also make a few English friends. Even if he does not make friends,

---

African movement, as interpreted and operated by Mr. Padmore and Dr. Nkrumah." See Philip W. Quigg (ed.) *Africa, A Foreign Affairs Reader* (New York: Frederick A. Praeger, 1961), p. 162.

[23] "Negritude and the Concept of Universal Civilization," *Présence Africaine*, Vol. 18, No. 26, Second Quarter, 1963, p. 10.

he is bound to find out that not all English people are "colonialist" in their sympathies. He might find himself marching with British radicals against this or that policy of the British government.

In addition, there is the element of anglicization which a student usually undergoes if he spends more than two years in England. The student might never grow to love England, but by being anglicized a little he would have rendered his anglophobia less pure psychologically. Perhaps even "British empiricism" might rub off on him—and he could become a gradualist in his attitude to decolonization.

An African from Francophone Africa educated in France might become even more ambivalent in his attitude to French colonial rule. He might make more French friends than his Anglophone counterpart might make English friends in England. And it might be even more effectively demonstrated in France than in England that colonialism was not universally applauded by the citizens of the colonial power. On the whole there have always been more French radicals in existence than there have been English radicals.

What emerges from these considerations is the fact that the imperial country itself was not conducive to single-minded nationalism in an African. There were factors which got in the way of total psychological hostility to the country concerned.

But unless he was prepared to learn a new language altogether the Francophone African did not have many alternatives to France as a source of higher education. At any rate he had before him no French-speaking equivalent of the United States—in terms of scholarships available.

What these factors added up to was this historical phenomenon. Firstly, English-speaking Africans were, on the whole, more nationalistic than French-speaking Africans. Secondly, among the English speakers those who were educated in the United States tended to be more single-minded in their nationalism that those educated in Great Britain. It was perhaps not accidental that the leadership in Ghana passed from British-educated personalities to the American-educated Nkrumah. Nor was it entirely a coincidence that the founding father of Nigerian nationalism was Nnamdi Azikiwe.

What made American-educated Africans more militant in their nationalism than British-educated ones? There was indeed the tradition of anti-imperialism which many Americans continued to subscribe to even if their governments did not always do so. There was also the factor that America was, in any case, a more ideological and more rhetorical country in its politics than Britain usually is. *The Observer* of London might have been overstating the case when it described Communist China and the United States as "the two most ideologically inspired States of the modern world."[24] But it is certainly true that political beliefs tend to be articulated with greater passion and more hyperbole by Americans than by British people. And exposure to such a climate could make an African educated in the United States more

[24] Editorial, *The Observer* (London), May 9, 1965.

ideological and more rhetorical in his own stand of anti-imperialism than his fellow African in the British Isles.

A third factor which made education in the United States conducive to militancy was the racial issue. In his book on Nigeria, James S. Coleman put the question in these terms:

> The special situation of the American Negro, into whose company an African student is inevitably thrown, was . . . an important conditioning factor. African students in America were perforce made acutely aware of color discrimination, in itself provocative of racial consciousness.

Coleman goes on to point out that West Africans did not meet in their own countries the highly institutionalized and omnipresent discrimination characteristic of Southern states, and to a degree also of Northern states, in America. Racial discrimination in Nigeria (formally outlawed in 1948) was irritating mainly as a symbol of European imperialism, but "it did not engulf the individual and plague him at every turn." Thus, Coleman tells us, many Nigerians encountered racial discrimination on a large scale for the first time when they arrived in the United States.[25]

Where Coleman was on less solid ground was when he went on to suggest that the same sort of racialistic cultural shock, though less pronounced, hit an African student studying in England. On the contrary, a reverse type of shock was more usual. In other words, what impressed African students in England in those early days was the apparent racial broadmindedness of the British people in England as compared with the type they encountered at home. Many a student came to draw a sharp distinction between those two types of Britons in his experience.

And so while African students studying in the United States found themselves in a more racialistic society than they had in their colonial homes, African students studying in England found themselves in a less. It is therefore not surprising that the American-educated African was the more single-minded in his nationalism.

On a broader linguistic plane this is another factor which spared Francophone Africa the passions which come with highly institutionalized racial discrimination. There was no French-speaking "Jim Crow." The United States within her own borders has contributed at least as much as British settlers in Africa to the racist image of the Anglo-Saxon peoples. Because of this general image of Anglo-American racial arrogance French-speaking Africans found it possible to congratulate themselves on having fallen under French imperial rule on the ground that it was a lesser evil. As for those occasions when even French policy betrayed signs of intolerance, the

[25] *Nigeria, Background to Nationalism* (Berkeley and Los Angeles: University of California Press, 1958), p. 245. This point is also analysed in my paper "Borrowed Theory and Original Practice in African Politics," *Patterns of African Development*, ed. Herbert Spiro (Englewood Cliffs, N.J.: Prentice-Hall, 1967).

nefarious influence could conceivably be traced to "the Anglo-Saxon example." It might be fitting here to conclude with a remark by Raphael Armattoe once again at that Pan-African Congress:

At one time all Africans born in the French Empire were citizens. It was only when the Anglo-Saxons brought their influence to bear on the French that the position changed and fewer Africans were regarded as citizens.[26]

In his own confused way Armattoe was making at least one valid point. He was alluding to the role of the British as pacesetters in matters of imperial conduct. Those who were ruled by the British became in turn pacesetters in the general movement against imperialism at large. Through their arrogance the British and the Americans had helped to arouse the Negro's pride. Through the paradox of their leadership in humanitarian ventures they had helped to restore the Negro's dignity. And through their language they had helped to detribalize the African's mind—and to give it a nationalistic dimension.

STUDY QUESTIONS

1. Mazrui suggests a contrast between "cosmopolitanism" and "nationalism." How does the use of French and English in Africa contribute to these two tendencies?
2. Does the following observation about African attitudes toward French and English support or refute Mazrui's hypothesis about the role the two languages have played in nationalistic movements:

   The French language is normally regarded, by those responsible for teaching it, as part of a complex which may be termed, the French way of life. This to an outside observer also appears to be generally accepted by French speakers as a quite proper attitude. English on the other hand is very frequently regarded as a tool to be acquired, without which it is impossible to make progress in other fields of knowledge. Put in its most crude form the difference between French and English in this respect would seem to be that the acquisition of French is normally regarded as an end in itself with certain valuable by-products, but the learning of English is a means to an end.[a]

3. Would you regard the growth of regional varieties of the international language as more likely in French- or in English-speaking areas of Africa?
4. Lambert reports that someone thoroughly skilled in a language not his own "can be disturbing to the natives . . . because he is a potential linguistic *spy* in the sense that he can get along too well with the intimacies and subtleties of their

---

[26] Padmore, *History of Pan-African Congress, op. cit.,* p. 36.

[a] Malcolm Guthrie, "Multilingualism and Cultural Factors," in *Symposium on Multilingualism: Second Meeting of the Inter-African Committee on Linguistics, Brazzaville 16–21 July 1962* (London: Scientific Council for Africa, nd), pp. 107–08.

dialects."[b] How would such feelings contribute to the rise of new national language varieties in former British colonies?

5. Treating some problems attending the use of English in Ghana, a university lecturer there writes:

> Improving the standard of English at the university level raises the controversial problem of what goal to aim at in spoken English. If English is the most important medium of communication within Ghana, and between Ghana and the outside world, it is well to aim at the kind of English most widely understood; which I understand is "southern English." Phonetically, it is utopian to expect even the very best Honors English student to cultivate a perfect "southern English" accent. But grammatically we must insist upon standard English, in so far as this is known, to increase the chances of mutual comprehension. "The best speakers of standard English are those whose pronunciation and language generally, least betray their locality," remarks Henry Sweet. We owe it to our students to make them good speakers and writers of standard English.[c]

Why is the question of standard English and of language standards so important in nations like Ghana? What criteria for the determination of standards does the writer of the preceding paragraph suggest? How would you test the notion that "southern English" is the kind most widely understood? What does Sweet mean, or does the lecturer imply that he means, by "the best speakers"—does the term refer to intelligibility or social acceptability?

An Indian scholar who has conducted tests of the intelligibility of Indian English among educated Indians from different regions and among Indians and British speakers writes:

> The view that "spoken English" is important in India has to be accepted, but it has to be noted that "Educated Indian English" is spoken very differently from British RP, and the view that the only suitable model for Indian teachers and pupils is British RP is not shared by the vast majority of the people in the country, not even by distinguished teachers of English.
>
> . . .
>
> Halliday, McIntosh, and Strevens suggest "two basic criteria to determine whether a variety of English is acceptable for use as an educational model. First, it must be a variety actually used by a reasonably large body of the population, in particular by a proportion of those whose level of education makes them in other respects desirable models . . . . Second, it must be mutually intelligible with other varieties of English used by similar professional and educated groups in other countries." It is suggested that imported forms of English should be excluded and mutual intelligibility should be attained by adopting "standard English grammar and lexis," and keeping "the number of phonological units . . . close to those of other educated accents."

This appears to be a very sensible view. It is impossible to change radically

[b] Wallace E. Lambert, "A Social Psychology of Bilingualism," *Journal of Social Issues*, **23**, ii(1967):92.

[c] R. F. Amonoo, "Problems of Ghanaian *Lingue Franche*," in *Language in Africa*, ed. John Spencer (Cambridge: Cambridge University Press, 1963), pp. 81–82.

the speech habits of 11 million Indian speakers of English, a number as large as the total population of Australia. Nor is it possible to impose an imported form of English which may be completely different from the prevalent usage among educated people in the country.[d]

Do the criteria offered here differ in any respect from those suggested by Amonoo? Why do both suggest a higher priority for grammar and lexis than for pronunciation?

6. All the quoted authors see as utopian any attempt to teach the precise accent of RP. Why? Contrast Amonoo's attitudes toward English with Gandhi's (see the preface of this article). Would it be similarly utopian to expect the speakers of nonstandard dialects in the United States to acquire the accent of standard American English?

7. Ayọ Bamgboṣe notes that in Nigeria: "One of the constant problems of the schoolteacher (especially the primary school teacher) is the limited opportunity his pupils have of using English. In most cases, the pupils speak only the vernacular in the home. Even in some boarding schools where pupils are fined a penny whenever they speak in the vernacular, the use of the vernacular outside the classroom is still quite common."[e] Why would this phenomenon occur, in spite of the prestige of English in Nigeria and its value for getting ahead in competition for jobs? Is the phenomenon likely to have any effect on the kind of English developing in Nigeria? Can similar phenomena be observed in the United States among schoolchildren who speak nonstandard dialects? What are some limits on the effectiveness of language planners?

8. The following is a selection from the opening address to a Seminar on Mass Media and Linguistic Communications in East Africa given by Milton Obote, former president of Uganda. It is a cogent statement of problems facing emergent nations as they formulate linguistic policy for education and administration.

Language and National Identification[f]

Milton Obote

I want to say briefly that Uganda finds difficulties in identifying herself, and that Uganda has a serious language problem. Our present policy as a Government is to teach more and more English in schools. We are not unmindful of disadvantages inherent in this policy. We know that English, before Independence was the language of the administrator. It was the language of the people who were rulers and by which Uganda was ruled. We also know that many of our people learned English in order to serve in the Administration, at least to serve our former masters. It would appear that we are doing exactly the same; our policy to teach more English could in the long run just develop more power in the hands of those who speak English, and better economic status for those who know English. We say this because we do not see any possibility of our being able to get English known by half the

[d] R. K. Bansal, *The Intelligibility of Indian English*, Central Institute of English, Hyderabad, India, Monograph No. 4 (Hyderabad, 1969), pp. 12–13.

[e] Ayọ Bamgboṣe, "The English Language in Nigeria," in *The English Language in West Africa*, ed. John Spencer (London, 1971), p. 46.

[f] Reprinted by permission of the publishers, East African Publishing House, from *East Africa Journal* (April 1967), pp. 3–6.

population of Uganda within the next fifteen years. English, therefore, remains the national language in Uganda when at the same time it is a language that the minority of our people can use for political purposes to improve their own political positions. Some of our people can use it in order to improve their economic status.

In spite of this reasoning, we find no alternative to English in Uganda's present position. We have, therefore, adopted English as our national language —in fact it is the political language. No Member of Parliament, for instance, is unable to speak English and indeed it is a qualification for membership to Parliament. Those in the Seminar will understand the challenge facing us. The Uganda National Assembly should be a place where Uganda problems are discussed by those best able to discuss them, and in our situation it would appear that those best able to discuss our problems are those who speak English. This is a reasoning which cannot be defended anywhere; there is no alternative at the present moment. We do also see that those amongst us in Uganda who speak English and have obtained important positions because of the power of the English language, are liable to be regarded by a section of our society as perpetrators of colonialism and imperialism; or at least as potential imperialists. This, fortunately, has not yet become a public issue in Uganda. Nevertheless there is a real possibility that as long as English is maintained as the official language, spoken by a minority, a charge against its use could be made on the ground that it is the language of the privileged group.

But the Government and the people of Uganda do realise that there are certain advantages in our learning English. We could not, for instance, adopt Lugbara—one of our Northern languages as our national language. It is clear that the task of teaching Lugbara itself would be beyond our capacity and ability, and since language has an economic power in that whoever in a country of this kind knows the official language is likely to get higher and higher in the Government service, the task of teaching Lugbara or adopting it could result in serious riots and instability.

I suggest that the same applies practically to every other language in Uganda. It is probably safe to say that Luganda and Lunyoro are spoken by the greatest number of our people but immediately we adopt either of them as the official language for administrative purposes or legislation, some of us will have to go out of the Government. I, for instance, would not be able to speak in Parliament in Luganda, neither could I do so in Lunyoro, and I think more than half the present National Assembly members would have to quit. The areas we now represent would not like to have just any person who speaks Luganda to represent them. They would feel unrepresented. So, there again, we find no alternative to English.

Then comes culture. The problem of culture is slightly different from the political problem and this is essentially a problem of how best we can maintain and develop the various cultural forms in Uganda through a common language. I have no answer to this. I am well aware that English cannot be the media to express Dingidingi songs. I have my doubts whether Lwo language can express in all its fineness Lusoga songs, and yet I consider that Uganda's policy to teach more and more English should be matched with the teaching of some other African language.

Currently we are thinking of what this African language should be. Already, of course, in Primary schools children learn in their own mother tongues but then it means that we have to find Primary School teachers and post them to each tribal area. This does not allow for the movement of teachers which may be a great disadvantage to the teachers themselves. The practical effect is that, having been to a Teacher Training College, teachers have no other place to go to except the tribal district. I consider this as something an Independent Uganda should not encourage.

There can be no doubt that time will come when some of these languages will lose meaning. We may today think that a tribe will lose very much if it loses its tribal language. I do not think so. Not at least two thousand years from now. I find it, therefore, easy to suggest that the teaching of an African language in Uganda schools today is difficult because of the lack of teachers. Someone may suggest that there are some two million people who speak Luganda and ask: "Why not recruit some fifty thousand to teach Luganda throughout Uganda"? I think the problem posed by languages like Runyoro/Rutoro and Luganda in the context of Uganda's geographical position is a different problem from that posed, for instance, by Swahili. The teaching of Runyoro/Rutoro or Luganda will assist Uganda in the years to come in that people of Uganda will be able to communicate with one another in one common language. But it will not assist Uganda in communicating with her neighbors. It would be difficult for those across the Sudanese border to be interested in learning Luganda or Runyoro/Rutoro when their contact with Uganda is really contact with East Africa. It would be difficult for the Congolese who already, by the way, speak some kind of Swahili to bother to learn our new national language when they know that across the borders of Uganda there are millions of people who speak a language they already know —which is Swahili.

So the adoption of any one of our present languages in Uganda may just go to endorse our isolation; we cannot afford any kind of isolation. We are surrounded by five countries. We can easily talk with them, and as they say here, walk across Rwanda village, walk across Congo village, walk across Sudan village, walk across Kenya and Tanzania and drink water by the simple words "mpa maji"—"give me water." It is possible today for the people of Uganda to communicate with the people in the neighboring countries in broken Swahili but it is not possible today for the people of Uganda to communicate with the neighboring countries in broken Luganda. If we cannot communicate with our neighbors in broken Luganda today, how much more difficult would it be to try and communicate in first-class Luganda.

I do think also that Swahili has its own problems within the context of Uganda. It is possible that one can learn a language without taking the culture that that language expresses. But the real question as I see it here is, Why should Uganda learn Swahili? Why should Kenya adopt Swahili as a national language, or for that matter, why has the Government of Tanzania announced the policy of the adoption of Swahili as a national language? I ask this question because I am not quite convinced that having adopted an African language as a national language, a tendency would not develop to discourage all other languages around the country. If that tendency developed and became the official policy, are we satisfied that my remarks regarding the inability of Luganda to express Dingidingi songs would be satisfied by Swahili? I am not satisfied, and here we are trying to think about a possible answer to the question of why we need an African language as a national language. Do we need it merely for political purposes, for addressing public meetings, for talking in Councils? Do we need it as the language of the workers, to enable them to talk and argue their terms with their employers? Do we need an African language for intellectual purposes? Do we need such a language to cover every aspect of our lives intellectually, politically, economically?

I would not attempt to answer that question but it appears to me that Uganda at least is faced with a difficult future on this matter and the future might confirm that a decision is necessary to push some language deliberately and to discourage the use of some other languages also deliberately.

Swahili was taken out of schools in the past for political reasons but I think there were also strong cultural reasons.

When Independence came, Radio Uganda was broadcasting in English, Luganda, Runyoro/Rutoro, Ateso, and Lwo. Today we have added another ten languages on the radio and this is a subject that interests me a great deal. Perhaps in this Seminar you will find an answer as to what is the objective in having a National Radio. I am in Government and I have to take political feelings of the people into account in formulating policies. I would not say that all our fourteen languages on the radio are in every case necessary but I would not also go as far as to say that they are there merely because of political reasons. I think to some extent—much as we would like to have one language—there is advantage in broadcasting in these various languages as things stand today. Our policy on Radio Uganda is to inform the public and that is our first task, first objective. We want to inform the people of Uganda. We find it exceedingly difficult to inform the Karamojong in Luganda or in any other language except their own, so we have Karamojong broadcast on the radio. Then we use the radio for educational purposes and we find that to assist those who never went to school at all, we must broadcast in their own mother tongues.

Then there is what is called entertainment which should actually be development of culture. Since the radio began broadcasting these various languages, there has been a new spirit in Uganda, simple composition of songs, dance teams, and various competitions around the countryside. Every village is eager to surpass the other in its cultural activities with a view that one day Radio Uganda recording vans will pass around the village and record the songs and the poems of a particular group. We find this useful although we are creating a problem of how to co-ordinate these activities in future.

The only aspect which I do not like on our radio but which I cannot do anything about, is the "Pop Song". But I understand that there are people who like pop, so that too has to stay.

When it comes to news, our National Radio is in the same weak position as many national radios in Africa. I will perhaps illustrate this by telling you that I know of a Minister in the Government of Uganda who followed the Sierra Leone trouble by tuning to the B.B.C. and to the Voice of America. He never tuned to Nairobi. He never tuned even to Kampala though he was in Kampala. When I asked him why he did so, he said he got more news about Sierra Leone on B.B.C. and the Voice of America. Certainly there was more news on the B.B.C. and the Voice of America about Sierra Leone—more than Radio Uganda could give. What news was it? And in any case what is news?

Well, we struggled for Independence. We have got it. There remains a problem in this context as to whom we should listen and what we want to hear. I find it extremely difficult here in Uganda to give the people of Uganda what I consider news. I find it difficult because first, we do not have enough trained manpower to collect what we consider news throughout Uganda every day and to present that news to the people of Uganda. Secondly, we have tremendous difficulties in broadcasting what is news in Kenya, or what is news in Tanzania—the happenings in Kenya or the happenings in Tanzania, or the happenings in any part of Africa. What comes to us as news very often turns out to be ideas of those they call "informed observers" and if you go to investigate as to who are the "informed observers" you will find their position extremely interesting and disturbing. So we are not giving the right type of news to our people first because of our own inability to collect the news within our territory.

This is because of lack of contact and lack of communication channels between one African capital and another. The O.A.U. has been talking about an African News Agency. This is the age of talking. We find it easier to talk about Union Government and to write the Constitution of that Government, than to talk about African News Agency or to talk about how to finance it, and yet the struggle goes on as to who should control the minds and the ears of Africa.

Today I have to, like all my colleagues in Africa, think in a foreign language in order to express myself to Africans on problems affecting Africans. When I move out of Kampala to talk to the people, I have to talk in English. Obviously I have no alternative but I lose a lot especially as far as the Party is concerned. The Party welcomes everybody and some of the greatest and most dedicated workers are those who do not speak English and yet the Party Leader cannot call this great dedicated worker alone and say "Thank you" in a language the man will understand. It has to be translated. There must always be a third party, and that is why it is said there are no secrets in Africa. This is our challenge. We are a young country and the vitality of youth should be able to lead us to greater days. I urge particularly the people of Uganda to turn the weaknesses of today into the strength of tomorrow.

What is Mr. Obote's attitude toward the continued use of English in Uganda? What advantage does he see in such use? What disadvantages? What problems would arise from a decision to adopt one of Uganda's native languages as the official language of education and administration? How is the question of what national language to adopt related to policy in mass media?

STANDARD AVERAGE FOREIGN IN PUERTO RICO
J. L. Dillard

The use of Spanish and English on the island of Puerto Rico presents a complex sociolinguistic picture. Limitations on home rule make the territory dependent on the United States, and both politics and economics encourage the use of English in the relations between Puerto Ricans and mainland Americans. Migration to and from the eastern seaboard makes a further contribution to the linguistic instability of the island, and nearly all Puerto Ricans agree that bilingualism in English and Spanish is particularly desirable. As Dillard shows in the following essay, English occupies a position of high status, and many speakers are eager to present themselves as bilinguals whatever their actual proficiency in English may be. One writer has even suggested that the social circumstances in Puerto Rico may be giving rise to a mixed language "whose intonation is Spanish, whose lexicon is drawn from English and Spanish, and whose morphology shares inflectional features of the two languages." [a] *The examples given by Dillard show some aspects of this language mixture, and it is interesting to compare the setting of linguistic variation in the island with the circumstances described by Brosnahan (pp. 40–54) and Hall (pp. 91–103) for other cases of language mixture and change.*

The case of Standard Average Foreign[1] in Puerto Rico is an unusually simple one because of a strong acculturative drive—toward the mainstream culture of the United States and toward American English—on the part of the majority of the island's population. In its present state, the island's language situation finds English and Spanish distributed in what would probably have become a classical diglossic state if it were not for some modifications due to conscious efforts to strengthen and restore the influence of Spanish. Politically, the Americanization tendencies (in language and

Reprinted by permission of the author from *Studies in Language, Literature, and Culture of the Middle Ages and Later*, eds. E. Bagby Atwood and Archibald A. Hill (Austin: The University of Texas Press, 1969). Written May 1964, revised 1971.

[a] David Lawton, "The Question of Creolization in Puerto Rican Spanish," in *Pidginization and Creolization of Languages*, ed. Dell Hymes (Cambridge: Cambridge University Press, 1971), p. 193.

[1] The term is an adaptation of Whorf's Standard Average European made by Fred W. Householder, Jr., in a review of Charles F. Hockett's *A Course in Modern Linguistics* (New York, 1958), in *Language*, 35(1959):524.

otherwise) are part of the movement toward statehood; the Hispanization tendencies of the *Independentista* movement. Nevertheless, English is to some degree the "high" language and Spanish the "low" language; and the use of Anglicisms is frequently a pretension factor. The use of at least some English is so all-pervading that it may be said to be characteristic of all Puerto Ricans except the very old and the very rural populations.[2]

The fullest description of English in Puerto Rico is that of Morgan E. Jones, who uses the term "hybrid" for the English of the island.[3] He refuses to call island English by the name "pidgin," and I would agree with him that it does not show pidgin characteristics.[4] Jones used two questionnaires, one given to 445 speakers, and the other to 27. He was not measuring average proficiency in English, since his informants were unusually fluent. He did not, however, use any "perfect" bilinguals.[5] In this paper, I shall consider a much wider and more varied group than those used by Jones, with greater variation in English proficiency. It will be seen, however, that most of those considered have a lower degree of English ability than do Jones's informants. "Perfect" or near-perfect bilinguals are not included, although several of the forms adduced were collected from people who teach English and who may have taught it for many years. Polyglots are rare indeed in Puerto Rico, and are virtually limited to immigrants; they are, of course, excluded. It is perhaps unfortunate that most of the materials contained herein were not collected by means of questionnaires; the result is a somewhat anecdotal

---

[2] A problem relevant to this study is how far Puerto Rican Spanish is intelligible elsewhere in the Spanish world. No clear answer is available. Joseph P. Matluck takes an extreme negative view in *Nueva Revista de la Filología Española*, **15**(1961):332–42. Ralph Robinett, in a mimeographed English pedagogical text, on the other hand, denies the often-stated thesis that Puerto Ricans must communicate with other Spanish speakers in English. His example, that Puerto Ricans communicate freely with inhabitants of the nearby island of Vieques, is perhaps deceptively favorable, with the intention of convincing the Department of Education. Perhaps typical is a complaint of court translators in New York, in an island newspaper:

> los interpretes son sudamericanos y no conocen las frases y modismos que se usan en Puerto Rico ["the interpreters are South American and don't understand the idioms used in Puerto Rico" *Eds.*]

[3] *A Phonological Study of English As Spoken by Puerto Ricans Contrasted with Puerto Rican Spanish and American English*. University of Michigan Dissertation (1962), typescript. In spite of the title, Jones gives valuable material other than phonological, particularly on social backgrounds affecting the two languages. That Puerto Rico participated in the general New World use of pidgin languages (especially Portuguese) in the contact situation of the sixteenth, seventeenth, and eighteenth centuries seems very likely. See footnote 19.

[4] Cf. my "Spanglish Store Names in San Juan, Puerto Rico," *Names*, **12**(1964):98–102.

[5] Janet Sawyer, "Aloofness from Spanish Influence in Texas," *Word*, **15**(1959):270–81, issues a convincing warning that bilingualism is never perfect. She cites the fact that her Latin informants did not know the localisms known to all Anglo speakers, even though their proficiency seemed otherwise complete. My own experience leads to the same conclusion for Puerto Ricans, even some born in New York. [See Sawyer's "Social Aspects of Bilingualism in San Antonio, Texas" on pp. 226–33 of this volume. *Eds.*]

approach. Puerto Ricans are, however, very defensive about the matters under discussion; and any overt questioning brings forth answers of a type which are of little value for this kind of study. In some cases, it has been possible to check against Jones's more methodologically orthodox procedures; and in a few cases incidental results of questionnaires designed for other purposes have been utilized.

It has frequently been noted that the Puerto Rican uses English as a status-symbol language.[6] Every traveler to the island observes this, and it is a rare one who does not comment upon it in writing. Perhaps the surest way of ascertaining that one is in Puerto Rico is to listen for the call "Meester [mihtel] I will traduce [wil tradus] for you." The unacculturated traveler or immigrant is likely to be incredulous that a person so little skilled in English should set up as an interpreter;[7] even in the Caribbean, where self-appointed interpreters abound, it is rare to find would-be guides with such a painfully poor command of English and such persistence. But the "traducer" whom one first meets at the airport will be encountered again and again throughout the island. The usual vehicle of these people is the hybrid as described by Jones, but much lower in performance quality. It leans heavily for vocabulary upon the creative device of dropping final vowels from nouns. One carries a *packet* < *paquete;* sees things manufactured in a *fabric* < *fabrica;* tells the student his *note* < *nota.* A partly sophisticated perception of Frenchification in the English vocabulary will produce a "meeting of the faculty cloister" < *claustro.* Where there is no final vowel, direct adoption into English (with whatever degree of phonetic approximation the speaker is capable of) is resorted to. Thus, "What direction you going to?" shows the Puerto Rican form (common elsewhere, of course) *direction* < *dirección* for "address." So in slightly differing manner, do *tiket* "check" and *six apples* "six blocks" (< *seis manzanas*). Most of these are, of course, merely false cognates; but there is an institutionalized quality about them (as Jones has noted), which does not always go with a Spanish accent. Among other devices, the ubiquitous "No got change" (again common Caribbean) phrased either as a statement meaning "I do not have any change" or as a question meaning "Don't you have any change?" or even "Do you have any change?" is typical of devices which are considered to be indispensable. Little attempt is made at grammatical approximation of English.

Although one desired result of this hybrid is communication with English-speaking people, it soon becomes clear that this is not the only motivation. Often, indeed, communication with the persistent speaker of the hybrid is

---

[6] Cf. E. Seda Bonilla, "Social Structures and Race Relations," *Social Forces,* **40**(1961): 146, for an extreme case. A related practice is that of dark-skinned Puerto Ricans in the United States who prefer to use Spanish to avoid being classed as Negro.

[7] Eager but unqualified would-be translators are widespread in Latin America, perhaps partly because of the belief that no American speaks or reads anything but English. The Puerto Rican practice seems commoner, and the degree of mastery lower than elsewhere in the Caribbean.

more difficult than with the Spanish monolingual. This is especially true if Spanish personal or place names are involved. It is difficult to estimate how much Anglicization a speaker of the hybrid is going to demand when dealing with San Germán, Loiza Aldea, *cuba libre*, Aguadilla (one such experience produced the nonceform [ægwədílyə]); even "Mahogany Street" for *Calle Caoba* may be demanded. Frequently, bilinguals who have insisted upon using English repeat "What? What?" to such names, while monolingual[8] bystanders, having understood, join in trying to explain the name to them. In some cases, institutionalized forms have been established: e.g., [sæn wan]. On the other hand, virtually anyone would know that his leg was being pulled if an American spoke of St. John on the island of Richport.

Travelers who know Spanish, even native speakers of nonisland Spanish, in special cases, and in extreme circumstances native Puerto Ricans, who naively decide to depart from this crude vehicle can meet some rude surprises. The Puerto Rican tends to resent the change: the hurt in the taxi driver's voice is probably real when he says, "Why you speak Espanish to me?" The Puerto Rican's insistence upon using English, even when it handicaps him as a medium of communication, has been noted frequently.[9] So far the particular qualities of his insistence have not been described in detail, and a partial description is one aim of this paper. It is quite noteworthy that the relationship between English and Spanish in Puerto Rico is, socially speaking, much like that between English and French Creole in St. Lucia as described by Mervin Alleyne,[10] although in Puerto Rico there are counterbalancing efforts of crusading Hispanists.

For the Puerto Rican, use of the hybrid arises out of the necessity of communicating with the *Americano*; and the island's mythos of language includes the statement that the speaker has tried many times to communicate with *Americanos* in Spanish and has failed, and has therefore resolved always to speak English to Americans. Undoubtedly, such instances occur; and any adult Puerto Rican may possibly have had one or two such experiences. But the fact that small children learning English in school shout phrases in English to passing *gringos* (some of them absolutely unanswerable, like "What's the mata for you, Meehtel?") and that Americans may be very frequently seen trying to induce Puerto Ricans to speak to them in Spanish, may be taken as effective refutation of any factual motivation for this particular attitude. Furthermore, even after the American has insisted upon Spanish and has conversed with the Puerto Rican in that language for an

[8] In this paper "bilingual" means one who habitually uses English in addressing foreigners, "monolingual" one who sticks to Spanish. No conclusions are given concerning proficiency of the two groups. It would be possible to set up grades of bilingualism, as Diebold does (*Language*, 37(1961):97–112), but only at the expense of unnecessary complication.

[9] Cf. Jones, p. 112. There is a voluminous travelers' correspondence on this insistence, often cited in such journals as *The Island Times*.

[10] *Caribbean Studies*, 1(1961).

hour or so, the Puerto Rican will frequently switch to English "so that the American can understand"; he may, after all that time, ask, "Do you speak Spanish?"[11] In a sense, the hybrid consists of what the Puerto Rican says to an "American"; he is somewhat inclined to define Spanish as that which he speaks to a Puerto Rican, no matter how heavily Anglicized, particularly in vocabulary.

A further complicating circumstance arises in consideration of what the term *Americano* means to the average Puerto Rican. The term is likely to fit any foreigner. This group includes, to my personal knowledge, Haitians, Hungarians, a Russian, a French Canadian, and one native of Curaçao (where Spanish is in daily use); it has been reported for a great variety of other nationalities. Furthermore, I am certain that Spaniards, Ecuadoreans, and Costa Ricans of my acquaintance are occasionally addressed in English by Puerto Ricans. Very many anecdotes of this type exist, but the "good story" aspect of the matter should probably inhibit their being considered as evidence. It would be worth something to substantiate the story that a Spanish lecturer (Ortega y Gasset, according to one version) who asked for directions to the *paraninfo* was told "Por favor, señor, no entiendo inglés" and, upon explaining in simpler words what he was looking for, was told "Eso, en español, llamamos el asemblijol." A native Spaniard who teaches Spanish on the island is reputed to have said that she used English for the first two years in Puerto Rico, until she learned the dialect; but, at best, such a story may carry elements of exaggeration. But it is certain that a foreigner like Mr. Joseph Charron, a French Canadian who keeps a guest house in Loiza Aldea, is consistently referred to as *el Americano*, and that the same kind of face-saving devices used to prove that the Puerto Rican knows some English are consistently used upon him,[12] although it is inconceivable that anyone should take Charron's English for that of a native speaker. A frequent sight on the University of Puerto Rico campus is that of a student trying to change the Spanish conversation into English when talking with one of the polyglot European professors of the faculty, even when the professor may manage Spanish somewhat better than English—and when the student's command of English may be rudimentary indeed.

The Puerto Rican obviously feels a great deal of discomfort when Spanish intrudes into his relations with an outsider. When the *Humanidades* staff of the English Department cooperated with Dwight L. Bolinger in submitting a questionnaire on Spanish usage to our students, my Structure of English class—consisting entirely of Puerto Ricans—was disturbed, indeed almost

---

[11] Cf. Jones, p. 189.

[12] A girl of my acquaintance often made a point of using [nekstaim] and [eniwe] as transitional devices, though in rapid conversation they would be replaced by *la próxima vez* and *de todos modos*. Sometimes these Spanish forms would be "corrected" to the hybrid forms. She and other Puerto Ricans occasionally spell with English letter-names, as in "El es un [pi ei ti o]." (*pato*, Puerto Rican for homosexual). Often times such forms are repeated, to allow the speaker to show his knowledge of English.

immobilized, by the fact that the questionnaire was written in Spanish. Several of them asked in what language they should answer, although the answers consisted largely of making check marks. The only actual writing came at the beginning, where the following questions were asked in Spanish.

Nombre:
Domicilio Actual:
Edad:
Ocupación:

For the first question, nobody managed to get any English into the answers. For the second, *Box* and *Street* were frequent; but these forms are regularly used in Puerto Rico. For the third question, two people wrote numbers followed by *years*; seven people wrote numbers with *años*; and the other twenty-three evaded the issue by using numbers only. For the last question, four answers were given in English

Elementary School Teacher
Teacher (twice)
English Teacher

and one person gave a bilingual answer

Teacher (Profesor)

It should be specified that there was no question of the comprehensibility of the Spanish of the questionnaire. And the numbers presented indicate nothing about the confusion, indecision, and time wasted because of disbelief that the instructions could have been written in Spanish. Likewise, giving the gloss *vds.* instead of *you* (*plural*) in a problem for an Introduction to Linguistics class resulted in such confusion that it had to be changed.

Another part of the Puerto Rican mythos of language is that such switching to English is motivated by perception of an English, or "American" accent.[13] There is undoubtedly some truth to this, yet it can easily be shown not to be the exclusively conditioning factor. The examples cited above, of speakers of European languages, none of them with a "good" English accent, may be taken as indication of this. A Puerto Rican girl of my acquaintance who has the habit of wearing slacks—not a traditional Puerto Rican behavior pattern, and not one which is tolerated in all parts of the island[14]—has told me that she is frequently addressed in English when so attired, particularly by people like ticket-sellers and waiters. I observed her efforts to address the waiters at

[13] Jones, p. 113, presents this perception of accent, real or fancied, as almost the unique motivation of switching. I believe that this is an exaggeration.

[14] As of 1971, the use of miniskirts, hot pants, and slacks by young women, especially in metropolitan areas, marks the accelerated pattern of acculturation.

the International Airport at Isla Verde in Spanish to be constantly rebuffed, although the waiters communicated among themselves in Spanish. A Puerto Rican employee of the English Department at the University reports that she is constantly addressed in the hybrid in local stores, the probable cause being her exceptionally fair skin. She speaks English virtually without accent, but she always approaches such people in Spanish.

Skin color is definitely a contributing factor, and it can frequently be observed that Puerto Ricans are more willing to speak Spanish to American Negroes than to their white-skinned compatriots, this is in spite of the fact that the oft-cited English accent may be clearly audible.[15] Even the presence of an overly white skin in a group may cause the Puerto Rican to switch into an English frame of mind; a Puerto Rican member of a group which was swimming with me on a beach at Loiza Aldea shouted something in Spanish to a passing Loizan and was answered "No entiendo inglés." Puerto Ricans who have attempted to attend meetings of secret societies in San Anton (*barrio*) in Ponce, where "African" (or Caribbean) customs, dances, etc., are believed to survive, have been told in English that they must leave or be killed.

In more general terms, it might be said that the Puerto Rican tends to use English to those persons who are not regarded as being part of his particular in-group.[16] In that respect, his attitude is very like that of the Antiguan to his more Creole-tinged English or of the resident of Port-au-Prince to the French Creole. This attitude conflicts with the Puerto Rican's belief that he is culturally closer to New York than to the Caribbean, and with his lack of knowledge about or interest in surrounding Caribbean Islands, with the possible exception of St. Thomas, Santo Domingo (not Haiti), and internationally prominent Cuba.

Thus, for most Puerto Ricans, the world is dichotomized into those who speak English and those who speak Spanish, and anything which is not Spanish is probably to be interpreted as English. On occasion, the converse also can be true. When Charron, in a hybrid-English conversation with a Puerto Rican professor, reported that he was going to get a cook from

---

[15] Although the subject is touchy, it must be stated that class distinctions have their effect. Spanish is, to some extent, the language of lower prestige, and unfortunately, black is the lower-class color in Puerto Rico as in the United States. Cf. Maria Teresa Babin, *Panorama de la Cultura Puertorriqueña*, New York, Las Americas Publishing Co., 1958. A colorful, bearded American Negro who gives his name as McLennon King has recently been peddling macaronic mimeographed sheets accusing Puerto Ricans of hypocrisy in declaring they are without prejudice against Negroes. It may or may not be significant that the *cantineras*, who are the only group which accepts me as a Spanish speaker, frequently address me as *Negro*. But for a more objective account of class and prejudice see Bonilla, *op. cit.*

[16] Phonological characteristics should not be overlooked. The educated Puerto Rican (who is apt to be genuinely bilingual in English), does not use [x] for *rr*, nor drop his *s*'s. (Cf. Matluck, *op. cit.*) To the speaker of the folk dialect, such a person may sound a little like a speaker of Spanish with an English accent.

Guadaloupe (using French phonology for the pronunciation of the name even more completely than he had been doing in his English), the Puerto Rican, obviously puzzled, asked, somewhat tentatively, "From the *pueblo*?" Clearly, he recognized something that was not English and assumed that it must be Spanish, although the general tenor of his conversation showed the familiar insistence upon English.

The international use of English, of course, parallels this kind of dichotomizing. The Puerto Rican is not the only person who sees English on all or most of the packages he buys, even though they may contain local products. But perhaps he is more likely than most to attend English films with Spanish subtitles and to find the books in his libraries arranged in English. (Cervantes comes under *S* for *Spanish*, not *E* for *Español*.) When he encounters something, like a movie, in French or German, he is inclined to think of it as somewhat ridiculous. The more uninhibited male members of the audiences at the cheaper movie houses—who are given to talking aloud to the characters in the pictures, whatever the language—frequently do satirical imitations of those strange noises when the language is neither Spanish nor English, although they do not do so for English. (Actually, the data for British English are incomplete. Toynbee, in his lectures to University professors and students, proved to be completely unintelligible. Mimeographed scripts were circulated after the first lecture, and it was obvious from the turning of pages that almost every member of the audience was depending upon the script. But they did not talk back to him.) At the university, "art" films (that is, films, often quite ordinary, in "foreign" languages) are usually presented with English subtitles; usually, announcements of such films are posted with the original title and an English translation. The presentation of the Bach St. Matthew Passion in English rather than in German at the 1963 Casals Festival is probably traceable to the performers (the Robert Shaw Chorale): but, whatever the cause, English intervenes between Spanish and other languages in a familiar pattern in Puerto Rico.

This is the expected state of affairs. When Georg[17] Demus played at the University *anfiteatro*, his announcing of encore titles in English was taken as a matter of course. When he announced one in clearly intelligible Spanish giggles ran through the audience. When a German philosophy professor gave a lecture, in German, under the auspices of the German Club, a mimeographed script, in German, was circulated; and it was announced that she would answer questions afterward in German, English, or Spanish. After one valiant attempt in German by an elderly man, the question period quickly turned to English, the principal questioner being a youth whose English was of the painful, word-at-a-time variety. The lady's Spanish, which may well be excellent, was not tested during the evening; and no one considered that there was anything strange in this. A student writing about a trip to

---

[17] The name appeared in announcements as both *Jorge* and *George*. At least one barber solves the difference by compromise, and gives his shop as *Gorge's*.

Germany reported upon her difficulties when she got into a taxicab with a driver who did not understand English. It is fairly certain that she did not even try Spanish; and, incidentally, her English is far from good. When Gagarin's famous landing declaration was a news item, *El Mundo* printed a cartoon showing him emerging from his capsule saying "I am eagle"; although the cartoon was supplied by a press agency, the Puerto Rican obviously found nothing strange in a Russian's speaking badly constructed English.

Under these circumstances, one is not surprised to find that a very high degree of Anglicization applies to words from the "foreign" languages which Puerto Ricans have to cope with. Johannes Brahms has his last name pronounced [bræmz] regularly at University concerts, and the speaker is likely to feel a little proud of such a pronunciation. When a newsreel, made in Puerto Rico, contains a reference to *la famosa academia St. Cyr*, the name is predictably pronounced [sent sir]. Camille St. Saens is, of course, [sent senz], although it is probable that Ogden Nash did not get his version of that pronunciation (verses to *Carnival of Animals*) in Puerto Rico. Still in the area of musicians, the pronunciations [mozart] and [bruno waltɛr] are not unexpected although perhaps the latter would be natural to any Spanish-speaking person. On Radio Station WIPR's opera programs, the announcer renders Hagen, of *Die Götterdämmerung*, as [hegɛn]. And when the "clase de dirección escénica" of the Facultad de Humanidades presented *Un Día de Octubre*, translated from the play by Georg Kaiser, the character known as Jean Marc Marien was frequently called [dʒan], often with an English-type affrication which exceeds the Puerto Rican tongue touching [j] in this position. A German like Kaiser or Demus, incidentally, is almost certain to have his name spelled *George*; this did not happen in the program for March 22, 23, 24, 1962; but it did happen in the notices of the play in *El Mundo*. And Frank Schubert turns up as a German composer in the same paper.

One's interpretation of typographical slips may condition his acceptance of some of this type of evidence. For example, when the Wiener Sängerknabe appeared at UPR (Nov. 13, 1961), the program contained, in addition to other difficulties in German, the mistake *Hoch bom Dachstein an* for *Hoch vom Dachstein an*. Of course this is a common mistake (*v* and *b* confusion) in spelling, even when dealing with monolingual Spanish materials; but practice in dealing with English in this manner (*Chebrolet* for *Chevrolet*) may well have contributed something. Certainly, such mistakes are less likely to arise from an [f] pronunciation. The audience at the concert chattered away during the vocal numbers much as they do at foreign movies with Spanish subtitles; a professor's shout, perhaps not in the very best of German accents, of "Schweigen Sie, bitte!" provoked nothing but laughter. Unusually, the singing of the boys in Spanish was greatly appreciated, and their "cuteness" was endlessly discussed. Of course, the Spanish number was balanced by one in English.

German, of course, turns up quite infrequently on this island, except when an occasional veteran student informs the class that Germans call their language *Dutch* [datʃ]. Löwenbräu, on the "Lista de Precios del Bar . . . efectiva el día 15 de Nov. de 1961" for the faculty club gets a double dose of anglicism and comes out

Lower Braun.

There can have been no mistake in identifying the beverage meant, for it has the same price as other imported beers and appears in the same section. The lion on the bottle would be no more effective than the umlaut mark on the last syllable in counteracting the Puerto Rican's tendency to regard such a form as English if at all possible. (Either English or Spanish influences could be responsible for ignoring the umlaut; [au] is the regular pronunciation of the syllable nucleus by, for example, all but the proprietress of a German restaurant in downtown Dallas, Texas.) Puerto Rican rums on the same list, as on the bottles, are

Don Q [dan kju] White
Don Q Gold, etc.

French names are treated in about the same way. Bordeaux comes out [bordəks] with a schwa in the final syllable which must have cost the radio announcer a great deal of trouble. So must the first vowel in [dʒæks ibɛrt] for the television announcer who pronounced it. Charles DeGaulle is regularly [tʃarlz digol] through both media, although people of lesser pretensions regularly pronounce that first name, wherever encountered, as [tʃarlɛs]. And the rare Puerto Rican who attempts a lecture in French must perform about as did the UPR professor who lectured on "Les Problèmes de l'Islam Contemporaine," with pronunciations like [rɛlidʒõ] for *religion* and [intɛlidʒãs] for *intelligence*. Students in French classes, as well as in other language classes, report that the teachers, especially when they are Puerto Ricans (and of course Americans) rather than Europeans, use a great deal of English and make constant reference to English. With the exception of the *Deutsch für Ausländer* series and a French elementary text which contains no words in any other language, foreign language textbooks are certain to be in English. And a store name like *Delia's Boutique* is very possibly not French at all, but a Puerto Rican use of an American name which just happens to come into American English through the feeling that French adds "tone" to a fashion store.

In a few cases, interpretation of the treatment of a foreign language form will depend upon one's attitudes toward such things as typographical errors.[18]

---

[18] Apart from mechanical blunders like hitting the wrong key, it seems to me that typographical errors in a bilingual situation at least, are interference phenomena like grammatical errors. When a Puerto Rican typist produces *Each student must occupy his own sit*, or *He told that it was true* in copying English texts, it is easy to see Spanish influence

With the attitude expressed above, I feel free to interpret the heading "Fact non verba" to a Spanish letter to the editor (*El Mundo*, June 9, 1962) as another example of hyper-Anglicism. It is tempting, but probably extreme, to interpret the form *Doming*, on a program giving dates for pictures for the local Cine Forum group, otherwise in Spanish, as interference from the hybrid's most common word-forming device.[19] Those who believe in mere "mistakes," unmotivated in any manner, are of course welcome to their opinions.

In very marked contrast to other languages, the Puerto Rican finds "English" (the hybrid, that is) very easily accessible; it requires neither a great deal of language learning to pass as a master of English nor a great deal of inconvenience to practice. The Puerto Rican feels, and expresses in public statements, that almost anything will fit into English—"*El inglés lo come todo.*" in the exact words of a speaker at the 1961 Conference on Language. Inasmuch as he has the accommodating cooperation of a great number of "continentals," he finds it quite easy to produce "English" through any one of the number of Anglicizing devices which he uses, whether they correspond to devices used by native speakers or not; indeed, he may institutionalize this hybrid and force continental children who attend the all-English schools of Puerto Rico to use one dialect in the home and another at school.

In addition, he finds small armies of dedicated—perhaps even over-dedicated—teachers armed with slogans of "They Need English!" and businessmen from the states assuring him that progress must come in the English language. This latter statement is a truism to anyone who knows the island, but a typical statement of the attitude may be found in Thomas C. Cochran, *The Puerto Rican Businessman*.[20] He is likely to think of lack of English as being unprogressive and uneducated, like the *público* driver whom

---

at work. Thus the hybrid process of word formation may be responsible for several occurrences of *numer* for *number* (< *numero*) in an English department test. Interference also affects printers, as it did those who rendered my "Caribbean Creole languages" as "Caribbean Creole *idioms*" (<*idiomas*), in accord with the hybrid practice of dropping the final vowel.

[19] An alternate explanation, though not one favored by Puerto Ricans, would derive these clipped forms through Papiamento. Thus Papiamento has *cerves, kas, kos* instead of *cerveza, casa, cosa*. If the hybrid forms have been passed through Papiamento, it would be necessary to accept Alleyne's concept of "decreolization." Clipped forms like *anoch, lech* have been cited in both student and popular Puerto Rican speech. Directly questioned on such matters, Puerto Ricans give defensive answers, such as "He was speaking English," or "He was speaking indistinctly," or even "Many of our people have speech defects." The "clipped forms" thus rank low on the social and stylistic scale, approximately *casual* or *intimate* in Joosian terms. Low prestige would be natural if these forms had passed through a creole stage. For decreolization, clipping, etc., cf. Mervyn Alleyne (review of Alvarez Nazario, *El Elemento Afronegroïde en el Español de Puerto Rico*), *Caribbean Studies*, 3(1693):96–98. Ruben del Rosario, "Estado Actual del Español en Puerto Rico," in *Presente y Futuro de la Lengua Española* (Madrid, 1964).

[20] (Philadelphia, 1958).

I heard marvelling about the two Spanish girls ("*muy bien educadas*") who did not speak a single word of English.

The street from one language to another is one way; English with heavy interference patterns from Spanish or from another language is English, but Spanish with unfamiliar characteristics is not Spanish. These linguistic facts, along with Puerto Rico's close social and economic ties to the United States and possible associations between class and language, make the Puerto Rican treat anything outside Puerto Rican Spanish patterns as though it were English. Thus, a process of rapid linguistic acculturation is obviously observable in Puerto Rico. If this process prevails, as it seems likely to do, over the competing Hispanism, there may someday be a new dialect of English, comparable to the English of the Pennsylvania "Dutch."

STUDY QUESTIONS

1. Some near bilinguals engage in elaborate patterns of "code-shifting" between one language and another, sometimes in an apparently unsystematic way. In the following passage, the narrative parts of the speaker's story tend to be in Spanish and the evaluative parts—for example, "it's nothing to be proud of"— in English.

> Por eso cada, you know it's nothing to be proud of, porque yo no estoy proud of it, as a matter of fact I hate it, pero viene Vierne y Sabado yo estoy, tu me ve haci a mi, sola with, aquí solita, a veces que Frankie me deja, you know a stick or something, y yo aquí solita, que es Judy no sabe y yo estoy haci, viendo television, but I rather, y cuando estoy con gente yo me . . . borracha porque me siento más, happy, más free, you know, pero si yo estoy con mucha gente yo no estoy, you know, high, more or less, I couldn't get along with anybody.[a]
>
> (*That's why*—you know it's nothing to be proud of, *because I'm not* proud of it, as a matter of fact I hate it—*whenever Friday and Saturday come, I'm alone* (*you see me like that*), here all alone; then Frankie leaves me, you know, a joint or something, *and I'm here all alone . . . that is, Judy doesn't know it and I'm like that* [high], *watching television*, but I rather; *and when I'm with people I . . . get high because I feel more* happy, *more* free, you know, *but if I'm with a lot of people I'm not*, you know, high, more or less; I couldn't get along with anybody.)

This kind of code-shifting also takes place in similar situations among speakers of one language. Imagine a context where the distance between two "codes" (or levels of style) would be great in your own speech.

2. The following quotation is from a "Spanish" conversation between three friends about current racial disturbances: (English speech underlined)

[a] Quoted by William Labov, "The Notion of 'System' in Creole Studies," in *Pidginization and Creolization of Languages*, ed. Dell Hymes (Cambridge, 1971), p. 457.

CP: Mira, este, Paul me dijo anoche que los amigos de él estaban allí en la barra y tenían esas cosas para protegerse la cabeza y con <u>shotgun</u> y todito d'eso y le dijeron, tu sabes, le dijeron, "ahora nosotros vamos a tirar a cualquiera que sea, que haga algo" le tiran enseguida. Le dijo que nunca le habían tirado a uno o habían matado a nadie pero que ahora si toda la gente de color estaban buscando por <u>trouble</u>, que ellos iban a buscar por <u>trouble</u> también.

AM: Esa gente de color, <u>they're not allowed to shoot at white people you know</u>.

AS: Tu sabes el <u>trouble they're making</u>. Yo creo que le tiraron, este, un tiro a un nene y le explotaron un ojo.

AM: O que lo mataron.

AS: Porque lo dijeron allá, este, <u>there where I work</u>, un <u>manager</u> lo dijo.

CP: Paul anoche me dijo, mira, que ahora mismo con los policías amigos míos lo trajeron hasta esta avenida. Dicen que le van a tirar, que le van a tirar enseguida. El dijo que <u>they're looking for trouble</u> . . . Que son todos jovencitos, <u>they're young</u>.[b]

(Translation:)

CP: Look, Paul told me last night that some friends were there in the bar and had those things to protect their heads and a <u>shotgun</u> and all, and they said to him, you know, they said, "now we're going to shoot at anything, anything that moves" and shot right away. He said they had never shot or killed anyone, but now if all the blacks were looking for <u>trouble</u>, they would look for <u>trouble</u>, too.

AM: Those blacks, <u>they're not allowed to shoot at white people, you know.</u>

AS: You know the <u>trouble they're making</u>. I think they shot at a kid and blasted his eye out.

AM: Or killed him.

AS: (Because) they said so there, <u>there where I work</u>, a <u>manager</u> said so.

CP: Paul told me last night, that right then my friends brought him to this street with the police. They said they're going to shoot, they're going to shoot immediately. He said that <u>they're looking for trouble</u> . . . that they're all kids, <u>they're young</u>.

Can the preceding example of code switching be explained systematically, or is it a sample of "free variation"? Compare the code switching among the three speakers. Do their code switching styles seem to differ?

3. Dillard illustrates the "anglicization" of proper names in Puerto Rican Spanish. How has this same process in American English altered the pronunciation of the following place names?

Des Moines	El Paso
Los Angeles	Berlin (New Hampshire)
Berkeley	Chevy Chase (Maryland)
New Orleans	Hanover (Pennsylvania)

[b] Quoted by Joshua A. Fishman, *Bilingualism in the Barrio* (Washington, D.C., 1968), p. 655.

4. On p. 85 Dillard gives several examples of "special" pronunciations of foreign
   words. What attempts have you heard (or can you find in your desk dictionary)
   that are sometimes used to give a "foreign" quality to the following?

Loch Ness	De Gaulle
Van Gogh	smorgasbord
Uruguay	Rheims

PIDGIN LANGUAGES
Robert A. Hall, Jr.

According to one estimate, languages known as pidgins and creoles are spoken by some ten million people around the world. Lacking documentary evidence to support a detailed historical account of most established creoles, linguists have had to develop generalizations based on recent investigations of multilingual communities and new contacts between speakers of different languages. The polygenetic *theory of creolization, described by Hall in the following essay, presumes two stages: first, contact between speakers of different languages is carried on in a rudimentary, pidgin vernacular that may contain elements contributed by the several languages of the speakers. Eventually this simplified language extends beyond the functions of trade or exploration that first gave rise to it and becomes the native language of some members of the community. Once the language reaches this second stage, it is considered a creole, and before long the process of* relexification *begins to take place as the structure of the simplified language is expanded by the introduction of new vocabulary. At this point in its development, a creole may be extended to all members of the community and thus begin the historical patterns of growth through borrowing and internal change characteristic of all human languages.*

The polygenetic theory described by Hall would suggest that creole languages vary extensively from region to region depending on the particular languages involved in the initial contact situation, but in fact certain traits are found in nearly all the creoles that owe their origin to one of the European languages. This observation has led to a monogenetic *theory of creole development, and some observers have claimed that Pidgin Portuguese gave rise to the many creoles now spoken around the world, even though this origin is obscured by the relexification of creoles from French, Spanish, English, Dutch, and other European languages. Although the monogenetic theory does not account for all creole languages, some of which have emerged in areas where Portuguese was never spoken, it nevertheless draws attention to the remarkable similarities of the best known creoles.*

The social status of a creole illustrates in a heightened form the interplay of attitude and style-shifting discussed by Labov, Tucker and Lambert, and Shuy in later sections of this book. Some creole speakers may be reluctant to admit the slightest knowledge of their "other" language to the outsider, whereas in other communities creole may act as a proud marker of nationality. In Sierra

From *Scientific American*, 1959, **200**(2), 124–34. Reprinted with permission of the author and publisher.

Leone, for example, some Krio speakers resist borrowings from current English and through a kind of "hypercreolization" assert their national solidarity. In Haiti, on the other hand, creole is rejected for governmental and cultural functions, and some disclaim knowledge of their native language and use only French in their contacts with outsiders.

Most pidgin languages are probably short-lived. The "Bamboo English" used by Americans and Koreans during the early 1950s virtually disappeared with the end of the Korean War. Even if contacts persist, the low social position usually assigned to pidgins may inhibit their development into creoles, particularly if some speakers decide to acquire fluency in one of the international languages rather than subject themselves to scorn by continuing to speak the makeshift vernacular. The development of an English-Japanese pidgin following the Second World War was arrested in this way by the Japanese decision to initiate a massive English-teaching program.[a] Linguistic history is doubtless full of cases where the cycle of pidgin → creole → national language begins but is arrested in some early stage. Linguists are beginning to recognize that pidginization may provide a useful insight into the history of all languages. Hall even suggests that the great European languages may have arisen by processes resembling the growth of pidgins and creoles, a hypothesis that makes the study of these apparently "marginal" languages of central interest to those interested in the growth of language.

Since the time of Columbus the course of history has largely been set by the growth of European commerce and power in the rest of the world. One much misunderstood by-product of this historical process has been the birth, in nearly every Oriental, African, and American region visited or colonized by Westerners, of a simplified form of speech, used in contacts with the native population: the so-called pidgin languages. Today, despite a certain amount of well-meant disapproval, the importance of some varieties of pidgin is increasing.

To those who speak European languages, pidgin sounds like a ludicrous mispronunciation of their own tongues; for that reason it is often castigated as a "bastard lingo" or "gibberish." Common parlance has made "pidgin" an opprobrious term for any formless speech, such as the broken-English "No tickee, no washee" attributed to Chinese laundrymen. I have even heard a professor apply the word to the language of his freshman students, simply because they wrote unimaginatively and overworked a few clichés. But investigations in Haiti, Melanesia, and elsewhere have shown that real pidgin languages are far more than half-learned versions of European speech. They are languages in their own right. Their sounds and grammar have the

---

[a] See John Stuart Goodman, "The Development of a Dialect of English-Japanese Pidgin," *Anthropological Linguistics*, **9**, vi(1967):43–55.

internal consistency requisite to any stable system of communication. And whether we like them or not they are probably here to stay, for they have their own humble, but useful, function in society.

Pidgin is not the only form of mixed language. To understand the stages through which such forms of speech develop, we must make a three-way distinction between the lingua franca, the pidgin language and the creolized language. A lingua franca is any tongue serving as a means of communication among groups that have no other language in common; for example, English in India and the Philippines. A pidgin language is a lingua franca that in the course of its adoption has become simplified and restructured. The reduced language which results from this process is nobody's native language, but the languages of its speakers considerably influence its vocabulary and other features. Occasionally users of a pidgin language will cease to speak their native tongue and come to rely upon the pidgin entirely. In such a community children will grow up speaking pidgin as their sole language. When a pidgin is pressed into service as a native language, its vocabulary must greatly expand to accommodate its users' everyday needs. A reduced language, when thus reexpanded, is called a creolized language (the creole languages of Haiti and other Caribbean areas are typical).

Pidgin and creolized languages have arisen many times in history. The earliest recorded pidgin, which has given its name to the whole genus of international languages, is the original Lingua Franca, based on southern French and the Ligurian dialect of Italian and used in the Middle Ages by western Europeans ("Franks") in the eastern Mediterranean. During the epoch of colonization, as Europeans came into contact with aboriginal populations, many pidgin forms of Portuguese, Spanish, French, and English became common. It is said that there was, or is, a Pidgin Portuguese in every region colonized by Portugal. Separate varieties of Pidgin English arose in North America, China, West Africa, Australia, and the Pacific; in the latter region subtypes have arisen in Hawaii, New Guinea, and the Solomon Islands. Pidginized varieties of French are found in North Africa and New Caledonia.

Pidginization has occurred not only with European but also with non-European languages, as in the case of the Chinook Jargon based on the Chinook Indian language and spoken in fur-trading days in the U.S. Northwest. We may also cite Bazaar Malay in Southeast Asia, Swahili in Central Africa, the Pidgin Motu of Papua, Tupí-Guaraní (the so-called Lingua Gêral or "general language") in Brazil, and the Fanaga-Lò or "Kitchen Kaffir" in South Africa.

The best-known creolized languages derive from French and are spoken in Louisiana, Haiti, the Lesser Antilles, Réunion, and Mauritius. English-based creole languages also exist: among them are the Gullah of the Sea Islands off South Carolina, the Taki-Taki of Dutch Guiana, and the Negro English of the West Indies. Pidgin Spanish, strongly influenced by Portuguese, gave rise to the Papiamentu Creole of Curaçao and neighboring islands. The Afrikaans or "Cape Dutch" of South Africa, which is much simpler than Netherlands

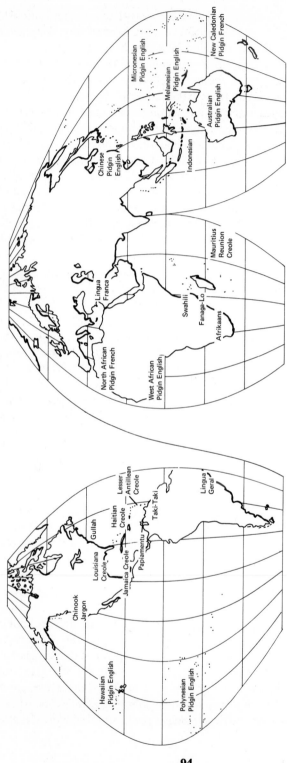

Pidgin and Creole languages are spoken at many points of contact between native peoples and colonial traders or rulers. Lingua Franca, the oldest known pidgin, was based on French and Italian. Lingua Géral, Chinook Jargon, Swahili, Fanaga-Lô, and Indonesian have a non-European basis. Gullah, Jamaica Creole, and Taki-Taki stem from English, Papiamentu from Spanish, and the creoles of Louisiana, Haiti, the Lesser Antilles, Mauritius-Réunion, and New Caledonia from French.

94

Dutch, may be another creolized language, arising out of an earlier Pidgin Dutch used between settlers and natives and adopted by white children growing up in South Africa.

People who wish to denigrate pidgin languages sometimes point out that they are not written, the implication being that any unwritten language is an unlicked bear cub, an unintelligible jargon never submitted to the necessary discipline of the schools. This reflects a basic misunderstanding of the nature of language. Most of the languages spoken by men throughout history (and before it) have never been reduced to writing, but they are no less languages. On the other hand, many modern pidgin and creole languages are quite regularly written and are even used in newspapers and education. Languages, pidgin or otherwise, are orderly by definition. Writing is no more than an external representation of most (not all) of the structure of a language.

The most orderly representation of a language is a spelling based on its phonemes, or functional units of sound. Nothing but confusion can result from attempts to render pidgin languages in a botched form of traditional English or French spelling. In this article I adhere strictly to phonemic spellings. For example, the Melanesian Pidgin English sentence meaning "I have three books" is "mi gat trifela buk," not "me got t'reefellow book." A Haitian Creole proverb meaning "He who gave the blow forgets, he who bears the scar remembers" would be "Bay-kal blié, pòté-mak sôjé," not the mock-French "Baille-calle 'blier, portermarque songer." Readers interested in the derivation of the pidgin and creole words that I have spelled phonemically will find them in the tables beginning on page 101. Phonemic spellings have been devised (mainly by missionaries) for a number of pidgin and creolized languages. This trend should be encouraged wherever possible, if only to enforce recognition of the fact that pidgin words and sounds are things in themselves and not bungled attempts to pronounce another language.

In general the phonemic systems of pidgin and creolized tongues show a certain amount of simplification. Vowel structure is often reduced to five vowels represented by "a," "e," "i," "o," "u" (pronounced as in Italian). Most French-based creoles have lost the group of French vowels pronounced with the lips rounded but with the tongue in the front of the mouth. In Haitian Creole the French word "culture" becomes "kilti" and "bleu" becomes "blé." Virtually all English-based pidgins lack the voiced and unvoiced sounds represented by "th" in English spelling: in Melanesian Pidgin "this" is "disfela" and "three" is "trifela." Similarly, the English "f" is replaced by "p," the "v" by "b," and the "sh" by "s." Thus "heavy" is "hebi" and "finish" becomes "pinis."

The pronunciation habits of a native language often carry over into a pidgin and survive, even for generations, in creoles. In the pidgin and creolized languages spoken in the Americas by the descendants of West African slaves the "r" at the end of a syllable is generally lost, as in the case of the Haitian "pòté" ("to carry," from the French "porter"). In Taki-Taki an older stratum of words has lost the "r" (e.g., "gódo" for "gourd"), but newer borrowings from the English or Dutch retain the "r" (e.g., "forku" for "fork"). The Cantonese Chinese merged "r" with "l," as in the Chinese Pidgin English "veli" ("very").

In Melanesian languages the consonants "b," "d," and "g" often begin with a nasal sound: "mb," "nd," "ng." Those who speak Melanesian carry this peculiarity over into Melanesian Pidgin, where "tabu" ("prohibition" or "forbidden") is usually "tambu," and "sidaun" ("sit" or "be located") is frequently "sindaun." Many combinations of consonants are difficult for the Melanesian, and he will insert an extra vowel into sound clusters such as "kl," "pl," "br," and "ls"; thus "klir" ("clear") often sounds like "kalír" or "kilír," and "olsem" ("so" or "thus") like "olasem." The younger generation, however, is learning to omit these interpolated vowels.

The same linguistic snobs who make sport of unwritten pidgin and creolized languages are likely to declare that these tongues have no grammar. Behind this criticism, too, lurks a misapprehension of the nature of language. Every language has a grammar; that is, a stock of linguistic forms and principles for using them. All men, no matter how primitive in other respects, speak fully structured languages. Grammar is a far older and more firmly established invention than the grammar book. One critic has asked: "How can it be said that pidgin has a grammar when it has no tenses, cases, or numbers?" It is true that many forms of pidgin lack these familiar features of European grammar, but they have other devices to make up for them.

Chinese Pidgin, for instance, adds the suffix "-pisi" ("piece") to all numerals, as in "tupisi man" ("two men") and "forpisi tebal" ("four tables"). In Chinese Pidgin the suffix "-said" indicates place where, and the suffix "-taim" indicates time when. Both are added to nouns and pronouns: "hi haussaid" ("at his house"), "doksaid" ("at the dock"), "maisaid" ("where I am"), "hwattaim?" ("when?"), "distaim" ("now"). In Melanesian Pidgin there are three suffixes that serve to indicate the form and function of words. The suffix "-fela," when added to the pronouns "mi" ("I" or "me") and "yu" ("you," singular), forms the plural: "mifela" ("we" or "us"), "yufela" ("you," plural). Another suffix, also pronounced "-fela" but distinct from the foregoing, characterizes demonstratives, indefinites, numerals, and one-syllable adjectives: "disfela" ("this"), "nadarfela" ("another"), "tufela" ("two"), "gudfela" ("good"). The suffix "-im" shows that a verb is transitive: "tok" means "speak," but "tokim" is "speak to" or "address"; "fait" is "fight," but "faitim" means "strike," "beat," "hit."

Some pidgin and creolized languages employ grammatical devices that appear quite peculiar to the Western mind. In languages with West African elements, prefixes replace suffixes as indicators of grammatical relationships. Haitian Creole, for instance, has no verb tenses in our sense. Instead verbs are distinguished by a set of prefixes indicating the continuity or completion of the action performed: while "mwê châté" means "I sing," mwê ap-châté" means "I am singing," and "mwê fèk-châté" means "I have just sung."

Sometimes parts of speech, as well as the process of adding suffixes or prefixes, derive from the original native language of the speakers. Consider the pronouns of Melanesian Pidgin. Those who speak this language distinguish between "yumi" ("we" or "us," including the hearer) and "mifela" ("we" or "us," excluding the hearer). This reflects the distinction between the "inclusive" and "exclusive" first-person plural found in native Melanesian languages. Melanesian Pidgin also employs phrases formed of pronoun plus numeral, such as "mi trifela" ("the three of us") and "yu tufela" ("the two of you"). These correspond to special forms in Melanesian languages called "dual" (referring to two) or "trial" (referring to three).

Pidgins and creoles, with their simplified use of grammatical endings, rely heavily on word order to indicate the relationship between words. Simple juxtaposition serves to characterize many types of phrases; in Melanesian Pidgin, for example, a noun following another noun serves to tell some characteristic or purpose of what is referred to by the first noun: "haus moni" is "house for money," i.e., "bank," and "tok gaman" is "talk characterized by deceit," i.e., "falsehood." A similar combination occurs in Haitian Creole, but with the second noun indicating a possessor: "pitit rwa" means "children of a king," and "lakay mwê" means "house of me" or "my house." In Melanesian Pidgin possession is indicated by a phrase introduced by the preposition "bilong" ("of"): "pikinini bilong king" means "a king's children," and "haus bilong mi" means "my house." In Chinese Pidgin possession is shown simply by a noun or pronoun preceding the noun modified: "dat master poni" ("that master's pony") or "yu legan" ("your legs").

Those who speak Western European languages expect every full sentence to contain a predicate whose main element is a verb. But in Melanesian Pidgin and Haitian Creole (as in many other languages) the core of the predicate may just as well be a noun, an adjective, or an adverb. In Melanesian Pidgin "mi plisboi" means "I am a policeman," "Yu redi?" means "Are you ready?," "tinktink bilong mi olsem" means "my opinion is thus." In Haitian Creole "li bô" means "he is good," "ou gasô" means "you are a regular fellow," and "yo isit" means "they are here." Some grammatical forms belong especially to predicates, such as the Melanesian Pidgin third-person predicate-marker "i-" in "disfela man i-gudfela" ("this man is good") and "ol i-hardwok" ("they work hard"). Other examples are the Haitian Creole tense markers "té-" (past), "va-" (future) and the negative particle "pa-": "li té-bô" ("he was good"), "yo va-isit" ("they will be here") and "ou pa-gasô" ("you're not a regular fellow").

Naive observers have been struck by three supposed characteristics of pidgin vocabularies: their poverty, bastard origin, and content of vulgar words. In all three of these respects, however, prevalent opinions concerning pidgin languages are erroneous. True, the ordinary pidgin language has a very small stock of words, say between 700 and 1,500, as contrasted with the 20,000 to 25,000 that even the most ignorant speaker of a "full-size" language knows. But though small, the pidgin vocabularies are not poor; the scarcity of individual words is counterbalanced by a wealth of combinations into which they may enter. These combinations often show considerable resourcefulness and ingenuity on the part of the speakers. The Melanesian Pidgin word "gras," for example, means not just "grass," but "anything growing bladelike out of a surface": "mustache" is "gras bilong maus." This restriction of vocabulary leads to semantic extensions and an increase of verbal allusiveness and color.

Curiously the vocabulary of any given pidgin language is usually less mixed in origin than that of the "full-sized" tongue on which it is based. Casual observers are struck by the presence of words from many sources in a pidgin language; Melanesian Pidgin, for example, has borrowings from German ("raus," meaning "get out"; "srank," meaning "chest of drawers"), from native languages ("kiau," meaning "egg"; "balus," meaning "pigeon" or "airplane"), from Malay ("karabau," meaning "water buffalo"), from Polynesian ("talatala," meaning "Protestant"). It even has a few Romance words ("save," meaning "know"; "pikinini," meaning "child"; "pato," meaning "duck"). But a count of the total lexicon reveals that roughly 80 per cent of the Melanesian Pidgin vocabulary is of English origin. In English itself over 50 per cent of the words are from French, Greek, Latin, and other non-English sources!

The vocabularies of pidgin languages often contain words revealing the lower-class origin of their first European speakers (Melanesian Pidgin "plantim," meaning "bury"; "kalabus," meaning "jail"), or their nautical calling (Melanesian Pidgin "haisimap," meaning "lift"; Haitian Creole "viré," meaning "turn" or "veer"). Other words seem, to fastidious Europeans, downright indecent: for example, the Melanesian Pidgin "ars," meaning "bottom"; "bagarimapim," meaning "wreck" or "ruin"; "godam," meaning "golly." In native cultures, however, European taboos are not relevant. Moreover, the meaning of the words themselves is often so greatly extended as to lose all inelegance. Thus "ars" not only means "bottom" but also "base," "cause," "reason," "source." The phrase "long ars bilong" is "because of," structurally an exact parallel to the French "à cause de."

The important feature of pidgin vocabularies is their ability to grow and their adequacy to the needs of the situations where they are used. When a pidgin becomes creolized, the vocabulary expands greatly, especially through borrowings from the language of the dominant nation in the region (e.g., Dutch in Taki-Taki and Papiamentu).

How do pidgin languages arise? Usually they spring from situations of casual contact, where a means of easy, informal communication is desired between a dominant foreign group and a subservient native population. No emphasis is laid on "correctness" or completeness. Members of the dominant group often assume that their interlocutors are childlike and must be addressed as children. Hence baby talk and similar simplifications enter into the original formation of a pidgin. Europeans are quick to assume that the native's first, broken imitation of the foreign speech represents his optimum performance; they reply in the same broken style. When the process of language learning is arrested at this stage, and the use of the resultant simplified structure and vocabulary is institutionalized, a pidgin has been born.

Pidgin languages do not always derive from this kind of master-and-servant relationship. Indeed, they may arise between groups (of traders, for example) that have more or less equal status. But when a pidgin survives beyond the initial stage of contact, when it persists for decades or centuries in intergroup dealings, we can assume that one group wishes to maintain social distance from the other. In the case of Chinese Pidgin English a standoffish attitude characterized both sides, for the Chinese more than matched the Europeans in their sense of national superiority. If only two language groups are involved, the side that feels it suffers loss of status because it speaks pidgin may come to insist on learning the other side's full language; this happened in China after 1900. But where those who speak many native tongues share a single pidgin, questions of status may be outweighed by an overpowering need for a means of communication. In New Guinea, with its multiplicity of tongues, Melanesian Pidgin has become a linguistic cement: without it labor relations and economic life would be impossible.

It is often assumed that a European language furnishes the pidgin vocabulary, while the "native" language supplies the pidgin grammatical structure. Chinese Pidgin English is sometimes called "Chinese spoken with English words." This notion is inexact. Close examination reveals that each form of pidgin adheres to the dominant language in grammar as well as vocabulary. The grammatical categories and types of phrase and clause in Taki-Taki, Chinese Pidgin and Melanesian Pidgin are English; those of the various creoles are North French; those of Papiamentu are Spanish. However, elements of all kinds—sounds, inflections and types of word order—can and do invade pidgin from the native tongues of the subservient group. I have already mentioned elements of Melanesian, Chinese, and West African pronunciation in certain pidgins and creoles. With respect to inflection the Chinese Pidgin suffix "-pisi" is clearly a translation of the Chinese itemizer or numeral classifier meaning "piece," and such a phrase as "Ning-Po mo far" ("beyond Ning-Po") reflects the native Chinese word order.

The creolization of a pidgin language can happen either voluntarily (as in certain modern villages in New Guinea), or involuntarily (as when Caribbean plantation owners deliberately separated slaves of the same language, in order to minimize the danger of conspiracy and revolt). In either case the children of the group speak pidgin as their first language. Thus they extend its range to meet everyday needs, either by developing its inner grammatical resources or by borrowing from outside sources, as Haitian and other creoles have done from French. Creolized languages are often subject to snobbish condemnation. This causes insecurity in their speakers, who in their anxiety commit malapropisms. For example, a Haitian Creole storyteller once said of his characters: "Yo pasé lanwit nâ-kôplézâs zétwal yo" ("they passed the night in the complaisance of the stars"); when what he meant was "kôtâ-plasyô" ("contemplation").

To date most creolized languages have remained on the level of despised vernaculars. Sometimes, though, a pidgin can become creolized and then, through the accidents of history, attain the status of a universally recognized national language. This is what happened in the case of Indonesian. On Java and elsewhere in the former Dutch East Indies a pidginized form of Malay, known as Bazaar Malay, was widely used as a trade language. With the help of extensive borrowings from classical Malay, Bazaar Malay became the linguistic vehicle for the new Indonesian nationalism; as such, it was renamed "Bahasa Indonesia" ("Indonesian Language"). Now a generation of native speakers is arising and Indonesian is developing a national standard, an official literature, and all the other appurtenances of a world language.

In recent years a new school of criticism has begun to condemn pidgin and creole languages because they often function as "status" languages, the use of which sets off a given group as socially inferior. For this reason the United Nations, in 1954, called on Australia to "eradicate" pidgin from New Guinea, saying: "Melanesian Pidgin is not only not suitable as a medium of instruction, but has characteristics derived from the circumstances in which it was invented which reflect now outmoded concepts of the relationships between indigenous inhabitants and immigrant groups."

The structures of pidgin languages, although reduced in contrast to "major" languages, are nonetheless clear and consistent once they are analyzed and described in their own terms. The lowly social origin of some vocabulary items is not a justifiable reason for condemnation or ridicule; otherwise we should have to ban such English words as "moist," "petulant," or "crepitate" because they come from inelegant Latin terms. The well-meaning diatribes of anticolonialists lose sight of the fact that, although pidgins often do serve as means of discrimination, this is not a necessary or essential part of their function. On the other hand, even if it were possible to "abolish" a language by some totalitarian fiat, a slow, costly, and immensely difficult process of reeducation would be required. Once creolized, pidgin has become a native language, with full rights to consideration and respect.

To remove the stigma associated with such terms as "pidgin" or "creole," it has been suggested that these languages be rebaptized with names such as "Neo-Melanesian," "Langue Haitienne," or, for Taki-Taki, "Sranan-Tongo" ("Surinam language"). This might be a wise concession. At any rate, it is evident that no amount of puristic or anticolonialistic condemnation will "eradicate" pidgin or creolized languages. We should be duly respectful of the role of pidgin as a source of social cohesion in multilingual regions. Quite possibly some current forms of pidgin are future national languages in embryo. In all likelihood new pidgins will continue to arise when the situation calls for them, and will either die out when the need is gone, or acquire longer life through the creative process of creolization.

Melanesian Pidgin	Derivation	Source Words	Meaning
ars	English	arse	bottom, base, cause, reason, source
bagarimap	English	bugger 'im up	wreck, ruin
balus	Gazelle Peninsula language	?	pigeon, airplane
bilong	English	belong	of, for
buk	English	book	book
disfela	English	this + fellow	this
fait	English	fight	fight
faitim	English	fight + 'im	strike, beat, hit
fes	English	face	face
gaman	English	gammon	deceit; deceive
gat	English	got	have
godam	English	god damn	golly
gras	English	grass	anything growing blade-like out of a surface; grass
gudfela	English	good + fellow	good
haisimap	English	h'ist + 'im + up	lift
hardwok	English	hard + work	work hard
haus	English	house	house; room
hebi	English	heavy	heavy
hed	English	head	head
i-	English	he	(predicate-marker)
kalabus	English	Calaboose (from Spanish calabozo)	jail
karabau	Malay	?	water-buffalo
kiau	Gazelle Peninsula language	?	egg
king	English	king	king
klir	English	clear	clear
long	English	along	to, at, with, by
maus	English	mouth	mouth
mi	English	me	I, me
mifela	English	me + fellow	we, us (not including the hearer)
moni	English	money	money
nadarfela	English	another + fellow	another
olsem	English	all the same	thus, so
pato	Portuguese	pato	duck
pikinini	Portuguese	pequenino (little)	child

Melanesian Pidgin	Derivation	Source Words	Meaning
pinis	English	finish	already
plantim	English	plant + 'im	bury
plisboi	English	police + boy	police-boy, native policeman
raus	German	raus (out!)	get out!
redi	English	ready	ready
save	Portuguese	sabe (he knows)	know
si(n)daun	English	sit down	sit, be located
srank	German	schrank	chest of drawers
talatala	Polynesian	(friend)	Protestant
ta(m)bu	Polynesian	tabu	prohibition; forbidden
tinktink	English	think-think	opinion, thought
tok	English	talk	speak; speech
tokim	English	talk + 'im	speak to, address
trifela	English	three + fellow	three
yu	English	you	you (sg.)
yufela	English	you + fellow	you (pl.)
yumi	English	you + me	we, us (including the hearer)

Chinese Pidgin	Derivation	Source Words	Meaning
dat	English	that	that
distaim	English	this time	now
doksaid	English	dock + side	at the dock(s)
far	English	far	far
forpisi	English	four + piece	four
haussaid	English	house + side	at the house
hi	English	he	he, him; she, her; it
hwattaim	English	what + time	when?
legan	English	leg + ?	leg
maisaid	English	my + side	where I am
man	English	man	man
master	English	master	master, European man
mo	English	more	more
poni	English	pony	pony
-said	English	side	at . . .
spoilim	English	spoil + 'im	rotten
-taim	English	time	(shows time when)
tebal	English	table	table
tupisi	English	two + piece	two
yu	English	you	you

Taki-Taki	Derivation	Source Words	Meaning
fórku	English	fork	fork
gó	English	go	go
gódo	English	gourd	gourd
mi	English	me	I, me
sa-	English	shall	(Future tense prefix)
torn	Dutch	torn	tower

Haitian Creole	Derivation	Source Words	Meaning
ap-châté	French	après (after) + chanter (sing)	be singing
bay	French	baille	give
blé	French	bleu	blue
blié	French	oublier	forget
bô	French	bon	good
châté	French	chanter	sing
fèk-châté	French	[ne] fait que chanter (only sings)	have just sung
gasô	French	garçon (boy)	young man; (regular) fellow
isit	French	ici	here
kal	(?)		blow
kilti	French	culture	cultivation
kôplézâs	French	complaisance	complaisance
kôtâplasyô	French	contemplation	contemplation
lakay	(?)		house
lanwit	French	la nuit (the night)	night
li	French	lui (him)	he, him; she, her; it
mak	French	marque	mark
mwê	French	moi	I, me
nâ	French	dans(?)	in
ou	French	vous	you
pa-	French	pas	not
pasé	French	passer	pass
pitit	French	petite	child, children
pôté	French	porter	carry
rwa	French	roi	king
sôjé	French	songer (think, dream)	remember
té-	French	était (was)	(past tense marker)
va-	French + West African	va (goes) + va- (sign of future)	(future tense marker)
viré	French	virer (veer)	turn
yo	French	(dialectal?)	they, them; (noun pluralizer)
zetwal	French	les étoiles (the stars)	star

Sample Texts: English-Based Pidgins and Creoles

1. Neo-Melanesian. A section of the autobiography of a workboy, Čavi, collected by Margaret Mead *ca.* 1936 and transcribed phonemically by Hall in 1942; reproduced from Hall, 1943, §7.62.4 (p. 62).

naw mi stap rabawl. mi stap ləŋ bıglajn, mi kətım kopra. naw wənfɛlə mastər bıləŋ kəmpəni ɛm i-kıčım mi, mi kuk ləŋ ɛm gɛn. mastər kıŋ. mi stap. naw əl mastər i-kık, naw əl i-kıkım ɛm, naw leg bıləŋ ɛm i-swɛləp. əl mastər tæsəl i-kık, naw əl i-kıkım ɛm. naw ɛm i-go ləŋ sıdni ləŋ haws sık. mi wənfɛlə mi stap lukawtım haws bıləŋ ɛm. əltəgɛdər səmtıŋ mi lukawtım, mi stap. ərajt, naw pæs i-kəm. naw kiap i-lukım, i-tək: "o, mastər bıləŋ ju i-no kæn kəm bæk." naw mastər—dısfɛlə ɛm i-kəməp —bıləŋ kəmpəni tu, ɛm i-save bajım nufɛlə bəj ləŋ əlgɛdər· ples—ɛm i-tək ləŋ mi: "ju no kæn go ləŋ bıglajn, maski, ju kuk ləŋ mi gɛn." mi stap ləŋ ɛm. stap stap stap stap. ɛm i-lajk go ləŋ kurili, naw mi no lajk. plɛnti bəj i-kuk ləŋ ɛm. mi no lajk go wəntajm əl, naw mi təkım mastər, mi spik: "o, mi no lajk go wəntajm ju. plɛnti bəj tuməč. maski, mi stap. mi kæn go bæk ləŋ bıglajn"ɛm i-tək: "ərajt. ju kæn stap." mi stap gɛn. ərajt. əl kəmpəni i-gowe, naw i-no mor. əltəgɛdər i-go sıdni. nəmbərwən bıləŋ əl, ɛm i-go tu. bipi kıčım stešən bıləŋ kəmpəni, bænıs bıləŋ ɛm. naw mifɛlə əl bəj hir. ərajt, naw mi tək ləŋ mastər bıləŋ mifɛlə: "a, ajtıŋk mi brokım tajm, mi go ləŋ ples." mastər bıləŋ bipi i-tək: "no, ɛm i-no holım wok bıləŋ jɛt." ərajt, naw mi stap naw ləŋ bipi. naw mastər bıləŋ bipi i-tək: "čavi, mi save ju. ju no wok ləŋ bıglajn, ju əltajm məŋki bıləŋ mastər." naw ɛm i-mekım pepər, naw mi go ləŋ mısıs bıləŋ dısfɛlə kæptɛn bıləŋ mirani bıfor.

Then I stayed in Rabaul. I was in the work-group, cutting copra. Then a white man from the company took me as a cook again. Mr. King. I stayed there. Now all the white men were playing football, and they kicked him, so that his leg swelled up. The white men were just kicking, and kicked him. So he went to Sydney, to the hospital. I stayed alone to look after his house. I looked after everything, and stayed there. Very well, then a letter arrived. Then the government official looked at it, and said: "Oh, your master cannot come back." Then the master—this one who had come—he too was of the company, he recruited new native laborers from all the villages—he said to me: "You cannot go to the work-group, rather you shall cook for me again." I stayed with him, and kept on staying. He wanted to go to Kurili, but I didn't want to. Many "boys" were cooking for him. I did not want to go with them, and I spoke to the master, saying: "Oh, I don't want to go with you. [You have] a great many 'boys.' I'd rather stay. I can go back to the work-group." He said: "Very well. You may stay." I stayed on again. Very well. All the company men went away, and they were not there any more. They all went to Sydney. Their chief went too. B. P. [Burns Philp & Co.] took over the company's plantation and its labor-line. Now we, the "boys," were there. Well, now I said to our master: "Ah, I think I will break my indenture, I shall go to my village." The B. P. master said: "No, he has not done work for me yet." Very well, then I stayed on with B. P. Then the B. P. master said: "Čavi, I know you. You did not work in the work-group, you were always the master's servant." Then he made an indenture, and I went to the wife of this former captain of the "Mirani."

2. Neo-Solomonic. The beginning of a story told to the author in 1954 by a native of Malaita.

ərajt. mifɛlə i-go go lɔŋ səlwatər, lʊkawtɪm fɪš, naw wɪn i-kəm, naw mifɛlə i-go ələbawt lɔŋ kinú, naw bɪgfɛlə wɪn i-kəm naw, mifɛlə i-fafasi ələbawtə, rɔŋ tuməs, mifɛlə go, no kæčɪm ɛni ples i-kwajtfɛlə. mifɛlə go ələbawt lɔŋ ɛvri ples, an mifɛlə go lɔŋ səlwatər, æn traj go, æn wɪn i-kəm hart, naw trifɛlə i-go, naw mifɛlə i-go slip ələbawt nomor lɔŋ antap lɔŋ sanbič, naw mifɛlə go go go, ən wɔnfɛlə man i-dajvən, wɔnfɛlə bɪgfɛlə šɛl lɔŋ səlwatɛr, an hɛm i-tekɪm lɔŋ šor, an mifɛlə askɪm hɛm, "blɔŋ wɔnem hir?". naw mifɛlə se, askɪm hɛm əlsem, an hɛm i-se: "blɔŋ kajkaj." "o, dɪswən ajtɪŋk bajmbaj kajkajm, man i-daj hir." na hɛm i-se, "a, hɛm i-ərajt. səmtɪŋ hir, ɛm i-gʊd hir, i-gʊdfɛlə fɪš." ɛm i-tək əlsem, naw mifɛlə i-go, livɪm hɛm, mifɛlə go ələwe. əl kæčɪm wɔnfɛlə ples mor, mifɛlə fajndɪm wɔnfɛlə wʊmən i-pɪkəp wɔnfɛlə šɛl ər tu lɔŋ səlwatər. mifɛlə askɪm ɛm, i-se: "hwičwe? ju save lʊkawtɪm šelə, na bajmbaj ju save go lɔŋ əlgɛdər wajtmæn fər bajɪm?" ɛm i-se, "no. i-blɔŋ mi fər kajkaj."

Very well. We kept going on the sea, hunting for fish, and a wind arose; now we were going in canoes, and an immense wind arose now, and we were thrown around and ran very fast [before the wind]. We went, and did not come to any place which was quiet. We went around to every place, and we went along on the sea, and tried to go, and the wind came hard, and three [canoes?] went, and we went and simply rested on the beach; then we kept going, and one man dived [for] a large shell in the sea, and he took it to the shore, and we asked him, "Why [do you do this] here?" Now we spoke [and] asked him thus, and he said "To eat." "Oh, this one, probably, if one eats it, one will die here." And he said: "Oh, it's all right. This thing here is good. It's a good fish." He spoke thus, and we went and left him, we went away. They came to another place, and we found a woman who was gathering a shell or two by the sea. We asked her, saying: "How come? Are you in the habit of looking for shells, and then of going to the Europeans to sell them?" She said, "No. They are mine, to eat."

3. Australian Pidgin English. Sentences dictated to the author in 1954 by Judge Norman Bell, a resident of the Northern Territory since 1907, and formerly a judge at West Arm. These sentences represent the type of utterances characteristic of an interrogation and a native's response.

tɔ́mi, jú bín sí ðǽtwən lúbra?

Tommy, did you see that native woman?

jú síɪm lɔŋ áj bɪlɔ́ŋ ju?

Did you see her with your own eyes?

jés, mí bín síɪm.

Yes, I saw her.

wɔ́tnem ší bín tɔ́k?

What did she say?

watsəmǽtər jú bín həmbəg lɔ́ŋə čájnə-mən?

Why did you cheat the Chinese?

ðís púr nígər, ðé bín wɔ́rk əlɔ́ŋə kɔ́tɪm wúd.

These poor black men, they worked at cutting wood.

ím bín kílɪm mí.

He struck me.

kílɪm ju? wɔ́tnem? kílɪm ju ər kílɪm jú déd?

Killed you? What? Struck you or killed you dead?

ó, ím bín kílɪm mi.

Oh he struck me.

jú nomór dú ðǽtwən.

Don't you do that.

wasəmǽrə jú həmbəg lɔ́ŋə ðǽt?

Why did you do wrongly with regard to that?

mí bín tɔ́kɪm jú dú ðíswən.

I told you to do this.

4. Chinese Pidgin English. A dialogue dictated to the author in 1944 by Mrs. Kathleen M. Merritt, native of Wu-Hu (middle Yangtze valley, Hankow region); the dialogue represents a conversation between a lady and her tailor.

MISTRESS: télər, máj hǽv kǽči wɔ́npisi plénti hǽnsəm sílka. máj wɔ́nči jú méki wən nájs ívniŋdrés.

Tailor, I have a very fine [piece of] silk. I want you to make a nice evening dress.

TAILOR: mísɪ hǽv gát búk?

Has missy a [fashion] book?

MISTRESS: máj nó hǽv kǽči'búk. pémi sí jú búk.

I haven't brought a book. Let me see your book.

TAILOR: máj búk blɔ́ŋ tú ólə.

My book is too old [out of date].

MISTRESS: máski, jú pémi lúk-sí.

Never mind, let me see it.

TAILOR: máj sǽvi mísi nó wɔ́nči ðísfǽšən. səpós mísɪ kǽn kǽči búk, máj kǽn méki. səpós mísi nó kǽn kǽči búk, máj nó kǽn dú. mísi kǽn kə́m tumɔ́lo?

I know missy doesn't want this kind [of dress]. If missy can get a book, I can make it. If missy can't get a book, I can't. Can missy come tomorrow?

MISTRESS: tumɔ́lo máj nó kǽn kə́m. máj lívi sílka ðíssajd, səpós máj kə́m tumɔ́rə néks dé.

Tomorrow I can't come. I'll leave the silk here, and possibly I'll come day after tomorrow.

TAILOR: ɔ́rajt, mísi, tumɔ́rə néks dé kǽn dú. máj méki véri pɔ́pa fɔ́ jú.

Very well, missy, day after tomorrow is all right. I'll make it just right for you.

MISTRESS: jú méki wɔ́npis ívniŋ-drés fɔ́r máj, háwmə́č jú wɔ́nči?

If you make an evening-dress for me, how much do you want?

TAILOR: spós blɔ́ŋ dǽnsɪŋ-drés, máj wɔ́nči twélv dɔ́lər.

If it is a dancing-dress, I want twelve dollars.

MISTRESS: twélv dɔ́lər blɔ́ŋ tumɔ́či.

Twelve dollars is too much.

TAILOR: háwfǽšən twélv dɔ́lər blɔ́ŋ tuməči? mástər hǽv kǽči plénti fájn plés, mísi tɔ́ki twélv dɔ́lər tumɔ́či. éni

How is it that twelve dollars is too much? The master has gotten a very fine job, [and yet] missy says twelve dollars is

mísi ğə́snaw kǽči hǽnsəm ívnɪŋ-drés, kǽn pémi twélv dólər.

MISTRESS: spós máj kǽči búk, kə́m ðíssajd tumə́rə néks dé, hwátajm jú kǽn fínɪš fər máj?

TAILOR: mísi, ğə́snaw máj plénti bɪ̀zi. məs wə́nči tén dé mór.

MISTRESS: tén dé mór blóŋ tú ləŋ tájm. máj wə́nči véli kwɪk.

TAILOR: fə́ jú, mìsi, máj kǽn dú wə́n wík.

MISTRESS: ðǽt blóŋ véli gúd.

too much. Any missy who gets a fine evening-dress at present can pay me twelve dollars. If I get the book and come here day after tomorrow, when can you finish it for me? Missy, at present I'm very busy. It'll take more than ten days. More than ten days is too long a time. I want it very quick. For you, missy, I can do it in a week. That is very good.

5. Sranan. Beginning of a folk tale taken down in Surinam by the Hersko-vitses, and reproduced in Herskovits, 1936 (p. 268).

wán kónde bén dé, en wán fóru bén dé bári. éf a bár só, na hér kóndre e trúbu. kónu pót táki, wán súma kír na-fóru, a-sa-tró náŋa wán úman pikín fo-éŋ.

anánsi jére. a-go táig kónu táki, éŋ sa-kíri na-fóru. mék kónu gí-em móni en bái sáni, dán éŋ sa-gó kír eŋ. dí anánsi gó, a-tán tú wíki. a-kír wán pómpom, a-tjár kóm. kónum nó bríbi eŋ táki na na-fóru dáti de-bár só. kónum táig hem, táki, éfu na-fóru nó bári báka wán mún, dán a-sa-tró náŋa na-pikín. ma bifós wán mún, dán na-fóru bári. dán kónum séni ték anánsi, mék srót eŋ.

There was once a kingdom, and there was a bird which screeched. If it screeched so, the whole kingdom was disturbed. The King announced that the person who killed the bird would marry a daughter of his. Anansi heard this. He went to tell the King that he would kill the bird. Let the King give him money to buy things, then he would go and kill it. When Anansi went, he remained away two weeks. He killed a Pompom and brought [it]. The King did not believe him, that this was the bird which screeched so. The King said to him that if the bird did not screech again within a month, then he could marry the girl. But before the month was up, the bird screeched. Then the King sent for Anansi and had him imprisoned.

6. Jamaican Creole. Beginning of a story entitled "William Saves His Sweetheart," transcribed by DeCamp and reproduced in LePage and DeCamp, 1960 (p. 143).

nóu, a úol táim anánsi-in stúori, wi gwáiŋ at nóu. nóu wánts dér wáz a úol wíč líedi lív, had wán són, níem av wíljəm. wíljəm wór ingjéj, tu a jóŋ líedi, frám a néks úol wíč sékšan húu waz hár mádar in láa. nóu dát gjól fáda, had dát gjól wid iz fós wáif. an áfta di wáif

Now, a old-time Anancying story we going at now. Now once there was a old witch-lady live, had one son, name of William. William were engage to a young lady from a next [another] old witch's section who was her mother-in-law [stepmother]. Now that girl's father had that girl with his first wife. And after the wife

disíis, hii iz mári a néks wúman, wíč is a úol wíč an dát wúman bíer túu dáataz bisáidz. nóu di tríi sístaz líviŋ gúd, bót di máda in láa dídn láik dat wán dáata atál, fi-di mán. him prefár fi-ar túu. bót jét di tríi gjól wor júobial wid wán anáda. wel dát wán gjól frénz wid dís jóŋ mán, níem av wíljam. wíljam máda iz a úold wíč. di gjól mádaanláa iz a úold wíč. súo, ju gwain fáin óut, wá de gó hápm nóu.

had that girl with his first wife. And after the wife decease, he is marry a next [another] woman, which is a old witch. And that woman bear two daughters besides. Now the three sisters living good [got along well together], but the mother-in-law didn't like that one daughter at all, the man's. She prefer her own two. But yet the three girls were jovial with one another. Well, that one girl was friends with this young man, name of William. William's mother is a old witch. The girl's mother-in-law is a old witch. So, you going to find out what is going to happen now.

7. Gullah. The first paragraph of a religious narrative,/sikɪn/, dictated to Turner by Hester Milligan (Edisto Island, South Carolina) and reproduced in Turner, 1949 (pp. 270–71). (For typographical reasons, upside-down ɒ has been replaced by ɔ, and his upside-down a by ə, as well as long ʃ by š.)

məi məsə šo mi əl kəin ə tiŋ. əi tiŋk ɪt bɪn e frəɪdɪ, in Ɉulɑɪ. i šo mi hɛl; i šo mi hɛwm; i šo mi həu tu Ɉɪt rɪlɪɈən. an wɛn i Jɪt tru, i ʌpm ə bɪg bəɪbl; an dɛn i blɛs məɪ sol. dɛn i tɛl mi—i sɛ: go in pis n sɪn no mo. unə sol də sɛt fri. an aftə wəɪl əɪ kʌm əut dɛ, an əl wɛrəs tiŋ əɪ si. dɪ morɪs əɪ si bɪn ə ɲəŋ manz, n ə Ɉal, n cɪlən, n məɪ farə, n pipl—əl ʌp in ə bəndl. de bɪn wʌk had. dɛn əɪ si ə Ɉadn n fləwəz wɪd ə fɛɲc rəuŋ. əɪ si fəɪw kəu n ə caf, səɪd ə pədl ə wətə. de də ɲam fərə. dɛn əɪ si hɛl; əɪ si hɛwm; əɪ si əl kəin ə tiŋ.

My Master show me all kind of thing. I think it been a Friday, in July. He show me hell; he show me heaven; he show me how to get religion. And when he get through, he open a big Bible; and then he bless my soul. Then he tell me— he say: "Go in peace and sin no more. Your soul is set free." And after while I come out there, and all various thing I see. The most I see been a young mans, and a girl, and children, and my father, and people—all up in a bundle. They been work hard. Then I see a garden and flowers with a fence round. I see five cow and a calf, beside a puddle of water. They were eating fodder. Then I see hell; I see heaven; I see all kind of thing.

REFERENCES

Robert A. Hall, Jr. *Melanesian Pidgin English: Grammar, Texts, Vocabulary.* Baltimore, 1943.

Melville J. Herskovits and Frances S. Herskovits. *Suriname Folklore.* New York, 1936.

Robert B. LePage and David DeCamp. *Jamaican Creole.* London, 1960.

Lorenzo Dow Turner. *Africanisms in the Gullah Dialect.* Chicago, 1949.

STUDY QUESTIONS

1. Distinguish *lingua franca*, *pidgin*, and *creole*.
2. Hall's description of the circumstances under which pidgins arise is now regarded as an oversimplification. What other factors than those he suggests would you consider important in the process?
3. What are the "objectionable" origins of *moist*, *petulant*, and *crepetate* alluded to by Hall (p. 100)?
4. Linguists sometimes categorize changes in word meaning as follows:
   a. *generalization:* development of a larger range of reference; for example, *delapidated*, as its etymology reveals, once was restricted to structures made from stone.
   b. *specialization:* narrowing of the range of reference; for example, *deer* once referred to a wide variety of animals and *meat* could be applied to nearly any solid food.
   c. *elevation:* a word of formerly neutral or low social meaning acquires a more elegant sense; for example, *knight*, once referring to any young man, has developed a more specialized and elevated sense.
   d. *degradation:* loss of "elevated" meaning; for example, *knave*, like *knight*, once was used to refer to a boy or young man but has undergone specialization and degradation.

   Examine the word lists given by Hall for examples of these categories of word change. Which types appear to be most common?
5. Roman Jakobson has suggested that a language "accepts foreign elements only when they correspond to its tendencies of development."[a] Examine the sample texts given by Hall and consider the hypothesis that pidginization extends the "tendencies of development" inherent in English.
6. Creole languages not only import vocabulary and grammatical structures from various source languages but also show the characteristic uses of language from the cultures in contact. In the following passage from *Veronica, My Daughter*, by the Nigerian writer Ogali A. Ogali, Chief Jombo feels that his daughter Veronica and his wife Pauline have been out-doing him in linguistic fluency through their superior knowledge of English. Because fluency and rhetorical display are important in the vernacular culture of Nigeria, he responds by bringing in "Bomber Billy" who is reputed to defeat his opponents in debate by throwing "word bombs." Examine the passage for examples of creole forms in Chief Jombo's speech and discuss the techniques by which Billy achieves his victory over Veronica and Pauline.

> CHIEF JOMBO: My pikin, you hear how my Misisi and Veronica my daughter dey talk grammarian for me?
> BOMBER BILLY: Madam, what's the meaning of all the hullabaloo that disturbed my capillary and tonsorial artist from discharging his duty efficiently, thus compelling me to have a pedestrian excursion to this place?
> PAULINA: (?) [sic] My husband does not want Vero to marry the man of her choice and I feel he is making a sad mistake.

[a] Roman Jakobson, "Sur la théorie des affinités des langues," in *Proceedings of the 4th International Congress of Linguists* (*1931*), tr. and quoted by Uriel Weinreich, *Languages in Contact* (New York, 1953), p. 25.

BOMBER BILLY: You are the person labouring under a delusion and not your husband.

VERO: What are you after? Are you hired to disturb us now?

BOMBER BILLY: If you talk to me again, I simply order your father to put you in a coffin of ostracism.

CHIEF JOMBO: Yes, make una talk grammarian. My pikin, talkam I dey hear.

PAULINA: You must know, Billy, that I am at least older than you and [you] *must* stop talking nonsense now.

VERO: Don't mind him. Does he know more than Mike [the man of her choice] who has his Inter BA.

BOMBER BILLY: Look here! Are you promulgating your exorditation or articulating superficial sentimentality and amicable philosophical observation, beware of platitudeness and ponderosity and learn to respect my integrity.

CHIEF JOMBO: Here! Here! [sic] (he claps and laughs) I hear you! Talkam, my pikin, for dem moth don closs.

VERO: My Mike will answer you well when he meets you.

PAULINA: Never mind that hopeless boy who is rather irresponsible.

BOMBER BILLY: Your statement, Veronica, indicates nothing but a psychological defeatism because you do not take into account the spirit of dynamism in my cerebrium and cerebellum.

PAULINA: I assure you that you are rather miscocopic [Microscopic?] to be noticed. A negligible pocket radio that utters useless words.

BOMBER BILLY: I must advice [sic] you madam, to let your conversational communications possess a cherified [clarified?] consciousness and cogency, let your entamporaneous discernment and unpermitted expectectation have intangibility, veroness and versity. Avoid pomposity, proticity, verbocity and rapacity.

CHIEF JOMBO: Talk now misiss! My pikin, go your way and when they talk too much again, I go callam you.

BOMBER BILLY: Thank you, Chief. Before I go, I must make your wife know that she, as a woman, is expected to maintain perfect tranquility whenever you talk to her. Well, goodbye all. I'll see you again.

CHIEF JOMBO: Salute your papa for me—O!

(EXIT BOMBER BILLY)[b]

7. Nearly all language communities develop a stylized dialect—one that may have little connection with the linguistic facts—to represent the speech of the outlander, the rustic who lacks the cultivated dialect of the social focal point of the community. Aristophanes made good use of the conventions of the stage rustic in *Lysistrata*, and his English translators have variously rendered the Doric language of such characters as thick Scots, a "never-never Devonshire," and uneducated Southern States speech to contrast with whatever *standard* they have chosen to assign to the Attic speech of the Athenian characters.

In the following translation—made for dramatic presentation in Nigeria—Aristophanes' Doric is rendered as Nigerian pidgin English. Examine the

[b] Ogali A. Ogali, *Veronica, My Daughter* (Onitsha: Appolos, 1956) as quoted by Donatus I. Nwoga, "Onitsha Market Literature," *Transition*, **19**(1965):29.

speeches of the Yoruba messenger for those traits that particularly distinguish him from Alkali, the sophisticated government official:

[*Enter Alkali to drums. He paces slowly, and uncomfortably. As he paces the Yoruba Messenger enters, in the same condition as Kwairanga, and bent almost double.*]

MESSENGER: [*breathlessly.*] Wusa ah go find una chiefs or wetin una de call dem leaders? Ah bring important news for dem.

ALKALI: News? You've a strange appearance for a herald.

MESSENGER: You tink say ah be strange? For South we done advance and modern.

ALKALI: [*regarding him closely.*] Advanced? And so I see.

MESSENGER: Na so all Yoruba messenger de look. Ah bin wan talk say ah come for talk of peace.

ALKALI: And yet you hide a spear beneath your clothes.
What sort of peace is that?

MESSENGER: [*turning to arrange his clothes.*] Ah no hide anyting.

ALKALI: Well, why squirm away. This is most strange
Behaviour; and your clothes stick out.

> [*He looks again.*]

> They do.
You've had some accident, poor fellow; don't be shy;
I know that road up from the South is rough;
You're hurt; your groin is swollen horribly.

MESSENGER: Ah swear by Shango, you tink say ah be fool, you ignorant nonsense.

ALKALI: *Look* at yourself.

MESSENGER: Ah well. Ah tell you ah done come makea talk important business.
Be serious.

ALKALI: I am quite serious. Very well,
Your news; let's hear it.

> [*He tries to look at the Messenger's groin again.*]
> But what is that thing?

MESSENGER: [*hurriedly.*] Dey done give me powa to say . . .

> [*He looks down at his groin.*]
Wetin? . . . Na Shango staff.

ALKALI: A Shango staff? A Shango staff? I've one myself,
But I've never heard it called a Shango staff.
Come, you can be quite frank with me, my lad.
How are the Yorubas? Quite happy? Eh?

> [*Pause.*]
Don't lie to me; I have my information.
Do they all sport those . . . Shango staffs?

MESSENGER: Makea talk true. Tings done hard for South. 'E no fit bad pass dis. De Ibos and de uddas 'e bad pass us.

ALKALI: I thought as much. A stricken nation. Can you
Diagnose what troubles you? Your ancestors, perhaps,
Are angry?

MESSENGER: Not our great fadas. Na one girl de cause all our troubles: Iyabo.

'E go for meetin for bush and return with nonsense ideas about peace. 'E collect all our women; and de shun us. When we talk fine words to dem or caress dem, den dey like wood.

ALKALI: How do you like it? It's the same with us.

MESSENGER: 'E done comeout de life from us. Dey fine fine, fit for eat, but dey de stare stare at us. Dey swear say no man go near am, till we done make peace. 'E done tay wey den dey do dis.

ALKALI: Why didn't you come to us before?

MESSENGER: Na de time wey we no fit bear am, na him we come. Den dey ask for mad tings. We bin de fight since man begin. Na de only work for man wey be propa man. Na so we bin tink. But now, na peace we want.

ALKALI: When women move together as one man
We just can't win. Run home and tell your chiefs
We'll meet an embassy with absolute power
To fix some treaty up, make peace. Go on.

MESSENGER: Ah wan talk to some *big* person.

ALKALI: [*glancing down at his own groin*]. I'm big enough. Run off and hurry.

MESSENGER: Make you no tell me hurry. Make you yourself no waste time. We no go tay.

[*He runs off at great speed, but again bent double.*]

ALKALI: [*shouting after him.*] Don't trip up on your . . . Shango staff.
[*Exit Alkali.*][c]

To clarify difficult points in the Nigerian translation, it may be helpful to you to examine an American and a British translation of the same passage. Comment on any stylistic or linguistic differences that you find striking in your comparison of the three versions. What varieties of English are used in place of the Nigerian Pidgin of the Yoruba messenger?

[*A Spartan Herald enters from the right, holding his cloak together in a futile attempt to conceal his condition.*]

HERALD: This Athens? Where-all kin I find the Council of Elders or else the Executive Board? I brung some news.

[*The Commissioner, swathed in his cloak, enters from the left.*]

COMMISSIONER: And what are you—a man? a signpost? a joint-stock company?

HERALD: A herald, sonny, a honest-to-Kastor herald. I come to chat 'bout thet-there truce.

COMMISSIONER: . . . carrying a concealed weapon? Pretty underhanded.

HERALD: [*Twisting to avoid the Commissioner's direct gaze.*] Hain't done no sech a thang!

COMMISSIONER: Very well, stand still. Your cloak's out of crease—hernia? Are the roads that bad?

SPARTAN: I swear this feller's plumb tetched in the haid!

COMMISSIONER: [*Throwing open the Spartan's cloak, exposing the phallus.*] You clown, you've got an erection!

SPARTAN: [*Wildly embarrassed.*] Hain't got no sech a thang! You stop this-hyer foolishment!

[c] *Aikin Mata: The Lysistrata of Aristophanes*, tr. T. W. Harrison and James Simmons (Ibadan: Oxford University Press, 1966), pp. 63–65. Used by permission of Oxford University Press, Nigerian Branch.

COMMISSIONER: What *have* you got there, then?

SPARTAN: Thet-thur's a Spartan *e*pistle. In code.

COMMISSIONER: I have the key. [*Throwing open his cloak.*] Behold another Spartan *e*pistle. In code. [*Tiring of teasing.*] Let's get down to cases. I know the score, so tell me the truth. How are things with you in Sparta?

HERALD: Thangs is up in the air. The whole Alliance is purt-near 'bout to explode. We-uns'll need buckets, 'stead of women.

COMMISSIONER: What was the cause of this outburst? The great god Pan?

HERALD: Nope. I'll lay 'twere Lampito, most likely. She begun, and then they was off and runnin' at the post in a bunch, every last little gal in Sparta, drivin' their menfolk away from the winner's circle.

COMMISSIONER: How are you taking this?

HERALD: Painful-like. Everyone's doubled up worse as a midget nursin' a wick in a midnight wind come moon-dark time. Cain't even tetch them little old gals on the moosey without we all agree to a Greece-wide Peace.

COMMISSIONER: Of course! A universal female plot—all Hellas risen in rebellion—I have should have known! Return to Sparta with this request: Have them despatch us a Plenipotentiary Commission, fully empowered to conclude an armistice. I have full confidence that I can persuade our Senate to do the same, without extending myself. The evidence is at hand.

HERALD: I'm a-flyin', Sir! I hev never heered your equal![d]

[*Exeunt hurriedly, the Commissioner to the left, the Herald to the right.*]

·   ·   ·

[*A Laconian herald is next seen approaching, and the Magistrate comes forward to meet him.*]

HERALD: Whaur sall a body fin' the Athanian senate,
  Or the gran' lairds? Ha' gotten news to tell.

MAG: News, have you, friend? And what in the world are you?

HER: A heralt, billie! jist a Spartian heralt,
  Come, by the Twa', anent a Peace, ye ken.

MAG: Ay, and how fare the Spartans? tell me that:
  And tell me truly, for I know the fact.

HER: They're bad eneugh, they canna weel be waur;
  They're sair bestead, Spartians, allies, an' a'.

MAG: And how and whence arose this trouble first?
  From Pan?

HER: Na, na, 'twer' Lampito, I ween,
  First set it gangin': then our hizzies, a'
  Risin' like rinners at ane signal word,
  Loupit, an' jibbed, an' dang the men awa'.

MAG: How like ye that?

HER: Och, we're in waefu' case.
  They stan' abeigh, the lassies do, an' vow
  They'll no be couthie wi' the laddies mair
  Till a' mak' Peace, and throughly en' the War.

[d] *Lysistrata,* tr. Douglass Parker (Ann Arbor: The University of Michigan Press, 1964), pp. 69–71. Used by permission of the University of Michigan Press. Copyright © by William Arrowsmith 1964. All rights reserved.

MAG: This is a plot they have everywhere been hatching,
     These villanous women: now I see it all.
     Run home, my man, and bid your people send
     Envoys with absolute powers to treat for peace,
     And I will off with all the speed I can,
     And get our Council here to do the same.
HER: Nebbut, I'se fly, ye rede me weel, I'm thinkin'.
[*The Herald leaves for Sparta; the Magistrate returns to the Senate; and the two
Choruses now advance for a final skirmish.*][e]

[e] *The Lysistrata of Aristophanes*, tr. Benjamin Bickley Rogers (London: G. Bell and Sons, Ltd., 1911), pp. 197–98.

THE LANGUAGE OF THE MASTER?
Kenneth Ramchand

We are as strangers here now, but the white tribe are the strangers.
We belong here, we are of the old ways.
We are the corroboree and the bora ground,
We are the old sacred ceremonies, the laws of the elders.
We are the wonder tales of Dreamtime, the tribal legends told.
We are the past, the hunts and the laughing games, the wandering camp
    fires,
We are the lightening-bolt over Gaphembah Hill
Quick and terrible,
And the Thunderer after him, that loud fellow.
We are the quiet daybreak paling the dark lagoon.
We are the shadow-ghosts creeping back as the camp fires burn low.[a]

The lines are by an Australian poet—not a descendant, however, of the English settlers who stayed on to dominate the continent at the antipodes, but of the aboriginal Australians whose physical and spiritual possession of the land is still echoed in Kath Walker's words, even though the words themselves are borrowed from the white tribe. In New Zealand, it is possible to find a new generation of Maori poets writing in English, their work complementing, as does Miss Walker's, that of Australian poets and novelists, the work done by men and women of Anglo-Saxon stock. In India, Ceylon, Pakistan; in Malaysia and Singapore; in East, Central, South, and particularly West Africa; and in the West Indies, writers can be found who announce their loyalties to the imposed language by choosing it as the medium of their work. There is no more hopeful omen of the continued use of English as an international medium, because language loyalty is a powerful and necessary force sustaining the use of any tongue. It is less hopeful, and a clear sign of the ethno-centrism of American readers and teachers, that many of the names of significant writers mentioned in the following selection are hardly known among the educated in the United States, particularly when these writers come from the Third World. It is perhaps ironic, perhaps indicative of a greater malice, that the two African writers best known in the West—Alan Paton and Nadine

Gordimer—are themselves white and come from South Africa where "the events of the last forty years have alienated every South African writer of any compassion or sensitivity from·the society developing around him. Most of them have taken refuge in exile, others are prematurely dead, banned, or in prison. Nadine Gordimer, the only white writer of real stature still working in the Republic, finds herself forced to write for an overseas audience, owing to the total banning of all her recent books within South Africa." [b]

Some historians of the use of English in the world speak of an international literature; and of course an international audience exists in the millions of persons of diverse nationalities who read English. But it is important to recognize, as Ramchand suggests, that each of the English literatures has its own national or regional identity; and each is written in a language suited to express that identity. The generalization made in the first essay of this collection: that "all speakers of English . . . agree more or less on the way it should be written" applies principally to the mechanics of getting it down on paper; that is, the writing conventions of English. With reference to more significant linguistic features, the generalization applies far more accurately to scientific and historical prose than it does to imaginative literature. In India, writers are perhaps more aware of an international audience for literature in English than in other countries where English serves as a second language. India possesses native languages traditionally put to literary uses in which an Indian writer may address his fellow countrymen. Yet in spite of this, Indian literature in English is written in a language expressive of Indian environment and experience, because most literature is about people and what they do. In Africa, a writer is more often required to speak to his fellow Africans in English if he is to be heard at all; and there a choice must sometimes be made between a form of language acceptable to the fussiest critic of the Times Literary Supplement *and one accessible and meaningful to a larger number of Africans than the elite who subscribe to* The Times. *In the West Indies, as Ramchand shows in his essay, an author is faced with other choices of audience and language because he is a native speaker of a form of English different from the standard English of expatriates.*

Oriented toward a different linguistic norm—West Indian Standard—and in contact with the considerable linguistic diversity in the islands, the West Indian writer exploits linguistic choices not available to the outsider. "West Indian literature," says Ramchand, "would seem to be the only substantial literature in which the dialect-speaking character is the central character," not the comic, peripheral, and stereotyped character of so much of English literature. "This characteristic feature of West Indian writing reflects the more obvious new event," he continues, "the centrality of the Black or Coloured character and the articulation of this hitherto obscure and stereotyped person." Black writers in the United States might contest the "newness" of the event; but many black writers are, nonetheless, calling for a new black

[b] Gerald Moore, *The Chosen Tongue* (London: Longmans, 1969), p. xv.

*voice expressive of character, person, and experience, and some are hearing it
in the black dialects of urban America. Because of the new call in America,
Ramchand's study has additional interest for those who read black literature
and, by contrast at least, raises suggestive questions about the linguistic choices
available to black writers in America who are, whether they like it or not,
participants in another linguistic community with its own loyalties, its own
beliefs and prejudices. They too must define an audience and divine a voice for
speaking to it.*

TERRANGLIA

An approach which has made the literature of the West Indies part of a
wider unit is conveniently illustrated by the publication *Terranglia: The
Case for English as World Literature.*[1] Professor Jones's project attempts to
cope with all the new literatures in English which have developed visibly in
the first half of the twentieth century:

When we talk about English (meaning British) literature, we are talking about a
segment. When we add American literature, we have added only another segment.
Until we are prepared to think of English as a world language expressing itself in a
world literature we shall be getting farther, and farther out of date. If we are to
study "English" literature—that is the literature of the English language—let us
study all of it; every bit of it that has legitimate claim to attention.[2]

This effort to make things bigger if not better is severely limited by arbitrary
regional groupings, and by an undiscriminating disposition of authors in
these groups. It is absurd to find Mabel M. A. Chan-Toon, Bankim Chandra
Chatterjee, and Sir Henry S. Cunningham in a region called "India-Pakistan-
Ceylon-Burma" for all the qualification that they are "older writers." It
serves no purpose to place Joseph Conrad, "Han Suyin," and Alec Waugh in
a section called "Malaysia-Hong Kong." But worse than *Terranglia's* biblio-
graphic follies are its serious misconceptions about what is meant by "the
use of English."

FIRST LANGUAGE OR SECOND LANGUAGE

It is necessary to make the distinction that in some areas like the West
Indies and Australia, English or a version of it is the first language, while in
places like Pakistan and Nigeria it is a learned or second language. In the
latter situation at least two kinds of possibilities have to be borne in mind.

---

[1] Joseph Jones, *Terranglia: The Case for English as World Literature* (N.Y., 1965).
[2] *Terranglia*, p. 20.

Firstly, there may be difficulties of expression arising from an inadequate grasp of basic features in the language—as when in Amos Tutuola's *The Palm–Wine Drinkard* (1954) the drinkard says "I lied down there awake" (p. 14). Although, in Tutuola's fiction, it is not always possible to distinguish between a deliberately ungrammatical usage and what might be just a mistake which happens to be effective ("they were rolling on the ground as if a thousand petrol drums were *pushing* along a hard road," p. 22), it is nevertheless necessary to be aware that the distinction sometimes can be made.

The "pushing" petrol drums above lead us into the second broad possibility that must be considered. An author who thinks in one language instinctively and can write in another is liable to modify the adopted language. A certain amount of this may be done unconsciously, but the Nigerian, Gabriel Okara, is all for a deliberate approach:

> As a writer who believes in the utilization of African ideas, African philosophy, and African folk-lore and imagery to the fullest extent possible, I am of the opinion the only way to use them effectively is to translate them almost literally from the African language native to the writer into whatever European language he is using as his medium of expression. I have endeavoured in my words to keep as close as possible to the vernacular expressions . . . a writer can use the idioms of his own language in a way that is understandable in English.[3]

In his novel, *The Voice* (1964), Okara puts this principle into practice, drawing upon his native Ijaw. Three quotations may help us to see some of the advantages and some of the limitations of the kind of dubbing Okara proposes. The first, from the end of the novel, does not seem to carry any marks necessarily derived from the native language:

> When day broke the following day it broke on a canoe aimlessly floating down the river. And in the canoe tied together back to back with their feet tied to the seats of the canoe, were Okolo and Tuere. Down they floated from one bank of the river to the other like debris, carried by the current. Then the canoe was drawn into a whirlpool. It spun round and round and was slowly drawn into the core and finally disappeared. And the water rolled over the top and the river flowed smoothly over it as if nothing had happened.
>
> (*The Voice*, p. 157)

From this, and other passages like it in the novel, it is evident that Okara does not follow his program as fanatically as the article in *Transition* suggests.

The next passage contains examples of the novel's most obtrusive translation feature. Most of the sentences have a verb form as their final word:

---

[3] Gabriel Okara, "African Speech . . . English Words," *Transition* 10, Vol. 3, 1963. Published from Ibadan, Nigeria.

It was the day's ending and Okolo by a window stood. Okolo stood looking at the sun behind the tree tops falling. The river was flowing, reflecting the finishing sun, like a dying away memory. It was like an idol's face, no one knowing what is behind. Okolo at the palm trees looked. They were like women with hair hanging down, dancing, possessed. Egrets, like white flower petals strung slackly across the river, swaying up and down, were returning home. And, on the river, canoes were crawling home with bent backs and tired hands, paddling.

(The Voice, p. 13)

It takes a while to get used to the grammar of Okara's novel to the point where a sentence like "Okolo at the palm trees looked" becomes normal, and it is arguable that a non-Ijaw reader cannot help being irritated by continuous exposure to such "abnormal" structures where no special effects are being aimed at, but on the credit side no reader can resist the aptness of "falling" in sentence two or fail to register the peculiar inevitability with which "paddling" completes the brilliant evocation of "canoes were crawling home with bent backs and tired hands."

In the next passage, Okolo is given protection in the hut of the girl, Tuere, who had been driven out of the town previously, on the allegation that she was a witch. With the mob outside, Okolo revolves past events in his mind:

Inside the hut Okolo stood, hearing all the spoken words *outside* and speaking with his *inside*. He spoke with his *inside* to find out why this woman there behaved thus. He knew her story only too well. She had been a girl of unusual habits, keeping to herself and speaking to herself. She did not flirt with boys though she had a hunger-killing beauty. So it was the *insides* of everyone that perhaps she had not the parts of a woman. They did not, because of these her strange behaviours, call her a witch. They openly called her a witch when her mother and father died one after the other within a few weeks and after every young man who proposed to her died one after the other. All these Okolo remembered. He also remembered how in a circle of strong eyes and strong faces she stood being accused of taking witchcraft to kill her father and mother. They then from the town drove her. His *inside* then smelled bad for the town's people and for himself for not being fit to do anything on her behalf.

(The Voice, p. 20)

Okara's "translation" principle seems to produce an extraordinarily vivid effect in the sentence "He also remembered how *in a circle of strong eyes and strong faces she stood being accused. . . .*" But the physical rightness of "inside" in the final sentence does not, I think, cancel out our impression that the word appears (my italics) only as a result of Okara's modish insistence. In sentence one it is impossible to avoid feeling that the author is being clever.

In Achebe's novels there is a tighter artistic control over the incursions from the native language into English, but I do not want to illustrate this at any length. I shall take a convenient and authoritative example from *Transition*

No. 18 (1965) where in an article "English and the African Writer," Chinua Achebe himself writes:

> Allow me to quote a small example from *Arrow of God* which may give some idea of how I approach the use of English. The Chief Priest is telling one of his sons why it is necessary to send him to church:
>> I want one of my sons to join these people and be my eyes there. If there is nothing in it you will come back. But if there is something there you will bring home my share. The world is like a Mask, dancing. If you want to see it well you do not stand in one place. My spirit tells me that those who do not befriend the white man today will be saying "had we known" tomorrow.
>
> Now supposing I had put it another way. Like this for instance:
>> I am sending you as my representative among those people—just to be on the safe side in case the new religion develops. One has to move with the times or else one is left behind. I have a hunch that those who fail to come to terms with the white man may well regret their lack of foresight.
>
> The material is the same. But the form of the one is in *character* and the other is not. It is largely a matter of instinct, but judgment comes into it too.

Tutuola, Okara, and Achebe differ from one another as artists, but these three writers are able to draw upon resources in their social situation which do not exist for writers whose only language is English.

In areas where English is a second language, the fiction produced in that tongue is not always the natural expression of a whole society. And it may be limited by local factors like the alternative literatures being produced in native languages; the number of people able to read English and what proportion of the total they represent; and the attitude of national governments to the foreign tongue. In Pakistan, to take one example, the existence of classics and highly developed written literatures in native languages has largely determined and fixed a process of compartmentalization:

> Though the English newspapers and journals print stories and poems at least once a week, generally writers like to write in Urdu and Bengali rather than in English. Our best writers do not like to write creative literature in English. English is reserved for journalism, official use, use in law-courts and, occasionally, for literary criticism. In other words, it is treated as a medium mainly for nonliterary communication and very rarely for creative self-expression.[4]

Pakistani writing in English is unlikely to become important at a national level. In Nigeria, on the other hand, in spite of some nationalistic demands in literary magazines that a local language should be used, the possibilities for the writer using English are enormous. "Nigeria," writes a professional linguist, "with a population of perhaps 48 million has according to conservative estimates, as many as 150 languages, none of which is spoken by

---

[4] S. A. Ashraf, "The Study of English Literature in Pakistan" in *Commonwealth Literature*, ed. John Press (London, 1965), p. 139.

more than six million people."[5] In this huge, artificial ex-colony, a Nigerian professional writer seeking a large audience, or a nationalist author committed to the task of helping to create a national consciousness, has the strongest of incentives to write in English. Because there is no indigenous literary tradition in written form to which the writer may be drawn to contribute, a tradition in English stands at least an equal chance with any other language, both for expressing modern Nigerian experience (Achebe and Ekwensi) or for the recasting of folk material (Tutuola).

Questions like these hardly arise in the West Indies. For the modern West Indian writer there is no possibility of a choice between English and another language. English is his native tongue and he uses it as a matter of course. I should like to look briefly at how this has come about.

ENGLISH IN THE WEST INDIES: "BAD ENGLISH"

A description by Edward Long in *The History of Jamaica* (1774) is a convenient point from which to look backward at the way in which English became established among Negroes in the West Indies during the seventeenth and eighteenth centuries. The same description has a shape which helps us to anticipate the fluidity of the twentieth-century situation:

The Africans speak their respective dialects, with some mixture of broken English. The language of the Creoles is bad English, larded with the Guiney dialect, owing to their adopting the African words, in order to make themselves understood by the imported slaves; which they find much easier than teaching these strangers to learn English. The better sort are very fond of improving their language, by catching at any hard word that the Whites happen to let fall in their hearing; and they alter and misapply it in a strange manner; but a tolerable collection of them gives an air of knowledge and importance in the eyes of their brethren, which tickles their vanity, and makes them more assiduous in stocking themselves with this unintelligible jargon. . . . This sort of gibberish likewise infects many of the white Creoles, who learn it from their nurses in infancy, and meet with much difficulty, as they advance in years, to shake it entirely off, and express themselves with correctness.[6]

To the three stages of "Englishness" outlined by Long we have to add a fourth—the standard English which he uses as a criterion of correctness. Individual Negroes had attained competence in this fourth type in the eighteenth and nineteenth centuries, but it is only in the twentieth century, as a result of the establishment of popular education in the islands, that we can speak of a class of educated speakers of English from among the Negroes and other Black elements in the population. I would like to argue later that when this happens we have to propose a category called West Indian Standard, but it is necessary first to look at the earlier periods.

---

[5] John Spencer in *Commonwealth Literature*, p. 116.
[6] Edward Long, *The History of Jamaica* (1774), Book III, Chapter 3, pp. 426–27.

The three stages contained in Long's description help us to reconstruct the process by which English displaced the African dialects and became the basis of the language of West Indian Negroes. As the quotation shows, the stages may coexist at any given time, especially in the pre-Emancipation period when there was a continuous supply of newly arrived Africans. But we might dispose them chronologically by focusing on the language of the groups among which, at each point in time, the process of substitution was most advanced. The farther back in time we go, the greater the number of Africanisms we find in the language of these groups; as we move forward, the degree of Englishness increases.

In the first stage, African dialects predominate with only a mixture of broken English. As there is little evidence, we have to speculate about how the stage actually began, and we have to set a hypothetical point at which a new stage would have begun. A fifty-year unit seems convenient since it covers at least two generations. With Jamaica as field, the first stage would stretch to the end of the seventeenth century. To make orders and instructions understood, the Whites would have had to invent a species of essential English, partly made up of a number of formulaic words and phrases, and in general, showing fewer inflexional variations than would occur in exchanges between Whites. There would, however, be a compensatory increase in the reliance upon the extralinguistic context, upon word order, and upon intonation to make necessary discriminations and to fill out meaning. One cannot help invoking the existence of an abbreviated language along these lines as one of the sources of the meagre inflexional content, and the heavy reliance upon syntactic directives in West Indian dialects of the twentieth century. However this may be, I would suggest that traces of a minimal English invented for practical purposes became lodged in the language of the slaves at an early period, and that in the slave context there would have been considerable motivation to pick up and practice the prestige language of the masters. We know that slavery was a scale by which all things African were devalued.

Only such pressure can account for the rapid transformation which had taken place by the early eighteenth century. Among the slaves born in the island, as the following quotation shows, stage two was well under way: "The Slaves are brought from several places in *Guiney*, which are different from one another in Language, and consequently they can't converse freely.... 'Tis true the *Creolian* Negroes are not of this Number: They all speak *English*."[7]

Although the plantation system restricted intercourse with the upper orders of the plantation hierarchy, there were areas of increased social contact, and consequently exposure to a wider range of English, between slaves and those Whites at the lower end of the social scale. In addition to general routine contact with the group and particular meetings with the

---

[7] Charles Leslie, *A New History of Jamaica*, 2d ed. (1740). Quotation from Letter XI, p. 310.

Negro "driver" for passing on instructions, there were intimacies contracted with slave women. Domestic slaves and personal attendants were exposed to a wider range of situations than field slaves, although it is worth remembering that not all the Creole ladies were literate. We can imagine that the individual contacts so far mentioned would have had some influence on the language of the participants and that the "improvement" made by the slave would have been transmitted in some form to his or her immediate circle. But the most significant contact, because it would appear to have been between groups, was that between the Negroes and the white indentured servants[8] (mainly Irish and Scottish) in the seventeenth century and in the first half of the eighteenth. Leslie writes of these servants being ruined by combining with the Negroes: "The great Thing which ruins most of these unfortunate Fellows, is the combining with the Negroes, who tell them many plausible Stories, to engage them to betray their Trust."[9] But Long (1774), describing them as "the very dregs of the three kingdoms," states that they used to seduce the wives of the slaves and that the "better sort of Creole Blacks disdain to associate with them."[10]

Since there was no formal teaching of any kind, and since the models from which the slaves picked up what they could were themselves degenerate ones, it is not surprising that slave English was "bad English." Imperfect learning, imperfect forgetting, and the necessary fraternization with newly arrived Africans ensured that this "bad English" would be "larded with Guiney dialect":

The Negroes seem very fond of reduplications, to express a greater or less quantity of anything; as *walky-walky, talky-talky, washy-washy, nappy-nappy, tie-tie, lilly-lilly, fum-fum:* so, *bug-a-bugs* (wood ants); *dab-a-dab* (an olio, made with maize, herrings, and pepper), *bra-bra* (another of their dishes), *grande-grande* (augmentative size, or grandeur), and so forth. In their conversations they confound all the moods, tenses, cases, and conjunctions, without mercy: for example, *I surprize* (for I am surprized), *me glad for see you* (I am glad to see you); *how you do* (for how d'ye do?), *me tank you; me ver well;* etc.[11]

The point to be emphasized, however, is that in stage two, in contrast to stage one, the base of the language is already English. Stage two seems to mark the period when we can begin to speak about Creole English, since the new combination is both English-based and literally island-born. From this point, however, the history of the Creole is a history of steady reduction in

---

[8] Leslie gives an account of the deficiency laws of 1703 which demanded *inter alia* that "Every Master of Slaves, for the first Five working Slaves, shall be obliged to keep One White Man-servant, Overseer or hired Man, for Three Months at least; and for Ten Slaves, two Whites, and for every Ten more, One; to be resident in the Plantation where the Negroes are employed..." (See p. 204.)

[9] Leslie, p. 304.

[10] Long, Book III, Chapter 3, p. 411 [sic.].

[11] Long, Book III, Chapter 3, p. 427.

the number of obvious Africanisms. According to F. G. Cassidy, an editor of the authoritative *Dictionary of Jamaican English* (1966):

... There is no real evidence ... that any articulate African speech survives in any community in the island today, and it is doubtful whether any has been spoken at all within the twentieth century. A few snatches of African or African-like words are preserved in some songs and some of the revivalist cults keep up a terminology among themselves that has African elements, but these are all vestiges in a structure that is not genuinely African, but Jamaican. ...[12]

For while Creole English was appearing to draw closer to Standard English in vocabulary, its grammar, as Thomas Russell observed, was taking its own shape:

Although it is evident that this, as every other corrupted form of language, is spoken by no previously well-planned system, yet as in course of time, every corruption resolves itself into certain very plain and distinct ones, which are, in not a few instances, in direct opposition to those of the pure parent language.[13]

Thomas Russell's *The Etymology of Jamaican Grammar* appeared in 1868. Russell is committed to a notion of correctness but his position was revolutionary in his time. More widely held than Russell's view in the eighteenth and nineteenth centuries, however, is the one, encouraged by the reduction of obvious Africanisms and by the closeness of vocabularies, that Creole English was simply "bad English," spoken mainly by Negroes but sometimes by uneducated White Creoles.

By the time that Lady Nugent was keeping her Jamaica journal indeed, we are told that

... The Creole language is not confined to the negroes. Many of the ladies, who have not been educated in England, speak a sort of broken English, with an indolent drawling out of their words, that is very tiresome if not disgusting. I stood next to a lady one night, near a window, and, by way of saying something, remarked that the air was much cooler than usual; to which she answered, "Yes, ma-am, him rail-ly too fra-ish."[14]

With Lady Nugent's comment we are reminded that however fluid the situation may in fact have been, the crude ruling generalization of pre-Emancipation society was that there were two main varieties of English— the language of the illiterate Negro and the language of the literate master. But it follows from the limited social contact of the eighteenth and early nineteenth centuries that the grammar of slave English could neither be recognized nor generated by nonspeakers of it. This gives great interest to

---

[12] F. G. Cassidy, *Jamaica Talk* (London, 1961), p. 20.
[13] Quoted by Cassidy in *Jamaica Talk*, p. 24.
[14] *Lady Nugent's Journal* (1839): entry for 24th April 1802. See p. 132 of 1907 edition.

the attempts of British writers in the eighteenth and early nineteenth centuries to represent "Negro English" in their fictions. The way in which "Negro English" became associated with certain stereotypes of the Negro is another concern of the next section. Both have bearings on modern West Indian writing.

"NEGRO ENGLISH" IN BRITISH FICTION OF THE EIGHTEENTH AND NINETEENTH CENTURIES

The first example I would like to look at comes from a work by a writer who had actually been to the West Indies. In *Tom Cringle's Log* (1829), the prying narrator describes the behavior of a Negro gravedigger left alone with a corpse and with the food and drink intended as an offering to the dead man's duppy (spirit):

I noticed he kept looking towards the east, watching, as I conjectured, the first appearance of the morning star, but it was as yet too early.

He lifted the gourd with the pork, and took a large mouthful.

"How is dis? I can't put dis meat in Quacco's coffin, dere is salt in de pork; Duppy can't bear salt."

Another large mouthful.

"Duppy hate salt too much."

Here he ate it all up, and placed the empty gourd in the coffin. He then took up the one with boiled yam in it, and tasted it also.

"Salt here too—who de debil do such a ting? Must not let Duppy taste dat."

He discussed this also, placing the empty vessel in the coffin as he had done with the other. He then came to the calabash with the rum. There is no salt here, thought I.

"Rum! ah, Duppy love rum—if it be well strong. Let me see—Massa Nigger, who put water in dis rum, eh? Duppy will never touch dat"—a long pull—"no, no, never touch dat."

Here he finished the whole, and placed the empty vessel beside the others; then gradually sunk back on his hams with his mouth open, and his eyes starting from the sockets, as he peered up into the tree, apparently at some terrible object.[15]

Scott's comic purpose is well served by his invented dialect. But there are two features of the passage that are of peculiar interest here. The first is the association of dialect with the stereotype of the comic Negro. The second has to do with the gap between the language of the narrator and the language of the fictional character. Bearing both of these in mind will help us to mark some significant points of growth in West Indian fiction. For as we shall see, the dialect is used in so many different human contexts by West Indian writers that it has been freed of the stereotype. And in different ways there

---

[15] Michael Scott, *Tom Cringle's Log* (1829). Quotation from Vol. 1, pp. 219–20, of the 1894 edition in two volumes by Gibbings and Co. Ltd. The incident quoted follows a hilarious account of a Negro funeral in which it is possible to trace African cultural survivals.

has been a steady closing of the gap between the language of the narrator and the language of the fictional characters.

Another example of the use of dialect comes from the work of a writer who never visited the West Indies. The consequence is not, perhaps, a necessary one, but in this passage the dialect is totally invented and it is unconvincing.

White man tie me mother, and force her and me brother Tankey board ship, and bring them and sell them to me master: me mother take sick, and no able to work; so she sit down; white man see her, and whip me mother, whip her very much, and make her work; when he turn away she so sick she no able to stand, she sit down again; but white man, cruel white man, again see her, and whip her much, very much, till blood run. Tankey see it, me see it; me cry; Tankey no bear it: he come softly behind white man, and with big hoe he knock him down; he make him dead; other white mans see Tankey and take him and hang him up by leg to tree, and whip him till he all bloody, and blood run upon the ground. . . .[16]

Dorothy Kilner's *The Rotchfords* (1786) from which the passage comes has elements of both antislavery and cult-of-feeling traditions, so its purpose should be evident. But there are again two features that I want to point out for the way in which they help us to measure the uses of dialect in West Indian writing. Miss Kilner's uncomplicated sentences with their monosyllabic words, their single tense, and their repetition to suggest paucity of vocabulary are intended to represent the simple speech of a simple man. It will be shown later how West Indian writers have complicated dialect to achieve less limited ends than this.

The two examples looked at reflect a limited knowledge of dialect and a limited conception of its possible artistic uses, the uses opted for coinciding with an external and stereotyped approach to the Negro. These were typical of British fictional representations in the eighteenth and nineteenth centuries. But that they were not inevitable may be argued from an interesting exception in William Godwin's *St. Leon* (1799), where the novelist-philosopher not only presents an unstereotyped Negro but protests against the habit of inventing a vulgar language to represent the socially inferior being. St. Leon, the hero, tries to bribe the jailer, Hector:

"My good friend, are not you poor?"
"Yes, sir."
"Would not you readily do me a kindness?"
"If my master give me leave, I will."
"You mistake me. Would you be my friend?"
"I do not know what you mean, sir. I have been used to call the man I love my friend. If you mean that, you know I cannot choose whether I will be a man's friend; it comes of itself."

---

[16] Cited by Wylie Sypher in *Guinea's Captive Kings* (University of North Carolina Press, 1942), see pp. 276–77.

"Can I not make you my friend?"

"That is, make me love you?"

I was surprised at the propriety of his answers. I am unable at this distance of time to recall the defects of his language: and I disdain the mimic toil of inventing a jargon for him suitable to the lowness of his condition: the sense of what he said I faithfully report.[17]

Although this is lifeless fiction, it is fiction conscious of the possibilities of life. But in 1799, it is still a hundred and fifty years before the folk become full human beings in literature. When they do so, the "jargon" invented for them will also have arrived. In the last part of this chapter there will be an examination of dialect in West Indian fiction. But first the ground must be prepared by a description of the contemporary linguistic situation.

THE CONTEMPORARY LINGUISTIC SITUATION

There are varieties of West Indian dialect from island to island, but there are certain broad features in common, and it is to these that one refers in speaking about a West Indian linguistic situation. Once this is said it is convenient to concentrate on one territory, and since recent discussions have focused on Jamaica it makes for some continuity of exploration to choose the same field.

In the twentieth century we have to give up the notion of separate languages (Creole English and Standard English) and we have to envisage a scale. At one end of the scale is what we have been calling "Standard English." In the strictest sense, Standard English (SE) is the language of British expatriates, but quite apart from whether it is actually practiced in the islands, it exercises a powerful influence. It exists as an ideal form to be aspired towards by mentally colonized West Indians, and it is the unknown norm by which even the illiterate measure social standing. An observant novelist, V. S. Naipaul, provides a comic illustration. In *The Mystic Masseur* (1957), Ganesh the mystic hero begins a small campaign:

One day he said, "Leela, is high time we realise that we living in a British country and I think we shouldn't be shame to talk the people language good."

Leela was squatting at the kitchen *chulha*, coaxing a fire from dry mango twigs. Her eyes were red and watery from the smoke. "All right, man."

"We starting now self, girl."

"As you say, man."

"Good. Let me see now. Ah, yes, Leela, have you lighted the fire? No, just gimme a chance. Is 'lighted' or 'lit' girl?"

"Look, ease me up, man. The smoke going in my eye."

"You ain't paying attention girl. You mean the smoke *is* going in your eye."

(*The Mystic Masseur*, p. 72)

[17] William Godwin, *St. Leon* (1799). Quotation from pp. 234–35 of the edition of 1831.

At this point in the novel, Leela is too concerned with life to bother about language, but with Ganesh's success and new importance Leela becomes a lady:

> Every day Leela became more refined. She often went to San Fernando to visit Soomintra, and to shop. She came back with expensive saris and much heavy jewellery. But the most important change was in her English. She used a private accent which softened all harsh vowel sounds; her grammar owed nothing to anybody, and included a highly personal conjugation of the verb to be.
> She told Suruj Mooma, "This house I are building, I doesn't want it to come like any erther Indian house. . . ."

> (*The Mystic Masseur*, p. 150)

Even beyond Leela and Ganesh, at the farthest end of the linguistic scale, and living in remote areas are the unschooled speakers of a number of closely related dialects that are the twentieth-century continuations of Creole English. The basic features are no different from those Thomas Russell had recognized in the language of the folk and had sought to describe in *The Etymology of Jamaican Grammar* (1868). But in the hundred-year interval, what was the language of the majority has become the language of a minority.

With the formal establishment of popular education in the latter half of the nineteenth century, we can trace the beginnings of a new connection on the grammatical level between the upper reaches of Creole English and Standard English. Once this connection was made, the long retreat of Creole as a separate language to its present minority position had begun. Another consequence of the connection was a multiplication of what I have called earlier "stages or degrees of Englishness." The emergent levels of dialect can be ranged in a continuous scale between Standard English and residual or hard-core Creole. At the opposite ends we seem to have two different languages but they move towards each other by mutually intelligible degrees.

It is hard-core Creole which is analyzed by Beryl Loftman Bailey in *Jamaican Creole Syntax: A Transformational Approach* (1966). Miss Bailey uses the term "Jamaican Creole" to cover what we have been calling "Creole English." Miss Bailey seems to be inconsistent, however, since she adopts more rigid criteria for purposes of pure grammatical analysis than in the more nationalistic activity of estimating the number of speakers of Jamaican Creole. The coherent system she produces in her analysis would have been impossible if she had seriously held the position declared in the "Introduction" to her grammar: "There is a hard core—the unschooled ranging from preschool children to the elderly . . . but if we take into consideration the fact that every native-born Jamaican understands some form of Creole, an estimate of a million speakers would not be extravagant. . . ." This seems to be an excessive estimate which can only be accounted for by Miss Bailey's commitment to a view of Creole today as the people's language, and to her belief in an ur-Creole, "some kind of Proto-Creole" whose "prior existence in the Old World" and relexification in the New has spawned a knot of related Creole languages in the Caribbean area:

By Jamaican Creole I mean the English-based Creole spoken throughout the island of Jamaica alongside the officially recognized English. It is a "*Mischsprache*" in which the syntax represents the mixing of two related syntactic types—one English, the other some kind of Proto-Creole—and the lexicon is predominantly English.[18]

In an earlier section I have proposed a theory of the origin of Creole English: I would suggest further, with Cassidy, that other Creoles developed under analogous conditions, hence their structural affinities:

But structure is not everything and even the marked differences of grammar and sounds are not enough to overbalance the large part of Jamaican folk speech that is English. If it is Creole, it is still English Creole as distinct from Spanish or French Creole. It coexists with English and the two have more in common than apart.[19]

I want therefore to return to the concept of a linguistic scale and the fluid situation which even Miss Bailey recognizes (see pp. 1–2 of *Jamaican Creole Syntax*) to explain what is meant by "West Indian Standard" and to suggest its significance for West Indian fiction.

West Indian Standard (WIS) lies nearest to Standard English (SE) on the linguistic scale in the islands. Its vocabulary is the same as that of SE but with the addition of a small number of West Indianisms[20] which have passed from the dialect into educated usage. The grammar of WIS is practically the same as that of SE. In their written forms, therefore, SE and WIS are almost indistinguishable. The most obvious differences between SE and WIS exist on the level of actual pronunciation. In *Jamaica Talk*, Cassidy equates Jamaican Standard (a variant of WIS) with the way educated Jamaicans pronounce Standard English. I will want to make the definition a little more exclusive than that, but Cassidy's impressionistic description of Jamaican pronunciation gives an idea of how one variant of WIS sounds:

The educated Jamaican pronounces Standard English as well as the educated man anywhere—that is to say, according to his personal lights and attitudes, his interests and the impression of himself that he may seek to establish. Like everybody else he will have his local differences, yet no more of those necessarily than the educated

[18] *Jamaican Creole Syntax* (Cambridge, 1966), p. 1.

[19] F. G. Cassidy, *Jamaica Talk*, p. 406.

[20] Formed by analogy from the term "Jamaicanism" used and defined by F. G. Cassidy in *Jamaica Talk* (1961) thus: "Most obviously this term would include any word, meaning or feature of grammar, idiom or pronunciation that has originated in Jamaica, or has been adopted here from a foreign source. It should also include any similar element that has survived in this island after dying elsewhere, or which has received a decidedly higher degree of use in Jamaica than elsewhere. Putting this into a more rational order, we may classify Jamaicanisms as belonging to five main types: preservations, borrowings, new formations, transferred meanings, and special preferences" (p. 3). The definition of "West Indianism" would run along the same lines.

Irishman, Welshman, or Scot—or for that matter, than the educated Englishman who is not from the "home counties." These local differences are heard in Jamaica in individual words and turns of phrase, but perhaps most strikingly as a pattern of intonation and accentuation that is often very different from the levelness of many Americans on the one hand, or the hilliness of many Englishmen on the other. Jamaican speech is more accidented: it goes up and down more frequently, and by sharper rises and falls. In short, it has a decided and characteristic lilt, the origin of which we shall discuss in a moment.[21]

In the next paragraph, Cassidy seems to recognize a connection between the pronunciation in WIS and the pronunciation of the dialects. The one is only a less accidented relation of the other. At the point therefore where WIS resembles SE least, it is closest to the dialects.

Using the resemblance in pronunciation as a starting point, it is tempting to argue that there is an organic connection between the dialects and WIS. But this is only an intuition which would need more evidence, more delicacy of analysis, and more expertise than can be mustered here. If such an organic connection did exist, however, we might have been able to attribute to it some of the features of repetition and other rhythmic effects which seem to occur spontaneously in the narrative sections of West Indian novels, for we could argue that these are natural incursions from the oral tradition of the dialects. But my interest is less to advocate a distinctive linguistic variety than to describe a new class of speakers in whose usage the notion of an organic connection between WIS and the dialects may be validated.

I would propose the following criteria for recognizing speakers of West Indian Standard: they have been sufficiently educated to control the grammar and lexis of Standard English; they may learn to pronounce in other ways, but they retain ability to pronounce in their natural WIS way; above all, however, they are more or less instinctive speakers of or thinkers in a West Indian dialect or dialects. The third criterion suggests that the speaker of West Indian Standard is an educated West Indian whose social origin is in the dialect-speaking group or whose social contacts make him a dialect speaker.

These criteria are not intended to increase nor diminish the number of speakers of WIS, but rather to help us to understand why the most distinctive speakers of West Indian Standard come from the Black or Colored educated classes; the criteria also helps us to see why such a class of speakers could not emerge as a class until the twentieth century. For until the effects of popular education could be felt, the numbers would be too small, and until there was a change in the social and psychological conditions, the Black or Colored West Indian who was educated would be more than likely to seek to eliminate his dialect facility and imitate SE.

The range of the speaker of WIS, and a summary of the West Indian linguistic situation, are represented in the following diagram. The divisions

[21] *Jamaica Talk*, p. 26.

Vertical lines mark off linguistic divisions but these are not mutually exclusive.
Horizontal lines indicate classes of speakers: broken portions indicate fluidity.
A = Speakers of Standard English   C = Speakers of Dialect
B = Speakers of West Indian Standard   D = Speakers of Creole

are arbitrary, but it is the general shape that I wish to impress. Speakers of WIS have a wide linguistic range. West Indian writers, as speakers of WIS, are also speakers of dialect.

A grammatical lapse which illustrates this in an accidental way is to be found in a short story *Afternoon in Trinidad*[22] by Alfred H. Mendes. At one point in the story, Dodo, a cab-man, suspects that his woman Queenie has been two-timing him:

One night he *ask* Queenie about it and she *denied* it so convincingly that all *he could say* was that *he had found* it strange that she was not on speaking terms with Corinne and Georgie.

"Why you carn' *axe* straight out whey you wants to know enh?" Queenie *said* indignantly. "We did have some high words and den she pull dong me clothes line. I has a good min' to bring she up, *oui*."

Mendes's grammatical lapse "he *ask*" (my italics) is made glaring by the correctness of his other verbs. The explanation would seem to be as follows: a tendency in West Indian dialects is to dispense with tense markers in the verb where context or where another grammatical feature is adequate. This tendency has passed into educated use to the extent that the speaker of West Indian Standard has to be on his guard (or thinks he has to be) when writing these forms. I would suggest that Mendes was tempted to say "axe" with his character, resisted it, but was so concerned about avoiding the most uneducated version that he slipped naturally into the intermediate form "ask."

But the West Indian writer's inwardness with the dialects is not revealed by accident in West Indian fiction. Although they do not have another language in the sense that Nigerians or Pakistanis do, West Indian writers have enriched their work by exploiting the possibilities of the folk dialect. How they do this is the subject of the next section of this chapter.

[22] In *Penguin New Writing 6*, ed. John Lehmann (Harmondsworth, Middlesex, 1941), pp. 69–82.

DIALECT IN WEST INDIAN FICTION

West Indian literature would seem to be the only substantial literature in which the dialect-speaking character is the central character. The conventional associations of dialect with comic characters, or with characters on the periphery, have not been eliminated, but they are disarmed of any stereo-typing appearances or effects by occurring among other contextualizations of dialect. This characteristic feature of West Indian writing reflects the more obviously new event—the centrality of the Black or Colored character and the articulation of this hitherto obscure and stereotyped person. It is important to add, however, that while the new contexts of dialect do not have a purely literary impulse in the way that Lawrence's use of dialect has in *Lady Chatterley's Lover*, neither are they to be accounted for in terms of the documentary demands of social realism. Most West Indian writers retain recognizable features of the dialects, but the literary inventions are shaped to meet wider expressive needs. In the works of a few writers dialect is put in for purposes of coarse realism, or to supply an anticipated exotic demand overseas; but the more interesting West Indian writers, like artists anywhere, are constantly opening up the possibilities of language, and in some of their works we can see the dialect being expanded in this exploratory way. It is at this growing process that I wish to look, but in order to clarify the discussion I would like to work under three main headings. In the first the focus will be on the relationship between the language of narration (the language of the implied author) and the language of the fictional character. In the second, the use of dialect to express the consciousness of the character will be looked at. In the third section, there will be a more rapid look at some other significant contexts where dialect is used by West Indian writers. The illustra-tions will be chosen in such a way as to reveal chronological developments, but I do not want to imply that each new possibility opened up eliminates an earlier usage. The emphasis must be on the variety of possibilities that have been created and that can still be drawn upon.

(a) Dialect and Distance

In the extract from *Tom Cringle's Log* quoted earlier, one of the sources of the comic effect was an incongruity between the language of the narrator (the implied author) and that of the fictional character. The incongruity was sharper for our awareness that the Standard English of the implied author belonged to a different social world from the world of the dialect-speaking character. We must begin therefore by making the observation that in West Indian fiction the two voices no longer reflect mutually exclusive social worlds. It increases the delicacy of our reading in fact if we can imagine the narrative sections in a West Indian Standard voice. This kind of delicacy is not always necessary, however, and is hardly called for, in the dialect novels of the white Creole, H. G. de Lisser, where the Negro is still a comic character and not much more, and where the author's attitude of withdrawal is reflected by an exaggerating of the distance between the narrator's language and that of the fictional character. An episode in *Jane's Career* (1914) is transitional in West Indian fiction in the way it combines an attitude of social superiority (recurrent in British presentations) with the West Indian's knowledge of the dialect. Jane is about to go to Kingston to pursue a career as a servant girl so she is taken to Daddy Buckram, the village sage. The description of the old man sets the scene in a revealing way:

> Like his audience, the Elder was black; he may have been about sixty years of age, and was intensely self-conscious. His close-cropped hair was turning grey; what chiefly distinguished him from all other men in the village was his glibness of tongue, his shoes, and his collar. Except on Sundays, everyone else went bare-footed and collarless; but this Daddy Buckram would never consent to do at any time, holding that one who preached "the Word" should be clothed in proper garments even though, as in his case, the shoes were usually down at heels and the collar dirty.
>
> *(Jane's Career,* p. 8)

Persuaded into an amused superiority, we witness next the recurrent device of writers handling the dialect-speaking character in a conventional way—a would-be impressive speech by the dialect-speaking character. Authorial markers of dissociation (my italics) are prominent, but de Lisser inscribes his dialect with obvious zest and with a dialect speaker's understanding of dialect's capacity to absorb miscellaneous material (in this case the Bible):

> "Jane," he continued *impressively* after a pause, "Kingston is a very big an' wicked city, an' a young girl like you, who de Lord has blessed wid a good figure an' a face, must be careful not to keep bad company. Satan goeth about like a roaring lion in Kingston seeking who he may devour. He will devour you if you do not take him to the Lord in prayer. Do you' work well. Write to you' moder often, for a chile who don't remember her parent cannot prosper. Don't stay out in de street in de night, go to church whenever you' employer allow you. If sinners entice thee, consent thou not. Now, tell me what I say to you."
>
> Jane hesitated a while, then answered.
>
> "You say I mus' behave myself, sah, an' go to church, an' don't keep bad company, an' dat de devil is a roarin' lion. An' . . . An' dat I must write mumma."
>
> The Elder *smiled his approval.* "I see," he *observed benignantly,* "that you have been giving my words attention. If you always remember dem like dat, you will conquer in de battle."
>
> *(Jane's Career,* p. 9)

As a speaker of WIS, de Lisser was capable of more varied uses of the dialect than he settled for. But his repeatedly comic purposes merely followed the convention of European writers. In his novels, for all his inwardness with the dialect, the two voices come from two different worlds.

Daddy Buckram is a peripheral character, so it would be unjust to make too much of the comparison between de Lisser's presentation and Samuel

Selvon's handling of a speech-making occasion by his peasant hero, Tiger, in *A Brighter Sun* (1952). But what I want to show is that social attitude has a great deal to do with the effects being pursued. Selvon is too involved with his character as an individual person to be distracted into superficial comedy. As a result, we find that the dialect is modified in the direction of the Standard, and the authorial voice slips in and out of the speech without drawing attention to its greater "correctness." The episode occurs when Tiger's parents come to visit him on the birth of Tiger and Urmilla's first child. There is a small party, and Joe, the neighbor, has proposed a toast:

Tiger saw a chance to prove he was getting to be a man. He said: "I is the man of the house, and I have to answer Joe toast."

Urmilla moved with a sixth sense and filled the glasses again. Tiger looked at her and smiled and she knew she had done the right thing.

But when he began to talk he found it wasn't going to be as easy as he thought, even with the rum in his head. "Well," he began waveringly, "—we—glad to have family and friends here today, especially as the baby born. Is true we not rich and we have only a small thing here, but still, is a good thing. So let we make a little merry for the baby. I should really begin different, I don't know what happen to me. I should say, "Ladies and gentlemens," and then make speech. But I cannot speechify very good. I would learn, though—." That was as far as he could go. He felt he would talk foolishness if he continued, and he gulped his drink.

He wanted everyone to make a speech, but all the elders shook their heads. And it became awkward, just standing and looking at one another, as if something had gone wrong.

(*A Brighter Sun*, p. 52)

Writers since de Lisser have taken a less restricted view of the dialect-speaking character, and consequently of the dialect itself. The closer involvement of the implied author with the low-life character is reflected by a closing of the gap between the language of narration and the language of the fictional character. Further examples of this may be found in the next section called "Dialect and Consciousness." This section continues with a discussion of some attempts to draw the two voices together by techniques of narration.

The use of a dialect-speaking narrator by V. S. Reid in the novel *New Day* (1949) and by John Hearne in a short story, *At the Stelling* (1960), remind us that few West Indian authors reproduce dialect precisely in their works. In these two cases invention is more obvious than in most. Both writers invent successfully, however, because they are intimate with the dialects out of which they are constructing, and have a keen eye for recognizable qualities and literary possibilities: As a result we feel that the language in the works is not a realistic reproduction of dialect as it may be spoken anywhere in fact, but it is a convincing extension of the familiar.

Reid's novel, which links the granting of a new constitution to Jamaica in 1944 with the Morant Bay Rebellion of 1865, is narrated by the old man

John Campbell who is a witness of the new and was an actor in the old. The novel opens in the later period and the new day unleashes the memory of the aged man. The whole is then unfolded more or less continuously from the earlier time to the later, but with regular returns to the present as the old man makes an interjection here or emphasizes a point there. Because the story is told as an oral performance by the reminiscing man, Reid is able to make a credible show of narrating in dialect. But what he actually does is to push WIS and dialect even closer together in the narrating voice of John Campbell:

Mas'r, is a heady night, this. Memory is pricking at me mind, and restlessness is a-ride me soul. I scent many things in the night-wind; night-wind is a-talk of days what pass and gone.

But the night-wind blows down from the mountains, touching only the high places as it comes; so then, 'member, I can remember only those places which stand high on the road we ha' traveled.

(New Day, p. 185)

Our sense of the speaking voice, rhythmic repetition, and personification imagery make this an impressive passage, but it is not dialect in the same way that the following from de Lisser is dialect:

"Who you gwine to send for policeman for?" demanded Sarah, also at the top of her voice and with arms akimbo. "Me! Y'u must be drunk! Look at the mallata [mulatto] ooman how she stand! Y'u t'ink I am a schoolgal, no? Y'u t'ink you can teck exvantage of me! If it wasn't for one t'ing, I would hold you in here an' gie y'u such a beaten dat you wouldn't walk for a week."

(Jane's Career, p. 118)

The stylized dialect in Reid's novel never sinks to such exotic vulgarity, although it does show signs of over-writing as in the pretentious homeliness of the following passage:

An old man now, me. Many years bank the flame that was John Campbell. And down the passages o' those years many doors have opened. Some o' them ha' let in rich barbecues o' joyousness, with good things covering the bottom of the pot o' life and no thorns there to give me pain. And others have opened into butteries of hell, and me soul has been scarred with the fires . . .

(New Day, p. 42)

On the whole, however, Reid's experiment is a successful one. Because the language of narration is pushed so close to the language of the characters, the reader is seldom jerked into awareness of two separate voices.

At less risk, since it is a much shorter piece, Hearne achieves vivid effects with his dialect-speaking narrator in *At the Stelling*:[23]

[23] In *West Indian Stories,* ed. Andrew Salkey (London, 1960).

I sink far down in that river and already, before it happen, I can feel *perai* chew at my fly button and tear off my cod, or alligator grab my leg to drag me to drowning. But God is good. When I come up the sun is still there and I strike out for the little island in the river opposite the *stelling*. The river is full of death that pass you by, but the *stelling* holds a walking death like the destruction of the Apocalypse.

I make ground at the island and draw myself into the mud and the bush and blood draw after me from between my legs. And when I look back at the *stelling*, I see Mister Cockburn lie down in him deck chair, as if fast asleep, and Mister Bailey lying on him face upon the boards. . . .

And John standing on the path, with the repeater still as the finger of God in him hands. . .

(*West Indian Stories*, p. 62)

The first point to be made is that it would be impossible to feel the full effect of this passage unless we imagine a speaking West Indian voice. Repetition, monosyllabic rhythm, and personification imagery make it resemble some in Reid's novel, but it is much less obviously a dialect passage than any in Reid. Little more than the pervasive present tense prevents it from being West Indian Standard.

Although both Reid and Hearne thus come close to making a modified form of dialect do the work both of narration and dialogue, their use of narrating characters is a conservative device. It is in Samuel Selvon's works that the language of the implied author boldly declares itself as dialect differing little from the language of the characters. In the story "Brackley and the Bed",[24] the author takes up the stance of the calypsonian or ballad maker and both SE and WIS are abolished:

Brackley hail from Tobago, which part they have it to say Robinson Crusoe used to hang out with Man Friday. Things was brown in that island and he make for England and manage to get a work and was just settling down when bam! he get a letter from his aunt saying Teena want to come to England too. . . .

Well, right away he write aunty and say no, no, because he have a feeling this girl would make botheration if she come England. The aunt write back to say she didn't mean to say that Teena want to come England, but that Teena left Tobago for England already.

Brackley hold his head and bawl. And the evening the boat train come in at Waterloo, he went there and start 'busing she right away not waiting to ask how the folks at home was or anything.

"What you doing in London?" Brackley ask as soon as Teena step off the train. "What you come here for, eh? Even though I write home to say things real hard?"

"What happen, you buy the country already?" Teena sheself giving tit for tat right away. "You ruling England now? The Queen abdicate?"

(*Ways of Sunlight*, p. 151)

This is as far as any West Indian author has gone towards closing the gap between the language of narration and the language of the fictional character.

[24] In his collection *Ways of Sunlight* (London, 1957).

It has been argued that social attitude has something to do with the closing of the gap. But this would be a misleading emphasis to end with. Writers like V. S. Naipaul achieve effects of incongruity by stressing differences between the two voices, and much of the fun of Alvin Bennett's *God the Stonebreaker* comes about in this way. A purely literary point on which to end, therefore, is that West Indian writers who possess WIS and dialect have a wide range within which to vary the distance between the voice of narration and the voice of the character. As we have seen, this can be of use in the hands of the artist who wishes to take advantage of it.

(b) Dialect and Consciousness

In *Corentyne Thunder* (1941), Edgar Mittelholzer's first novel, one of the centers of interest is Ramgolall the cowminder:

A tale we are about to tell of Ramgolall, the cowminder, who lived on the Corentyne coast of British Guiana, the only British colony on the mainland of South America. Ramgolall was small in body and rather short and very thin. He was an East Indian who had arrived in British Guiana in 1898 as an immigrant indentured to a sugar estate. He had worked very hard. He had faithfully served out the period of his indenture, and now at sixty-three years of age he minded cows on the savannah of the Corentyne coast, his own lord and guide.

(Corentyne Thunder, p. 7)

It is an unpromising start, with the West Indian author doing his best to accommodate his prospective British reader by providing the geographical and historical background. The tone of the tourist guide combines with the stance of the superior omniscient novelist. But the work recovers from this disastrous beginning as Mittelholzer moves into his tale of fragile human endeavor in a vast, inscrutable landscape.

Mittelholzer handles his dialect-speaking peasants with great compassion, but his use of dialect is in accordance with a strict realistic criterion of appropriateness to the character. This means that if he wishes to express anything complicated about the character, he has to work not directly through the character's consciousness, or in the character's language, but by a mediating omniscience.

I would like therefore to look at an episode in *Corentyne Thunder*, where an attempt is made to express Ramgolall's overwhelming sense of desolation. This will be followed by two examples from later West Indian novels where dialect is used, and the character's consciousness articulated in similarly complicated situations. There is no wish to imply that one method is necessarily better than the other. The purpose is to show by comparison how dialect offers alternative artistic possibilities to the West Indian writer.

Ramgolall and his daughter are returning home from work when the girl Beena is seized by pain:

Beena moaned softly and her breathing came in heavy gusts *as though her soul were fatigued with the things of this life and wished to leave her body in gasp after gasp of wind.* And Ramgolall, weak in body and in mind, could only look about him at a loss. His dark eyes seemed to appeal to the savannah and then to the sky. But the savannah remained still and grey-green, quiet and immobile *in its philosophy.* And the sky, too, would do nothing to aid him. Pale purple in the failing light and streaked with feathery brown and yellow clouds, *the sky watched like a statue of Buddha.*

"Ow! Bettay, you na go dead. Eh? Bettay? Talk, na? Is wha' wrong, bettay?"
But Beena moaned in reply, doubled up.
"Talk, na, bettay? Try. You' belly a-hurt?"
The moan came again *like a portent, like the echo of a horn sounded in the depth of the earth. "The Dark gathers,"* it seemed to tell the soul of Ramgolall, *"and Death cometh with the Dark. Be resigned, my son."*
Ramgolall stood up in a panic, looking all around him. He saw the cows, a group of moving spots, headed for their pen and getting smaller as they went. He could smell their dung mingled with the iodine in the air. He could see the tiny mud-house, with its dry palm-leaf roof, where he and Beena and Kattree lived. It stood far off, a mere speck.

(Corentyne Thunder, p. 11)

I have italicized some phrases which seem to be too crudely intrusive and which get in the way of the reader's imagination. But Mittelholzer works in other more acceptable ways. The evocation of empty savannah and vast sky against Ramgolall's appealing eyes is brought home in the final paragraph. Here distant objects express his desolation and panic at being cut off; and the faint smell in the air seems to suggest his wobbly hold upon existence.

But however effective Mittelholzer's indirect method may be, it remains an indirect method at its best. Ramgolall is little more than a figure of pathos: while *we* become aware of the meaning of his panic Ramgolall himself remains without consciousness. For, all the effects of the passage are achieved through devices in Standard English or in the West Indian Standard voice of the author. In this light, Ramgolall's words and dialect are flat counters out of touch with the experience he has undergone.

Because of Mittelholzer's limited view of Ramgolall's possibilities, *Corentyne Thunder* never really becomes the tale of a cowminder that it sets out to be. The peasant becomes increasingly peripheral as the novel advances. The peasant character is emphatically a central character in Samuel Selvon's *A Brighter Sun* (1952). And it is in this novel that dialect first becomes the language of consciousness in West Indian fiction. For Tiger is an introspective character and a dialect-speaking one. As we follow his development from premature Hindu wedding to turbulent fatherhood and responsible domestic anxiety, from Indian legacy to Trinidadian citizenship, and from obscure youth to naive inquiring manhood, dialect becomes saturated with inner experience. Selvon does not present Tiger's consciousness exclusively through dialect; but authorial comment, reportage of the character's thought processes, and reproduction of these processes directly in dialect modulate into one another so smoothly that the impression given is of direct access to the dialect-speaker's raw consciousness:

Life was beginning to get complicated, now that he was beginning to learn things. Sookdeo had promised to teach him to read. Boysie was going to show him many things in Port of Spain. Where was his life going to fit in? Perhaps, if he liked the city, he could get a job there, and give up the garden. Or Urmilla could keep it while he was at work. Anyway, he wasn't sure. He wasn't sure about anything. . . . When Urmilla and the baby were asleep he looked up at the roof and felt revulsion for his wife and child. They were to blame for all his worry. If he were alone he could be like Boysie, not caring a damn. He would go to the city and get a job. . . . He would even go to school in the night and learn to read and write. . . . Look at Sookdeo, he argued, you think I want to be like he when I get old? Is only old age that I respect in him. All he could do is read and drink rum. When I learn to read, you think is only *Guardian* I going to read? I going to read plenty books, about America and England, and all them places. Man, I will go and live in Port of Spain; this village too small, you can't learn anything except how to plant crop.

(*A Brighter Sun*, pp. 90–91)

If Tiger's thought processes are naive, they are at least spread over a wide area of experience. In following the character's inner workings in a credible modification of dialect, Selvon helps to make dialect a more flexible instrument.

In Wilson Harris's *The Far Journey of Oudin* (1961), which also takes East Indians in the West Indies for its raw material, dialect becomes the dramatic language for articulating a complex process in consciousness. Mohammed and his brothers Hassan and Kaiser had deprived their crazy half-brother of his legacy and murdered him. After an initial period of prosperity the three brothers begin to feel their possessions crumbling and they become the prey of the ruthless money-lender, Ram. The strange materialization of a wandering laborer called Oudin presents Ram with a longed-for accomplice and a willing slave. Ram sends Oudin to Mohammed, ostensibly as a useful helper, but in fact Oudin's mission is to steal Mohammed's cattle, thus driving Mohammed even further into economic dependence upon the demonic money-lender. Oudin's resemblance to the murdered half-brother causes consternation in the Mohammed household and from this point Mohammed begins to feel himself visited by a curse:

"Is like if some kind of thing circulating me." He paused.

"What you mean?" Ram was involved and interested.

"I don't know exactly how to explain. But time itself change since he come. Is like if I starting to grow conscious after a long time, that time itself is a forerunner to something. But Ah learning me lesson so late, is like it is a curse, and things that could have gone smooth now cracking up in haste around me. I so bewilder I can't place nothing no more. What I used to value and what I used not to value overlapping. Two, three, four face looking at me. Every face so different. I don't know which is private, which is public, which is past, which is future. And yet all is one, understand me?"

"I do," Ram said softly, and almost inaudibly.

"I suppose I is an ignorant man. Ah lose me grip long ago. I wish to God Ah could accept the fact that I changing. Ah feel that I, *me*, then is just a piece of moving furniture, and something else, bigger by far, pushing me about until I don't know whether I standing 'pon me head, me backside, or me foot."

(The Far Journey of Oudin, pp. 91–92)

The process of breakup of the known substances in the character's life under the weight of an intuition of something beyond complacent existence is a crucial stage in the experience of a Harris character. By boldly allowing the crumbling character to describe his condition in dialect, Harris enlists the urgency of the rhythmic speaking voice in suggesting the urgency of the experience. Here too, as throughout Harris's first five novels, the recognizable elements in the character's language offer the reader a foothold for coming to closer grips with a disturbing and unfamiliar state of consciousness. The successful use of dialect in a context like this in West Indian writing carried the conventionally simple language of the simple character to new levels of profoundity.

(c) Some More Contexts of Dialect

In the last two sections, there has been an attempt to show that dialect is a natural part of the equipment of the West Indian novelist, used as a means of narration, and for expressing the consciousness of the peasant character in a wide range of situations. It has been suggested that such a subtle and flexible use of dialect on such a large scale is probably unique in literature. In this section, it is proposed to consolidate the argument by providing some more examples of the varying contexts of dialect. It has possibly begun to appear already that the degree of Englishness of the dialect varies from situation to situation in the novels, and this impression will be confirmed by the passages to follow. But certain common features which have also emerged from previous examples will again be in evidence. These are improvisation in syntax and lexis; direct and pithy expression; a strong tendency towards the use of image, especially of the personification type; and various kinds of repetition of syntactic structure and lexis combining with the spoken voice to produce highly rhythmic effects. It would be repetitive to accompany each extract below with a full description, and since my main purpose is simply to provide telling examples of the use of dialect in various contexts, analytic remarks will be restricted to a minimum.

Two examples of dialect used in a broadly political situation may be taken from works by George Lamming. Lamming's second novel, *The Emigrants* (1954), brings together, on a ship bound for England, a collection of West Indians from different islands and of different social and educational levels. This gives Lamming scope to exercise a wide range of linguistic skills in differentiating the various dialects of his characters. For they all find themselves drawn into frequent council in which they discover the sameness of the islands and the sameness of their human quest for something better—national identity or personal freedom. The many discussions in the work are carried on in dialect. The example I want to quote is from a long speech by a Jamaican who begins with the generalization that "West Indies people whatever islan' you bring them from, them want to prove something." An account of the settling of the islands from different sources, and the state of disorientation this has produced, leads to this universal understanding:

> ... Them is West Indians. Not Jamaicans or Trinidadians. 'Cause the bigger the better.... An' is the reason West Indies may out o' dat vomit produce a great people, 'cause them provin' that them want to be something. Some people say them have no hope for people who doan' know exactly w'at them want or who them is, but that is a lot of rassclot talk. The interpretation me give hist'ry is people the world over always searchin' an' feelin', from time immemorial, them keep searchin' an' feelin'. Them ain't know w'at is wrong 'cause them ain't know w'at is right, but them keep searchin' an' feelin', an' when them dead an' gone, hist'ry write things 'bout them that them themself would not have know or understand. Them wouldn't know themself if them see themself in hist'ry. 'Cause w'at them was tryin' to prove them leave to hist'ry to give a name.
>
> *(The Emigrants*, p. 66)

Lamming's "Jamaican dialect" is not only credible as that, it is made to carry an extremely sophisticated notion—the kernel of the novel—without signs of strain or unnaturalness, and without announcing itself as dialect.

In the same author's *Season of Adventure* (1960), a novel concerned with different levels of freedom and the ways in which the political is also deeply personal, the following conversation takes place between Crim, who is grateful that the colonial powers have given freedom at last to San Cristobal, and Powell, who sees the matter in a different light:

> "I say it was a real freedom happen when the tourist army went away," Crim said. "It look a real freedom they give San Cristobal."
>
> "It don't have that kind o' givin'," said Powell, trying to restrain his anger. "Is wrong to say that, 'cause free is free an' it don't have no givin'. Free is how you is from the start, an' when it look different you got to move, just move, an' when you movin' say that is a natural freedom make you move. You can't move to freedom, Crim, 'cause freedom is what you is, an' where you start, an' where you always got to stand."
>
> *(Season of Adventure*, p. 18)

It is worth pointing out not only that the dialect is convincing and that it is being made to work in the context of a political philosophy but also that the emphatic and categorical quality of the language being used by Powell is appropriate to his character. Powell is in fact a passionate fanatic, a man who will not be handed his freedom by anyone and who has a violent distrustful attitude to the liberal gesture. Towards the end of the novel, when the white-skinned West Indian girl, Fola, wishes to free herself from the traditional denial by her class of its West Indianness, it is Powell the uncompromising fanatical victim of the history of his time who makes a murderous assault upon her:

"No noise," he said, rubbing his hand inside his shirt, "no more than a sandfly can make, I warn you, no noise."

"But . . . but . . . but what have I done?" Fola stammered.

"Enough," said Powell, "You an' your lot done do enough."

"Why? Why?" Fola's voice dribbled.

"It too late," said Powell, rubbing the hand inside his shirt, "it too late to explain, just as it too late for you an' your lot to make your peace with me."

"You don't understand", she cried, "You don't understand."

"Exact, exact," said Powell, "I don't understand. An' what's more, I don't want to. Where you an' your lot concern, I hope I never live to understand."

Now Powell's hand emerged slowly from inside his shirt; but his fist was still hidden as it rubbed against his chest.

"What I do I do alone," said Powell, "no help from you an' your lot, 'cause I learn, I learn how any playing 'bout with your lot bound to end. You know the rules too good, an' it too late, it too late for me to learn what rules you have for murderin' me. So is me go murder first. Otherwise is you what will murder me, or make me murder myself."

(Season of Adventure, p. 328)

The extraordinary power of the emotion in this incident might prevent us from realizing that Powell is a dialect speaker whose way of speaking is precisely appropriate to his highly personal condition.

The advance which Lamming's artistic use of dialect represents may be illustrated by a quotation from an early West Indian writer who invested in the common language. In Alfred Mendes' *Black Fauns* (1935), set in a barrackyard in Trinidad, the women of the yard meet daily and have long conversations in dialect on miscellaneous subjects. An admiring remark about White people, and a denigration of Africans by one of the fauns prompts the following rejoinder from Ethelrida:

"I don't know why you say that, old lady," Ethelrida retorted, "I see all the white people in civilised lands behaving worse than savage an' heathen. Look at de war in nineteen-fourteen. You ever see people made in God's image cut up and shoot up an' mash up each other like dat? I see Mister Pompom does like to go to the teeayter. What for? To see white girl upon white sheet behave like dressed-up worthless women. I hear white priest an' white parson does go to Africa in the forest to teach our own colour about Christ an' God. Day does call demself mission-ary. It look to me they got more than enough people in their own land to teach about Christ an' God. It look to me like niggers in Africa happy when white people leave them alone. As soon as white people, with Bible an' chaplet in hand go to our own people in Africa like they does bring trouble and unhappiness an' misery."

(Black Fauns, p. 194)

Although Mendes' usage is not as dynamic as Lamming's, the passage, a product of the 1930s, was a sign of things to come.

In Austin Clarke's *Amongst Thistles and Thorns* (1965), a sonorous dialect is used simultaneously for comic effect and to register social protest. In one episode, Nathan feels that he is qualified to describe the limiting society to his woman Ruby: "I have come to a damn serious understanding during my travels in and around this blasted past-tense village." The conversation occurs when Nathan and Ruby are considering sending their son to the high school. Nathan argues that there is no hope of any but the least-considered white-collar jobs for the educated Black man:

> . . . He could even come out a saniterry inspector and walk all through this blasted village in a khaki suit and white cork hat with a white enamel ladle in his hand' to dip down inside the poor people shitty closets with. But be-Christ! after all them school fees I pay out, and all them dollars spend on books, I hopes, I hopes to-hell that Milton do not come out as no damn inspector, looking for a million and one larvees in no blasted person' outdoor closet, or to see if they have young mosquitoes in their drinking-water buckets. That Ruby . . . that, Rube, is the lengths and advantages Milton could go in this kiss-me-arse island after he find himself in the possession of a high-school eddication.
>
> (*Amongst Thistles and Thorns*, p. 105)

The zest with which Nathan puts this case and the rhythmic insistence of his language might be thought to distract from the force of the protest. But this would be true if direct protest were Clarke's sole intention. In fact, Nathan is an irresponsible character and his intention is to regain the favor of Ruby by attacking the things that threaten to thwart the boy. There is a protest element in his speech which is part of an authorial intention, but it is emphatically in the background.

The full measure of Nathan's deceptive oratory comes out when having argued against the futility of becoming educated, he insists that Milton must be sent to school. Aware of Ruby's vulnerability on this question, and of her yearnings for a better life for the boy, Nathan sweeps her along with the rhetoric of dialect:

> "And if Milton is a boy what have a singing voice in his head, I want him to sing in the cathedral' choirs 'pon a Sundee. Oh Christ, I could see that bastard now, Rube, darling love! I could see Milton right this very now before my eye' wearing them red robes and that thing 'round his neck. . . .
>
> Yeah . . . and walking up and down that cathedral' aisle with the choirs, and the Bishop o' the islan', and singing them psalms and carols and songs ancient and modernt so damn sweet, more sweeter than if he was a blasted humming bird!"
>
> "That is our son, Nathan."
>
> "Be-Christ, Ruby, you have just say a mouthful! Milton is our son. Our own-own flesh-and-blood possession!"
>
> (*Amongst Thistles and Thorns*, p. 105)

What I am trying to suggest with the quotations from Clarke, is that dialect has traveled so far in West Indian fiction that it is used to produce different effects simultaneously and that it can even go beyond lyricism to fake lyricism.

A fine example of the lyricism of dialect occurs in Jan Carew's *Black*

Midas (1958). The novel as a whole is remarkable for the way it uses the vivid immediate qualities of dialect to suggest the speech of outdoor men, and to invoke a staggering landscape, but I shall confine myself to a lush moment when Rhodius and Shark (the Black Midas) are traveling up-river and Rhodius sees Shark sitting quietly:

"You hear the voices?" he asked.

"Which voices?"

"The river, man, the river. This water got more talk than the tongue in Babel. When night-time come all the dead man under the river does talk." He spoke quietly, with his eyes on John Pye's shadow in the bow all the time. "They got good people and bad one under the river, and me travel up and down so often me know them all. Me travel when star was bright, when moon hang low, when dark so heavy me couldn't spit through it. The good people does say 'Rhodius, Rhodius, don't take no chance with the power-god; Kusewayo sitting stony-still in he big chair. Steer clear of the living rock; they get tentacle-hand to pull you down . . . don't take no risk by Topoco, the green spirit of the quiet water got whirlpool to suck you in . . . don't make mistake at the Looking Glass, is time of the year for sacrifice, that water deep with hungrying for you.' But the bad ones does say, 'Come down, Rhodius. Come down, Rhodius. We will make you bones flute like weeping wood! Come down, Rhodius; the river bottom smooth and we will roll you eye from here to Macharee.' You hear them?" he said. "You hear them?" And I pressed my ear against the gunwale, but all I heard was tongueless lisping and all I saw when I sat up was starlight dancing on the rim of whirlpools.

(Black Midas, pp. 177–178)

In passages like this, Carew is able to suggest the haunting qualities of his massive landscape, thus making credible the central faith of the novel, upon which much of its tension is built, that the pork-knocking characters are literally possessed, that the jungle is in their veins. In the final sentence we have an instance, I think, of WIS more than usually suffused with dialect rhythm and expressiveness.

The final example comes from Wilson Harris's *Palace of the Peacock* (1960). In his five Guyana novels, Harris follows a vision which demands to be worked out in unconventional ways: his characters do not exist in a recognizable social context; he is not concerned with the portrayal in realistic terms of the individual character; and there is a collapsing of our usual constitutive categories of time, person, and place. We find in his novels, therefore, that the living and the dead, and people from different times and places coexist. Further, persons are constantly collapsing into one another and they frequently collapse into place and thing. Harris's vision is a vision of universality and transcendence running against our everyday notions about the nature of reality.

This means, taking the word in its common sense, that there is an air of unreality in these Guyana novels. There are two main ways in which Harris gives initial credibility to his strange fictions. The first is by the sensuous rendering of an intimate, felt Guyanese landscape. The second is by the use of dialect. This is true in general in the novels, but it is more sharply apparent at critical moments. At a time when characters are undergoing the most bizarre or extraordinary experiences, they express themselves in dialect.

In *Palace of the Peacock*, the crew of dead men pursuing their journey up-river beyond Mariella become aware of a flock of birds wheeling overhead. Each of the men has been dead once before, and they are all approaching their second death. Since da Silva is the first to go, he "sees" the most, and between him and Cameron who is still "alive" (only once dead) there is a tense exchange:

"What in heaven name really preying on you sight and mind, Boy?" Cameron suddenly became curious. "I only seeing vulture bird. Where the parrot what eating you?"

"Ah telling you Ah dream the boat sink with all of we", da Silva said speaking to himself as if he had forgotten Cameron's presence. "Ah drowned dead and Ah float. All of we expose and float. . . ."

"Is vulture bird you really feeling and seeing" shouted Cameron. His voice was a croak in the air. Da Silva continued—a man grown deaf and blind with sleep— "Ah dream Ah get another chance to live me life over from the very start. Live me life over from the very start, you hear?" He paused and the thought sank back into the stream. "The impossible start to happen. Ah lose me own image and time like if I forget is where me sex really start. . . ."

"Fool, stop it," Cameron hissed.

"Don't pick at me," da Silva said. "The impossible start happen I tell you. Water start dream, rock and stone start dream, tree trunk and tree root dreaming, bird and beast dreaming. . . ."

"You is a menagerie and a jungle of a fool", Cameron's black tongue laughed and twisted.

(*Palace of the Peacock*, pp. 110–111)

Harris modulates the language in this passage so subtly that we might miss the way that we are made to move between Cameron's invective, da Silva's exultation, and the discreet organizing touches of the implied author. Strange as the experience may be, and no matter how undifferentiated the two men in a conventional way, the tension betweem them is laid bare, and da Silva's sense of a new beginning makes a vivid impression. Harris's use of the dialect in his novels is quite crucial from the point of view of their readability. Because the folk language is involved in such a complex imaginative world, the range and flexibility of the dialect are made greater.

To understand properly the certainty with which West Indian writers have turned the dialects to such literary account as I have tried to illustrate, we must remember that coexisting with the new literary growth in the West Indies, and predating it, is a long oral tradition of storytelling and folk poetry in the dialect. A modern representative of this tradition is Louise Bennett of Jamaica, whose dialect poems produced over the last twenty-five years have recently been published as *Jamaica Labrish: Jamaica Dialect Poems* (1967). In Trinidad, the oral tradition flourishes in the calypso whose

most skilful exponent is Francisco Slinger, called "The Mighty Sparrow."
What we are seeing in the West Indian novel, and in very recent West Indian
poetry, is the assimilation of linguistic properties that have long been
established in the oral usages of the folk. It is to be lamented that while local
audiences have made Sparrow a millionaire and a popular hero because of
his use of dialect, those who read either fail to recognize its subtle pervasive
influence, or as Naipaul relates, "object to its use in books which are read
abroad. 'They must be does talk so by you', one woman said to me. 'They
don't talk so by me'."[25]

STUDY QUESTIONS

1. How does the status of English as a literary language differ in the West Indies
   from its status in West Africa? In India? In answering, you might think about
   the following quotation from Gerald Moore's *The Chosen Tongue:*

   > Nevertheless the language did slowly make its way into the life of these
   > tropical communities, inhabiting climates and landscapes infinitely removed
   > from its origin. In the British West Indies, as successive waves of African,
   > Indian, and Chinese immigration spent themselves upon the shore, forgetting
   > in a generation or two the very provinces whence they had come, English in a
   > variety of dialect forms gradually established itself as the unique language of
   > the region. In Asia and Africa it became, at least temporarily, the language of
   > government, of higher education and, more important still, of higher status.
   > In Asia, however, the withdrawal of imperial control revealed how precarious
   > the situation of the language really was. The volume of literary activity in
   > languages such as Bengali, Tamil, Gujarati, Malay, and Urdu, together with
   > the gradual decline of English usage in public life, suggests that ultimately
   > the imperial language may prove as marginal as the English presence itself;
   > whilst in tropical Africa only the recent spread of mass education has offered
   > it the possibility of escape from an equally marginal role. For historical
   > experience confirms that a language which remains the property of a small elite
   > cannot provide the basis for a national culture.[a]

   If English were to cease to be used as an official language in Africa, would
   authors continue to write in it?
2. What will be the factors involved in the choice of a literary language by a writer
   in Nigeria? Are the factors different for an Indian writer? What might prompt a
   serious Ghanaian novelist to employ a form of English closer to the form used in
   the Onitsha market fiction than to international or standard English?
3. What special knowledge would a critic need to be able to discriminate "between
   a deliberately ungrammatical usage and what might be just a mistake which
   happens to be effective"? Is such a discrimination important? Have you
   encountered any American writers who use "translation features" like those
   pointed out in the work of Gabriel Okara (pp. 118–19)?

[25] V. S. Naipaul, *The Middle Passage* (London, 1962), p. 69.
[a] (London: Longmans, 1969), p. xi.

4. Does Ramchand's account of the development of West Indian Creole support the polygenetic or the monogenetic theory of creole development? Is his criticism of Beryl Bailey's *Jamaican Creole Syntax* consistent with his theory and assumptions?

5. It has been argued[b] that some dialects spoken by blacks in the United States have derived from an earlier creole gradually relexified and influenced by standard English and nonstandard white dialects; and that only such a theory can account for features found in black dialects some of which are shared by West Indian and Sea Island Creole (Gullah). What evidence would be needed to prove such a hypothesis? Does such a hypothesis agree with Ramchand's account of the development of West Indian English?

6. Compare linguistic features—phonology (that is, as you can deduce from the spelling), morphology, syntax, and lexicon of the selections from *Tom Cringle's Log* (p. 125); de Lisser's *Jane's Career* (p. 133); Hearne's *At the Stelling* (p. 136); and Selvon's *Ways of Sunlight* (p. 136). Does such an analysis support Ramchand's differentiation of artificial and natural representations of dialect? Can you find linguistic evidence supporting his generalizations about the uses to which dialect is put?

7. In the story that follows, Ram (a West Indian) uses several schemes to convince a landlord that he is Indian, *not* West Indian. How would you characterize the changes in Ram's speech whenever he talks to the landlord? Compare the language of the narrator in this story and in the second excerpt from *Season of Adventure* (p. 142). What differences in effect are produced? From the following story, extract those features which differ from your own concept of standard English features. Do the same for several example passages in Ramchand's essay, and make comparisons.

When Greek Meets Greek

Samuel Selvon

One morning Ramkilawansingh (after this, we calling this man Ram) was making a study of the notice-boards along Westbourne Grove what does advertise rooms to let. Every now and then he writing down an address or a telephone number, though most of the time his eyes colliding up with *No Colours, Please,* or *Sorry, No Kolors.*

"Red, white and blue, all out but you," Ram was humming a little ditty what children say when they playing whoop. Just as he get down by Bradley's Corner he met Fraser.

"You look like a man who looking for a place to live." Fraser say.

"You look like a man who could tell me the right place to go," Ram say.

"You try down by Ladbroke Grove?" Fraser ask.

"I don't want to go down in that criminal area," Ram say, "at least, not until they find the man who kill Kelso."

Reprinted by permission of the author, who is now continuing his career as a novelist and short story writer in London. Among Mr. Selvon's novels in which West Indian English gets its fullest use are *Ways of Sunlight* (New York: St. Martin's Press, 1957), *The Lonely Londoners* (New York: St. Martin's Press, 1957), and *The Housing Lark* (London: MacGibbon & Kee 1965).

[b] William A. Stewart, "Toward a History of American Negro Dialect," in *Language and Poverty: Perspectives on a Theme*, ed. Frederick Williams (Chicago, 1970), pp. 351–79.

"Then you will never live in the Grove," Fraser say.

"You are a contact man," Ram say, "which part you think I could get a room, boy?"

Fraser scratch his head. "I know of a landlord up the road who vow that he ain't ever taking anybody who come from the West Indies. But he don't mind taking Indians. He wouldn't know the difference when he see you is a Indian . . . them English people so foolish they believe every Indian come from India."

"You think I stand a chance?" Ram ask.

"Sure, you stand a chance. All you have to do is put on a turban."

"I never wear a turban in my life; I am a born Trinidadian, a real Creole. All the same, you best hads give me the address, I will pass around there later."

So Fraser give him the address, and Ram went on reading a few more boards, but he got discourage after a while and went to see the landlord.

The first thing the landlord ask him was: "What part of the world do you come from?"

"I am an Untouchable from the heart of India," Ram say. "I am looking for a single room. I dwelt on the banks of the Ganges. Not too expensive."

"But you are not in your national garments," the landlord say.

"When you are in Rome," Ram say, making it sound like an original statement, "do as the Romans do."

While the landlord sizing up Ram, an Indian tenant come up the steps to go inside. This fellar was Chandrilaboodoo (after this, we calling this man Chan) and he had a big beard with a hair net over it, and he was wearing a turban. When he see Ram, he clasp his hands with the palms touching across his chest by way of greeting.

The old Ram catch on quick and do the same thing.

"*Acha, Hindustani,*" Chan say.

"*Acha, pilau, papadom, chickenvindaloo,*" Ram say desperately, hoping for the best.

Chan nod his head, say good morning to the landlord and went inside.

"That was a narrow shave," Ram thought, "I have to watch out for that man."

"That was Mr. Chan," the landlord say, "he is the only other Indian tenant I have at the moment. I have a single room for two pounds. Are you a student?"

"Who is not a student?" Ram say, getting into the mood of the thing. "Man is for ever studying ways and means until he passes into the hands of Allah."

Well, to cut a long story short, Ram get a room on the first floor, right next door to Chan, and he move in that same evening.

But as the days going by, Ram had to live like cat-and-mouse with Chan. Every time he see Chan, he have to hide in case this man start up this Hindustani talk again, or start to ask him questions about Mother India. In fact, it begin to get on Ram nerves, and he decide that he had to do something.

"This house too small for the two of we," Ram say to himself, "one will have to go."

So Ram went down in the basement to see the landlord.

"I have the powers of the Occult," Ram say, "and I have come to warn you of this man Chan. He is not a good tenant. He keeps the bathroom dirty, he does not tidy up his room at all, and he is always chanting and saying his prayers loudly and disturbing the other tenants."

"I have had no complaints," the landlord say.

"But I am living next door to him," Ram say, "and if I concentrate my powers I can see through the wall. That man is a menace, and the best thing you can do is to give him notice. You have a good house here and it would be a pity to let one man spoil it for the other tenants."

"I will have a word with him about it," the landlord say.

Well, the next evening Ram was in his room when he hear a knock at the door. He run in the corner quick and stand upon his head, and say, "Come in."

The landlord come in.

"I am just practising my yoghourt," Ram say.

"I have had a word with Mr. Chan," the landlord say, "and I have reason to suspect that you have deceived me. You are not from India, you are from the West Indies."

Ram turn right-side up. "I am a citizen of the world," he say.

"You are flying false colours," the landlord say. "You do not burn incense like Mr. Chan, you do not dress like Mr. Chan, and you do not talk like Mr. Chan."

"Give me a break, old man," Ram say, falling back on the good old West Indian dialect.

"It is too late. You have already started to make trouble. You must go."

Well, the very next week find Ram out scouting again, giving the boards a perusal, and who he should chance to meet but Fraser.

He start to tell Fraser how life hard, how he had to keep dodging from this Chan fellar all the time, and it was pure torture.

"Listen," Fraser say, "you don't mean a big fellar with a beard, and he always wearing a turban?"

"That sound like him," Ram say. "You know him?"

"Know him!" Fraser say. "Man, that is a fellar from Jamaica who I send to that house to get a room!"

Part II

English in America

"I couldn't live here and talk like that."

— NEW YORK CITY SCHOOLBOY

American English dialects have been the object of strong feeling from the earliest days of settlement along the Atlantic seaboard. Although it might seem that the frontier spirit and democratic vistas would encourage tolerance and diversity of ways of speaking, the best evidence we have suggests that language— then as now—was a means of asserting unity within parts of the community: rustic backwoodsmen scorned the fancy talk of towns and villages, society folk agreed with English visitors in looking with amused contempt on the speech of the unlettered. From the sometimes uneasy interaction of the settled and the unsettled in colonial days emerged some of the differences that came to distinguish American from British English. Some terms came to be accepted by both groups of pioneers and remain in the language; many of these were derived from the new environment: squash *and* raccoon *adapted from American Indian languages;* portage, kill, *and* canyon *borrowed through contact with other Europeans on the American scene;* robin *and* corn *applied in America in a way different from the traditional English use.*

Contact with the new land and the languages in it produced other changes in the English the immigrants brought from Britain. In New England, where most settlers had emigrated from East Anglia, the prestige dialect had much in common with one of the local standards of Great Britain, but farther south and westward other influences came into play. In the South, the Atlantic Creole

151

spoken by traders to the West Indies and particularly by the black slaves newly arrived from Africa blended with the dialects of south-eastern England to produce a greater heterogeneity in speech and consequently greater change in the English of that region than was evidenced in New England. In the West, contacts with long-established French trappers and traders in the upper reaches of the Mississippi and St. Lawrence watersheds had an impact on spoken English, though an effect that is apparent today only in the place names along the waterways connecting Quebec and New Orleans with the interior. Farther west, contacts with the Spanish culture in missions and ranches strung out along the Pacific influenced the kind of English spoken by Americans, but most of the distinctive features of this dialect were smothered in the deluge of migrants from other dialect regions during the Gold Rush of 1849.

In many of these regions, the distinctive varieties of English that grew up through language contact were short-lived, for just as the notion of manifest destiny led to the political uprooting of French, Spanish, and Indian communities, so the contact languages that developed along the frontier disappeared with the influx of new settlers. But the social dynamics of the rise or fall of such contact languages is instructive in our own day, because the motives that affect language mixture also influence the retention or leveling of dialects.

Language differences that have resulted from the varying sources just mentioned—particularly the American varieties derived from several local dialects in Great Britain—have been the subject of interest from the earliest days of our nation and of scholarly research since the founding of the American Dialect Society in 1889. The best of these studies have resulted from the systematic investigation of a representative selection of communities by scholars armed with an extensive questionnaire containing items thought to be distinctive of regional dialects. Typical of the results derived from such studies is the map here reproduced showing the distribution of chesterfield—*a term for what is elsewhere known as a* sofa *or* couch—*in California and Nevada. Once the information gathered by the field worker has been tabulated in this way, it is usual for the dialectologist to draw an* isogloss *or boundary between the area where the linguistic feature is dominant and the area where it is only occasionally heard. Such lines typically are related to social and historical factors; in the case of* chesterfield, *the map shows the region focused on the San Francisco Bay area and the area of its influence in the great interior valley of California.*

When a great number of linguistic features like chesterfield *are investigated, certain general traits emerge. Taken together, these differences mark off the major dialect areas of the United States; a recent representation of this general picture is given in the map below. As C.-J. Bailey argues in the following essay, maps of this kind have many shortcomings, particularly in their failure to show that nearly all Americans speak mixed dialects—mixed by the geographical mobility of the American people and by the way that the speech of others influences our own language behavior. Nevertheless, maps like these do show certain general trends that Americans recognize as salient features of the*

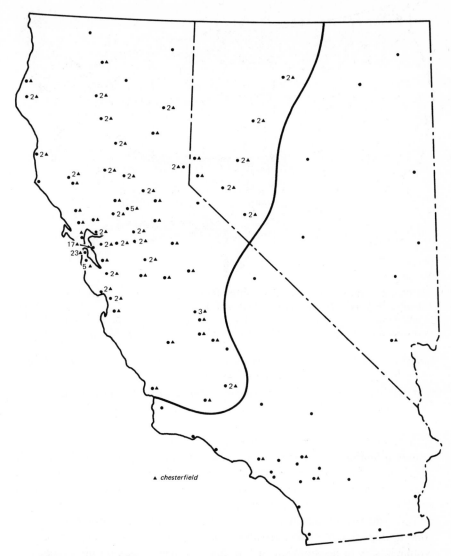

The distribution of *chesterfield* in California and Nevada. [SOURCE: Elizabeth S. Bright, *A Word Geography of California and Nevada* (Berkeley, Calif.: University of California Publications, Linguistics 69, 1971), p. 78. Originally published by the University of California Press; reprinted by permission of the Regents of the University of California and of the author.]

linguistic diversity of the nation. If such maps could be made to reflect more clearly areas of overlap and the focal influences of cities as urbanization produces dialect mixture, their value would be greatly enhanced. Furthermore, most such maps now available reflect a way of life now disappearing under the influence of broadcasting and nation-wide advertising campaigns. The question-

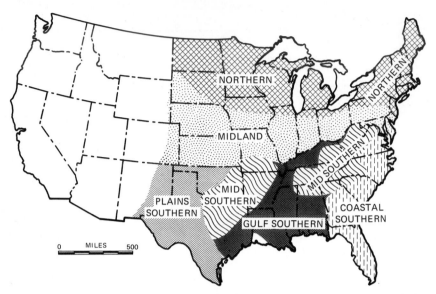

Major dialect areas of the United States. [SOURCE: Gordon R. Wood, *Vocabulary Change: A Study of Variation in Regional Words in Eight of the Southern States* (Carbondale, Ill.: Southern Illinois University Press, 1972), p. 358. Reprinted by permission of the author and of Southern Illinois University Press.]

naires on which such maps are based emphasize terms typical of rural life: calls to cows and sheep; names for the implements and practices of forestry, fishing, and agriculture now antiquated and remembered only by older citizens.

It would be a mistake, however, to suppose that dialect differences are disappearing, for in all sorts of ways the tendencies that produced the American regional dialects recorded on the map are still in operation. Subtle variations in pronunciation are the most systematic indicators of regional variation, but the vocabulary of modern life continues to be differentiated along geographical lines. Americans from various parts of the country may take time out for a snack, piece, bite, *or* nosh *consisting, perhaps, of* pop, soda, *or* tonic *and a* hoagy, grinder, submarine, *or* hero. *Depending on his regional origin, an American may suffer the consequence of such a meal in being* sick at his stomach, sick to his stomach, sick in his stomach, *or* sick on his stomach.

The impact of other languages on American English has been carefully investigated, not only in pronunciation, vocabulary, and syntax but also in the place names that show the history of American settlement. But the social dynamics of language interaction are only now beginning to be understood. What causes a word to be borrowed when the receiving language is already well supplied with similar terms? Such borrowings may fill a gap in the lexicon, but the adoption of a newly borrowed word into the language of the community may result from other-motives, particularly the prestige of the source language among speakers of the receiving language. Glissmeyer and Sawyer show some of these motives in their discussion of language contact in Hawaii and Texas.

In both cases, group solidarity is the determining factor in the retention of "foreign" elements coupled with the desire to speak "naturally" at home and with one's friends, however much that variety of English may conflict with the prestige norms asserted elsewhere in the community. The differences between dialects in vocabulary, pronunciation, and syntax that are important for "natural" speech in formal and informal situations, and the norms that maintain them are tacitly understood by all members of the community. The sanctions against breaking these norms are oftentimes severe; as McDavid shows, the formal speech of Southerners in Northern settings may cause misunderstanding, prejudice, and linguistic insecurity—the latter, as Labov notes in his discussion of New York speech, the consequence of feeling that one's English is somehow out of line with what the speaker feels it ought to be.

Linguists are now beginning to recognize that description does not end with an inventory of linguistic features that characterize a language or dialect and that real understanding must also account for the feelings that are current in the community about language varieties. Such feelings are often based on stereotypes associated with speech: "patrician speakers" are unlikely to accept bribes, "nonstandard varieties" of English typically lack logic, clarity, and cogency. News reports may refute the former belief, but the stereotype persists. The latter is perhaps more insidious because it leads, as Shuy shows, to the waste of talents and abilities. Labov, by examining such beliefs in light of the real language behavior of Americans, shows the role of these stereotypes in the fabric of American society. His investigations, reported in the essay that concludes Part II, suggest some of the directions that will be the subject of future accounts of American English.

THE PATTERNING OF LANGUAGE VARIATION
Charles-James N. Bailey

The proliferation of linguistic theories in recent years is a testimony to the considerable enthusiasm aroused in the field by the work of younger scholars and by the tendency toward interdisciplinary studies that has brought together in a common pursuit scholars from various languages, from the social sciences, and from philosophy. These developments, however, have only exacerbated the differences that have always existed between those whose empirical bias draws them to the complexity of linguistic data and those who prefer a more selective approach that makes data amenable to speculation about the nature of the human mind. The difference between the two positions has something in common with the artist who escapes his studio to draw nature as it really is, and the artist who prefers to remain indoors refining and exploring the tradition in the hope of some deeper insight.

Yet the opposition between the two tendencies is never really clear, and today's naturalist may be tomorrow's academician. Nevertheless, as far as dialect studies are concerned, it is apparent that the study of the full range of language behavior has only begun to participate in present-day interest in explanatory theories that may bring the apparent chaos of language differences into harmony with more developed views of social interaction and mental capacities. What such a theory must entail is the subject to which C.-J. Bailey addresses himself in the following essay.

Until quite recently, prevailing American linguistic theories have assumed a *static* framework, which has in practice obliged linguists to abstract from the variation and on-going change inherent in all language data and use instead artificially homogeneous data—a decision that has excluded the study of variation from the purview of descriptive linguistics. The dominance of this framework has consequently inhibited past work in *dialectology*, the study of language variation in the horizontal or geographical dimension. Dialectologists have been forced either to work in a theoretical vacuum or to bend their analyses into the procrustean straightjacket of very hostile premises.

This report, printed by permission of the author, is part of the research efforts of the Sociolinguistics Program, School of Languages and Linguistics, Georgetown University, made possible by a grant from the National Science Foundation, whose support is gratefully acknowledged. The writer is also grateful to James Fidelholtz, Ralph Fasold, and Richard W. Bailey for helpful suggestions. Copyright © 1973 by Charles-James N. Bailey.

The emerging emphasis today is on the study of variation in the vertical or social dimension—differences among styles, classes, special-interest groups, the sexes, age groupings, and the like. This new trend has led to profound changes in the assumptions held by those involved in what I shall call the new *lectology*. While both structural and generative linguists hold a static form up to view, the dynamic framework of lectology adds function to form and variable data to categorical generalizations. In place of the behaviorism typical of structuralism and the mentalism which characterizes the Chomskian point of view, the dynamic framework espouses both naturalism and mentalism. As we shall see, the descriptive apparatus of our approach is time-based, and the *variable rules* that are employed to formalize variation differentiate earlier and later manifestations of a change in the speech patterns of a *language community* (which is defined as the collection of speakers who can communicate in the language under analysis).[1]

Before entering on detailed discussions of variation in the social dimension, we should take notice of discoveries concerning the spread of language changes in the geographical dimension that have been made by advocates of the new lectology. Table 1 represents an idealization of data collected by Labov (see Labov 1971:427). The change depicted here begins variably rather than categorically; that is, it begins as a rule that sometimes operates and sometimes does not.[2] Moreover, as schematized in Table 1, the environments of the change form an implicational series, such that the nonvariable presence of the change at any point in the (a)–(i) sequence *implies* that the change is also categorically present in any of the heavier-weighted environments on the left. Moving leftward of the entry point, we find that the environments become increasingly *more* favorable to the change in question. The categorical absence of the change in any environment *implies* its absence also in the lighter-weighted environment to the right. These lighter-weighted environments are increasingly *less* favorable to the operation of the change. Any *variable* change in this particular table *implies* the categorical presence

---

[1] It should be noted that Jakobson (1941) and Greenberg (1966) succeeded in escaping many of the confining aspects of the static framework in their studies of cross-language implications. Many sociolinguists have contributed insights, suggestions, and the data with which the new models have been constructed and verified. Particularly important work in this connection has been done by William Bright, Charles Ferguson, Paul Friedrich, John Gumperz, Marvin Herzog, and Dell Hymes, to mention only a few.

Work that has had a direct bearing on the development of models and assumptions of the new framework includes Labov 1963, 1966, 1969, 1970, 1971, MSa, MSb; Weinreich, Labov, and Herzog 1968; Labov *et al.* 1968; DeCamp 1971; Bailey 1968c, 1970, 1971a, MSc, and other work alluded to in general terms below; Elliott, Legum, and Thompson 1969; Carden 1970; Fasold 1970; Bickerton 1971, MS; Bhat 1970; Ferguson 1971; Chen and Hsieh 1971; Chen 1971a, 1971b; not to mention the writings of pioneer Romance dialectologists who antedated the static framework.

[2] Labov MSa has cited data from a study by L. Gauchat in a Swiss village in 1905, showing a pattern like that of Table 1, but spread out in time across the generations in the same locale.

Table 1. Schematized illustration of the spread of the change that raises the vowel nucleus of words like *ham* to that of *hem* (and eventually to that of *hymn*) in the different environments shown. (From Labov 1971.) A minus sign denotes the categorical nonoperation of the rule for the change; × denotes the variable operation of the rule; a plus sign denotes its categorical operation. An asterisk denotes a thus far unattested, but presumably discoverable, pattern. The change is presumed to originate in locale 10, where it is complete in the vernacular style of speaking—the style illustrated in this table.

Locales		m n (a)	f θ s (b)	d (c)	b (d)	š (e)	g (f)	v z (g)	p t k (h)	l (i)
		Sound environments differentiated according to the following consonant:								
0	*	−	−	−	−	−	−	−	−	−
1	*	×	−	−	−	−	−	−	−	−
2	Birdsboro	+	×	−	−	−	−	−	−	−
3	Philadelphia	+	+	×	−	−	−	−	−	−
4	Mammouth Junction	+	+	+	×	−	−	−	−	−
5	Ringoes	+	+	+	+	×	−	−	−	−
6	Jackson	+	+	+	+	+	×	−	−	−
7	New York City	+	+	+	+	+	+	×	−	−
8	*	+	+	+	+	+	+	+	×	−
9	*	+	+	+	+	+	+	+	+	×
10	Buffalo	+	+	+	+	+	+	+	+	+

of the change in any environment to the left and the categorical absence of the change in any environment to the right. The variable rules discussed and illustrated later use weightings to differentiate the environments of a change.

If linguistic variation within the environments of Table 1 took place randomly, 362,880 combinations of environments would be mathematically possible (9!). The human brain could hardly be expected to cope with such a vast pattern of possibilities without some general principles of organization. The most natural patterning would seem to result from an arrangement in which larger sets are implied by smaller ones. Even though the data in Table 1 are not entirely attested, we may assume that further studies will verify the patterns shown—excepting, of course, minor deviations which may be attributed to accidents of speaking performance.

The obvious reason for the implicational patterning of language variation lies in the wave-like manner in which a change gradually spreads through social space, slowing down at class, geographical, and other barriers to communication. The change depicted in Table 1 begins variably in environment (a), the heaviest-weighted or most favorable environment. Figure 1 shows that at the second time step, this variety of the language (1), has spread out, and variety (2) in Table 1 is now found at the origin. Here the change is categorical in environment (a) and beginning variably in environment (b). At the third time step, variety (3) is found at the origin; (2) has overlapped

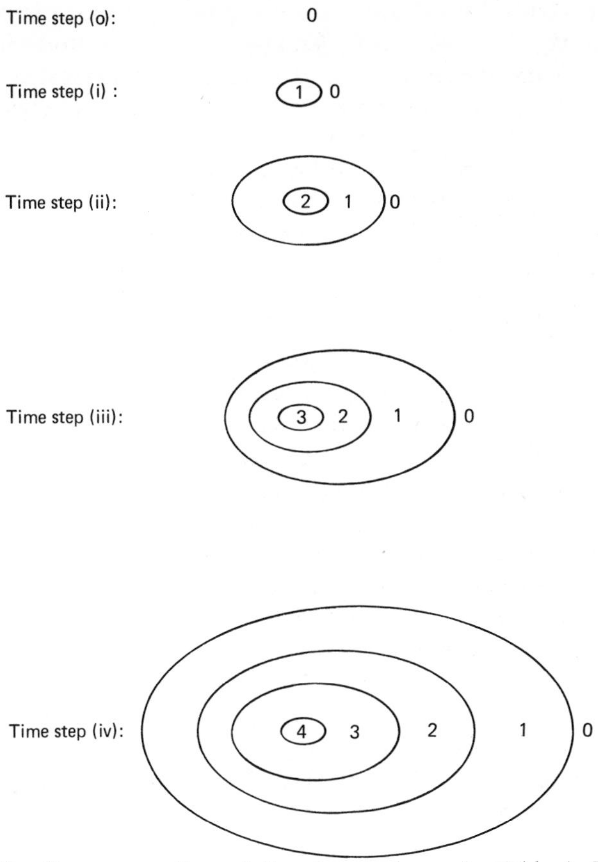

Time step (o):   0

Time step (i) :   ① 0

Time step (ii):   (② 1) 0

Time step (iii):   ((③ 2) 1) 0

Time step (iv):   (((④ 3) 2) 1) 0

Figure 1. Wavelike propagation of the change shown in Table 1. The Arabic numerals represent the same varieties of the language here as in Table 1. The time steps are defined by the changes themselves.

where (1) was in the previous time step; and (1) has now moved farther out. Only a temporal, dynamic framework can handle such patterning, which went largely unrecognized in the old dialectology. Table 1 makes clear how the rule begins variably in each successive environment, before operating categorically in that environment. If a rule survives long enough, it eventually may become *unconditioned*; that is, not limited to specific environments, but heard categorically in all environments in which the affected sound occurs.

What differentiates the new lectology from former work is the discovery of *linguistic* patternings in place of the older emphasis on *geographical* patternings. It makes little difference where the locales in Table 1 are placed relative to one another on a map. On the contrary, the distribution of linguistic patterns in geographical space is, more often than not, fairly chaotic.[3]

[3] In an area of India investigated by him, Bhat 1970 found that regional isoglosses do not always exhibit the neat patterning found with caste isoglosses. Bhat offers explanations for this phenomenon.

Looking at Kolb's maps showing the distribution of the pronunciations of the vowel in *sky*, *time*, *wife*, *died*, *flies*, *night*, and similar words in the North of England, we find the craziest of crazy-quilt patterns in most instances. Yet, this irregular distribution does not prevent a high degree of regularity in the purely linguistic patterning (see Bailey MSc). An implicational series of environments, arranged from heaviest to lightest, appears in the data: (a) *sky*, (b) *time*, (c) *wife*, (d) *Friday*, (e) *writing*, (f) *-wright* (as in *wheelwright*), (g) *died*, *flies*, (h) *night*. Later environments in this list imply the preceding environments. These environments depend on whether a consonant follows the vowel, and on what kind of consonant it is.[4]

As we have pointed out, a change in a lighter-weighted environment would imply the same change in the heavier-weighted environments. But it might also imply an *earlier* change in those heavier environments. To understand what this means, we should note that underlying //ī// in the words extracted from Kolb's survey passes through several stages of chronological development in the North of England: When unchanged, it sounds like the vowel in *feed* (phonetic [i]). The next stage shows it pronounced as a diphthong beginning with a vowel, like that of *met* or *cut* and gliding to the vowel of *feed* (respectively transcribed in phonetic symbols as [ɛⁱ] and [əⁱ]). A further change has the diphthong [aᵉ] (or [ɑᵉ]), as in most American pronunciations of *wife*. A final development deletes the satellite of the diphthong, leaving the vowel [a], which is typically heard in Southern states *died* (or Bostonian *card*). Since these changes are *successive* in the fixed order just given—minor deviations aside—the pronunciation [a] implies earlier [aᵉ] in a given environment; this implies earlier [ɛⁱ] or [əⁱ]; and this implies the original [i], still heard in some of the words in some of the locales. So there are two implications, side by side, and a given change in any environment both implies prior changes in that environment and also the same or prior changes in the heavier-weighted environments.

No geographical mapping would be expected to have any regularity of patterning unless differences of age, sex, and class are held rigidly constant—a matter not always systematically acknowledged in older dialectology. But Kolb's maps are based on data gathered with the aim of eliminating such differences. Even so, neat patterns are absent, by and large. This does not

---

[4] A probable environment, not attested in the data, would be represented by mid-accented *side* as in *right-side*; this would come between (e) and (f). The lexical //t// in *writing* is not changed to [d] in the North of England, as in America. In the present essay, double slants enclose underlying lexical segments, from which the phonetic output (enclosed in square brackets) is eventually derived. Middle stages of the derivation are enclosed in single slants.

The term *feature* is employed in various passages that follow. A *feature* designates a *natural class* of sounds or other linguistic phenomena, that is, a class required for writing linguistic rules of the sort that properly capture the generalizations of the language data involved. Thus, the feature [nasal] would designate the class of nasal segments. Note that feature names are put into square brackets.

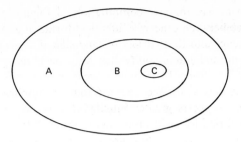

(a) No bundling of lines (isoglosses) separating the regions where A, B, and C are heard.

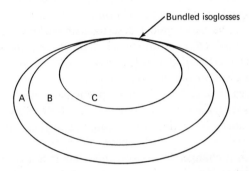

(b) Bundling of lines (isoglosses) separating the regions where A, B, and C are heard.

Figure 2. Geographical distributions of a pattern in which linguistic feature A implies B, and B implies C—but not vice versa.

upset the new lectologist, for he realizes that the pattern that is linguistically relevant—namely, A ⊃ B ⊃ C—is the same in Figures 2a and 2b. This is unaffected by whether the lines—technically known as *isoglosses*—separating the regions in which the linguistic features A, B, and C are found occur in a bundle (as in Figure 2b) or not (Figure 2a).

In view of the foregoing, the traditional definition of *dialects*—mutually intelligible forms of a language delimited by isoglossic bundles—appears to have little value for linguists. Since such dialects are rarely found, refuge has often been taken in other notions, which have not, however, proved sufficient to rehabilitate the traditional point of view. What are found are crisscrossing isoglosses; and this is vastly more evident if vertical (or social) differences are added to horizontal (or geographical) ones. Everyone speaks what traditional dialectologists have called *transitional* dialects. If dialects exist, they will have to be provided with a more realistic characterization than in the past.[5] Until that time, it will be more prudent to make use of the more

[5] I am at present working on a possible characterization of the term *dialect*. Since it is still too early to know whether my intimations are valid, I will refrain from presenting the

noncommittal term, *lect* for any combination of linguistic differences.[6] A minimal difference between otherwise identical forms of a language is called an *isolectal* difference and that variety of language an *isolect*. The futility of the criterion of mutual intelligibility has long been recognized, but only quite recently (Bailey 1968c, 1970) have there been put forward reasons that might explain why this is so. We now see that the implicational nature of linguistic variation suggests greater intelligibility in one direction than in the other. Further, one lect will often merge things which a sister lect will keep distinct, a merger technically known as a *neutralization*. A lect with more neutralizations than another is said to be more *leveled* than that other. We can now offer for empirical testing two theses: one, that lects which are more leveled than others can be more readily understood by those others than conversely, and the other that lects like (4) in Table 1 are more readily understood by speakers of lects like (7) than conversely.

Let us see how the wave model described above obviates the inevitable paradox (Becker 1967:64) in a framework that rules out the time dimension: Some authors have claimed that rules "peter out" (become less general) as they spread and develop; others, that rules can only become more general by losing features that restrict them to particular environments. Figure 1 resolves both issues by adding the dimension of time. Since the earliest and least general changes have time to spread the farthest, there is indeed a petering out at the points of social space which are most remote from the point of origin of a change. Moreover, this view is not contradicted by the increasing generalization of a rule to more environments at a given point in social space, since successively more general forms of a rule overlap one another as the wave spreads from the origin in both time and space.

Some particular examples drawn from familiar features of American lects may help to clarify the theoretical position that we have outlined:

1. A few speakers of English have the vowel heard in *cute* in their pronunciation of *lute*, but this vowel is rare after [r] as in *rude* and after [1] clustered with a preceding consonant in the same syllable as in *flute* or *blue*. But if the speaker has it in *rude, flute*, and *blue*, he will by implication have it

---

hypothesis here. For the present, the concept of *lect* seems to be of more use to the linguist. Previous work in dialectology has not submitted its methods to controlled testing of the sort that would adequately reveal the extent to which those methods are valid. The testing of the predictions of any theory that might underlie past methods seems to be largely wanting, as are the tests of the replicability of the results. While one must not denigrate past work for not knowing what we know today, one is, on the other hand, to be warned against today's employment of methods which are now known to be inadequate.

[6] Sometimes *subsystem* will be used for lect. For a characterization of a language system, see Bailey MSb. Dialectologists have never tested what sort of isoglosses and how many of them need to be bundled to form a dialect; cf. Bailey 1968b, 1968c. Although I once proposed that the depth of the applicational ordering of a rule might weight it, I now think that the place of a rule in the implicational ordering of all the rules in the language will be more relevant.

in *lute*; and if he has it in *lute*, he will also have it in accented syllables following [θ, s, z, n, t, d] in *enthusiasm, suit, presume, news, tune,* and *duty,* respectively. Note that the converse is not true: the appearance of this vowel in *tune* does not imply its occurrence in *lute*. However, if it appears in any of the words just mentioned, it will occur in other sound environments where most speakers of English have it: *cute, fume, view, mute, putrid, beautiful,* and *useful*.

2. David Stampe has informed me that the deletion of [h] in *his henhouse* in sloppy speech follows a fixed, implicational pattern. The [h] before the unaccented vowel in *his* is the first to go. Only when it has disappeared there will the third [h] (in mid-accented *-house*) be deleted. The last to be lost is the [h] standing before the fully accented vowel of *hen-*, and the deletion of this //h// implies the deletion of the others.

3. DeCamp (1959:60) found that in San Francisco the vowel in *naughty* (where the following syllable in the same word is unaccented) merged with that of *knotty*, while the distinction between *caught* and *cot* (where no syllable follows in the word) was maintained. Humphrey Johnson, a native and present resident of Washington, D.C., has [ɑ] in *foggy* but [ɔ] in *fog*, an example exactly parallel with the situation in San Francisco.

4. The presence of unaccented [ɪ]—rather than the [ə] heard at the end of *sofa*—in *moment* and *tunnel*—implies the presence of unaccented [ɪ] in *towel*; its presence here implies its presence in *duel* and *Joel*; its presence here implies [ɪ] in the second syllables of *mountain* and *satin*; its presence here implies [ɪ] in the middle syllable of *delegate*; its presence here implies [ɪ] in the final syllables of *tempest, Horace, salad, marriage,* and the noun, *delegate*; and its presence in these words implies it in the unaccented second syllables of *Bethlehem* and *archaism*. Each of these words is taken as representative of the sound environments illustrated in it.

5. If a Southerner has the diphthong [æⁱ] before [d, nd, mb, dᶻ]—as in *bad, band, gamble, badge*—he will have the same diphthong before another class of sounds, namely [v, ð, z]—as in the nouns *salve, lathe, jazz*—in the same or a less formal style. The presence of the diphthong in these environments implies it in the same style before //nt, mp, f, θ, s//—as in *slant, camp, raft, path, pass, past*. Its presence in these environments implies it before [g, ŋ, š]—as in *hag, hang,* and *hash*—in any style.

6. It is clear that for speakers who merge *pen* with *pin*, in at least some styles, *pen* implies *pin*, but not conversely. That is, *pin* is never pronounced with the vowel of *pen* heard in lects or styles where they are distinct.

7. For American speakers who pronounce *utter* like *udder* or *metal* like *medal*, the first word in each pair implies the latter but not vice versa. *Medal* is never pronounced with a [t], as *metal* is in some styles.

8. For speakers who merge *which* with *witch* in some or all styles, the implication is (like example 7) a unidirectional one, since *witch* is never "corrected" to *which*.

9. In northern New Jersey, Labov (p.c.) found that *wagon*—normally

[ˈwægən], where [æ] represents the vowel in most English pronunciations of *back*—could be pronounced just like *waggin'*, which is [ˈwɛᵊgən] in the locale in question. However, *waggin'* could not be rendered as [ˈwægən].

10. For nonstandard speakers who say *bof* for *both* [boθ], the [θ] following a vowel in the same syllable implies [f]. Again, the implication is unidirectional since *off* is never pronounced as *oth*.

Some syntactic examples further suggest the force of the theory we have sketched at the opening of this paper:

1. In 1969, this writer presented the following sentences in various combinations of their variables to twenty undergraduate and graduate students who were native speakers of English. They represented twelve states and two foreign countries.

1. There are several people $\begin{Bmatrix} \text{who(m)} \\ \text{that} \end{Bmatrix}$ I (don't) like $\begin{Bmatrix} \text{who} \\ \text{that} \end{Bmatrix}$ (don't) like me.

2. There are several people $\begin{Bmatrix} \text{who} \\ \text{that} \end{Bmatrix}$ (don't) like me $\begin{Bmatrix} \text{who(m)} \\ \text{that} \end{Bmatrix}$ I (don't) like (them).

At the beginning of this investigation, it was predicted that (1) would be the more "natural"—technically, *unmarked*—of the two orderings of the relative clauses modifying *people*. The results of the investigation confirmed the prediction: All speakers tested accepted the order shown in (1). When eighteen combinations of the variables in the two sentences—if *who* or *that* was used in one clause, it was used in the other also—were presented to the twenty native speakers of English in random order, only four deviations from an implicational patterning of the results occurred.[7] All testees who accepted the redundant pronoun at the end of (2) also accepted its omission. With only one exception in each instance, the acceptance of negatives in both relative clauses implied the acceptance of the negative in either one alone, and the acceptance of a sentence with *who* implied the acceptance of it with *that*.

2. The writer administered a test in 1971 to determine whether he could corroborate the claims by Bever and Langendoen (1971:439, 442, 443) that "for most speakers of English" the omission of the relative pronoun in sentences like (3) and (4) is "not grammatically acceptable."

3. There is a man wants to see the boss downstairs.
4. It was low wages and poor working conditions caused the workers to strike.

These are respectively called *existential* and *cleft* sentences. Bever and Langendoen (446) also maintained that interrogative sentences like (6) are,

---

[7] Fewer acceptances of the data and more deviations occurred when the verb was *know* instead of *like*; this had been predicted by the testers.

according to the data collected by them, somewhat more acceptable than noninterrogative ones like (5):

5. It's/There's a boy wants to see you.
6. Who is there/ it wants to see me?[8]

This claim was also investigated.

The test was given in a Midwestern university to thirty-eight native speakers of English from Maine, Massachusetts, New York, New Jersey, North Carolina, South Carolina, Tennessee, Texas, West Virginia, Pennsylvania, Illinois, Michigan, Minnesota, Indiana, Ohio, Montana, Nebraska, and Oregon (the last-named subject patterned quite deviantly). The subjects were mostly undergraduates. Although the sentences tested were not the same as those in Bever and Langendoen (1971), they had the structures for which Bever and Langendoen's claims were made. Testees were asked to grade the sentences on the basis of their naturalness, without deferring to supposed grammarian's views of correctness. Of the sixteen sentences tested, the six most acceptable ones, in the order of decreasing acceptability, were

7. I know a man will help you.
8. I wonder who it was didn't like our neighbors.
9. It's health should make a man happy.
10. He asked me who it was defined man as a featherless two-legged animal.
11. It's carelessness kills many drivers.
12. Who's the one never gets there on time?

There was only an 8 per cent performance deviation from a completely regular implicational pattern—that is, the acceptance of (12) implied the acceptance of (11); this implied the acceptance of (10), and so on. In explaining even this quite small deviation, one must allow for possible semantic factors that may have interfered with the results. Some testees might have unconsciously rejected a sentence because of the unlikelihood of its meaning rather than its syntactic structure. On the other hand, the high acceptability of (7) is doubtless owing to the reading, "I know (that) a man will help you," since (13) was ranked next-to-least acceptable:

13. I met a woman never gets up before noon.

It is doubtful that the negative in (13) makes it that much less acceptable than (7). However, the modal *should* in (9) may have made that sentence

---

[8] These writers admit (in their fn. 17) that the intuitions which they are following in their discussion are "relatively evanescent." They suggest that readers ask themselves whether they agree with the authors that the insertion of *who* or *that* before *wants* makes (5) more acceptable, but not clearly so in the case of (6).

more acceptable than (14), which ranked fourth from the bottom in acceptability:

14. It's wealth never makes a man content.

The investigation just conducted does not confirm the claims which Bever and Langendoen make for "most Americans."

3. Another test by the writer in 1971 attempted to assess the statements by Ross (1970:228) on the acceptability of the following sentences:

15. This paper was written by Ann and myself.
16. ??This paper was written by myself.
17. ?Ann and myself wrote this paper.
18. *Myself wrote this paper.
19. ?The lioness may attack Ann and myself.
20. *The lioness may attack myself.

The asterisk denotes a "completely unacceptable" sentence; the single question mark means "doubtful"; the double question mark means "very doubtful"; and no mark means acceptable. While Ross (1970:228) admits, concerning parallel examples, that "no doubt most readers would assign different degrees of acceptability to the sentences . . . than I have, especially in the intermediate cases," he nonetheless avers that the intensive reflexives "are invariably better if conjoined than if they occur alone, and that such reflexives are more acceptable as agent phrases [as in (15)] than as subjects or direct objects." He notes in addition, however: "Doubtless there are many other conditions . . . which interrelate in a complex manner with those just stated, and which are of some intrinsic interest."

My test was given to the same group of testees as in the study of Bever and Langendoen's claims. I augmented the examples from Ross with a number of others containing *yourself, herself,* and *himself* in place of *myself.* Twenty-one sentences were tested, but four obviously unacceptable sentences beginning with subject reflexives (like [18])—which no one accepted—were omitted from the results, so as not to bias them unduly in favor of a clear pattern. The resultant pattern has only 7.4 per cent deviations from a regular implicational patterning; if the thirteen testees who accepted none of the sentences are eliminated, 11.5 per cent of the results are deviant from a regular implicational pattern. The results do not confirm Ross's gradings of the acceptability of the sentences, except that there was a consensus among those who did not reject every sentence that (15) was the most acceptable of all. Second in acceptability was the same sentence with *yourself* in place of *myself.* (Third-person reflexives had low acceptability in these data.) Example (16) was third-most acceptable, and was followed by (19). Next in order of decreasing acceptability followed (21), which differs from (16) only in the reflexive pronoun:

21. This paper was written by yourself.

Sixth-highest in acceptability was (17), which Ross ranked above (16).

The foregoing studies show the weakness of previous methods of gathering linguistic data. Labov in many studies has shown that monitored data often deviate from systematic patterning in a manner which casual vernacular speech does not. The studies by Ross and by Bever and Langendoen suffer no doubt from this very weakness. In the second of the three studies, two control sentences were included among the sixteen tested, but were not included in the computation percentages of deviations from the implicational patterning—though their inclusion would have enhanced the results, making a lower percentage of deviations. These sentences, whose grammatical properties were different from the property being tested in the remaining sentences, despite similarities in the appearances of both groups, were

22. Who's the one so happy he can't stop singing?
23. There are some people so dumb they like cold weather.

Although these are perfectly grammatical examples, eight native speakers rejected both, and another rejected (23).

In the study of Ross's data by the present writer there were included two instances of the same sentence at different places in the sequence of the data tested. Two testees accepted one instance of the sentence, but not the other. One such acceptance had already been marked as deviant in formulating the pattern, but the other discrepancy is unaccounted for. In this same study, a lone testee accepted the obviously unnatural (20), but the very process of schematizing in the pattern automatically marked this as a performance deviation.

These cautions are not meant to cast doubt on the method employed in these studies, provided the person carrying out the test is aware of the difficulties and exercises care in his research. The study to be described now has in fact been replicated by the author several times since it was first reported by Elliott, Legum, and Thompson (1969). Their investigation concerned the acceptability of the following examples:

24. Sophia was seen by the people while enjoying herself.
25. The people saw Sophia Loren while enjoying themselves.
26. Judy was seen by the people while enjoying themselves.
27. The people saw Karen while enjoying herself.

Elliott, Legum, and Thompson discovered that the mathematically possible number of variations among speakers using one or more of these sentences—that is twenty-five counting speakers who say none of these—did not occur. When twenty-seven speakers were checked, they found—with only six exceptions ascribable to performance errors—just four combinations, in addition to the zero combination for speakers rejecting all four sentences. The four combinations can be reduced to a single implicational pattern:

Acceptance of (27) implies acceptance of (26); this implies acceptance of (25); and this, acceptance of (24).

But the *implicational order* of these data make no sense without an understanding of *applicational order* of the rules that generate them. Let us assume that the abstract semantic structure of (28) underlies these sentences. The structure underlying (24) would be (29):

28. SENTENCE *ACCOMPANY* SENTENCE.
29. [Sophia Loren enjoy Sophia Loren] ACCOMPANIED
    [the people see Sophia Loren].

To generate (24)–(27) from an abstract underlying semantic structure like (28), we need

  i. a passivization rule to convert the active *the people saw Sophia Loren* to the passive *Sophia Loren was seen by the people.*
 ii. a rule which puts *while* before the subject clause of (28), deletes underlying *ACCOMPANY*, and inverts the order of the clauses. (Actually the foregrounding of the *while* clause is a separate rule of a more general character.)
iii. a rule to delete the subject of *while* clauses.

Other rules, like the one needed to reflexivize the object of *enjoy* will of course also be required for these data. Rule i and rule iii are technically known as optional rules and may or may not apply.[9] Furthermore—and this is an important restriction for what follows—there is for speakers producing only (24, 25, 26) and not (27) a condition attached to rule iii that restricts its operation to instances in which the subject of the *while* clause is the same as the subject of the main clause. For speakers having this restriction, "*The people saw Karen while enjoying herself*" is completely unacceptable. Although "*Judy was seen by the people while enjoying themselves*" appears to violate the restriction, it is nevertheless acceptable to some speakers who have the restriction on the rule for forming *while* clauses. To understand why this is so, let us go a bit more deeply into the analysis of these four sentences.

To generate (24), the relevant rules are, in order of application:

  i. passivization
 ii. *while* formation
iii. subject deletion

If the application of (i) did not precede (iii), the condition restricting subject deletion would prevent the operation of (iii). To generate (25) the same ordering applies except that the optional rule for passivization does not

---

[9] Probably very few so-called optional rules are really equipollent. Most will have a directionality which increases or decreases their operation in defined circumstances.

operate. But in the derivation of (26), rule iii precedes rule i, which does operate in the generation of this sentence, but with the consequence that the condition or restriction on rule iii appears to have been violated. This results from the new ordering of the rules, since before the operation of the passivization rule, the while formation rule operated without any violation of the restriction on it. After the passivization rule changes the grammatical subject of example (26), it no longer agrees with the deleted subject of the while clause. This accounts for the grammaticality of (26) for some testees. In the derivation of (27), rule iii again applies before rule i is considered—it does not operate in this case—and now with a real violation of the condition on it.

Without an understanding of the rules involved, it would be impossible to interpret the results reported by Elliott, Legum, and Thompson. First, the applicational ordering of rules i and iii accounts for the difference between (24) and (25), on the one hand, and (26) on the other. As we shall see, applicational differences of this sort may also be invoked to account for differences in lects. Second, the rules clarify the implicational patterning: As a result of the newer ordering found in (26), the acceptance of (26) implies the acceptance of (24), generated with the older ordering of the rules in question. Since the acceptance of (27) also implies the acceptance of (26), we may conclude further that a less restricted formulation of a rule (such as rule iii) implies a more restricted form of the same rule.

Scholars who should know better have confused personal differences of the sort found in the acceptability of (24) through (27) with so-called dialect differences. Such differences could not be regarded as dialect differences unless they correlated and bundled with several other differences. They are in fact not dialect differences, for they occur among speakers of similar backgrounds and even among different styles of one speaker. I grew up in a place where we did not "drop the *h*" in most words beginning with *wh-* (such as *when, where, why,* and *which*) except in compounds (such as *anywhere*). We differentiated *wheel* from *weal,* and *whale* from *wail.* But I had a close friend of my same age who lived a block from me—we were both natives of the town—who habitually "dropped his *h*'s"! This was not a dialectal difference, but a personal idiosyncrasy, perhaps due to some peculiarity in the way this friend learned English.

We have just suggested that speakers of a language may differ simply in the applicational ordering of rules common to them all; a phonological example should now clarify this point. With further details not relevant to the issue, contemporary English has

i. a rule that, *inter alia,* changes unaccented lax /i/ to the consonant /y/ when an unaccented vowel follows

ii. a rule that changes the underlying lateral consonant //1// to the satellite of a diphthong when a consonant follows—this satellite (phonetic [ᴵ] is heard in *will* [wɪᵆ:]).

When these rules are applied to such words as *familiar, brilliant, million, William, valiant,* and the like, rule i creates the consonant /y/ and rule ii then applies to create the satellite. Hence the northern states pronunciation of *brilliant* as [ˈbrɨˑyə̃t] (where [ə̃] is a nasalized vowel). This is the so-called *unmarked* ordering of the rules.[10] When rule ii is applied first—the *marked* or less expected order—there is no consonant following //l// and hence the conditions for rule ii are not met. Rule i then changes the unaccented short /i/ to /y/; hence the southern states pronunciation of *brilliant* as [ˈbrɨ(l)yə̃t]. In some lects or styles, a later rule in southern states English eliminates the /l/ before /y/ plus unaccented vowel.

Note that all natural language is equally rule-governed. The rules of so-called nonstandard varieties of English may differ in various ways from those of the different varieties of standard English, but they are no less imperative. Such rules are not the *prescriptive* rules of school grammars, but the *descriptive* rules that characterize actual usage. In fact, there is reason to believe that the unmonitored vernacular speech of nonstandard speakers forms the most coherent system of speech in any language.

At this juncture, the reader should be well convinced by the examples that have been adduced that lectal patterns within a given language are implicational. So striking is this that the present writer (Bailey 1970) has proposed lining up all the isolects of a language on an implicational scale and designating each lect by its characterizing phenomenon that stands highest on that scale. Characterizing phenomena would be the categorical presence, variable presence, or absence of a given rule; or various differences in the generality or ordering of a given rule. Preliminary research has indicated the feasibility and validity of this approach. If future work continues to corroborate its validity, the isolects so characterized will prove far more useful than the currently useless notion of dialects.

II

Although the inception of dialectological studies was marked by a concern for linguistic theory, this concern was eventually replaced[11] with an antiquarian interest in filling up the language museum with well-classified curiosities, often predominantly rustic.[12] Moreover, the data that have been

---

[10] When two rules are in an order in which one of them does not apply to a given linguistic form, the rules have a marked ordering relative to one another, provided that there is another order in which both do apply to the form in question. The order in which both apply is called the unmarked ordering. It gives the rules greater generality; cf. Kiparsky 1968, Stampe 1969, Anderson 1969, and Kiparsky 1971.

[11] A notable exception is Moulton's 1962 careful study of vowel positions in Swiss German.

[12] This issue and the alleged "midland" dialect are discussed by Bailey 1968b. See now also Wood 1971. As the writer pointed out (in Bailey 1968b), many of the rustic data used to establish dialect boundaries in the United States would not be known to most people; for example, *sook, sugar tree, whipple tree, stone boat, snake feeder.* The effects of this observation on such studies go without saying.

gathered have frequently been from "monitored" speech produced by the knowledge that it is destined for a linguistic use, and such speech normally loses the regularity of the casual vernacular. Corrections and normative pronunciations are found in such monitored speech to a degree that inevitably renders it inconsistent. The newer approach has devised ingenious ways of obtaining vernacular speech samples. It has been learned that speakers consistently make distinctions in casual speech which they deny they make when questioned about the matter, and which they sometimes cannot even hear when tested. For example, Labov found an older speaker in Pennsylvania who kept *hawk* and *hock* quite distinct in his casual speech, but, when asked to say them both, pronounced them alike. He lived in an area where the young people normally merged *hawk* with *hock*. The variation in the pronunciations of *hawk* poses no problems for an adequate theory of variation though very serious ones for a theory involving the elicitation of "minimal pair" differences.

The newer investigations have abandoned former attempts to link variation patterns too intimately with the patterns of migration. An example will illustrate what is meant. English arrived on the Atlantic Coast in the southern states with the diphthongs [əⁱ] in *wife* and *wine*, and [ɵᵘ] or [əᵘ] in *out* and *down* (where [ɵ] represents [ə] pronounced with the addition of the lip rounding seen in blowing out a candle), and these diphthongs are still heard in *wife* and *out* in some southeastern locales. A new change started much further inland, lowering both parts of the diphthongs one step further, yielding [aᵉ] in *wife* and [aᵒ] or [æᵒ] ([æ] is the vowel in *back*) in *out* and *down*. In *wine*, the inland change went even further and dediphthongized the nucleus to [a]. These inland changes eventually backed up—in a direction *opposite* to that of migration—into some areas between the coastal regions and the inland regions where the changes seem to have begun. The coastal areas seem to have gotten [ɑᵉ] in *wine* (but [əⁱ] in *wife*) and [ɑᵒ] in *down* (but [əᵘ] in *out*) through an independent development in Caribbean English, of which their lects are variants. Areas slightly inland from the coast do not show the same sound distribution as that which is heard in the other regions.[13] Such lects may possibly be the result of overlapping waves (like those discussed in Bailey MSc).

Such examples reveal the true complexity of all attempts to prepare so-called dialect maps. Maps cannot be valid in most instances for more than one combination of social parameters—age, sex, class, style, the rural-urban difference, and so on. Hence students would be well advised to treat such maps with almost total skepticism. Even where parameters are kept distinct, it should be noted that settlers often move from city to city, leaving the intermediate rural areas unaffected. A map of lectal distributions in the

---

[13] Some speakers in America and Great Britain have other patterns (in addition to the pattern heard for //ī// in the North of England that has been discussed above). In Scotland one can hear *tide* with [əⁱ], but *tie#d* has [aᵉ]. In Batavia, N.Y., *fiber* has [əⁱ], but *briber* has [aᵉ] (Gary J. Parker, p.c.). David Johns has [əⁱ] in *spider* and *cider*, but [aᵉ] in *rider*. Some speakers from Richmond, Va., have [ɵᵘ] in *down* and *loud*.

United States would show northern speech in cities lying within the southern speech area if the latter were mapped on the basis of rural speech.

Conversely, many southerners have migrated to northern cities. Another problem is suggested by the fact that older, upper-class speech of the inner-southern "r-less" type is found in central Kentucky where other classes and other age groups in the upper class have outer-southern "r-ful" speech.

A further case involves the English lects found in the midwestern states. These resulted from overlapping migrations from New England, from the central Atlantic Coast, from Virginia and Kentucky, and later, Texas. The result of such overlapping bears many resemblances to the results of creolization or mixing of different language systems, in that extensive leveling—merging of distinctions preserved elsewhere—occurs. *Inter alia*, the intonational tune for plain *yes-no* questions has changed from those heard in the other lects to the very neutral one which in English and many languages can convert any statement into an interrogation (for example, *He's reading a novel?*). But it was an error in the old dialectology to suppose that the neutralization of *Mary*, *marry*, *merry*, and even *Murray* in midwestern states English was due to a neutralization that does not take place also in those lects keeping all these words distinct. Bailey 1968a has shown that a more important factor is a difference in the syllabication of *y*, *w*, *l*, and *r* between vowels in "r-less" English.[14] All kinds of English neutralize the non-high front vowels—those underlying the accented vowels heard in *Mary*, *marry*, and *merry*—before an *r* in the same syllable (that is, when *r* is followed by a consonant or is word-final). This illustration shows with great clarity the care which must be taken in studying variation, if error is to be avoided.

The current emphasis in the new framework is on formulating polylectal and eventually panlectal grammars of languages like English. The rules of the grammar would have to be set up on an implicational scale so that the lects could be defined as suggested earlier. Past studies which have depended on defining language varieties in terms of bundled isoglosses have in practice side-stepped the problem of looking for objective, testable criteria that would determine how to weight isoglosses relatively to one another. Presumably, there are single isoglosses of sufficient importance as to outweigh several less weighty ones. In America, the whole problem has frequently been side-stepped by an overvaluation of geography in comparison with other approaches.

Aside from the lack of neatness in the patterns emerging from such

---

[14] "*R*-less" lects are those in which speakers "drop their *r*'s." They have [ə] in *bare* ['bæəː] and [ə] in the second syllable of *butter*, while "*r*-ful" lects have [ɚ] and [ɚ] in these environments. Bailey (1968a) claimed that the syllabication differences among American lects with respect to *l* and the glides (*y*, *w*, *h*) between vowels is the main differentiator of northern states and southern states lects, though it had not been noticed by older dialectologists. Ferguson (1971:16 fn. 8) notes that his speech—from the border area between the two treatments of //l// between vowels—shows syllabication of the //l// in *daily* with the preceding vowel but of the //l// in *gaily* with the following vowel.

studies, there are a number of theoretical problems with the approach of word geography. As every layman knows, words can be borrowed from one form of English into another without affecting the pronunciation or syntax. This can occur through various means of communicating with other regions or classes. This is because the *lexicon* is, technically speaking, a listing of exceptional and unpredictable matter; the generalizations of predictable aspects of a language are formulated in the *rules* of its grammar. For example, every American can give evidence of his "knowledge" that *underlying* (lexical) //t// between vowels ends up in informal speech as [d] if the following vowel is not accented (cf. *greet* [ˈgrit]: *greeter* [ˈgridɚ]). The evidence that a speaker could provide for this "knowledge" would result from telling him that there is a word *croot* (meaning such-and-such) and asking him to form the agent in *-er*; the speaker would say *crooter* with [d] between vowels (if the following vowel is unaccented, as here). The independence of the lexicon from the rest of the language has been amply attested in the study of creoles. Without any theoretical reasoning, few would assume that their lect had been changed by borrowing a word or two (for example, *sputnik*) heard on television. Finally, there is the fact that the word geographers have been able to adduce only a small handful of words to shore up their claims about the patterning of variation. No reason has been alleged why so few words (or any other given number) could provide adequate evidence for the patterns of variation claimed to exist.[15]

One can find implicational relations among English words. The "broad-*a*" pronunciation of *plastic, catholic,* and *trans-* implies the same pronunciation of the large class of words including *pass, raft,* and *path*; if a speaker has "broad-*a*" in these words, he will by implication have it in the same style, or in a more formal style, in *half* and *calf* (but not necessarily conversely [Kurath et al. 1939:30]); if here, also in *aunt* and *rather*; if here, also in *drama*; if here, also in *pajamas*; if here, also in *plaza*; if here, also in *-alm* words like *calm* and *almond*; and if here, finally in *mama* and *father*. There is probably also an implicational series of "broad-*a*" pronunciations of words ending in *-ade*. There are areas of the English-language community where, for given classes and styles, the loss of *h* in *whip* implies a similar loss in *wheelbarrow*; and the loss here implies it in *whinny*. (Map 174 in Kurath and McDavid 1961 shows a patterning whose lack of consistency is doubtless due to a failure to keep class and style differences constant.) There are probably implications among the uses or nonuses of [ʉᵘ] or [u] (heard in *food* and *tomb*) in words of the class including *gloom, soon, stoop, proof, groom, spook, broom, room, roost(er), root, whoop, hoop, coop, Cooper, Buddha, worsted, boogieman, roof, toots, soot, hoof, woof, bosom, hood, nook,*

---

[15] The situation is not, however, now quite so bleak as just portrayed. Recent work has shown that there are patterns among lexical items. They are not describable by rules but only by listing, and they are linguistic rather than regional per se. Most of this work has been carried out on Chinese by the associates of William S.-Y. Wang: see Wang and Cheng 1970, Chen and Hsieh 1971, Hsieh 1971. See also Ferguson 1971.

and *rook*. Students of the writer's are currently investigating the implications in these words.[16] Past studies of the vowels in many words of the *cog, fog, dog,* and *hog* classes, together with other related classes, were carried out prior to the advent of the newer systematic approach.[17]

Kolb's maps of the North of England indicate that [d^ž] (instead of [g] in *bridge* implies the same sound in *ridge*; that this implies [t^š] (not [k]) for "ch" in *church, birch, such, chaff,* and *flitch*. Moreover, it seems that [k] in *kirk* implies [k] for "ch" in *birch* and *such*; and that [k] here implies it in *chaff* and *flitch*. Such patterns need further study by future students of language variation.[18]

Lexical residues form a special problem. Why did *steak, great, break, yea, drain,* and *-tain* not come to rhyme with *deed,* like *bleak* and other words with the same vowel in most forms of English outside of Ireland? (At least *break* and *-tain* were peculiar in that their vowel alternated with [ɛ], as in *breakfast* and *contents*; cf. Irish *mean,* which rhymes with *contain,* and *meant,* which rhymes with *intent.*) Why in the Philadelphia area do only *mad, bad,* and *glad* (not, e.g., *sad* [Ferguson 1971:9]), of all the words in environment (c) in Table 1, get affected by the rule affecting their vowel? Why do *took, soot,* and *put* not come to have the vowel of *tuck* in standard English, as they do in many nonstandard lects? Why do *bulk* and *bulge* get pronounced in the southern states as [ˈbl̵ːk] and [ˈbl̵ːd^ž] (where [l̵ː] is the lengthened form of the vowel heard at the end of *table* [ˈtheˈbl̵]), while *bulb* and *pulp* are [ˈbʌˈːb] and [ˈp^{h}ʌˈːp])? Why does northern *pulpit* vary between the two pronunciations? Why does only *whip*—and then only in humorous

---

[16] Local factors cause [u] in *hood* [=" hoodlum"] in Chicago, [ɯ] in *Wooster* in Massachusetts, and [ɪ] in *Chattanooga* in Tennessee.

[17] From the statistics in McDavid (1940), one might guess that [ɔ] in certain lexical items implies the same sound in others, but this is not clear from McDavid's presentation. It seems clear from these data, however, that by and large, [ɔ] before [θ] and [ŋ] implicates [ɔ] before [f] and [š]. And certainly, [ɔ] or [ɒ°] in *Gothic* would implicate the same nucleus in *cloth, moth, broth,* and so on. Note that if the rule changing the underlying //ɒ// to [ɔ] before /ŋ/ applies before underlying //n// becomes /ŋ/ before /k/ in the same syllable, (as in *conquer*), then there will be no [ɔ] in *conquer.* If, however, the opposite, unmarked (see fn. 10) rule order applies (for example, in weary speech), then [ɔ] will be heard in *conquer.* These problems have been discussed in Bailey MSa. The failure to cope with reordering has held past dialectological studies back. Of course, reordering was not generally known until Kiparsky's 1968 discussion; but since then dialectologists have not made adequate use of this valuable tool for studying variation.

[18] Past studies have been impeded by a lack of adequate phonetic knowledge. Wang 1969:22n.22 showed the importance of the grooved articulation (the author calls the feature *sulcality*) for understanding certain sound changes in languages. The change of *train* to *chrain* (Hawaiian *chain*) and of *drop* to *jrop* (Hawaiian *jop*) is due to an assimilation of //t// and //d// to the sulcal articulation of the following [r].

The pronunciation of *bird* as [ˈbɜ³ˈːd] or [ˈbɵˈːd] by older Southerners from Kentucky to Alabama and from South Carolina to Louisiana is due to the sulcality of [ˈ] and [ɚ] (the latter is the vowel heard in this word in the English spoken in the midwestern states, Charleston, S.C., and elsewhere). Without sophisticated transcriptions of linguistic data, it is impossible to have sophisticated analyses.

pronunciations, in standard speech—have the vowel [ʊ] in most of the southern states?[19] Such questions make the lexicon a much less satisfactory focus for studying lectal patterns than the grammar.

Another problem is the incommensurability of lexical differences with grammatical differences. Carol Odo found that the stylistic indexes of lexicon, syntax, and phonology could vary independently in the speech of young Hawaiian children. For instance, words and grammar of a lower style (such as dropping the copula *is* or *are*) could coexist with "*r-ful*" school pronunciation, the mark of a more formal style. Odo MS established (at least for young lower-middle-class children in Honolulu) that the use of *get* for "there is" implies the use of *one* for the indefinite article; and that *one* for the indefinite article is also implied by the deletion of the copula in sentences like the following:

30. Lani (one) pretty wahine.

Richard Day, in a detailed study of twenty speakers of Hawaiian English, tells me that he found that for a given style (and with only one performance deviation) the omission of the copula before a predicate noun implied a like omission before a predicate adjective; the omission here implied the same omission before a place expression (for example, *[in] Honolulu, [on the] Big Island*); and the omission of the copula here implied its omission also in progressive verbs like *(is/are) running*.

III

If a socially disfavored (stigmatized) phenomenon begins to spread from the casual style of the lower class—or some other class—the change will begin with males and then spread, first to females, and then to other classes. In each class it will spread to more formal styles later, and the younger age groups will show the change in a more advanced stage than their elders. A dynamic grammar, but not a static one, is capable of generating the implicational steps of the change; and sociolinguistic algorithms (such as those found in Bailey MSc) assign the isolects thus generated to the different combinations of social variables in the speech community. A *speech com-*

[19] In Kurath and McDavid (1961), the transcriptions on Maps 4, 5, 6, 7, and 84 of *wool* ['wɪː], *push* ['pʰɪš], and *bulge* ['bɫːdž] are not correct; nor is it evident that the authors correctly transcribed the back vowel in the vulgar pronunciation of *whip* ['hʊup], since [ʊ] does not appear on the map. The important difference between ['skuᵘl] and ['skuɫ] *school* seems to be unknown to these authors.

This may be the best place to point out the absence in the local Hawaiian standard pronunciation of the names *Caucasian* and *Beretania* (a major thoroughfare in Honolulu) of the English rule that would make the accented vowels in these words the same as the accented vowel in *gymnasium*. Note that in Appalachia, this word is [ˌæpɫˈlætˢə].

munity is a group of speakers among whom lectal patterns—these may even be bilingual or multilingual—are socially allocated and evaluated in a comparable manner.[20] If in such a community a socially favored (prestige) change spreads from the most formal style of the highest class, it will reach the more casual styles and probably the males (cf. Labov MSb) later in each class. As before, the young will show more advanced stages of the change than their elders in each class-style category. The pattern will be somewhat skewed by the general phenomenon called the *crossover of the second-highest class*, which, in the highly formal style used in reading lists of words, will show more favored, or fewer disfavored, phenomena than the highest class will show in that style. The reason for the extremist speech of the second-

Table 2. An illustrative wave-like spread through social space of a disfavored linguistic change that begins in the most casual style of the lowest class. The change depicted in this Table is that which occurs in Table 1. Roman numerals designate the time steps that are defined by the successive changes in the pattern. Arabic numerals designate regional lects, as in Table 1. The plus, ×, and minus signs have the same values as in Table 1. A, B, C, and D may represent successively more formal styles, successively higher social classes, or successively older age groupings.

	A B C D		A B C D		A B C D		A B C D
(o) 1	− − − −	(i)	− − − −	(ii)	− − − −	(iii)	− − − −
2	− − − −		− − − −		− − − −		× − − −
3	− − − −		− − − −		× − − −		× × − −
4	− − − −		× − − −		× × − −		× × × −
(iv)	× − − −	(v)	× × − −	(vi)	× × × −	(vii)	× × × ×
	× × − −		× × × −		× × × ×		× × × ×
	× × × −		× × × ×		× × × ×		+ × × ×
	× × × ×		× × × ×		+ × × ×		+ + × ×
(viii)	× × × ×	(ix)	+ × × ×	(x)	+ + × ×	(xi)	+ + + ×
	+ × × ×		+ + × ×		+ + + ×		+ + + +
	+ + × ×		+ + + ×		+ + + +		+ + + +
	+ + + ×		+ + + +		+ + + +		+ + + +
(xii)	+ + + +						
	+ + + +						
	+ + + +						
	+ + + +						

[20] Despite their own varied "*r*-less" and "*r*-ful" pronunciations, New Yorkers between eighteen and forty years of age judged with 100 per cent consistency (Labov 1966:432) recorded tapes which had been doctored for different amounts of "*r*-fulness." ("*R*-ful" speakers do not apply the late rule that desulcalizes /ɜ/.) Labov shows that a reevaluation of "*r*-lessness" had occurred at the time persons of about forty years of age were approaching the age when an awareness of the community's evaluation of speech differences has matured—ca. eighteen or nineteen.

highest class in their most monitored style is that they occupy the position of greatest linguistic insecurity.

Table 2 schematizes the spread of a change in a given linguistic environment (for example, [b] in Table 1) through social space. In order to understand why all of the cells marked × at a given time step in Table 2 do not constitute a single isolect, it is necessary to look at Table 3, where the stepwise *covariation of class and style isolects*, first discovered by Labov 1966, is depicted: Moving up a class in the *same style* is equivalent to moving up to a more formal style in the *same class*; and moving down a class in the *same style* is equivalent to moving down to a more casual style in the *same class*. But in the second-highest class, there is the crossover exception already referred to: Style D

Table 3. Covariation of style and class lects in the spread of a disfavored change through social space; the cross-over of the second-highest class in reading style is marked with an exclamation point. Style A is the casual vernacular; style B is more careful speech, that heard in interviews; style C is heard in reading passages; and style D is heard in reading word lists. Roman and Arabic numerals have the same uses as in Table 2. Environments (a) through (i) correspond with those similarly designated in Table 1. The blocks designated with Arabic numerals here correspond to locales having similar numbers in Table 1 (but in Table 1 the lect of each locale is the style A lect).

0 = (0)	Style A	Style B	Style C	Style D
Upper class	—	—	—	—
Upper middle class	—	—	—	—
Lower middle class	—	—	—	—
Lower class	—	—	—	—

	i = (1)	ii = (2)	iii = (3)	iv = (4)	v = (5)
U	– – – –	– – – –	– – – –	a – – –	b a – –
UM	– – – –	– – – –	a – – –	b a – –	c b a –
LM	– – – –	a – – –	b a – –	c b a –	d c b a
L	a – – –	b a – –	c b a –	d c b a	e d c b

	vi = (6)	vii = (7)	viii = (8)	ix = (9)	x = (10)
U	c b a –	d c b a	e d c b	f e d c	g f e d
UM	d c b –!	e d c –!	f e d a!	g f e b!	h g f c!
LM	e d c b	f e d c	g f e d	h g f e	i h g f
L	f e d c	g f e d	h g f e	i h g f	+ i h g

	xi = (11)	xii = (12)	xiii = (13)	xiv = (14)	xv = (15)
U	h g f e	i h g f	+ i h g	+ + i h	+ + + i
UM	i h g d!	+ i h e!	+ + i f!	+ + + g!	+ + + h!
LM	+ i h g	+ + i h	+ + + i	+ + + +	+ + + +
L	+ + i h	+ + + i	+ + + +	+ + + +	+ + + +

	xvi = (16)	xvii = (17)
U	+ + + +	+ + + +
UM	+ + + i!	+ + + +
LM	+ + + +	+ + + +
L	+ + + +	+ + + +

shows fewer disfavored forms than the same style in the highest class. Note also that Table 3 preserves the implicational relation in which a given change in a given environment implies—for the cell in question—the prior existence of the change in the next heavier environment.[21] When Tables 2 and 3 are compared, it is clear that there is a directionality in the ×'s in Table 2 which only becomes explicit in the breakdown shown in Table 3.

It should be observed that group (for example, ethnic) solidarity frequently operates in the opposite direction from social prestige. Moving in one direction may be socially prestigious, but it alienates a speaker further from his in-group. Conversely, moving away from what is socially favored may enhance solidarity with a speaker's in-group. Thus, group solidarity may effect a reversal in the plus and minus values of the prestige feature and result in a speaker's ambiguous feelings about his manner of speaking.

Despite the general nature of many implications within a language, part of a given speech community may, because of being stigmatized as speaking incorrectly, misinterpret the character of an "error." It is not the well-known phenomenon of overcorrection that is being referred to—saying *for she and I* after being corrected for saying, "Her and me did it"; spelling pronunciations like *of[t]en*; recompoundings like *forehead* for [ˈfɒrɪd]; and so on. Such overcorrections are not peculiar to given speech communities, but are general in English. Some reinterpretations, however, appear to occur only within speech communities. For example, it seems that the lower middle class and the classes below it in New York City have reinterpreted the character of the error involved in saying *dese* and *dose* for *these* and *those*. Whereas the rest of the country judges the correctness and incorrectness of the pronunciations of syllable-initial *th*, *f*, and *v* on the basis of their *place* of articulation (whether or not the tip of the tongue or the lower lip touches the edges of the upper row of teeth), New Yorkers of the social levels in question (Labov 1966) now judge the correctness of these articulations on the basis of the *manner* of articulation (whether the air stream is momentarily stopped or allowed to flow without stoppage). Since the upper middle class does not pattern like the classes lower than it, it must be that they have retained the criterion of correctness that prevails elsewhere. This would be a reasonable expectation, in view of the unlikelihood that the upper social levels have been subjected to the corrective processes undergone by the lower echelons of society.

IV

Of all the differences between the new and the old frameworks that I have mentioned, none is more important than the new concern to describe variation patterns by means of rules that generate or characterize them in a

---

[21] A more technical version of the wave model is found in Bailey MSc. Cf. also the smaller model in Labov MSa.

precise manner. The scope of the present survey entails limiting the remaining pages to a single example of variable rules; that is, rules that generate outputs stacked in an implicational series. In these rules, a lighter-weighted input or output implies the prior operation of the rule in connection with heavier input or output (respectively) in a given environment.

The example to follow is based on data from Labov MSa. What will be shown is a simplified version of a variable rule which deletes underlying //t// or //d// in the environments illustrated by: (1) *past* standing before a nonvowel (that is, before a consonant or at the end of a clause); (2) *past* standing before a vowel; (3) *passed* before a nonvowel; and (4) *passed* before a vowel. The reader should note that in *passed* but not in *past*, the [t]—which is spelled "-ed"—is preceded by a boundary between an inflection and the word to which it is added. This *internal word boundary* is symbolized as # below; the *external word boundary*, ##, denotes the end of an entire word, inflection and all. The rule formulated below will ignore several complications irrelevant to this illustration; for instance, the rule operates more often to delete input //t// and //d// when they end an unaccented syllable (as in *breakfas'*, *dentis'*, and *fastes'*).

The rule required for the deletion of //d// and //t// has two variables that must be considered:

i. the presence or absence of an internal word boundary preceding the consonants; and
ii. the presence or absence of a vowel at the beginning of a following word.

In addition, the data provided by Labov *et al.* (1968:149) show that for one group of black males the presence of a preceding internal word boundary is *more* heavily weighted than the presence of a following vowel—this situation is represented in rule 31b below. For another group of black males, the reverse is true; the preceding internal word boundary is *less* heavily weighted than the following vowel—this situation is represented in rule 31a:[22]

31a. $d, t \twoheadrightarrow \emptyset/C$ [−1 word boundary]____ ## [−2 nuclear]
31b. $d, t \twoheadrightarrow \emptyset/C$ [−2 word boundary]____ ## [−1 nuclear]

---

[22] The minus sign preceding the number is irrelevant to the weighting itself. It merely means that the minus value of the feature in question is favored over its plus value. Thus, [−2 word boundary] means that [+w.b.] is weighted as −2, while [−w.b.] (denoting the absence of a word boundary immediately before the input //t// or //d//) is weighted as +2 (where minus times minus yields a positive product).

Rules 31a,b utilize the following additional conventions and abbreviations: the input or affected item stands to the left of the arrow. The double head on the arrow indicates that the rule is a variable one; that is, it sometimes changes the input to the output and sometimes not. The output is shown to the immediate right of the arrow. In rules 31a,b the zero (∅) output means a change to zero—that is, a deletion. The slant means "in the environment of." The place of the affected input in the environment is indicated by the solid underline. Preceding it, *C* stands for a consonant or non-nuclear phonological segment. Following it, ## denotes an external word boundary, as noted earlier.

Rule 31 is to be read: //d// or //t// is variably changed to zero (that is, deleted) in the environment of a preceding consonant and one, or no, internal word boundary, if there follows an external word boundary plus a vowel or non-vowel (that is, consonant or nothing.) Most groups favor rule 31a in casual speech. But in the style used when a speaker was alone with the interviewer, Labov and his associates found that in New York City teen-age and adult working-class black males who had mostly lived in the North used version (31b) of the rule while preadolescent black youths and adult black males who had lived in the South during their preadolescent years had rule 31a. Isolated black preadolescents who did not belong to peer groups (the so-called *lames*) preferred rule 31b in the interview style, as did middle-class adult black males.

If the word boundary is present in rule 31, the variable feature [word boundary] is plus-valued and multiplied by −2 or −1, depending on whether (31b) or (31a) is under consideration. If a vowel comes at the end, the [nuclear] is plus-valued and multiplied by −1 or −2, depending on which formulation is under consideration. Note that positive values of the two variable features inhibit the operation of the rule, while negative values enhance it. The weightings insure that the rule will operate more often in the heavier environments than in the lighter ones. To see how this comes about, it is necessary to make a calculus of the four weighting combinations—either of the two variables may be present or absent—in each version of the rule. For this purpose the four environments are abbreviated as *past* or *pass#ed* followed by a vowel or a consonant.

32a. Calculus of variables in rule 31a:

	[−1 w.b.]	[−2 nuc]		Total weight
past +C	+1	+2	=	+3
pass#ed +C	−1	+2	=	+1
past +V	+1	−2	=	−1
pass#ed +V	−1	−2	=	−3

32b. Calculus of variables in rule 31b:

	[−2 w.b.]	[−1 nuc]		Total weight
past +C	+2	+1	=	+3
past +V	+2	−1	=	+1
pass#ed +C	−2	+1	=	−1
pass#ed +V	−2	−1	=	−3

The application of either form of the rule in a lighter environment implies its operation also in any heavier-weighted environment. Note that the heaviest and lightest environments are the same for (31a) and (31b): *past* $+C$ and *passed* $+V$ respectively. The two middle-weighted environments are reversed in the two variants of the rule. But in both forms of (31) any $+C$ environment is heavier than any $+V$ environment, and in either of these two environments *past* outweighs *pass ‡ed*. All speakers of English delete *t* or *d* in the heaviest environment (cf. the loss of *t* in *last night, wastepaper,* and the loss of *d* in *handbag, windmill*). But only in very rapid or fatigued speech (which is not infrequent) do speakers of standard English delete *t* in *jus' a minute.*

Various studies have confirmed what common sense dictates: Children begin with language practices that are easier for them to acquire, before graduating to the more difficult items of fully developed adult language.[23] This has the consequence that, if adult speech has become too difficult, or *marked*, for children as the result of mixture in the language, children may fail to acquire a given marked phenomenon. Or children may fail to learn a constraint on a rule—the heaviest-weighted one—so that their rule applies more generally than the rule in their parents' speech. Such failures of children to acquire marked or less general forms of a rule result in changes from marked to unmarked phenomena, or from more restricted to more general applications of a rule, across the generations. Feature unmarking is a regular language change,[24] although it may be overruled by well-known kinds of

---

[23] In technical parlance, the child begins with *unmarked* phenomena—that is, those more easily acquired and, from the universal point of view, more expected and "natural"— and later graduates to those that are more *marked*—that is, those more difficult to acquire and less expected or "natural." Linguistic change proceeds in the opposite direction, for reasons given below. When adults suffer brain injuries, they often lose linguistic phenomena in an order which is the opposite of that in which children learn them. A change from marked to unmarked often occurs also in adult speech which has deteriorated because of fatigue, rapidity, or extreme emotion. Presumably, all phenomena are marked for adults and have to be learned by them.

[24] This is only true of *natural* languages—that is, those which are subject to the constraints that govern the process of language acquisition in children. *Pidgins* are artificial constructs made by adults to communicate among languages. Lacking native speakers, they are not subject to the constraints of natural acquisition (cf. Bailey MSb). When pidgins are *naturalized* (i.e. acquire native speakers) as *creoles*, they subsequently develop as natural languages, unless they become satellites to a more prestigious parent remaining on the scene (Bailey MSb). An example of the former type of creole was Middle English, a mixture of Old English and the French of that period, itself a creole. The satellite species of creole in time usually loses most of the elements of parents other than the language of which they have become satellites. A third type of creole, which never passed through a pidgin stage, is discussed in Gumperz and Wilson (1971). It has a relatively unmixed lexicon and differs in other ways from a naturalized pidgin.

Adult changes, besides those due to borrowing, frequently belong to the category of *overcorrection* (for example, spelling pronunciations, like putting [ˡ] in *calm* or [t] in *often*— though not in *soften*) and are lacking in the regularity of change which occurs in the acquisition of language by children, as Labov has emphasized in various writings. Over-corrections often manifest themselves in the neglect of very late rules in the rule ordering; cf. Kazazis (1968), with which may be compared the deletion of the last stage of the rule

higher-level unmarking.[25] In view of these considerations, rule 31a—found in preadolescent black vernacular and some older white nonstandard and lower-class black vernacular in the southern states—would appear to be more unmarked than (31b). And (31a) would then be the later or more developed version of rule 31. This conclusion would follow from the presence of (31a) in preadolescent speech, whether because the younger children have not yet learned a more complex adult rule, or whether—as seems more likely—they have moved to a later and more developed state of the language than the lames and the older blacks (whether middle-class or northern-reared lower-class adults and teenagers). Note also that the more well-developed form of the rule—(31a)—prevails in casual, unmonitored discourse (as expected).

Given the correctness of the foregoing account, the relative weightings of the variable features in (31a) are the unmarked ones, and those in (31b) are the more marked.[26] A further significance of this observation in the dynamic framework will be discussed later. Here it will suffice to point out that a variable rule utilizing conventions like those of rule 31 can be formulated for the changes of $//\bar{\imath}//$ in the North of England discussed earlier, so that the rule will have the correct implicational hierarchy of environments for its operation (Bailey MSc).

In describing English as a whole—that is, in writing a grammar of the English language—a given rule is to be formulated in its most marked as well as least general version (for example, environment [a] in the rule depicted in Table 1). This is done because unmarked or more general variants of a rule can be predicted from more marked or less general formulations, on the view that language change proceeds in this direction. The unmarked (universally expected) relative weighting of two features can be predicted from a given marked relative weighting, but not vice versa. Implications go in the opposite direction, since the use of an unmarked or more general version of a rule implies one's acceptance of more marked and less general formulations.

Marking phenomena including the relative weightings of features, the

---

changing $/\partial^{\imath}/$ to $[a^e]$ in *wife*, and so on, among many speakers on the island of Martha's Vineyard (for the data, see Labov [1963], who posited the wrong directionality for the change; see also Labov MSa).

[25] It is clear that there are levels of unmarkedness which can overrule lower levels. Generalization (the so-called *crazy rules* of Bach and Harms MS), assimilation, rule reordering, deletion and epenthesis, polarization, and chain shifts—as well as morphologized processes—overrule feature markings. Thus, Hawaiian unmarked syllable-initial *t* becomes *k* (more marked) because of the polarization with *p*, after *k* has become a glottal stop. There is also the feature-stripping process that reduces voiceless stops to [ʔ] and voiceless fricatives to [h]. These glides are more unmarked than other consonants, but in a peculiar way not clearly understood at present. Evidence for marking includes the order of acquisition by children, linguistic change, neutralizations, and statistical universals.

[26] Reweighting changes were first discovered by Labov (1969). The interpretation of this discovery in terms of the theory of marking is the present author's.

relative ordering of two rules, and marked and unmarked values of the features that describe languages. As for the marked values of features that describe the sounds of languages, the present writer has proposed that the unmarked stop (a consonant with a silent interval) or nasal following an accented vowel in the same syllable is [k] or [ŋ] (heard in *sing*), but [t] or [n] in other environments.[27] This is because the tip of the tongue, used for [t] and [n], has the least inertia of any articulator in the mouth, while the back of the tongue, used for [k] and [ŋ], has the most. If a signal of syllable length is sent from the brain to the articulating organs, it would naturally first activate [t] before a vowel and then [k] after a vowel. Evidence also comes from language changes of various sorts[28] and the metathesis of /tk/ to /kt/ in many languages. Here it will be of interest to note, in connection with language variation, that the present writer has recorded *streak* for *street*, *whike* for *white*, *strike* for *stripe*, *tike* for *type*, and *take* for *tape* in his own or others' careless or fatigued enunciation.[29] Note also the well-attested change of syllable-final *t* to *k* in *turtle* and *turkle*.

That syllable-final [f, v] are more unmarked than [θ, ð] is shown by *bof* for *both* and *b(r)uvvah* for *brother* in nonstandard English; likewise *Marfa* for *Martha* in children's pronunciation. When two obstruents (consonants, excluding nasals, liquids, and glides like *y*, *w*, and *h*) occur together, the first tends to be a continuant (cf. Modern Greek *eftá* for ancient *heptá* "seven"), and the second tends to be a stop. An example of the latter is [t] for "-th" in *fifth* and *sixth*, both in Old English and in various contemporary pronunciations. The difference between [s] in the southern states and [š] (usually spelled "sh") in the northern states at the beginning of words like *shrimp* and *shrub*, where [r] follows, may be a marking difference.

The importance of such observations is that they offer the means for analysts to describe diverse lects in a single grammar. Given a marked phenomenon, the unmarked one is predictable from it and can be taken for granted: If it is not attested now, that may be due to an accidental omission in the data; unmarked lects are predictable and may turn up soon. A theory that permits us to predict possible lects with confidence offers an excellent discovery method; it tells us what to go looking for—what we may have previously overlooked.

It would carry us beyond the limited scope of the present discussion to describe successes already accomplished in predicting possible and impossible

---

[27] In the "special position" immediately following an accented vowel which is in the same syllable, nasals are more expected than liquids; [r] more than [l]; the last, more than sibilants like [s, z, š, ž] ([š] is heard in *shoe* and [ž] in *azure*); these, more than other continuant obstruents ([f], [v], [θ], as in *thin*, [ð] as in *then*, and so on); and these more than noncontinuants (stops like [k, g, p, b, t, d]). Note that after unaccented vowels in the same syllable, it is [n], not [ŋ], that is unmarked—for example, *singin'*.

[28] Note also the evidence from child speech. Hsin-I. Hsieh (1971) gives evidence of a Chinese child's substituting *tuk* for *kut* "bone."

[29] Ralph Fasold's small son was heard to change *apart* to *apark*.

lects and in formalizing rules which build into our linguistic descriptions the directionality and relative rate of changes which differentiate contemporary varieties of a language. But it is now even possible to formalize and predict language patterns resulting from accelerations of later aspects of a change over earlier ones. Indeed, the new work is advancing with such rapid strides that what was impossible to formulate in the static framework of a few years ago is now either at hand or just around the corner.

REFERENCES

ANDERSON, STEPHEN R. 1969. *West Scandinavian Vowel Systems and the Ordering of Phonological Rules*. Bloomington: Indiana University Linguistics Club.

BACH, EMMON, AND ROBERT T. HARMS. MS. "How Do Languages Get Crazy Rules?" to appear in *Historical Linguistics in the Light of Generative Grammar*, ed. Robert P. Stockwell. Bloomington: Indiana University Press.*

BAILEY, CHARLES-JAMES N. 1968a. "Dialectal Differences in the Syllabification of Non-nasal Sonorants in American English," *General Linguistics*, 8:79–81.

_____. 1968b. "Is There a 'Midland' Dialect of American English?" (Available from the ERIC Document Reproduction Service, ED 021 240.)

_____. 1968c. "Optimality, Positivism, and Pandialectal Grammars." (Available from the ERIC Document Reproduction Service, PEGS paper 30.)

_____. 1970 [to appear]. "The Integration of Linguistic Theory: Internal Reconstruction and the Comparative Method in Descriptive Analysis," to appear in *Historical Linguistics in the Light of Generative Grammar*, ed. Robert P. Stockwell. Bloomington: Indiana University Press.*

_____. 1971. "Trying to Talk in the New Paradigm," *Papers in Linguistics*, **4**, ii:312–38.

_____. MSa. "Southern States Phonetics."

_____. MSb. "Toward Characterizing a Language System."

_____. MSc. "Variation and Linguistic Theory."

BECKER, DONALD A. 1967. *Generative Phonology and Dialect Study: An Investigation of Three Modern German Dialects*. Ann Arbor: University Microfilms.

BEVER, T. G. AND D. T. LANGENDOEN. 1971. "A Dynamic Model of the Evolution of Language," *Linguistic Inquiry*, 2:433–63.

BHAT, D. N. S. 1970. "A New Hypothesis of Language Change," *Indian Linguistics*, 31:1–13.

BICKERTON, DEREK. 1971. "Inherent Variability and Variable Rules," *Foundations of Language*, 7:457–92.

_____. MS. "On the Nature of a Creole Continuum."

CARDEN, GUY. 1970. *Logical Predicates and Idiolectal Variation in English*. Cambridge, Mass.: The Aiken Computation Laboratory, Harvard University, Report NSF-25.

CHEN, MATTHEW. 1971a. *The Time Dimension: Contribution Toward a Theory of Sound Change*. Berkeley: Phonology Laboratory, University of California, POLA II, 12:1–63.

_____. 1971b. *Metarules and Universal Constraints in Phonological Theory*. Berkeley: Phonology Laboratory, University of California, POLA II, **13**:1–56.

————, AND HSIN-I. HSIEH. 1971. "The Time Variable in Phonological Change," *Journal of Linguistics*, **7**:1–13.

DeCAMP, DAVID. 1959. "The Pronunciation of English in San Francisco, Second Part," *Orbis*, **8**:54–77.

————. 1971. "Toward a Generative Analysis of a Post-Creole Speech Continuum," in *Pidginization and Creolization of Languages: Proceedings of a Conference Held at the University of the West Indies, Mona, Jamaica, April, 1968*, ed. Dell Hymes. Cambridge, England: At the University Press. Pp. 349–70.

ELLIOTT, DALE, STANLEY LEGUM, AND SANDRA ANNEAR THOMPSON. 1969. "Syntactic Variation As Linguistic Data," in *Papers from the Fifth Regional Meeting, Chicago Linguistic Society, April 18–19, 1969*, eds. Robert I. Binnick *et al.* Chicago: Department of Linguistics, The University of Chicago. Pp. 52–59.

FASOLD, RALPH W. 1970. "Two Models of Socially Significant Linguistic Variation," *Language*, **46**:551–63.

FERGUSON, C. A. 1971. "'Short A' in Philadelphia English," *Stanford Occasional Papers in Linguistics*, **1**:2–27.

GREENBERG, JOSEPH H. 1966. "Some Universals of Grammar with Particular Reference to the Order of Meaningful Elements," in *Universals of Language*, 2nd edition, ed. Joseph H. Greenberg. Cambridge, Mass.: MIT Press. Pp. 73–113.

GUMPERZ, JOHN J., AND ROBERT WILSON. 1971. "Convergence and Creolization: A Case from the Indo-Aryan/Dravidian Border in India," in *Pidginization and Creolization of Languages: Proceedings of a Conference Held at the University of the West Indies, Mona, Jamaica, April 1968*, ed. Dell Hymes. Cambridge: At the University Press. Pp. 151–67.

HSIEH, HSIN-I. 1971. *Lexical Diffusion: Evidence from Child Language Acquisition*. Berkeley: Phonology Laboratory, University of California, POLA II, **15**:1–12.

JAKOBSON, ROMAN. 1941 [1968]. *Child Language, Aphasia, and Phonological Universals*. The Hague: Mouton.

KAZAZIS, KOSTAS. 1968. "Sunday Greek," in *Papers from the Fourth Regional Meeting, Chicago Linguistic Society, April 19–20, 1968*, eds. Bill J. Darden, *et al.* Chicago: Department of Linguistics, University of Chicago. Pp. 130–40.

KIPARSKY, PAUL. 1968. "Linguistic Universals and Linguistic Change," in *Universals in Linguistic Theory*, eds. Emmon Bach and Robert T. Harms. New York: Holt, Rinehart and Winston, Inc. Pp. 170–202.

————. 1971. "Historical Linguistics," in *A Survey of Linguistic Science*, ed. William O. Dingwall. College Park: Linguistics Program, University of Maryland. Pp. 576–642.

KOLB, EDUARD. 1966. *Phonological Atlas of the Northern Region: The Six Northern Counties, North Lincolnshire, and the Isle of Man*. Bern: Francke Verlag.

KURATH, HANS, with the collaboration of MARCUS L. HANSEN, JULIA BLOCH, AND BERNARD BLOCH. 1939. *Handbook of the Linguistic Geography of New England*. Providence, R.I.: Brown University.

————, AND RAVEN I. McDAVID, JR. 1961. *The Pronunciation of English in the Atlantic States*. Ann Arbor: The University of Michigan Press.

LABOV, WILLIAM. 1963. "The Social Motivation of a Sound Change," *Word*, **19**:273–309.

————. 1966. *The Social Stratification of English in New York City*. Washington D.C.: Center for Applied Linguistics, Urban Language Series I.

————. 1969. "Contraction, Deletion, and Inherent Variability of the English Copula," *Language*, 45:715–62.

————. 1971. "Methodology," in *A Survey of Linguistic Science*, ed. William O. Dingwall. College Park: Linguistics Program, The University of Maryland. Pp. 412–91.

————. MSa. "The Internal Evolution of Linguistic Rules," to appear in *Historical Linguistics in the Light of Generative Grammar*, ed. Robert P. Stockwell. Bloomington: Indiana University Press.*

————. MSb. "The Social Setting of Linguistic Change," to appear in *Current Trends in Linguistics*. The Hague: Mouton. Vol. 11.

————, PAUL COHEN, CLARENCE ROBINS, AND JOHN LEWIS. 1968. *A Study of the Non-Standard English of Negro and Puerto Rican Speakers in New York City: Phonological and Grammatical Analysis*, Vol. I. Washington, D.C.: Office of Education, Final Report, Cooperative Research Project 3288.

MCDAVID, RAVEN I., JR. 1940. "Low-Back Vowels in the South Carolina Piedmont," *American Speech*, 15:144–48.

MOULTON, WILLIAM G. 1962. "Dialect Geography and the Concept of Phonological Space," *Word*, 18:23–32.

ODO, CAROL. MS. "Some Implications in Hawaiian English."

PARKER, GARY J. 1971. "Comparative Quechua Phonology and Grammar V: The Evolution of Quechua B," *University of Hawaii Working Papers in Linguistics*, 3,iii:45–109.

ROSS, JOHN ROBERT. 1970. "On Declarative Sentences," in *Readings in English Transformational Grammar*, eds. Roderick A. Jacobs and Peter S. Rosenbaum. Waltham, Mass.: Ginn and Company. Pp. 222–72.

SAPORTA, SOL. 1965. "Ordered Rules, Dialect Differences, and Historical Processes," *Language*, 41:218–24.

STAMPE, DAVID. 1969. "The Acquisition of Phonetic Representation," in *Papers from the Fifth Regional Meeting, Chicago Linguistic Society, April 18–19, 1969*, eds. Robert I. Binnick *et al.* Chicago: Department of Linguistics, University of Chicago. Pp. 443–54.

WANG, WILLIAM S.-Y. 1969. "Competing Changes as a Cause of Residue," *Language*, 45:9–25.

————, AND CHIN-CHUAN CHENG. 1970. "Implementation of Phonological Change: The Shuāng-fēng Chinese Case," in *Papers from the Sixth Regional Meeting, Chicago Linguistic Society, April 16–18, 1970*. Chicago: Chicago Linguistic Society. Pp. 552–59.

WEINREICH, URIEL, WILLIAM LABOV, AND MARVIN I. HERZOG. 1968. "Empirical Foundations for a Theory of Language Change," in *Directions for Historical Linguistics: A Symposium*, eds. W. P. Lehmann and Yakov Malkiel. Austin: University of Texas Press. Pp. 95–195.

WOOD, GORDON R. 1971. *Vocabulary Change: A Study of Variation in Regional Words in Eight of the Southern States*. Carbondale: The Southern Illinois University Press.

---

* Since Bailey's essay was written this collection has appeared as *Linguistic Change and Generative Theory*, eds. R. P. Stockwell and R. K. S. Macaulay (Bloomington: Indiana University Press, 1972). *Eds.*

STUDY QUESTIONS

1. Summarize Bailey's argument for favoring the new *lectology* over the old *dialectology*. Consider in particular the contrasting views of: (a) patterning by region, style, sex, and age grouping; (b) dialect change through time; and (c) methods of data collection.

2. Define the following terms used in Bailey's essay:

categorical rule	conditioned rules
variable rule	unconditioned rules
language community	isolect
isogloss	neutralization
bundle of isoglosses	weighting

3. In example 2 on p. 163, Bailey suggests that the three [h]'s of *his henhouse* form an implicational series such that they disappear in rapid or careless speech in a fixed sequence: first in the least stressed syllable (in *his*), then in the mid-stressed syllable (*-house*), and finally in the fully stressed syllable (*hen-*). Later (p. 183) he argues that the unmarked stop following an accented vowel in the same syllable is [k] and in other environments [t].

   Both of these proposals can be tested using the familiar tongue twister,

   Peter Piper picked a peck of pickled peppers,

   which contains both a hierarchy of stressed and unstressed syllables and a series of stop consonants. First, mark the syllables of the tongue twister for three degrees of stress as the sentence would be heard in speech at a normal rate. Then mark all the stop consonants, noting which appear following stressed vowels in the same syllable and which occur elsewhere.

   Ask a friend to repeat the tongue twister several times. Which syllables degenerate first; the stressed or the unstressed? How does Bailey's assertion about the unmarked stops explain the fact that your friend is likely to say *Peter Piker* after a few repetitions of the sentence? What other errors crop up?

4. As Bailey notes, "a theory that permits us to predict possible lects with confidence offers an excellent discovery method" (p. 183). As an illustration of this method, examine the following data from O. F. Emerson's pioneering study of old-fashioned speech in Ithaca, New York, for the raising of the vowel of *ham* to that of *hem* [ɛ]:[a]

m n (a)	f θ s (b)	d (c)	b (d)	š (e)	g (g)	v z (g)	p t k (h)	l (i)
	*						[čɛpmən] "Chapman"	
*						[hɛv] "have"		[ɛlɪk]
		*	[hɛd] "had"	*	*	*	[hɛtš] "hatch"	"Alec"
[džɛnəwəri] "January"	*					[hɛz] "has"	[ɛkwɪdək] "aqueduct"	

[a] Oliver Farrar Emerson, *The Ithaca Dialect: A Study of Present English* (Boston: *Dialect Notes*, Vol. 1, Part 3, 1891), §80. The editors wish to thank Professor James Walker Downer for bringing these data to their attention.

Note that as in Table 1 (p. 158) the data from Emerson's study are arranged according to the consonant following the vowel in question; asterisks indicate possible items not mentioned in the study.

Assuming that C.-J. Bailey's scale reflects the implicational patterning of the Ithaca dialect:

a. How would you expect speakers of this dialect to pronounce *jam, staff, math, Cass, crab, hash, sag*?

b. Which vowel raisings are likely to be categorical and which variable (assuming that the data given does not contain lexical exceptions or performance variations)?

c. What locale listed in the left-hand column of Table 1 most closely resembles the patterning of this feature in Ithaca?

5. Arthur J. Bronstein says of the following two groups of words that the vowel sound is slightly higher, toward [ɛ], in the words in Group I.

Group I			*Group II*		
last	ham	cash	hat	rat	sat
master	hand	badge	fat	nap	map
dance	bag	bad	gap	rack	back
cram	sag	bath	stack	shack	catch
handle	fancy		hatch	batch	latch

"The raised vowel for the words in Group I," he writes, "is common to educated persons throughout the country."[b] Is there a distinction between the two groups in your own speech?

Arrange the words in both groups along the implicational scale given in Table 1 (p. 158). Does the patterning confirm the arrangement of environments given by Bailey? Which of the environments—(a) through (i)—is likely to be categorical and which variable? No data are given by Bronstein for words with following [l]—such as *gal* and *pal*; how would you expect a speaker who retains [æ] in Group II words to pronounce such words? What changes would have to take place before such speakers began to pronounce *pal* as [pɛl]?

6. Test your intuition about the acceptability of the sentences given in examples 1 (p. 164), 2 (pp. 164–66), and 3 (pp. 166–67). Do you agree with the intuitions reported by Bailey? Do others in your class make the same judgments?

7. What objections does Bailey raise against the "monitored data" that forms the basis of many dialect studies?

8. Explain the difference between the *applicational ordering* of a set of rules and the *implicational order* of a series of environments. Why does Bailey argue that "a less restricted formulation of a rule implies a more restricted form of the same rule" (p. 169).

9. In his study of Detroit Negro speech, Wolfram discovered that the absence of [r] in word-medial and word-final positions was stratified by class and by style:[c]

	Interview style	*Reading style*
Upper middle class	25.0%	15.2%
Lower middle class	38.1%	23.2%
Working class	66.2%	55.5%

[b] Arthur J. Bronstein, *The Pronunciation of American English: An Introduction to Phonetics* (New York, 1960), p. 155.

[c] Walter A. Wolfram, *A Sociolinguistic Description of Detroit Negro Speech* (Washington, D.C., 1969), p. 116.

As the data show, this linguistic feature is variable and not categorical for the speakers investigated. To help extract a pattern, we can set a threshold for this variable at 30 per cent, assigning a one to speakers below the threshold and a zero to speakers above it.[d]

	Interview style	Reading style
Upper middle class	1	1
Lower middle class	0	1
Working class	0	0

Consider this data in light of Bailey's discussion (pp. 175–78) and his Tables 2 and 3. Suppose that the absence of [r] in these positions is a *disfavored* change in the linguistic community; what sequence of change would you expect in the dispersion of the zeroes and ones in the display here? What pattern would you expect if the absence of [r] is a *favored* change?

What pattern in the display would be expected to develop in response to the phenomenon Bailey calls "the crossover of the second-highest class" (p. 176)? How would this phenomenon reveal itself if the feature in question is disfavored? If it is favored?

[d] Both the general form of the display and the problem of establishing a threshold are discussed by Ralph W. Fasold, "Two Models of Socially Significant Linguistic Variation," *Language*, **46**(1970):551–63. Further data and proposals for such a model are found in Walter Stolz and Garland Bills, *An Investigation of the Standard-Nonstandard Dimension of Central Texan English* (Austin: Child Development Evaluation and Research Center, The University of Texas, Part of the Final Report to the Office of Economic Opportunity, contract OEO–4115, 1968).

SOME CHARACTERISTICS OF ENGLISH IN HAWAII
Gloria Glissmeyer

. . because the beauty part of the Islands is to listen to a guy talk pidgin like Neki and Freddie sometimes.

NEKI KAUHI
Keaukaha, July 1966

English in Hawaii shows many of the features present in other varieties of the world language: equational sentences (for example, "she sick"), like those identified by McDavid and Labov in mainland dialects; devoiced final consonants (in such words as leg *and* five), *similarly found in many speech styles throughout the English-speaking world; and adopted foreign words* (aloha, hula, ukulele), *which have characterized English throughout its history. As Glissmeyer shows in her careful exploration of the dialect, Hawaiian English has some unique traits, but its most distinctive features depend mainly on a change in emphasis: Rules and structures rare in other varieties are more frequent in the language of the Islands, making its speakers largely intelligible to outsiders but marking them as a homogeneous linguistic group.*

The social conditions that have given rise to Hawaiian English are similarly unique in some respects, for nowhere else in the world have Chinese, Japanese, Portuguese, Puerto Rican Spanish, Philippine languages—and of course the Hawaiian language itself—combined with American English dialects in just the same way. And yet the process of pidginization imposes many of the same traits found in other places where plantation agriculture and international trade have had a formative influence.

Perhaps even more critical are the effects of the present social role of Hawaiian English. Its speakers are confronted by conflicting forces—the impulse toward dialect maintenance on one hand, and the attempt by the schools to eradicate a supposedly nonstandard dialect on the other. Just as the New York schoolboy quoted by Labov (p. 284) found it impossible to survive in his peer culture with schoolroom English, so the speaker of Hawaiian English finds himself in the dilemma of making a linguistic choice:

One day when a boy and I were talking. We were not speaking good English, so, another person heard the boy speaking poor English. The person tried to correct the boy, but what did the boy do? Correct

190

himself or not? What do you think his answer was? The boy's answer was, "I talk how I like, you no boss me, you not my teacher."[a]

Even though this dialogue took place nearly forty years ago, the conflict between dialects prevails: "'There are three thousand students in this school, which is supposed to preserve the Hawaiian culture—whatever that's supposed to mean,'" says a student in the 1970s. "'Ever since Kam [Kamehameha School] was founded, students have been forbidden to speak Hawaiian, or even pidgin.'"[b]

HISTORY OF ENGLISH IN HAWAII

The arrival, in 1820, of the first missionary group from New England signaled the beginning of large-scale contact of many language systems in Hawaii, including English. There had been earlier contact, of course. For thirty or more years before the missionaries' time, sailors had been leaving ships and bringing their English where Hawaiian had been spoken for 800, and possibly 1,800, years.[1] And Hawaiian was being heard on British and American vessels calling at Hawaii, both in port and out, because Hawaiians were even then leaving as sailors (Kuykendall & Day 1948:44). Among these one young Hawaiian linked his people irrevocably with the Connecticut and other New England missionaries. In 1809, Opukahaia (Henry Obookiah) swam out to Captain Caleb Brintnall's *Triumph*, in the same bay, Kealakekua, where Cook's vessels had lain offshore thirty years earlier still. At the end of the voyage that took Opukahaia first to the Seal Islands of northwest America, to Hawaii again, then China and around the Cape of Good Hope to New York, he went with Brintnall to his home in New Haven. There he met a son of a minister from Torringford, Connecticut, and went to live with his family. He continued learning to read and write English (and studied arithmetic, geometry, geography, some Hebrew and Latin) at different locations in New England. He became a member of the religion and the Mission, and, before dying of typhus fever in 1818 at Cornwall, wrote the *Memoirs* credited with launching the *Thaddeus*, which brought the first missionary group within sight of Mauna Kea on "the Big Island" of the chain, the island now called Hawaii.

Within thirty years or so following 1820, the New Englanders learned Hawaiian, devised a Hawaiian orthography (Wise and Hervey 1952: 313–325),

[a]John E. Reinecke, *Language and Dialect in Hawaii: A Sociolinguistic History* (Honolulu, 1969), p. 178.

[b] Francine du Plessix Gray, "The Sugar-Coated Fortress," *The New Yorker* (March 4, 1972), pp. 43–44.

[1] Suggs 1960:152, 155, 227. Radiocarbon dates so far obtained: South Point, Hawaii, A.D. 120 ± 120 years; Kuli'ou'ou Valley, Oahu, A.D. 1005 ± 180; Ha'ele'ele, Kauai, A.D. 1239 ± 200; Moomomi, Molokai, A.D. 1408 ± 300.

and in the earliest part of this period began teaching Hawaiian adults and children to read and write Hawaiian. But almost from the beginning this sixty-year period belonged linguistically to both English and Hawaiian. Although the first sheet printed on Elisha Loomis' press in 1822 was part of an eight-page spelling book in Hawaiian, it is reported that "government documents, reports, laws, and papers generally" were printed bilingually, and English increasingly became the main language of trade and government (Reinecke 1969:32; Lind 1967:87). It was in this period, in the middle half of the century, that there is report of a mixed language known as *hapa haole* (Reinecke 1969:34–35, 87–89, 91, 92, 109–110, 144, 194). There is no certainty about it, however, except that the Hawaiian term for it means "half English." In the 1930s Reinecke encountered hints that a mixture of Hawaiian and English had been in existence during whaling days, though no record of what it was like has yet been found. There is likewise considerable uncertainty generally about the early origin of English dialects in Hawaii, but according to old-time Islanders a "'pidgin[2] English' did not arise until after the Chinese and Portuguese immigration" (Reinecke 1969:35). Chinese workers were first brought to the cane fields in 1852, so it is possible that the language systems of the years immediately following included *hapa haole* and Chinese pidgin (besides Hawaiian, English, and the Chinese dialects). According to Reinecke (1969:92) the formation of plantation pidgin English was precipitated when the Portuguese came in the 1880s and 1890s. Many became supervisors on the plantations, and in the role of "day-to-day buffers" between the plantation owners and laborers, the Portuguese *lunas* must logically have contributed to the emergence of pidgin (Fuchs 1961:57). In addition, the contracts with the Portuguese (who came from the Madeiras and the Azores) had guaranteed free schools for their children. Some intelligible linguistic compromise was a necessity in the schools, and from 1876 on, there was an immense increase of "English" instruction. By 1890, Hawaiian was all but supplanted as the language of instruction (Reinecke 1969:49–50).

In the second half of the nineteenth century even more languages than the Chinese and Portuguese dialects were added to the Hawaiian and English on the sugar cane and later the pineapple plantations. Most numerous of all the groups were Japanese, of whom the strongest inflow was between 1885 and 1907 (Reinecke 1969:58). The next largest group were speakers of Philippine languages, mainly Ilocano, but also Visayan, who came after 1907 (Reinecke 1969:63). Others were Puerto Ricans, South Sea Islanders,

---

[2] My use of the term *pidgin* follows Hall, whose definition (1966:xii) is ". . . language . . . whose grammar and vocabulary are very much reduced in extent and which is native to neither side."

In Hawaii the term can have this restricted meaning, but it also ranges to full coverage of all varieties of language which contain characteristics different from U.S. Mainland speech, and which are used by native speakers of English in Hawaii.

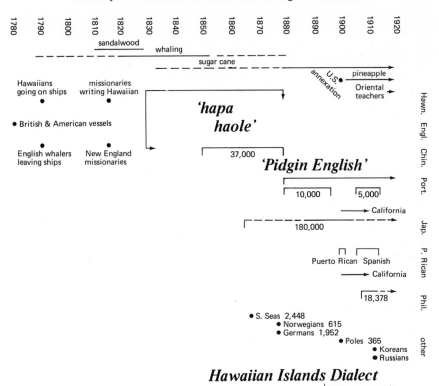

Thumbnail sketch of Hawaiian language history.

Spanish, Norwegians, Germans, Galician Poles, Koreans, and Russians (Reinecke 1969:59–67).

The preceding thumbnail sketch (abstracted from Reinecke 1969, Chapters 3 and 7) brings this language history into focus. In the left-hand columns are sociohistorical items. The remaining columns, beginning with "Hawaiian," contain information pertinent to each language. Solid lines signal full-scale activity, and dotted lines, minimal activity, extending over periods of time. For instance, the sandalwood trade was at its height in the years after 1810, but did not last until 1830; whaling activity accelerated during and after the sandalwood trade, and was practically over by 1880. The numerical figures which are listed are those given by Reinecke, and they approximate the number of individuals speaking a given language who emigrated to Hawaii. Of the Portuguese, for example, 10,000 are said to have arrived in the 1880s, and about 5,000 who emigrated from 1906–1913 later went to California. Fuchs' recent social history of Hawaii estimates the Hawaiian population in 1780 at 300,000 (Fuchs 1961:4), in 1850 at 70,000, and in 1920 at 24,000 (*ibid.*:68).

The highlights as Reinecke presents them are that

a. Between 1820 and 1880
   hapa haole, possibly a Hawaiian-based pidgin, arose, at the same time that Hawaiian, English, and Chinese were the languages of the land.
b. From 1880 on
   an English-based pidgin developed among the speakers of all the various languages on the scene.
c. By about 1910
   a Hawaiian English dialect was established (Reinecke 1969:166).

Reinecke points out that the plantation speech was a lingua franca that supplemented but did not supplant the language of each group of speakers— as long as they maintained an ethnic spirit and community life of their own (Reinecke 1969:143). But public school experience, begun in 1840 and broadly extended in the 1880s, as well as growing economic opportunities, led to the increased use of a "dialectal" English (Lind 1967:90; Reinecke 1969:69–82).

At this time it is possible only to speculate about the proportionate contributions made by different varieties of English to that spoken in Hawaii. Beginning with the days of Cook, the dominant foreign influence had been British, and continued so to 1830, but declined in the subsequent thirty years with the increased commercial activities of the American "sugar missionaries" (Fuchs 1961:11, 18–19). Even so, British dialects were varied and numerous throughout the nineteenth century. Theo H. Davies, a Welshman from Liverpool, founder of the corporation that bears his name, "imported many Scots to run his Honolulu agencies and its plantations" and "by 1905, almost two out of every five plantation managers were of Scotch descent." Scots were also hired as bank clerks and tellers (Fuchs 1961:54–55). Christopher Lewers came from Dublin, opened a lumber-yard, and with a cousin founded what is today Hawaii's largest construction firm. Alan S. Davis, whose father was English and mother Irish, became president and chairman of the board of the Brewer Company. Henry M. Greenwell, Kona coast rancher, and the powerful Robinsons were of English descent.

In the nineteenth century, American dialects were mainly those of the missionaries from Massachusetts, Connecticut, Vermont, and the Finger Lakes region of New York, and of the whalers, many of whom were from the Boston area. Then beginning around 1900 came teachers, businessmen, politicians, and union leaders from other parts of the U.S. Mainland, but principally from the West Coast, and since the 1940s residents of Hawaii have heard speakers from every region of the United States, among the military and the tourists. Our knowledge of the development of the various English systems in Hawaii is almost wholly speculative, but contemporary Hawaii English does show traces of the complex linguistic situation of the last century and a half.

AN ACCOUNT OF RESEARCH REGARDING ENGLISH DIALECTS IN HAWAII

The accompanying table indicates briefly the extent and nature of systematic investigation that has been made up to the present concerning different aspects of English in Hawaii. When the annotated bibliography *English in Hawaii* was published in 1966, it was the opinion of its editors that most of the best technical writing on the subject had been sociological, and they noted that the theses that approach a scientific description of the Island dialect have been mostly phonologically oriented (Tsuzaki & Reinecke 1966:vii).

Systematic analysis/description of English in Hawaii

Date	Author(s)	Subject
1934	Reinecke & Tokimasa	General phonology, lexicon, syntax
1935	Chun*	Chinese-related syntax
1942	Larry	Hawaiian-, Chinese-, Portuguese-, Japanese-, and Filipino-related phonology
1951	Costa*	Hawaiian-, Chinese-, and Japanese-related phonology
1958	Hayes*	Japanese-related phonology
1960	Kindig*	Puerto Rican-related phonology, lexicon, syntax
1960	Knowlton	Portuguese-related lexicon, syntax
1961	Shun*	General phonology, syntax
1966	Pukui & Elbert	Hawaiian dictionary
1967	Knowlton	Portuguese-related phonology, lexicon, syntax
1967	Vanderslice & Pierson	General phonology
1967	Reinecke & Tsuzaki	Hawaiian-related lexicon
1967a	Tsuzaki	General syntax
1967b	Tsuzaki	Hawaiian-related lexicon
1967	Glissmeyer	Hawaiian-related phonology
1968	Tsuzaki	Hawaiian-related lexicon
1968	Tsuzaki & Elbert	Hawaiian-related lexicon
1969	Nagara	Japanese-related phonology, syntax
1969	Reinecke	General lexicon, syntax
1970	Glissmeyer	Hawaiian-related syntax
1971	Tsuzaki	General syntax
1971	Odo	General phonology
1971	ms Labov	General syntax, phonology

* M.A. thesis, Department of Speech, University of Hawaii.

Of the studies listed in the table, the following are published:

Date	Author(s)*	Subject
1934	Reinecke & Tokimasa	General phonology, lexicon, syntax
1960	Knowlton	Portuguese-related lexicon, syntax
1966	Pukui & Elbert	Hawaiian dictionary
1967	Knowlton	Portuguese-related phonology, lexicon, syntax
1967	Vanderslice & Pierson	General phonology
1967	Reinecke & Tsuzaki	Hawaiian-related lexicon
1967a	Tsuzaki	General syntax
1967b	Tsuzaki	Hawaiian-related lexicon
1967	Glissmeyer	Hawaiian-related phonology
1968	Tsuzaki	Hawaiian-related lexicon
1968	Tsuzaki & Elbert	Hawaiian-related lexicon
1969 (1935)	Reinecke	General lexicon, syntax
1971	Tsuzaki	General syntax

* The works by John E. Reinecke and Aiko Tokimasa are the sociological writings referred to in the text.

PHONOLOGY

Linguistically oriented reports on phonology are to be found in the paper on segmentals by Glissmeyer[3] and in the short, but pioneering and significant account of suprasegmentals in Hawaii English by Vanderslice & Pierson.

My study was limited to the region known as Keaukaha,[4] an area of about four square miles in Hilo, on the island of Hawaii. The 1960 census lists the population of Hilo at 25,966. Sugar, coffee, fruits, and macadamia nuts are exported from the harbor on Hilo Bay, on the eastern coast of Hawaii. The town has a public library, customs house, courthouse, public school system, and the Lyman Museum on Hawaiiana. Heavily forested areas of tropical ferns and trees are in close proximity, and the lava fields of Kilauea and Mauna Loa are only about thirty miles away. Keaukaha is immediately adjacent to the Hilo airport and the hotel-resort area, so that people living there have some contact with tourists, at least on the open "sampan" buses that serve Hilo generally. Residents of all ages are also regular viewers of national television.

According to firsthand report, Keaukaha was settled in the early 1920s. It

---

[3] From 1963 to 1970, I was instructor and assistant professor of English at the University of Hawaii, and received a Ph.D in linguistics there in December 1970. My research in Keaukaha was carried out over a 14-month period in 1965–66. Salt Lake City (Utah), Bakersfield (California), Zurich (Switzerland), Palo Alto, Berkeley and Chico (California) are other places besides Honolulu where during extended periods of time I have heard English spoken.

[4] *Keaukaha* is generally pronounced /kèòkáhà/. But when a ten-year-old boy said, "I play for Keaukaha Warriors," I heard /ké:kà/.

is one of the so-called Hawaiian Homes areas, where residents must be of at least part Hawaiian ancestry. Historical documentation of particulars regarding the people, or of information possibly related to the origin of their dialect, has been to date impossible to find. Beyond the background indicated in the first section of this essay, it may be added that English is at least one of the first languages of Keaukaha residents. Parents and children sing songs in Hawaiian, but the children generally do not translate Hawaiian songs into English.

My 1967 analysis, which remains preliminary, included seven speakers ranging in age from 8 to 14 years. Forms were elicited using the Swadesh 200-word list, and the individuals were encouraged to use the words in the first or most usual way that came to mind. Though the inventory of consonant phonemes in Keaukaha English (hereafter sometimes referred to as KE) matches that of mainland dialects, the incidence and nature of these phonemes differ in several respects.

I noted instances of aspiration initially after /p, f, s/ in *play*, *float*, and *sleep*, also after /p/ in *spit*. In final position, /p, t, k, g/ were sometimes aspirated in *rope*, *fight*, *lake*, and *big*. Devoicing of /d, g, v, ð, z, m, n, l/ could occur finally in *blood*, *leg*, *five*, *smooth*, *eggs*, *come*, *one*, *all*. The phenomenon commonly known as back clipping was observed on occasion in *that*, *float*, *and*, *old*, *stand*, *dog*, *animal*, *far*. Such deletion of /d/ happens in most other dialects too, but in KE the process is extended to include /t, g, l, r/. Another change in final phonemes, namely, to a glottal stop (which is phonemic in Hawaiian), is recorded for some instances of *count*, *fight*, *float*, *night*, *salt*, *short*, *that*, *what*, *while*, *drink*, *cloud*, *five*, *rain*, *all*, *fall*, involving /t, k, d, v, n, l/. (These last two processes raise questions of analysis and explanation still to be solved.) A variety of final consonants (/p, t, k, b, d, g, f, v, θ/) occasionally exhibited prolonged articulation (reminiscent of double consonants in Japanese), in *rope*, *at*, *back*, *rub*, *blood*, *big*, *fife*, *five*, *tooth*. Another feature notable in Keaukaha English and quite general in Hawaii English is the aspiration of the intervocalic voiceless consonant in *kíttèn*, *moúntàin*, *róttèn*, *búttèr*, *búttòn*, *and waitèr*, accompanied by an upward gradation in stressing the second syllable, and a fronting of the vowel in the second syllable to /ɪ/ or occasionally to /ɛ/ before final /n/ (compare Vanderslice & Pierson 1967:159, [kʰɪtʰɛn]).

The vowels remain to be dealt with in published research. A major feature here is a predominant shift from the more usual simple /ɪ/ to a higher diphthong /iy/. A list of some of the words affected contains many which are used very frequently: big, did, different, dinner, fifty, finish, fish, give, him, his, hit, if, in, is, it, kick, knit, live, pick, picture, pig, river, sister, sit, six, think, this, win, with.

Besides the foregoing significant differences between Keaukaha English and most mainland dialects, this Hawaii dialect shares certain variant features with some other varieties of English. As Reinecke & Tokimasa mention (1934:131), in Hawaii there is alternation between /d/ and /ð/ in

words like *the, this, that, them, they, their, there,* and *together,* and between
/t/ and /θ/ in examples like *think, thing, three, third, thirties, thought, through,
thousand,* and *anything.* (Pederson and Labov have recently reported on the
same characteristics in Chicago and New York City.)

In the words *what, when, where* and *white,* initial /w/ (in contrast to /hw/)
occurred in 29 out of 30 instances in the Keaukaha study. As to this feature,
the Hawaii dialect is similar to American usage reported in Rhode Island,
Massachusetts, Maine, Connecticut (Thomas 1961:64), the Pacific Northwest (Reed 1961a:119), Pennsylvania German (Reed 1961b:278), and
Charleston (McDavid 1946:360), and to British Received Standard (McDavid
1946:359).

In view of the history of early British involvement and of the predominance
of New England speech in Hawaii until the twentieth century, it may not
be surprising that many varieties of Hawaii English are generally "r-less" as
are Standard British English (Kurath 1964a:266) and dialects in eastern
Massachusetts, Vermont, and Connecticut (Thomas 1961:64). As a matter
of fact, "r-lessness" is even more widely attested, namely in New Hampshire,
Rhode Island, Maine (Thomas 1961:64), in metropolitan N w York City,
the lower Hudson Valley, eastern Virginia, adjoining Maryland and north-
central North Carolina, the South Carolina-Georgia coast, Florida and the
states on the Gulf of Mexico (Kurath 1964a:266–267; 1964b:368), in southeast Texas (Norman 1956:148) and San Antonio (Sawyer 1964:227), in
Chicago (Pederson 1964:407), and in the south and west of England as well
as the eastern counties north of the Thames (Kurath 1964a:266–267). As
Kurath says, "approximately three-fourths of the American people use /r/
in all positions, but about forty million living in the areas mentioned above do
not" (Kurath 1964a:267). The present usage of both "r-less" and "r-ful"
speech in Hawaii raises questions similar to those put by Kurath regarding
these divergent features in American, British, Irish, and Scotch English. Was
"r-lessness" established in the speech of some or all of the British colonizers?
Was it a feature brought by some or all of the New England missionaries? To
what extent is the introduction of postvocalic /r/ in Hawaii to be credited to
"r-ful" American speech or to that of newcomers from Scotland? Were both
features possibly in competition throughout much of the history of English
in Hawaii? Questions like these are applicable to almost all of the differences
of segmentals in Keaukaha English and in Hawaii English generally.

Both segmentals and suprasegmentals are involved in a tendency of
syllables in Hawaii English "to have equal prominence in terms of loudness
and duration" (Vanderslice & Pierson 1967:157). The upgrading of stress
and the fronting of the vowel (before /n/ and /d/) in the second syllable of
words like *kitten* are examples of this aspect. Similar upgrading and fronting
in noninitial syllables occur in *Japanese* /jǽpæ̀nìyz/, *Helen* /hélìn/, *Islands*
/áylìnz/, *Mainland* /méynlìn/, *couldn't* /kúdìn/, *rugged* /rǝ́gìd/, *students*
/stúwdìns/, *river* /ríyvìr/, *sentence* /séntìns/, *husband* /hǝ́zbìn/, *even* /íyvìn/,
certain /sɨ́rtʰìn/, *chicken* /číkìn/, *wouldn't* /wúdìn/, *Boston* /bástìn/, *New*

England /nʊ íyŋlìn/, *Rhode Island* /ròwʔ áylìn/. Fronting also occurred in the initial of *Japan*, both /jǽpæ̀n/ and /jǽpæ̀n/, and of *traditional* /træ̀díšnìl/. As Vanderslice & Pierson note, this tendency to eliminate contrast between strong and weak stresses in syllables also has a leveling effect between content and function words (Vanderslice & Pierson 1967:157). The rhythm of a statement in Keaukaha English therefore contrasts with a mainland dialect somewhat as follows:

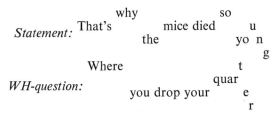

They take the cattle to the ship.

KE: ♪ ♪ ♪ ♪♪ ♪♪ ♪♪ ♩

Mainland: ♪ ♪. ♪ ♪♪ ♪♪ ♪♪ ♩

   Along with upgrading of stress in function words, there is a strong tendency to maintain back vowels in *to, you, for,* and the front vowel in *at,* and to keep the lower central quality of vowels in *of, from,* and *the.*
   In the realm of pitch, both range and intonation patterns are interesting. Vanderslice & Pierson noted that the characteristic range is generally wider than in other American dialects, and that frequent use is made of the higher pitch (158). One pitch pattern that seems to be special in Hawaii is called *scoop* by Vanderslice & Pierson. They extend Hockett's term to mean a rise in pitch, in or after an accented syllable, as part of a contour that then falls (160–161). Two of their examples show this.

                         why   so
        Statement: That's   mice died   u
                              the   yo n
                                                   g
                      Where   t
        WH-question: quar
                         you drop your   e
                                              r

Vanderslice & Pierson note that "a closely similar intonation is described by Jones (Daniel Jones, *The Pronunciation of English*, 4th edition, 1966: 159, 161–162) as used sometimes in southern England and especially in Wales" (161).
   An intonation pattern that sounds markedly different to mainland speakers is that described by Vanderslice & Pierson for general (yes-no) questions (162–163). It consists of general high pitch, initially and medially in the question, with a wide drop to low pitch either to or in the accented syllable, and then a terminal steadying or slight rise.

        going home
   You   n   (drop in the accented syllable;
             o   steadying terminal)
          w →
        need a general cata
   You   (drop to the accented syllable;
             log ↑   slight rise)

In Hawaii English this ordinary yes-no question posed in a declarative syntactic pattern seems to occur with a very high frequency.[5] Bolinger, speaking of American English (1957:11), guessed that "possibly half of the total of yes-no Qs are syntactically and morphemically unmarked." An approximation of the frequency of the interrogative intonation just described in Keaukaha English questions is much higher, totaling approximately 75 per cent of the total recorded yes-no questions. Therefore the frequency of this feature, which differentiates Hawaii English from some other American varieties, is felt by visitors to be distinctive though it is not a characteristic unique to Hawaiian English. During the 1969–1970 ETV season I heard two questions which I would transcribe as follows:

```
                                     to
                           to wear it
              Do you want
                                         morrow →
                           to
                    want
              Do you
                         see it ↑
```

These were in the contemporary British production of the *Forsyte Saga*.

My further observations regarding interrogative intonation are that in Keaukaha English there is not one distinctive pattern for yes-no and another for WH-questions, but that a pattern similar to the above is used for both types as in:

```
                          ing
              Is the thing go

                                 on →
and

                                  their
                  How over there

                             luaus ↑
```

Also at least another further pattern is used for both types of questions (Glissmeyer 1970:130–131; 228–230):

```
              Taught
                       someplace →

              Where you was
                           going tomorrow →
```

[5] Knowlton (1967:230) notes the use of interrogatives using the same order as declarative clauses as a feature in common between Hawaii English and Chinese Pidgin English.

This second type maintains a lower than ordinary pitch for most of the question, and drops to a still lower pitch shortly before the ending. A fairly long example of this pattern occurred with a tag:

If they put it in cast, don't heal, no
good, eh →

It is evident that Hawaii English is similar to other dialects of English in not distinguishing the two types of questions by intonation.

LEXICON

Reinecke-Tokimasa indicated in the 1930s that English in Hawaii included a very small number of borrowings from Cantonese, Japanese, and Portuguese, and a considerable number of borrowings from Hawaiian. According to Tsuzaki's recent statements, even with a decrease of the Hawaiian vocabulary over the past years, there is still a notable proportion of Hawaiian words in use among English speakers. A count made in 1938 of the Hawaiian words which Reinecke considered in frequent or very frequent use yields a total of 172. In 1967, Tsuzaki found among a sampling of 26 informants that elementary school children were familiar with 48 Hawaiian loanwords; secondary school students with 83; and adults with 109 (Reinecke & Tsuzaki 1967:81, 83, 90, 90–112). Based on a limited check with 50 students at the University of Hawaii in 1970, I estimate that there are between 75 and 100 Hawaiian borrowings in ordinary usage in Hawaii, not generally understood elsewhere. Some of these are *haole* "Caucasian," *pau* "finished," *mauka* "toward the mountains," *makai* "toward the sea," *pilikia* "trouble," *kuleana* "bailiwick," *wikiwiki* "quickly," *huhu* "angry," *make* "dead," *ulu* "breadfruit," *imu* "underground oven," *malihini* "newcomer," *kama aina* "person born to the land." I know of no study aimed at distinguishing borrowings generally in use in Hawaii and those restricted to some of the more divergent dialects popularly called "pidgin." It is natural to expect that, among each different language group, borrowings from the lexicon of the respective language will number more than among the population as a whole. Also, some borrowings in Hawaii have no doubt spread to other English dialects. Many mainlanders probably understand *aloha, hula, luau, lei, lanai, ukulele,* and perhaps *poi,* borrowed from Hawaiian. From Japanese, *tsunami* "tidal wave," *sashimi* "prepared fresh fish," and *-san* "Mr., Mrs." may have some distribution beyond Hawaii, but these and the combined lists from Hawaiian, along with *kaukau* "food" and *pake* "Chinese person" from Cantonese, play an integral part in everyday speech in Hawaii.

Among special interpretations of the English lexicon in Hawaii there is a phrase which is put to widespread use and marks Hawaii English. It is *the kind,* often written *da kine.* Apparent meanings are "the kind, that particular one, some, a sort of, and roughly that class." It is a useful general label for any definite or indefinite subject of reference. Examples of its occurrence in compound phrases follow in the next section in connection with double nominal and reverse nominal phrases.

SYNTAX

At the present time very little is in print that gives authentic evidence of the syntax of spoken English in Hawaii. In the *Memoirs* of Opukahaia one can find a few instances of purported speech in the early nineteenth century. But the editor lets it be known that even Opukahaia's writing has been altered, so that only "in general, his own language will be preserved" (*Memoirs* 1968:3). The "Examples of Makeshift and Dialectal English Used in the Hawaiian Islands" (in the 22-page Appendix of Reinecke's *Language and Dialect in Hawaii*) date from Opukahaia's time to the 1930s, but are taken partly from letters, newspaper reports, and other written material, while including short passages credited to the speech of a Chinese woman, a Portuguese girl, a Japanese boy, and Portuguese and Japanese adults.[6] In my description of Keaukaha English, at present available only on microfilm, is a 34-page transcription of adult conversations made in 1966. My study as a whole was based on more than three thousand clauses extracted from recorded conversations of twenty-three children (under 12 years of age) and nine adults (over 12 years), all of whom are of at least part Hawaiian ancestry. The aim was to report actual human speech, and, over a fourteen-month period in 1965–1966, recordings were made of ordinary exchanges in homes, in a car, at the beach, at a restaurant, or at small group get-togethers in a motel around Christmas time. In the tapes can be heard the continual bubbling up of laughter which Labov (1966:110) notes as one of the "channel cues" of casual style, as well as some of the spontaneous singing by both boys and girls. What is presented here relies on material in all three of these sources and upon the few published reports of syntactic features.

Two processes affecting predication in Hawaii English are deletion and permutation. Copula deletion is documented beginning with Opukahaia.

Who dis? (1968:16)
Hawaii gods! they wood . . . (17)

---

[6] Holt's work contains a small amount of purported local speech, probably from the 1930s through the 1950s. None of his examples contradict the material in this article.

Labov's forthcoming article presents approximately eighteen "pidgin" sentences and about 150 "Hawaiian Creole" sentences from tape recordings made in 1968 and 1970 with people of different ages from various locations in Hawaii, using the basic technique for participant-observation of peer groups summarized in "The Study of Language in Its Social Context," *Studium Generale*, 23 (1970): pp. 30–87.

When I at home ... but my thought no there ... then I very
happy. (33)
You fraid? (34)
I sorry ... God ready, Christ ready—all ready. (38)

Reinecke's examples are from the late 1920s (1969:218)

... money	all pau ("finished")
ikane ("friend")	pau
kaukau	pau
everything	pau

and from the early 30s of this century (1967:204).

kaukau	no good
lady	all same dog
I	too much happy
she	wild
I	no sick one day
I	too happy
kanaka ("Hawaiian man")	all same pake ("Chinese")

The following are instances from the 1960s.[7]

you	a newcomer	
you	a kamaaina	now
you	the right person	for this
he	sure a midget	
his mother	the coach	
it	the steam	
whoever made this	sure a ugly	
I	pau	
you	lucky	
you	better off	
you	righthanded	
Batman	weak	
she	sick	
it	flat	
it	easier	for you
this	mine	
that	out	
everything	just like how we eating	
the tire	flat	
the game	pau about 11 o'clock	
this kind car	better	

[7] Examples not otherwise credited are extracted from my research in Keaukaha.

we	still little	
they	very stricky	
they	clumsy	
they	very huge	
they	young	
they all	real friendly	
the feathers	just round	
you	on the wave	good
you	in the home of a full-blooded Hawaiian	
all you have to do	insert a quarter	
how	you,	brother?
what	your name?	
the lessons 'at they had	the same?	

This deletion results in the "copulaless equational clause" referred to by Tsuzaki (1971:330) and others. Robert A. Hall ascribes this structure in pidgins to intentional simplification (1966:86), but he recalls an advertisement in Australia in 1954 which began "You a woman?" As he states, such constructions are less infrequent in many dialects than we sometimes seem to think, for instance, in a sports broadcast, "Horton on third." The existence of this construction in questions in American English has also been noted by Bolinger in 1957 (65),

John	a lawyer?
an American	a traitor?

and in 1970 (355).

John	sick?

If one wishes to account for the fairly frequent occurrence of this deletion in Hawaii English, he needs to include the fact that the grammars of both Hawaiian and Chinese have this same kind of predication.[8] Here it should also be remarked that though copula deletion especially characterizes Keaukaha English, this system otherwise displays the same full variety of declarative (including active and passive constructions), interrogative, and imperative clause structures as do other English dialects.[9]

Subject deletion is possible in KE clauses with transitive, intransitive, and equational verb phrases in which the contextual meaning of the subject is *I*, *you, he, we, it.*

Took him up to the principal.
So then, then, go by the street there.

---

[8] Hawaiian: Judd & Pukui 1945:10, 24; Pukui & Elbert 1965:xxvi. Chinese: Kratochvil 1968:130; Rand 1969:14–19.

[9] See "Nuclear Clause Types in Keaukaha English" on pages 218–19.

Is too much money!
Is the capital.
To us is *pelehuu.* ("turkey")
Is nice, really nice.
When I saw that I say is so funny, different from our way of kaluing.
Could be that.
What time wanna leave and go pick down there?

Reinecke cited "Hurt" as a reply to "Doesn't it hurt?" (1934:128). In Opukahaia's "Hawaii god! they wood, burn" (1968:17) *they* would be the substitute. As to this deletion elsewhere, Bolinger has reported four different kinds of questions in which it is possible in current American English (1957:24, 30, 36–37, 38, 63):

> General yes-no question
> > Tired?
> > Like a taste?
> General yes-no question plus tag
> > Get there, will they?
> > Want it, did he?
> Yes-no question with implied assertion
> > Likes it?
> > Might break?
> Yes-no question with implied assertion plus tag
> > Wanted it, did he?
> > Couldn't wait, could you?

Speculation about the provenience of this feature in declarative as well as interrogative clauses in Hawaii English needs to take into account three possible influences. It is reported (Pukui & Elbert 1965:xx) that subject pronouns in Hawaiian are commonly omitted unless there is ambiguity. Chinese Pidgin English used predicates without subjects when the latter were implied by context (Knowlton 1967:230). In Japanese, too, the subject is an optional clause unit (Nagara 1969:164).

Object deletion, also occurring in Japanese (Nagara 1969:165), is represented in these examples from Keaukaha, which suggest *it* as a general substitute.

> I don't believe. ("it")
> I give you! ("I did give it to you!")
> Somebody else will bring. ("food")
> Well, you see somebody told me and I never believe. ("that")

This and the other types of deletion invite much more study, among all varieties of English, in Hawaii and throughout the world. Many dialects may not share the above examples, but some no doubt make use of a similarly small inventory of verbs (for example, *quote, think, consider, know, play*) with which a contextually unambiguous object may be deleted.

Permutation appears to function mostly, but not entirely, as a means of foregrounding or topicalizing, and the specific types of permutation sometimes coincide with those of dialects elsewhere, and sometimes do not. Speakers in different parts of the world say things like:

Object	Subject	Verb
Gloria, this one	I	already passed.
Eleven	we	do.
Hawaiian	I	don't even know.
Spanish	I	know a little.

and

Equation	Equational verb	Subject
Here	's	the cards.
There	is	goose.
Here	are	the people here, right here, outside here.
Over here	is	the melting pot.

The structural model for the second type is of course the same as for Opukahaia's expression "Poor boy am I" (1968:6) in the early nineteenth century, and for the Hawaiian woman's "Dumb are you!" which Reinecke heard one hundred or more years later (1969:197). The differences lie in the choice of a noun phrase or an adjective rather than a locative adverb in the "Equation" position.

Similarly, the following examples share syntactic symmetry as permutations of the constituents resulting from copula deletion.

Equation	Subject
Here	the sun.
Here	the earth.
Here	the moon.
Here	the ugly moon.
Here	a rabbit.
There	the people.
Right on this portion in here	the Niihau.
Favorite story	this.
Maybe not good	speak of the kind rocks.
Nice	that one.
Better for you	to lie down.

In contrast to the Equation-Equational Verb-Subject examples, in this case the choice of locative characterizes Hawaii English more than the choice of noun phrase or adjective. I imagine that before hearing KE I might have said, or not have been too surprised if someone else said, "Good, this kind" (Reinecke 1934:128) or "Favorite story, this" or "Better for you to lie down." It may be that the regular possibility in a given dialect of "Here's the sun" inhibits the acceptability of "Here the sun," and such a likelihood suggests that permutation takes precedence over copula deletion in such a dialect.

But in the Keaukaha dialect not only can permutation or copula deletion operate with the identical structure, but examples seem to present permutation with both copula and subject deletion.

Location	*Equation*
Over there	good.

Condition	*Equation*
If she was whole Hawaiian	better.

This view assumes initial *It*-Equational verb-Equation-Location and *It*-Equational verb-Equation-Condition.

The means of foregrounding or topicalizing in Hawaii English questions and subordinate structures include (a) initial positioning of the questioned element only, followed by the remainder of the clause,

> What I mean?
> Annette, where you went, in Honolulu?
> What he say then?
> How many she get?
> What kind word they use?
>
> What I'm talking about is the preparation. . . .
> What you call *laulau* it's a kind. . . .
> That's what I been eating.
> You know what *kahuna* means?

and (b) both initial positioning of the questioned element and transposition of the subject with the auxiliary or single verb.

> What does that mean?
> What's that for?
> What went I done with that, the picture?
>
> Know who's the lady?
> What should we do, we should have mix up the words. . . .
> . . . and you read, Rosina, which part do you like best.
> They don't have any watch so they don't know what time is it.
> You know Hilo High School where is it?

Knowlton mentioned the second type as a feature similar to Portuguese (1967:234), and took his examples from Reinecke-Tokimasa (1934:128):

> What means "irony"?
> Where was Gabriel she did not know.

In Keaukaha I heard type (a) in much more frequent use than type (b). It is also the only type in Opukahaia's *Memoirs* (1968:27, 34).

> How you spell?
> What our Savior mean?
> What he mean?

Laura Shun's study, in 1961, reveals only one example of type (b) in a total of 47 WH-questions. "Why don't you go work for him then?" (183–191) corresponds to the examples from Keaukaha in that the verbal element involved is either a form of *be* or an auxiliary, never a single transitive verb. It is possible that the comparative usage of these two types has changed in thirty years. This is another aspect for investigation.[10]

Additional research is extremely desirable to confirm the fact and to explore the extent of the topicalization being conjectured here. I found permutations not seeming to effect any obvious foregrounding as I conceive it.

Equational verb	Subject	Equation
Is	only Hawaiian	there

	Verb	Subject
...	come	this out the water.
... then	come	her.

The second type inverts subject and verb, but does not have the emphatic *here* as in other dialects with *come* and as in these instances from Keaukaha:

---

[10] I list here additional features which demand more extensive explanation than space in the text allows and which I believe are also becoming much less important in characterizing Hawaii English than they might have been even thirty-five years ago. Future research concerning them would be of definite interest.
   1. *for* in place of *to* with the infinitive (Reinecke–Tokimasa 1934:125; Reinecke 1968:216; Knowlton 1967:234)
   2. unusual use of *a*, *the*, and Ø preceding nouns (Reinecke–Tokimasa 1934:126; Knowlton 1967:235)
   3. *a* and *the* with an adjective to constitute a nominal phrase (Reinecke–Tokimasa 1934:55; Knowlton 1960:216; Knowlton 1967:235)
   4. noun + *side* as locative element (Knowlton 1967:230)
   5. noun + *time* as temporal element (Knowlton 1967:230)
   6. double negative (Knowlton 1967:235)

Direction	Verb	Subject
Here	come	another one.
Here	come	my mother.

Additional permutations that are divergent from many dialects, but which seem to have questionable topicalizing effect are these:

Time
> I ate *last night* the poi.
> I phoned *yesterday* Mitchell.

Location
> They have *at Punahou* the pool.

Co-action
> I was playing *with my cousin* baseball after school.

Direction
> Bernard, you have to *back* put em over here.

Here permutation of the elements labeled Time, Location, Co-action, and Direction to initial position would accomplish the most definite foregrounding. Perhaps these are examples of a step-move toward fronting from an original position after the object, this partially forward position indicating a partial degree of topicalizing.

A somewhat different kind of topicalization is evidenced in some of the structures I have called discontinuous appositives, which result from the duplication of a clause or phrase element. Fronting of the copied element constitutes the topicalizing.

Subject	Subject	Verb	Manner
The front, you know,	it	jumps	like that.

Subject	Subject	Equational verb	Equation
The taro leave ...	it	's	a foot deep.

Equation	Subject	Equational verb	Equation
Far	it	's	really far.

Object	Subject	Verb	Object
Eel	you	have to clean	it really good.
Rabbit	you	better not take	my rabbit.
Moray eel	you	can spear	it.

Subject	Object	Subject	Verb	Object
My mother um	four	she	had	four.

Here again partial fronting was also observed.

	Subject	Object	Verb	Object
Let	him	his	open	it.

These seem to differentiate Hawaii English from many varieties. Perhaps such constructions are one means forged by some speakers of languages like English and Spanish, which do not have a formalized topicalizing device such as *wa* in Japanese.

But some discontinuous appositives turn up in final position, or at least are not fronted in the clause.

	Subject	Equational verb	Equation	Subject
	That	's	your house	this?
	That	's	Hawaiian name	Kelelani.
But	the runner	was	slow	runner, the one.
Ooh	he	's	some tall	Mr. Crowley

Equational verb	Subject	Equation	Subject
Are	they	contented	the people?

Subject	Verb	Ditransitive	Object	Verb
These haoles	ask	me	"Nik, you kanaka?"	ask.

Subject	Verb (Direction)	Subject
This guy from the Mainland	came over	professor ...
He	went	this boy

Subject	Verb	Object Modifier	Noun	Location	Modifier	Location
He	has	some	hair	on he	a little bit	right up here.

...	Verb	Object	Preposition	Object	Preposition	...
and	put	it	on	your weight	on	the left side of the board.

...	Preposition	Prep. object	Prep. object
What went I done	with	that	the picture?

These are more similar than the first set to other American dialects I am acquainted with. They also recall some constructions said to occur in Mexican Spanish (Brend 1968:72).

... ya después entonces pues nos casi juntaron, las dos familias.
(... then, after, then well, we almost joined—the two families.)

... porque ya se puede mover para todos lados, ella con sus muletas.
(... because now she can move all over—she with her crutches.)

Both English and Spanish examples seem to serve, as the previous discontinuous appositives also do, a disambiguating end. Beyond the intrinsic interest of discontinuous appositives in general, the feature is worth attention because a mainland speaker aware of the first set of these variations will avoid misinterpretation of an expression like "Cheat now, no cheatin!" This is not a contradiction, but merely a discontinuous appositive, and the following is a single imperative: "Try again, let me try again!" As a matter of fact, perhaps when more data are in from many other studies it may be found that discontinuous appositives are regularly used by a good many of us. I have heard myself explaining how to put waffle batter in the iron in this way: "In the middle, you put one spoon in the middle."

The remainder of this essay considers verb, noun, and prepositional phrases. Tsuzaki has presented an analysis of a verbal phrase in Hawaii English which resembles other creoles (1971:332–33). The sequence of the component categories and their markers follows the order here.

1. Negative (*no/never*)
2. Auxiliary (*can/might/must*/etc.)
3. Past tense (*been/went/had*)
4. Future or contingent mood (*go*)
5. Progressive aspect (*stay*)
6. Habitual aspect (∅[= unmarked stem])
7. Verb stem, nucleus, or base

Tsuzaki's comment at this point (333) is as follows:

All of the prestem particles do not seem to occur within a single verbal construction, suggesting cooccurrence restrictions. For example, (1) (*never*) and (3) are usually mutually exclusive, since *never*, which is usually used as a past negator, indicates past time. Similarly categories (2) and (3), (4), and (5) are usually mutually exclusive. The use of up to three preposed particles in any given verbal construction is the rule (e.g., *I no eat*, "I don't eat"; *I no go eat*, "I am not going to eat/I will not eat"; *I no go stay eat*, "I am not going to be eating/I will not be eating"). Four particles are possible, but unusual (e.g., *I no been go stay eat*, "I wasn't/hadn't been eating"); five seem to be impossible (i.e., sentences of the type **I no could been go stay eat* are not grammatical sequences).

In a relevant footnote (336) he states:

The data presented here are taken from an ongoing study of the verbal system of HE begun in the summer of 1968. Since the study has not been completed as of this writing, the results should be treated cautiously.

My present view of KE is that single verbs most regularly constitute verb phrases. Uninflected bases and *-ing* forms are used for past, present, and future time. Those inflected for past seem to be used unambiguously. An abstract sequence for components in Keaukaha English active verb phrases, when they are used, would be as follows.

1. Negative (*no/never/not*)
2. Auxiliary ∼ Past tense ∼ Future ∼ Progressive
3. Verb stem, nucleus or base

Examples of Auxiliaries: *can, could, might, must, have to, gotta, better, will, would, shall, should, do, does, did*
Examples of Past tense: *been, went, have, has, have been, use to*
Examples of Future: *going, are gonna*
Examples of Progressive: *am, is, was, were*

In all instances except with *have, been, have been* and the Progressive, the verb stem is uninflected. *Have* takes a past participle, and with the other special cases *-ing* forms occur.

The sole exception in my recorded research to this sequence is *should have mix* (see page 207). I did not observe usage similar to that noted in Reinecke's work in the 1930s:

been come (1969:204, 215, 216)
no go marry (214)
been go stay tell (214)

Further research will clarify the picture, but it appears that in KE the verb phrase is reduced as to components beyond that described by Tsuzaki, while being generally elaborated beyond his possible fillers for each of the particle classes.[11]

Usage regarding the KE fillers for Negative can be outlined in this way.

$\left.\begin{array}{l} \text{no} \\ \text{never} \end{array}\right\}$ occur in the environment Subject ____ (Aux) Verb

not occurs in the environments Subject ____ (Aux) Verb

Subject ____ Equation
Aux $^{\text{1st or only}}$ ____ Verb ^{remaining}
Adverb ____ Equation

n't occurs in the environments Aux $^{\text{1st or only}}$ ____ Verb ^{remaining}

Equ. verb ____ Equation
Aux ____ Adverb Verb ^{remaining}

Examples:

I no like poi.
I no can place that name.
They never see the other part.
They never did us like that.
I not make em button.
. . . they not gonna learn anything about it.
No, this not VISTA

---

[11] According to Labov's research, a verb phrase like *wen go hug* is in free variation with one like *wen walk* (forthcoming: 47–48).

... she's not taking this English study.
Otherwise I cannot be there.
... they're just not a hit. ...
You shouldn't go in there.
It ain't a fiberboard.
I can't always tell too good.

To summarize, there is

1. over-all identically restricted distribution of *no* and *never*,
2. overlapping distribution of *not* with *no* and *never* (/Subject _____ (Aux) Verb),
3. overlapping distribution of *not* with *n't* (/First or only Aux _____ Remaining Verb Phrase),
4. distinctive distribution of *not* (/Subject _____ Equation; Adverb _____ Equation), and
5. distinctive distribution of *n't* (/Equational verb _____ Equation; Aux _____ Adverb Remaining Verb Phrase).

Historical evidence shows *no* in Opukahaia's verb phrases (*Memoirs*, 1968:17, 38), and *no* along with two instances of *n't* (used with *did* and *do*) in Hawaiian speech of the 1930s (Reinecke 1969:204, 214–17). In addition, Holt represents *never* in Portuguese Hawaiian English of the 1950s (1965:36).[12]

Among noun phrases there is a type I am calling double nominal. In such phrases the head may be a determiner noun phrase, and the modifier itself may be a determiner or possessive noun phrase. In these examples the modifier precedes the head; that is, the first member is the more specific, the second one the more general. Keaukaha English does not differ from other dialects in some examples:

you	folks
you	guys
haole type	music

In some other varieties, the alternative or equivalent of the third example might be "haole type of music." The preference in Hawaii for the first structure is shown by such other instances as these:

some	the basics
two case	coke
only about sixty pound	poi
south end	Italy

[12] Labov analyzes *never* as "simply the preterit negative" (forthcoming: 29). "The past is always signalled by *never* when the negative is present" (51).

one	the kind
the kind	tree
the kind	rocks
this kind	car
some kind	impression
another kind	alcohol
the music kind	school teachers

KE innovations on this model also include

Kali sister	(the sister identified as Kali),
the kind left field	(that particular left field player),
my mother dem	(that group of people identified by my mother), and
Lee folks	(those people identified by Lee).

Another type of noun phrase in which the subcomponents have been rather freely enlarged beyond the possibilities which exist in most other American English dialects is the "reverse nominal phrase." Here the head precedes the modifier. The second member is the one which is more specific, the first one being more general.

they	all
somebody	else
my sister	Lily
the Club	Kontiki
Mr.	Kauhi
a kind	made in ti leaf

These of course could be found elsewhere among English speakers. There is a further variety of this kind similar to the second subset in double nominal phrases, in that Keaukaha examples would be matched elsewhere with a linking *of*.

copy   your

And again still additional innovations appear.

a Hawaiian every taste	(a Hawaiian in every way)
em my wife here	(someone, particularly my wife here)
em button	(something, namely button)
em this thing	(something, namely this thing)

Keaukaha English possessive noun phrases manifest similar expansive or improvisational tendencies, going beyond examples of this kind

my		auntie
my	little	girl
their	own	club
Pearlie's		godfather

to others like these:

my	both parents
mine's	one
my mother's	one
Lee folks	house
my sister	friends
Gloria Glissmeyer	name
we	kalu

Prepositions are likely to have divergent use across dialects, and within a dialect or even an idiolect there may be some variant choices of prepositions for given situations and meanings. (He's on third base; he's at third base. Ask her/his whereabouts; ask of her/his whereabouts. The aim was to report actual human speech; the aim was to report upon actual human speech.) So in Keaukaha English it is in the expected nature of things linguistic to find "I want everybody to meet together for our house" or "I wanna stand on a pole" where I might have said "I want everybody to meet together at our house" or "I wanna stand by the pole." Further, if one remembers the examples of double nominal and reverse nominal phrases in which *of* is an alternate in other dialects, there seems to be consistency as to the optional nonuse of certain prepositions in additional ways. I list them as follows.

a. *for*   I want to see you great while (Opukahaia 1968:79).

b. *as*   Lady all same dog (Reinecke 1969:204).

c. at_1 My husband house kaukau no good (Reinecke 1969:204).
Kalapana a boy ran across the street.
Kendall, stop playing with it other people's place.
Makaha there, the waves aren't consistent.

d. at_2 She came home 8 o'clock.

e. at_3 I didn't look it exactly.

f. to_1 By'm-bye my husband he go Honolulu (Reinecke 1969:204).
. . . he speak for me come Honolulu (Reinecke 1969:204).
So queek I make da sireen and go da scene. . . . (Reinecke 1969: 217).
Whats da matter dis Japanee more betta take heem poleece stations (Reinecke 1969:217).
When I was fourteen I came Honolulu. (spoken in Hilo)

g. to_2 We lost Cardinals.

h. *to₃*   I going fifth grade.
           She go Kam School.
           Johnna and Bryan em go same school.
           She go a different school.
           I go different.
           I go a Haili church.
i. *in*   My auntie she's living Kona, my grandmother, but now she's
           living Honolulu.
           I went stay Honolulu more long than you.
j. *with*   My auntie she's living Kona, my grandmother. . . .

As in the case of both types of nominal phrases, there are one or two models
in other dialects for corresponding usage.

a. I've wanted to see you these many months.
d. That moment I knew what to do.

And of course *home, here, there, yesterday, today, tomorrow, then, now,* and
thus are references to location, time, and manner which would otherwise be
specifically realized in prepositional phrases. For a given dialect, the
particular constellation of these case-like elements involving prepositions no
doubt presents one means of identifying that dialect and could serve to
differentiate it from others.

CODA

Having considered this much information, we have arrived at a perspective
possibly allowing some observations and speculation.

Hawaii English is unique among American English dialects in its history of
contact with non-Indo-European as well as European languages. With a time
span of little more than 150 years, it ranks among the younger, or more
recent, of the world's English dialect systems. The material gathered here
might be taken as support for Tsuzaki's view (1971) that there are "coexistent" systems in Hawaii English. At least one can say that in some
phonetic processes and in nuclear clause types, copula deletion, subject
deletion, object deletion, permutations to Object-Subject-Verb, Equation-
Equational Verb-Subject, perhaps Equation-Subject, Direction-Verb-Subject,
some discontinuous appositives, verb phrases, negative, as well as double
nominal, reverse nominal, possessive, and prepositional phrases, Keaukaha
English has more in common than not when it is compared with other
dialects, and that for most of the divergent features there are minimal
counterparts elsewhere. Tsuzaki's hypothesis of four coexistent systems will
probably prove difficult to confirm because many people in Hawaii are so
linguistically versatile as to be able to use features of Hawaiian Pidgin
English, Hawaiian Creole English, Non-Standard Hawaiian English, and

Standard Hawaiian English (Tsuzaki's terms). At this time Tsuzaki's comment is that "there seem to be no convincing examples of the component systems occurring in their pure forms, or as completely discrete systems occurring independently of one another" (1971:334). As he indicates (1971:336), all of Hawaii English would have to be submitted to a fairly complete analysis before the question could be resolved. A reasonable statement is still that Hawaii English manifests "systems which in part include but which are also more manifold than those of a monodialectal speaker from the United States mainland" (Glissmeyer 1967:146).

Hawaii English typifies quite impressively the hospitable characteristic of English in relation to innovations. Robert A. Hall pointed this quality out in connection with derivational patterns and the extensive morphophonemic alternation that has developed from the time of borrowings from Old French. As he says,

our derivational pattern is richer, but far more irregular, than that of Old English. Probably the very presence of such a large amount of morphophonemic variation makes us, as speakers of present-day English, more ready to accept aberrant morphological characteristics in new loan words, and hence more open to all kinds of borrowings, than are speakers of languages with a greater degree of regularity in their derivational patterns such as Italian and Spanish (1964:337).

But it seems that both the richness and the irregularity of the one grammatical domain exist also in other realms.

Possibilities for research in Hawaii call for response in a comprehensive series of descriptions, entailing lifetimes of attention on the part of many students. If living speech is the object of knowledge, it will be desirable and necessary for work to be done by native speakers as well as non-native. In order for the term *Hawaii English* to be used with any fair amount of reliability we will need to know something at least about the speech of each of the major linguistic groups; that is, of those whose other-language backgrounds are Hawaiian, Cantonese, Portuguese, Japanese, Ilocano, and Visayan. Then, if similar information were available from most of the multilingual communities throughout the United States, we would have in view a sufficient body of information so that we could speak with some understanding of "creole" and "dialect" in the country. At present it seems to me premature to generalize very definitely in a comprehensive way regarding Keaukaha English or Hawaii English and other varieties. As Roger W. Shuy states in the introduction to the Urban Language Series (1968:v), "historically, linguists have formulated theory from individual rather than group performance. They have had to generalize about what constitutes 'standard' or 'nonstandard' from intuitive judgments or from very limited data." If some such directions and dimensions of research could become actuality, even more might be accomplished than establishing solid ground for the use of the terms *Keaukaha English*, *Hawaii English*, or *standard English* and the like. Extended and comprehensive studies in a situation with the linguistic multiplicity of Hawaii should add immeasurably to our understanding of language variation throughout the world. Hawaii invites large scale research because Japanese, Chinese, some of the Philippine languages, and possibly Hawaiian, in addition to English, are now to be observed in the actual processes of change.

Perhaps such research may also get closer to an answer about the theory, as stated by DeCamp, suggesting a possible relationship between English in Hawaii and Sabir (the remarkable lingua franca of the Mediterranean which lasted from the Crusades until the twentieth century).

It is very possible that a predominantly Portuguese version of Sabir (or a Portuguese relexification of it) was indeed that pidgin which in the sixteenth century was carried to the Far East, where it developed into the Portuguese and so-called Spanish creoles and perhaps also pidgin English, and was carried to West Africa, where its creole descendant is still spoken on Cape Verde and other islands, and thence to the New World, where it formed the basis not only of Papiamento but also of the English, French, and Dutch creoles (DeCamp 1971:23).

At present, of course, the theory remains a question for research.

Nuclear clause types in Keaukaha English

Declarative Types			
Active Type Al:	Subj^{actor}	Trans VP	Object
	They	*haul*	*sheep, cattle and honey*
Ala:	Subj^{actor}	Trans VP	Ditransitive	Object
	They	*present*	*me*	*lei*
Alb:	Subj^{actor}	Trans VP	Object	Attributive
	You	*call*	*it*	*sea urchins*
A2:	Subj^{actor}	Intrans VP		
	I	*'m going*		
A3:	Subj^{item}	Equational VP	Equation	
	Mehameha	*is*	*"lonely"*	

Passive: (A1 T^r 1) =	Object	PassAux	VP^{-en}	(*by* Subj)	. . .
	We	*are*	*known*	. . .
(Ala₁ T^r 2) =	Object	PassAux	VP^{-en}	(*to* Ditr)	(*by* Subj) . . .
	It	*was*	*given*	*to her*
(Ala₂ T^r 3) =	Ditr	PassAux	VP^{-en}	Object	(*by* Subj) . . .
	I	*was*	*told*	*it*
(Alb T^r 4) =	Object	PassAux	VP^{-en}	Attributive	. . .
	He	*was*	*named*	*king*

Expletive: (A2 T^r 5) =	*There*	Intrans VP	Subj	. . .
	There	*'ll come*	*a time*	. . .
(A3 T^r 6) =	*There*	Equ VP	Subj	. . .
	There	*were*	*lots of brothers*	. . .
(Passive A1 T^r 7) =	*There*	Pass VP	Pass Subj	. . .
	There	*was conducted*	*a school*	*over there.*

Interrogative Types

$QConf_1$: (A1, A2, A3, A3^{deletion}) = Declarative + Q Intonation
Oh, my baby, Grandma take your food?
They pau?

$QConf_2$: (A1, A2, A3, A3^{deletion}) = Declarative   Tag$^{eh, no...}$
That's a steep pali,   yeah?

$QConf_3$: (A1, A1a, A2, A3 T^r 8) = *be*
Aux   Subject   ...
do
Is   the thing   going on?

$QInfo_{1a}$: (A1, A2 T^r 9) = QSubj   Predicate
Who   get money?

$QInfo_{1b}$: (A1, A1b, A2, A3, = Q(Object, Attributive, Location,   (clause residue)
A3^{deletion} T^r 9)   Manner, Time, Duration,
Cause, Equation)

What	*you got?*
What	*you call this?*
Where	*you was going to-morrow?*
How long	*you been in the Islands now?*
Where	*the icebox?*

$QInfo_{1c}$: (A3, Expl^{A3} T^r 10) = Q Equ   Subj^{item}
Equ VP

Q Expl Subj		*there*
What	*is*	*that?*
How much kings	*are*	*there?*

$QInfo_2$: (A1, A1b, A2 T^r 11) = Q(Obj, Attr,   *do*   Subj   V   Pred$^{-Q'ed\ item}$
Loc, Man,
T)

What	*does*	*that*	*mean?*	
What time	*did*	*you*	*go*	*over there?*
How	*do*	*you*	*like*	*that?*

Imperative Types

$Imper_1$: (A1, A1a, A2, A3) = (*You*)   V^{infinitive} ...
You   *listen*   *to Neki*
Tell   *me what beach*

$Imper_2$: (A1, A2 T^{r}12) = (*You*)   *let*   Declarative$^{Subj-Obj\ pronoun}$
You   *let*   *her read that*
Let   *her rest*

REFERENCES

BOLINGER, D. L. 1957. *Interrogative Structures of American English. Publication of the American Dialect Society*, No. 28. University of Alabama Press.
_____. 1970. "The Imperative in English." *To Honor Roman Jakobson*. The Hague: Mouton.

BREND, RUTH. 1968. *A Tagmemic Analysis of Mexican Spanish Clauses*. The Hague: Mouton.

CHUN, ELINOR Y. L. 1935. "A Study of the Use of Sentences by the Bilingual Children of Chinese Ancestry in Honolulu." Unpub. M.A. thesis, University of Hawaii.

COSTA, ROBERT. 1951. "Beginning Studies in Linguistic Geography in Hawaii." Unpub. M.A. thesis, University of Hawaii.

DECAMP, DAVID. 1971. "Introduction: The Study of Pidgin and Creole Languages," *Pidginization & Creolization of Languages*. Cambridge: Cambridge University Press.

FUCHS, LAURENCE H. 1961. *Hawaii Pono (A Social History)*. New York: Harcourt Brace Jovanovich, Inc.

GLISSMEYER, GLORIA. 1967. "In-progress Analysis of English Idiolects, Keaukaha, Hilo, Hawaii." *Proceedings of Tenth International Congress of Linguists, Bucharest*, Vol. II, 143–50.

———. 1970. "A Tagmemic Analysis of Hawaii English Clauses." Unpub. Ph.D. dissertation, University of Hawaii.

HALL, ROBERT A., JR. 1964. *Introductory Linguistics*. Philadelphia: Chilton Books.

———. 1966. *Pidgin and Creole Languages*. Ithaca, N.Y.: Cornell University Press.

HAYES, ROBERT W. 1958. "A Phonological Study of the English Speech of Selected Japanese Speakers in Hawaii." Unpub. M.A. thesis, University of Hawaii.

HOLT, JOHN DOMINIS. 1965. *Today Ees Sad-dy Night and Other Stories*. Honolulu: Star-Bulletin Printing Company.

JUDD, H. P., MARY K. PUKUI, AND J. F. G. STOKES. 1945. *Introduction to the Hawaiian Language*. Honolulu: Tongg Publishing Company.

KINDIG, MAITA M. 1960. "A Phonological Study of the English Speech of Selected Speakers of Puerto Rican Spanish in Honolulu." Unpub. M.A. thesis, University of Hawaii.

KNOWLTON, E. C., JR. 1960. "Portuguese in Hawaii," *Kentucky Foreign Language Quarterly*, 7:212–18.

———. 1967. *Pidgin English and Portuguese. Proceedings of the Symposium on Historical, Archaeological, and Linguistic Studies on Southern China, S.E. Asia and the Hong Kong Region*. Hong Kong University Press.

KRATOCHVIL, PAUL. 1968. *The Chinese Language Today*. London: Hutchinson University Library.

KURATH, HANS. 1968. "The Investigation of Urban Speech," *Publications of the American Dialect Society*, 49:1–7.

———. 1964a. "British Sources of Selected Features of American Pronunciation: Problems and Methods," in *Readings in American Dialectology*. New York. Appleton-Century-Crofts, 1971.

———. 1964b. "Interrelation between Regional and Social Dialects," in *Readings in American Dialectology*. New York. Appleton-Century-Crofts, 1971.

KUYKENDALL, RALPH S. AND A. GROVE DAY. 1948. *Hawaii: A History*. New York: Prentice-Hall, Inc.

LABOV, WILLIAM. 1966. *The Social Stratification of English in New York City*. Washington, D.C.: Center for Applied Linguistics.

———. 1964. "Stages in the Acquisition of Standard English," in *Readings in American Dialectology*. New York: Appleton-Century-Crofts, 1971.

──────. Forthcoming (1971 MS). On the Adequacy of Natural Languages: I. The Development of Tense. (Expanded version of paper given at the Symposium on Language and Change, annual meeting LSA, December 1970).

LARRY, ETTA CYNTHIA. 1942. "A Study of the Sounds of the English Language As Spoken by Five Racial Groups in the Hawaiian Islands." Unpub. Ph.D. dissertation, Columbia University.

LIND, ANDREW W. 1967. *Hawaii's People*, 3rd edition. Honolulu: University of Hawaii Press.

McDAVID, RAVEN I., JR. 1946. "Dialect Geography and Social Science Problems," in *Readings in American Dialectology*. New York: Appleton-Century-Crofts, 1971.

NAGARA, SUSUMU. 1969. "A Bilingual Description of Some Linguistic Features of Pidgin English Used by Japanese Immigrants on the Plantations of Hawaii: A Case Study in Bilingualism." Unpub. Ph.D. dissertation, University of Wisconsin.

NORMAN, ARTHUR M. Z. 1956. "A Southeast Texas Dialect Study," in *Readings in American Dialectology*. New York: Appleton-Century-Crofts, 1971.

OBOOKIAH, HENRY. 1968. *Memoirs*, ed., Edwin Dwight. Honolulu Woman's Board of Missions for the Pacific Islands, Hawaii Conference, United Church of Christ.

ODO, CAROL. 1971 "Variation in Hawaiian English: Underlying R.," *Working Papers in Linguistics*, Department of Linguistics, University of Hawaii, **III** ii.

PEDERSON, LEE A. 1964. "Some Structural Differences in the Speech of Chicago Negroes," in *Readings in American Dialectology*. New York: Appleton-Century-Crofts, 1971.

PUKUI, MARY KAWENA AND SAMUEL H. ELBERT. 1965. *Hawaiian-English Dictionary*, 3rd edition. Honolulu: University of Hawaii Press.

RAND, EARL. 1969. *The Syntax of Mandarin Interrogatives*. Berkeley: University of California Press.

REED, CARROLL E. 1961a. "The Pronunciation of English in the Pacific Northwest," in *Readings in American Dialectology*. New York: Appleton-Century-Crofts, 1971.

──────. 1961b. "Double Dialect Geography," in *Readings in American Dialectology*. New York: Appleton-Century-Crofts, 1971.

REINECKE, JOHN E. 1969. *Language and Dialect in Hawaii*, ed. Stanley M. Tsuzaki. Honolulu: University Press of Hawaii.

──────, AND AIKO TOKIMASA. 1934. "The English Dialect of Hawaii," *American Speech* **IX** 48–58, 122–31.

──────, AND STANLEY M. TSUZAKI. 1967. "Hawaiian Loanwords in Hawaiian English of the '30s," *Oceanic Linguistics* **6**:80–115.

SAWYER, JANET B. 1964. "Social Aspects of Bilingualism in San Antonio, Texas," reprinted in this volume, pp. 226–33.

SHUN, LAURA L. 1961. "A Study of Selected Bilingual Speakers of English in the Hawaiian Islands." Unpub. M.A. thesis, University of Hawaii.

SHUY, ROGER W., WALTER A. WOLFRAM, AND WILLIAM K. RILEY. 1968. *Field Techniques in an Urban Language Study*. Washington, D.C.: Center for Applied Linguistics.

SUGGS, ROBERT C. 1960. *The Island Civilizations of Polynesia*. New York: Mentor Books.

THOMAS, C. K. 1961. "The Phonology of New England English," in *Readings in American Dialectology*. New York: Appleton-Century-Crofts, 1971.

TSUZAKI, STANLEY M. 1967a. "Hawaiian English: A Note on Grammatical Categories," *Pacific Speech*, **2**:7–12.

———. 1967b. *Common Hawaiian Loanwords in English*. Hilo Language Development Project.

———. 1968. "Common Hawaiian Words and Phrases Used in English," *Journal of English Linguistics*, **2**:78–85. Bellingham, Wash.

———. 1971. "Coexistent Systems in Language Variation: The Case of Hawaiian English," in *Pidginization and Creolization of Languages*. Cambridge: Cambridge University Press.

———, AND S. H. ELBERT. 1968. "Hawaiian Loanwords in English." *General Linguistics*, **9**:22–40.

———, AND JOHN E. REINECKE. 1966. *English in Hawaii: An Annotated Bibliography*. *Oceanic Linguistics Special Publication No. 1*. Honolulu, Pacific and Asian Linguistics Institute.

VANDERSLICE, RALPH AND LAURA SHUN PIERSON. 1967. "Prosodic Features of Hawaiian English," *The Quarterly Journal of Speech*, **53**:156–66.

WISE, CLAUDE M. AND WESLEY D. HERVEY. 1952. "The Evolution of Hawaiian Orthography," *The Quarterly Journal of Speech*, **38**:311–25.

STUDY QUESTIONS

1. The following story was written by a seventh-grade schoolgirl. What aspects of its language distinguish it from other dialects of English? Use Glissmeyer's analysis to help clarify those traits that might not be understood by someone with no experience of Hawaiian English.

> Once upon a time there lived two brothers, who lived near the river. Every day they would go for a walk.
>
> One day they took a walk, and saw three beautiful girls.
>
> They went home and sported up themselfs. John was very silly in his work. He was dressing when his brother said, "What I tell little, tell plenty." John said, "OK." They went to the girls' house. John had a girl too.
>
> When they reached there. She welcomed them in. She said, "Please seat down." The two brothers said, "Thank you." They sat down. Jack said, "Ah! I forgot to feed my little chicken." "Your little chicken! you get thousands of chickens." The youngest [girl] said, "Gee! rich men."
>
> Then Jack said, "Ah! I forgot to feed my little cow." "Your little cow! you get thousands of cows." Then the same girl said, "Gee! I'll marry him then."
>
> Jack was glad and didn't say anything. Then Jack just happened to scratch where the fly has flown.
>
> Then the same girl said, "What you get?" "Ah! only one little sore." "One little sore! You get thousands of sores."
>
> "Ah! I no go marry you then."
>
> Jack was angry and went off the house.
>
> When he saw John he said, "What for you been go stay tell that?"

John said, "Well you said when you tell little tell plenty. So I been go stay tell what you said."[a]

2. What resemblances do you see between the following analysis of problems of language choice faced by speakers in Hawaii and the choices faced by other speakers of "nonstandard" dialects:

When a non-Caucasian in Hawaii refuses to continue talking the substandard dialect of English to his classmates during recess but instead practices what he has learned of standard English in class by addressing his peers in that dialect, he may be called contemptuously a "yellow Haole." This gives rise to feelings of guilt, impedes the learning of standard English by non-Haole children, and just about guarantees the continuation of substandard English in Hawaii, with all its emotional identifications with everything that is "home" in the still diverse non-Haole cultures. There are three different paths that a non-Haole may take in response to the constant insistence by Haoles in Hawaii that standard English is better than substandard English. Of these three paths, the last listed is the more interesting than the other two: (1) resist the prodding of Haole educators, maintain a sullen silence in class, and try to avoid speaking at all unless it is possible to speak in the substandard dialect of English with other non-Haole speakers; (2) yield to the prodding of Haole educators, and thereby learn to switch from substandard to standard English by refusing to say anything in the substandard dialect that was the only dialect spoken before going to school; (3) speak the standard English with Haole friends and the substandard with non-Haole friends."[b]

3. In the fall of 1931, Mrs. Thalia Massie was allegedly raped by a gang of Hawaiians in Honolulu. In the subsequent trial, the accused men were not convicted but, in the days that followed, one of them, Joseph Kahahawai, was murdered. For this second crime, Mrs. Massie's mother, her husband, and two sailors were found guilty of manslaughter and were given the mandatory ten-year sentence to be served at hard labor. Under the pressure of political and journalistic outrage from the mainland, the territorial governor commuted the sentences to one hour, which the four convicts served while chatting with their attorney, Clarence Darrow, and newspaper men in the Governor's office.[c]

In the course of these dramatic events, the police obtained a sworn statement from Philip Kemp concerning the alleged rape. Examine the following selection from this statement for features of "Hawaiian English" as described by Glissmeyer; give particular attention to negation, structures of topicalization, and elements of the verb phrase.

---

[a] Quoted by John E. Reinecke, *Language and Dialect in Hawaii: A Sociolinguistic History to 1935* (Honolulu, 1969), p. 214. Used by permission of the University Press of Hawaii © 1969.

[b] C. F. and F. M. Voegelin, "Hawaiian Pidgin and Mother Tongue," *Anthropological Linguistics*, **6**,vii(1964):27–28.

[c] Further details concerning these events may be found in Theon Wright's, *Rape in Paradise* (New York, 1966) and in Peter Van Slingerland's *Something Terrible Has Happened* (New York, 1966).

1   When we came back to town we went up to the joint in a taxi. When we
2   were inside the taxi, he said he want make a trip to the states. He said
3   he want me go with him to the states. I told him I have no money to go up
4   there and he said he pay my way. I told him "All right" and we went
5   up the joint—that's the time I saw him get the money from the wahine up
6   there. When ———— got the money, the wahine she said "Well, baby,
7   you going get out of this town and out of this trouble." ———— he said
8   "yes." We came outside the joint and ———— showed me the $72. I
9   counted the money and said "No nuf for us to go." He said "That's
10 all right—I get some money home and can get some more from the
11 wahine on the 16th." We came back to town in the taxi and he dropped
12 me off at Bethel Street and he tell me wait there. He went away and came
13 back walking and that is the time he gave me $6.00 and told me "You
14 can go show." I went in H. Afong store to buy one silk shirt, $5.00—
15 one dollar left. I went to the room, changed clothes, came to town and
16 went to the show.
17   The next day I meet him behind Hawaii Theatre where he was supposed
18 to meet me. I meet him there and was talking inside there and he gave
19 me $1.00. I told him when he gave me the $1.00 to let us go to Empire
20 Grill on Bethel Street. He no want to go. In the afternoon about 2 o'clock,
21 he came pick me up and we went up to Joe Hoke's place. We parked the
22 car there and I saw a fellow walk out. ———— he got out of the car and
23 went to meet the fellow in front of the house. The fellow who came to
24 meet ———— had something wrapped in a piece of paper. When ————
25 got in the car, I saw one gun. I looked at it and ———— said, "Don't show
26 it too much, somebody might spot it." When we came back to town, he
27 tell me we go get some shot. I tell him go police station and ask for
28 paper and he tell me he no want go there. Afterward he said we go E. O.
29 Hall. He went E. O. Hall and he showed them a fountain pen gun and
30 they give us one blanket shot. We went out Ala Moana and he tell me I
31 shoot and I shoot myself and gun was all right. We went back to store but
32 store was closed. Then we went up to ————'s house that night and
33 sleep out there. He said, "All right, sleep inside this room," and I said,
34 "All right." He locked the door from the outside. I looked at the win-
35 dow in case there was anything wrong I would jump through the window.
36   Next day, we came back in town and he said, "Let's go in town and
37 eat," but we did not go in town—we went to Barbecue and eat. Afterward,
38 we came in town to Hall & Son for one box real shot—fifty in a box at
39 $1.75. We went to Ala Moana when he got the shot. He signed a paper
40 in Hall & Son. We tried the gun at Ala Moana again. I fired one shot
41 over there and I told him, "All right." We went up his house and he
42 fired two shots over there. Then we cleaned the sister's car which took
43 about two hours. Afterward we came back in town. I asked him why he
44 need the gun and he tell me "If you know any Navy officer or sailor try
45 make trouble for me, I let him have it." A couple of days after, we hear
46 Kahahawai get killed. When Kahahawai got killed by the haoles, I was
47 with ———— up his house on Olu Street. When we hear Kahahawai was
48 killed, I got worried because I go around with ———— and I tell him I
49 don't want go with him. ———— was nervous. I grabbed the gun which

50   was on the table and I tell him, "I feel like shooting you," and he tell me
51   "Please don't—you know well we going shove off and you know well
52   only three of us over here now—Shorty, the Filipino-Hawaiian, and
53   myself." He said if I report him, only three of them get the blame because
54   "Bull" he went away already, and I tell him it is none of my business,
55   but I feel like let him have it because I was nervous too. I take off one
56   shot from the gun and one shot was on the table. I picked them up and
57   shoved off. I came in town. He ring me up again at Empire Grill and when
58   he ring me up and I said, "What you want," he said "Please come up,
59   I want see you." I went up there and he asked me if I report and I said,
60   "No I no report." He asked me sleep out there and I said I no want sleep
61   out there. When I left there, he tell me no report on him; I tell him all
62   right. When I came in town, I was worried because all the boys he see me
63   go with ———— and if ———— got caught, they might take me too. From
64   that time on, ———— drank heavy because he was nervous and he make
65   me drink up with him, then I get drunk and paralyzed. He said he must
66   drink to forget about the case. He tell me, too, "Please no squawk," and
67   he begged me no tell nobody.[d]

4. Only a few words derived from the Hawaiian language have found general
   acceptance in mainland varieties of English. For definitions of any of the following words you do not know, see *Webster's Third New International Dictionary*.
   What areas of human experience are represented by these words? What is
   suggested about the relationship between English speakers and Hawaiians in
   the fact that these and only a few others have become generally current?

aloha	lei
haole	muumuu
hula	pau
kanaka	ukulele
malihine	wahine

[d] The editors wish to thank Miss Agnes C. Conrad, State Archivist of Hawaii, for sup-
plying them with a copy of Kemp's testimony.

SOCIAL ASPECTS OF BILINGUALISM IN SAN ANTONIO, TEXAS

Janet B. Sawyer

The position of those who live on the interface between two cultures can sometimes prove to be extremely difficult. Many Mexican-Americans in the Southwest suffer from the rebuffs of the dominant Anglo culture, but at the same time find themselves outsiders in the Spanish-speaking culture from which they come. The stresses of the community are clearly reflected in language and language attitudes; as a member of the Texas State Senate characterizes the situation, "we hear a great deal about the chicanos (those Mexican-Americans who cling to their ethnic tradition and use Spanish whenever possible), the pochos (who attempt to identify with the dominant culture and speak primarily English), and the pachuco (who rejects both and who speaks an argot which is neither Spanish nor English . . . and who, by the way, doesn't give a damn). These terms although arbitrarily chosen do illustrate basic differences of acceptance and rejection of another man's language and culture." [a]

As Sawyer shows in the following essay, these basic differences of acceptance and rejection underlie the development of a distinct variety of American English. While some feel that maintaining Spanish is necessary to their ethnic identity, others argue for mastery of English: "Excellence in English is emphasized by those Mexican-Americans concerned with fighting discrimination and with rising in the class hierarchy. Thus, the more socially mobile as well as the more socially conscious may refrain from using their ethnic mother tongue to avoid being taken for ignorant 'Mexs'!" [b] *Yet a more militant position is reflected in the view that "a Hispano who does not speak Spanish must choke on his chili."* [c] *All of these views affect the choice of language in the community.*

At the same time, non-Spanish speakers respond in their use of English to the same forces in the social matrix. There is a pervasive feeling among Anglos that American English should not sound like Spanish, and pronunciations that elsewhere in America have no social implications are foregrounded in the linguistic value system of the region. David W. Reed found, for instance, that

Reprinted, by permission of the author and the University of Alabama Press, from *Publications of the American Dialect Society*, 41 (1964): 7–15.

[a] "Statement of Joe Bernal, Member, Texas State Senate from San Antonio, Bexar County, Tex.," *Hearings before the Special Subcommittee on Bilingual Education of the Committee on Labor and Public Welfare, United States Senate, 90th Cong. 1st sess. on S. 428,* Part 1, May 26, 1967, pp. 327–28.

[b] Robert G. Hayden, "Some Community Dynamics of Language Maintenance," in *Language Loyalty in the United States*, ed. Joshua A. Fishman *et al.* (The Hague, 1966), p. 202.

[c] Quoted by Stan Steiner, *La Raza: The Mexican Americans* (New York, 1970), p. 220.

patio *with the vowel of* father [ɑ] *occurs everywhere in the United States—perhaps side by side with* patio *with the vowel of* hat [æ]. *Only in the Southwest is the* [ɑ] *pronunciation scrupulously avoided by middle-class Anglos who seem to want to distance themselves from the Spanish pronunciation of the word.*[d]

A recent dialect survey of English in San Antonio Texas,[1] a community where over 40 per cent of the people are Spanish-speaking immigrants from Mexico, yielded two important types of data: first, interviews with native speakers of English provided knowledge of the pronunciation features and vocabulary of a relatively unstudied part of Texas;[2] second, a study of the English spoken in the same community by Spanish-speaking informants revealed at least two degrees of second-language skill and unexpected evidence of the social stresses felt by speakers from a low-status culture who found no advantage in being identified as members of the Spanish-speaking minority.

The study of the pronunciation and vocabulary of the English-speaking informants, whom we will call *Anglos* in this report, following the custom of the community, was helpful in establishing the predominant influences upon the regional dialect. The informants were selected from various age, education and culture groups within the Anglo community, and the tabulated records[3] gave the following pronunciation features as characteristic of San Antonio:

1. "Vocalized /r/": *here* [hɪə].
2. Diphthongal /æy/: *pass* [pæys].
3. Monophthongal "long i": *five* [fa·v].
4. Diphthongal /ɔw/: *fought* [fɔwt].
5. /ɪ/ in certain unstressed syllables: *Dallas, wanted.*
6. /iw/ or /yuw/ after /t/, /d/, /n/: *tune, due.*

A comparison of these features with the known features of the dialect areas studied in the East[4] proved that such features are typical of the Southern dia-

---

[d] David W. Reed, personal communication.

[1] Janet B. Sawyer, "A Dialect Study of San Antonio, Texas, a Bilingual Community" (University of Texas diss., 1957).

[2] See E. Bagby Atwood, *The Regional Vocabulary of Texas* (Austin: University of Texas Press, 1962), for a more recent analysis of the larger dialect area.

[3] The items used for this study are those included in the worksheets made by Hans Kurath in 1939 (see note 4 below), as revised by E. Bagby Atwood for the Southwest regional study. The worksheets were supplemented by taped readings of Dagwood comic strips and other selections which provided additional information about pronunciation features in various styles of speech. For example, although in citation forms [aɪ] (in *five*) was often heard in the speech of certain Anglo speakers, in the reading of the comic strip, monophthongal [a·] was more frequent for these same speakers.

[4] Hans Kurath, M. L. Hanley, B. Bloch, G. S. Lowman, Jr., and M. L. Hansen, *Linguistic Atlas of New England* (3 vols. in 6 parts. Providence: Brown University, 1939–43); Hans

lect area, a somewhat surprising fact since a study of the immigration to San Antonio during the critical years between 1865 and 1880[5] states that 47 per cent of the Anglo immigrants were from the Midland and South Midland speech areas, and only 44 per cent were from the Gulf states. The prestige of the Southern settlers must have been high, judging from the persistence of the Southern speech characteristics. Of the six features listed above, only (1) is receding sharply in the speech of the youngest Anglo informants; (4) may be receding slightly.

In matters of lexicon, the survey disclosed that San Antonio English is not so strikingly Southern, partially because many of the words known to be characteristic of the South, such as *light-wood, chittling*, and *co-wench*, are obsolescent in this urban community. Words which spread from the South into the South Midland area appear with the greatest frequency in San Antonio. Terms such as *pully bone* and *clabber* are known to all the Anglo informants. Thus, in the Anglo community of San Antonio, we find a frequency of 53 per cent for words common to the South and South Midland.

The English vocabulary of San Antonio has its distinctive regional flavor because of a continual contact with the Spanish culture and language during the early settlement years. We found numerous Spanish words pertaining particularly to Southwestern ranching and cattle raising: *burro, lariat, hackamore, tank, norther, acequia, arroyo, chaps, corral*, and *mesa* are in very common usage; however, others such as *nopal, guajilla, tuna, piñata, yobero*, and *potro* were known only by the older members of the Anglo community, since the items they name are characteristic terms in a receding rural way of life.

The comparison of the English of seven Spanish-speaking informants, who will be referred to as *Latin* informants, since the name *Latin-Americans* is the term preferred by this group, with the English of the seven Anglo informants made it possible to distinguish varying degrees of second-language skill. We were able to classify three informants as basically *unilingual* Spanish speakers, since they spoke Spanish exclusively at home and whenever possible away from home. (All of them were native second-generation residents of San Antonio with grade school educations.) Their English was characterized by constant interference from the phonological structure of Spanish, numerous errors in basic grammatical contrasts, and a limited, inaccurate use of English vocabu-

----

Kurath, *A Word Geography of the Eastern United States* (Ann Arbor: University of Michigan Press, 1949); and E. Bagby Atwood, "Outline of the Principal Speech Areas of the Eastern United States" (mimeographed pamphlet, Austin, 1950) [printed in *English Linguistics: An Introductory Reader*, eds. Harold Hungerford, Jay Robinson, and James Sledd (Glenview, Ill., 1970), pp. 204–14. *Eds.*]. A book which gives detailed information on the Linguistic Atlas materials was not available at the time that this dialect study of San Antonio, Texas, was made: Hans Kurath and Raven I. McDavid, Jr., *The Pronunciation of English in the Atlantic States* (Ann Arbor: University of Michigan Press, 1961).

[5] Homer Lee Kerr, "Migration into Texas 1865–1880" (University of Texas diss., 1953).

lary. These informants were L2, a female midwife, 53 years old; L3, a male gardener, 46 years old; and L5, a female actress, 41 years old.

The remaining four Latin informants were classified as *bilinguals*, because their English was extremely competent. Very few errors occurred in their speech in either phonology or grammar, and they were able to respond to eight or more hours of interviewing in fluent English. These informants were L1, a retired female seamstress, 74 years old; L4, a female saleslady and housewife, 45 years old; L6, a male university graduate, 32 years old; and L7, a male university student, 21 years old.

In classifying these four informants as bilinguals, we do not mean that they had completely mastered English. Anyone speaking to either of the two women informants would immediately recognize the fact that English was not their native language. But they were competent within a limited vocabulary, and they had no difficulty making their ideas clear in English. Neither had had more than an elementary school education, but their jobs, which brought them into contact with English speakers, made it possible and even necessary for them to speak English well. The two male informants were much superior to them in the range and relative perfection of their English; L6, at least, was near the dividing line between bilingual Spanish and bilingual English, since he felt some embarrassment when speaking Spanish to anyone outside of San Antonio. Of course, neither L6 nor any of the other bilinguals felt completely at ease in English either.

The unilinguals experienced greater embarrassment and frustration when speaking English. However, L5, the unilingual actress, criticized the Spanish spoken in San Antonio, calling it "Tex.-Mex." Having been well-educated in cultured Spanish, thanks to the training of her Cuban husband and years in the Spanish theater, she disapproved of the way the Spanish speakers of the area interspersed English words among the Spanish words when speaking Spanish.

In order to ascertain the actual features of this Tex.-Mex., we also recorded the Spanish of the Latin informants and compared these records with those of Spanish students studying at the University of Texas from various parts of Mexico and the rest of the Spanish-speaking world. And no matter how diverse Tex.-Mex. may be in its vocabulary, the records proved that it is almost identical in its phonology to Mexican Spanish, so this dialect of Spanish was used in the comparative study of the two languages.[6]

The phonology of standard Southern English as spoken by the Anglo informants of San Antonio was the dialect of English used in judging the skill of the Latin informants since it seems reasonable to assume that the model they were striving to attain in English was not Northern or New England speech, or even "General American," but simply that variety of American English found in the Anglo community into which they were striving to in-

[6] Harold V. King, "Outline of Mexican Spanish Phonology," *Studies in Linguistics*, X (1952), 51–62.

tegrate. Therefore, in making the analysis of the bilinguals' achievement, we did not consider them to be skilled if they used [ɑu] in *cow*, even if these phones happened to be found in this word in many varieties of American English, since the Anglo informants of San Antonio used only [æu] or [au] in such words.

The English phonology of the unilingual Latins and the bilingual Latins can be briefly summarized:

Several vowel contrasts caused particular difficulty for the unilinguals:

1. /i/ and /ɪ/. The unilinguals commonly substituted Spanish /i/ (which lacks the high off-glide of English /i/) for English /ɪ/ in such words as *pig*.
2. /u/ and /ʊ/. The unilinguals commonly substituted Spanish /u/ (which lacks the lip-rounding off-glide of English for English /ʊ/ in such words as *pull*).
3. /æ/. This phoneme does not occur in Spanish, and the unilinguals commonly substituted either the close [e] or the open [ɛ] allophone of the Spanish /e/ in such words as *man*.
4. /ə/ also does not occur in Spanish. The unilingual Spanish speakers substitute (in words such as *one*) either the [ɑ] of Spanish /ɑ/ or the [ɔ] allophone of Spanish /o/.

The bilingual informants very seldom had difficulty with the simple vowel contrasts. The most difficult vowel qualities for them were the [æu] (in *cow*), the monophthongal [aˑ] (in *five*), and the fronted [ʉ] (in *school*). L6, the university graduate, was the only Latin informant who had mastered these regional features.

A variety of errors occurred in the attempt of the Latins to produce the English consonant system. Those of highest incidence in the records of the San Antonio unilingual informants were the following:

1. Fricative allophones of Spanish stops such as [β] often occurred in place of the labiodental [v] of English, following the Spanish distributional pattern. There is no /v/ phoneme in Spanish.
2. Final voiced consonants are often devoiced following the Spanish pattern, which permits only a few consonants to occur in word-final position and commonly devoices those that do occur. Example: [wepʻ] for *web*; [pikʻ] for *pig*.
3. The fricatives and affricates /š/, /č/, and /ǰ/ often replace each other in a form of free variation. *Sheep* [čiˑp], *chair* [šɛr], *jump* [čəmp], and *fudge* [fəš] are typical occurrences in unilingual Latin speech.

Such phenomena were typical of unilingual speech. But such interference by the Spanish consonant system was rare in bilingual English. Apparently, the bilinguals had mastered the essential contrasts between the voiced and voiceless consonants and had learned the new phonemes which occur only as allophones in Spanish. The most difficult pattern for the bilinguals to master seemed to be the contrast between /s/ and /z/, which are separate phonemes in English. In Spanish, however, the [z] is an allophone of /s/, occurring only when /s/ is followed by a voiced consonant in close transition. In the speech of L5, one of the unilinguals, an example of this Spanish distributional pattern occurred: In the phrase "twice better," *twice* was pronounced as [twɑɪz], but when *twice* occurred before pause, it was pronounced as [twɑɪs]. Although the bilinguals never made a total transfer of the Spanish pattern, the most persistent feature of "accent" in their speech (as well as in the speech of the unilinguals) is the occurrence of the tense voiceless [s] or the only partially voiced [z̥] in final position where [z] should occur in English. The high frequency of /s/ in both languages as a plural suffix and as a verb inflexional suffix may be one of the causes of the persistence of the difficulty in mastering the phoneme /z/ in English. It is a feature of the speech of even L6, who has attained most of the features of Texas English.

An interesting and unexpected feature of the pronunciation of the San Antonian bilinguals can be directly linked to the social pressures of the bilingual community, rather than to the interference of Spanish language habits. It became obvious after even the most superficial study of the community that the Latin-American population, commonly called *Mexicans,* or more derogatory terms such as *Meskans, pilau, greasers,* or *wetbacks,* were regarded as inferior. One of the Anglo informants of a prominent San Antonio family commented, "Many of my friends and relatives don't think Negroes and Mexicans are human beings—just animals. I didn't even know we had many Mexicans in San Antonio until I came back from college in Virginia." The Latin informants were well aware of the situation. The granddaughter of L1, herself a skilled bilingual, talked of her difficulty in getting a job upon her return from a good position in a psychiatrist's office in a western city. "Every ad for a good job here in San Antonio says 'Only *Anglos* need apply'!"

How this almost insurmountable pressure would affect the language achievement of the bilinguals was not immediately clear. It would seem logical that the ultimate degree of their effort would be the mastery of English as spoken in San Antonio. But the bilinguals interviewed for this survey (and others observed at various times before and after this survey) had gone even further. So determined were they to erase any influence of their low-prestige language upon their use of English that they treated Spanish words in two very special ways. First, Spanish words that they could not avoid in English received different pronunciations depending upon who was listening. Second, Spanish words that could be avoided were not used even though they were the typical regional terms in the English-speaking community.

Let us illustrate each of these facets of bilingual behavior in greater detail. Whenever a Spanish word could not be avoided in English, for example, when a bilingual speaker had to pronounce a Spanish personal name or a Spanish place name, he pronounced it in two different ways. If the listener was also a bilingual speaker, he gave the word a Spanish pronunciation. If the listener was a member of the English-speaking prestige group, the bilingual gave the word an Anglicized pronunciation. The bilingual informants even pronounced their own names in two different ways in English: *Lorenzo*: [lořɛnso] to other bilinguals; [lowrɛnzow] to Anglos. Other examples follow: (In each case, the Spanish pronunciation has been given first.) *Dolores*: [dolóřɛs] or [dəlórɛs]; *San Antonio*: [Sanantónio] or [sænæntówniə]; *burro*: [búřo] or [bɔ́row]; *plaza* [plásɑ] or [plǽzə]; *corral* [kořál] or [kərǽl]. The bilinguals gave the same double treatment for other indispensable borrowings from Spanish. It must be emphasized that this is not the way a speaker of Spanish from any Latin-American country or from Spain would treat Spanish words when speaking English. It would be a matter of pride to pronounce them in the true Spanish way and even to correct English speakers who mispronounced them. This writer remembers the horror of a bilingual from one South American country when he heard a San Antonio bilingual mispronounce his own Spanish name. The South American took an instant dislike to the Texan solely on the basis of this strange linguistic behavior.

As we mentioned above, if a Spanish word could be avoided in English, the bilinguals would not use it at all. In this they were like the unilinguals, who never used Spanish words in English. This was in direct contrast to the freedom with which all the Latin informants used *English* words in *Spanish*, the main distinguishing feature of San Antonio Spanish, according to various informants. (Examples: "Dame mi *pokebuk*." [Give me my *pocket book*.], or "Es un *eswamp*." [It's a *swamp*.].) Some of the Spanish words rejected in English by all the Latin informants were used normally by the Anglo informants: *corral, lariat, cinch, remuda, pilon, frijoles, chaps, hackamore, quirt.* Other words, which may have been borrowed from Latin or French rather than from Spanish, were also rejected by some of the Latin informants, because they were so similar to Spanish words: *gallery, melon, rancid.*

This rejection of the typical regional vocabulary of the English-speaking community illustrates the cultural isolation of even the bilingual speakers. In fact, if a Northern term happened to be more common in print, the Latin informants were likely to use that instead of the term preferred by all age levels in the Anglo group. Words such as *light bread, clabber,* and *corn shuck* were unknown to the Latin informants. They used the terms *corn husk* and *wish bone* rather than *corn shuck* and *pully bone*. The phrase *setting hen* was not known by even the most skilled bilingual Latin, L6, because such items are commonly learned in the home, and in the homes of the Latins only Spanish words for such things were used. Other terms typical of the regional English culture such as *Christmas Gift* or *snap beans* were unknown to the Latins, who used instead the general greeting, *Merry Christmas* and the commercial term *string beans*.

In evaluating our findings, we must remember that the number of bilinguals interviewed for this survey is out of all proportion to their number in the Spanish-speaking community, since it was our intent to study bilingualism.

Actually only a small number of people attempt to break through their isolation into the larger, prestige culture. Generally, they are content to consider themselves part of the Mexican culture and to live out their lives in relative security. Those who are more ambitious are called *agringados*, from the term *gringo*, with no compliment intended. Even members of the younger generation in the public schools generally stick together and talk Spanish outside of class. This is a sort of voluntary segregation; yet they would be the first to protest any actual segregation for the purpose of teaching them English as it should be taught to speakers of a second language. As a result, they are taught English along with the native speakers who need to learn the special kind of English known as formal written style. Those students who wish to become competent bilinguals adopt the "book words" and formal usage rules of this special style for ordinary English speech situations, and this precise, elegant style often sets off a bilingual from the English-speaking community quite as much as the "errors" of the unilinguals do.

The isolation of the Latin American results in a series of social isoglosses separating their speech from that of the Anglo community. Although these lines cannot be drawn on the map like the geographical isoglosses which separate one dialect from another, they are quite as real and as enduring. In the long run, the acquiring of the regional standard speech depends upon acculturation, which means the elimination of social barriers. Only when this is achieved (a necessity, from the point of view of democracy) can social isoglosses be eliminated.

STUDY QUESTIONS

1. It has been suggested that the most widespread and substantial change in American English is the merging of long open *o* in *caught*, *hawk*, and *dawn* with short *o* in *cot*, *hock*, and *don*. According to Labov, "this merger is spreading geographically and through younger age levels in northeastern New England, western Pennsylvania, scattered areas in the Midwest, and throughout the western United States with residual resistance in Los Angeles and San Francisco."[a]

   In the same essay, Labov notes that the distribution of this change in the Southwest is somewhat different: "we find that in Phoenix, Arizona, the incomplete merger of long open *o* and short *o* is a variable: for some speakers, the pairs *cot* and *caught*, *stock* and *stalk* are homonyms, and for others they are not. There is a strong tendency for the Anglos to show the one-phoneme, merged pattern, while Spanish and Negro groups tend to retain the two-phoneme system. But no one is aware of this fact, and very few know of the merger at all. As a rule, speakers show no shift in their use of this variable from their most casual to their most careful speech."[b]

   [a] William Labov, "Variation in Language," in *The Learning of Language*, ed. Carroll E. Reed (New York, 1971), p. 211.
   [b] *Ibid.* p. 197.

What internal and external forces would prevent Mexican-Americans from attaining the full range of English styles characteristic of the local Anglo community?

2. Sawyer discusses the "two different ways" in which Spanish speakers pronounce personal and place names (p. 231). Study the following exchange between former Senator Yarborough of Texas and Richard Villarreal, a social worker from Corpus Christi. What social pressures discussed by Sawyer are apparent in this exchange? Evaluate the Senator's claim that "it works in both directions."

> RICHARD VILLARREAL: I would like to say that my name is José Ricardo Villarreal, but because of the implications of our Great Society, oftentimes it is finer to say Richard Villarreal, and this also may be the essence of why we need the [bilingual education] program. . . .
>
> SENATOR YARBOROUGH: I noticed what you said about your name, that changing Ricardo to Richard. You know, that was the experience of some of the early Anglo settlers in Texas. When Stephen F. Austin started the first Anglo colony, he immediately changed his name to Esteban F. Austin, and Peter Ellis Dinn was captured down in Mexico while he was fighting with the Mexican revolutionary force against Spain. Spain kept him in prison for years before Mexico got their independence and then he became a colonel in Mexico, at which time he changed his name to Pedro Alias Dinn. I have seen his signature. He was Pedro Alias Dinn. So it works in both directions.[c]

3. The following anecdote from another bilingual community—Montreal—suggests that the problems described by Sawyer are widespread:

> One day while driving her to school, a lycée run by teachers from France, I stopped to pick up one of my daughter's friends and they were immediately involved in conversation, *French-Canadian* French style. A block or two farther I slowed down to pick up a second girlfriend when my daughter excitedly told me, in English, to drive on. At school I asked what the trouble was and she explained that there actually was no trouble although there might have been if the second girl, who was from France, and who spoke another dialect of French, had got in the car because then my daughter would have been forced to show a linguistic preference for one girl or the other. Normally she could escape this conflict by interacting with each girl separately, and, inadvertently, I had almost put her on the spot.[d]

What parallel problems do you see between this story and the situation in San Antonio? Do such difficulties present themselves to speakers in a community where several dialects of English are spoken?

4. Examine the following list of American English words mentioned by Sawyer. Which of them do you use yourself?

[c] *Hearings before the Special Subcommittee on Bilingual Education of the Committee on Labor and Public Welfare, United States Senate, 90th Cong., 1st sess. on S. 428*, Part 1, May 26, 1967, pp. 260–61.

[d] Wallace E. Lambert, "A Social Psychology of Bilingualism," *Journal of Social Issues*, **23**(1967):93.

burro	mesa
lariat	nopal
hackamore	guajilla
acequia	tuna
arroyo	piñata
chaps	potro
corral	

Most of these words are not recent borrowings. What social pressures mentioned by Sawyer might reduce the flow of borrowings from Spanish into English?

These same pressures cause changes in the variety of Spanish spoken in the American Southwest, not only in pronunciation but in vocabulary as well. Such forces lead to the development of a mixed language, as Dillard and Hall show in other essays in this collection. Consider the social factors that contribute to this kind of language mixture and in light of the growth of English meanings in the "*Pachuco*" variety of Spanish in the American Southwest.

	Spanish meaning	*Pachuco meaning*
birria	a meat dish	beer
dátil	fruit of the date palm	date (social engagement)
ganga	a bargain	gang
mecha	a wick	match
chanza	an amusing saying or act	chance
carro	a cart	car[e]

[e] Examples from Rafael Jesús González, "*Pachuco*: The Birth of a Creole Language," *Arizona Quarterly*, **23**(1967):353.

SOME FEATURES OF THE ENGLISH OF BLACK AMERICANS

William Labov

Between the two world wars, the interest of American dialectologists centered on regional dialects. Although they paid some attention to the speech of cities and to social differences in items of usage, the makers of the Linguistic Atlas of the United States and Canada were more concerned with those features of language that are related to home and homestead and reflect early settlement patterns of colonists and immigrants. Events of the past thirty years, however, have shifted attention from rural to urban American and have given a new urgency to research into social differences in the speech of Americans. Dialectologists are now more likely to write about nonstandard English than the English of Maumee, Ohio; and an overwhelming majority of them write about black English, a term usually referring to the speech of poor, underemployed, and uneducated urban Negroes.

Several events account for the massive research interest of social scientists in the language and life styles of urban or urbanized blacks: migration by unprecedented numbers of blacks to industrial centers in search of jobs opened by the Second World War and the postwar boom; movements for civil rights; agitations of more violent sorts, typically in the North, forcing on all but the most ostrichlike a clear view of the deep and dangerous alienation felt by the black ghetto dweller toward an affluent and white-dominated society. Faced with civil disturbance bordering on rebellion, a government eager to purchase tranquility has offered liberal funding for research into the causes of alienation. And some causes have been easily discovered: blacks are fed up with white hatred and patronizing benevolence in what is still a strongly racist society; blacks need jobs, particularly jobs that bring good pay and dignity; blacks need better education to fit them for better jobs. But such findings reveal only the need, or the seeming need, for further research. Why, for example, are black urban children not getting an adequate education? Are the urban schools failing them, as some have claimed? Or does failure result from some more covert source—from something in these children's upbringing, their culture, their ways of thinking and perceiving, perhaps from their language itself? For linguists, money was available to study the speech of urban blacks—to find out whether, and if so how, the dialects of blacks differ from those spoken by whites, particularly middle-class whites.

Is there a black English? As Labov says in the following article, the debate is loud, often angry, and not always well informed. Earlier researchers thought not:

By and large the Southern Negro speaks the language of the white man of his locality or area and of his education . . . As far as the speech of uneducated Negroes is concerned, it differs little from that of the illiterate white; that is, it exhibits the same regional and local variations as that of the simple white folk.[a]

Some scholars presently working on contemporary varieties of American English would agree in the main with Hans Kurath's early appraisal.[b] Others, however, would trace black nonstandard English to a source quite different from the British dialects that are the ancestors of all other American dialects: to a creole ancestor—a slave language based on English, developed first as a pidgin, then learned as a native tongue (that is, creolized), and then gradually undergoing decreolization through contact with American English dialects.

Indeed, the nonstandard speech of present-day American Negroes still seems to exhibit structural traces of a creole predecessor, and this is probably a reason why it is in some ways more deviant from standard English than is the nonstandard speech of even the most uneducated American whites.[c]

Those who accept the creolist position posit deep structure differences of considerable scope between black and white English; and their research seems to be the basis of claims (when there is a basis) that black nonstandard English is an entirely different language from standard English. William Labov, who with his colleagues has conducted the most extensive study yet done of the speech of urban Negroes,[d] takes a more moderate position on structural differences between black and white varieties, stating elsewhere that differences between

---

[a] Hans Kurath. *A Word Geography of the Eastern United States* (Ann Arbor, Mich., 1949), p. 6.

[b] See Juanita V. Williamson, "A Phonological and Morphological Study of the Speech of the Negro of Memphis, Tennessee." Unpublished doctoral dissertation, University of Michigan, 1961; and "A Look at Black English," *The Crisis*, **78**, 6(1971): 169–73, 185. See also Raven I. McDavid, Jr., "American Social Dialects," *College English*, **26**(1965): 254–60; Raven I. and Virginia Glenn McDavid, "The Relationship of the Speech of American Negroes to the Speech of Whites," *American Speech*, **26**(1951): 3–17.

[c] William A. Stewart, "Continuity and Change in American Negro Dialects," *The Florida FL Reporter*, **6**, 1(1968): 3–4, 14–16, 18.

[d] William Labov, Paul Cohen, Clarence Robins, and John Lewis. *A Study of the Non-Standard English of Negro and Puerto Rican Speakers in New York City*, Vols. I and II. Final Report, Cooperative Research Project No. 3288 (Washington, D.C., 1968). (Available through ERIC.)

black nonstandard and standard English "*are largely confined to superficial, rather low-level processes which have little effect upon meaning.*" [e]

Definitive answers to questions about the structure and origins of the nonstandard dialects spoken by blacks must await more extensive and intensive research. In the meantime, readers of presently available research into black English should be aware that most of it is fragmentary—focused on severely restricted lists of features often recorded from the speech of only a handful of informants; and much of it is biased by the pressure for quick, easy, and general application. Labov's work suffers the least of any yet done from such faults, and his following short sketch of some characterizing features of black nonstandard dialects gains authority from the scope of his work in New York City and from his concern with general and explanatory linguistic theory.

One of the most extraordinary failures in the history of American education is the failure of the public school system to teach black children in the urban ghettos to read. The fact of reading failure is so general, and so widespread, that no one school system, no one method, and no one teacher can be considered responsible. We are plainly dealing with social and cultural events of considerable magnitude, in which the linguistic factors are the focal points of trouble or centers of difficulty rather than the primary causes. Before considering specific linguistic problems, it will be helpful to look at the general reading problem of disadvantaged blacks in its cultural setting.

Since 1965, research has been conducted into the structural and functional differences between the nonstandard vernacular used by black speakers in the urban ghettos and the standard English of the classroom.[1] One of the first studies was a series of seventy-five interviews with black boys in randomly selected "Vacation Day Camps" in Harlem in the summer of 1965. These day camps were conducted in recreation centers and schools, and each child's

[e] William Labov. *The Study of Nonstandard English* (Champaign, Ill., 1970), p. 40.

[1] The research reported here was supported by the United States Office of Education as Cooperative Research Projects 3091 and 3288. The most complete report is provided in W. Labov, P. Cohen, C. Robins, and J. Lewis. *A Study of the Non-Standard English of Negro and Puerto Rican Speakers in New York City*, Final Report on Cooperative Research Project 3288 (Washington, D.C., 1968; available through ERIC, Center for Applied Linguistics, Washington, D.C.). The sections of this essay entitled "The Problem of Black Dialect," "Relevant Patterns of Black Speech," "Some Phonological Variables and Their Grammatical Consequences," "Changes in the Shapes of Words," and "Grammatical Correlates of the Phonological Variables," and "Consequences for the Teaching of Reading" were adapted from William Labov, "Some Sources of Reading Problems for Negro Speakers of Nonstandard English," in A. Frazier, ed., *New Directions in Elementary English* (Champaign, Ill.: NCTE, 1967), pp. 140–67, and are used by permission of the National Council of Teachers of English. Some of the treatment in this essay is derived from William Labov, "A Note on the Relation of Reading Failure to Peer Group Status," *Teachers College Record*, Vol. 70 (1969), pp. 395–405.

parents had to enroll him personally in the program; there was therefore a large factor of selection for intact homes and favorable family attitudes. In these interviews we found that the great majority of these boys, aged ten to twelve, had considerable difficulty in reading second- or third-grade-level sentences such as the following:

> Last month I read five books.
> When I passed by, I read the posters.
> When I liked a story, I read every word.

In the course of the next two years, the language and behavior of a number of preadolescent and adolescent peer groups in South Central Harlem were systematically investigated. The researchers avoided contact with the home and the school, the adult-dominated environments; instead, they worked through participant-observers in the area to reach the boys on the streets, in their own territories, in environments dominated by peer-group interaction. In the same areas, marginal members of the groups and isolated individuals were studied. The latter included boys from the Vacation Day Camps and boys from the immediate neighborhood of the peer groups, who were "lames" —definitely not participants in the vernacular street culture. Reading tests showed that reading skills were very low for most boys—close to zero for many. More important, reading was truly irrelevant to the daily life of these boys. For example, two boys who were best friends and saw each other every day had very different reading abilities. One could read the last page in Gray's Oral Reading Test, and the other could not read the second-grade-level sentences; the first was astonished to find that his friend could not read, and the second was even more surprised to find that the first boy could read so well.

With the cooperation of the New York City Board of Education, the school records were examined for most of the individuals studied.[2] Figure 1 shows the relation of reading level to grade level for thirty-two isolated individuals. The horizontal axis is the actual grade at the time the investigators were in contact with the boys; the vertical axis is the average Metropolitan Achievement Test score. The central diagonal, from lower left to upper right, represents reading on grade: the pair of symbols at the upper right of the diagram, for example, shows two boys in the eighth grade reading at the eighth-grade level.

In Figure 1, we see that most of the children studied from South Central Harlem are indeed below grade in reading, though there are some who are doing quite well. The general movement of the population from lower left to upper right indicates that learning is taking place.

We can contrast Figure 1 with Figure 2, which shows the same relations

---

[2] Data given here are based on a relatively small sample of seventy-five boys, since many had moved or been transferred, suspended, or discharged during this period.

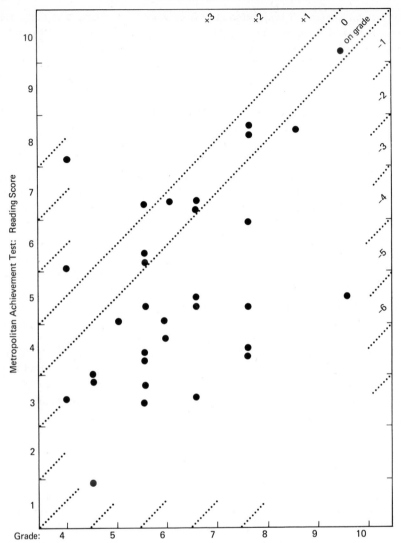

Figure 1. Grade and reading achievement of thirty-two nonmembers of street groups in south central Harlem.

for forty-six children who are members of various gangs, clubs, or hang-out groups—fully participating members of the street cultures. The over-all pattern is very different from Figure 1: only one person is reading on grade, and the great majority are not learning to read at all. Year by year, the boys belonging to these groups fall further below grade—four, five, or six years, until they finally drop out.

The sharp difference between these two figures represents information that could not have been gathered by research within the schools, since teachers have no means of knowing which children are indeed fully identified with the

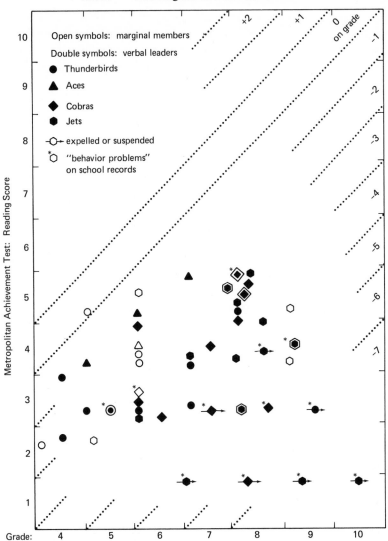

Figure 2. Grade and reading achievement of forty-six members of street groups in Harlem.

street culture. The linguistic differences between the two groups are minor, but the difference in acceptance or rejection of school as an institution is very great indeed.

These figures make it fairly evident that there are factors operating that are more important than native intelligence or verbal ability—culturally determined values and attitudes that interfere with the process of learning to read. The fundamental problem revealed in Figures 1 and 2 should be kept in mind so that the relative importance of functional and structural problems is not obscured. At the present time we can give a number of concrete suggestions on linguistic problems and some of these are presented in the following pages. As helpful as these may be, it should be clear that they deal with only one (and certainly not the major) problem interfering with the learning of reading.

THE PROBLEM OF BLACK DIALECT

One of the first questions to which we must address ourselves is whether or not there is a single definite pattern of speech used by blacks in urban ghetto areas. This question has provoked a great deal of discussion in the last few years, much more than it deserves. At many meetings on educational problems of ghetto areas, time that could have been spent in constructive discussion has been devoted to arguing the question as to whether black dialect exists. The debates have not been conducted with any large body of factual information in view, but rather in terms of what the speakers wish to be so, or what they fear might follow in the political arena.

For those who have not participated in such debates, it may be difficult to imagine how great are the pressures against the recognition, description, or even mention of black speech patterns. For various reasons, many teachers, principals, and civil rights leaders wish to deny that the existence of patterns of black speech is a linguistic and social reality in the United States today. The most careful statement of the situation as it actually exists might read as follows: *Many features of pronunciation, grammar, and lexicon are closely associated with black speakers—so closely as to identify the great majority of black people in the northern cities by their speech alone.*

The correspondence between this speech pattern and membership in the black ethnic group is of course far from complete. Many black speakers have none—or almost none—of these features. Many northern whites, living in close proximity to blacks, have these features in their own speech. But this overlap does not prevent the features from being identified with black speech by most listeners: we are dealing with a stereotype that provides correct identification in the great majority of cases, and therefore with a firm base in social reality. Such stereotypes are the social basis of language perception; this is merely one of many cases where listeners generalize from the variable data to categorical perception in absolute terms. Someone who uses a stigmatized form 20 to 30 per cent of the time will be heard as using this form all the time. It may be socially useful to correct these stereotypes in a certain number of individual cases, so that people learn to limit their generalizations to the precise degree that their experience warrants; but the over-all tendency is based upon very regular principles of human behavior, and people will continue to identify as black speech the pattern that they hear from the great majority of the black people they meet.

The existence of a black speech pattern must not be confused of course with the myth of a biologically, racially, exclusively black speech. The idea that dialect differences are due to some form of laziness or carelessness must be rejected with equal firmness. Anyone who continues to endorse such myths can be refuted easily by such subjective-reaction tests as the Family Background Test, which we are using in our current research in Harlem. Sizable extracts from the speech of fourteen individuals are played in sequence for listeners who are asked to identify the family backgrounds of each. So far, we find no one who can even come close to a correct identification of black and white speakers. This result does not contradict the statement that there exists a socially based black speech pattern; it supports everything that I have said above on this point. The voices heard on the test are the exceptional cases: blacks raised without any black friends in solidly white areas; whites raised in areas dominated by black cultural values; white southerners raised in predominantly black areas; blacks from small northern communities untouched by recent migrations; college-educated blacks who reject the northern ghetto and the South alike. The speech of these individuals does not identify them as black or white because they do not use the speech patterns that are characteristically black or white for northern listeners. The identifications made by these listeners, often in violation of actual ethnic membership categories, show that they respond to black speech patterns as a social reality.

RELEVANT PATTERNS OF BLACK SPEECH

One approach to the study of nonstandard black speech is to attempt a complete description of this form of language without direct reference to standard English. This approach can be quite revealing, and can save us from many pitfalls in the easy identification of forms that are only apparently similar. But as an over-all plan, it is not realistic. We are far from achieving a complete description of standard English, to begin with; the differences between nonstandard black speech and standard English are slight compared to their similarities; and, finally, some of these differences are far more relevant to reading problems than others. Let us therefore consider some of the most relevant patterns of black speech from the point of view of reading problems.

Some black-white differences are plainly marked and easy for any observer to note. In the following examples, the black forms are patterns that frequently occur in our recordings of individual and group sessions with boys from ten to seventeen years old—ranging from careful speech in face-to-face interaction with adults to the most excited and spontaneous activity within the primary (closed network) group:

Black	*White*
It don't all be her fault.	It isn't always her fault.
Hit him upside the head.	Hit him in the head.
The rock say "Shhh!"	The rock went "Shhh!"

Black	White
I'm a shoot you.	I'm g'na shoot you.
I wanna be a police.	I wanna be a policeman.
Ah 'on' know. [a o no]	I d'know. [aᴵdnoᵁ]

(Black pitch marks: 2 4 3; White pitch marks: 2 3 1)

Now consider the following examples, in which black-white differences are less plainly marked and very difficult for most people to hear:

Black	White
He [pæsɪm] yesterday.	He [pæsḓɪm] yesterday.
Give him [ðeᴵ] book.	Give him [ðɛə:] book.
This [jɔːɫ] place?	This [jɔːᵊ] place?
[ðæs] Nick boy.	[ðæᵗs] Nick's boy.
He say, [kæːᵊɫ] is.	He says, [kærəl] is.
My name is [bu].	My name is [buˀ].

This second series represents a set of slight phonetic differences, sometimes prominent, but more often unnoticed by the casual listener. These differences are much more significant than the first set in terms of learning and reading standard English. In truth, the differences are so significant that they will be the focus of our attention. The slight phonetic signals observed here indicate systematic differences that can lead to reading problems and problems of being understood.

Corresponding to the phonetic transcriptions on the left, we can and do infer such grammatical constructions and lexical forms as

> He pass him yesterday.
> Give him they book.
> This you-all place?
> That's Nick boy.
> He say, Ca'ol is.
> My name is Boo.

Each of these sentences is representative of a large class of phonological and grammatical differences that distinguish nonstandard black speech from standard English. The most important are those in which large-scale phonological differences coincide with important grammatical differences. The result of this coincidence is the existence of a large number of homonyms in the speech of black children that are different from the set of homonyms in the speech system used by the teacher. If the teacher knows about this different set of homonyms, no serious problems in the teaching of reading need occur; but if the teacher does not know about it, there are bound to be difficulties.

The simplest way to organize this information seems to be under the headings of the important rules of the sound system that are affected. By using lists of homonyms as examples, it will be possible to avoid a great deal of phonetic notation and to stay with the essential linguistic facts. In many cases, the actual phonetic form is irrelevant: it is the presence or absence of a distinction that is relevant. Thus, for example, it makes no difference whether a child says [pɪn] or [prⁱn] or [peːⁱn] or [pɛn] for the word *pen*; what counts is whether or not this word is distinct from *pin*. The linguistic fact of interest is the existence of contrast, not the particular phonetic forms that are heard from one time to another. A child might seem to distinguish [pɪn] and [pɛn] in northern style in one pair of sentences, but if the basic phonemic contrast is not present, the same child might reverse the forms in the next sentence, and say [pɪn] for *ink pen* and [pɛn] for *safety pin*. A linguistic orientation will not supply teachers with a battery of phonetic symbols, but rather encourage them to observe what words can or cannot be distinguished by the children they are teaching.

SOME PHONOLOGICAL VARIABLES AND THEIR GRAMMATICAL CONSEQUENCES

R-Lessness

There are three major dialect areas in the eastern United States where the *r* of spelling is not pronounced as a consonant before other consonants or at the ends of words: eastern New England, New York City, and the South (upper and lower). Thus white speakers from Boston, New York, Richmond, Charleston, or Atlanta will show only a lengthened vowel in *car*, *guard*, *for*, and usually an obscure centering glide (schwa) in place of *r* in *fear*, *feared*, *care*, *cared*, *moor*, *moored*, *bore*, *bored*, and so on. This is what we mean by *r*-less pronunciation. Most of these areas have been strongly influenced in recent years by the *r*-pronouncing pattern that is predominant in broadcasting so that educated speakers, especially young people, will show a mixed pattern in their careful speech. When the original *r*-less pattern is preserved, we can obtain such homonyms as the following:

guard	= god	par	= pa
nor	= gnaw	fort	= fought
sore	= saw	court	= caught

and we find that *yeah* can rhyme with *fair*, *idea* with *fear*.

Black speakers show an even higher degree of *r*-lessness than white New Yorkers or Bostonians. The *r* of spelling becomes a schwa or disappears before vowels as well as before consonants and pauses. Thus in the speech of most white New Yorkers, *r* is pronounced when a vowel follows, as in *four o'clock*; even though the *r* is found at the end of a word, if the next word begins with a vowel, it is pronounced as a consonantal [r]. For most black speakers, *r* is still not pronounced in this position, and so never heard at the end of the word *four*. The white speaker is helped in his reading or spelling by the existence of the alternation in which the underlying *r* comes out before a vowel, as in fou*r* o'clock, but the black speaker has no such clue to the underlying (spelling) form of the word *four*. Furthermore, the same black speaker will often not pronounce intervocalic *r* in the middle of a word, as indicated in the dialect spelling *inte'ested, Ca'ol*. He has no clue, in his own speech, to the correct spelling form of such words, and may have another set of homonyms besides those listed above:

$$
\begin{array}{ll}
\text{Carol} & = \text{Cal} \\
\text{Paris} & = \text{pass} \\
\text{terrace} & = \text{test}
\end{array}
$$

L-Lessness

The consonant *l* is a liquid very similar to *r* in its phonetic nature. The chief difference is that with *l* the center of the tongue is up and the sides are down, whereas with *r* the sides are up but the center does not touch the roof of the mouth. The pattern of *l*-dropping is very similar to that of *r*, except that it has never affected entire dialect areas in the same sweeping style. When *l* disappears, it is often replaced by a back unrounded glide, sometimes symbolized [ɰ], instead of the center glide that replaces *r*; in many cases, *l* disappears entirely, especially after the back rounded vowels. The loss of *l* is much more marked among the black speakers we have interviewed than among whites in northern cities, and one therefore finds much greater tendencies toward such homonyms as

$$
\begin{array}{llll}
\text{toll} & = \text{toe} & \text{all} & = \text{awe} \\
\text{help} & = \text{hep} & \text{Saul} & = \text{saw} \\
\text{tool} & = \text{too} & \text{fault} & = \text{fought}
\end{array}
$$

Simplification of Consonant Clusters

One of the most complex variables appearing in black speech is the general tendency toward the simplification of consonant clusters at the ends of words. A great many clusters are involved, primarily those ending in /-t/ or /-d/, /-s/ or /-z/.[3] We are actually dealing with two distinct tendencies: (1) a general tendency to reduce clusters of consonants at the ends of words to single consonants, and (2) a more general process of reducing the amount of information provided after stressed vowels, so that individual final consonants are affected

---

[3] When the /-t/ or /-d/ represents a grammatical inflection these consonants are usually automatic alternants of the same abstract form *-ed*. Phonetic rules delete the vowel (except after stems ending in /-t/ or /-d/), and we then have [t] following voiceless consonants such as /p, s, t, k/ and [d] in all other cases. In the same way, [s] and [z] are coupled as voiceless and voiced alternants of the same *-s* inflections, but in clusters that are a part of the root word we do not have such automatic alternations.

as well. The first process is more regular and requires more intensive study in order to understand the conditioning factors involved.

The chief /-t, -d/ clusters that are affected are (roughly in order of frequency) /-st, -ft, -nt, -nd, -ld, -zd, -md/. Here they are given in phonemic notation; in conventional spelling we have words such as *past, passed, lift, laughed, bent, bend, fined, hold, poled, old, called, raised, aimed.* In all these cases, if the cluster is simplified, it is the last element that is dropped. Thus we have homonyms such as

past	= pass	mend	= men
rift	= riff	wind	= wine
meant	= men	hold	= hole

If we combine the effect of *-ld* simplification, loss of *-l*, and monophthongization of /ay/ and /aw/, we obtain

[ʃi wa: ɫ] She wow! = She wild!

and this equivalence has in fact been found in our data. It is important to bear in mind that the combined effect of several rules will add to the total number of homonyms, and even more, to the unexpected character of the final result:

told = toll = toe

The /-s, -z/ clusters that are often simplified occur in such words as *axe* /æks/, *six* /siks/, *box* /baks/, *parts* /parts/, *aims* /eymz/, *rolls* /rowlz/, *leads* /liydz/, *besides* /bisaydz/, *John's* /džanz/, *that's* /ðæts/, *it's* /its/, *its* /its/. The situation here is more complex than with the /-t, -d/ clusters, since in some cases the first element of the cluster is lost, and in other cases the second element.[4]

In one sense, there are a great many homonyms produced by this form of consonant-cluster simplification, as we shall see when we consider grammatical consequences. But many of these can also be considered grammatical differences rather than changes in the shapes of words. The /-t, -d/ simplification gives us a great many irreducible homonyms, so that a child has no clue to the standard spelling differences from his own speech pattern. Though this is less common in the case of /-s, -z/ clusters, we can occasionally have

six	= sick	Max	= Mack
box	= bock	mix	= Mick

as possible homonyms in the speech of many black children.

---

[4] The loss of the first element—that is, assimilation to the following *s*—is most common in forms where the *-s* represents the verb *is* or the pronoun *us* in *it's, that's* and *let's*. In none of these cases is there a problem of homonymy.

Weakening of Final Consonants

It was noted above that the simplification of final consonant clusters was part of a more general tendency to produce less information after stressed vowels, so that final consonants, unstressed final vowels, and weak syllables show fewer distinctions and more reduced phonetic forms than initial consonants and stressed vowels. This is a perfectly natural process in terms of the amount of information required for effective communication, since the number of possible words that must be distinguished declines sharply after we select the first consonant and vowel. German and Russian, for example, do not distinguish voiced and voiceless consonants at the ends of words. However, when this tendency is carried to extremes (and a nonstandard dialect differs radically from the standard language in this respect), it may produce serious problems in learning to read and spell.

This weakening of final consonants is by no means as regular as the other phonological variables described above. Some individuals appear to have generalized the process to the point where most of their syllables are of the CV type; that is, consonant plus vowel, and those we have interviewed in this category seem to have the most serious reading problems of all. In general, final /-t/ and /-d/ are the most affected by the process. Final /-d/ may be devoiced to a [t]-like form or disappear entirely. Final /-t/ is often realized as glottal stop, as in many English dialects, but more often disappears entirely. Less often, final /-g/ and /-k/ follow the same route as /-d/ and /-t/: /-g/ is devoiced or disappears, and /-k/ is replaced by glottal stop or disappears. Final /-m/ and /-n/ usually remain in the form of various degrees of nasalization of the preceding vowel. Rarely, sibilants /-s/ and /-z/ are weakened after vowels to the point where no consonant is heard at all. As a result of these processes, it is possible to have such homonyms as

Boot = Boo	seat = seed = see
road = row	poor = poke = pope
feed = feet	bit = bid = big

It is evident that the loss of final /-l/ and /-r/, discussed above, is another aspect of this general weakening of final consonants, though of a much more regular nature than the cases considered in this section.

Other Phonological Variables

In addition to the types of homonymy singled out in the preceding discussion, there are a great many others that may be mentioned. They are of less importance for reading problems in general, since they have little impact on inflectional rules, but they do affect the shapes of words in the speech of black children. There is no distinction between /i/ and /e/ before nasals in the great majority of cases. In the parallel case before /-r/, and sometimes /-l/, we frequently find no distinction between the vowels /ih/ and /eh/. The corresponding pair of back vowels before /-r/ are seldom distinguished; that is, /uh/ and /oh/ fall together. The diphthongs /ay/ and /aw/ are often monoph-thongized, so that they are not distinguished from /ah/. The diphthong /oy/ is often a monophthong, especially before /-l/, and sometimes cannot be dis-tinguished from the vowel /oh/, so that *oil = all*.

Among other consonant variables, we find the final fricative /-θ/ is fre-quently merged with /f/, and similarly final /-ð/ with /v/. Less frequently, /θ/ and /ð/ become /f/ and /v/ in intervocalic position. Initial consonant clusters that involve /r/ show considerable variation: /str/ is often heard as /skr/; /ʃr/ as [sw, sr, sφ]. In a more complex series of shifts, /r/ is frequently lost as the final element of an initial cluster.

As a result of these various phonological processes, we find that the follow-ing series of possible homonyms are characteristic of the speech of many black children:

pin	= pen	beer	= bear	poor	= pour
tin	= ten	cheer	= chair	sure	= shore
since	= cents	steer	= stair	moor	= more
		peel	= pail		
Ruth	= roof	stream	= scream	boil	= ball
death	= deaf	strap	= scrap	oil	= all
find	= found = fond				
time	= Tom				
	pound = pond				

CHANGES IN THE SHAPES OF WORDS

The series of potential homonyms given in the preceding sections indicate that black children may have difficulty in recognizing many words in their standard spellings. They may look up words under the wrong spellings in dictionaries and be unable to distinguish words that are plainly different for the teacher. If the teacher is aware of these sources of confusion, he may be able to anticipate a great many of the children's difficulties. But if neither the teacher nor the children are aware of the great differences in their sets of homonyms, it is obvious that confusion will occur in every reading assign-ment.

However, the existence of homonyms on the level of a phonetic output does not prove that the speakers have the same sets of mergers on the more ab-stract level that corresponds to the spelling system. For instance, many white New Yorkers merge *guard* and *god* in casual speech, but in reading style they have no difficulty in pronouncing the /r/ where it belongs. Since the /r/ in *car* reappears before a following vowel, it is evident that an abstract *r* occurs in their lexical understanding of the word. Thus the standard spelling system finds support in the learned patterns of careful speech and in the alternations that exist within any given style of speech.

The phonetic processes discussed above are often considered to be "low level" rules—that is, they do not affect the underlying or abstract representations of words. One piece of evidence for this view is that the deletable final /-r, -l, -s, -z, -t, -d/ tend to be retained when a vowel follows at the beginning of the next word. This effect of a following vowel would seem to be a phonetic factor, restricting the operation of a phonetic rule; in any case, it is plain that the final consonant must "be there" in some abstract sense if it appears in this prevocalic position. If this were not the case, we would find a variety of odd final consonants appearing, with no fixed relation to the standard form.

For all major variables that we have considered, there is a definite and pronounced effect of a following vowel in realizing the standard form.

The same argument, however, can be applied to show that black speakers have underlying forms considerably different from those of white speakers. The white speakers showed almost as much over-all simplification of the clusters before a following consonant, but none at all before a following vowel; in other words, their abstract forms were effectively equivalent to the spelling forms. The black speakers showed only a limited reduction in the degree of simplification when a vowel followed.

GRAMMATICAL CORRELATES OF THE PHONOLOGICAL VARIABLES

As we examine the various final consonants affected by the phonological processes, we find that these are the same consonants that represent the principal English inflections. The shifts in the sound system therefore often coincide with grammatical differences between nonstandard and standard English, and it is usually difficult to decide whether we are dealing with a grammatical or a phonological rule. In any case, we can add a great number of homonyms to the lists given above when we consider the consequences of deleting final /-r, -l, -s, -z, -t, -d/.

The Possessive

In many cases, the absence of the possessive s can be interpreted as a reduction of consonant clusters, although this is not the most likely interpretation. The -s is absent just as frequently after vowels as after consonants for many speakers. Nevertheless, we can say that the over-all simplification pattern is favored by the absence of the -s inflection. In the case of -r, we find more direct phonological influence: two possessive pronouns that end in /-r/ have become identical with the personal pronoun:

[ðeɪ] book   not [ðɛ·ə] book

In rapid speech, one can not distinguish *you* from *your* from *you-all*. This seems to be a shift in grammatical forms, but the relation to the phonological variables is plain when we consider that *my*, *his*, *her*, and *our* remain as

possessive pronouns. Only in areas under strong creole influence will one hear
I book, *she book*, or *we book*, for there is no phonological process that would
bring the possessives into near-identity with the personal pronouns.

The Future

The loss of final /-1/ has a serious effect on the realization of future forms:

you'll = you	he'll = he
they'll = they	she'll = she

In many cases, therefore, the colloquial future is identical with the colloquial
present. The form *will* is still used in its emphatic or full form, and various
reductions of *going to* are frequent, so there is no question about the grammatical category of the future. One contracted form of the future heard only
among black speakers is in the first person, *I'm a shoot you*; there is no general
process for the deletion of this *m*.

The Copula

The finite verb forms of *be* are frequently not realized in sentences such as *you
tired* and *he in the way*. If we examine the paradigm as a whole, we find that
phonological processes have obviously been at work. In the first person, we
find that either the full or contracted form is normal; such forms as *I here* or *I
is here* are extremely rare, except perhaps among very young children, but
because they are so striking many casual observers have reported them as
common. The third-person form *is* represents a true variable for all vernacular speakers. We have found that the deletion of *is* ranges from 20 or 30 per
cent to 70 or 80 per cent, but it is never absent entirely even in the most casual
speech. On the other hand, the second-person singular and plural form *are*
is deleted much more frequently and is almost completely absent for many
speakers. It is evident that the phonological processes that affect *are* are much
stronger than those that affect *is*.

It may seem strange at first to speak of phonological processes operating to
effect the deletion of a whole word. However, our recent studies of the copula
have revealed that in every situation in which standard English cannot contract to '*s*, the nonstandard vernacular does not permit deletion of *is*.[5] Thus
contraction precedes deletion in the rules operating here; the rules of consonant-cluster simplification, discussed above, apply in part to this situation.

The Past

Again, there is no doubt that phonological processes are active in reducing
the frequency of occurrence of the /-t, -d/ inflection.

[5] Thus in *He is here, He ain't here, is he? Yes, he is, I'm smarter than he is, That's what it is*,
and many other cases we find that *is* can neither be contracted nor deleted. See William
Labov, "Contraction, Deletion and Inherent Variability of the English Copula," *Language*,
Vol. 44 (1969), pp. 718–22.

pass = past = passed   pick = picked
miss = mist = missed   loan = loaned
fine = find = fined   raise = raised

At the same time, there is no question about the existence of a past-tense category. The irregular past-tense forms, which are very frequent in ordinary conversation, are plainly marked as past no matter what final simplification takes place.

I told him [atoɪm]   he kept mine [hikɛpmaˈn]

The problem that confronts us concerns the form of the regular suffix -ed. Is there such an abstract form in the structure of the nonstandard English spoken by black children? The answer will make a considerable difference both to teaching strategy and to our understanding of the reading problems that children face. We have carried out a number of quantitative studies of consonant clusters and the -ed suffix on this point.[6] The behavior of speakers in spontaneous group interaction has been studied, as well as their ability to recognize -ed in reading as a past-tense signal and to detect nonstandard forms in printed material. Our conclusion is that there are many black children who do not have enough support in their linguistic system to identify -ed as a past-tense signal, and they must be taught the meaning of this form from the outset. There are many others who have no difficulty in *reading -ed* even though they do not pronounce it. In our investigations, we use test sentences such as

1. Tom read all the time.
2. Last month I read five books.
3. Now I read and write better than my brother.
4. When I passed by, I read the sign.

The unique homograph *read* helps us to discover the status of the -ed suffix for the reader. If he correctly reads aloud sentences 1 and 2 with the past-tense form [rɛd], and sentence 3 in the present-tense form [riːd], then we know that he can interpret this homograph in a standard manner depending on whether it is placed in a past or present context. Then in sentence 4, he should give us the pronunciation [rɛd] *if* he deciphers the -ed in *passed* as a signal of the past tense, whether or not he pronounces it.

An Overview of the Nonstandard Vernacular

We have contrasted the casual speech of peer groups of ten- to twelve-year-olds with that of groups of fourteen- to sixteen-year-olds. We find that

---

[6] See "Some Sources of Reading Problems" cited in note 1 and Cooperative Research Report 3288 for quantitative data.

the rules for the basic vernacular become more consistent and regular rather than more mixed with standard English. Some phonological conditions become more consistent, and the spelling forms of individual words, such as *box*, come closer to the standard forms. But the basic grammatical patterns (no third-person singular -*s*, no possessive -*s*, weak -*ed* suffix, stylistic deletion of the copula, and so on) remain well fixed. Whereas the dropping of the plural -*s* is never more than an occasional feature, the third-person singular -*s* has no more support among sixteen-year-olds than among twelve-year-olds.

The most striking evidence of these underlying grammatical facts is the effect of a following vowel on the consonant cluster concerned. When a vowel follows -*ed*, as in *messed up*, the percentage of simplified forms drops moderately. When a vowel follows clusters that are a part of a word, as in *act* or *box*, we see a regular decrease in simplification. This effect becomes stronger with the increasing age of the speakers; and when a vowel follows plural clusters, as in *books*, there is a marked decrease in simplification as well. But when a vowel follows the third-person singular -*s*, as in *works*, or possessive -*s*, as in *John's*, we do not find the -*s* remaining more often. On the contrary, it appears *less* often than when a consonant follows. For this reason, we can argue that there is no phonological process involved here at all. In the underlying grammar, there simply is no morpheme -*s* representing the third-person singular of the verb, and no morpheme -*s* representing the possessive. To be sure, there is a possessive category in *my*, *our*, *his*, and *mine*, and so on, but the particular use of -*s* to mean the possessive after nouns must be taught from the beginning.

CONSEQUENCES FOR THE TEACHING OF READING

Let us consider the problem of teaching a youngster to read who has the general phonological and grammatical characteristics just described. The most immediate way of analyzing his difficulties is through the interpretation of his oral reading. As we have seen, there are many phonological rules that affect his pronunciation, but not necessarily his understanding of the grammatical signals or his grasp of the underlying lexical forms. The two questions are distinct: the relations between grammar and pronunciation are complex and require careful interpretation.

If a pupil is given a certain sentence to read, say *He passed by both of them*, he may say [hi pæs baɪ bof ə dɛm]. The teacher may wish to correct this bad reading, perhaps by saying, "No, it isn't [hi pæs baɪ bof ə dɛm], it's [hi pæst baɪ boθ əv ðɛm]." One difficulty is that these two utterances may sound the same to many children—both the reader and those listening—and they may be utterly confused by the correction. Others may be able to hear the difference, but have no idea of the significance of the extra [t] and the interdental forms of *th*-. The most embarrassing fact is that the child who first read the sentence may have performed his reading task correctly, and understood the -*ed* suffix just as it was intended. In that case, the teacher's correction is completely beside the point.

We have two distinct cases to consider. In one case, the deviation in reading may be only a difference in pronunciation on the part of a child who has a different set of homonyms from the teacher. Here, correction might be quite unnecessary. In the second case, we may be dealing with a child who has no concept of *-ed* as a past-tense marker, who considers the *-ed* a meaningless set of silent letters. Obviously the correct teaching strategy would involve distinguishing between these two cases and treating them quite differently.

How such a strategy might be put into practice is a problem that educators may be able to solve by using information provided by linguists. As a linguist, I can suggest several basic principles derived from our work that may be helpful in further curriculum research and application.

1. In the analysis and correction of oral reading, teachers must begin to make the basic distinction between differences in pronunciation and mistakes in reading. Information on the dialect patterns of black children should be helpful toward this end.

2. In the early stages of teaching reading and spelling it may be necessary to spend much more time on the grammatical function of certain inflections that may have no function in the dialect of some of the children. In the same way, it may be necessary to treat the final elements of certain clusters with the special attention given to silent letters such as *b* in *lamb*.

3. A certain amount of attention given to perception training in the first few years of school may be extremely helpful in teaching children to hear and make standard English distinctions. But perception training need not be complete in order to teach children to read. On the contrary, most of the differences between standard and nonstandard English described here can be taken as differences in the sets of homonyms that must be accepted in reading patterns. On the face of it, there is no reason why a person cannot learn to read standard English texts quite well in a nonstandard pronunciation. Eventually, the school may wish to teach the child an alternative system of pronunciation. But the key to the situation in the early grades is for the teacher to know the system of homonyms of nonstandard English and to know the grammatical differences that separate her own speech from that of the child. The teacher must be prepared to accept the system of homonyms for the moment if this will advance the basic process of learning to read, but not the grammatical differences. Thus the task of teaching the child to read *-ed* is clearly that of getting him to recognize the graphic symbols as a marker of the past tense, quite distinct from the task of getting him to say [pæst] for *passed*.

If the teacher has no understanding of the child's grammar and set of homonyms, she may be arguing with him at cross purposes. Over and over again, the teacher may insist that *cold* and *coal* are different, without realizing that the child perceives this as only a difference in meaning, not in sound. She will not be able to understand why he makes so many odd mistakes in reading, and he will experience only a vague confusion, somehow connected with the ends of words. Eventually, he may stop trying to analyze the shapes of letters that follow the vowel and guess wildly at each word after he deciphers the first few letters. Or he may completely lose confidence in the alphabetic principle and try to recognize each word as a whole. This loss of confidence seems to occur frequently in the third and fourth grades, and it is characteristic of many children who are effectively nonreaders.

The sources of reading problems discussed here are only a few of the causes of poor reading in black ghetto schools. But they are quite specific and easily isolated. The information provided here may have immediate application in the over-all program of improving the teaching of reading to children in these urban areas.

STUDY QUESTIONS

1. Why does Labov feel justified in identifying such an entity as a *black speech pattern* or *black dialect*? Is such an entity necessarily connected with race? In identifying black dialect, Labov speaks of a linguistic reality and a social reality; does the italicized sentence defining black dialect (p. 242) refer more to one than to another? Why does he feel that the inability of subjects to make accurate identification of a speaker's race on the Family Background Test (p. 243) proves his contention that black dialect exists? Compare Labov's results with those reported in the essay by Tucker and Lambert (pp. 293–302).

2. What forces might oppose the recognition of a black dialect? What forces might urge its recognition? Is there any danger that the study of black dialect in the context of educational failure might exaggerate the differences between it and standard English? One student has written, "In regard to the supposed substandard language of lower-class Negroes, school investigators are just beginning to recognize that Negro speech is a language system unto itself which differs from 'standard' English in everything but vocabulary."[a] Would Labov agree with that characterization?

3. It has been observed that features in nonstandard dialects often merely extend tendencies present as well in the standard language. How do such features as the treatment of /r/ and consonant cluster simplification in black dialect exemplify this generalization? If you have studied the history of English from Anglo-Saxon to the modern period, to what would you connect the tendency Labov reports for nonstandard black English "of reducing the amount of information provided after stressed vowels." (p. 246)?

4. If a phonetic rule deletes final consonants, giving the form /pæs/ *passed* rather than /pæst/, does this mean that the nonstandard speaker does not distinguish between present and past time? that he is unable to communicate such a differ-

[a] Roger D. Abrahams, "Black Talk and Black Education," in *Linguistic-Cultural Differences and American Education*, A. C. Aarons, *et al.*, eds. Special Anthology Issue, *The Florida FL Reporter*, 7, 1(1969): 11.

ence? What does Labov mean when he says (p. 252): "There are many [black children] who have no difficulty in *reading -ed* even though they do not pronounce it"? What is the difference between an underlying grammatical category and an underlying morpheme for realizing a grammatical category? What is the difference between a misreading and an accurate reading in a nonstandard pronunciation?

5. A linguistic variable is a single feature of language realized in different, but systematically different ways: for example, the final cluster in *burned* //-nd//, is sometimes realized in standard English speech as /-nd/, sometimes as /-n/, depending on speech style and context (compare "The house burned down" in careful and in casual speech; compare "The house burned down" with "The house burned up" in casual speech). Why do variable features have to be taken into account in comparing nonstandard and standard English? What is the significance for the descriptive linguist of the fact that in black dialect *be* is sometimes realized in copulative sentences, sometimes not (p. 251)? Is this fact pedagogically significant? Can you think of any copulative sentences, subordinate or main, in standard English that lack the copula?

6. What conclusions about the causes of reading failure can be drawn from a comparison of Figures 1 and 2 (pp. 240–41)? How much weight does Labov assign to linguistic causes? Would he agree with the following statement:

> . . . the one major fault of our urban educational system is its failure to understand why teaching an urban child to read is so difficult. But the explanation is really quite simple. A cultural variable is at work which is basic to the difficulty that the Negro child experiences in attempting to learn to read. Evidence has been accumulating that the Negro ghetto child has a different language system (call it Negro nonstandard dialect) which is part of his culture and which interferes with his learning to read. Unless and until this variable is considered, and specific educational innovation based on it, the majority of the inner-city Negro children will continue to fail despite the introduction of all sorts of social improvements to the educational setting.[b]

7. In representing speech, dialect writers usually represent a dialect partly by imitating the actual features of language and partly through "eye dialect"— spellings that have the look but not the substance of dialect. "Wimmin" and "wuz" are both examples of "eye dialect" because they reflect the nearly universal pronunciation of "women" and "was" in English and not the special pronunciation characteristic of a regional or social dialect. As readers, however, we accept a sentence like, "Eye wuz ekspekting sum wimmin" as reflecting some dialect other than our own.

Most dialect writers seek a wider audience than a single group of speakers by liberal use of "eye dialect" mixed with a few instances of "real dialect." After you have studied Labov's list of linguistic features associated with black Americans, examine the following poem by Paul Laurence Dunbar and determine which spellings represent "eye dialect" and which real dialect features. Identify instances where Dunbar might have used a dialect spelling but instead adhered to the usual conventions of written English.

---

[b] Stephen S. Baratz and Joan C. Baratz, "Negro Ghetto Children and Urban Education: A Cultural Solution," in Aarons, *et al.*, *ibid.*, p. 13.

Little Brown Baby

Little brown baby wif spa'klin' eyes,
    Come to yo' pappy an' set on his knee.
What you been doin', suh—makin' san' pies?
    Look at dat bib—you's ez du'ty ez me.
Look at dat mouf—dat's merlasses, I bet;
    Come hyeah, Maria, an' wipe off his han's.
Bees gwine to ketch you an' eat you up yit,
    Bein' so sticky an' sweet—goodness lan's!

Little brown baby wif spa'klin' eyes,
    Who's pappy's darlin' an' who's pappy's chile?
Who is it all de day nevah once tries
    Fu' to be cross, er once loses dat smile?
Whah did you git dem teef? My, you's a scamp!
    Whah did dat dimple come f'om in yo' chin?
Pappy do' know yo—I b'lieves you's a tramp;
    Mammy, dis hyeah's some ol' straggler got in!

Let's th'ow him outen de do' in de san',
    We do' want stragglers a-layin' 'roun' hyeah;
Let's gin him 'way to de big buggah-man;
    I know he's hidin' erroun' hyeah right neah.
Buggah-man, buggah-man, come in de do',
    Hyeah's a bad boy you kin have fu' to eat.
Mammy an' pappy do' want him no mo',
    Swaller him down f'om his haid to his feet!

Dah, now, I t'ought dat you'd hug me up close.
    Go back, ol' buggah, you sha'n't have dis boy.
He ain't no tramp, ner no straggler, of co'se;
    He's pappy's pa'dner an' playmate an' joy.
Come to you' pallet now—go to yo' res';
    Wisht you could allus know ease an' cleah skies;
Wisht you could stay jes' a chile on my breas'—
    Little brown baby wif spa'klin' eyes!°

° Reprinted by permission of Dodd, Mead & Company, from *The Complete Poems of Paul Laurence Dunbar* (New York, 1922), pp. 134–35.

GO SLOW IN ETHNIC ATTRIBUTIONS:
GEOGRAPHIC MOBILITY AND DIALECT PREJUDICES

Raven I. McDavid, Jr.

In the great novel of American migrants, The Grapes of Wrath, *John Steinbeck draws attention to the regional dialect boundaries that divide American English:*

> By the tent a little embarrassment had set in, and social intercourse had paused before it started. Pa said, "You ain't Oklahomy folks?"
>
> And Al, who stood near the car, looked at the license plates. "Kansas," he said.
>
> The lean man said, "Galena, or right about there. Wilson, Ivy Wilson."
>
> "We're Joads," said Pa. "We come from right near Sallisaw."
>
> "Well, we're proud to meet you folks," said Ivy Wilson. "Sairy, these is Joads."
>
> "I knowed you wasn't Oklahomy folks. You talk queer kinda—that ain't no blame, you understan'."
>
> "Ever'body says words different," said Ivy. "Arkansas folks says 'em different, and Oklahomy folks says 'em different. And we seen a lady from Massachusetts, an' she said 'em differentest of all. Couldn' hardly make out what she was sayin'."[a]

As McDavid shows in the following essay, contact between speakers of different regional dialects may cause "a little embarrassment" at first, even among those well-disposed to friendship, or may act as the pretext for stereotyped and prejudicial attitudes among those not so disposed. In addition to the overt linguistic signals that mark dialect differences, the extralinguistic patterns of gesture and the beliefs about appropriate language behavior may also contribute to suspicion, misunderstanding, or hostility. Although understanding these differences may contribute toward harmony, "there is no substitute," as McDavid says (p. 270), "for respect for every mode of speaking."

Anyone who has seriously studied the history of the English language— or indeed of any other language—will realize that what happens to be a

[a] John Steinbeck, *The Grapes of Wrath* (New York: Modern Library, nd), p. 184.

prestigious form of language at a given time is largely the result of a series of historical accidents. Though some have hinted that a language may have special virtues—Benjamin Lee Whorf, for instance, suggested that Hopi might be better than English for dealing with vibration phenomena—one can conclude that all languages have the same potentiality for expressing all the range of human experience, and that any language (given the right kind of creative genius to use it) can be the vehicle of what we sometimes call "great literature." The reverence we feel for Greek as a language is associated with the culture of the Hellenic, Alexandrian, and Byzantine civilizations, not with anything intrinsic in any period of the Greek language itself. Our linguistic and cultural isolation prevents us from realizing that Arabic was the vehicle of the greatest civilization in the Mediterranean world from the seventh till the twelfth century. We are but dimly aware that since 1800 the achievements of Western civilization have been made available to monolinguals who speak such tongues as Indonesian, Turkish, Czech, and Finnish; we are more familiar with the technological success of the Israelis whose national tongue was fitted for modern civilization after more than two thousand years of disuse except as a liturgical language and has proved itself adequate for everything from aeronautics to zoology. As we become more sophisticated, we realize that what is the prestigious variety of a given tongue may vary from one century to another. English was the language of barbarians when it was first carried to the British Isles; shortly afterward, however, the northern variety—Northumbrian—became the vehicle of a distinguished culture. Then, with Northumbria overrun by the Northmen, prestige shifted southward to Mercia; a little later, to Wessex in the southwest; and finally, after all varieties of English lost prestige under the Norman Conquest, to London where still a further prestige variety arose. And with the exception of Scots—and not a complete exception at that—every variety of standard English since that time has borne the imprint of what has become standard in London.

There are two qualifications that we need to make to clarify the influence of the London standard. First of all, London English itself has changed in many ways since its preeminence was established. All of the long vowels and diphthongs have changed; some have fallen together and others have arisen. The inflections have been greatly simplified, with some categories disappearing altogether and others becoming more uniform in their expression. New syntactic devices have developed; if English does not have—and it never has had—the variety of verb inflections for tense that Latin possessed, it has developed a much more complicated system of verb phrases than anything we find on the European continent. English has lost many words and gained many more. The half-million entries in a so-called "unabridged" dictionary are but the tip of the lexicographical iceberg, for it is estimated that fifty thousand chemical compounds are discovered and named every year. There is not—and may never be—a complete inventory of all the slang words that have been used in English since printing was developed. Moreover, it is a hopeless task to consider what went on in the thousand previous years of

English, for few words of what we would now call slang found their way into the limited records set down by those few who had mastered the arcane skill of writing. Of the words that do survive in the language from the fifth century onward, almost every one has somehow changed its range of meaning—even such verbal auxiliaries as *can* and *may*, *shall* and *will*, or such prepositions as *of* and *with*.

The other qualification to our reflections on the influence of London English is that there is no single variety of English that we can call standard to the exclusion of other varieties. In a review of Mark M. Orkin's *Speaking Canadian English*, I have taken the author to task for setting up a contrast between "Standard English" and "General American." Leaving the latter term aside, I observe that to him "Standard English" seems to be restricted not merely to what is sometimes referred to as "Received Standard," Southern British, or "Public School English," but to the subspecies of it that A. S. C. Ross, Nancy Mitford, and their journalistic playmates chose to designate as *U*, the usage of the hereditary aristocracy. I had to remind Orkin —or at least the readers of the journal for which I was writing the review— that *U* was not coterminous in its application with even the body of speakers of Received Standard, and that many people in England have excellent cultural credentials, excellent education, and often titles of nobility, but do not speak that subvariety of the standard usage of Southern Britain, much less command the ineffable subtleties attributed by Ross and Miss Mitford to *U*.

If we go elsewhere in the world, we discover that there is even less reason to regard one variety of the language as the unique bearer of a culture. In Canada and the United States, in Australia and New Zealand and South Africa, and in dozens of areas within these grander subdivisions of the English-speaking world, there are people who grow up acquiring the best usage of the best representatives of local cultural traditions. Leaving aside the usage of other nations, the cultural facts are that there is inherently nothing to place the usage of Massachusetts (eastern or western) above that of Minnesota, that of New York above that of New Orleans, that of Texas above that of Tennessee, that of Virginia above that of California. The American presidency has spoken in the accents of the Virginia Piedmont, of central Ohio, of Vermont, of Iowa transplanted to the San Francisco Bay area, of the Hudson Valley, of Western Missouri, of Boston, of southeast Texas, and of Southern California—all within the last half century when broadcasting has made a candidate's accent instantly accessible to a national audience.

Yet the intellectual demonstration that any variety of language is intrinsically as good as any other, for all human purposes, is not always matched by visceral acceptance of this argument. Of the presidential worthies we have mentioned, every one had his way of speaking severely criticized by his countrymen, sometimes by members of the opposition party, sometimes by his nominal followers. Possibly the most cruel ridicule in recent years was that which Eastern and Middle-Western newspapers bestowed on the speech of Lyndon B. Johnson; "Old Cornpone" was one of the more printable epithets used to describe his speech, which was compared unfavorably to that of his more glamorous predecessor, John Kennedy. Yet Kennedy's own speech was not above criticism; in a discussion with students at the University of Kentucky, Albert H. Marckwardt discovered that they responded favorably to Johnson's speech as that of a familiar, sincere type of person with whom they could feel at ease; they distrusted the speech of the Kennedy clan as that of cold, arrogant, ruthless manipulators. It is simply the speech to which one has become accustomed that inspires the favorable reaction. The reactions of the Kentucky students were not dissimilar to those I once had toward the speech of other regions than my native South Carolina; indeed, within South Carolina itself, we of the Piedmont region were frequently amused and bewildered by the exotic speech of the Charleston area, even though we knew that the social order of Charleston—and hence the speech of representatives of that social order—was something to be admired by all those with any feeling for standards. For outsiders we had other feelings, rare as were our contacts. New Englanders we adjudged—as the Kentucky students did the Kennedys—as cold and calculating and arrogant; New Yorkers as unpleasantly aggressive; eastern Virginians as a bit pompous. For Middle Westerners we had little to say, perhaps because the routes of travel brought few of them into our neighborhood; but the feeling could hardly have been one of respect, since one of the folk comments in South Carolina is that the educated Middle Westerner talks like the uneducated Southerner— both of them having the strongly constricted postvocalic /-r/ that has been lacking in the educated speech of London and Boston and Richmond and Charleston and (until recently) New York.

As geographic mobility has increased, it has not always been a blessing, even to the educated migrant, since he has to wrestle with the prejudices his new neighbors have toward his way of speaking. And if he is white and a native speaker of English, he has none of the obvious cues of race or ethnicity to win the sympathetic ear of teachers or counselors who suspect that only willfulness prevents him from instantly adopting local speechways. That he may himself come from a cultural environment with traditions quite different from those of his new community is rarely admitted; Middle Westerners are often astounded that schoolchildren in the South are expected to use *sir* or *ma'am* in addressing teachers or older people; and Southern parents may become enraged on learning that their children have been reprimanded by Michigan teachers for using these normal tokens of respect. No matter how sure one is of his identity and cultural credentials, it is traumatic to have his normal speech made the butt of alleged professorial humor, as mine was in my first summer in Ann Arbor, two years after I received my Ph.D.; equally traumatic—perhaps even more so—would be the playground mockery that a Virginian might encounter in Nebraska, or a Wisconsinite in the cracker precincts of Florida.

The understanding of speechways different from one's own should start with groups whose overt status is close enough for the differences in cues and reactions to be subtle ones. Then one can expand his view to include groups where the divergences are greater and are reinforced by more striking differences in race or religion or ethnic background. In other words, for many in the United States it is easier to start with the speech of educated whites of long-term residence, then progress through the speech of the uneducated native monolingual whites to white groups with foreign-language background and finally to other races. And since for the first two categories, speakers of Southern background are the most numerous and perhaps most strikingly different from the inland Northerners and Far Westerners, we may start with these.[1] It is also an advantage for me to start this way since my family has lived (on one side) for six generations in the same upland county of South Carolina, and since I have been constantly reminded—as fieldworker, teacher, and citizen—of differences between my own habits of communication and those of the people among whom I have spent the greater part of my professional career. It is almost certain that I have partially assimilated to the Middle-Western mode after thirty years of living in the region, though I question the validity of my sister's judgment when she asserts that I have been living in the North so long I speak "just like a Yankee." (But then her definition of what constitutes a Yankee is hardly one that would satisfy New Englanders or York Staters).

One of the first differences recognized between the speech of Southerners and that of other Americans is a difference in range. A good deal of this kind of difference can be equated with specific parts of the linguistic system, particularly stress and pitch. We can assume that Southern varieties of American English agree with those of other regions in having four pitch levels and four degrees of stress (and though the testing of the theories of Pike and Wells and Trager has not yet provided us with a definite answer, the fact that all three approaches agree in the number of levels they posit is enough to justify our adopting them as a working hypothesis). Nevertheless the intervals are greater in the Southern varieties; the highest Southern pitch is higher than its

---

[1] There are other reasons for starting with the speech of the South and its cultural dependencies. These regions have differed strikingly from others in that their population has grown, if at all, largely as the result of natural increase rather than of immigration; in fact, population is one of the principal export crops of the South, and is responsible for the growth, say, of Detroit as a manufacturing center, much like the iron of the Mesabi Range and the coal of southern Ohio.

In the South, there has been no sizeable influx of foreign-language speakers except for scattered urban colonies of middle-class Germans, and the Spanish-Americans in south Florida and the southern and southwestern corners of Texas. In this way, perhaps, one may see the kernel of truth in the venerable myth that certain Southerners—mountaineers or islanders—continue to speak "pure Elizabethan English."

The relationships of the speech of white Southerners and that of their black neighbors is an extremely complex question, which will not concern us here. The emphasis is generally on those features that are found widely spread, including such areas as the Appalachians where African influence is unlikely.

Midwestern counterpart, and its lowest is probably lower; likewise, the strongest stress in the speech of Southerners is relatively stronger, and the weakest is relatively weaker. Prolongation of the stressed vowels under these conditions gives the illusion of drawl, of relatively slow speech, though in all probability the tempo of even the slowest Southern speech is somewhat faster than Midwestern, thanks to the shortening of the weak-stressed syllables. Other varieties of Southern, such as those along the South Carolina and Georgia coast, do not even create an illusion of languor; and among these the English of the Gullah coast—spoken by the black people of the Sea Islands and necks, isolated for generations from the prestige patterns of the mainland—is notorious for its speed, even among urban speakers of the same region and race.

But perhaps even more important—and more susceptible of misinterpretation by others—is the difference in the modalities of communication, even among the most highly educated Southerners. Everybody has long recognized—and such scholars as Martin Joos and Harold Allen have pointed out for more than a decade—that what we call Standard English is not monolithic, even in the usage of a single speaker. None of us writes exactly the way he talks; none of us uses the same kinds of locutions on informal occasions that he uses on formal ones. But the difference between written and spoken usage, between informal and formal, can vary a great deal. Here, it seems, the educated Southerner has a far greater range than his analog in other regions. Almost proverbially, sometimes even to the occasion of mild ridicule, the Southerner can indulge in flights of formal rhetoric or deferential manners that one does not meet in Michigan or Vermont; yet the same Southerner, in intimate conversation with his equals, can engage in banter and in the free use of the most scornfully condemned grammatical features. In some of the most class–conscious Southern communities, the use of *ain't* by educated speakers in informal situations is a signal to the stranger that he has been accepted as a social equal. The educated speaker from other regions, who doesn't use *ain't* at all—who may, in the words of James H. Sledd, consider it slightly more reprehensible than incest—cannot make so dramatic a shift even if he understands the cue. So the Southerner gets the reputation for speaking sloppily, and the person from other regions gets that of being stiff if not pompous. Since the subculture of schoolteachers, even in the South, is infected with the notion of monolithic correctness, the Southerner—especially the male one—may have a hard time in the classroom, even in his own region. Transplanted, whatever his ethnic background, he is likely to encounter even greater prejudices. Nor is the Midwesterner transplanted to the South sure of escaping traumata; his new associates may interpret his natural speechways as standoffish at best, patronizing at worst.

This entire problem is perhaps not so much linguistic as ethnographic. Probably no one can provide a student or teacher or traveler with a full range of the cues that may differ from one region to another. What is needed, rather, is some elementary cultural anthropology, with an emphasis on respecting the habitual mode of speaking of the other person, wherever you encounter him, and a skepticism about any kinds of generalities, however eloquently stated or whoever states them. And particularly a person should be skeptical of anyone who claims to speak for an entire region or social group.

In pronunciation, there are relatively few differences between cultivated Southern speech and that of other regions, so far as the system of the language is concerned. If the Southerner sometimes lacks an active contrast between such pairs of words as *pin* and *pen*, this is a tendency that is old in the Germanic languages; and it is no more exotic than the lack of contrast between *cot* and *caught*, *collar* and *caller*, that one finds in northeastern New England, including Boston, in the Pittsburgh area, in parts of the Ohio and middle Mississippi valleys, in much of the Rocky Mountain area, and in most of Canada from Toronto west. The Southerner often has many contrasts that speakers in some other regions lack. He is likely to have such initial clusters as /tj-, dj-, nj-, stj-/, as in *tube, due, new, student*, which contrast with the initials of *tool, do, noodle,* and *stool*. He often contrasts such pairs as *hoarse/ horse, mourning/morning, boarder/border*, with the former member of each pair having a higher vowel than the latter. He usually has an initial /hw-/ cluster in such words as *whales* and *whit*, contrasting with /w-/ in *wails* and *wit*. And he may have a three-way contrast between *Mary, merry,* and *marry*, respectively, with the vowels of *bait, bet,* and *bat*. He sometimes has lost the postvocalic /r-/ in *barn* and the like, but not always; in either event, he has company in other regions. But in many parts of the South, the presence of a strong /-r/ has been associated with poor-white speech, and the Southerner who hears the Midwestern /-r/ from speakers who do not make the vowel contrasts he normally makes is perhaps inclined toward the ethnocentric observation that the Middlewestern form of English is somehow inferior. Such an observation, of course, is based on imperfect information, but it is no more naive than other observations about regional speech patterns that ostensibly educated men have made in the past.

The educated Southerner is likely to simplify many final consonant clusters, and the less formal his speech, the greater the extent of the simplification. The simplification is most likely to occur before a following consonant, as in *act mad*, where the final /-t/ of *act* will disappear in educated speech in other regions too; but in the South, it may also occur before vowels, as in *ac' alive*. Along with the vocalization of postvocalic /-r/, which we have already mentioned, we have a similar vocalization of preconsonantal /-l/, as in *help yourself*, which becomes *he'p yourse'f*; but there are many instances of similar vocalization in standard English, whether of the native word stock, as in *talk*, or of borrowings, as *palm*. That many of these (such as *vault*) have seen the /-l/ restored under the influence of spelling pronunciation does not alter the fact that it is an old phenomenon, and one that occurs often without stigmatization. Less common in educated Southern speech, and often highly conditioned by the informality of the speaking situation, are the loss of /r/

in /θr-/, as in *throw* and *through,* and the replacement of /θ, ð/ by /t, d/ so that there is no contrast between *thinker* and *tinker* or between *then* and *den.*

The phonic realization of vowels and diphthongs in the South is often very different from that to which Midwesterners are accustomed. The diphthong of *oil,* for instance, sometimes becomes a monophthong, or glides toward the position of the weak-stressed vowel in *sofa;* most Southerners still contrast such words with, say, *all* where the diphthong is up-gliding, but since Southern *oil* often sounds like Midwestern *all,* there is much opportunity for confusion. More notorious is the /ai/ diphthong, which in most varieties of Southern speech becomes a low-front monophthong finally and before voiced consonants—as in *lie* and *live*—and in an increasing number of educated speakers is now heard in all positions where [ai] is heard elsewhere. This leads to confusion among outside observers. Some Philadelphians, for instance, confuse Southern *ride* with their own *rod;* Detroiters notoriously confuse Southern *right* with their own *rat*—and both groups, assuming their own norms as the truth, accuse the Southerners of articulatory or auditory deficiencies. The deficiency, of course, is in the experience of the Northern observer. A group of Chicago teachers, tested on contrasts that occur regularly in Southern speech, predictably scored low in "auditory discrimination."

Less troublesome, perhaps, is the Virginia and Charleston alternation between the phonic shapes of /ai/ and /au/ according to their environments— [əɪ] [əʊ] before voiceless consonants as in *tight* and *house* (n.) but [ai] and [au] elsewhere as in *tide* and *house* (v.)—since these variants also occur in Canadian speech. The Charlestonian ingliding /e/ and /o/, as in *date* and *boat,* sound peculiar to the outsider but are not likely to cause trouble.

The Southern stress patterns are sometimes misappreciated; strong stress and the reduction of weak syllables prosper the tendency to reduce final vowels in *Tuesday* and *borrow,* where various influences—spelling pronunciation in particular—have spread the full vowels /e/ and /o/ in the Middle West. There is also much greater tendency among Southerners than elsewhere (and not just among the uneducated) to drop weak-stressed pretonic syllables, so that *professor* may become *fessor.* Even educated Southerners show greater persistence of the tradition of front-shifting English stress in loan words, giving *pólice, hótel, guítar,* and the like, and, though the more sophisticated Southerners deride it, there is some favoring by the recently risen of secondary stresses in such words as *séttlemènt, présidènt, évidènce.* Both of these phenomena are heard elsewhere, and reached national notoriety when used by President Eisenhower.

Among the grammatical features of educated Southern speech, in its informal modes particularly, are several that have sometimes been taken as stigmata of nonstandard English, or even of particular ethnic varieties of nonstandard. One of the most common is the *-in* in the present participle, popularly known as "dropping the *-g,*" but actually the substitution of one nasal consonant /n/ for another /ŋ/. Southerners also have the participle *done,* emphatic or otherwise, as *I('ve) done told you that three times.* They often omit the auxiliary *have*, as in *I been thinking about it*, and the copula *be* before participles, adjectives, and predicate nouns, as *We going to vote for him, they all dead, you worn out, you a good girl*. The informal discourse of the educated Southerner also includes many compound auxiliaries not often met in other regions, for instance, *might could, used to could*, and *used to didn't*. Depending on the speed of utterance and the degree of intimacy between speaker and hearer, the future auxiliary may be reduced down to the nasalized vowel [õ], as [a·m õ go], "I'm going to go." *He don't* is not uncommon. There are occasional multiple negatives; like the use of *ain't*, this practice serves as a social cue indicating that the occasion is one for relaxed speech. Not dependent on an intimate situation is the occasional use of the article *a* before vowels, as in *give me a apple*. There is frequently an appositive pronoun after a noun subject, as *my brother John he told me this*. Indirect questions may have the inverted word order associated with direct ones, as *I want to know can you come over next week*. And there are various omissions of the relative pronoun in subject or object position, such as *He's a man thinks well of himself* and *that's a dog I'd like to own*. All of these usages, to be sure, are well attested earlier, in informal literary texts; in fact, one may say that the colloquial mode of educated Southern speech is reminiscent of the relaxation of its British counterpart of the colonial period, indicating that in this as in other ways the South has lagged behind cultural developments of the rest of the English-speaking world.[2]

All of these features may be heard from Southerners whose social credentials are impeccable—persons of the assured social position that comes with approved lineage, good education, and long exposure to books and some amounts of inherited wealth. They are not, we must reiterate, characteristic of all the discourse of such people. These forms would never appear in writing, except by way of joking, nor would they be likely to show up in a formal address, except perhaps by way of illustration (though the audience, while smiling at such speech forms, would be perfectly aware that anyone present could use them in less formal situations). The tradition of decorum, again perhaps a carry-over from the seventeenth and eighteenth centuries, argues that one adapts one's speech to the social occasion. If we have emphasized so far the kinds of things that educated Southerners will use in the spirit of informal discourse, we must indicate that they are also aware of the needs of the formal situation. The Southerner also likes to dress up—in language as

[2] These forms have been generally documented in the archives of the Linguistic Atlas of the Middle and South Atlantic States, for eight years at the University of Chicago, and are of course accessible to reputable scholars; but as yet they have never been consulted by those who have made the generalizations about ethnic varieties of nonstandard speech. Most of these have been documented from my own speech; here I rely on the observations of my Minnesota-reared wife and of our various non-Southern colleagues, since even the most objective mind can be bamboozled in intuitive observations of grammaticality. Most have also been observed in six decades of association with educated Southerners, especially in recent business and social visits to the South.

well as in clothes and behavior. If a planter's son like Eugene Talmadge could shift into the vernacular of poor whites so well that he could be adopted as their spokesman, so could the son of a poor white like Huey Long master the most courtly traditions of Southern formal oratory and use this mastery when the occasion demanded, as at the Democratic convention of 1932.

What happens is that this linguistic versatility is—or has been—the property of a relatively small class, of a near-hereditary élite, and of a relative few who have assimilated the full range of the rhetorical tradition. This assimilation is not confined to any one race; Jesse Jackson and Martin Luther King have had a wide range of styles suitable for various audiences and their expectations. But those who have not had or acquired the social background to develop the full repertoire of modalities find themselves at a disadvantage in using some of them—the modality of writing as opposed to that of speaking, the formal modality as opposed to the informal. Most Southerners—educated and uneducated alike—will have such homonyms as *six* and *sixth* and *sixths* or *mind* and *mine*; but the educated will know the conventions of writing. They will know that there are certain cues necessary in writing that are not necessary in speech, and they will know that formal speech demands a number of things that are not needed in informal. Those who do not know these conventions—and very often their knowledge is less a matter of formal schooling than of long exposure to a cultural environment—will try to make the switch simply by using bigger words and longer sentences with a greater number of modifiers. That these misdirected attempts often result in the ludicrous is also in keeping with a long English tradition, represented by Mrs. Malaprop of *The Rivals* and the grocer's wife of *The Knight of the Burning Pestle*.

What makes the problem more acute in the South than in other regions is again the matter of greater spread. Because the social order and the accidents of history have provided, until very recently, fewer economic and educational advantages in the South than elsewhere, and have given those advantages to a smaller part of the population, there has been a wider gap between educated and uneducated speech in the South than in other regions. Thus while almost all Southerners have the relaxed, informal mode of speech, relatively few know how to shift to the practices of the formal mode of speech or to the conventions of writing. The others, as we have already mentioned, generalize the informal to all circumstances; when this mode is used by transplanted Southerners in an alien Northern environment—especially in classrooms staffed by teachers who do not understand the Southern tradition and its cues—the result may often be harsh condemnation from the teacher and ridicule from classmates.[3] And this unsympathetic reaction may result

---

[3] One may point out that the rites of passage of the pedagog, especially those in the elementary school, are so traumatic as to instill antipathy toward one's native speech forms that do not conform to the schoolbook knowledge of propriety. Since the generality of public school teachers come most largely from the upper working class or lower middle class, where social insecurity is most acute, they tend to rely on their new status and to shun

regardless of the race of the migrant student or of his social standing in his native habitat. According to the conventions of his new environment—conventions which may not even accurately reflect local speechways—these forms which most Southerners share are simply not recognized as part of educated usage.

Though a large part of the difficulties of the white speaker of a divergent dialect comes from the fact that his native culture and that into which he has moved have different beliefs about what constitutes cultivated speech, some of them are due to his having more of what are everywhere regarded as non-standard forms of English and his using them more frequently. We have indicated some of the cultural forces—economic and educational—that have produced a cultural lag in much of the South; we might here mention as well the greater proportion of the Southerners who heretofore grew up in rural areas and spent their lives in an environment of subsistence agriculture and consequently poorer opportunities for travel and encounters with speakers from other regions. Of course this cuts both ways; the Midwesterner who has never known an educated Southerner is at a disadvantage as well, and for both kinds of deprivation, the radio and television are a poor substitute for face-to-face contacts. All of these forces promote the kind of cultural isolation in which nonstandard forms thrive—whether archaisms that have been lost elsewhere or neologisms that have simply not spread. A person who knows the history of English will recognize both tendencies as we summarize some characteristics of speech characteristic of the uneducated in the South.

There are only a few differences in noun plurals. Even the uninflected plurals of nouns of measure (*forty bushel, ten mile, five ton,* and the like) are not solely identified with the South, for they occur widely in other regions. A special group of plurals are those of nouns ending in *-sp, -sk,* and *-st* (such as *wasp, desk, post*). In the American South and South Midland, such nouns often have plurals in /-iz/, sometimes added directly to the base form and sometimes with the /-p, -t, -k/ lost. Both types of plural for these nouns are found in Southern England, except for the East Anglian region where most New England settlers came from. Hence it is in the different historical antecedents of Northern and Southern dialects that the explanation for these differences should be sought.

Among the personal pronouns there are some differences in the use of subject and object forms in educated and uneducated Southern usage, a difference confounded by the interference of pedagogs who teach students to avoid *it's me* and adopt *between you and I.* On a more fundamental level—particularly in the South Midland—there is some persistence of the *-n* forms

---

linguistic forms that remind them embarrassingly of the class from which they came. This is true of teachers with Southern origins, who have lacked economic and social prestige. It is also true of the urban teacher of recent central or southern European descent, who has no exposure to the colloquial tradition of English and is hence incapable of appreciating the language of children of Southern American descent.

of absolute genitives: *it's yourn, ourn, hisn, hern, theirn.* The historical merger of singular and plural in the second person—there is no survival of the old second singular (*thou, thee, thy, thine*) in the folk speech of continental North America (their preservation among the Society of Friends is a learned affectation)—has induced the development of several new plural forms: *you-all* (chiefly Southern), *youse* (associated with metropolitan proletarians), *you-uns* (South Midland), *mongst-ye* (eastern shore of Chesapeake Bay), *oona* (Gullah). That all of these show some tendency to become used as polite singulars is a repetition of linguistic history; that none of these is found in standard writing, and only *you-all* in cultivated speech, suggests that the innovations are not likely to be a problem unless teachers set out to create one. From the point of view of consistency, such forms as *hisself* and *their-selves* complete the pattern of *myself, ourselves, yourself, yourselves—herself* and *itself* are ambiguous—but they are unlikely to overcome their association with uneducated speech and become standard.

With the comparison of adjectives and adverbs, there is some tendency among uneducated speakers in the South to use more inflected comparisons (such as *beautifuller, lovinger,* and *grown-uppest*) and some emphatic double comparisons (such as *more prettier*). These represent an archaic trait in English—everyone who has read *Julius Caesar* has noted "the *most unkindest* cut of all"—but the construction lost its lodgment in standard English before the end of the seventeenth century.

Most of the strictly nonstandard forms are found among the verbs. The zero third singular (*he do,* and the like) is found not only on the Southern coast but in the mountains as well, and occasionally further north in native white speech; it is old in English folk speech, and is still widely distributed in the south of England. A parallel is the generalization of the *-s* ending for all persons and both numbers (*I says, we works*), which also has its origins in Britain, this time in the north and as far back as 1300. With the process of dialect mixture in all of the original colonies, to say nothing of their derivations westward, we might expect to find vacillation in local usage and even in a given speaker. In some communities of Newfoundland, this has resulted in an aspectual distinction, formally signaled, but nothing of the kind has been attested in white speech in the United States.

Be as a finite verb (as in *He be miner*) still flourishes in dialects of the West Country of England, but in white speech in the United States it is definitely a relic, generally confined to a few items. However, its relic distribution is wide: New England, the inland North, the Appalachians, the coastal South, to say nothing of a well-attested use among black Americans.

Among principal parts of verbs, there are three kinds of differences between standard and nonstandard usage, all of which may appear in the same speaker.

1. A difference in the irregular preterite or participle: *He give it to me; we seen him; it's brang.* Sometimes this involves the extension of the preterite form to the past participle: *the post must be drove in, the road is tore up.*

2. The use of an irregular form, whether archaic or innovating, in the non-standard: *I drug it away, we clumb* (or *clim* or *clome*) *the tree.*
3. The use of a regular form (usually innovative) where the standard form is irregular: *the wind blowed hard, he drawed a bucket of water.*

Needless to say, there are different kinds of verb phrases in nonstandard speech from what one finds in standard. Most multiple negatives, for instance, revolve around predication, including something as intricate as *there ain't nobody never makes no pound cake no more.* But the number of differences generally turns out to be fewer than we would anticipate; many forms that have been put under the schoolmaster's taboo turn out to have some currency in cultured usage—the language of those who by family and education and social standing have the right to be considered cultured—as well as in non-standard usage. *I'm been thinking* seems exotic to most Americans, yet it has currency among educated speakers of the Chesapeake Bay area. *Hadn't ought* has been assailed for generations, though it is used by many educated Northerners, especially in the covert form, *I ought to do it, hadn't I?* Such compounded auxiliaries as *might could, used to could,* and *used to didn't* are more frequent in the mouths of the uneducated but, as we have noted earlier, they also occur in the informal speech of cultivated Southerners.

Perhaps this is where we should end, almost where we began. There is a great deal of variety within cultivated English usage, and the person who works with a restricted definition of what is cultivated is only limiting himself. It is such restricted definitions of the cultivated—accompanied most of the time by unfamiliarity with the history of the English language and with the wide range of folk speech among the native stock of English-speaking North America (to say nothing of the British Isles)—that are responsible for many popular and profitable pronouncements about the peculiar ethnicity of many speech forms. Most of the time, they turn out to be things widely distributed in the language, but not in the speech of the observer and his associates. One could of course have a field day deploring such information, but what is more important is to encourage the habit of observation. Perhaps the slogan might be: "Go slow in ethnic attributions; the usage you label might be your own." From the long-term point of view, there is no substitute for respect for every mode of speaking as an adequate system, for compassion toward students who must master other modalities from those habitual to them, and for painstaking accumulation of data whether or not it fits conveniently into eloquent (and transient) theories of language behavior.

STUDY QUESTIONS

1. As McDavid notes, "the relationships of the speech of white Southerners and that of their black neighbors is an extremely complex question" (p. 262n). While there is no clear agreement among scholars on the answer to this ques-

tion, it is clear from the masses of linguistic data accumulated by the field-workers for the Linguistic Atlas of the United States and Canada that there are many points of resemblance. Compare the account given by Labov in the previous selection with the sketch of Southern speech presented by McDavid. What common features do you find?

2. McDavid points out that in addition to specific features of phonology, morphology, and syntax, dialects differ in how widely they range from formal to informal usage, in the use of particular styles for particular occasions, and in the expectations of their speakers regarding the language behavior of others. In what respects have these differences contributed to misunderstandings between Northerners and Southerners? Can you add additional examples of the difficulties that speakers encounter in communicating successfully in a dialect region new to them?

3. In a previous study question, we pointed out the difference between "eye dialect" and the attempt to imitate the features genuinely characteristic of a regional or social variety. Examine the following passage from a newspaper story about Governor George Wallace and determine which features of the dialect described by McDavid are represented here and which spellings represent the informal speech of nearly all Americans, Southern and Northern alike.

> During lunch at the mansion one day last summer, the Governor cringed when he saw a fly buzzing near the food. "They's a fly," he said darkly, got up and swatted at it vainly.
>
> "Don't worry with it, George," Cornelia said with a small smile. "It shouldn't bother you. It oughta remind you of home in Barbour County."
>
> "Don't say somethin' like that with him here," Wallace sputtered, jerking a thumb in my direction. "He'll think they's nothin' but dirt in Barbour County. . . ."
>
> "You watch," he cautioned Cornelia between mouthfuls. "Whatever I say, he's gonna make it come out 'aincha,' 'doncha,' 'gonna.' An' he'll have *you* sayin', 'Yawl come back now, heunh?' . . . An' he's gonna have me wipin' off my mouth with the back of my hand and suckin' through my teeth."
>
> "Yeah, they smooth, these newsboys—but they'll getcha. When they quote Wallace, it always comes out bad grammar. But Martin Luther King and [Ralph] Abernathy? They always come out speakin' the King's English."[a]

4. McDavid suggests that a failure to understand the "modalities of communication" may inhibit human relationships (p. 263). Examine the following account of a West Virginian's experiences in Chicago and describe the assumptions that the Southerner and the Northerner bring to a casual encounter.

> Those people down there, they eat good and they feed you good, too. You don't just get by the way they do up here. I get well taken care of down there, you better believe it. I get offered a lot more food than I can eat—for a short spell, you know, anyways. They're a lot friendlier in West Virginia than they are out here.

[a] Stephen Lesher, "Who Knows What Frustrations Lurk in the Hearts of X Million Americans? George Wallace Knows," *The New York Times Magazine* (January 2, 1972), p. 35.

I went back to West Virginia and was talkin with a guy.
He said, "Well, Ras," he said, "how you gettin along out there?"
I said, "Oh, gettin along good," I said, "you only have one problem."
He said, "What's that?"
I said, "To find somebody to talk to."
He said, "Why is that?"
I said, "Everybody talks to theirself out there," I said, "They go along the street talkin to theirself."

You notice em doin that lots of times, you know. These original ones from here, you know. I told im, "Now if you find somebody from West Virginia, or the South somewhere, down in Alabama or someplace like that, they're ready to talk to you." But the original ones that live here, you can ask em anything. Maybe they'll say something or they'll turn their head and look the other way. I had em do me that way lots a times. Settin in a beer garden, you know, drinkin. Maybe I'll go in and get me a mug o' beer, say somethin-or-other to a guy: it's pretty cold out there, or somethin, or pretty warm, or somethin like 'at. "Yep"—he'll just turn his head over, turn right on the stool, turn and look the other way. They won't talk to you. I dunno for why, but they won't. They sure won't talk to you.[b]

5. McDavid suggests (p. 266) that the English characteristic of the educated Southerner is conservative, retaining many archaic traits that have not survived in other parts of the United States. Evaluate this statement in light of the following sample from an interview with a representative of one of the most conservative dialects of English, the English of the isolated island of Tristan da Cunha in the South Atlantic. From its settlement in the early nineteenth century until the volcanic eruption that displaced the islanders in 1961, Tristan da Cunha was largely isolated from linguistic and cultural developments taking place elsewhere in the world; its language, although resembling British dialects more than American ones, is especially archaic and traditional. In examining the speech, look particularly for features typical of the dialect that McDavid describes.

Gordon Glass (=GG) Age: 63

Interviewer: René Cutforth, B.B.C. (=RC).

1 RC: What's the difference between the time when you were twenty and just before now?

2 GG: ou ɛs ə ˈlɒd ə ˈdifrəns biˈtwin ˈdɛn →| wən ˈai wəs
    Oh, there's a lot of difference between then, when I was

3 ˈtwɛnti n →| sins də ˈfæktri kʌm ʌp →|| n wɛn ˈai wəs əbaut
    twenty, and, since the factory come up. And when I was about

4 ˈtwenti(j) →| twɛniˈfaiv jə ˈsiː →| jᵊu æd ə ˈpɛn ən s ˈpɑːsn
    twenty— twenty-five, you see, you had to depend on passing

5 ˈʃips fər ˈɛvriθiŋ →| ðɛn sʌmˈtaims it bi əbaut ə ˈjiːᵊ fɔː ju ˈgid ə
    ships for everything, then, sometimes it be about a year 'fore you get a

---

[b] Quoted by Todd Gitlin and Nanci Hollander, *Uptown: Poor Whites in Chicago* (New York, 1970), pp. 197–98.

6 ʃip → | ˈsʌmtɑims ˈmə: ↑ | eitin   ˈmʌns ↑ ‖
   ship . . . sometimes more— eighteen months.

7 RC: And what did you live on then?

8 GG: wəl [. . .] wi ˈgruː arˈoum pˈteitəs → | n   ˈɛːgs ˈmiːt n   ˈmilk
   Well, [. . .] we grew our own potatoes   and eggs, meat and milk

9 n   wət ət jᵊu ˈgɛt frəm → | wi jus tˈpɛnd   ən ˈðæt fə ˈnʌθiŋ
   and what that you get from . . . we used to depend on that for nothing

10 ↓ | ju ˈgɛt æt jəˈsɛlf ↓ ‖ bʌt ˈflɑuə səmtaims ə wəs ə ˈjiːᵊ fɔr   ju
                                                                      gɛd i ↓ ‖
   . . . you get that yourself.   But flour, sometimes it was a year 'fore you
                                                                      get it.

11 RC: Now what about the birds—did you get any of those?

12 GG: jɛːs ju ˈgɛt ðə ˈsiːbʌds →| ju ˈgɛt ə ˈpɛrəwins →| wət ˈwi ˈkɔːl
   Yes, you get the sea-birds—you get the periwins—   what we call

13 ə ˈpɛriwin →‖ ai ˈspɛk ju ˈgɛt əm →| ju   gɛt ˈpɛriwin ˈɛːgs →| gɛd
   a periwin . . . I 'spect you get 'em . . . you get periwin   eggs . . . get

14 ə ˈməlisməks ˈɛːgs →| ðeisə ˈsimlə tu ˈælb⁽ᵊ⁾trəs ↓ ‖
   mollymocks' eggs,   they's similar to albatross.

15 RC: And do they still eat them a lot on Tristan?

16 GG: ˈjɛː ðei ˈstil du →| bʌt ˈnaitiŋgeil ɛs   ˈmɔːr ˈmʌtʃ s ən
                                                           ˈtristən →|
   Yeah, they still do,   but Nightingale there's more much as on
                                                           Tristan . . .

17 ˈðɛn ðə   ˈɑː fə ˈjiːs ˈpɑːs ˈðei stə   gou tə ˈnᵊaitiŋgeil fər ˈɛːgs →‖
   then the . . . ah, for years past they used to go to Nightingale for eggs.

18 n   ðɛn ju gɛ ˈpɛtrəls →| wəˀ ju ˈkɔːl ə ˈpɛtrls ˈɛːg ↓ ‖ ən
                                                           ˈnᵊaitiŋgeil→|
   And then you get petrels,   what you call a petrel's egg.   On
                                                           Nightingale

19 əs   ˈθɑusns əv m ↓ ‖ ət ˈnaitaim juː   if ju ˈwɔːk [. . .] i
                                                           ˈailən →|
   there's thousands of 'em.   At night-time, you . . . if you walk [. . .] the
                                                           island,

20 ˈnᵊaitngeil ət ˈnait →| ju ˈluk aut ðei doun ˈnək ju ˈdaun ↑ |
                                                           ˈjɛː →‖
   Nightingale, at night,   you look out, they don't knock you down,
                                                           yeah.°

° Transcribed by Arne Zettersten, *The English of Tristan da Cunha* (Lund: Lund Studies in English **37**, 1969), pp. 33–34.

GENERAL ATTITUDES TOWARDS THE SPEECH OF NEW YORK CITY

William Labov

Labov's The Social Stratification of English in New York City, *from which the following selection is taken, marked a new departure in American dialectology. Carried out under the name of "The American Language Survey" (ALS), the study was one of the first to profit from modern sociological techniques in the selection and classification of informants. Where earlier work was primarily concerned with geographical variations in language, Labov set out to examine in systematic fashion the social dimensions of language variation within a restricted community, the Lower East Side of New York City. In addition, Labov recognized the shortcomings of trying to elicit a single style of speech and investigated the variation of styles ranging from informal conversation to the reading of word lists. Rather than attempt a complete study of the speech of the area, Labov limited himself to five phonological variables—listed on pp. 280–81—that a pilot study had proved to be salient markers of social class in New York. Finally, Labov enlarged his data to include the subjective reactions and attitudes of speakers toward variation in the speech of New York City. Although Labov recognized, with earlier linguists, that the comments of untrained informants are often factually misleading, he argued that these "tertiary" responses to language, properly analyzed, provide important clues to the role that language plays in the community. In fact, Labov argues that norms of subjective evaluation are more clearly definitive of a linguistic community than overt linguistic behavior and are, moreover, as demonstrably factual. In the selection that follows, Labov identifies some of the attitudes that make New York City "a great sink of negative prestige" for its inhabitants—attitudes that may be more intense in New York City than elsewhere, but that are nonetheless characteristic of the national devotion to some external norm different from one's own native speech.*

At many points in the course of this study, it has been emphasized that the behavior which we are studying lies below the level of conscious awareness. Very few of the informants perceive or report their own variant usage of the phonological variables, and fewer still perceive it accurately. This does not mean that New Yorkers do not give a great deal of conscious attention to their language. Most of the informants in our survey have strong opinions about language, and they do not hesitate to express them. But their attention focuses only on those items which have risen to the surface of social consciousness and have entered the general folklore of language. Just as the reporting of usage in the self-evaluation test is essentially inaccurate, so most perception of language is not perception of sense experience, but of socially accepted statements about language.

It was common for our informants to condemn the language of a person, a group, or a whole city in very general terms: "sloppy," "careless," "hurried," "loud," or "harsh." When we asked for particular features in this style of speech which were offensive, most of the respondents could not think of any; the few examples which were given were morphological variants, such as *ain't* for *isn't*, *gonna* for *going to*, *whatcha* [wʌtšə] for *what are you*, or *aks* [æks] for *ask*. The only phonological form that was mentioned frequently and spontaneously was the stigmatized upgliding vowel in *bird, work, shirt*.[1] Most voice qualities which the listener did not like were termed "nasal"; in New York City, this most frequently refers to a denasalized voice quality of lower-class speech.

In this chapter, we will be concerned with general attitudes toward New York City English, the kind of information which can be obtained from any informant directly: general approval or disapproval, comparisons with other regional dialects, feelings about correctness, and the need to change one's language. The data will concern emotional attitudes rather than cognitive statements; most of these attitudes may be seen as expressions of the linguistic insecurity of the New York City speech community.

METHODS AND THE POPULATION STUDIED

The questions on linguistic attitudes which were used in the survey of the Lower East Side are given on p. 291. This section of the interview was not applied with formal rigor: for some informants, the discussions were long, and for others, very brief. In many cases, the interview had already lasted an hour or more before this section was reached, and the strenuous effort of the subjective reaction test[2] had left the subjects in no state of mind for extended

---

[1] Other phonological variables which were mentioned occasionally are the following: a strongly voiced [g] following [ŋ] in words such as *wrong, ringer, singer, Long Island*, called the "*ng click*" in college speech classes; "hard *t*, *d*, and *g*" in initial position (usually referring to velarized initial consonants); and the variables (eh) and (r), which have been considered in this study.

[2 The "subjective reaction test" mentioned here is described in Chapter 9 of *The Social Stratification of English in New York City*. The subjects were asked to listen to brief recorded speech samples and to suggest which of a series of jobs—ranging from "television personality" to "factory worker"—the speaker might be expected to hold. Though the particular phonological features that differentiated the samples were not always consciously

formal questioning. The linguistic attitudes section was therefore administered as if it were not a part of the formal interview, and the completion rate for various questions was somewhat irregular. If the informant had only a limited amount of time, other sections of the interview were given priority.

As a result of these limitations, only 68 of the 93 adult New York City informants gave responses to the section on linguistic attitudes, and there are usually only 40 to 50 responses for a given question. Twenty-eight of the 38 out-of-town respondents participated in this section of the survey, with comparable rates for particular questions.

There is a class bias in the losses, as Table 1 shows. A breakdown by classes

Table 1. NYC Respondents participating in the linguistic attitudes section by class[3]

	Socioeconomic Class			
	0–2	3–5	6–8	9
Total ALS adult informants	27	32	22	12
Participating in linguistic attitudes section	15	24	18	11

will therefore be required to assess the effect of the bias on the over-all results. Since the data consists of single answers, and lacks the quantitative reliability of the phonological indexes, only obvious and large-scale trends will be considered here.

The numerical data for the discussion are given in Table 2. In the following pages, the results will be discussed in general terms, with references to the figures in Table 2 only where necessary.

RECOGNITION OF NEW YORKERS BY OUTSIDERS

The informants were asked if they had ever traveled outside of New York City, and if they had ever been recognized as New Yorkers by their speech. Some had never been outside of the city limits, even on a vacation; but for those who had left the city at times, it seems to have been a common experience to be recognized as New Yorkers by the evidence of their speech alone.

---

apparent to the subjects, the widespread agreement caused Labov to conclude that "subjective reactions to phonological variables form a deeply embedded structure which is recognized by the entire speech community" (p. 450). *Eds.*]

[3 Following the lead of the "Mobilization for Youth" survey of the Lower East Side, Labov makes use of a ten-point socioeconomic index combining three objective characteristics—occupation, education, and family income—into a single linear scale. In Tables 2 and 3, this scale is reduced to show the upper (6–9), middle (3–5), and lower (0–2) categories. *Eds.*]

Table 2. Responses to questions on linguistic attitudes[4]

| | Adult New York Respondents | | | | | | | | | | | Out-of-town Respondents | |
| | | Socioeconomic Class | | | Ethnic group | | | Sex | | Age | | | |
	Total	0–2	3–5	6–9	I	J	N	M	F	20–39	40–	W	N
Recognition by outsiders as New Yorker													
Yes	24	8	9	7	10	9	—	8	16	7	17	6	4
No	8	2	3	3	—	6	1	—	8	2	6	4	—
As non-New Yorker	4	—	—	4	1	—	1	1	3	1	3		
Opinion on outsiders' view of NYC speech													
Not negative	15	4	6	5	6	6	2	7	8	6	9	6	4
Negative	30	5	10	15	5	15	2	11	19	11	19	4	—
Own attitude towards NYC speech													
Positive	14	2	4	8	3	5	4	7	7	7	7	5	5
Negative	23	6	6	11	6	13	1	5	18	4	19	6	2
Neutral	9	2	6	1	1	6	1	6	3	2	7	2	7
Own attitude towards Southern speech													
Positive	8	2	3	3	2	4	—	2	6	1	7	—	—
Negative	12	2	3	7	3	3	4	5	7	4	8	3	7
Neutral	4	1	2	1	—	3	—	2	2	1	3	—	—
Efforts to change own speech													
Yes	32	4	9	19	5	19	3	10	22	14	18	4	5
No	14	3	6	5	3	6	—	8	6	4	10	3	—

[4 In addition to the socioeconomic categories already described in note 3, the abbreviations at the head of this table categorize the responses of Italian (I), Jewish (J), White (W), and Negro (N) adults. *Eds.*]

277

"It's the first thing you open your mouth," reported one of the oldest ALS informants, a 73-year-old Irishman. A middle-class Jewish housewife admitted ruefully, "I know I sound like a New Yorker. I've been spotted instantly, innumerable times." A young Italian woman from a working-class family had the same experience: "Oh definitely, wherever I go."

Three quarters of the lower-class and working-class informants reported that they had been recognized as New Yorkers, but only half of the middle-class informants did so. All but one of the Italian respondents had been identified by outsiders as New Yorkers, but only three-fifths of the Jewish group. But there were no Jewish respondents among the four middle-class speakers who could say that someone outside of the city had thought that they were *not* New Yorkers. Those who made this report took considerable pride in doing so, for the overwhelming majority of respondents felt that recognition as a New Yorker was tantamount to stigmatization as a New Yorker.

OPINIONS ON HOW OUTSIDERS VIEW NEW YORK CITY SPEECH

Immediately after the question on recognition, the subjects were asked if people who lived outside of the city liked New York City speech, and why these outsiders felt as they did. (We will refer to such outside residents as *outsiders*, in contrast to the ALS informants who were raised outside of the city and who are designated *out-of-towners* in this study.)

Two-thirds of the New York City respondents thought that outsiders did not like New York City speech. Only three thought that the speech of the city was looked on with interest or approval by outsiders; the balance thought that the outsiders were neutral, or didn't care much one way or the other. Among the working-class respondents, there was a higher proportion of respondents who felt that outsiders were neutral than for any other class. Yet even a majority of them voted for "dislike."

"They think we're all murderers," said the old Irish working man. "To be recognized as a New Yorker—" thought a middle-class Jewish woman, "that would be a terrible slap in the face!" An older Jewish woman put it this way: "Somehow, the way they say, 'Are you a New Yorker?', they don't care so much for it."

Sometimes the New Yorker will pretend to be ignorant of the ridicule directed at his local speech pattern, but no one is deceived. An Italian girl in her early twenties, from a working-class family, gave the following view of her identification as a New Yorker by her husband's friends.

Bill's college alumni group—we have a party once a month in Philadelphia. Well, now I know them about two years and every time we're there—at a wedding, at a party, a shower—they say, if someone new is in the group: "Listen to Jo Ann talk!" I sit there and I babble on, and they say, "Doesn't she have a ridiculous accent!" and "It's so New Yorkerish and all!" [laughter]

I don't have the accent. I'm in a room with fifty people that have accents, and . . . I don't mind it, but I *never* take it as a compliment. And I can tell by the way people say it, they don't mean it complimentary.

Although the general consensus is that outsiders do condemn New York City speech, there is an opposing point of view held by some New Yorkers. Most of these are men, and the experience they draw upon was usually obtained in the armed services.

A thirty-year-old Jewish truck driver denied that other servicemen disliked New York City speech.

Some got quite a kick out of it. . . . I used to put on "thoity thoid 'n' thoid" [θɔɪti θɔɪdntθɔɪd] but I didn't really talk that way—I spoke that way because it was expected of me. Kidding, you know.

This minority point of view is stated even more strongly by Steve K., the ex-philosophy student.[5]

The people in the army—respected New York. They liked New York. They were fascinated by it, all from Ohio, Chicago—they enjoyed the fact that I was from New York. It was never said as a put-down . . . it was a matter of curiosity.

VIEWS OF THE OUT-OF-TOWN ALS INFORMANTS

What do the out-of-town informants in our survey actually think about New York City speech? Their view is almost exactly the contrary of the New York respondents. Only one in four reported that outsiders disliked New York City speech; most of the out-of-town informants believed that outsiders were neutral towards New York City speech, neither admiring it nor despising it. This was true for the white respondents as well as the Negroes, although Negroes lean even more heavily in favor of New York City.

When the out-of-town respondents reported their own feelings about New York City, the result was still more favorable. Ten liked the speech of the city,

[5 See *The Social Stratification of English in New York City*, pp. 120ff: "Steve K. might be considered a deviant case in many ways. He studied philosophy for four years at Brooklyn College, but left without graduating; he has turned away from the academic point of view, and as an intense student of the psychologist Wilhelm Reich, seeks self-fulfillment in awareness of himself as a sexual person. His attitude towards language is much more explicit than that of most people. He was unique among the informants in being aware of all five of the chief variables, and believed that he was able to control, or at least influence, his own usage. He has consciously tried to reverse his college-trained tendency towards formal speech, and to reinstate the natural speech pattern of his earlier years. . . . Steve K.'s inability to deal with a few sentences containing only thirteen (r)'s suggests that the original reading score of 38 is probably very close to the pattern which was solidified in his college days. Despite his profound shift in ideology, the speech pattern dictated by equally profound forces remains constant. It is not likely that he could, by his own efforts, return to zero or reach much higher than 38 in extended reading style." *Eds.*]

nine were neutral, and less than a third said that they disliked it. Again, this tendency was strongest among Negroes: 12 out of 14 Negro out-of-town respondents said that they liked the speech of the city or were neutral towards it. (For all Negro respondents, the figure is 17 out of 20.)

Sometimes the leaning towards New York was a part of a reaction against the respondents' own native region or town. "I don't like that Midwestern drawl," said a post office clerk who was raised in Indiana. Some of the lower-class subjects from Eastern Pennsylvania found little to admire in the declining fortunes of the coal mining towns from which they came.

Pennsylvania? I wouldn't give five cents—too dead. I'm out of that graveyard. There's a lot of excitement in New York City.

But there is also the sincere desire to sound like a New Yorker. One woman who came to work in New York City as a young girl said: "When I came to New York City, I tried to talk like that, but I couldn't because my accent was too much Pennsylvania." When her aunt back home said that she spoke like a New Yorker, she took it as a compliment, which a true New Yorker would never have done.

There are some respondents who have spent most of their lives in New York City without showing any significant change in their native speech pattern. A teacher who had worked for thirty years in the New York City school system seemed to have preserved intact the phonological pattern of Beverly, Massachusetts, where she was raised. She said that when she was a little girl, a boy from New York City used to visit her:

He was always talking about his *aunt* [eh-3] Nelly—had to take a *bath* [eh-3]—we took the wrong *path* [eh-4] in the woods, and so forth. I just didn't like it, and when I came, I just made an effort not to change.[6]

[6 Labov's study focused on five phonological variables, several of which are mentioned in this selection. They are (1) *r.* presence or absence of final and preconsonantal /r/; (2) *eh.* the height of the front vowel in a set of words including *bad, bag, ask, pass, cash,* and *dance*; (3) *oh.* the character of the mid-back rounded vowel heard in *caught, talk, awed, dog, off, lost, all*; (4) and (5). the initial consonants of words like *thing* and *then.* In Labov's notation, parentheses enclose variables: (r), (eh). Numbers within the parentheses (or within brackets [ ]) indicate the phonetic value of an instance of the variable; e.g., (eh-3) or [eh-3] translates to a particular point on the phonetic scale for the variable ((eh-3) = [æ⁻]). Numbers outside parentheses are index scores indicating average values for the variants used by a particular speaker; thus (r)-00 would indicate complete absence of preconsonantal /r/ in a piece of discourse; (r)-75 would indicate that in 75 per cent of the possible contexts an /r/ occurred. The following more detailed comments are intended to explain Labov's notations in the selection.

1. (r). A simple dichotomy between the presence or absence of final and preconsonantal /r/ in such words as *car* or *card, bare* or *bared, bore* or *bored, Saturday, November, fire* or *fired, flower* or *flowered.* (r-1) notes the presence of some form of constriction; (r-0) its absence. Indexes, for example (r)-50, are percentages of occurrence of /r/ for a speaker or group of speakers.

As a rule, upper-middle-class respondents from out-of-town showed the most resistance to the speech of the city, and lower-class and working-class subjects showed a more favorable response.

ATTITUDES OF NEW YORK RESPONDENTS TOWARDS NEW YORK SPEECH

When most New Yorkers say that outsiders dislike New York City speech, they are describing an attitude which is actually their own. Whether or not their opinion about outsiders' views is a projection of their own feelings, New Yorkers show a general hostility toward New York City speech which emerges in countless ways. The term "linguistic self-hatred" is not too extreme to apply to the situation which emerges from the interviews. Only 14 New Yorkers expressed themselves favorably towards New York City; 9 were neutral, and 23 expressed dislike quite plainly. These overt reactions are the correlates of the phonological behavior and the unconscious subjective reactions which have been studied in the various chapters of the present work.

The terms which New Yorkers apply to the speech of the city give some indications of the violence of their reactions: "It's terrible." "Distorted." "Terribly careless." "Sloppy." "It's horrible." "Lou-zay!"

Again, we find that men express much less of this attitude than women. As Table 2 shows, a minority of the men expressed themselves negatively about New York City speech, but a large majority of the women respondents did so. Since our survey population is weighted somewhat in favor of women, it is possible that this aspect of the city's attitudes has been stressed too heavily. Yet it should be emphasized that men follow the same general pattern of

---

2. (eh). The height of the front or retracted front vowel in a set of words having as their final environments: (i) voiceless stops or liquids (*cap, bat, pal, batch*): (ii) voiced fricatives (*salve, jazz*) or the velar nasal (*bang*); (iii) voiced stops (*cab, bad, bag, badge*), voiceless fricatives (*half, pass, cash, bath*), or the other nasals (*ham, dance*). In actuality, the vowel height forms a continuum but is broken for reference into six points or categories: (eh-1) = [ɪə]; (eh-2) = [ɛə]; (eh-3) = [æ˔]; (eh-4) = [æː]; (eh-5) = [aː]; (eh-6) = [ɑː]. The values (eh-3) and (eh-4) typify most American dialects; the raised values (eh-1 and eh-2) characterize certain forms of New York City speech and are subject to correction. The lower the index number, for example (eh)-20 vs. (eh)-40, the higher the average vowel height.

3. (oh). Again a vowel continuum is broken into six categories characterized in this case by height and degree of rounding for the mid-back vowel. The values are, roughly: (oh-1) = [ʊə]; (oh-2) = [ɔ˔, ˔ə]; (oh-3) = [ɔ˔ə]; (oh-4) = [ɔː]; (oh-5) = [ɒ]; (oh-6) = [ɑ]. (oh-1) and (oh-2) are, according to Labov, peculiar to NYC and are, like the higher values of (eh), subject to correction. Index scores are as in (eh).

4-5. (th) and (dh). There are three values: (th-1) (dh-1) = [θ] [ð]; (th-2) (dh-2) = [tθ] [dð]; (th-3) (dh-3) = [t] [d] (lenis stops). The index (th)-00 would indicate the use only of the fricative values; (th)-200 indicates the use only of stops. The fricative values (th-1) (dh-1) are the prestige forms in NYC and throughout the United States.

For further details, see *The Social Stratification of English in New York City*, pp. 50–56, from which the material in this note is taken. *Eds.*]

stylistic variation and subjective reaction as women; their reactions are simply more moderate, and in this case, there is a third force which modifies their behavior even further in comparison to that of women. We will return to this discussion below.

The negative attitude towards New York City speech seems to have penetrated even to those who have never been outside of the city. An old Italian woman who had been only to the fifth grade, cannot read even today, and had never been outside the city limits, remarked in answer to the interviewer's question, "Out of town they speak more refined."

A more neutral attitude characteristic of working-class men may be heard in a quotation from a working-class Italian man, raised in Williamsburg: "I was brought up in New York, and if I would talk any other way it would seem strange."

One may wonder how the ALS interview question could be asked in terms of "New York City speech" in general. It would seem natural for the respondents to distinguish between many kinds of New York City speech, since they did distinguish sharply the usage of various informants in the subjective reaction test. However, very few respondents felt the need for such equivocation. There seemed to be a general understanding that there was such a thing as "New York City speech," and whatever the respondent perceived as that entity was the object of the statements quoted above.

INFORMANTS' DISLIKE OF THEIR OWN SPEECH

Pressures from Above

We find the negative attitude towards the city speech in general is directed by the respondent towards himself as well. More than half of the respondents thought poorly of their own speech, and two thirds had attempted to change their speech in some way or another.

The pressures towards conformity with middle-class norms of speech are very strong. We have seen objective evidence of this tendency; in the course of the survey, respondents reported many incidents which showed the social contexts in which such pressures occur. A Negro man reported the following situation among his immediate friends:

I have some friends that speak very rough—when we are all together, with the careful group, we all try to be more careful.

Some fellas never come down—they stay up all the time—and you find that the ones that don't speak well—are more or less quiet.

Another form of correction comes from the respondents' children. A number of the oldest informants, especially among the lower-class subjects, had suffered for many years under the sharp corrections of their own children. A frequent comment is, "My son always laughs at me." One older Italian woman was particularly embarrassed at her own inability to distinguish *earl* and *oil*, which had apparently been a point of ridicule for many years in her own family. She cheered up considerably when she learned that this was once the prestige pronunciation of the highest levels of society.

As a rule, our informants show little tendency to respect the speech of their elders. "Lots of these words, they laugh at me," said one old Jewish woman. Another woman took a more hopeful view:

I'll tell you, you see, my son is always correcting me. He speaks very well—the one that went to [two years of] college. And I'm glad that he corrects me—because it shows me that there are many times when I don't pronounce my words correctly.

Under such pressures, a tendency towards linguistic insecurity on the part of older New Yorkers is not difficult to understand.

Pressures from Below

A great deal of the present study is devoted towards delineating the effect of pressures from above upon language. It has been pointed out that equally powerful pressures must be exerted from below, since the pattern of class stratification of language is becoming sharper rather than tending to disappear. Many New Yorkers are conscious of the need for the style shifts that we have observed by means of the phonological indexes. One respondent who is the owner of a small advertising agency shows the effects of pressures from above and below, and is himself aware of both influences on his own language. He was very conscious of the need for correct speech for his office staff: he said that he would have refused to hire any of the speakers on the subjective reaction test tape except Speaker UMC [upper middle class]. "I think people have to have some respect for the way the language is written. Even if we all make mistakes, I think we can't say *'cause* 'n' *dat* 'n' *di udda ting* [oh-1, dh-3, th-3]. It's no longer our language. I'm vehement about this." Yet he also said of himself:

As a performer—I change my style of speech. I will do a kind of gutsy talk, that's very different. It will not include four letter words, but I change the pattern almost entirely, 'cause I'm very good at that, and I enjoy it.

In the examples that he offered ["I'm gonna talk plain . . ."], he used (r-0), (th-3), (dh-3), (oh-2). He found this style essential for dealing with customers:

I said, "Thank you" for something, and he was annoyed, 'cause I thanked him—'cause he's a rough, tough kinda guy, y'know. So he says, "Aaah, ya fuckin' gentleman you!" 'Cause basically I am—he resents the fact that I'm courteous to him. So what I did was to put my head back in the door and say to him, "You know Jack, you're quite a character." He had a bunch of people—they're all close people, and he had made the remark in front of them. "What would you want me to do, take that thing from you, and call you a dirty name? Would that [dh-3] be a sign of respect to you?" . . . So he smiled and says, "Go on, kiddo, I'll see ya."

A lawyer explained to the interviewer why he made no effort to change his own speech, and why his speech had actually "deteriorated" in recent years.

. . . most of the people I associate with in this area are men with very little schooling . . . mostly Italian-American . . . so that these are the men I've gone out drinking with, the ones I go out to dinner with, and when I talk to them, my speech even deteriorates a little more, because I speak the way they speak . . . .

This speaker had preserved the traditional r-less pattern, with raised (eh), more consistently than any other class 9 speaker. He showed the mixture of feelings that are produced in any New Yorker who tries to go against the tide—yet the pressure from below was strong enough to allow him to resist the opposing pressure from his wife, his children, and their friends.

The people that I represent never criticize my speech—the only criticism I receive is primarily from my wife—I get it there—my children also . . . self-criticism when I listen to myself. I find it important to be natural in my speech—I can express myself faster and clearer.

Pressure towards conformity with the native speech pattern is very strong among schoolchildren. Those who come to the city from out of town are quickly compelled to drop their own regional accents. One woman who had come from Atlanta as a ten-year-old, fifty years ago, could still remember how she had cried when the others made fun of her Southern accent. The pressure is greatest against those who would attempt to use an acquired prestige pattern too early. A teacher who conducted a class of gifted children told me:

I had a boy of Greek parentage, and oh! he spoke beautifully in class, and I happened to hear him on the street one day. He sounded just like everybody else in Chelsea, and when I mentioned it to him—the next day—he said that he knew which was correct, but he said: "I couldn't live here and talk like that."

One of the reasons for the resistance of children to the middle-class norms is that their teachers advocate a language, and an attitude towards language, which is quite remote from everyday life. The teacher quoted above told me of her difficulties in explaining to children the importance of pronouncing the word *length* as [lɛŋθ] and not [lɛnθ].

Some children, you correct them—and they aren't anxious. They say, "What difference does it make?" And I try to tell them that it does make [a difference]. There might be two people applying for a position, and someone might talk about the length [lɛŋθ] of the room, and someone else about the [lɛnθ] of a dress, and I said the one who spoke correctly, probably, in many instances *would* get the position.

The phonological variables we have been studying are seldom discussed by teachers. Instead, many of them concentrate on individual words that have become major issues in their own thinking. One young man, of Polish background, who now worked in a furniture warehouse, remembered two rules of pronunciation on which the speech teacher had drilled his high school class.

I never paid attention to the rules of grammar until she started teaching to me, and I was so surprised at the way stuff is supposed to be pronounced. . . . She wrote the word *butter* on the board, and she asked me how to pronounce it, and I said [bʌtʃ]. She told me that was wrong, and that's when I learned to pronounce *t*'s like a *t*—I used to pronounce them as *d*'s all the time.

The pronunciation he used with me was exactly the same pronunciation of *butter* which almost all Americans use—with a semivoiced intervocalic consonant. When I asked him how the teacher had taught him to pronounce the word, he couldn't remember what it was supposed to sound like.

I haven't been in school for a while, and I'm reverting back to the *d*'s again.

The only other rule of pronunciation which the teacher had stressed was the use of [hw] as the initial consonant of *when* and *where*, instead of the normal [w] which is used by New Yorkers of all classes and age levels. This young man used a high percentage of stops and affricates in his careful conversation —(th)-95, (dh)-47—but the teacher had never brought this feature to his attention.

Almost everyone in the sample agreed that the speech of their high school English teachers was a remote and special dialect which had no utility for everyday life. A few looked rather wistfully back at the lost possibility of "improving" their own speech in those days, but hardly a word was raised in defense of the English teacher.

A Negro man gave me this view of the pressure exerted against working-class children who adopt middle-class standards of speech:

When I was small and going to school, if you talked that way, the kids would kid you, but we had a few kids that would do it, and we always kid them. . . . There was a girl who was always very proper . . . so, she'd always walk up and say, "Pardon me." We'd all laugh, we knew it was correct, but we'd still laugh. Today, she end up successful.

One of the main factors which contribute support to the working-class speech pattern of the city is its association with cultural norms of masculinity. A middle-aged Italian man who was raised in Massachusetts explained why he lost his outside speech pattern very quickly when he came to the city:

To me, I think [th-3] I got the [dh-3] New York speech. At one time, I had a good speech, and vocabulary too, when I first came from Massachusetts. But I lost it. When I first came here, to New York, they used to say, "You speak like a fairy—like they do in Massachusetts." When I kept going back to Massachusetts, they said, "Gee, you got the New York lingo."

The masculinity attributed to New York City working-class speech is described directly in Steve K.'s account of a primitive painter who had abandoned his earlier career as an archaeologist, and with it, his middle-class speech pattern.

> If E. has consciously gone back to Brooklyn for his language—his reasons are not social, they're sexual. Because his vulgarity was sexual: he's aware of himself sexually, as a sexual person. His idea of success isn't the American idea of success—it's not the money. . . . If he's gone back to Brooklyn, it's for the same reason, he wants to be there grappling.

DIFFERENCES IN LINGUISTIC ATTITUDES OF VARIOUS SUB-GROUPS

Men vs. Women

As we compare the sexes' reports of linguistic attitudes, we find a series of significant differences. Only one man reported that he had not been recognized as a New Yorker when he left the city, but 11 out of 16 women made this statement. Both men and women share the view that outsiders dislike New York speech, but women were more consistent in this respect. As we have seen, the sexes are opposed in their personal attitudes towards the speech of the city, with men favoring it slightly, and women heavily against. In the reports of efforts to change, women also show a more consistent tendency in this direction.[7] On every count, women show much greater linguistic insecurity than men. The masculine values associated with the working-class speech pattern used by men do not seem to be counterbalanced by any similar positive values with which women endow their native speech pattern.

Class Differences

We have noted that only a few New Yorkers reported that they had been identified as *not* being from New York, and all of these were middle class. The linguistic goal of most of the middle-class speakers is to lose all resemblance to New Yorkers; almost all of them stated that they would be complimented if someone told them they did not sound like New Yorkers. There are also class differences in the perception of outsiders' views: three quarters of the middle-class respondents thought that out-of-towners disliked New York speech, but smaller percentages of working-class respondents thought so, and even fewer from the lower class. In New Yorkers' attitudes towards their own speech, we find that the working class showed the smallest percentage of respondents who reacted negatively. This finding correlates with the results of the ILI index, where working-class speakers showed the least

---

[7] There were three women who reported that their speech had "deteriorated" in their present surroundings, and who felt that they could do little about it. We may place these respondents among the ones who showed the most linguistic insecurity.

linguistic insecurity.[8] In the tendency to change one's language, again we find that the middle class led the others,[9] while the lower class showed the least effort in this direction.

We can summarize these findings by saying that the middle class shows the greatest linguistic insecurity, and the working class the least. But when we consider the recognition of norms imposed from above by the socio-economic hierarchy, which we have called the social significance of the variables, the class groups are ranked in order: middle class highest, working class next, and lower class least. Despite their good knowledge of these unifying norms, the working-class speakers show the least tendency to reject their native speech pattern in favor of the prestige pattern. The lower class shows less ability to recognize middle-class norms, and less confidence in the native speech pattern. Thus the lower class forms an outside group in two senses: (1) many lower-class subjects fall outside the influence of the unifying norms which make New York City a single speech community, and (2) many seem to lack the cultural values which maintain the working-class pattern of speech in opposition to massive pressure from above.

Ethnic Differences

We have already noted that Italians were almost unanimous in their report that they had been recognized as New Yorkers, while the Jews showed some exceptions to this rule. As far as our limited numbers of replies indicate, the Jews showed more tendency to think that outsiders disliked New York City speech, and to dislike it themselves. However, both groups showed equal dislike of their own speech, and equal effort to change their own speech.

The Negro informants, on the other hand, are separated from the rest of the sample population by more than a quantitative difference in trends. In almost all respects, the Negroes reverse the pattern of attitudes shown by the others. The numbers of New York City Negro respondents are too small to give us a very reliable report by themselves, but they seem to conform quite closely to the pattern shown by the out-of-town Negro respondents, and the two subgroups will be discussed together.

While most white New Yorkers thought that outsiders disliked New York City speech, almost all of the Negroes who expressed an opinion thought that out-of-town residents did not dislike the speech of the city. While most

[8 The index of linguistic insecurity (ILI) mentioned here is fully described in Chapter 12 of *The Social Stratification of English in New York City*. Eighteen different words were listed on a questionnaire and the interviewer gave two pronunciations for each. The subject was asked to indicate which pronunciation he believed to be correct and which he used himself. The number of instances where the subject acknowledges a disparity between "correctness" and his own performance forms the basis of the index. *Eds.*]

9 The upper-middle-class respondents showed as great a tendency in this direction as the lower middle class. The reason is probably that most of the upper middle class had been required to take speech courses for the city school system and other academic work. The difference between these two groups is that the upper-middle-class respondents had usually made the changes earlier, and with more consistent results.

white New Yorkers showed negative attitudes towards the New York speech pattern themselves only three out of twenty Negro respondents expressed this opinion, and nine reported that they liked it.

The sharpest opposition between Negro and white occurred when the respondents were asked to compare their feelings about New York City speech with their feelings about Southern speech. Eight white informants said they liked Southern speech better, four were neutral, and only eight liked New York City speech better. As far as the Negroes were concerned, none liked Southern speech better than New York City speech.

A typical white attitude towards Southern speech was expressed by a woman white-collar worker:

[Southern speech?] I like the sound of it. A girl in the office comes from Kentucky, and people get me mixed up with her.

An old Jewish lady had grandchildren in Texas: "They sound adorable—I love to hear them talk."

A Negro woman, fifty years old, born and raised in the Bronx, said this about Southern speech:

When I was very young, and used to hear about some of the things that happened in the South, I had a physical reaction, as if my hair was standing on end . . . and if I would hear a white Southerner talk, I was immediately alerted to danger, and so I never could see anything pleasant in it.

Although Negro speakers share the white attitudes towards correctness, and are even more anxious to change their own speech, they reverse white attitudes towards the cultural values of New York City speech. For most Negro speakers, any feature of speech associated with Northern regional dialects [such as (r-1)], is considered good, cultivated, and educated usage, as opposed to Southern dialect features, which are considered uneducated and "rough." But in the same way that many younger New Yorkers prefer the rough outlines of the working-class dialect, so many young Negro speakers lean towards Southern characteristics in their casual speech. Many older Negro respondents told me that they were quite puzzled to find young Negro people, raised in the North, of Northern parents, talking "rough" just like Southerners. For the older Negro subjects, the sound of New York City English is a good sound, and the very qualities which make white New Yorkers shudder, seem perfectly acceptable Northern speech to many Negroes. Thus in the subjective reaction test, about half of the New York City Negro respondents showed (oh)-positive response, and two thirds of the out-of-town Negro respondents did so. In the case of (eh), the majority showed negative response to (eh-2), but there was a much larger number of Negro respondents who showed (eh)-positive response than white respondents.

Thus the Negroes of New York City react primarily against features of Southern English—the regional dialect speakers from the Lower South form a negative reference group for them.[10] The white New Yorkers react against their own speech, and their image of it: to many of them, Southern speech appears as attractively remote and not without glamor as compared to the everyday sound of New York City speech.

Age Differences

In the limited data which we have available, there were no differences by age in the respondents' reports of being recognized as New Yorkers, nor in their views of outsiders' evaluations of New York City speech. The younger respondents did not seem to have absorbed as much negative feeling about New York City speech as the older subjects. Finally, we may note that the younger people reported more efforts to change their language; this may reflect the greater number who have been required to take speech courses at one time or another.

The primary observation to be drawn from the data is that attitudes towards New York City speech have not changed radically in recent years. The strong feeling against the native speech pattern of the city seems to be shared by all age levels of the community.

THE NEGATIVE PRESTIGE OF NEW YORK CITY SPEECH

Preceding chapters have dealt with patterns of behavior which revealed negative evaluations of New York City speech. In this chapter, we have brought forward a relatively small body of evidence from conscious reactions which illustrate the same orientation. As far as language is concerned, New York City may be characterized as a great sink of negative prestige. The reasons for this cultural bias fall outside of the province of the linguist. However, we can present some evidence to indicate that the pattern is not a new one, but originated well before the arrival of the immigrants from Southern and Eastern Europe whose descendents occupy the Lower East Side today.

In the earlier history of New York City, New England influence and New England immigration preceded the influx of Europeans. The prestige dialect which is reflected in the speech of cultivated Atlas informants shows heavy borrowings from Eastern New England.[11] There has been a long-standing tendency for New Yorkers to borrow prestige dialects from other regions, rather than develop a prestige dialect of their own. In the current situation, we see that the New England influence has retreated, and in its place, a new prestige dialect has been borrowed from Northern and Midwestern speech patterns. We have seen that for most of our informants, the effort to escape

[10] This term is used in the technical sense developed by Robert K. Merton, *Social Theory and Social Structure* (Glencoe, Ill.: The Free Press, 1957), p. 300.

[11] Evidence for both migration patterns and dialect influence is provided by Yakira A. Frank, "The Speech of New York City" (unpublished dissertation, the University of Michigan, 1948), chapter 1 and *passim*.

identification as a New Yorker by one's own speech provides a motivating force for phonological shifts and changes.

The failure of the New York City speech pattern to expand into its own hinterland is another aspect of the process of negative evaluation which we have been studying. Most of the important dialect boundaries of the eastern United States fall along lines which are natural troughs in the network of communication.[12] The speech patterns of Boston, Philadelphia, Richmond and Charleston expanded throughout the eighteenth and nineteenth centuries to a radius of 75 to 150 miles around each of these influential cities; today we find that the limits of dialect regions which surround them are located in the more or less remote mountainous areas that impede the flow of communication. But the New York City dialect area is an exception to this pattern, and a radical exception. The influence of New York City speech is confined to a narrow radius, hardly beyond the suburbs that form the "inner ring" of the city; and even today the speech pattern fails to expand as New Yorkers move in large numbers into the outer ring.[13] The dialect boundary which surrounds New York City is crossed every day by at least a million people: it has no relation to any minimal lines in the pattern of communication.

Thus we see that most other dialect boundaries of the eastern United States represent the limits of the expansion of prestige patterns, while the New York City boundary represents a circumscription of an area of negative prestige. This is not a recent pattern, but rather one which must date from at least the early part of the nineteenth century.

SUMMARY

With this chapter, we have concluded our study of the subjective evaluation of the speech of New York City. In this study, we have seen that subjective evaluation often precedes and outruns changes in speech itself. Our view is

---

[12] This statement is based on the dialect boundaries shown in Hans Kurath, *A Word Geography of the Eastern United States* (Ann Arbor: The University of Michigan Press, 1949), and in Hans Kurath and Raven I. McDavid, Jr., *The Pronunciation of English in the Atlantic States* (Ann Arbor: The University of Michigan Press, 1961), and calculations from traffic flow maps provided by the highway departments of all Eastern states. An example of such a minimum line in the communication network is the line which divides Northern speech from Midland speech. It runs across Pennsylvania from East to West, separating the northern tier of counties from the rest. Even today, very few travelers go from Pittsburgh to Buffalo, or from Philadelphia to Schenectady, compared to the number that go from Albany to Buffalo, or from Philadelphia to Pittsburgh.

[13] For the delineation of the terms *inner ring* and *outer ring*, see Edgar M. Hoover and Raymond Vernon, *Anatomy of a Metropolis* (Cambridge, Mass.: Harvard University Press, 1959). The process in which the New York pattern is rejected, and children follow the pattern of an *r*-pronouncing dialect despite the presence of a very large number of r-less New York City adults, may be seen in the area of Bergen County where I live. In the elementary schools of Closter, New Jersey, one can hardly find a single instance of an (r-0) form spoken by the children; among their parents, (r-0) forms predominate.

that New York City is a single speech community, united by a common set of evaluative norms, though divergent in the application of these norms. The structures of fine stratification, sharp stratification, and ethnic diversity which have been found in the objective indexes of the variables were correlated with a uniform pattern of subjective reactions. Changes in apparent time, however, appeared with greater clarity in subjective reactions to particular variables than they did in the evidence of speech itself.

We have seen that the dominant theme in the subjective evaluation of speech by New Yorkers is a profound linguistic insecurity, which is connected with a long-standing pattern of negative prestige for New York City speech.

In this chapter, we have also touched on some of the less obvious sources of pressure from below, which maintain the structure of stylistic and social variation, and even seem to be leading towards increased stratification of speech performance within the city. The preponderance of some stigmatized speech forms among male speakers, despite their clear recognition of the social significance assigned by pressure from above, reinforces the suggestion that masculinity is unconsciously attributed to the unmodified native speech pattern of the city, as it is used by men. Thus the pressure exerted in conformity with the socioeconomic hierarchy is counterbalanced by a cultural tradition which we have described as pressure from below. The exact description of the covert values associated with the native speech pattern is one of the unfinished tasks which remain for future studies.

QUESTIONNAIRE: LINGUISTIC ATTITUDES

1. What do you think of your own speech?
2. Have you ever tried to change your speech? What particular things about it?
3. Have you ever taken any courses in speech? What did the teacher mention in connection with pronunciation?
4. a. What do you think of New York City speech?
   b. Have you traveled outside of New York City? (If so) did people pick you up as a New Yorker by your speech?
   c. Do you think that out-of-towners like New York City speech? Why?
   d. What do you think of Southern speech as compared to New York City speech? (If Negro, distinguish Negro versus white speech.)
   e. Have you heard Mayor Wagner talk? As far as his speech is concerned, not his politics, but his way of talking, how do you like it? (same question for Rockefeller). Which do you like better? (Probe if time permits for opinions on other speakers the informant thinks are good or bad.)
5. Going back to the time when you were growing up, I'd like to get some idea of the kind of speech that your friends used. Were most of your friends (same race or religion as informant)? Did you have any friends who were (other races and religions)?
6. (If time permits, probe for any incidents in which speech was a factor in disagreements of the group.)

STUDY QUESTIONS

1. Labov suggests that "most perception of language is not perception of sense experience, but of socially accepted statements about language" (p. 275). How does the claim that New York City speech is "nasal" reflect this situation?

2. List the apparently descriptive terms that you have heard applied to various dialects or styles—for example, *nasal, twang, drawl,* and so on. What is the linguistic situation that these terms represent? The social situation?

3. Has anyone ever recognized your dialect when you have traveled outside your home community? If so, what attitude toward your dialect did they seem to express? Has such an experience influenced your feeling about your own speech?

4. Standard English is often defined as the speech of the dominant social class in a linguistic community—as C. C. Fries put it, "that set of language habits in which the most important affairs of our country are carried on, the dialect of the socially acceptable in most of our communities."[a] Would Labov think this an adequate definition of the prestige norm for New York City? If, as Labov says, "subjective evaluation often precedes and outruns changes in speech itself," can standard English be defined with reference to overt linguistic behavior alone?

5. Labov found that in New York City "the pattern of class stratification of language is becoming sharper rather than tending to disappear." What "pressures" does he describe that contribute to this development?

6. Labov says (p. 287) that the lower class in New York City "forms an outside group in two senses": they fall outside the influences of middle-class prestige norms and also lack "the cultural values which maintain the working-class pattern of speech." Can you speculate on the causes of this linguistic isolation? Can you speculate on how the isolation might be cured?

7. "Almost everyone in the sample agreed that the speech of their high school English teachers was a remote and special dialect which had no utility for everyday life." Would your own experience lead you to agree with this view? What "pressures" might lead to the isolation of the teacher's dialect?

8. Labov notes that present-day attitudes of New Yorkers toward their speech continue long-standing traditions. Do you know of any other such traditions that favor or disfavor certain American dialects?

[a] *American English Grammar* (New York: D. Appleton-Century Co., 1940), p. 14.

WHITE AND NEGRO LISTENERS' REACTIONS TO VARIOUS AMERICAN-ENGLISH DIALECTS*

G. Richard Tucker and Wallace E. Lambert

Varieties of American English provide subtle but salient clues to the social status and sometimes the race of speakers, and very brief samples of speech are often enough to evoke (if not always accurately) widespread agreement about these matters. Such judgments depend entirely on stereotyped beliefs about language and class in the community—beliefs often perpetuated in the usage drills in English classes—and about the supposed personal traits of individual speakers. As the results reported in the following essay show, the so-called "Network English" of broadcasting is generally regarded as attractive and its speakers as intelligent, trustworthy, determined, and considerate. Less favored dialects attract to their speakers less genial adjectives, reflecting the stereotypes and prejudices of class and racial antagonisms, judgments that vary from one group to another. As Tucker and Lambert show, "speech styles which are pleasing to one social group will not necessarily be so perceived by another."

Stereotypes of the kind that come into play in such judgments are extraordinarily durable and long-lasting; they seem to persist against even repeated encounters with individuals who, for example, speak the "Network" dialect but lack the revered traits associated with it, or who speak a despised dialect but are widely admired. The study of these stereotypes is only now being recognized as an important aspect of the broader connections of language and social class in America, and the interdisciplinary cooperation called for by Tucker and Lambert can be expected to produce results that will contribute to a clearer understanding of the role that language plays in American social life.

In recent years, a useful technique has been developed at McGill University to measure, in an indirect fashion, the views that members of one social group have of representatives of some other contrasting group. Described briefly, a sample of "judges" is asked to listen to a series of taped recordings of different speakers reading a standard passage, and to evaluate relevant

Reprinted from *Social Forces*, **47**:463–68 by permission of the authors and publisher. Copyright, 1969, by The University of North Carolina Press.

* An earlier version of this study was presented at the EPA meetings in Boston, 1967. This research was financed in part by research grants from the Canadian Defense Research Board and from the Canada Council, and by a grant from the Rockefeller Foundation to W. N. Francis at Brown University.

personality characteristics of each speaker, using only voice characteristics and speech style as cues. The technique appears to expose the listeners' more private feelings and stereotyped attitudes toward a contrasting group or groups whose language, accent, or dialect is distinctive, and it appears to be reliable in that the same profile of reactions emerges on repeated sampling from a particular social group. The procedure has been used to compare the reactions of judges listening to the two guises of bilingual speakers presenting (a) contrasting languages, (b) contrasting dialects, or (c) contrasting accents.[1]

The present research extends the basic technique and focuses on the reactions of white and Negro college students to various exemplars of white and Negro American-English speech. The study was guided by the practical and theoretical significance of two questions: (1) Are both white and Negro subjects sensitive enough to dialect variations to make reliable differentiations? (2) If so, will there emerge a meaningful pattern of dialect preferences, that is, some particularly favored and others disfavored?

METHOD

Development of Rating Scales

To be most useful, the rating scales provided listeners for evaluating speakers should be developed specifically for the samples of subjects to be examined. In this case,[2] scales were chosen with two ends in mind: (a) positive ratings should indicate that the listener believes the speakers could attain or have already attained "success," and (b) that speakers are "friendly." Thus, success should not imply separation from or mobility out of the group represented by the speaker.

With this purpose in mind, students from a small southern Negro college were asked to indicate those traits which they considered important for friendship and those important for success. Their responses were tabulated

---

[1] M. Anisfeld, N. Bogo, and W. E. Lambert, "Evaluational Reactions to Accented English Speech," *Journal of Abnormal and Social Psychology*, 65 (1962), pp. 223–31; Elizabeth Anisfeld and W. E. Lambert, "Evaluational Reactions of Bilingual and Monolingual Children to Spoken Languages," *Journal of Abnormal and Social Psychology*, 69 (1964), pp. 89–97; W. E. Lambert, R. C. Hodgson, R. C. Gardner, and S. Fillenbaum, "Evaluational Reactions to Spoken Languages," *Journal of Abnormal and Social Psychology*, 60 (1960), pp. 44–51; W. E. Lambert, M. Anisfeld, and Grace Yeni-Komshian, "Evaluational Reactions of Jewish and Arab Adolescents to Dialect and Language Variations," *Journal of Personality and Social Psychology*, 2 (1965), pp. 84–90; W. E. Lambert, Hannah Frankel, and G. R. Tucker, "Judging Personality Through Speech: A French-Canadian Example," *The Journal of Communications*, 4 (1966), pp. 305–21; N. N. Markel, R. M. Eisler, and H. W. Reese, "Judging Personality From Dialect," *Journal of Verbal Learning and Verbal Behavior*, 6 (1967), pp. 33–35; and M. S. Preston, "Evaluational Reactions to English, Canadian French and European French Voices," unpublished M.A. thesis, McGill University, 1963.

[2] Miss Marilen Picard, now a graduate student at the University of Western Ontario, assisted us in this phase of the study.

and the traits ranked in order of popularity. They were then asked to give free associations to and synonyms for some of the trait names, and finally to choose, from a larger list of traits drawn from previous research using the same technique, those they considered important for friendship and those important for success. The rating scales finally used were selected on the basis of this initial survey. Bipolar rating scales were constructed by pairing a positive and a negative adjective with each trait (e.g., good upbringing, poor upbringing; good disposition, bad disposition; considerate, inconsiderate). Two of the traits, speaking ability and good upbringing, were not spontaneously suggested by the students, but were added because we believed they were appropriate for our purposes. Similar pilot work with traits suggested by white college students permitted us to decide on a set of scales useful for all three groups.

Selection of Stimulus Voices

The dialect samples were selected by trained dialectologists, who specialized in variations in American speech styles. Recordings were made of 4 representatives of each of 6 dialect groups: (1) speakers of *Network* English (the typical mode of speaking of national newscasters); (2) college-*Educated White Southern* speakers; (3) college-*Educated Negro Southern* speakers; (4) college-Educated Negro speakers from Mississippi presently attending *Howard University* in Washington, D.C.; (5) southern Negro students, referred to as the *Mississippi Peer* group, who spoke a dialect similar to that used by most students at the Negro college where the actual testing was carried out; and (6) alumni from this college who have since lived for several years in New York City—*New York Alumni*. All speakers in groups 1 and 2 were white, while those in groups 3, 4, 5, and 6 were Negro.

Each speaker read aloud the same passage, a short one requiring about forty-five seconds to read. The context of the passage was simple and neutral as to emotional value. Both male and female speakers were chosen to represent each dialect group except for the *Educated White Southern* group which, because of an oversight, included only males. The 24 recordings (6 dialects and 4 representatives of each) were placed on two separate tapes, making two groups of 12 recordings each, with each dialect group represented by two voices on each tape. A "practice" voice was also added at the beginning of each tape.

Subjects

The subjects were 150 male and female freshmen from a southern Negro college, 40 white male and female students from a New England university, and 68 white male and female students from a southern university.

Experimental Procedure

The testing was carried out on the three campuses, and the procedure was the same for all groups. The students serving as "judges" were asked to

Table 1. Mean ratings* and ranks of mean ratings† of each dialect type by northern white university students

Dialect Groups	Upbringing	Intelligent	Friendly	Educated	Disposition	Speech	Trustworthy	Ambitious	Faith-God	Talented	Character	Determination	Honest	Personality	Considerate	Sum
Network	6.8 [1]	6.7 [1]	5.8 [2]	7.2 [1]	6.0 [1]	6.7 [1]	6.3 [1]	5.8 [1]	5.3 [2]	6.1 [1]	6.4 [1]	5.9 [2]	6.2 [1]	6.1 [1]	6.3 [1]	[18]
Educated Negro Southern	5.4 [3]	5.5 [3]	5.7 [3]	5.1 [3]	5.4 [4]	4.7 [3]	5.8 [2]	5.6 [2]	5.8 [1]	5.2 [3]	6.0 [2]	6.0 [1]	5.9 [2]	5.3 [4]	5.7 [3]	[39]
Educated White Southern	6.0 [2]	5.8 [2]	5.6 [4]	5.7 [2]	5.5 [3]	5.5 [2]	5.6 [3]	5.2 [3]	5.2 [3]	5.3 [2]	5.7 [4]	5.5 [3]	5.6 [4]	5.5 [3]	5.6 [4]	[44]
Howard University	5.2 [4]	5.4 [4]	6.0 [1]	4.6 [4]	5.9 [2]	4.6 [4]	5.6 [3]	5.1 [4]	5.2 [4]	5.1 [4]	5.9 [3]	5.2 [4]	5.8 [3]	5.9 [2]	5.7 [2]	[48]
New York Alumni	4.6 [5]	4.5 [5]	5.3 [5]	3.5 [5]	5.0 [5]	3.1 [6]	5.2 [5]	4.5 [5]	5.1 [5]	3.9 [6]	5.2 [5]	4.9 [5]	5.5 [5]	5.0 [5]	5.3 [5]	[80]
Mississippi Peer	4.3 [6]	5.0 [6]	5.1 [6]	3.9 [6]	5.0 [6]	3.3 [5]	4.9 [6]	4.4 [6]	4.9 [6]	4.1 [5]	5.0 [6]	4.5 [6]	5.1 [6]	5.1 [6]	4.8 [6]	[85]
Dialect difference, F ratios: (df = 5.175)‡	22.5	14.3	2.0	35.1	4.9	35.7	6.5	5.5	3.0	14.5	6.1	7.3	4.6	3.4	3.9	

* Mean ratings are rounded to one decimal place.
† Ranks of mean ratings are set in brackets.
‡ All F ratios except that for the trait "Friendly" are significant at or beyond the .05 level of confidence.

296

listen to the voices on one of the two tapes and to evaluate each speaker in terms of the traits listed in Table 1. A separate rating sheet was provided for the evaluation of each speaker, and the order of adjective placement on the sheet was alternated. Standard instructions and examples were given to explain the testing procedure and the use of the 8-point rating scales.

First, the practice voice was played and the judges made their ratings. All questions were answered and the formal testing session began. Each speaker's taped passage was played twice, separated by a five-second pause, and thirty seconds were given for judges to complete their evaluations before the next speaker's recording was played. Each judge evaluated 12 speakers in addition to the practice voice.

Method of Data Analysis

A number from 1 to 8 was assigned to each rating. The positive end of each scale was arbitrarily given the value 8, and the negative end the value 1. The ratings produced by the two groups of male judges were combined as were those of the female judges. This was done for each of the dialect groups and for each of the 15 traits, making it possible to determine, for instance, how favorably the southern Negro male in contrast to the female judges rated any one of the 6 dialect groups on any particular trait.

A three-way analysis of variance, repeated measures design with corrections for unequal sample size,[3] was performed separately on the responses of the southern Negro and northern white judging groups for each of the 15 traits. A separate analysis was performed for the responses of the southern white group of judges. This statistical analysis indicates (1) whether the dialects were rated differentially (e.g., whether different ratings were given to the *Network* speakers than to the *Howard University* speakers), (2) whether male and female judges responded differently, and (3) whether there were differences in the reactions to the members of the dialect groups separated on the two tapes.

RESULTS AND DISCUSSION

The results are summarized in Tables 1, 2, and 3 where the ratings by each group of judges for the 15 traits are presented. The column marked "total" provides an index of the over-all ranking of each group over all traits. In these comparisons, the ratings of male and female judges are combined since there were, for the most part, no sex differences in patterns of response. In the few instances where sex differences in responding did occur, the females tended to rate the speakers slightly more favorably.

The statistical analyses show that each group of judges clearly differentiates the various dialects. The most pronounced trend noted for all three

[3] B. J. Winer, *Statistical Principles in Experimental Design* (New York: McGraw-Hill Book Co., 1962).

Table 2. Mean ratings* and ranks of mean ratings† of each dialect type by southern Negro college students

Dialect Groups	Traits															Sum
	Upbringing	Intelligent	Friendly	Educated	Disposition	Speech	Trustworthy	Ambitious	Faith-God	Talented	Character	Determination	Honest	Personality	Considerate	
Network	6.4 [1]	6.5 [1]	6.2 [1]	6.6 [1]	6.2 [1]	6.3 [1]	6.3 [1]	6.0 [1]	6.0 [1]	6.0 [1]	6.4 [1]	5.9 [1]	6.3 [1]	6.4 [1]	6.3 [1]	[15]
Educated Negro Southern	5.8 [2]	5.8 [2]	5.5 [3]	5.8 [2]	5.2 [3]	5.1 [2]	5.7 [3]	5.4 [2]	5.6 [2]	5.3 [2]	5.5 [3]	5.4 [2]	5.6 [3]	5.4 [3]	5.3 [3]	[37]
Howard University	5.3 [3]	5.4 [3]	5.7 [2]	5.2 [3]	5.6 [2]	4.2 [3]	5.7 [2]	5.0 [3]	5.4 [3]	4.7 [3]	5.8 [2]	4.9 [3]	5.8 [2]	5.8 [2]	5.7 [2]	[38]
Mississippi Peer	4.9 [4]	4.8 [4]	5.4 [4]	4.4 [4]	4.9 [4]	3.4 [4]	5.2 [4]	4.6 [4]	5.2 [4]	4.1 [4]	5.0 [4]	4.4 [4]	5.4 [4]	5.0 [4]	4.7 [4]	[60]
New York Alumni	4.9 [5]	4.8 [5]	5.0 [5]	4.3 [5]	4.6 [5]	3.4 [5]	5.0 [5]	4.6 [4]	4.9 [5]	3.9 [5]	4.8 [5]	4.2 [5]	5.2 [5]	4.7 [5]	4.4 [5]	[74]
Educated White Southern	4.4 [6]	4.4 [6]	4.2 [6]	4.2 [6]	4.1 [6]	3.3 [6]	4.6 [6]	4.0 [6]	4.8 [6]	3.7 [6]	4.4 [6]	4.0 [6]	5.1 [6]	4.1 [6]	4.2 [6]	[90]
Dialect differences, F ratios (df = 5.720)‡	42.7	56.2	26.6	77.7	39.3	107.7	29.5	32.2	14.6	60.9	38.1	41.0	16.7	37.9	37.8	

* Mean ratings are rounded to one decimal place.
† Ranks of mean ratings are set in brackets.
‡ All these F ratios are significant beyond the .01 level of significance.

298

Table 3. Mean ratings* and ranks of mean ratings† of each dialect type by southern white college students

Dialect Groups	Traits															Sum
	Upbringing	Intelligent	Friendly	Educated	Disposition	Speech	Trustworthy	Ambitious	Faith-God	Talented	Character	Determination	Honest	Personality	Considerate	
Network	6.7 [1]	6.6 [1]	5.9 [1]	7.0 [1]	6.1 [1]	6.8 [1]	6.2 [1]	6.3 [1]	5.4 [1]	6.3 [1]	6.4 [1]	6.0 [1]	6.2 [1]	6.1 [1]	6.2 [1]	[15]
Educated White Southern	6.2 [2]	6.2 [2]	5.8 [2]	6.5 [2]	5.9 [2]	5.4 [2]	6.1 [2]	5.8 [3]	5.1 [3]	5.6 [2]	6.0 [2]	5.6 [3]	6.0 [2]	5.8 [2]	5.8 [2]	[33]
Educated Negro Southern	5.9 [3]	5.9 [3]	5.5 [4]	6.1 [3]	5.5 [4]	5.2 [3]	5.6 [3]	5.9 [2]	5.3 [2]	5.3 [3]	5.8 [3]	5.7 [2]	5.9 [3]	5.6 [3]	5.7 [3]	[44]
Howard University	4.9 [4]	5.0 [4]	5.6 [3]	4.8 [4]	5.6 [3]	3.8 [4]	5.4 [4]	5.1 [4]	5.1 [5]	4.4 [4]	5.4 [4]	4.7 [5]	5.4 [4]	5.5 [4]	5.6 [4]	[60]
New York Alumni	4.6 [5]	4.5 [5]	4.8 [6]	4.2 [5]	4.8 [6]	3.0 [4]	5.0 [5]	4.6 [5]	5.1 [4]	3.8 [6]	5.3 [5]	4.7 [4]	5.3 [5]	4.7 [6]	4.8 [4]	[78]
Mississippi Peer	4.0 [6]	4.2 [6]	5.2 [5]	3.9 [6]	4.9 [5]	3.0 [5]	4.8 [6]	4.3 [6]	4.8 [6]	3.9 [5]	4.9 [6]	4.4 [6]	5.0 [6]	5.0 [5]	4.8 [5]	[84]
Dialect differences, F ratios: (df = 5.63)‡	53.1	40.8	7.6	65.1	12.6	78.2	15.6	26.7	1.3	41.1	16.7	17.4	10.4	12.3	16.1	

* Mean ratings are rounded to one decimal place.
† Ranks of mean ratings are set in brackets.
‡ All these F ratios are reliable at or beyond the .05 level of significance except that for the trait *Faith in God*.

299

groups of judges was the nearly unanimous perception of the *Network* speakers as having the most favorable profile of traits. This dialect group was considered as most favorable by the Negro judges *and* by the southern white judges on every trait, and by the northern white judges on 12 of the 15 traits.

The dialect group rated next most favorably by both northern white and southern Negro judges was the *Educated Negro Southern*. In fact, the northern white judges thought that the *Educated Negro Southern* speakers had slightly more "faith in God" and were more "determined" than the *Network* speakers. The Negro judges, however, rated these speakers only slightly more favorably than the *Howard University* group. The southern white judges, on the other hand, rated speakers belonging to their own peer group (i.e., *Educated White Southern*) in the second position followed by the *Educated Negro Southern* speakers.

A very interesting contrast emerges in the choice of the least favored group. The Negro judges rated the *Educated White Southern* speakers least favorably on every one of the 15 traits, whereas the white judges, both northern and southern, rated the *Mississippi Peer* speakers least favorably, and the *New York Alumni* speakers only slightly higher.

The two groups of white judges were also asked to indicate what they thought the race of each speaker was.[4] The following percentages indicate the northern white judges' estimates of the race of the speakers representing each dialect group: *Network*, 95 per cent white; *Educated White Southern*, 87 per cent white; *New York Alumni*, 49 per cent Negro; *Educated Negro Southern*, 49 per cent Negro; *Howard University*, 84 per cent Negro; and *Mississippi Peer*, 94 per cent Negro. The following percentages indicate the southern white judges' estimates: *Network*, 98 per cent white; *Educated White Southern*, 96 per cent white; *Educated Negro Southern*, 47 per cent Negro; *New York Alumni*, 54 per cent Negro; *Howard University*, 70 per cent Negro; and *Mississippi Peer*, 89 per cent Negro.

Although incidental to the central theme of this study, these results indicate that further research on judges' estimates of a speaker's race would be valuable. There is here an interesting relation between the perceived favorableness of a speaker and his perceived race. From a consideration of the extreme cases, e.g., the *Network* in contrast to the *Mississippi Peer* group, it might appear that speakers thought of as being white are judged favorably while those perceived as Negro are judged relatively unfavorably. But this generalization doesn't hold since the *New York Alumni* group is seen as being more likely white than is the *Howard University* group, and yet the *New York Alumni* group is less favorably rated. One might then argue that the *New York Alumni* group is looked on suspiciously because racial background is not clear from speech style in this case, but this explanation doesn't hold since the *Educated Negro Southern* group is also ambiguous as to

---

[4] In the context of the experiment, it would have been inappropriate to ask this question of the Negro students.

race and yet it is clearly regarded more favorably than the *New York Alumni* by both groups of white judges.

In summary, several instructive results have come to light. First, subjects were able to reliably differentiate the dialect groups and they clearly favored the *Network* style of spoken English in comparison with the other styles. There are, of course, limits to the generalizability of this finding because of the sampling of stimulus voices. Many speakers could have been selected for each of the 6 dialect groups, and we used only small samples. Thus, the reliability of these results can only be determined through repeat studies, using new samples of stimulus speakers.

The second noteworthy finding concerns the different perspectives of the white and Negro judges regarding the least favorable of the dialects. These differences in views likely reflect basic comparisons in affectively toned attitudes that representatives of America's major ethnic groups hold toward one another. The contrasts also make it evident that speech styles which are pleasing to one social group will not necessarily be so perceived by another.

In the third place, the results indicate that white judges can, in certain instances at least, distinguish white from Negro speakers. Much more research is needed, of course, to examine this question in depth. This finding, however, suggests some interesting next steps in research, calling for cooperation of dialectologists and psychologists. For instance, certain *combinations* of dialect features might enhance or depress the perceived pleasantness of speech styles. A fusion of *Network* and *Educated Southern White* characteristics might be particularly attractive for certain listeners, say southern whites, whereas *Network-Educated Southern Negro* mixtures might be most appealing to southern and northern Negro listeners.

STUDY QUESTIONS

1. Examine the results given by Tucker and Lambert for the identification of the race of the speakers whose voices were heard (p. 300). Which group of judges was most often correct in identifying race? What reason would you give for this result? Could reasons be deduced to explain those cases where judges had the least success in identifying race?
2. Concerning the ability of listeners to identify the race of a speaker, Labov reports in an earlier selection (p. 243) that in his Family Background Test: "Sizable extracts from the speech of fourteen individuals are played in sequence for listeners who are asked to identify the family backgrounds of each. So far, we find no one who can even come close to a correct identification of black and white speakers." Do Labov's findings contradict those of Tucker and Lambert? If not, why not? How might subjectivity or bias be introduced in attitude tests by the initial choice of the speakers to be heard, for example by selecting Negro speakers only with southern backgrounds?
3. What difference in attitudes toward dialects did Tucker and Lambert discover

among the three groups of judges? What do the differences tell us about differences in the preconceptions or stereotypes held by the judges?

4. Tucker and Lambert asked for judgments about the personality traits of the recorded speakers. Would it be accurate to say that the judgments made involve stereotyped beliefs held by the judges concerning the relationship between dialect and social status? How would you describe the stereotypes that are associated with the varieties of American English included in the study?

5. A number of virtues are associated with "Network English"—logicality, clarity, precision, and so on. Are these traits inherent in that variety of English, or are they merely believed to belong to it? In formulating your answer, consider the following observation about a variety of Akan (an African language) called *adehye kasa*, the speech style of royals. "Its main feature is deliberate stutter and a slight nasality. When a child wishing to have his own way speaks with a pronounced nasality, he is said to be showing off or trying to behave falsely in the manner of royalty."[a]

6. Comment on the following definition of "standard English" formulated by members of the International Reading Association in 1968:

> A socially unmarked variety of spoken American English used as a reference point in school language instruction to increase the individual's repertoire of important and useful ways of communicating. This variety of American English is often heard on network radio and television newscasts.[b]

Do the results reported by Tucker and Lambert support the idea that Network English is "socially unmarked"? Should Network English be adopted as a model variety to be learned by everyone?

[a] J. H. Kwabena Nketia, "The Linguistic Aspect of Style in African Languages," in *Current Trends in Linguistics: Linguistics in Sub-Saharan Africa* (The Hague: Mouton, 1971), p. 733.
[b] Thomas D. Horn, ed., *Reading for the Disadvantaged: Problems of Linguistically Different Learners* (New York: Harcourt, Brace and World 1970), p. 4.

LANGUAGE AND SUCCESS:
WHO ARE THE JUDGES?

Roger W. Shuy

Every linguistic community shares a commonly held set of beliefs about language, and, as Shuy points out in the following essay, its members act decisively out of these beliefs however little they are able to talk about them or justify their decisions. Because language is often taken as a defining characteristic of man, those who are regarded as somewhat less than fully developed human beings are also believed to have inadequate linguistic abilities. Hence when the eradication of the American Indian was regarded as essential to "manifest destiny," the "savages" were widely assumed to communicate only by inarticulate grunts. The landowners of nineteenth-century England were quite willing to believe that the peasant had a vocabulary of only a hundred words, and even an expert on ancient languages, the Right Honorable Professor F. Max Müller, K.M., of Oxford University, could write in 1861 that "the average man uses about five hundred words," adding "it is appalling to think how pitiably we have degenerated from the copiousness of our ancestors." [a]

What might be called the myth of the miniscule vocabulary persists today in much the same form as in the past. In response to questioning about "the major problems your children have with vocabulary, grammar, and pronunciation," one Detroit school teacher replied:

> Some had a vocabulary of about a hundred and some words, I'd say; no more than that. They got along fine with what they knew. They didn't have any trouble expressing themselves. They knew the important words for them to get along okay. Some could talk your foot off. I mean, they just knew everything. The quieter ones were the ones who didn't have a large vocabulary. [b]

This confusion of the nonvocal with the nonverbal child persists into adulthood; writers of letters of recommendation feel obliged to explain that quiet students are really thoughtful and reflective, as if outward silence reflects inner vacuity.

This paper was originally presented at a conference on "Language and Cultural Diversity" held at the University of Minnesota in 1971 and is published here by permission of the author. Copyright 1971 by Roger W. Shuy.

[a] Quoted and discussed with similar examples by Otto Jespersen, *Growth and Structure of the English Language* (Garden City, N.Y., Doubleday, nd), pp. 225–27.

[b] Roger W. Shuy, Walter A. Wolfram, and William K. Riley, *Linguistic Correlates of Social Stratification in Detroit Speech* (East Lansing: Cooperative Research Project No. 6–1347 [mimeographed], 1967), Part IV, p. 4.

As Shuy and his associates note in discussing the Detroit teacher's remarks, "the absurdity of assuming that a child has only a hundred words or so is one of the curious stereotypes of the teaching profession." [c]

Much of the justification for teaching students their native language has rested in the past on the supposed correlation between "good English" and "good jobs." Little research has been carried out to date on the place of facility in English in decisions about employment. Shuy's investigation of the beliefs of those responsible for some 40,000 jobs in the Washington area is an important first step toward a clear understanding of the issues involved.

Back in the days when I was working my way through college on a six-to-midnight general labor job at the Firestone Tire and Rubber Company, the importance of language in relating to one's fellow employees was never more clear to me. My job involved manufacturing tire treads on a machine which engaged a crew of five other men. My pay was based on how much we as a crew produced in a given evening while my fellow workers were paid at a constant hourly rate, regardless of what we produced. Since I was also a graduate student in English at that time, my role was obviously precarious from the perspective of the other members of my crew, none of whom had finished high school. Whatever else could be deduced from the situation, it was clear beyond words that it was necessary for me to speak something other than grad school English. Since my paycheck was at their mercy, it was obvious that the speech of a grad student simply would not do on the assembly line. This was not a new situation for me, however, for almost all males who grew up in working-class communities can probably remember their adolescent need to speak with masculinity, particularly if there was any question whatsoever about their physical prowess, their ability as athletes, or if they were tortured by the anomaly of a relatively late development of facial hair and a deeper voice. Masculinity, they discovered, could be expressed by a choice of vocabulary, grammar, and pronunciation even after their bodies had unceremoniously failed them.

HOW IMPORTANT IS LANGUAGE USE IN JUDGING SUCCESS?

Here we can see two legitimate evidences of a need to speak something other than "schoolroom English" at work in a society which at least outwardly claims that its values are to be placed on entirely different forms. It cannot be denied that a man must adjust to the social needs of his environment, particularly if he gains physically or psychologically from that adjustment. The good intention of the school frequently causes the boy to produce

[c] *Ibid.*

standard English, not realizing what the ramification of such usage might be in an entirely different context. The school might consider itself a failure, furthermore, if it produced graduate students in English who say "bring them crates over here," despite the fact that such a locution might seem more appropriate in the factory than "bring those crates over here" or the hyperstandard, "gentlemen would you kindly convey these containers to this portion of the edifice." Such good intentions generally are characterized by tunnel vision, failing to recognize the complexity or multitude of the forces which constantly operate in a person's life.

If we are to deal at all with the question of language and success, therefore, we must make some sort of heroic effort to define success and we must try desperately to determine who it is that makes this judgment. In the preceding example the definition of linguistic success must be viewed as a relative term, depending on any number of circumstances involving the relationship of the speaker and the listener in real time and real space.

HOW IS THE CORRELATION OF LANGUAGE USE AND SUCCESS JUDGED?

Historically the schools have viewed success as causing the learner to behave-perform-produce in a way which is consonant with what teachers said should be done. Recent years have produced enough awareness of this in the education profession to enable us to say this sort of thing publicly, and people like Silberman and Holt are saying it as loud as anyone. But even the non-education world is on to us by now and in such recent noneducation books as Charles Reich's, *The Greening of America* we read:

School is intensely concerned with training students to stop thinking and start obeying. Any course that starts with a textbook and a teacher and ends with an examination runs this danger unless great pains are taken to show students that they are supposed to think for themselves; in most school and college classes, on the other hand, thinking for oneself is actually penalized, and the student learns the value of repeating what he is told. Public school is "obedience school"; the student is taught to accept authority without question, to respect authority simply because of its position, to obey not merely in the area of school regulations but in the area of facts and ideas as well. . . .

One of the great purposes of the school is to indoctrinate the inmates. Vast powers are set to work on remolding their thinking. Indoctrination is not the same as teaching. The purpose of teaching is to help the student to think for himself. The purpose of indoctrination is to compel him to accept someone else's ideas, someone else's version of the facts. It is indoctrination whenever the student can get a bad mark for disagreeing. Indoctrination may take many forms. There may be a blatant course entitled, "Democracy versus Communism." Even if there is not, the usual courses in American studies, history, and civics will present a strongly biased point of view. As we have just begun to learn, the bias may not only be political, it often is racial as well. The school tries to force-feed a whole set of values and attitudes: about advertising, business, competition, success, and the American way of life. And this is carried on amid a pervasive atmosphere of dishonesty and hypocrisy. No one will admit that America might be a bad country, that the textbooks might be boring and stupid, that much of what the school does may not be in the best interests of students, that there could be other ways of doing what routine requires.[1]

This view of the school as the leader of blind authority has also characterized the language arts and English classrooms of our country.

It is not a well-guarded secret that the schools have had very few sources of motivation to cause students to want to speak standard English. One classic motivation has been that of pleasing the teacher, obtaining a tangible or abstract reward from the instructor. This might be called a contiguous, or short-range motivation. Its long-range counterpart requires the student to project into the misty future, seeking out the abstraction of his potential life work as the motivation for learning acceptable schoolroom English. At least by the onset of junior high school (usually even earlier) students are barraged with statements about the importance of learning standard English if ever they are to make something of their lives.

The question some of us recently asked is as follows, "Is speech really an important criterion in employability?" In an effort to answer this question we produced a tape recording of sixteen samples of Washington, D.C. Negro male adults and teen-agers from the complete range of socioeconomic status groups in the city. The tape included two adult (21–25) and two teen-age (14–17) speakers to represent each of four social classes. The passages chosen for the study were taken from the discourse section of the interview conducted as a part of the Washington Dialect Study. The passages selected for the tape were based on two criteria: (1) the linguistic features in the passage should represent the particular social group of the informant and (2) the passage should be as culturally unmarked as possible, since we wanted the people who listened to the tapes to react solely on the basis of linguistic criteria.

This tape was played individually to sixteen persons who actually do the hiring for various Washington employers. These people represent approximately 40,000 jobs of all sorts in this area. Nine of the sixteen employers claimed that on the basis of the speech sample which they heard they considered all sixteen men employable.

These nine people represented employment in the hotel, telephone, dry-cleaning, baking, lumber, drug, and newspaper businesses. Representatives of a large department store and a printing business found only one person unemployable, while employers from a men's clothing store, another printing company, the telephone company, and a large automotive repair business found three of the taped speakers unemployable.

On the whole, the reactions of these employers to the taped speech samples were fairly consonant with the idea generally perpetrated by the classrooms

[1] Charles Reich, *The Greening of America* (New York: 1970), pp. 123–24.

of America; namely, that speech is directly proportionate to employability. Of the four lower working-class tape speech samples, the representative of the men's clothing store picked two as unemployable. The other two he would hire as porters, or as receiving-room workers with no public contact. The other employers gave comparable answers.

On the other hand, when asked to comment in writing on the extent to which they are influenced by the speech of a prospective employee, many employers denied that any such influence took place. The representative of one of Washington's largest hotels, in fact, observed "I would say that speech plays a relatively minor part in hiring an employee . . . general presentation, knowledge, and appearance weigh most heavily." Likewise the employment supervisor of a large chain drug company which employs 9,000 Washingtonians observed that the most important speech criterion for his employees is that they be . . . "able to express themselfs [sic] in a way that is understood by our customers." The only employers who expressed much interest in speech as a criterion for selection were, predictably, those from the telephone company and the men's clothing store and, much less predictably, the one in the automotive repair business.

The general liberality of our employers when asked to comment on the significance of a job applicant's speech may have resulted from their attempt to bend over backward toward utter fairness, perhaps even a bit defensively. This liberality was generally not as evident, however, in a follow-up study in which the same employers were asked to rank each speaker on the same tape by job categories. Seven job categories were established, ranging from the highest (doctor, professor, architect) to the lowest (laborer, janitor, bus boy). The professional, well-educated speakers of the highest actual category were consistently ranked in the fourth and fifth categories (salesmen, policemen, mechanics), indicating a general unwillingness to believe that such persons could be as highly placed as they actually were.

What, then, are we to say about the importance of speech as a criterion for opportunity? It appears that it operates differently on different points of a continuum of awareness. Most of the employers in our study consciously denied that speech is a consideration, but they unconsciously reacted with amazing uniformity in assigning jobs on the basis of very few linguistic clues. The better jobs invariably went to the standard speakers. Those who were judged unemployable were invariably those with a lesser degree of standard English. One might say that employers seem better able *to use* linguistic clues as a criterion for employment than they are *to talk about them*. This is not at all surprising to linguists who have been working in this area, for it is also generally true of English teachers, especially those with little or no training in the nature of the English language.

Although this generally uniform ability to assign jobs from the clues provided by a small sample of speech seems encouraging, there are a number of pitfalls which many of our Washington employers illustrate. One employer, for example, observed that speech tells ". . . an unmistakable story about a person's background, training, and mental alertness." We may agree that speech reveals interesting information about his geographical origins, his social status, his education, and even his race. But in no way can it be considered a useful index to his mental alertness or intelligence. In his recent article on the logic of nonstandard English, [reprinted on pp. 319–54], William Labov puts to sleep for good the widely held but totally erroneous notion that nonstandard speech is a signal of mental inadequacy. For far too many years now the general public and the schools have assumed the position currently espoused by Carl Bereiter, who observes: ". . . the language of culturally deprived children . . . is not merely an underdeveloped version of standard English, but is a basically nonlogical mode of expressive behavior."[2] In order to overcome this illogicality and underdevelopment, this psychologist urges teachers to proceed as though the children have no language at all and to train children to speak in fully explicit formal language. The absurdity of these admonitions becomes evident when we examine the solutions to the illogicality and underdevelopment. Bereiter argues for unelliptical responses to questions (for example, *The squirrel is in the tree* is preferred over *in the tree*) as though, somehow, the full unelliptical form is the well-developed and logical version from which all other versions diverge. Current linguistics clearly argues that the semantics of each of these sentences is the same and that there are superficial surface-structure differences between them. In his recent overview of the assumptions of linguists who work with social dialects Walt Wolfram observed: "All languages adequately provide for the conceptualization and expression of logical propositions, but the particular mode . . . for conceptualizing may differ drastically between language systems. The linguist, therefore, assumes that different surface forms for expression have nothing to do with the underlying logic of a sentence."[3] It is safe to assert that linguists are unanimous in this position.

In clear terms of the relationship of a person's use of language and employability, then, it can be concluded that it is dangerous to infer anything about a speaker's logic or intelligence on the basis of his use of the language. Far more revealing might be the person's social status, his education, or his geographical origins. Furthermore, however tempting it may be to use a prospective employee's nonstandard grammar, pronunciation, and vocabulary as a sign of his motivation or trainability, chances are that all one can accurately infer is that the candidate has grown up in a nonstandard English speaking environment.

[2] Carl Bereiter, Siegfried Engelmann, *et al.*, "An Academically Oriented Pre-School for Culturally Deprived Children," in *Pre-School Education Today* (Garden City, N.Y.: Random House, 1966), pp. 112–13.

[3] Walt Wolfram, "Social Dialects from a Linguistic Perspective: Assumptions, Current Research, and Future Directions," in *Developmental Studies of Communicative Competence and Social Dialects from a Linguistic Perspective* (Washington, D.C.: National Center for Educational Research and Development [mimeographed], 1970), p. 97.

Clear evidence of how dangerous it can be for the nonlinguistically sensitized employment manager to speculate about the clues language provides may be found in the previously cited study of Washington employers. The vice-president of one of the city's largest dry cleaning companies, for example, expressed a theory that the efficiency of his truck drivers is directly related to their speech tempo. It is of some interest, also, that this gentleman himself speaks at a very rapid rate, suggesting, perhaps, that he has either a personal or cultural bias against people unlike himself, at least with regard to speech tempo. Regardless of the source of his feeling, however, he is convinced that his drivers who speak slowly take longer to deliver their goods and, for whatever it is worth, they take too much time, as he put it, "commuting with customers."

Another employment manager's observations about language also seem to be widely held. After listening to our tape-recorded speech samples, this department store executive expressed the opinion that the people who came into his office had much worse speech than any of the samples on the tape (our tape, of course, contained samples from all levels of Washington society) and that he couldn't hire many people because they couldn't make themselves well enough understood to give any pertinent information to the interviewer.

Linguists who have worked with educators have faced this situation for many years. Teachers bitterly complain that their students have a very limited vocabulary. They assume, quite wrongly, that the lack of vocabulary used in school settings is equivalent to lack of over-all vocabulary. Teachers also indicate little or no understanding of the slum child's grammar, often paying great heed to features which are actually of little consequence in terms of social stigmatization. Many are utterly unaware of what recent sociolinguistic research has indicated about the relative importance of grammatical features in social stigmatization as opposed to nonstandard pronunciations. That is, they fail to understand that English speakers tend to tolerate or accept pronunciation differences much more than grammatical variations. If teachers fail to respond to these clues, how can we expect employment managers to do so? For they, like teachers, hear English spoken in very specialized and, in some ways, tense situations. A person seeking employment, like a schoolchild, is apt to be guarded, nervous, and timid in an obviously intimidating situation. Employment interviewers, like teachers, are apt to forget how used to their jobs they have become. They are apt to forget that their subjects are not at all used to such interviewing or that they are aware of being judged at all times. The child in the first grade soon learns that the point of the game of education is to be wrong as seldom as possible and to be right as often as possible. He may determine, quite properly, that his best defense is a retreat into silence. If the teacher corrects his speech enough times when he responds with the right answer, the child may logically assume that his answer is really wrong, or quite possibly that this school business doesn't make a whole lot of sense anyway.

WHAT ARE THE MISCONCEPTIONS ABOUT LANGUAGE USE AND SUCCESS?

To this point we have observed that the traditional view of language success in the classroom has centered around two motivations:

1. Pleasing the teacher, conforming to the school norm, or basically being good.
2. Getting a good job.

We have dismissed the first motivation rather cavalierly, since the world of education seems bent, at long last, on dismissing it itself. The second motivation, economic success, is a bit more tricky and deserves considerably more attention than we have given it so far. Several dangerous assumptions may be noted in the reactions of our Washington employers, as noted previously:

1. There is *one* best form of English which should be spoken at all times.
2. A person's language use reflects his logic and intelligence.
3. Nonstandard speech should be eradicated.
4. That making mistakes is always bad.

The employers did not dream up these assumptions—they inherited them naturally, probably from their own teachers. Recent sociolinguistic research has been making clear the facts of our need for stylistic variation, making a lie of the feeling that one best form of English should be saved for all occasions. The exact description of when who speaks what dialect to whom, sometimes referred to as an ethnography of communication, is a current focus of much sociolinguistic research. This sort of information is gradually legitimizing the use of a variety of linguistic systems—even from the viewpoint of classroom teachers, some of whom are now even accepting the fact that it may be quite inappropriate to play football in standard English. Likewise, certain strides have been made in disseminating known information about the lack of connection between language and intelligence. We are beginning to see realism creep into some of the classrooms of America in which it is admitted that nonstandard speech may be useful to a speaker not only in certain well-defined contexts but also as a part of a pedagogical strategy for pointing out contrasts between language use in different appropriate situations. That is, instead of hiding behind the widely held fear of negative reinforcement, some teachers are boldly making use of the nonstandard dialect in the classroom as a way of implementing another widely acclaimed pedagogical strategy, that of learning by contrast. Such teachers cannot be characterized as seeing burglars under the bed at every conceivable opportunity. They recognize that children have peer-group pressures to speak one way and school pressures to speak another. These teachers are content to help their students learn to cope effectively with both sets of pressures. Curiously enough, this has been an avowed goal of our English classes for many years (remember such topics as Writing with a Purpose, Speaking the Language of Your Audience, and the like), although it seems to have broken down outside the realm of written English.

One last common misconception about the correlation of language and success may be observed in the reactions of teachers, employers, and people in general to certain supposed errors. It has long been recognized that there is some sort of linguistic tolerance toward the mistakes of foreign language learners and children. At some fuzzy, unspecified time in a child's life, however, the school turns on him and he is no longer smiled at for his cute near-misses. It is odd that we have learned to expect those who acquire language non-natively to make mistakes. In fact, the foreign language classroom that does not allow for the making of mistakes is one in which relatively little is likely to be learned. It is seldom uttered aloud, but language learning is in many ways a mistake-processing operation. And good teachers know this, but the transfer of this idea to second dialect acquisition has not been obvious. In fact, it has not been obvious in much of any sort of education process, where right is right and wrong is always wrong, regardless of whether or not permissive liberals think that there are different degrees of wrongness and that these degrees may suggest entirely different teaching strategies. For example, a child who misspells *basement* as *basemint* has an entirely different learning problem from the one who spells it *bslefrmt* or *bosemetn*. We have hardly begun to think about different teaching strategies for mistakes of these sorts, but if my younger son's recent experience is typical, the problem is even deeper than I suspected. He came home from school with a paper on antonyms in which his response to the stimulus word, *came*, was marked wrong. The teacher wanted *went*. He was either audacious or creative enough to offer *left* as the opposite of *came*. Obviously he was wrong.

Recent research in learning theory by psycholinguists such as Thomas Bever has revealed some interesting insights that may prove helpful to us in learning to understand such phenomena as hypercorrection. It appears that as the four-year-old child acquires knowledge of the law of conservation (larger spaces tend to contain more things than smaller spaces), this knowledge causes him some temporary problems. That is, once he learns this law he is, at least for a time, trapped by it. When shown two rows of M and M's, one short row containing five, and one long row containing four, he may decide that the long row contains the most candies. He will not do this forever; only for a few months until he learns to process two kinds of data at once: The law of conservation and the exact number of M and M's.

This sort of behavior has long been observed in language contexts. My son Joel recently discovered *-en* participles and began tagging them on to all sorts of non-*en* participle words such as *have satten down, have walken, has readen the book,* and so on. Recent research in ghetto speech seems to indicate that the child who says *deskes* for *desks* is somewhere beyond the *desses* speaker in the acquisition of standard English. It appears that he realizes the need for a full consonant cluster -SK but still hangs on to the same -EZ morpheme which he quite appropriately attached to the word when he thought it ended in a single consonant, -S.

In general then, one aspect of language and success almost totally over-looked by the education world involves the stages in the acquisition of the standard form. We have myopically chosen to view the process as polar rather than as a continuum.

WHAT ARE THE JUDGES JUDGING?

If we can say with confidence that the spoken use of language is corre-lated with success, one obvious thing to do, perhaps the next logical one, is to get a clear research description of the parameters of the success-fail matrix. What aspects of language lead to failure? Which aspects signify success? Labov's important article, "The Logic of Non-Standard English," shows that at least a part of the success markers in language use are rather superficial and vague: "The accumulating flow of words buries rather than strikes the target. It is this verbosity which is most easily taught and most easily learned, so that words take the place of thoughts, and nothing can be found behind them."[4] While Labov has been examining the presumed characteristics of successful language, several of us have been also involved in determining what the exact points of tension are. That is, we need to know exactly what con-tributes to stigmatization in the success-fail judgment process.

DISCOVERING CRUCIALITY

Insight of this sort has been revealed in what might be called a hierarchy of cruciality concerning the three generally recognized categories of language: lexicon, phonology, and grammar. Much of the currently available oral language material for poor black children focuses on matters of pronuncia-tion.[5] This is perhaps excusable, for the demand for materials always pre-cedes the demand for research upon which materials are based. At the time in which this demand first began to be satisfied it appeared to many people that teaching standard English to nonstandard speakers involved primarily teaching them to pronounce English in a standard manner. Once sociolin-guistic research into nonstandard English began, however, it became clear

[4] See p. 336.

[5] For example, Ruth Golden, "Instructional Record for Changing Regional Speech Patterns" (*Folkway Scholastic*, No. 9323, 1965); Charles Hurst, *Phonological Correlates in Dialectolalia* (Washington, D.C.: Howard University, 1965); San-Su Lin, *Pattern Practice in the Teaching of Standard English to Students with a Non-Standard Dialect* (New York: Teachers College Press, 1965).

that the mainstream of American society tolerates phonological variation considerably more than it tolerates grammatical variation.[6]

This measure of the tolerance range of social acceptability for linguistic features is extremely difficult to calculate and, at present, we can do little more than speculate about how it might be established.

As linguistic geographers have long observed, it is not enough to point out where the speech of one group differs from that of another. We must also try to discover how crucial that difference is, particularly if we intend to use such information as a basis for shaping classroom activities. It has long been known, for example, that some people use relatively little aspiration at the beginnings of words with an initial *wh* spelling. Consequently, *witch* and *which* are homophonous in their dialects. This minor pronunciation difference carries relatively little social consequence even for those who produce a contrast between these two words. Those who pronounce them the same are often not even aware that some speakers produce a contrast. There are several reasons for the lack of social stigmatization attached to either side of the issue, not the least of which involves the relatively light functional load which the sounds carry. In isolation, there is potential ambiguity between *which* and *witch*, but in real-life speech there are obvious syntactic clues which prevent confusion. That is, one seldom utters sentences like, **Look, there goes a relative pronoun* (witch) *on a broom!* or **This is the story old hag* (which) *I heard last night.*

Considerable attention has been given this matter of relative cruciality, of late, by sociolinguists who are concerned about which linguistic features are not stigmatized. The most comprehensive treatment of this issue to date is Wolfram's set of criteria for ranking such features:[7]

1. *Sharp versus gradient stratification.* Since all features do not correlate with social status in the same manner, it is obvious that those features which show sharp breaks between social classes are more crucial than those which show only slight differences across social-status groups. Wolfram's research clearly shows that verb third-person singular *-s* absence (*My sister go to school every day*) stratifies sharply, whereas pronominal apposition (*My brother he came home late*) has only gradient (gradual) stratification across social class.

2. *The generality of the rule.* "Some nonstandard forms affect only a small subset of words or a single item, whereas others involve general rules that operate on the form of every sentence of a particular structural type."[8] The Black English rule of multiple negation, for example, is a general rule that affects all negative sentences with an indefinite pronoun, determiner, or

---

[6] It would appear, in addition, that lexical variations tend to be the most tolerated of all.

[7] See "Sociolinguistic Implications for Educational Sequencing," in *Teaching Standard English in the Inner City*, eds. Ralph W. Fasold and Roger W. Shuy (Washington, D.C.: Center for Applied Linguistics, 1970), pp. 105–19.

[8] Wolfram, "Sociolinguistic Implications," p. 110.

adverb. On the other hand, the Black English equivalent of the *there is–there are* construction, *it is*, concerns only one item.

3. *Grammatical versus phonological.* It has already been pointed out how important this difference can be to the development of materials. Nonstandard grammatical features, which tend to show sharp stratification between socioeconomic groups, are generally considered more stigmatizing than most phonological features by sociolinguists working in this area.

4. *Social versus regional significance.* Although some features which are perfectly acceptable in one part of the country become stigmatized in another, other features have negative social values everywhere. It has been discovered that the latter, the generally stigmatized features, tend to be the most crucial, for they always display sharper stratification than the regionally distributed items and they do not run the risk of developing regional snobbery.

5. *The relative frequency of the items.* Since some Black English patterns occur infrequently, they take less precedence than those which occur often. It is obvious that features which occur frequently are more crucial than those with low frequency.

To be sure, considerably more research needs to be done to refine our current knowledge in this area, but considerably more is now known than ever before about the relative values placed on socially stigmatized differences.

CONCLUSION

In this paper, I have painted in some of the gross details of the nature of judging failure or success on the basis of a person's use of language. I have urged that, regardless of whether we like it or not, language seems to be of great importance in the kinds of success usually sought in terms of education, economics, and acceptance among one's peers. This does not mean, of course, that the same kinds of language are always used to measure that success. Peer acceptance of preteen-age males, for example, sometimes seems to demand a degree of nonstandardness which runs counter to the schoolroom norms. And we must recognize the data presented by Labov several years ago when he documented a correlation between gang leadership and illiteracy in New York City [see pp. 238–42]. This paper has focused only on spoken language, but it is certain that the importance of language for success must also be noted in other language realms such as writing and reading. There is not much demand for people who read nonstandardly (however that might be defined), or who write that way.

I have also noted that most people not only *think* they relate language to success—they also do it quite well. Our research into the subjective reactions of people of all ages to tape-recorded samples of speech revealed that they were amazingly accurate in their judgment of race, occupation, and education. This seems to tell us that people not only *think* language is important; they also behave as though it is.

Despite all this, however, people maintain some rather surprising folk beliefs about the correlation of language and success. Employers seem to be hung up on an unproved assumption that language correlates with intelligence (and in one case, that it correlates with working speed and efficiency). Nor are teachers immune to this folk belief or to many other myths perpetrated upon them by the establishment. Teachers preserve the notion, for example, that inner-city children are nonverbal, primarily because tradition seems to have it that way and despite the outbursts of pure verbality that overcome our children once they escape the all too frequent joyless silence of the schoolroom. Perhaps the greatest misconception about language and success, however, involves the purity theory, which seems to say that everyone should speak school English at all times, a notion as absurd as saying that everyone should always wear formal clothing.

We now know some of the things that the judges seem to be judging. We know that they judge grammar more than pronunciation and we have little reason to believe that vocabulary stigmatizes much at all. In fact, lexicon seems to be one of the plus-markers, unless, of course, the word is a malapropism. We have still not isolated the stigmatizing grammatical and phonological markers as well as we would wish, however, and a great deal remains to be done. In addition, we know very little about the social stigmatization which may come about from intonation or voice quality. What little we do know, however, seems to be at odds with much of the textbook focus on language and success routines. For example, absolutely no commercial material exists, to my knowledge, which addresses itself to the special composition problems posed for ghetto children whose grammar and phonology cause interference in their writing. In typical educational fashion, the problems of the general learners are assumed to be the problems of the ghetto kids.

The matter of developing special materials for the special problems of ghetto children, of course, is obvious. Once you have isolated a problem as characteristic of a given racial group, you cannot isolate the group for special teaching without risking the label of segregationist. This is a serious problem which deserves considerably more attention than it has been given so far.

My assigned topic was "Language and Success: Who Are the Judges?" The world of education has too long run the risk of ignoring the realities of this problem. Our tradition was to teach to the problems that we assumed existed, regardless of the views of the general public. In recent years the situation has shifted drastically. Today we are becoming sensitive to the pressures of groups of all sizes and shapes. Few will argue against the healthy change in position. Yet we now run the risk of trying to be everything to everybody while one thing seems to remain constant: people go on judging or assessing each other because of their use of language. Some critics will continue to argue that we should leave our language alone. They argue that one person's speech is as inherently good as another and that we should do *nothing* about helping nonstandard speakers acquire standard English if they choose not to do so.

Strangely enough, these arguments are always conducted in perfectly standard English, suggesting that if the millenium is ever to come, if linguistic lambs and lions are ever to lie down together, it will take a new view of humanity on the part of those who argue from this position as well as from those who are supposedly exerting their racial or social biases on nonstandard-English-speaking children. I have yet to hear a black parent argue that we should not help his child learn standard English. I have met few if any black teachers who will have any truck with this idea. I *have* met black researchers and professors who hold this position and I ask them, as I ask myself, "Language and Success: Who *Are* the Judges?"

STUDY QUESTIONS

1. Shuy discusses views that employers in Washington hold about the relationship between jobs and language. Are those views compatible with the assumptions suggested in the following news report (from the *Detroit Free Press*, September 23, 1971):

Student Protests State Test

LANSING.—A Michigan State University student says that he is being fired from his job as a Capitol tour guide because he doesn't know Negro ghetto slang.

Leo Forster contends new State Civil Service Commission tests for guide jobs are rigged to favor those who understand the patois of the inner city and consequently blacks are favored over whites.

Questions on the test ask the definition of a "punk" (a homosexual), the meaning of "the man" (authority), and how one would refer to Negro tourists —as blacks or colored people.

"I would call them ladies and gentlemen, and that wasn't even one of the (multiple) choices," said Forster, who is white.

State Senator David A. Plawecki, D-Dearborn Heights, said he had seen the test and agreed 15 of its 67 questions require a knowledge of inner-city slang.

Plawecki's office said the senator had a number of complaints from applicants from his district.

The tour guide job is prized by college students because it requires employees to work only up to four hours a day. The top pay is $3.47 an hour.

The guides shepherd student groups and tourists through the Capitol building. A large proportion of those taking the tour are Negro school students from inner-city areas.

Forster has been a guide for six months. He faces dismissal Oct. 9.

The Civil Service Commission inaugurated its new test recently as a result of a U.S. Supreme Court ruling. That ruling, in effect, set down new Civil Service guidelines aimed at opening state jobs to Negroes.

So far, under the new tests, only four persons have been hired as Capitol tour guides. Two are white and two are black.

Because of the complaints, the commission said it had rescored the 286 applicants including Forster, deleting the 15 questions under complaint.

Forster, under the rescoring, still did not make the top 50, the commission said.

Foster has asked for a Civil Service appeal hearing in the case.

2. Shuy reports that some teachers are becoming receptive to the use of non-standard English in the classroom. Consider the advantages and disadvantages of such a practice in light of the following result from a survey of linguistic attitudes among parents of school-age children in Washington:

> An overwhelming majority of parents (mostly black and Spanish-speaking) see the teaching of Standard English as an important responsibility of the school and consider Standard English to be one prerequisite for moving up the socioeconomic ladder. They hold this view despite the opinion of many [that] nonstandard speech is not inferior, is appropriate at times, and can express some things better than Standard English. This traditional conservative stance toward Standard English is virtually uncompromising among parents who have only elementary school educations and perform unskilled labor. A minority view (especially among blacks) was revealed, however, which, while sharing the majority view, admits various elements of compromise. These elements of compromise center around receptivity to new ideas and innovations in schools, especially for those that see the young learner as an individual, with hopes and needs, and above all, feelings, dignity, and pride. This receptivity toward innovation increases with increasing education.[a]

3. Shuy twice refers to "black English" in the course of his discussion. Read the essays by McDavid (pp. 258–70) and Glissmeyer (pp. 190–222) and, citing the evidence given there, argue for or against the existence of a dialect of English restricted to black people.

4. Shuy speaks of "elliptical responses" to questions. Contrast the elliptical and unelliptical answers that might be given to the following:
   a. What time is it?
   b. Where did Bill go yesterday?
   c. Did Ann find herself a job?
   Discuss any differences in style and content that you find among the possible alternatives. Consider further uses of ellipsis in English and what effect they have.

5. What factors of the interview setting might lead employment officers to assign the speakers they heard on Shuy's tape to a lower job category than the ones they actually held. How could the "folk beliefs about the correlation of language and success" (p. 315) become self-fulfilling prophecies?

6. In the selection from *The Greening of America* quoted by Shuy (pp. 305–06), Charles Reich suggests that schools are designed to indoctrinate rather than to "help the student think for himself." Consider the following dialogue between a teacher (T) and the pupils (P) in a British secondary school. How does the interaction illustrated here support Reich's claim.

---

[a] Alfred S. Hayes and Orlando L. Taylor, "A Summary of the Center's 'BALA' Project," *The Linguistic Reporter*, 13, iv (1971):3.

T   Sand dunes. They're usually in an unusual . . . a specific shape . . . a special shape. . . . Does anybody know what shape they are? Not in straight lines . . . .

P   They're like hills.

T   Yes, they're like low hills.

P   They're all humpy up and down.

T   Yes, they're all humpy up and down.

P   They're like waves.

T   Good, they're like waves.

P   They're like . . . .

T   They're a special shape.

P   They're like boulders . . . sort of go up and down getting higher and higher.

T   I don't know about getting higher and higher.

P   Something like pyramids.

T   Mm . . . wouldn't call them pyramids, no.

P   They're in a semicircle.

T   Ah, that's getting a bit nearer. They're often in a semicircle and nearly always . . . we call them . . . well, it's part of a semicircle. . . . What do we call part of a semicircle? You think of the moon . . . perhaps you'll get the shape.

P   Water.

T   No, not shaped like water. . . . Yes?

P   An arc.

T   An arc . . . oh, we're getting ever so much nearer.

P   Crescent.

T   A crescent shape. Have you heard that expression . . . a crescent shape? I wonder if anybody could draw me a crescent shape on the board. Yes, they're nearly all that shape. . . .[b]

7. Why should Shuy regard it as "strange" that arguments against intervention by the schools in changing dialects should be "conducted in perfectly standard English" (p. 316)?

---

[b] Quoted by Douglas Barnes, "Language in the Secondary Classroom," in *Language, the Learner and the School* (Harmondsworth: Penguin Books, 1971), p. 43.

THE LOGIC OF NONSTANDARD ENGLISH
William Labov

A nonstandard dialect is a language variety spoken by the outs—by a group on the lower rungs of the social ladder. The older, near-mythic conception of such dialects held them to be corruptions of or deviations from some higher form of language created by imperfect learning characteristic of the natural sloth and stupidity of the lower classes. Long and painstaking work has corrected such a view for those who prefer science to religion. We now know that nonstandard dialects have histories as long as those for standard languages; that similar, although not identical, historical forces operate to shape the spoken forms of standard and nonstandard; that standardized literary languages have peculiarities of development all their own and exert only sporadic and minimal influence on the development of spoken varieties.

As Labov argues in the following selection, some educationists do appear to prefer religion to science, and the mythic view of the nature of nonstandard may be discerned in some of the fundamental assumptions on which their interventionist programs have been built: The assumption that logic can be defined on the basis of usages in the standard language; the assumption that deviations from standard usage can be termed illogical without supportive analysis; the assumption that alternate surface forms inevitably reflect semantic and cognitive differences; the assumption that performance exemplifies cognitive ability. The issues treated in Labov's paper are of the greatest importance to educational strategy, for concepts of the nature of nonstandard affect decisions about what must be taught. If, as the deprivation theorists maintain, a nonstandard dialect is cognitively deficient—primitive, unsystematic, lacking in abstract vocabulary or the means for manipulating abstract vocabulary—learning such a dialect will not fit the child for success in school, for handling the mainly cognitive tasks he will be asked to perform. If on the other hand, Labov is right in saying that nonstandard speakers "have the same basic vocabulary, possess the same capacity for conceptual learning, and use the same logic as anyone else who learns to speak and understand English," our teaching task is not to introduce a new language but to make use of the one the student has, helping him as we would any other student to expand his native and innate linguistic resources. In this particular debate, as Sledd points out in a later selection, someone has got to be wrong, because the nature of nonstandard is not a matter of opinion but of empirical fact. Teachers will prefer the facts.

Reprinted with the author's corrections from *Report of the Twentieth Annual Round Table Meeting on Linguistics and Language Studies*, ed. James E. Alatis, Georgetown University Press, Washington, D.C., pp. 1–43. Copyright 1970.

In the past decade, a great deal of federally sponsored research has been devoted to the educational problems of children in ghetto schools. In order to account for the poor performance of children in these schools, educational psychologists have attempted to discover what kind of disadvantage or defect the children are suffering from. The viewpoint that has been widely accepted and used as the basis for large-scale intervention programs is that the children show a cultural deficit as a result of an impoverished environment in their early years. Considerable attention has been given to language. In this area the deficit theory appears as the concept of verbal deprivation. Negro children from the ghetto area are said to receive little verbal stimulation, to hear very little well-formed language, and as a result are impoverished in their means of verbal expression. They cannot speak complete sentences, do not know the names of common objects, cannot form concepts or convey logical thoughts.

Unfortunately, these notions are based upon the work of educational psychologists who know very little about language and even less about Negro children. The concept of verbal deprivation has no basis in social reality. In fact, Negro children in the urban ghettos receive a great deal of verbal stimulation, hear more well-formed sentences than middle-class children, and participate fully in a highly verbal culture. They have the same basic vocabulary, possess the same capacity for conceptual learning, and use the same logic as anyone else who learns to speak and understand English.

The notion of verbal deprivation is a part of the modern mythology of educational psychology, typical of the unfounded notions which tend to expand rapidly in our educational system. In past decades linguists have been as guilty as others in promoting such intellectual fashions at the expense of both teachers and children. But the myth of verbal deprivation is particularly dangerous, because it diverts attention from real defects of our educational system to imaginary defects of the child. As we shall see, it leads its sponsors inevitably to the hypothesis of the genetic inferiority of Negro children that it was originally designed to avoid.

The most useful service which linguists can perform today is to clear away the illusion of verbal deprivation and to provide a more adequate notion of the relations between standard and nonstandard dialects. In the writings of many prominent educational psychologists, we find very poor understanding of the nature of language. Children are treated as if they have no language of their own in the preschool programs put forward by Bereiter and Engelmann (1966). The linguistic behavior of ghetto children in test situations is the principal evidence of genetic inferiority in the view of Jensen (1969). In this paper, we will examine critically both of these approaches to the language and intelligence of the populations labeled "verbally deprived" and "culturally deprived,"[1] and attempt to explain how the myth of verbal deprivation has

---

[1] I am indebted to Rosalind Weiner of the Early Childhood Education group of Operation Head Start in New York City, and to Joan Baratz of the Education Study Center, Washington, D.C., for pointing out to me the scope and seriousness of the educational issues involved here, and the ways in which the cultural deprivation theory has affected federal intervention programs in recent years.

arisen, bringing to bear the methodological findings of sociolinguistic work and some substantive facts about language which are known to all linguists. Of particular concern is the relation between concept formation on the one hand, and dialect differences on the other, since it is in this area that the most dangerous misunderstandings are to be found.

VERBALITY

The general setting in which the deficit theory arises consists of a number of facts which are known to all of us. One is that Negro children in the central urban ghettos do badly in all school subjects, including arithmetic and reading. In reading, they average more than two years behind the national norm (see *The New York Times*, December 3, 1968). Furthermore, this lag is cumulative, so that they do worse comparatively in the fifth grade than in the first grade. Reports in the literature show that this poor performance is correlated most closely with socioeconomic status. Segregated ethnic groups seem to do worse than others—in particular, Indian, Mexican-American, and Negro children. Our own work in New York City confirms that most Negro children read very poorly; however, studies in the speech community show that the situation is even worse than has been reported. If one separates the isolated and peripheral individuals from members of central peer groups, the peer-group members show even worse reading records, and to all intents and purposes are not learning to read at all during the time they spend in school (see Labov, *et al.* 1968).

In speaking of children in the urban ghetto areas, the term *lower class* frequently is used, as opposed to *middle class.* In the several sociolinguistic studies we have carried out, and in many parallel studies, it has been useful to distinguish a lower-class group from a working-class one. Lower-class families are typically female-based, or matrifocal, with no father present to provide steady economic support, whereas for the working-class there is typically an intact nuclear family with the father holding a semiskilled or skilled job. The educational problems of ghetto areas run across this important class distinction. There is no evidence, for example, that the father's presence or absence is closely correlated with educational achievement (e.g., Langer and Michaels 1963; Coleman, *et al.* 1966). The peer groups we have studied in south-central Harlem, representing the basic vernacular culture, include members from both family types. The attack against cultural deprivation in the ghetto is overtly directed at family structures typical of lower-class families, but the educational failure we have been discussing is characteristic of both working-class and lower-class children.

This paper, therefore, will refer to children from urban ghetto areas rather than lower-class children. The population we are concerned with comprises those who participate fully in the vernacular culture of the street and who have been alienated from the school system.[2] We are obviously dealing with the effects of the caste system of American society—essentially a color-marking system. Everyone recognizes this. The question is: By what mechanism does the color bar prevent children from learning to read? One answer is the notion of cultural deprivation put forward by Martin Deutsch and others (Deutsch and associates 1967; Deutsch, Katz, and Jensen 1968). Negro children are said to lack the favorable factors in their home environment which enable middle-class children to do well in school. These factors involve the development of various cognitive skills through verbal interaction with adults, including the ability to reason abstractly, speak fluently, and focus upon long-range goals. In their publications, these psychologists also recognize broader social factors.[3] However, the deficit theory does not focus upon the interaction of the Negro child with white society so much as on his failure to interact with his mother at home. In the literature we find very little direct observation of verbal interaction in the Negro home. Most typically, the investigators ask the child if he has dinner with his parents, if he engages in dinner-table conversation with them, if his family takes him on trips to museums and other cultural activities, and so on. This slender thread of evidence is used to explain and interpret the large body of tests carried out in the laboratory and in the school.

The most extreme view which proceeds from this orientation—and one that is now being widely accepted—is that lower-class Negro children have no language at all. The notion is first drawn from Basil Bernstein's writings that "much of lower-class language consists of a kind of incidental 'emotional' accompaniment to action here and now" (Jensen 1968, p. 118). Bernstein's views are filtered through a strong bias against all forms of working-class behavior, so that middle-class language is seen as superior in every respect— as "more abstract, and necessarily somewhat more flexible, detailed and subtle" (p. 119). One can proceed through a range of such views until he comes to the preschool programs of Bereiter and Engelmann (1966; Bereiter, et al. 1966). Bereiter's program for an academically oriented preschool is based upon the premise that Negro children must have a language with which they can learn and the empirical finding that these children come to school without such a language. In his work with four-year-old Negro children from Urbana, Bereiter (et al. 1966, pp. 113 ff.) reports that their communication was by gestures, single words, and "a series of badly connected words or phrases," such as *They mine* and *Me got juice*. He reports that Negro children could not

[2] The concept of nonstandard Negro English (NNE) and the vernacular culture in which it is embedded is presented in detail in Labov, et al. (1968, sections 1.2.3 and 4.1). See volume 2, section 4.3 for the linguistic traits which distinguish speakers who participate fully in the NNE culture from marginal and isolated individuals.

[3] For example, in Deutsch, Katz, and Jensen (1968) there is a section on Social and Psychological Perspectives which includes a chapter by Proshansky and Newton on "The Nature and Meaning of Negro Self-Identity," and one by Rosenthal and Jacobson on "Self-Fulfilling Prophecies in the Classroom."

ask questions, that "without exaggerating . . . these four-year-olds could make no statements of any kind." Furthermore, when these children were asked "Where is the book?" they did not know enough to look at the table where the book was lying in order to answer. Thus Bereiter concludes that these children's speech forms are nothing more than a series of emotional cries, and he decides to treat them "as if the children had no language at all." He identifies their speech with his interpretation of Bernstein's restricted code: "the language of culturally deprived children . . . is not merely an under-developed version of standard English, but is a basically nonlogical mode of expressive behavior" (Bereiter, *et al.* 1966, pp. 112–13). The basic program of his preschool is to teach them a new language devised by Engelmann, which consists of a limited series of questions and answers such as "Where is the squirrel?" "The squirrel is in the tree." The children will not be punished if they use their vernacular speech on the playground, but they will not be allowed to use it in the schoolroom. If they should answer the question, "Where is the squirrel?" with the illogical vernacular form "In the tree" they will be reprehended by various means and made to say, "The squirrel is in the tree."

Linguists and psycholinguists who have worked with Negro children are apt to dismiss this view of their language as utter nonsense. Yet there is no reason to reject Bereiter's observations as spurious. They were certainly not made up. On the contrary, they give us a very clear view of the behavior of student and teacher which can be duplicated in any classroom. In our own work outside of adult-dominated environments of school and home, we have not observed Negro children behaving like this.[4] However, on many occasions we have been asked to help analyze the results of research into verbal deprivation conducted in such test situations.

Here, for example, is a complete interview with a Negro boy, one of hundreds carried out in a New York City school. The boy enters a room where there is a large, friendly, white interviewer, who puts on the table in front of him a toy and says: "Tell me everything you can about this." (The interviewer's further remarks are in parentheses.)

[12 seconds of silence]
(What would you say it looks like?)
    [8 seconds of silence]
A space ship.
(Hmmmm.)
    [13 seconds of silence]
Like a je-et.
    [12 seconds of silence]

[4] The research cited here was carried out in south-central Harlem and other ghetto areas in 1965–1968 to describe the structural and functional differences between Negro nonstandard English and standard English in the classroom. It was supported by the Office of Education as Cooperative Research Projects 3091 and 3288. Detailed reports are given in Labov, *et al.* (1965), Labov (1967), and Labov, *et al.* (1968).

Like a plane.
　　[20 seconds of silence]
(What color is it?)
Orange. (2 seconds) An' whi-ite. (2 seconds) An' green.
　　[6 seconds of silence]
(An' what could you use it for?)
　　[8 seconds of silence]
A je-et.
　　[6 seconds of silence]
(If you had two of them, what would you do with them?)
　　[6 seconds of silence]
Give one to some-body.
(Hmmm. Who do you think would like to have it?)
　　[10 seconds of silence]
Cla-rence.
(Mm. Where do you think we could get another one of these?)
At the store.
(Oh ka-ay!)

We have here the same kind of defensive, monosyllabic behavior which
is reported in Bereiter's work. What is the situation that produces it? The
child is in an asymmetrical situation where anything he says can literally be
held against him. He has learned a number of devices to avoid saying anything
in this situation, and he works very hard to achieve this end. One may observe
the intonation patterns of

$$^3 \text{'o'}$$
$$^2 a \qquad ^2 \text{know}$$

and

$$^3 \text{ip}$$
$$a \, ^2 \text{space} \, ^2 \text{sh}$$

which Negro children often use when they are asked a question to which the
answer is obvious. The answer may be read as: "Will this satisfy you?"

If one takes this interview as a measure of the verbal capacity of the child,
it must be as his capacity to defend himself in a hostile and threatening
situation. But unfortunately, thousands of such interviews are used as evidence
of the child's total verbal capacity, or more simply his verbality. It is argued
that this lack of verbality explains his poor performance in school. Operation
Head Start and other intervention programs have largely been based upon
the deficit theory—the notions that such interviews give us a measure of the
child's verbal capacity and that the verbal stimulation which he has been
missing can be supplied in a preschool environment.

The verbal behavior which is shown by the child in the situation quoted
above is not the result of the ineptness of the interviewer. It is rather the result

of regular sociolinguistic factors operating upon adult and child in this asymmetrical situation. In our work in urban ghetto areas, we have often encountered such behavior. Ordinarily we worked with boys ten to seventeen years old, and whenever we extended our approach downward to eight- or nine-year-olds, we began to see the need for different techniques to explore the verbal capacity of the child. At one point we began a series of interviews with younger brothers of the Thunderbirds in 1390 Fifth Avenue. Clarence Robins (CR) returned after an interview with eight-year-old Leon L., who showed the following minimal response to topics which arouse intense interest in other interviews with older boys.

CR: What if you saw somebody kickin' somebody else on the ground, or was using
   a stick, what would you do if you saw that?
LEON: Mmmm.
CR: If it was supposed to be a fair fight—
LEON: I don' know.
CR: You don' know? Would you do anything?... huh? I can't hear you.
LEON: No.
CR: Did you ever see somebody got beat up real bad?
LEON: ... Nope ...
CR: Well—uh—did you ever get into a fight with a guy?
LEON: Nope.
CR: That was bigger than you?
LEON: Nope ...
CR: You never been in a fight?
LEON: Nope.
CR: Nobody ever pick on you?
LEON: Nope.
CR: Nobody ever hit you?
LEON: Nope.
CR: How come?
LEON: Ah 'on' know.
CR: Didn't you ever hit somebody?
LEON: Nope.
CR: (incredulously) You never hit nobody?
LEON: Mhm.
CR: Aww, ba-a-a-be, you ain't gonna tell me that!

It may be that Leon is here defending himself against accusations of wrongdoing, since Clarence knows that Leon has been in fights, that he has been taking pencils away from little boys, and so on. But if we turn to a more neutral subject, we find the same pattern:

CR: You watch—you like to watch television?... Hey, Leon ... you like to watch
   television? (Leon nods) What's your favorite program?
LEON: Uhhmmmm ... I look at cartoons,
CR: Well, what's your favorite one? What's your favorite program?

LEON: Superman . . .

CR: Yeah? Did you see Superman—ah—yesterday, or day before yesterday? When's the last time you saw Superman?

LEON: Sa-aturday . . .

CR: You rem—you saw it Saturday? What was the story all about? You remember the story?

LEON: M-m.

CR: You don't remember the story of what—that you saw of Superman?

LEON: Nope.

CR: You don't remember what happened, huh?

LEON: Hm-m.

CR: I see—ah—what other stories do you like to watch on TV?

LEON: Mmmm? . . . umm . . . (glottalization)

CR: Hmm? (four seconds)

LEON: Hh?

CR: What's th' other stories that you like to watch?

LEON: Mi-ighty Mouse . . .

CR: And what else?

LEON: Ummmm . . . ahm . . .

This nonverbal behavior occurs in a relatively favorable context for adult-child interaction. The adult is a Negro man raised in Harlem, who knows this particular neighborhood and these boys very well. He is a skilled interviewer who has obtained a very high level of verbal response with techniques developed for a different age level, and he has an extraordinary advantage over most teachers or experimenters in these respects. But even his skills and personality are ineffective in breaking down the social constraints that prevail here.

When we reviewed the record of this interview with Leon, we decided to use it as a test of our own knowledge of the sociolinguistic factors which control speech. In the next interview with Leon we made the following changes in the social situation:

1. Clarence brought along a supply of potato chips, changing the interview into something more in the nature of a party.
2. He brought along Leon's best friend, eight-year-old Gregory.
3. We reduced the height in balance by having Clarence get down on the floor of Leon's room; he dropped from six feet, two inches to three feet, six inches.
4. Clarence introduced taboo words and taboo topics, and proved, to Leon's surprise, that one can say anything into our microphone without any fear of retaliation. The result of these changes is a striking difference in the volume and style of speech. (The tape is punctuated throughout by the sound of potato chips.)

CR: Is there anybody who says *your momma drink pee?*

{LEON: (rapidly and breathlessly) Yee-ah!
{GREG: Yup!

LEON: And *your father eat doo-doo for breakfas'!*

CR: Ohhh! ! (laughs)

LEON: And they say your father—*your father eat doo-doo for dinner!*

GREG: When they sound on me, I say *CBS.*

CR: What that mean?

⎧LEON: Congo booger-snatch! (laughs)
⎩GREG: Congo booger-snatcher! (laughs)

GREG: And sometimes I'll curse with *BB.*

CR: What that?

GREG: Black boy! (Leon crunching on potato chips) Oh that's a *MBB.*

CR: *MBB.* What's that?

GREG: 'Merican Black Boy.

CR: Ohh . . .

GREG: Anyway, 'Mericans is same like white people, right?

LEON: And they talk about Allah.

CR: Oh yeah?

GREG: Yeah.

CR: What they say about Allah?

⎧LEON: Ailah—Allah is God.
⎩GREG: Allah—

CR: And what else?

LEON: I don' know the res'.

GREG: Allah i—Allah is God, Allah is the only God, Allah . . .

LEON: Allah is the *son* of God.

GREG: But can he make magic?

LEON: Nope.

GREG: I know who can make magic.

CR: Who can?

LEON: The God, the *real* one.

CR: Who can make magic?

GREG: The son of po'—(CR: Hm?) I'm sayin' the po'k chop God![5] He only a po'k chop God! (Leon chuckles).

(The "nonverbal" Leon is now competing actively for the floor; Gregory and Leon talk to each other as much as they do to the interviewer.)

We can make a more direct comparison of the two interviews by examining the section on fighting. Leon persists in denying that he fights, but he can no longer use monosyllabic answers, and Gregory cuts through his facade in a way that Clarence Robins alone was unable to do.

CR: Now, you said you had this fight now; but I wanted you to tell me about the fight that you had.

LEON: I ain't had no fight.

⎧GREG: Yes you did! He said Barry . . .
⎩CR: You said you had one! you had a fight with Butchie,

---

[5] The reference to the *pork chop God* condenses several concepts of black nationalism current in the Harlem community. A *pork chop* is a Negro who has not lost the traditional subservient ideology of the South, who has no knowledge of himself in Muslim terms, and the *pork chop God* would be the traditional God of Southern Baptists. He and His followers may be pork chops, but He still holds the power in Leon and Gregory's world.

⎰ GREG: An he say Garland! . . . an' Michael!
⎱ CR: an' Barry . . .
⎰ LEON: I di'n'; you said that, Gregory!
⎱ GREG: You did!
⎰ LEON: You know you said that!
⎱ GREG: You said Garland, remember that?
⎰ GREG: You said Garland! Yes you did!
⎱ CR: You said Garland, that's right.
GREG: He said Mich—an' I say Michael.
⎰ CR: Did you have a fight with Garland?
⎱ LEON: Uh-Uh.
CR: You had one, and he beat you up, too!
GREG: Yes he did!
LEON: No, I di—I never had a fight with Butch! . . .

The same pattern can be seen on other local topics, where the interviewer brings neighborhood gossip to bear on Leon, and Gregory acts as a witness.

CR: . . . Hey Gregory! I heard that around here . . . and I'm 'on' tell you who said it, too . . .
LEON: Who?
CR: About you . . .
⎰ LEON: Who?
⎱ GREG: I'd say it!
CR: They said that—they say that the only person you play with is David Gilbert.
⎰ LEON: Yee-ah! yee-ah! yee-ah! . . .
⎱ GREG: That's who you play with!
⎰ LEON: I 'on' play with him no more!
⎱ GREG: Yes you do!
LEON: I 'on' play with him no more!
GREG: But remember, about me and Robbie?
LEON: So that's not—
GREG: and you went to Petey and Gilbert's house, 'member? *Ah haah!!*
LEON: So that's—so—but I would—I had came back out, an' I ain't go to his house no more . . . .

The observer must now draw a very different conclusion about the verbal capacity of Leon. The monosyllabic speaker who had nothing to say about anything and cannot remember what he did yesterday has disappeared. Instead, we have two boys who have so much to say they keep interrupting each other, and who seem to have no difficulty in using the English language to express themselves. In turn we obtain the volume of speech and the rich array of grammatical devices which we need for analyzing the structure of nonstandard Negro English; for example: negative concord ("I 'on' play with him no more"), the pluperfect ("had came back out"), negative perfect ("I ain't had"), the negative preterite ("I ain't go"), and so on.

We can now transfer this demonstration of the sociolinguistic control of speech to other test situations, including IQ and reading tests in school. It should be immediately apparent that none of the standard tests will come anywhere near measuring Leon's verbal capacity. On these tests he will show up as very much the monosyllabic, inept, ignorant, bumbling child of our first interview. The teacher has far less ability than Clarence Robins to elicit speech from this child. Clarence knows the community, the things that Leon has been doing, and the things that Leon would like to talk about. But the power relationships in a one-to-one confrontation between adult and child are too asymmetrical. This does not mean that some Negro children will not talk a great deal when alone with an adult, or that an adult cannot get close to any child. It means that the social situation is the most powerful determinant of verbal behavior and that an adult must enter into the right social relation with a child if he wants to find out what a child can do. This is just what many teachers cannot do.

The view of the Negro speech community which we obtain from our work in the ghetto areas is precisely the opposite from that reported by Deutsch or by Bereiter and Engelmann. We see a child bathed in verbal stimulation from morning to night. We see many speech events which depend upon the competitive exhibition of verbal skills—sounding, singing, toasts, rifting, louding —a whole range of activities in which the individual gains status through his use of language (see Labov, *et al.* 1968, section 4.2). We see the younger child trying to acquire these skills from older children, hanging around on the outskirts of older peer groups, and imitating this behavior to the best of his ability. We see no connection between verbal skill in the speech events characteristic of the street culture and success in the schoolroom.

VERBOSITY

There are undoubtedly many verbal skills which children from ghetto areas must learn in order to do well in the school situation, and some of these are indeed characteristic of middle-class verbal behavior. Precision in spelling, practice in handling abstract symbols, the ability to state explicitly the meaning of words, and a richer knowledge of the Latinate vocabulary, may all be useful acquisitions. But is it true that all of the middle-class verbal habits are functional and desirable in the school situation? Before we impose middle-class verbal style upon children from other cultural groups, we should find out how much of this is useful for the main work of analyzing and generalizing, and how much is merely stylistic—or even dysfunctional. In high school and college, middle-class children spontaneously complicate their syntax to the point that instructors despair of getting them to make their language simpler and clearer. In every learned journal one can find examples of jargon and empty elaboration, as well as complaints about it. Is the elaborated code of Bernstein really so "flexible, detailed, and subtle" as some psychologists (for example Jensen 1969, p. 119) believe? Isn't it also turgid, redundant, bombastic, and empty? Is it not simply an elaborated style, rather than a superior code or system?[6]

Our work in the speech community makes it painfully obvious that in many ways working-class speakers are more effective narrators, reasoners, and debaters than many middle-class speakers who temporize, qualify, and lose their argument in a mass of irrelevant detail. Many academic writers try to rid themselves of that part of middle-class style that is empty pretension, and keep that part that is needed for precision. But the average middle-class speaker that we encounter makes no such effort; he is enmeshed in verbiage, the victim of sociolinguistic factors beyond his control.

I will not attempt to support this argument here with systematic quantitative evidence, although it is possible to develop measures which show how far middle-class speakers can wander from the point. I would like to contrast two speakers dealing with roughly the same topic—matters of belief. The first is Larry H., a fifteen-year-old core member of the Jets, being interviewed by John Lewis. Larry is one of the loudest and roughest members of the Jets, one who gives the least recognition to the conventional rules of politeness.[7] For most readers of this paper, first contact with Larry would produce some fairly negative reactions on both sides. It is probable that you would not like him any more than his teachers do. Larry causes trouble in and out of school. He was put back from the eleventh grade to the ninth, and has been threatened with further action by the school authorities.

JL: What happens to you after you die? Do you know?
LARRY: Yeah, I know. (What?) After they put you in the ground, your body turns into—ah—bones, an' shit.
JL: What happens to your spirit?
LARRY: Your spirit—soon as you die, your spirit leaves you. (And where does the spirit go?) Well, it all depends . . . (On what?) You know, like some people say if you're good an' shit, your spirit goin' t'heaven . . . 'n' if you bad, your spirit goin' to hell. Well, bullshit! Your spirit goin' to hell anyway, good or bad.
JL: Why?
LARRY: Why? I'll tell you why. 'Cause, you see, doesn' nobody really know that it's a God, y'know, 'cause I mean I have seen black gods, pink gods, white gods, all color gods, and don't nobody know it's really a God. An' when they be sayin' if

---

[6] The term *code* is central in Bernstein's (1966) description of the differences between working-class and middle-class styles of speech. The restrictions and elaborations of speech observed are labeled as codes to indicate the principles governing selection from the range of possible English sentences. No rules or detailed description of the operation of such codes are provided as yet, so that this central concept remains to be specified.

[7] A direct view of Larry's verbal style in a hostile encounter is given in Labov, *et al.* (1968, volume 2, pp. 39–43). Gray's Oral Reading Test was being given to a group of Jets on the steps of a brownstone house in Harlem, and the landlord tried unsuccessfully to make the Jets move. Larry's verbal style in this encounter matches the reports he gives of himself in a number of narratives cited in section 4.8 of the foregoing report.

you good, you goin' t'heaven, tha's bullshit, 'cause you ain't goin' to no heaven, 'cause it ain't no heaven for you to go to.

Larry is a paradigmatic speaker of nonstandard Negro English (NNE) as opposed to standard English. His grammar shows a high concentration of such characteristic NNE forms as negative inversion ("don't nobody know . . ."), negative concord ("you ain't goin' to no heaven . . ."), invariant *be* ("when they be sayin' . . ."), dummy *it* for standard *there* ("it ain't no heaven . . ."), optional copula deletion ("if you're good . . . if you bad . . .") and full forms of auxiliaries ("I have seen . . ."). The only standard English influence in this passage is the one case of "doesn't" instead of the invariant "don't" of NNE. Larry also provides a paradigmatic example of the rhetorical style of NNE: he can sum up a complex argument in a few words, and the full force of his opinions come through without qualification or reservation. He is eminently quotable, and his interviews give us many concise statements of the NNE point of view. One can almost say that Larry speaks the NNE culture (see Labov, *et al.* 1968, vol. 2, pp. 38, 71–73, 291–92).

It is the logical form of this passage which is of particular interest here. Larry presents a complex set of interdependent propositions which can be explicated by setting out the standard English equivalents in linear order. The basic argument is to deny the twin propositions:

> (*A*) If you are good, (*B*) then your spirit will go to heaven.
> (~*A*) If you are bad, (*C*) then your spirit will go to hell.

Larry denies (*B*) and asserts that if (*A*) or (~*A*), then (*C*). His argument may be outlined as follows:

1. Everyone has a different idea of what God is like.
2. Therefore nobody really knows that God exists.
3. If there is a heaven, it was made by God.
4. If God doesn't exist, he couldn't have made heaven.
5. Therefore heaven does not exist.
6. You can't go somewhere that doesn't exist.

> (~*B*) Therefore you can't go to heaven.
> (*C*) Therefore you are going to hell.

The argument is presented in the order: (*C*), because (2) because (1), therefore (2), therefore (~*B*) because (5) and (6). Part of the argument is implicit: the connection (2) therefore (~*B*) leaves unstated the connecting links (3) and (4), and in this interval Larry strengthens the propositions from the form (2) "Nobody knows if there is . . ." to (5) "There is no . . . ." Otherwise, the case is presented explicitly as well as economically. The complex argument is summed up in Larry's last sentence, which shows formally the dependence of (~*B*) on (5) and (6):

An' when they be sayin' if you good, you goin' t'heaven, (The proposition, if A, then B)

Tha's bullshit (is absurd)
'cause you ain't goin' to no heaven (because B)
'cause it ain't no heaven for you to go to (because (5) and (6)).

This hypothetical argument is not carried on at a high level of seriousness. It is a game played with ideas as counters, in which opponents use a wide variety of verbal devices to win. There is no personal commitment to any of these propositions, and no reluctance to strengthen one's argument by bending the rules of logic as in the (2)-(5) sequence. But if the opponent invokes the rules of logic, they hold. In John Lewis's interviews, he often makes this move, and the force of his argument is always acknowledged and countered within the rules of logic. In this case, he pointed out the fallacy that the argument (2)-(3)-(4)-(5)-(6) leads to ($\sim C$) as well as ($\sim B$), so it cannot be used to support Larry's assertion (C):

JL: Well, if there's no heaven, how could there be a hell?
LARRY: I mean—ye-eah. Well, let me tell you, it ain't no hell, 'cause this is hell right here, y'know! (This is hell?) Yeah, this is hell right here!

Larry's answer is quick, ingenious, and decisive. The application of the (3)-(4)-(5) argument to hell is denied, since hell is here, and therefore conclusion (C) stands. These are not ready-made or preconceived opinions, but new propositions devised to win the logical argument in the game being played. The reader will note the speed and precision of Larry's mental operations. He does not wander, or insert meaningless verbiage. The only repetition is (2), placed before and after (1) in his original statement. It is often said that the nonstandard vernacular is not suited for dealing with abstract or hypothetical questions, but in fact speakers from the NNE community take great delight in exercising their wit and logic on the most improbable and problematical matters. Despite the fact that Larry H. does not believe in God, and has just denied all knowledge of him, John Lewis advances the following hypothetical question:

JL: . . . but, just say that there is a God, what color is he? White or black?
LARRY: Well, if it is a God . . . I wouldn' know what color, I couldn' say,—couldn' nobody say what color he is or really *would* be.
JL: But now, jus' suppose there was a God—
LARRY: Unless'n they say . . .
JL: No, I was jus' sayin' jus' suppose there is a God, would he be white or black?
LARRY: . . . He'd be white, man.
JL: Why?
LARRY: Why? I'll tell you why. 'Cause the average whitey out here got everything, you dig? And the nigger ain't got shit, y'know? Y'unnerstan'? So—um—for—in order for *that* to happen, you know it ain't no black God that's doin' that bullshit.

No one can hear Larry's answer to this question without being convinced that he is in the presence of a skilled speaker with great "verbal presence of mind," who can use the English language expertly for many purposes. Larry's answer to John Lewis is again a complex argument. The formulation is not standard English, but it is clear and effective even for those not familiar with the vernacular. The nearest standard English equivalent might be: "So you know that God isn't black, because if he was, he wouldn't have arranged things like that."

The reader will have noted that this analysis is being carried out in standard English, and the inevitable challenge is: why not write in NNE, then, or in your own nonstandard dialect? The fundamental reason is, of course, one of firmly fixed social conventions. All communities agree that standard English is the proper medium for formal writing and public communication. Furthermore, it seems likely that standard English has an advantage over NNE in explicit analysis of surface forms, which is what we are doing here. We will return to this opposition between explicitness and logical statement in subsequent sections on grammaticality and logic. First, however, it will be helpful to examine standard English in its primary natural setting, as the medium for informal spoken communication of middle-class speakers.

Let us now turn to the second speaker, an upper-middle-class, college-educated Negro (Charles M.) being interviewed by Clarence Robins in our survey of adults in Central Harlem.

CR: Do you know of anything that someone can do, to have someone who has passed on visit him in a dream?

CHARLES: Well, I even heard my parents say that there is such a thing as something in dreams some things like that, and sometimes dreams do come true. I have personally never had a dream come true. I've never dreamt that somebody was dying and they actually died, (Mhm) or that I was going to have ten dollars the next day and somehow I got ten dollars in my pocket. (Mhm). I don't particularly believe in that, I don't think it's true. I do feel, though, that there is such a thing as—ah—witchcraft. I do feel that in certain cultures there is such a thing as witchcraft, or some sort of *science* of witchcraft; I don't think that it's just a matter of believing hard enough that there is such a thing as witchcraft. I do believe that there is such a thing that a person can put himself in a state of *mind* (Mhm), or that—er—something could be given them to intoxicate them in a certain—to a certain frame of mind—that—that could actually be considered witchcraft.

Charles M. is obviously a good speaker who strikes the listener as well-educated, intelligent, and sincere. He is a likeable and attractive person, the kind of person that middle-class listeners rate very high on a scale of job suitability and equally high as a potential friend.[8] His language is more moderate and tempered than Larry's; he makes every effort to qualify his opinions,

---

[8] For a description of subjective reaction tests which utilize these evaluative dimensions see Labov, *et al.* (1968, section 4.6).

and seems anxious to avoid any misstatements or overstatements. From these qualities emerge the primary characteristic of this passage—its verbosity. Words multiply, some modifying and qualifying, others repeating or padding the main argument. The first half of this extract is a response to the initial question on dreams, basically:

1. Some people say that dreams sometimes come true.
2. I have never had a dream come true.
3. Therefore I don't believe (1).

Some characteristic filler phrases appear here: *such a thing as, some things like that,* and *particularly.* Two examples of dreams given after (2) are afterthoughts that might have been given after (1). Proposition (3) is stated twice for no obvious reason. Nevertheless, this much of Charles M.'s response is well-directed to the point of the question. He then volunteers a statement of his beliefs about witchcraft which shows the difficulty of middle-class speakers who (a) want to express a belief in something but (b) want to show themselves as judicious, rational, and free from superstitions. The basic proposition can be stated simply in five words:

"But I believe in witchcraft."

However, the idea is enlarged to exactly 100 words, and it is difficult to see what else is being said. In the following quotations, padding which can be removed without change in meaning is shown in parentheses.

1. "I (do) feel, though, that there is (such a thing as) witchcraft." *Feel* seems to be a euphemism for "believe."

2. "(I do feel that) in certain cultures (there is such a thing as witchcraft)." This repetition seems designed only to introduce the word *culture,* which lets us know that the speaker knows about anthropology. Does *certain cultures* mean "not in ours" or "not in all"?

3. "(or some sort of *science* of witchcraft.)" This addition seems to have no clear meaning at all. What is a "science" of witchcraft as opposed to just plain witchcraft?[9] The main function is to introduce the word *science,* though it seems to have no connection to what follows.

4. "I don't think that it's just (a matter of) believing hard enough that (there is such a thing as) witchcraft." The speaker argues that witchcraft is not merely a belief; there is more to it.

5. "I (do) believe that (there is such a thing that) a person can put himself in a state of mind . . . that (could actually be considered) witchcraft." Is witchcraft as a state of mind different from the state of belief, denied in (4)?

6. "or that something could be given them to intoxicate them (to a certain frame of mind) . . . ." The third learned word, *intoxicate,* is introduced by

---

[9] Several middle-class readers of this passage have suggested that *science* here refers to some form of control as opposed to belief. The science of witchcraft would then be a kind of engineering of mental states. Other interpretations can of course be provided. The fact remains that no such difficulties of interpretation are needed to understand Larry's remarks.

this addition. The vacuity of this passage becomes more evident if we remove repetitions, fashionable words and stylistic decorations:

> But I believe in witchcraft.
> I don't think witchcraft is just a belief.
> A person can put himself or be put in a state of mind that is witchcraft.

Without the extra verbiage and the "OK" words like *science, culture,* and *intoxicate,* Charles M. appears as something less than a first-rate thinker. The initial impression of him as a good speaker is simply our long-conditioned reaction to middle-class verbosity. We know that people who use these stylistic devices are educated people, and we are inclined to credit them with saying something intelligent. Our reactions are accurate in one sense. Charles M. is more educated than Larry. But is he more rational, more logical, more intelligent? Is he any better at thinking out a problem to its solution? Does he deal more easily with abstractions? There is no reason to think so. Charles M. succeeds in letting us know that he is educated, but in the end we do not know what he is trying to say, and neither does he.

In the previous section I have attempted to explain the origin of the myth that lower-class Negro children are nonverbal. The examples just given may help to account for the corresponding myth that middle-class language is in itself better suited for dealing with abstract, logically complex, or hypothetical questions. These examples are intended to have a certain negative force. They are not controlled experiments. On the contrary, this and the preceding section are designed to convince the reader that the controlled experiments that have been offered in evidence are misleading. The only thing that is controlled is the superficial form of the stimulus. All children are asked, "What do you think of capital punishment?" or "Tell me everything you can about this." But the speaker's interpretation of these requests and the action he believes are appropriate in response are completely uncontrolled. One can view these test stimuli as requests for information, commands for action, threats of punishment, or meaningless sequences of words. They are probably intended as something altogether different—as requests for display,[10] but in any case the experimenter is normally unaware of the problem of interpretation. The methods of educational psychologists such as used by Deutsch, Jensen, and Bereiter follow the pattern designed for animal experiments where motivation is controlled by simple methods as withholding food until a certain weight reduction is reached. With human subjects, it is absurd to believe that identical stimuli are obtained by asking everyone the same question.

Since the crucial intervening variables of interpretation and motivation are uncontrolled, most of the literature on verbal deprivation tells us nothing about the capacities of children. They are only the trappings of science, approaches which substitute the formal procedures of the scientific method for

---

[10] The concept of a request for verbal display is here drawn from a treatment of the therapeutic interview given by Blum (1970).

the activity itself. With our present limited grasp of these problems, the best we can do to understand the verbal capacities of children is to study them within the cultural context in which they were developed.

It is not only the NNE vernacular which should be studied in this way, but also the language of middle-class children. The explicitness and precision which we hope to gain from copying middle-class forms are often the product of the test situation, and limited to it. For example, it was stated in the first part of this paper that working-class children hear more well-formed sentences than middle-class children. This statement may seem extraordinary in the light of the current belief of many linguists that most people do not speak in well-formed sentences, and that their actual speech production, or performance, is ungrammatical.[11] But those who have worked with any body of natural speech know that this is not the case. Our own studies (Labov 1966) of the grammaticality of everyday speech show that the great majority of utterances in all contexts are complete sentences, and most of the rest can be reduced to grammatical form by a small set of editing rules. The proportions of grammatical sentences vary with class backgrounds and styles. The highest percentage of well-formed sentences are found in casual speech, and working-class speakers use more well-formed sentences than middle-class speakers. The widespread myth that most speech is ungrammatical is no doubt based upon tapes made at learned conferences, where we obtain the maximum number of irreducibly ungrammatical sequences.

It is true that technical and scientific books are written in a style which is markedly middle-class. But unfortunately, we often fail to achieve the explicitness and precision which we look for in such writing, and the speech of many middle-class people departs maximally from this target. All too often, standard English is represented by a style that is simultaneously overparticular and vague. The accumulating flow of words buries rather than strikes the target. It is this verbosity which is most easily taught and most easily learned, so that words take the place of thoughts, and nothing can be found behind them.

When Bernstein (for example,1966) describes his elaborated code in general terms, it emerges as a subtle and sophisticated mode of planning utterances, where the speaker is achieving structural variety, taking the other person's knowledge into account, and so on. But when it comes to describing the actual difference between middle-class and working-class speakers (Bernstein 1966), we are presented with a proliferation of "I think," of the passive, of modals and auxiliaries, of the first-person pronoun, of uncommon words, and so on.

---

[11] In several presentations, Chomsky has asserted that the great majority (95 per cent) of the sentences which a child hears are ungrammatical. Chomsky (1965, p. 58) presents this notion as one of the arguments in his general statement of the nativist position: "A consideration of the character of the grammar that is acquired, *the degenerate quality and narrowly limited extent of the available data* [my emphasis], the striking uniformity of the resulting grammars, and their independence of intelligence, motivation, and emotional state, over wide ranges of variation, leave little hope that much of the structure of the language can be learned . . . ."

But these are the bench marks of hemming and hawing, backing, and filling, that are used by Charles M., the devices which so often obscure whatever positive contribution education can make to our use of language. When we have discovered how much of middle-class style is a matter of fashion and how much actually helps us express ideas clearly, we will have done ourselves a great service. We will then be in a position to say what standard grammatical rules must be taught to nonstandard speakers in the early grades.

GRAMMATICALITY

Let us now examine Bereiter's own data on the verbal behavior of the children he dealt with. The expressions *They mine* and *Me got juice* are cited as examples of a language which lacks the means for expressing logical relations, in this case characterized as "a series of badly connected words" (Bereiter, *et al.* 1966, p. 113). In the case of *They mine*, it is apparent that Bereiter confuses the notions of logic and explicitness. We know that there are many languages of the world which do not have a present copula, and which conjoin subject and predicate complement without a verb. Russian, Hungarian, and Arabic may be foreign, but they are not by that same token illogical. In the case of NNE we are not dealing with even this superficial grammatical difference, but rather with a low-level rule which carries contraction one step farther to delete single consonants representing the verbs *is, have* or *will* (Labov 1969). We have yet to find any children who do not sometimes use the full forms of *is* and *will*, even though they may frequently delete them. Our recent studies with Negro children four to seven years old indicate that they use the full form of the copula more often than preadolescents ten to twelve years old, or the adolescents fourteen to seventeen years old.[12]

Furthermore, the delection of the *is* or *are* in NNE is not the result of erratic or illogical behavior; it follows the same regular rules as standard English contraction. Wherever standard English can contract, Negro children use either the contracted form or (more commonly) the deleted zero form. Thus *They mine* corresponds to standard *They're mine*, not to the full form *They are mine*. On the other hand, no such deletion is possible in positions where standard English cannot contract. Just as one cannot say, "*That's what they're*" in standard English, "*That's what they*" is impossible in the vernacular we are considering. The internal constraints upon both of these rules show that we are dealing with a phonological process like contraction—one sensitive to such phonetic conditions as whether the next word begins with a vowel or a consonant. The appropriate use of the deletion rule, like the contraction rule, requires a deep and intimate knowledge of English grammar

---

[12] This is from work on the grammars and comprehension of Negro children, four to eight years old, being carried out by Prof. Jane Torrey of Connecticut College in extension of the research cited above in Labov, *et al.* (1968).

and phonology. Such knowledge is not available for conscious inspection by native speakers. The rules we have recently worked out for standard contraction (Labov 1969) have never appeared in any grammar, and are certainly not a part of the conscious knowledge of any standard English speakers. Nevertheless, the adult or child who uses these rules must have formed at some level of psychological organization, clear concepts of tense marker, verb phrase, rule ordering, sentence embedding, pronoun, and many other grammatical categories which are essential parts of any logical system.

Bereiter's reaction to the sentence *Me got juice* is even more puzzling. If Bereiter believes that " Me got juice" is not a logical expression, it can only be that he interprets the use of the objective pronoun *me* as representing a difference in logical relationship to the verb—that the child is in fact saying that "the juice got him" rather than "he got the juice"! If on the other hand, the child means "I got juice" then this sentence shows only that he has not learned the formal rules for the use of the subjective form *I* and oblique form *me*. We have in fact encountered many children who do not have these formal rules in order at the ages of four, five, six, or even eight. It is extremely difficult to construct a minimal pair to show that the difference between *he* and *him*, or *she* and *her* carries cognitive meaning. In almost every case, it is the context which tells us who is the agent and who is acted upon. We must then ask: What differences in cognitive, structural orientation are signaled by the child's not knowing this formal rule? In the tests carried out by Jane Torrey, it is evident that the children concerned do understand the difference in meaning between *she* and *her* when another person uses the forms. All that remains, then, is that the children themselves do not use the two forms. Our knowledge of the cognitive correlates of grammatical differences is certainly in its infancy, for this is one of very many questions which we simply cannot answer. At the moment we do not know how to construct any kind of experiment which would lead to an answer; we do not even know what type of cognitive correlate we would be looking for.

Bereiter shows even more profound ignorance of the rules of discourse and of syntax when he rejects "In the tree" as an illogical, or badly formed answer to "Where is the squirrel?" Such elliptical answers are, of course, used by everyone. They show the appropriate deletion of subject and main verb, leaving the locative which is questioned by *wh* + *there*. The reply "In the tree" demonstrates that the listener has been attentive to and apprehended the syntax of the speaker.[13] Whatever formal structure we wish to write for expressions such as *Yes* or *Home* or *In the tree*, it is obvious that they cannot be interpreted without knowing the structure of the question which preceded them, and that they presuppose an understanding of the syntax of the question. Thus if you ask me, "Where is the squirrel?" it is necessary for me to under-

---

[13] The attention to the speaker's syntax required of the listener is analyzed in detail in a series of unpublished lectures by Prof. Harvey Sacks, Department of Sociology, University of California–Irvine.

stand the processes of *wh*-attachment, *wh*-attraction to front of the sentence, and flip-flop of auxiliary and subject to produce this sentence from an underlying form which would otherwise have produced "The squirrel is there." If the child has answered "The tree," or "Squirrel the tree," or "The in tree," we would then assume that he did not understand the syntax of the full form, "The squirrel is in the tree." Given the data that Bereiter presents, we cannot conclude that the child has no grammar, but only that the investigator does not understand the rules of grammar. It does not necessarily do any harm to use the full form "The squirrel is in the tree," if one wants to make fully explicit the rules of grammar which the child has internalized. Much of logical analysis consists of making explicit just that kind of internalized rule. But it is hard to believe that any good can come from a program which begins with so many misconceptions about the input data. Bereiter and Engelmann believe that in teaching the child to say "The squirrel is in the tree" or "This is a box" and "This is not a box" they are teaching him an entirely new language, whereas in fact, they are only teaching him to produce slightly different forms of the language he already has.

LOGIC

For many generations, American schoolteachers have devoted themselves to correcting a small number of nonstandard English rules to their standard equivalents, under the impression that they were teaching logic. This view has been reinforced and given theoretical justification by the claim that NNE lacks the means for the expression of logical thought.

Let us consider for a moment the possibility that Negro children do not operate with the same logic that middle-class adults display. This would inevitably mean that sentences of a certain grammatical form would have different truth values for the two types of speakers. One of the most obvious places to look for such a difference is in the handling of the negative, and here we encounter one of the nonstandard items which has been stigmatized as illogical by schoolteachers—the double negative, or as we term it, *negative concord*. A child who says "He don't know nothing" is often said to be making an illogical statement without knowing it. According to the teacher, the child wants to say "He knows nothing" but puts in an extra negative without realizing it, and so conveys the opposite meaning, "He does not know nothing," which reduces to "He knows something." I need not emphasize that this is an absurd interpretation. If a nonstandard speaker wishes to say that "He does not know *nothing*." he does so by simply placing contrastive stress on both negatives as I have done here ("He *don't* know *nothing*") indicating that they are derived from two underlying negatives in the deep structure. But note that the middle-class speaker does exactly the same thing when he wants to signal the existence of two underlying negatives: "He *doesn't* know *nothing*."

In the standard form with one underlying negative ("He doesn't know anything"), the indefinite *anything* contains the same superficial reference to a preceding negative in the surface structure as the nonstandard *nothing* does. In the corresponding positive sentences, the indefinite *something* is used. The dialect difference, like most of the differences between the standard and nonstandard forms, is one of surface form, and has nothing to do with the underlying logic of the sentence.

We can summarize the ways in which the two dialects differ:

	Standard English, SE	Nonstandard Negro English, NNE
Positive:	He knows something.	He know something.
Negative:	He doesn't know anything.	He don't know nothing.
Double Negative:	He *doesn't* know *nothing*.	He *don't* know *nothing*.

This array makes it plain that the only difference between the two dialects is in superficial form. When a single negative is found in the deep structure, standard English converts *something* to the indefinite *anything*, NNE converts it to *nothing*. When speakers want to signal the presence of two negatives, they do it in the same way. No one would have any difficulty constructing the same table of truth values for both dialects. English is a rare language in its insistence that the negative particle be incorporated in the first indefinite only. The Anglo-Saxon authors of the Peterborough Chronicle were surely not illogical when they wrote *For ne wæren nævre nan martyrs swa pined alse hi wæron*, literally, "For never weren't no martyrs so tortured as these were." The "logical" forms of current standard English are simply the accepted conventions of our present-day formal style. Russian, Spanish, French, and Hungarian show the same negative concord as nonstandard English, and they are surely not illogical in this. What is termed "logical" in standard English is of course the conventions which are habitual. The distribution of negative concord in English dialects can be summarized in this way (Labov, *et al.* 1968, section 3.6; Labov 1968):

1. In all dialects of English, the negative is attracted to a lone indefinite before the verb: "Nobody knows anything," not "*Anybody doesn't know anything."
2. In some nonstandard white dialects, the negative also combines optionally with all other indefinites: "Nobody knows nothing," "He never took none of them."
3. In other white nonstandard dialects, the negative may also appear in preverbal position in the same clause: "Nobody doesn't know nothing."

4. In nonstandard Negro English, negative concord is obligatory to all indefinites within the clause, and it may even be added to preverbal position in following clauses: "Nobody didn't know he didn't" (meaning, "Nobody knew he did").

Thus all dialects of English share a categorical rule which attracts the negative to an indefinite subject, and they merely differ in the extent to which the negative particle is also distributed to other indefinites in preverbal position. It would have been impossible for us to arrive at this analysis if we did not know that Negro speakers are using the same underlying logic as everyone else.

Negative concord is more firmly established in nonstandard Negro English than in other nonstandard dialects. The white nonstandard speaker shows variation in this rule, saying one time, "Nobody ever goes there" and the next, "Nobody never goes there." Core speakers of the NNE vernacular consistently use the latter form. In repetition tests which we conducted with adolescent Negro boys (Labov, *et al.* 1968, section 3.9), standard forms were repeated with negative concord. Here, for example, are three trials by two thirteen-year-old members (Boot and David) of the Thunderbirds:

MODEL BY INTERVIEWER: "Nobody ever sat at any of those desks, anyhow."
BOOT:
1. Nobody never sa—No [whitey] never sat at any o' tho' dess, anyhow.
2. Nobody never sat any any o' tho' dess, anyhow.
3. Nobody as ever sat at no desses, anyhow.
DAVID:
1. Nobody ever sat in-in-in-in- none o'—say it again?
2. Nobody never sat in none o' tho' desses anyhow.
3. Nobody—aww! Nobody never ex—Dawg!

It can certainly be said that Boot and David fail the test; they have not repeated the sentence correctly—that is, word for word. But have they failed because they could not grasp the meaning of the sentence? The situation is in fact just the opposite; they failed because they perceived only the meaning and not the superficial form. Boot and David are typical of many speakers who do not perceive the surface details of the utterance so much as the underlying semantic structure, which they unhesitatingly translate into the vernacular form. Thus they have an asymmetrical system:

PERCEPTION	Standard	Nonstandard
PRODUCTION	Nonstandard	

This tendency to process the semantic components directly can be seen even more dramatically in responses to sentences with embedded questions; for example:

MODEL:
  I asked Alvin if he knows how to play basketball.
BOOT:
  I ax Alvin do he know how to play basketball.
MONEY:
  I ax Alvin if—do he know how to play basketball.
MODEL:
  I asked Alvin whether he knows how to play basketball.
LARRY F:
  1. I axt Alvin does he know how to play basketball.
  2. I axt Alvin does he know how to play basketball.

Here the difference between the words used in the model sentence and in the repetition is striking. Again, there is a failure to pass the test. But it is also true that these boys understand the standard sentence, and translate it with extraordinary speed into the NNE form, which is here the regular Southern colloquial form. This form retains the inverted order to signal the underlying meaning of the question, instead of the complementizer *if* or *whether* which standard English uses for this purpose. Thus Boot, Money, and Larry perceive the deep structure of the model sentence (Figure 1). The complementizers *if* or

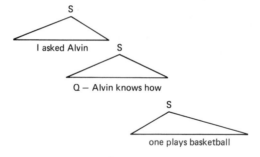

Figure 1.

whether are not required to express this underlying meaning. They are merely two of the formal options which one dialect selects to signal the embedded question. The colloquial Southern form utilizes a different device—preserving the order of the direct question. To say that this dialect lacks the means for logical expression is to confuse logic with surface detail.

    To pass the repetition test, Boot and the others have to learn to listen to surface detail. They do not need a new logic; they need practice in paying attention to the explicit form of an utterance rather than its meaning. Careful attention to surface features is a temporary skill needed for language learning —and neglected thereafter by competent speakers. Nothing more than this is involved in the language training in the Bereiter and Engelmann program, or in most methods of teaching English. There is of course nothing wrong with learning to be explicit. As we have seen, that is one of the main advantages of standard English at its best; but it is important that we recognize what is actually taking place, and what teachers are in fact trying to do.

I doubt if we can teach people to be logical, though we can teach them to recognize the logic that they use. Piaget has shown us that in middle-class children logic develops much more slowly than grammar, and that we cannot expect four-year-olds to have mastered the conservation of quantity, let alone syllogistic reasoning. The problems working-class children may have in handling logical operations are not to be blamed on the structure of their language. There is nothing in the vernacular which will interfere with the development of logical thought, for the logic of standard English cannot be distinguished from the logic of any other dialect of English by any test that we can find.

WHAT'S WRONG WITH BEING WRONG?

If there is a failure of logic involved here, it is surely in the approach of the verbal deprivation theorists, rather than in the mental abilities of the children concerned. We can isolate six distinct steps in the reasoning which has led to positions such as those of Deutsch, or Bereiter and Engelmann:

1. The lower-class child's verbal response to a formal and threatening situation is used to demonstrate his lack of verbal capacity, or verbal deficit.
2. This verbal deficit is declared to be a major cause of the lower-class child's poor performance in school.
3. Since middle-class children do better in school, middle-class speech habits are seen to be necessary for learning.
4. Class and ethnic differences in grammatical form are equated with differences in the capacity for logical analysis.
5. Teaching the child to mimic certain formal speech patterns used by middle-class teachers is seen as teaching him to think logically.
6. Children who learn these formal speech patterns are then said to be thinking logically and it is predicted that they will do much better in reading and arithmetic in the years to follow.

In the preceding sections of this paper I have tried to show that the above propositions are wrong, concentrating on 1, 4, and 5. Proposition 3 is the primary logical fallacy which illicitly identifies a form of speech as the cause of middle-class achievement in school. Proposition 6 is the one which is most easily shown to be wrong in fact, as we will note below.

However, it is not too naive to ask: "What is wrong with being wrong?" There is no competing educational theory which is being dismantled by this program, and there does not seem to be any great harm in having children repeat, "This is not a box" for twenty minutes a day. We have already conceded that NNE children need help in analyzing language into its surface components, and in being more explicit. But there are serious and damaging consequences of the verbal deprivation theory which may be considered under two headings: theoretical bias, and consequences of failure.

Theoretical Bias

It is widely recognized that the teacher's attitude toward the child is an important factor in his success or failure. The work of Rosenthal and Jacobson (1968) on self-fulfilling prophecies shows that the progress of children in the early grades can be dramatically affected by a single random labeling of certain children as "intellectual bloomers."[*] When the everyday language of Negro children is stigmatized as "not a language at all" and "not possessing the means for logical thought," the effect of such a labeling is repeated many times during each day of the school year. Every time that a child uses a form of NNE without the copula or with negative concord, he will be labeling himself for the teacher's benefit as "illogical," as a "nonconceptual thinker." Bereiter and Engelmann, Deutsch, and Jensen are giving teachers a ready-made, theoretical basis for the prejudice they already feel against the lower-class Negro child and his language. When teachers hear him say "I don't want none" or "They mine," they will be hearing through the bias provided by the verbal deprivation theory—not an English dialect different from theirs, but the "primitive mentality of the savage mind."

But what if the teacher succeeds in training the child to use the new language consistently? The verbal deprivation theory holds that this will lead to a whole chain of successes in school, and that the child will be drawn away from the vernacular culture into the middle-class world. Undoubtedly this will happen with a few isolated individuals, just as it happens for a few children in every school system today. But we are concerned not with the few but the many, and for the majority of Negro children the distance between them and the school is bound to widen under this approach.

Proponents of the deficit theory have a strange view of social organization outside of the classroom. They see the attraction of the peer group as a substitute for success and gratification normally provided by the school. For example, Whiteman and Deutsch (1968, pp. 86–87) introduce their account of the deprivation hypothesis with an eyewitness account of a child who accidentally dropped his school notebook into a puddle of water and walked away without picking it up: "A policeman who had been standing nearby walked over to the puddle and stared at the notebook with some degree of disbelief." The child's alienation from school is explained as the result of his coming to school without the "verbal, conceptual, attentional, and learning skills requisite to school success." The authors see the child as "suffering from

---

[*]See, however, the critique of measures used by Rosenthal and Jacobson in the review by Robert L. Thorndike, *American Educational Research Journal* 15 (1968): 708-11. *Eds.*

feelings of inferiority because he is failing; he withdraws or becomes hostile, finding gratification elsewhere, such as in his peer group."

To view the peer group as a mere substitute for school shows an extraordinary lack of knowledge of adolescent culture. In our studies in south-central Harlem we have seen the reverse situation—the children who are rejected by the peer group are most likely to succeed in school. Although in middle-class suburban areas, many children do fail in school because of their personal deficiencies, in ghetto areas it is the healthy, vigorous, popular child with normal intelligence who cannot read and fails all along the line. It is not necessary to document here the influence of the peer group upon the behavior of youth in our society, but we may note that somewhere between the time that children first learn to talk and puberty, their language is restructured to fit the rules used by their peer group. From a linguistic viewpoint, the peer group is certainly a more powerful influence than the family (e.g., Gans 1962). Less directly, the pressures of peer-group activity are also felt within the school. Many children, particularly those who are not doing well in school, show a sudden sharp downward turn in the fourth and fifth grades, and children in the ghetto schools are no exception. It is at the same age, at nine or ten years old, that the influence of the vernacular peer group becomes predominant (see Wilmott 1966). Instead of dealing with isolated individuals, the school is then dealing with children who are integrated into groups of their own, with rewards and value systems which oppose those of the school. Those who know the sociolinguistic situation cannot doubt that reaction against the Bereiter-Engelmann approach in later years will be even more violent on the part of the students involved, and their rejection of the school system will be even more categorical.

The essential fallacy of the verbal deprivation theory lies in tracing the educational failure of the child to his personal deficiencies. At present, these deficiencies are said to be caused by his home environment. It is traditional to explain a child's failure in school by his inadequacy. But when failure reaches such massive proportions, it seems to us necessary to look at the social and cultural obstacles to learning, and the inability of the school to adjust to the social situation. Operation Head Start is designed to repair the child, rather than the school; to the extent that it is based upon this inverted logic, it is bound to fail.

Consequences of Failure

The second area in which the verbal deprivation theory is doing serious harm to our educational system is in the consequences of this failure, and the reaction to it. As failures are reported of Operation Head Start, the interpretations which we receive will be from the same educational psychologists who designed this program. The fault will be found not in the data, the theory, nor in the methods used, but rather in the children who have failed to respond to the opportunities offered to them. When Negro children fail to show the significant advance which the deprivation theory predicts, it will be taken as further proof of the profound gulf which separates their mental processes from those of "civilized," middle-class mankind.

A sense of the failure of Head Start is already in the air. Some prominent figures in the program are reacting to this situation by saying that intervention did not take place early enough. Caldwell (1967, p. 16) notes that:

... the research literature of the last decade dealing with social-class differences has made abundantly clear that all parents are not qualified to provide even the basic essentials of physical and psychological care to their children.

The deficit theory now begins to focus on the "long-standing patterns of parental deficit" which fill the literature. "There is, perhaps unfortunately," writes Caldwell (1967, p. 17), "no literary test for motherhood." Failing such eugenic measures, she has proposed "educationally oriented day care for culturally deprived children between six months and three years of age." The children are returned home each evening to "maintain primary emotional relationships with their own families," but during the day they are removed to "hopefully prevent the deceleration in rate of development which seems to occur in many deprived children around the age of two to three years."

There are others who feel that even the best of the intervention programs, such as those of Bereiter and Engelmann, will not help the Negro child no matter when such programs are applied—that we are faced once again with the "inevitable hypothesis" of the genetic inferiority of the Negro people. Many readers of this paper are undoubtedly familiar with the paper of Arthur Jensen in the *Harvard Educational Review* (1969) which received immediate and widespread publicity. Jensen (p. 3) begins with the following quotation from the United States Commission on Civil Rights as evidence of the failure of compensatory education:

The fact remains, however, that none of the programs appear to have raised significantly the achievement of participating pupils, as a group, within the period evaluated by the Commission. (U.S. Commission on Civil Rights 1967, p. 138)

Jensen believes that the verbal-deprivation theorists with whom he had been associated—Deutsch, Whiteman, Katz, Bereiter—have been given every opportunity to prove their case, and have failed. This opinion is part of the argument which leads him to the over-all conclusion (p. 82) that "the preponderance of the evidence is ... less consistent with a strictly environmental hypothesis than with the genetic hypothesis." In other words, racism—the belief in the genetic inferiority of Negroes—is the most correct view in the light of the present evidence.

Jensen argues that the middle-class white population is differentiated from the working-class white and Negro population in the ability for "cognitive or conceptual learning," which Jensen calls Level II intelligence as against mere "associative learning" or Level I intelligence:

. . . certain neural structures must also be available for Level II abilities to develop, and these are conceived of as being different from the neural structures underlying Level I. The genetic factors involved in each of these types of ability are presumed to have become differentially distributed in the population as a function of social class, since Level II has been most important for scholastic performance under the traditional methods of instruction. (Jensen 1969, p. 114)

Jensen found, for example, that one group of middle-class children were helped by their concept-forming ability to recall twenty familiar objects that could be classified into four categories: animals, furniture, clothing, or foods. Lower-class Negro children did just as well as middle-class children with a miscellaneous set, but showed no improvement with objects that could be so categorized.

The research of the educational psychologists cited here is presented by them in formal and objective style, and is widely received as impartial scientific evidence. Jensen's paper has been reported by Joseph Alsop and William F. Buckley, Jr. (*New York Post*, March 20, 1969) as "massive, apparently authoritative . . . ." It is not my intention to examine these materials in detail, but it is important to realize that we are dealing with special pleading by those who have a strong personal commitment. Jensen is concerned with class differences in cognitive style and verbal learning. His earlier papers incorporated the cultural deprivation theory which he now rejects as a basic explanation.[14] Jensen (1968, p. 167) classified the Negro children who fail in school as "slow learners" and "mentally retarded" and urged that we find out how much their retardation is due to environmental factors and how much is due to "more basic biological factors." His conviction that the problem must be located in the child leads him to accept and reprint some truly extraordinary data. To support the genetic hypothesis Jensen (1969, p. 83) cites the following percentage estimates by Heber (1968) of the racial distribution of mental retardation (based upon IQs below 75) in the general population:[15] These estimates, that almost half of lower-class Negro children are mentally retarded, could be accepted only by someone who has no knowledge of the children or the community. If he had wished to, Jensen could easily have

---

[14] In Deutsch, *et al.* (1968), Jensen expounds the verbal deprivation theory in considerable detail, for example (p. 119): "During this 'labeling' period . . . some very important social-class differences may exert their effects on verbal learning. Lower-class parents engage in relatively little of this naming or 'labeling' play with their children . . . . That words are discrete labels for things seems to be better known by the middle-class child entering first grade than by the lower-class child. Much of this knowledge is gained in the parent-child interaction, as when the parent looks at a picture book with the child . . ."

[15] Heber's (esp. 1968) studies of eighty-eight Negro mothers in Milwaukee are cited frequently throughout Jensen's paper. The estimates in this table are not given in relation to a particular Milwaukee sample, but for the general United States population. Heber's study was specifically designed to cover an area of Milwaukee which was known to contain a large concentration of retarded children, Negro and white, and he has stated that his findings were "grossly misinterpreted" by Jensen (*Milwaukee Sentinel*, June 11, 1969).

Socioeconomic Status	Per Cent of Whites	Per Cent of Negroes
1 (highest)	0.5	3.1
2	0.8	14.5
3	2.1	22.8
4	3.1	37.8
5 (lowest)	7.8	42.9

checked this against the records of any school in any urban ghetto area. Taking IQ tests at their face value, there is no correspondence between these figures and the communities we know. For example, among seventy-five boys we worked with in central Harlem who would fall into status categories 4 or 5 above, there were only three with IQs below 75. One spoke very little English; one could barely see; the third was emotionally disturbed. When the second was retested, he scored 91, and the third retested at 87.[16] There are of course hundreds of realistic reports available to Jensen. He simply selected one which would strengthen his case for the genetic inferiority of Negro children.

The frequent use of tables and statistics by educational psychologists serves to give outside readers the impression that this field is a science and that the opinions of the authors should be given the same attention and respect that we give to the conclusions of physicists or chemists. But careful examination of the input data will often show that there is no direct relationship between the conclusions and the evidence (in Jensen's case between IQ tests in a specially selected district of Milwaukee and intelligence of lower-class Negro children). Furthermore, the operations performed upon the data frequently carry us very far from the common-sense experience which is our only safeguard against conclusions heavily weighted by the author's theory. As another example, we may take some of the evidence presented by Whiteman and Deutsch for the cultural deprivation hypothesis.

The core of Deutsch's environmental explanation of poor performance in school is the Deprivation Index, a numerical scale based on six dichotomized variables. One variable is "the educational aspirational level of the parent for the child." Most people would agree that a parent who did not care if a child finished high school would be a disadvantageous factor in the child's educational career. In dichotomizing this variable Deutsch was faced with the fact that the educational aspiration of Negro parents is in fact very high, higher than for the white population, as he shows in other papers.[17] In order to fit

---

[16] The IQ scores given here are from group rather than individual tests and must therefore not be weighed heavily; the scores are from the Pintner-Cunningham test, usually given in the first grade in New York City schools in the 1950s.

[17] In Table 15–1 in Deutsch and associates (1967, p. 312), section C shows that some degree of college training was desired by 96, 97, and 100 per cent of Negro parents in class levels I, II, and III, respectively. The corresponding figures for whites were 79, 95, and 97

this data into the Deprivation Index, he therefore set the cutting point for the deprived group as "college or less" (see Whiteman and Deutsch 1968, p. 100). Thus if a Negro child's father says that he wants his son to go all the way through college, the child will fall into the "deprived" class on this variable. In order to receive the two points given to the "less deprived" on the index, it would be necessary for the child's parent to insist on graduate school or medical school! This decision is not discussed by the author; it simply stands as a *fait accompli* in the tables. Readers of this literature who are not committed to one point of view would be wise to look as carefully as possible at the original data which lies behind each statement, and check the conclusions against their own knowledge of the people and community being described.

No one can doubt that the reported inadequacy of Operation Head Start and of the verbal deprivation hypothesis has now become a crucial issue in our society.[18] The controversy which has arisen over Jensen's article typically assumes that programs such as Bereiter and Engelmann's have tested and measured the verbal capacity of the ghetto child. The cultural sociolinguistic obstacles to this intervention program are not considered, and the argument proceeds upon the data provided by the large, friendly interviewers whom we have seen at work in the extracts given above.

THE LINGUISTIC VIEW

Linguists are in an excellent position to demonstrate the fallacies of the verbal deprivation theory. All linguists agree that nonstandard dialects are highly structured systems. They do not see these dialects as accumulations of errors caused by the failure of their speakers to master standard English. When linguists hear Negro children saying "He crazy" or "Her my friend,"

---

per cent. In an earlier version of this paper, this discussion could be interpreted as implying that Whiteman and Deutsch had used data in the same way as Jensen: to rate the Negro group as low as possible. As they point out [personal communication], the inclusion of this item in the Deprivation Index had the opposite effect, and it could easily have been omitted if that had been their intention. They also argue that they had sound statistical grounds for dichotomizing as they did. The criticism which I intended to make is that there is something drastically wrong with operations which produce definitions of deprivation such as the one cited here. It should of course be noted that Whiteman and Deutsch have strongly opposed Jensen's genetic hypothesis and vigorously criticized his logic and data.

[18] The negative report of the Westinghouse Learning Corporation and Ohio University on Operation Head Start was published in *The New York Times* (April 13, 1969). The evidence of the failure of the program is accepted by many, and it seems likely that the report's discouraging conclusions will be used by conservative Congressmen as a weapon against any kind of expenditure for disadvantaged children, especially Negroes. The two hypotheses mentioned to account for this failure are that the impact of Head Start is lost through poor teaching later on, and more recently, that poor children have been so badly damaged in infancy by their lower-class environment that Head Start cannot make much difference. The third "inevitable" hypothesis of Jensen is not reported here.

they do not hear a primitive language. Nor do they believe that the speech of working-class people is merely a form of emotional expression, incapable of expressing logical thought.

All linguists who work with NNE recognize that it is a separate system, closely related to standard English but set apart from the surrounding white dialects by a number of persistent and systematic differences. Differences in analysis by various linguists in recent years are the inevitable products of differing theoretical approaches and perspectives as we explore these dialect patterns by different routes—differences which are rapidly diminishing as we exchange our findings. For example, Stewart differs with me on how deeply the invariant *be* of "She be always messin' around" is integrated into the semantics of the copula system with *am, is, are,* and so on. The position and meaning of *have. . . . ed* in NNE is very unclear, and there are a variety of positions on this point. But the grammatical features involved are not the fundamental predicators of the logical system. They are optional ways of contrasting, foregrounding, emphasizing, or deleting elements of the under-lying sentence. There are a few semantic features of NNE grammar which may be unique to this system. But the semantic features we are talking about here are items such as "habitual," "general," "intensive." These linguistic markers are essentially *points of view*—different ways of looking at the same events, and they do not determine the truth values of propositions upon which all speakers of English agree.

The great majority of the differences between NNE and standard English do not even represent such subtle semantic features as those, but rather extensions and restrictions of certain formal rules, and different choices of redundant elements. For example, standard English uses two signals to express the progressive, *be* and *-ing,* while NNE often drops the former. Standard English signals the third person in the present by the subject noun phrase and by a third singular *-s;* NNE does not have this second redundant feature. On the other hand, NNE uses redundant negative elements in negative concord, in possessives like *mines,* uses *or either* where standard English uses a simple *or,* and so on.

When linguists say that NNE is a system, we mean that it differs from other dialects in regular and rule-governed ways, so that it has equivalent ways of expressing the same logical content. When we say that it is a separate sub-system, we mean that there are compensating sets of rules which combine in different ways to preserve the distinctions found in other dialects. Thus as noted above NNE does not use the *if* or *whether* complementizer in embedded questions, but the meaning is preserved by the formal device of reversing the order of subject and auxiliary.

Linguists therefore speak with a single voice in condemning Bereiter's view that the vernacular can be disregarded. I exchanged views on this matter with all of the participants in the Twentieth Annual Georgetown Round Table where this paper was first presented, and their responses were in complete agreement in rejecting the verbal deprivation theory and its misapprehension of the nature of language. The other papers in the report (Alatis 1970) of that conference testified to the strength of the linguistic view in this area. It was William Stewart who first pointed out that Negro English should be studied as a coherent system, and in this all of us follow his lead. Dialectologists like Raven McDavid, Albert Marckwardt, and Roger Shuy have been working for years against the notion that vernacular dialects are inferior and illogical means of communication. Linguists now agree that teachers must know as much as possible about Negro nonstandard English as a communicative system.

The exact nature and relative importance of the structural differences between NNE and standard English are not in question here. It is agreed that the teacher must approach the teaching of the standard through a knowledge of the child's own system. The methods used in teaching English as a foreign language are recommended, not to declare that NNE is a foreign language, but to underline the importance of studying the native dialect as a coherent system for communication. This is in fact the method that should be applied in any English class.

Linguists are also in an excellent position to assess Jensen's claim that the middle-class white population is superior to the working-class and Negro populations in the distribution of Level II, or conceptual, intelligence. The notion that large numbers of children have no capacity for conceptual thinking would inevitably mean that they speak a primitive language, for even the simplest linguistic rules we discussed above involve conceptual operations more complex than those used in the experiment Jensen cites. Let us consider what is involved in the use of the general English rule that incorporates the negative with the first indefinite. To learn and use this rule, one must first identify the class of indefinites involved—*any, one, ever*, which are formally quite diverse. How is this done? These indefinites share a number of common properties which can be expressed as the concepts "indefinite," "hypothetical," and "nonpartitive." One might argue that these indefinites are learned as a simple list, by association learning. But this is only one of the many syntactic rules involving indefinites—rules known to every speaker of English, which could not be learned except by an understanding of their common, abstract properties. For example, everyone knows, unconsciously, that *anyone* cannot be used with preterit verbs or progressives. One does not say, "*Anyone went to the party" or "*Anyone is going to the party." The rule which operates here is sensitive to the property [+ hypothetical] of the indefinites. Whenever the proposition is not inconsistent with this feature, *anyone* can be used. Everyone knows, therefore, that one can say "Anyone who was anyone went to the party" or "If anyone went to the party . . ." or "Before anyone went to the party . . ." There is another property of *anyone* which is grasped unconsciously by all native speakers of English; it is [+ distributive]. Thus if we need one more man for a game of bridge or basketball, and there is a crowd outside, we ask, "Do any of you want to play?" not "Do some of you want to play?" In both cases, we are considering a plurality, but with *any*, we consider them one at a time, or distributively.

What are we then to make of Jensen's contention that Level I thinkers cannot make use of the concept *animal* to group together a miscellaneous set of toy animals? It is one thing to say that someone is not in the habit of using a certain skill. But to say that his failure to use it is genetically determined implies dramatic consequences for other forms of behavior, which are not found in experience. The knowledge of what people must do in order to learn language makes Jensen's theories seem more and more distant from the realities of human behavior. Like Bereiter and Engelmann, Jensen is handicapped by his ignorance of the most basic facts about human language and the people who speak it.

There is no reason to believe that any nonstandard vernacular is in itself an obstacle to learning. The chief problem is ignorance of language on the part of all concerned. Our job as linguists is to remedy this ignorance; but Bereiter and Engelmann want to reinforce it and justify it. Teachers are now being told to ignore the language of Negro children as unworthy of attention and useless for learning. They are being taught to hear every natural utterance of the child as evidence of his mental inferiority. As linguists we are unanimous in condemning this view as bad observation, bad theory, and bad practice.

That educational psychology should be strongly influenced by a theory so false to the facts of language is unfortunate; but that children should be the victims of this ignorance is intolerable. It may seem that the fallacies of the verbal deprivation theory are so obvious that they are hardly worth exposing. I have tried to show that such exposure is an important job for us to undertake. If linguists can contribute some of their available knowledge and energy toward this end, we will have done a great deal to justify the support that society has given to basic research in our field.

REFERENCES

ALATIS, J., ed. *Georgetown Monographs in Language and Linguistics*, No. 22. Washington, D.C.: Georgetown University Press, 1970.

BEREITER, C., AND ENGELMANN, S. *Teaching Disadvantaged Children in the Preschool*. Englewood Cliffs, N.J.: Prentice-Hall, 1966.

BEREITER, C.; ENGELMANN, S.; OSBORN, JEAN; AND REIDFORD, P. A. An academically oriented preschool for culturally deprived children. In F. Hechinger, ed., *Pre-school Education Today*. New York: Doubleday, 1966.

BERNSTEIN, B. Elaborated and restricted codes: Their social origins and some consequences. In A. G. SMITH, ed., *Communication and Culture*. New York: Holt, Rinehart & Winston, 1966.

BLUM, A. The sociology of mental illness. In J. Douglas, ed., *Deviance and Respectability*. New York: Basic Books, 1970.

CALDWELL, BETTYE M. What is the optimal learning environment for the young child? *American J. Orthopsychiatry* 1967, 37: 8–21.

CHOMSKY, N. *Aspects of the Theory of Syntax*. Cambridge, Mass.: MIT Press, 1965.

COLEMAN, J. S., *et al. Equality of Educational Opportunity*. Washington, D.C.: U.S. Office of Education, 1966.

DEUTSCH, M., and associates. *The Disadvantaged Child*. New York: Basic Books, 1967.

DEUTSCH, M.; KATZ, I.; AND JENSEN, A. R., eds., *Social Class, Race, and Psychological Development*. New York: Holt, Rinehart & Winston, 1968.

GANS, H. *The Urban Villagers*. New York: Free Press, 1962.

HEBER, R. Research on education and habilitation of the mentally retarded. Paper read at Conference on Sociocultural Aspects of Mental Retardation, June 1968, Peabody College, Nashville, Tenn.

JENSEN, A. R. Social class and verbal learning. In M. DEUTSCH, *et al.*, eds., *Social Class, Race, and Psychological Development*. New York: Holt, Rinehart & Winston, 1968.

————. How much can we boost IQ and scholastic achievement? *Harvard Educational Review* 1969, 39: 1–123.

LABOV, W. On the grammaticality of everyday speech. Paper presented at the annual meeting of the Linguistic Society of America, December 1966, New York.

————. Some sources of reading problems for Negro speakers of nonstandard English. In A. Frazier, ed., *New Directions in Elementary English*. Champaign, Ill.: National Council of Teachers of English, 1967. Also reprinted in J. C. BARATZ and R. W. SHUY, eds., *Teaching Black Children to Read*. Washington, D.C.: Center for Applied Linguistics, 1969.

————. Negative attraction and negative concord in four English dialects. Paper presented at the annual meeting of the Linguistic Society of America, December 1968, New York.

————. Contraction, deletion, and inherent variability of the English copula. *Language*, 1969, 45: 715–62.

LABOV, W.; COHEN, P.; ROBINS, C. A preliminary study of the structure of English used by Negro and Puerto Rican speakers in New York City. Final report, U.S. Office of Education Cooperative Research Project No. 3091, 1965.

LABOV, W.; COHEN, P.; ROBINS, C.; AND LEWIS, J. A study of the nonstandard English of Negro and Puerto Rican speakers in New York City. Final report, U.S. Office of Education Cooperative Research Project No. 3288 Vols. 1, 2. Mimeographed. Columbia University, 1968.

LABOV, W., AND ROBINS, C. A note on the relation of reading failure to peer-group status in urban ghettos. *The Teachers College Record* 1969, 70: 396–405.

LANGER, T. S., AND MICHAELS, S. T. *Life Stress and Mental Health*. New York: Free Press, 1963.

ROSENTHAL, R., AND JACOBSON, LENORE. Self-fulfilling prophecies in the classroom: teachers' expectations as unintended determinants of pupils' intellectual competence. In M. DEUTSCH, *et al.*, eds., *Social Class, Race, and Psychological Development*. New York: Holt, Rinehart & Winston, 1968.

United States Commission on Civil Rights. *Racial Isolation in the Public Schools*, Vol. 1. Washington, D.C.: U.S. Government Printing Office, 1967.

WHITEMAN, M., AND DEUTSCH, M. Social disadvantage as related to intellective and language development. In M. DEUTSCH, *et al.*, eds., *Social Class, Race and Psychological Development*. New York: Holt, Rinehart & Winston, 1968.

WILMOTT, P. *Adolescent Boys of East London.* London: Routledge & Kegan Paul, 1966.

STUDY QUESTIONS

1. Linguists commonly distinguish between language as a system and the uses of language by individuals. Is logic, as the term is used by Labov, a matter of language per se or of language use? If a claim were made that a given language system is illogical, how might that claim be substantiated?

2. Labov charges (p. 320) that: "In the writings of many prominent educational psychologists, we find a very poor understanding of the nature of language." How does his assertion apply to the concept of verbal deprivation? To the language programs of Bereiter and Engelmann?

3. Is "middle-class verbal behavior" the same thing as standard English? What distinction would Labov make between dialect and style? How might an investigator set out to discover "how much middle-class style is a matter of fashion and how much actually helps us to express our ideas clearly" (pp. 337)?

4. Identify the nonstandard grammatical features in Larry's dialogue (pp. 330–32). Using these features, demonstrate the claim that NNE is fully as systematic and grammatical as standard English.

5. The following is a possible standard English version of a portion of Larry's argument. Which of its features are matters of dialect? Which are matters of style?

> Some people say that if you are good, your spirit will go to heaven; and if you are bad, your spirit will go to hell. I deny the first proposition since it is based on an unproven or unproveable assumption; and I assert emphatically that your spirit will go to hell in any case.
>
> Those who make such a proposition have many ideas about what God is. Because their conceptions are multiple, different, and often contradictory, they cannot prove that God exists since they cannot clearly comprehend or communicate His nature. If there is a heaven, God must have made it; but if God does not exist, He cannot have made a heaven. If heaven does not exist, it is obvious that your spirit cannot go there. Consequently, your spirit will go to hell, since that is the only permitted alternative.

6. Labov says "Many academic writers try to rid themselves of that part of middle-class style that is empty pretension, and keep that part that is needed for precision" (p. 330). Does this describe a useful aim for a composition class? Does it have anything to do with the teaching of standard English?

7. What does Labov mean when he says (p. 333): "it seems likely that standard English has an advantage over NNE in explicit analysis of surface forms . . ."? Is he talking about dialect? Verbal habits? Style?

8. Labov argues that the primary responsibility of the linguist is to remedy ignorance about the nature of language, dialect, and dialect difference. Does the English teacher have a similar responsibility? What is the responsibility of the teacher concerned with effective language use?

9. Labov asserts that the most pernicious effect of the concept of verbal deprivation is the way it shapes the teacher's perception of the abilities and character of the child who speaks nonstandard English. Do you agree that such perceptions have an effect on the ability of a teacher to teach or of a child to learn? What might be some such effects?

Part III

English in the Classroom

"That's all very well, but what do I do?"

—*Vox Magistri*

Children from lower- and working-class backgrounds do less well in school as a group than do middle-class children; children from some of America's racial and ethnic minorities do less well in school than their fellows from the majority culture. These are facts easily documented, and have been so well publicized and so frequently commented on they are a fixed part of our current educational lore. Why they should be facts, however, is less transparent. Why should children of low socioeconomic status fail when free schools dedicated to universal education are available to them? Why do black urban children lag behind national norms for reading achievement, or sometimes fail to learn to read at all? Why do Puerto Rican and Indian children leave school at the earliest opportunity still not speaking English? Why do the children of immigrants from Appalachia to such cities as Chicago drop out of school with such alarming frequency? Why do all such children do as badly as they do in arithmetic, in social studies, in science? Questions like these have dominated educational research during the past few years; educational researchers argue violently over the separate answers they have offered.

For many researchers, the causes of educational failure lie in the child, or more often in the sub- or different culture that has shaped the child. Such investigators have coined the terminology of disadvantage *or* deprivation; *and they speak of* impoverished culture, cultural deprivation, cultural deficit, cultural lag, disadvantaged environments, *lacking toys, lacking books, lacking fathers, lacking human contact and conversation. When the subject is language and its development, we hear of* language deprivation *or of the* nonverbal child, *silent because he lacks names for things around him; deprived because his language does not fit him for conceptualization or logic. For other researchers, the causes of failure lie in the schools and not in the children who attend them: in the squalor and dirt of badly maintained and ill-equipped slum school buildings; in the apathy, cynicism, or broken idealism of teachers consigned to teach in such buildings; in the cultural and racial biases of teachers and administrators drawn largely from the middle class. From these investigators and commentators we hear of the* culturally different, *not the culturally deprived; of the* ethnocentrism *of American schools and the curative powers of* bi- and multicultural *outlooks and programs; of culturally biased tests and of self-fulfilling prophesies. When the subject is language, we hear of different systems of English, cognitively like, but socially and functionally differentiated into hierarchies of status and use. The deprivation theorists look to compensatory education to solve failure by repairing the cultural loss suffered by children disadvantaged by their native environments; the difference theorists look for changed and improved schools and for teachers better trained to react intelligently and sensitively to cultural difference and the special needs of special learners.*

A second dichotomy separates current projectors—one based on more subjective but no less cogent grounds: conceptions of how American society does and should work; conceptions of how schools should function in preparing students for life in American society. Some see the hope of the future in assimilation and leveling—in the adaptation or at least partial adaptation of minority life styles to the dominant norms of American life. Thus are classes arranged for assembly-line workers recruited out of the ghetto to teach middle-class virtues of punctuality and attention to job duties; thus are courses instituted in business curricula to teach the pronunciation and usages of standard English. On the other side, some projectors foresee a future only if Americans can learn to accept, respect, and coexist with cultural diversity. Classes appear in black literature and black culture, bilingual programs are encouraged in which anglo and hispano alike are taught Spanish and English, black dialect is taught as something other than usages to be scorned.

Among the disputants, linguists have been nearly unanimous in rejecting the concept of cultural and linguistic deprivation. But they are split into contentious groups by this second dichotomy, some falling on one side, some on the other, some into the chasm gaping in the middle. Some linguists and appliers of linguistics would have the schools strenuously teach the dominant linguistic norms—standard English—arguing that all children must be equipped for struggle in the market place where the middle class guards the till. Some urge bidialectalism—the teaching of standard English for certain purposes without disturbing the student's native dialect. Still others reject dialect tinkering entirely, arguing that the acquisition of dominant norms can be confidently left to natural processes if teachers will teach humanely those matters that do count.

Most of the major controversies now raging are touched on in the following selections. James Sledd offers the term doublespeak *in place of "biloquialism" or "bidialectalism" as more connotatively accurate of the linguistic engineering proposed by bidialectalists. A humanist scholar and an English teacher as well as a linguist, Sledd questions the ethical and moral bases of the biloquial principle, sensing the presence of "big brother" behind arguments that schools bear a particular responsibility for teaching all students middle-class norms. Richard Bailey comments on implications of the social stratification of English in the United States and suggests a reordering of priorities in composition classes from a too-intense concern with "correct" sentences to a more proper and productive concern with larger organizational structures. Robinson returns to a discussion of prevailing conceptions of the nature of nonstandard dialects, arguing that classroom practice must be guided by sound and substantial research into the nature of language, language difference, and language development. He is concerned with attitudes, prejudices, and the prejudging of students as well as the limits and relevant domains for the application of linguistic knowledge in the English classroom.*

DOUBLESPEAK: DIALECTOLOGY IN THE
SERVICE OF BIG BROTHER

James Sledd

The doctrine of bidialectalism starts with the innocuous observation that speech is variable in its several uses, and goes on to incorporate findings from sociolinguistics that stylistic levels correlate to some extent with dialect differences to urge the systematic teaching of prestige norms. But the dialect an individual speaks has powerful symbolic value. A man's speech is as personal and as personally identifying as his appearance; it is expressive of group loyalties and antagonisms, linking the individual with kindred humans who "speak his language," connotative of intimate relations with family, friends, and colleagues, and of the face to face relations that all humans seek and value. To distinct forms of speech attach the sometimes benign, sometimes malignant, stereotypes of class and caste. When we speak of standard and nonstandard dialects we enter the realm of class stratification and class conflict; the realms of value judgments, preferences, and prejudices. Because dialect is expressive of personality, class, and class attitudes; because class and class attitudes involve questions of power and money; because policies of language and dialect intervention involve some people urging or forcing other people to change or modify their speech, politics and ethics are not separable from educational questions about what dialect to teach and how it should be taught.

James Sledd's plea is for an evaluation of educational proposals—in this case of a mode of teaching standard English—in terms of ultimate social and philosophical aims and humane values. What kind of society do we wish to build? What kind of man does that society need in order to survive and flourish? What are the proper functions of educational institutions? What are the societal and human responsibilities of teachers? The questions are almost embarrassing in a world that runs to a time clock and the hum of generators; but they are being asked, if often in different language, by numbers of young people or by parents pushing for local control of schools that seem no longer to meet their community and personal needs. Sledd's argument is not for acceptance of a program, an approach, or a method; it is an argument less for acquiescence than for thought. His ultimate hope is for informed, humane, and free teachers—teachers who will be able to make decisions on the basis of their own philosophical commitments and the needs of their students; teachers courageous enough to submit their decisions to criticism while maintaining against corporate opposition what seems true to them.

From *College English*, 33(1972):439–56. Copyright © 1972 by the National Council of Teachers of English. Reprinted by permission of the publisher and James Sledd.

A SHORT HISTORY OF DOUBLESPEAK

It was only a few years ago that Professor Dr. Roger W. Shuy, then of Michigan State University, discovered American dialects.[1] In a little book which James R. Squire, Executive Secretary of the National Council of Teachers of English, described as "a valuable resource" for teachers increasingly concerned with "the study of the English language in our schools,"[2] Dr. Shuy informed the profession that in Illinois "a male sheep was known as a *buck* only to farmers who had at some time raised sheep"[3] and that "the Minneapolis term *rubber-binder* (for rubber band)" was spreading into Wisconsin.[4] He also declared that Southerners pronounce *marry* as if it were spelled *merry*, that they pronounce *fog* and *hog* like *fawg* and *hawg*, that they have a final /r/ in *humor*, that they make *which* identical with *witch* and rhyme *Miss* with *his*, etc.[5]

But one does not expect high scholarship from a popularizing textbook, and though Dr. Shuy's discoveries made no great noise in the world of dialectology, the fault was not his alone. As he himself pointed out, American dialect studies were becoming "both more complex and more interesting," and new questions were being asked.

Twenty or thirty years ago dialect geographers were mainly concerned with relating current pronunciations, vocabulary, and grammar to settlement history and geography. In the sixties, the problems of urban living have attracted attention, including social dialects and styles which need to be learned and used to meet different situations. We need more precise information about the dialects which set one social group apart from another.[6]

One might say metaphorically that the dialectologists, like millions of their compatriots, had left the farm for the big city. There they had discovered the blacks—and were making the best of it. In September, 1967, Dr. Roger W. Shuy was no longer a teacher in East Lansing, Michigan, but a Director of Urban Language Study in Washington, D.C.

The trouble with the blacks, as it seemed to the nabobs of the National Council, was that they didn't talk right and weren't doing very well in school. But they were also raising considerable hell with the police; and since the traditional self-righteous pontification against the South showed little promise of quelling riots in Chicago, Detroit, or New York, the greater Powers of the North had assumed a beneficent air and (as one stratagem) had

---

[1] Roger W. Shuy, *Discovering American Dialects*. Champaign, Ill: National Council of Teachers of English, 1967.

[2] *Discovering American Dialects*, "Foreword."

[3] *Ibid.*, p. 15.

[4] *Ibid.*, pp. 36–37.

[5] *Ibid.*, pp. 12–13.

[6] *Ibid.*, p. 63.

employed a band of linguists and quasilinguists who would pretend to help black folks talk like white folks on all occasions which the Northern Powers thought it worth their while to regulate. This was the origin of bidialectalism, biloquialism, or—in "good plain Anglo-Saxon"—doublespeak. No missionary enterprise of recent times has been more profitable—for the evangelists.

Readers in search of a longer and more reverential history may find it in many sources, including at least six volumes in the Urban Language Series, under the general editorship of Dr. Roger W. Shuy, now Director of the Sociolinguistics Program of the Center for Applied Linguistics. They are particularly directed to the volume entitled *Teaching Standard English in the Inner City*, which Dr. Shuy has edited with his colleague Ralph W. Fasold.[7] Further light is shed by other collections of essays, notably the special anthology issue of *The Florida FL Reporter* which appeared in 1969 under the title *Linguistic-Cultural Differences and American Education*; the report of the twentieth annual Round Table Meeting at Georgetown, *Linguistics and the Teaching of Standard English to Speakers of Other Languages or Dialects*; and Frederick Williams' anthology, *Language and Poverty: Perspectives on a Theme*. Professor Williams includes a recent essay by the British sociologist Basil Bernstein, who in his own way is also somewhat critical of doublespeak; and readers interested in Bernstein's earlier work will find it reviewed by Denis Lawton in *Social Class, Language and Education*. By all odds the best of the bidialectalists is the genuinely distinguished linguist William Labov of the University of Pennsylvania whose little book *The Study of Nonstandard English* includes a selected bibliography. Recently, the apostles of doublespeak have been vexed by more numerous and more vocal objectors, and perhaps there is just a hint of admitted failure in the shifting of attention by some biloquialists from doublespeak to the teaching of reading. Linguists, educationists, and others have addressed themselves to reading problems in memorial volumes like *Reading for the Disadvantaged*, edited by Thomas D. Horn, and *Language & Reading*, compiled by Doris V. Gunderson.[8]

---

[7] Ralph W. Fasold and Roger W. Shuy, eds., *Teaching Standard English in the Inner City*. Washington, D.C.: Center for Applied Linguistics, 1970.

[8] To list the cited works more formally: Alfred C. Aarons, Barbara Y. Gordon, and William A. Stewart, eds., *Linguistic-Cultural Differences and American Education*. Special anthology issue of *The Florida FL Reporter*, Vol. 7, No. 1 (Spring/Summer, 1969). James E. Alatis, ed., *Linguistics and the Teaching of Standard English to Speakers of Other Languages or Dialects*. Report of the Twentieth Annual Round Table Meeting on Linguistics and Language Studies. Washington, D.C.: Georgetown University Press, 1970. Frederick Williams, ed., *Language and Poverty: Perspectives on a Theme*. Chicago: Markham Publishing Company, 1970. Denis Lawton, *Social Class, Language and Education*. New York: Schocken Books, 1968. William Labov, *The Study of Nonstandard English*. Champaign, Ill.: National Council of Teachers of English, 1970. Thomas D. Horn, ed., *Reading for the Disadvantaged: Problems of Linguistically Different Learners*. New York: Harcourt, Brace & World, 1970. Doris V. Gunderson, compiler, *Language & Reading: An Interdisciplinary Approach*. Washington, D.C.: Center for Applied Linguistics, 1970.

THE MONEYED BANKRUPT

It is sad to report that the results of such vast activity have been disproportionately small. The biloquialists themselves do not claim to have produced substantial numbers of psychologically undamaged doublespeakers, whose mastery of whitey's talk has won them jobs which otherwise would have been denied them. In fact, the complete bidialectal, with undiminished control of his vernacular and a good mastery of the standard language, is apparently as mythical as the unicorn: no authenticated specimens have been reported.[9] Even the means to approximate the ideal of doublespeaking are admittedly lacking, for "the need for teaching materials preceded any strongly felt need for theoretical bases or empirical research upon which such materials could be based."[10] Consequently, there are relatively few teaching materials available,[11] and those that do exist differ in theory, method, content, and arrangement.[12] In the words of Director, Dr. Shuy

A majority of the materials currently available for teaching standard English to nonstandard speakers rest on the uneasy assumption that TESOL techniques [for teaching English as a second language] are valid for learning a second dialect. They do this without any solid proof. We do not have a viable evaluation tool at this time, nor are we likely to get one until the linguists complete their analysis of the language system of nonstandard speakers. Most current materials deal with pronunciations although it has long been accepted that grammatical differences count more heavily toward social judgments than phonological or lexical differences.[13]

Taken literally, that confession would mean that the biloquialists will never be able to tell their patrons whether or not their costly teaching materials are any good, because a complete analysis of any language, standard or nonstandard, is another unattainable ideal. The best of existing descriptions of what is called Black English are only fragments, sketches of bits and pieces which have caught the eye of Northern linguists unfamiliar with Southern

[9] Labov has repeatedly said as much, most recently in "The Study of Language in its Social Context," *Studium Generale*, 23 (1970), p. 52: "We have not encountered any nonstandard speakers who gained good control of a standard language, and still retained control of the nonstandard vernacular." The goodness of the acquired control of the standard language will not easily be assumed by students of hypercorrection, readers of H. C. Wyld on "Modified Standard," or teachers of Freshman English in state universities.

[10] Roger W. Shuy, "Teacher Training and Urban Language Problems," in Fasold and Shuy, *Teaching Standard English*, p. 126.

[11] *Ibid.*, p. 128.

[12] Walt Wolfram, "Sociolinguistic Implications for Educational Sequencing," in Fasold and Shuy, p. 105.

[13] Roger W. Shuy, "Bonnie and Clyde Tactics in English Teaching," in Aarons, Gordon, and Stewart, *Linguistic-Cultural Differences and American Education*, p. 83.

speech.[14] Advocates of doublespeak must therefore admit that they have still not produced the "absolutely necessary prerequisite to English teaching in such situations, . . . the linguistic analysis and description of the nonstandard dialect."[15]

CAUSES OF FAILURE

At this juncture the irreverent might be tempted to ask a question. If happy, accomplished, and fully employed doublespeakers are not swarming in Northern cities, if tried and tested materials for teaching more of them remain scarce, and if complete descriptions of the relevant dialects are not going to exist while we do, then one might ask just what the biloquialists have been doing with the money and manpower which the Establishment has provided them or whether (more suspiciously) the Establishment really wants them to do anything or just to give the impression of a great society on the march toward new frontiers.

One naughty answer would be that the biloquialists have been so busy convening, conferring, organizing, advertising, and asking for more that their intellectual activities have suffered. There is even some expert testimony to this effect:

A recent national conference on educating the disadvantaged devoted less than 5 per cent of its attention during the two days of meetings to the content of such education. Practically all of the papers and discussion centered on funding such programs, administrating them and evaluating them.[16]

But so elementary a naughtiness is only a partial answer, and in part unfair. It is unfair specifically to William Labov and his associates, who have taught us a great deal, not just about current American English, but about the theory and practice of descriptive and historical grammar; and it does not sufficiently emphasize the extenuating circumstance that well-meaning sloganeers may be trapped by their own slogans as they try to do in a few years a job that would take a generation.

[14] Readers may satisfy themselves of the truth of this proposition by examining the table of contents in Walter A. Wolfram's *Sociolinguistic Description of Detroit Negro Speech* (Washington, D.C.: Center for Applied Linguistics, 1969) or by reading Wolfram and Fasold, "Some Linguistic Features of Negro Dialect," in Fasold and Shuy, *Teaching Standard English*, pp. 41 ff. A much more extensive work is the *Study of the Non-Standard English of Negro and Puerto Rican Speakers in New York City* by Labov, Paul Cohen, Clarence Robins, and John Lewis (2 vols.; Columbia University, 1968); but Chapter III of their first volume, "Structural Differences between Non-Standard Negro English and Standard English," is very far from a "complete" grammar of either dialect.

[15] William A. Stewart, "Urban Negro Speech: Sociolinguistic Factors Affecting English Teaching," in Aarons, Gordon, and Stewart, *Linguistic-Cultural Differences*, p. 53.

[16] Roger W. Shuy, "Teacher Training and Urban Language Problems," in Fasold and Shuy, *Teaching Standard English*, p. 127.

Since the Powers prefer the appearance of social change to the reality, it was not hard to hook governments and foundations on the alleged potentialities of doublespeak as if those potentialities had been realized already or would be on a bright tomorrow; but when the advertisements had brought the customers, the delivery of the actual goods turned out impossible. Nobody knows what the biloquialists admit they would have to know about dialects of English to make doublespeak succeed; and besides this general ignorance (which some of them have manfully attacked), the biloquialists are working under some special disadvantages. It is always hard for people who have not taught much to talk about teaching (though ingenious youths like Dr. Peter S. Rosenbaum can sometimes manage it),[17] and it is hard for linguists who have not heard much Southern speech to talk about speech which is basically Southern: they are constantly discovering distinctive characteristics of "the Negro vernacular," like "dummy *it* for *there*," which the most benighted caucasian Christian spinster in Milledgeville, Georgia, could assure them are commonplace among poor whites.[18]

There are other difficulties, too, which hamper not only the biloquialists but all practitioners of large-scale linguistic engineering (the jargon is contagious). Linguistics in the 60s and early 70s has been unsettled by new theories, whose advocates are openly skeptical of oversold "applications"; and even in favorable circumstances "interdisciplinary" efforts like biloquialism are always slow to take effect, often hampered by disagreements among the congregation of prima donnas, and sometimes disappointingly unproductive.

Quite as loud as the general lamentation over the failure of "interventionist" programs for the disadvantaged are the debates among the interveners. Thus, to the devotees of applied linguistics, both the Englishman Bernstein

[17] Dr. Rosenbaum's oration in the twentieth Round Table report deserves special attention, but lack of space forbids an attractive excursus. A couple of quotations will suggest the orientation of this already eminent "linguistic engineer." (1) "*Learning* means acquiring new or improved control over one's environment. *Teaching* means structuring or manipulating an environment so that a learner through experience in this environment can with facility acquire the desired control" (p. 112). Just how this statement applies to a class in *Beowulf* may be left to Dr. Rosenbaum to explain. (2) "In experimental computerized versions of such an environment being developed by IBM Research, the tutor is a computer itself, communicating with a student by means of a terminal station equipped with a typewriter, tape recorder, and image projector" (p. 116). It would be unkind to blame the tutor computer for Dr. Rosenbaum's prose, since it is well known that he received conventional humanistic instruction at MIT; but even acknowledged masters of inanity might envy the following sentence: "As is understood by all, some students are weaker than others" (p. 114). An antiquated antiquarian (perhaps unduly vexed by the "structuring or manipulating" of the now well-oiled Gulf beaches) must ask forgiveness for doubting that a man who can write like that is likely "to devise a new classroom regime capable of satisfying all major language learning environment criteria" (p. 117).

[18] William Labov, *The Study of Nonstandard English*, p. 27; Flannery O'Connor, "A Good Man Is Hard to Find," in *Three by Flannery O'Connor* (New York: New American Library, n d), pp. 133, 139, 142, 143.

and the American partners Engelmann and Bereiter are sinners against the light,[19] but neither Bernstein nor Engelmann has rushed headlong to confession. On the contrary, both are recalcitrant.

For all his talk about restricted and elaborated codes (talk which has won him a retinue of American disciples), Bernstein still sees no reason to interfere with nonstandard dialects:

> That the culture or subculture through its forms of social integration generates a restricted code, does not mean that the resultant speech and meaning system is linguistically or culturally deprived, that its children have nothing to offer the school, that their imaginings are not significant. It does not mean that we have to teach these children formal grammar, nor does it mean that we have to interfere with their dialect. There is nothing, but nothing, in dialect as such, which prevents a child from internalizing and learning to use universalistic meanings.[20]

Obviously, Bernstein has little in common with the biloquialists except the tendency to talk smugly about *we* and *they* and what *we* have to do to *them*. Engelmann, equally godlike, ranks "The Linguistic and Psycholinguistic Approaches" under "Abuses in Program Construction" and dismisses both:

> It is not possible to imply statements about teaching from the premises upon which the linguist and the psycholinguist operate. Attempts to use linguistic analysis as the basis for teaching reading have produced the full range of programs, from paragraph reading to single-sound variations. The linguist's entire theoretical preamble, in other words, is nothing more than an appeal used to sanction an approach that derives from personal preferences, not from linguistic principles.[21]

Unless the Powers are willing to subsidize all interveners equally, such disagreement indicates that at least some seekers of funds should get no more funding for the evaluating of their administrating; and the unfunded (to close this selective catalogue of disagreements) are likely to include some linguists, for linguist can differ with linguist as vigorously as with psychologist or sociologist. Marvin D. Loflin, for example, transmogrifies all Southern whites to pluriglots when he finds "Nonstandard Negro English" so unlike the standard speech of whites "that a fuller description . . . will show a grammatical system which must be treated as a foreign language."[22] Similarly, William A. Stewart finds enough "unique . . . structural characteristics" in "American Negro dialects" to justify the bold historical speculation that the Negro dialects "probably derived from a creolized form

---

[19] See Labov's "Logic of Nonstandard English," reprinted on pp. 319–54.

[20] Basil Bernstein, "A Sociolinguistic Approach to Socialization: With Some Reference to Educability," in *Language and Poverty*, p. 57.

[21] Siegfried Engelmann, "How to Construct Effective Language Programs for the Poverty Child," in *Language and Poverty*, p. 118.

[22] "A Teaching Problem in Nonstandard Negro English," *English Journal*, 56.1312–1314, quoted by Wolfram, *A Sociolinguistic Description of Detroit Negro Speech*, p. 13.

of English, once spoken on American plantations by Negro slaves and seemingly related to creolized forms of English which are still spoken by Negroes in Jamaica and other parts of the Caribbean."[23]

Perhaps it may be so. At any rate, when Stewart's theory is questioned he is quick to denounce what he calls "the blatant intrusion of sociopolitical issues into the scientific study of Negro speech";[24] and his sociopolitical rhetoric, if not his linguistic evidence, has been so convincing that his conclusions are sometimes confidently repeated by persons whose linguistic sophistication is considerably less than his.[25]

Yet Loflin and Stewart have not had everything their own way among the linguists. Raven McDavid is presumably one of Stewart's blatant intruders of sociopolitical issues into virginal science:

Even where a particular feature is popularly assigned to one racial group, like the uninflected third-singular present (*he do, she have, it make*)—a shibboleth for Negro nonstandard speech in urban areas—it often turns out to be old in the British dialects, and to be widely distributed in the eastern United States among speakers of all races. It is only the accidents of cultural, economic, and educational history that have made such older linguistic features more common in the South than in the Midland and the North, and more common among Negro speakers than among whites.[26]

William Labov is equally firm in rejecting Loflin's theory of nonstandard Negro English as a foreign language:

In dealing with the structure of NNE, we do not find a foreign language with syntax and semantics radically different from SE [Standard English]: instead, we find a dialect of English, with certain extensions and modifications of rules to be found in other dialects. . . . Striking differences in surface structure were frequently the result of late phonological and transformational rules.[27]

No amount of funding can conceal the fact that somebody, in arguments like these, has got to be wrong.

THE SHIFT TO READING

If the shift from doublespeak to interdisciplinary assaults on reading does hint at some sense of failure among the disunited sloganeers of overambitious biloquialism, their choice of a second front will not redeem their reputation

[23] "Toward a History of American Negro Dialect," in Williams, *Language and Poverty*, p. 351.

[24] "Sociopolitical Issues in the Linguistic Treatment of Negro Dialect," in Alatis, *Linguistics and the Teaching of Standard English*, p. 215.

[25] For example, Muriel R. Saville, "Language and the Disadvantaged," in Horn, *Reading for the Disadvantaged*, p. 124.

[26] Raven I. McDavid, Jr., "Language Characteristics of Specific Groups: Native Whites," in *Reading for the Disadvantaged*, p. 136.

[27] Labov, *et al.*, *A Study of the Non-Standard English of Negro and Puerto Rican Speakers in New York City*, II. 339, 343.

as skilful strategists. The familiar tactic of concealing the failure to keep one promise by making another is unlikely to succeed if the second promise is less plausible than the first; and promises to give everyone "the right to read" are notoriously hard to make good on, even for the linguist in his favorite role of universal expert.

The perusal of books on reading like those edited by Horn and Gunderson leaves one considerably sadder, therefore, but little wiser, than when he began. The inquisitive amateur soon accepts the experts' repeated assertion that little is known—and gets tired of their plea for more research and full employment:

After decades of debate and expenditures of millions of research dollars, the teaching of reading remains on questionable psychological and linguistic grounds.

When one looks at the research on reading over the past half century, the sheer volume of the literature and the welter of topics and findings (and lack of findings) is incredible. Yet, we are sore put to name even a few trustworthy generalizations or research based guides to educational practice.

Eleven widely different methods, represented by a variety of materials, were tested in some five hundred classrooms of first grade children during 1964–1965. Summary reports . . . revealed that by and large methods and materials were not the crucial elements in teaching first grade children to read.

At the present time we need research into every aspect of the education of the disadvantaged.[28]

If the amateur educationist is already an amateur linguist, he probably already knows Labov's opinion that "the major problem responsible for reading failure" in the ghettos "is a cultural conflict," not dialect interference.[29] He is thus surprised only by the source of Dr. Roger W. Shuy's quite unsurprising statement "that learning to read has little or nothing to do with a child's ability to handle standard English phonology."[30] A Southern amateur who has consorted with Australians, for example, or vacationed among Lake Country farmers, hardly needs linguistic enlightenment to know that the oddest speech is perfectly compatible with the reading of internationally acceptable English. And the mere happy innocent who cares nothing for either linguistics or pedagogy, if he has reflected at all on what he does when he reads, will know that reading is not just a "language art." The essential processes, even in reading parrotlike without understanding, are inference and judgment in what Kenneth S. Goodman has

[28] Richard L. Venezky, *et al.*, Harry Levin, and William D. Sheldon, in Gunderson, *Language & Reading*, pp. 37, 123, 266, 271.

[29] William Labov and Clarence Robins, "A Note on the Relation of Reading Failure to Peer-Group Status in Urban Ghettos," in *Language & Reading*, p. 214.

[30] "Some Language and Cultural Differences in a Theory of Reading," *Language & Reading*, p. 80.

called "a psycholinguistic guessing game";[31] and most of the linguistic entrepreneurs can claim no special competence in such matters.

SOMNIGRAPHY AND EUPHEMISM

To anyone with a normal dislike for solemn inanity, the contribution of linguistics to the teaching of reading is thus a less promising subject than the sleep-writing and professional euphemism which mark the work of the biloquialists and the inhabitants of schools of education. The name *biloquialism* is itself as fine an instance of verbal magic as one could want. Because nobody likes to admit that his speech makes other people laugh at him or despise him, *dialect* has become a dirty word. Hence its compounds and derivatives, like the older *bidialectalism*, must go too—the hope being, one imagines, that if the name goes the thing will vanish with it. For such wizardry, *doublespeak* is the perfect label.

Educationists make as much fuss over the euphemism *the disadvantaged* as the linguists do over *biloquialism*. They have not contented themselves with the one weasel-word, but have matched it with a number of others: *the culturally different, the linguistically different, the culturally deprived, the intellectually deprived, the culturally antagonized.*[32] It is a touch of genius that after choosing a word to obscure his meaning, a writer can then debate what he means by it. Thomas D. Horn concludes that anybody can be disadvantaged, even when he thinks he is in the catbird seat:

Any individual may be disadvantaged socially, economically, psychologically, and/or linguistically, depending upon the particular social milieu in which he is attempting to function at a given time. Indeed, he may be completely oblivious to his disadvantaged condition and perceive others in the group as being disadvantaged rather than himself.[33]

Horn's readers will not deny their intellectual deprivation.

Somnigraphy, the art of writing as if one were asleep, is as zealously cultivated by biloquialists and educationists as euphemism. Sleep-writing must be distinguished from New High Bureaucratian (NHB), which is grammatical and has a meaning but obscures it by jargon. At its best, somnigraphy is neither grammatical nor meaningful; but no sentence can qualify as somnigraphic unless either its meaning or its grammar is somehow deviant. The following statement approaches the degree of vacuity necessary to somnigraphy; but since its distinctive feature is pompous scientism, it is probably to be treated as NHB:

---

[31] "Reading: A Psycholinguistic Guessing Game," *Language & Reading*, pp. 107–119.

[32] Horn, *Reading for the Disadvantaged*, pp.: v, 11.

[33] *Reading for the Disadvantaged*, p. 2. Observe the opening for the educationist to decide who gets the works in school because he's disadvantaged without knowing it.

Commands or requests for action are essentially instructions from a person A to a person B to carry out some action X at a time T.

$$A \rightarrow B: X!/T$$

Somnigraphy in the pure state is more easily recognizable:

Illogical comparison: "The selection of informants in this study is more rigid than the original study."

Tautology rampant: "Before a nonconsonantal environment the presence of the cluster-final stop, for all practical purposes, is categorically present in SE."

Failure of agreement: "The difference between the Negro classes appear to be largely quantitative for monomorphemic clusters."

The dying fall: "That we see linguists, psychologists, sociologists, educators, and others exercising varying definitions of language and language behavior, is important to know."

Chaos and Old Night: "Much of the attention given to the sociocultural aspects of poverty can be seen in the kinds of causes and cures for poverty which are often linked as parts of an over-all *poverty cycle* (Figure 1)." [But neither the attention to poverty, nor the cures for it, can be found in the cycle itself.]

The *like/as* syndrome: "English, as most languages, has a variety of dialects."

Self-contradiction: "The nativist position carries with it the concept of a distinction between a child's linguistic knowledge and all of the varied facets and factors of his actual speaking and listening behaviors, one factor of which is the aforementioned knowledge." [That is, the child's knowledge both is and is not a part of his behavior.]

Scrambled metaphor: "In brief the strategy is to prepare the child for candidacy into the economic mainstream." [Sooner or later, we will read about the aridity of the mainstream culture—probably sooner.]

Fractured idiom: "Goodman (1965) and Bailey (1965), along with Stewart (esp. 1969), have all discussed the possibility of interference from the dialect on acquiring the ability to read." [And let no man interfere on their discussion.]

The unconscious absurd: ". . . both the linguists and sociologists . . . were relatively free from . . . cross-fertilization. . . ."

Lexical indiscretion: "As long as one operates in terms of languages and cultures conceived as isolates, internally discreet, ..."

Flatus: "Middle-class children emitted a larger number of . . . self-corrections than the lower-class children did."

The cancerous modifier: "Mrs. Golden's program, as with most of the teaching English as a second language to Negro nonstandard English speakers programs, relies on pattern practice. . . ." [Sounds like somebody needs it.]

Confusion of map with territory: "The rule for the absence of d occurs more frequently when d is followed by a consonant than when followed by a vowel."

The genteel thing: "To improve one's social acceptability to a middle-class society, working-class people should focus primarily on vocabulary development."

The intense inane: "Reading is a process of recognizing that printed words represent spoken words and is a part of the total language spectrum."

The shipwrecked question: "How do the separate and disparate experiences of individuals lead to a common acceptance of general meaning but which also permit differences of interpretation?" [God only knows.]

Circumblundering a meaning: "The educational world has generally thought of language as lexicon and it is not surprising that they would equate cultural adjustment to the words of the city. . . ."

The undefining definition: "By underlying structure here I mean that ability which even beginning readers have which enables them to avoid misreading via any other manner than by the phonological, and grammatical rules of their native language."

The arresting title: "Economic, Geographic, and Ethnic Breakdown of Disadvantaged Children"

Opposites reconciled: "One obstacle, lack of skill in the use of standard American English, has increasingly been recognized as a major contributing factor to the success of a child beginning his formal education."

WHY THE POWERS PAY

That exhibit, which could be enlarged at will, is neither cruel nor insolent nor joking. The insolence is that the perpetrators of such writing should set themselves up as linguists and teachers of standard English. The cruelty is that people who think and write so badly should be turned loose upon children. The level of simple competence in the use of words is simply low among biloquialists, and to the old-fashioned English professor who still believes that a man's sentences (not his dialect) are a good index to his intelligence, that fact demands an explanation.

The obvious answer is that governments and foundations have put up so much money for doublespeak that they have not been able to find good people to spend it; but that answer simply shifts the question to another level. Why do our rulers act like that? Why should they employ verbicides in the impossible and immoral pursuit of biloquialism? Well-meaning incompetence may characterize many biloquialists; but incompetence has no direction, follows no party line unless some other force is guiding—and the drift of biloquialism is too plain to be accidental. There must be, somewhere, an inhumanity that shapes its ends.

The explanation does not require that inhumanity should be reified in a body of conspirators or that the making of educational policy, at any level, should be viewed as the conscious, intelligent adaptation of public means to private ends. In their dealings with black people, most middle-class white linguists in the United States may be expected to act like most other middle-class whites. Their probable motivations include a real desire to do good, some hidden dislike, some fear, and the love of money and status. Foundation men, bureaucrats, and politicians may be expected to share those foibles; and precisely because the whole conglomerate is shaped and moved by the same forces, it cannot move beyond its limits.

The appeal of doublespeak is that it promises beneficent change without threat to existing power or privilege. If doublespeak were to succeed, the restive communities of the poor and ignorant would be tamed; for potential revolutionaries would be transformed into the subservient, scrambling, anxious underlings who constitute the lower middle class in a technological society. Their children, if there should be a next generation, would rise to be its linguists, its English teachers, and its petty bureaucrats; and doublespeak would be justified by Progress. If doublespeak should fail, as it must, large numbers of young blacks can still be assured that it was they who failed, and not their white superiors; and the blacks' presumed failure in not doing what they could not and should not do can be used against them as a psychological and political weapon.[34] In either event, the white Powers have nothing to lose by their exercise in cosmetology. Both their conscience and their supremacy will be clear.

THE FORM OF THE ARGUMENT

The essential argument for such an explanation should be stated formally enough to keep the issues plain. As a hypothetical syllogism, the argument would look like this:

Unless the biloquialists and their sponsors were misled by their presumed self-interest, they would not pursue the impossible and immoral end of doublespeak so vigorously—or defend themselves for doing it.

But they do pursue, etc.

Therefore they are misled. . . .

Less pedantically, nobody insists on trying to do what he can't and shouldn't unless there's something in it for him somewhere.

It is the consequent of the major premise that needs attention.

THE IMPOSSIBILITY OF DOUBLESPEAK

The impossibility of establishing doublespeak in the real world has already been argued: the necessary descriptions of standard and nonstandard dialects are nonexistent, and materials and methods of teaching are dubious

---

[34] See Wayne O'Neil, "The Politics of Bi-dialectalism," *College English* **33**(1972):433–38, from which I have borrowed the ingenious idea that educational failure might still be political success for the backers of doublespeak.

at best. It may be added here that competent teachers of doublespeak are a contradiction in terms. For tough young blacks, the worst possible teacher is a middle-class white female; and a middle-class black female may not be much better, since she is nearly as likely as her white counterpart to look down on her lower-class students. Such condescending culture-vendors have no chance whatever of neutralizing the influence of the world outside the classroom, a world where ghetto youngsters have few occasions to use such standard English as they may have learned and where, if they did use it, they might find the effort unrewarding. Their peers would blame them for trying to talk like white people, and they would hardly be compensated for such isolation by any real increase in "upward mobility." The black college graduate who makes less money than a white dropout is a sad familiar figure.

Teachers of standard English may be sure, then, of resistance from teen-age students in the ghettos, and unless they are more tactful than the biloquialists, they may be sure of resistance from black adults as well. On the issue of doublespeak the black community is undoubtedly divided. Blacks who have made it into the middle and upper classes, and many black parents, want to see young people make it too. They consider the ability to use "good English" a part of making it (though in reality good English is far less important to success on the job than a great many other qualifications). At the other extreme are the tough teen-agers, the adults who secretly or openly share their values, and some of the more militant community leaders; while in between there are probably a good many blacks of various ages for whom the white world's insistence on its standard English sets off an internal conflict between pride and self-hate.

But the black community is not at all divided in its opposition to doctrines of white supremacy, whether politely veiled or publicly announced. No black of any age is likely to be much pleased by condescension and the calm assumption of superiority:

First, there has been the general attitude, common even among some linguists, that nonstandard speech is less worthy of interest and study than varieties of speech with high prestige. . . . As this relates to the speech of Negroes, it has been reinforced by a commendable desire to emphasize the potential of the Negro to be identical to white Americans. . . .[35]

Even if it were possible to "stamp out" nonstandard English, changing the students' language behavior completely might be detrimental to their social well-being. They may need the nonstandard for social situations in which it is appropriate.[36]

More than the foreign-language student, more than the native speaker of Standard

[35] William A. Stewart, "Urban Negro Speech," in Aarons, Gordon, and Stewart, *Linguistic-Cultural Differences*, p. 51.
[36] Irwin Feigenbaum, "The Use of Nonstandard English in Teaching Standard," in Fasold and Shuy, *Teaching Standard English*, p. 89.

English, the second-dialect student needs to know his teacher considers him truly "worth revising."[37]

The neighbor-loving speech which ended with the last quotation was soon followed, understandably, by an angry outburst from a black auditor:

I am outraged and insulted by this meeting. . . . I would like to know why white people can determine for black people what is standard and what is nonstandard.

But two of the linguists present did not get the message—the plain message that it must no longer be whites only who "conduct the important affairs of the community." The first of them rebuked the young lady rudely, once in the meeting and once in a "subsequent written comment": he rapped about "rapping" on sociolinguists and using phony ploys "in political confrontations." The second, in a display of caucasian tact, congratulated her on expressing herself "in perfectly standard grammar."

If those who set themselves up as teachers of teachers behave like that, they may succeed in uniting the divided black community—uniting it against the advocates of doublespeak. Whatever the black community does want, it does not want to be led by the nose.

THE IMMORALITY OF DOUBLESPEAK

The biloquialist, of course, makes a great fuss about giving the child of the poor and ignorant, whether black or white, the choice of using or not using standard English. "He should be allowed to make that decision as he shapes his decisions in life."[38] But the biloquialist obviously sees himself as the determiner of the decisions which other people may decide, and the choice he deigns to give is really not much choice after all. In the name of social realism, he begins by imposing a false scheme of values, of which "upward mobility" is the highest; and he then sets out to make the child "upwardly mobile" by requiring hours of stultifying drill on arbitrary matters of usage, so that in situations where standard English is deemed appropriate the child may choose between "Ain't nobody gon' love you" and "Nobody is going to love you." *Appropriate* will be defined by the white world, which will also fix the punishment if the liberated doublespeaker prefers his own definition. Ain't nobody gon' love him if he does that.

The immorality of biloquialism is amply illustrated by such hypocrisy. Assuring the child that his speech is as good as anybody else's, publicly forswearing all attempts to eradicate it, and vigorously defending the individual's free choice, the biloquialist would actually force the speech and

---

[37] Virginia F. Allen, "A Second Dialect Is Not a Foreign Language," in Alatis, *Linguistics and the Teaching of Standard English*, p. 194.

[38] John C. Maxwell in "Riposte," *English Journal*, 59 (November, 1970), p. 1159.

values of the middle-class white world on children of every class and color. By *upward mobility* he means getting and spending more money, wasting more of the world's irreplaceable resources in unnecessary display, and turning one's back on family and friends who are unable or unwilling to join in that high enterprise. Every day, by his loud-voiced actions, the biloquialist would tell the child to build his life on that rotten foundation.

But *tell* is too mild a word: *force* is more accurate. Force is more accurate because the schoolchild would not have a choice between wasting his precious days (with the biloquialists) in the study of socially graded synonyms and (with intelligent teachers) learning something serious about himself and the world he lives in; and besides, when schooldays were over, the young double-speaker could not really choose between his vernacular and his imperfectly mastered standard English. In every serious transaction of an upwardly mobile life, the use of standard English would be enforced by the giving or withholding of the social and economic goodies which define upward mobility. The upwardly mobile doublespeaker would be expected to eradicate his vernacular except in some darkly secret areas of his private life, of which eventually he would learn to be ashamed; and his likely reward for such self-mutilation would be just enough mobility to get him stranded between the worlds of white and black. There he could happily reflect on the humanitarianism of the Great White Expert, who saves the oppressed from militancy and sends them in pursuit of money and status, which literature, philosophy, religion, and the millennial experience of mankind have exposed as unfit ends for human life. "That doesn't seem very humane from where I sit."[39]

ON NOT LOVING BIG BROTHER

But the present argument against biloquialism is not a militant argument (though biloquialists have called it one in the attempt to discredit it with a label which they think is frightening), and it is not primarily a humanitarian argument (though biloquialists have called it inhumane). Our new teachers of reading cannot read well enough to tell Mill from a militant. The argument here is the argument of an unashamed conservative individualist. With his own eyes the arguer has seen British working people, and chicanos, and black Americans humiliated by contempt for their language and twisted by their unhappy efforts to talk like their exploiters. An expert is no more needed to prove that such humiliation is damaging or such efforts an expense of spirit than a meteorologist is needed to warn of the dangers of urinating against the wind; but the weight of the argument rests mainly on the fact that if any man can be so shamed and bullied for so intimate a part of his own being as his language, then every man is fully subject to the unhampered tyrants of the

[39] *Loc. cit.* But I bet you guessed.

materialist majority. To resist the biloquialist is to resist Big Brother, and to resist him for oneself as well as others. Big Brother is not always white.

In all the variety of his disguises, Big Brother is very near at hand today. In one form he is Basil Bernstein, whose notions about restricted and elaborated codes (as they are interpreted or misinterpreted by Bernstein's American disciples) might vulgarly be taken as supporting an injunction to get the pickaninnies away from their black mammies; in another form he is the arrogant dogmatist Siegfried Engelmann, the amoral educational technologist with a big stick.

The biloquialist follows neither Engelmann nor Bernstein, but his own high-sounding talk should not be taken at face value, either. Doublespeak is not necessary to communication between users of different dialects, since speakers of nonstandard English generally have passive control of standard, if only through their exposure to television; the biloquialist himself assures us that no dialect is intrinsically better than any other; and his announced devotion to freedom of choice has already been exposed as phony, like his promise of social mobility through unnatural speech. When the biloquialist's guard is down, he too can talk the language of dialect eradication, which he officially abhors:

attempting to eliminate this kind of auxiliary deletion from the speech of inner-city Negro children would be a low-priority task.[40]

Behind the mandarin's jargon and self-praise lies the quiet assumption that it is his right and duty to run other people's lives.

The mandarin will go a long way to make other people see that his good is theirs, so that his values may prevail among the faceless multitude. As educator, his aims are not always educational, but may be as simple as keeping young people off the labor market by keeping them in school, though he tacitly admits that he has planned nothing to teach them there:

The problems of finding suitable programs will be complicated if, as educators anticipate, education is made compulsory for students until they reach the age of eighteen. Educators will be forced to adapt programs for the group of young people from sixteen to eighteen who under the present system have dropped out of school.[41]

Yet the mandarin's ends, he thinks, justify almost any means.

Intelligence and verbal skills within the culture of the street is prized just as highly as it is within the school: but the use of such skills is more often to manipulate and control other people than to convey information to them. Of course it is the school's

[40] Fasold and Wolfram, "Some Linguistic Features of Negro Dialect," in Fasold and Shuy, *Teaching Standard English*, p. 80.

[41] Robert J. Havighurst, "Social Backgrounds: Their Impact on Schoolchildren," in Horn, *Reading for the Disadvantaged*, p. 12.

task to emphasize the value of language in cognitive purposes. But in order to motivate adolescent and preadolescent children to learn standard English, it would be wise to emphasize its value for handling social situations, avoiding conflict (or provoking conflict when desired), for influencing and controlling other people.[42]

Between 5 and 10 per cent of the 62,000 schoolchildren in this city in the American midlands are taking "behavior modification" drugs prescribed by local doctors to improve classroom deportment and increase learning potential. The children being given the drugs have been identified by their teachers as "hyperactive" and unmanageable to the point of disrupting regular classroom activity.[43]

Bettye M. Caldwell . . . has proposed "educationally oriented day care for culturally deprived children between six months and three years of age." The children are returned home each evening to "maintain primary emotional relationships with their own families," but during the day they are removed to "hopefully prevent the deceleration in rate of development which seems to occur in many deprived children around the age of two to three years."[44]

The Defense Department has been quietly effective in educating some of the casualties of our present public schools. It is hereby suggested that they now go into the business of repairing hundreds of thousands of these human casualties with affirmation rather than apology. Schools for adolescent dropouts or educational rejects could be set up by the Defense Department adjacent to camps—but not necessarily as an integral part of the military. If this is necessary, it should not block the attainment of the goal of rescuing as many of these young people as possible.[45]

In June the Camden (N.J.) Board of Education hired *Radio Corporation of America* to reorganize its entire school system. According to *Education Summary* (July 17, 1970), the management contract for the first year of the USOE pilot project requires that RCA "be responsible for identifying Camden's educational needs; specifying priorities; organizing demonstration projects; training school personnel for functions they can't perform adequately now; organizing the system on a cost-effectiveness basis; and arranging for objective valuation of results."[46]

[42] William Labov, "The Non-Standard Vernacular of the Negro Community: Some Practical Suggestions," ED 016 947, p. 10.

[43] Robert M. Maynard, "Children Controlled by Drugs," dispatch from Omaha to *The Washington Post*, in *The Austin American*, June 29, 1970, p. 1. Yet they jail the kids for smoking pot.

[44] Labov, "The Logic of Nonstandard English," reprinted on pp. 319–54 above. Labov, who here as usual is much above his fellow biloquialists, is criticizing Bettye M. Caldwell's article "What Is the Optimal Learning Environment for the Young Child?" in the *American Journal of Orthopsychiatry*, 37 (1967), pp. 8–21. *Ortho-* is a bit optimistic when the proposal is to disrupt the families of mothers whom Bettye M. Caldwell has judged inadequate.

[45] Kenneth B. Clark, quoted by George H. Henry in reviewing Alvin C. Eurich's *High School 1980* in the *English Journal*, 59 (1970), p. 1165. Henry's review is a splendid denunciation of manipulators inside and outside the NCTE.

[46] Edmund J. Farrell, "Industry and the Schools," NCTE *Council-Grams*, 31 (Special Issue for November, 1970), pp. 1–3. Farrell takes a strong stand against the takeover by industry—with the natural consequence that Robert F. Hogan, Executive Secretary of the

There is not much doubt that the use of such means will corrupt whatever end is said to justify them. It is not, for example, a superabundance of new teachers which now keeps them from finding jobs, but the government's decision to pay for war in Viet Nam and not for education. To solve this financial problem, school boards are encouraged to choose education on the cheap. When they make their bargains with the big corporations, the corporations get direct control both of education and of whatever money the school boards do spend. The corporations can thus keep up their profits; teachers are made subservient automatons; and the country is delivered from the danger that either teachers or students might occasionally think. Disrupted families, drugged students, schools run by business or the military—these are the typical products of Big Brother's machinations.

The role of the biloquialist in our educational skin flick is not outstanding: he is not a madam, just a working girl. His commitment, however, to the corrupt values of a corrupt society makes him quite at house with the other manipulators, and his particular manipulations have their special dangers because a standard language can be made a dangerous weapon in class warfare.

Standard English in the United States is a principal means of preserving the existing power structure, for it builds the system of class distinctions into the most inward reaches of each child's humanity: the language whose mastery makes the child human makes him also a member of a social class. Even rebellion demands a kind of allegiance to the class system, because effective rebellion, as the world goes now, requires the use of the standard language, and the rebel is not likely to master the standard language without absorbing some of the prejudice that it embodies. In the United States, the child "knows his place" before he knows he knows it, and the rebellious adult is either co-opted into the ruling class or has to fight to get a hearing. Biloquialism makes capital of this situation.

Big Brother and his flunkies are in control now; there is no doubt of that. But they have not won the last battle as long as resistance is possible, and resistance is possible until Big Brother makes us love him—if he can. If resistance saves nothing else, it saves the manhood of the unbrainwashed resister. The conservative individualist opposes biloquialism just because he does believe in individuality, to which liberty is prerequisite. "Tell the English," a bad poem says, "that man is a spirit." He is; and he does not live by beer alone; and the *radix malorum* is the businessman's morality of "getting ahead," which the biloquialist espouses when he argues that "right

Council, warns readers to "keep in mind that the point of view is Mr. Farrell's, not a reflection of Council policy or position." When George Henry called it likely "that English will find itself taken over by the USO—Foundation—Big Business—Pentagon Axis," he also said that the appeasing executives of the Council complain only mildly of such barbarian invasions, "because by virtue of being high in the Council one is eligible for a place in the Axis" (Henry, *op. cit.*, pp. 1168–69). But unlike RCA, Henry is not an objective evaluator.

now, tomorrow, the youngster needs tools to 'make it' in the larger world."[47]

Both physically and spiritually, *that* "larger world" is unfit for human habitation.

WHAT TO DO

The biloquialist's favorite counterpunch, when he is backed into a corner, is the question "If not biloquialism, what?" and he pretends, if his critic does not spin out a detailed scheme for curing all the ills of education, that in the absence of such a scheme doublespeak remains the best available policy for English teachers. The pretense is foolish, like doublespeak itself. Whatever English teachers ought to do, they ought not to follow the biloquialist, and the mere establishment of that fact is a positive contribution. To know what's not good is part of knowing what is.

The cornered biloquialist will often make his question more specific. It's all very well, he will concede, to expose linguistic prejudice as an instrument of repression and to work for social justice, though he himself may not be notably active in either cause; but in the meantime, he asks, what will become of students who don't learn standard English?

The beginning of a sufficient reply is that the advocate of doublespeak must answer the question too, since there are probably more biloquialists than doublespeakers whom they have trained. In the foreseeable future there will always be distinctions in speech between leaders and followers, between workers at different jobs, residents of different areas. And in a healthy society there would be no great harm in that. Millions of people in this country today do not speak standard English, and millions of them, if they are white, have very good incomes. But in job hunting in America, pigmentation is more important than pronunciation.

There is not, moreover, and there never has been, a serious proposal that standard English should not be taught at all, if for no other reason than because its teaching is inevitable. Most teachers of English speak it (or try to speak it); most books are written in it (somnigraphy being sadly typical); and since every child, if it is possible, should learn to read, schoolchildren will see and hear standard English in the schools as they also see and hear it on TV. Inevitably, their own linguistic competence will be affected.

The effect will be best if teachers consciously recognize the frustrations and contradictions which life in a sick world imposes on them. Because our ruling class is unfit to rule, our standard language lacks authority; and because our society has been corrupted by the profit seeking of technology run wild, an honest teacher cannot exercise his normal function of transmitting to the young the knowledge and values of their elders. In fact, the time may come, and soon come, when an honest teacher can't keep his honesty

[47] Right again: John C. Maxwell, *EJ*, 59 (1970), p. 1159.

and keep teaching. At that point, he must make his choice—and take the consequences. So long, however, as he stays in the classroom, he must do his imperfect best while recognizing its imperfection, and must find in that effort itself his escape from alienation.

Specifically, and without pretense:

1. We English teachers must have—and teach—some higher ambition than to "get ahead." We have the whole body of the world's best thought to draw on. The daringly old-fashioned amongst us might even recommend the Ten Commandments.

2. We should do all we can to decentralize power, to demand for ourselves and for other common men some voice in shaping our own lives. Reason enough to say so is the truism that men are not men unless they are free; but if the practical must have practical reasons, we all can see that in education as in everything else, conditions vary so much from state to state, from city to city, from city to country, from neighborhood to neighborhood, that no one policy for the whole nation can possibly work. Decisions about our teaching must *not* be passed down, as they now are, from a tired little mediocre in-group, who in the best of circumstances are so involved in the operation of the professional machinery that they can't see beyond its operation. A useful rule of thumb might be to never trust a "leader in the profession."

3. As politically active citizens, we must do whatever we can to end the social isolation of "substandard speakers," so that differences in speech, if they do not disappear of themselves, will lose their stigmatizing quality.[48]

4. As English teachers we should teach our students (and if necessary, our colleagues) how society uses language as its most insidious means of control, how we are led to judge others—and ourselves—by criteria which have no real bearing on actual worth. We must stigmatize people who use dialects as stigmatizing; and if that means that we as correctness-mongers get blasted too, then we deserve it.[49]

---

[48] For such suggestions I have been told both that I believe that English teachers can change the world by political action, perhaps by revolution, and at the same time (because I oppose biloquialism), that I advocate "do-nothingness." Though I hope I have more awareness of human tragedy than to believe that the NCTE, or RCA, or even an Educational Laboratory can abolish pain, I would certainly not teach English if I did not believe that to some small extent English teachers indeed can change the world. If I did not believe that English teachers can act politically for good, by parity of reasoning I would not bother to attack the evil politics of doublespeak. On the subject of revolution, I wrote in the essay which has been criticized as perhaps inciting to revolt that "the only revolution we are likely to see is the continued subversion, by the dominant white businessman, of the political and religious principles on which the nation was founded" (*EJ*, 58:1312). I leave it to the objecting and objectionable biloquialist to reconcile the conflicting charges of do-nothingism and political activism, but I do resent the suggestion that I consider English teachers brave enough to start a revolution. I have never entertained such a false and subversive idea in my life.

[49] This suggestion has nothing to do with the self-seeking proposal by foolish linguists that the English language should be made the center of the English curriculum. I would

5. We should teach ourselves and our white students something about the lives and language of black people. For communication between dialects, receptive control is what matters. In the United States, most black children are already likely to understand most kinds of English that they hear from whites. Presumably white people have the intelligence to learn to understand the blacks. The Center for Applied Linguistics may even be capable of learning that white ignorance is a bigger obstacle to social justice than Black English is.

6. In teaching our students to read and write, our aim should be to educate them, to open and enrich their minds, not to make them into usefully interchangeable parts in the materialists' insane machine. We should know and respect our children's language as we demand that they know and respect our own. And we should make no harsh, head-on attempt to *change* their language, to make them speak and write like us. If they value our world and what it offers, then they will take the initiative in change, and we can cautiously help them. But we must stop acting as the watchdogs of middle-class correctness and start barking at somnigraphy.

7. As teachers and as citizens, we must defend the freedom of inquiry and the freedom of expression. Neither is absolute, and it is often hard to strike a balance between the demands of the society that pays us and the intellectual duties of our calling. It is clear, however, that subservience to government and indifference to social need will alike corrupt inquirer and inquiry and thus endanger the freedoms that no one else will cherish if we don't. When we allow our choice of studies to be governed by government subsidy, we have committed ourselves to the ends of the subsidizers. When pure curiosity guides us, we tacitly assert that the satisfaction of that curiosity is more important than any other purpose that our research might serve. Along both roads we are likely to meet the amoral intellectual, whether for hire or self-employed. The prime contention of this indirect review is that the biloquialist, by his acquiescence in the abuse of standard English as a weapon, forfeits some part of the respect which otherwise would be inspired by achievements which are sometimes brilliant, like Labov's. For despite the politician's scholar who says that scholarship is politicized when scholars question his privy politics, scholars *are* teachers, and scholar-teachers citizens.

STUDY QUESTIONS

1. What would successful doublespeaking consist of? Can you think of reasons (other than lack of teaching materials) to explain why linguists like Labov should find *no* speakers "who gained good control of a standard language,

---

indeed teach prospective teachers of English in the schools a good deal more about their language than they are usually taught now: but only a biloquialist would believe—or pretend to believe—that to suggest a college curriculum in English for prospective English teachers is to suggest the same curriculum for every schoolchild. A "language-centered curriculum" for the schools would be a disaster.

and still retained control of the nonstandard vernacular?" Does this statement mean that a speaker whose native vernacular is a nonstandard dialect is incapable of learning standard English? Would Sledd maintain such a position?

2. In the first essay of this anthology (p. 17) it is reported that in many places in the world: "It is quite normal for members of a language community which has a standard language to continue to use both the native and the learnt (standard) dialect in different situations throughout their lives." It is also reported on the same page that when a speaker learns a second dialect: "He generally speaks it with 'an accent': that is, with phonetic features of his native dialect. ... Most speakers, learning the standard language of their community, continue to speak with the phonetics of their native dialect, and there is usually no loss in intelligibility." Do these reports describe double-speak? If the aim of bidialectalism is to erase socially proscribed features, or to teach nonstandard speakers to avoid using such features in certain circumstances, will an accented standard serve? Do the reports contradict Sledd's assertion that doublespeak is an impossibility?

3. Why and how might doublespeak lead to psychological damage? Does it make a difference whether the need for alternate speech forms is discovered by a child or forced on him in the classroom? How would you react if on moving to a new community you found yourself excluded from certain groups or jobs by your speech? Will a person's reactions in such situations depend on his personality and beliefs?

4. Why does Sledd prefer the term *doublespeak* to the term *biloquialism?* Why does he consider not only the advocates of biloquialism but also the agencies that support them? Is such consideration justified or is it merely motive hunting or *ad hominem?* Does Sledd feel that political motives do or should underlie all scholarship? Why does he identify his own political and philosophical orientation?

5. Sledd charges (p. 372) that the doctrine of bidialectalism is predicated on preserving the status quo. Do you agree? If so, why should that be the case?

6. Why does Sledd assert that doublespeak is immoral? Why and in what ways are moral and ethical questions involved in the issue of how to teach standard English? Are they relevant?

7. Sledd makes harsh judgments about writing done by several bidialectalists. What are the bases of his judgments? How does one apply the principle "that a man's sentences (not his dialect) are a good index to his intelligence"? Would Sledd want to give a prospective teacher a method for making such judgments?

8. What evidence could you gather, from preceding essays in this collection and elsewhere, to support the following of Sledd's assertions:
   a. ". . . society uses language as its most insidious means of control . . . we are led to judge others—and ourselves—by criteria which have no real bearing on actual worth."
   b. "In the United States, most black children are already likely to understand most kinds of English that they hear from whites."
   c. "If [students] value our world and what it offers, then they will take the initiative in change, and we can cautiously help them."

9. What can an English teacher do to accomplish the third goal stated by Sledd on p. 380?

10. In an attack on Sledd's position, Melvin J. Hoffman asks: "What does the student of the language-permissive teacher have to look forward to while discrimination continues?"[a] Reread Sledd's seven imperatives for English teachers (pp. 380–81) and suggest how he might answer Hoffman's question.

11. Hoffman goes on to make observations which he "invites the reader to consider and to be on the alert for:

> most opponents of bidialectalism have not only a passable command of some regional standard as well as control of standard written English. I wonder whether the opponents of bidialectalism permit their own children to attend schools taught by teachers who do not believe in teaching standard English. Further, why don't the opponents of bidialectalism permit their own children to attend schools taught by teachers who do not believe in teaching standard English. Further, why don't the opponents of bidialectalism write their articles in the colloquial language of their dialect area if personality and content—not form—are to be the important considerations of the future?"[b]

Comment on Hoffman's damned-if-they-do/damned-if-they-don't view of his opponents' decision about the schooling of their children. Does Sledd believe that "teachers who do not believe in teaching Standard English" exist? that such teachers ought to exist? What does Hoffman mean by "personality" in his final question? Why should he expect Sledd to write "in the colloquial language of his dialect area"? Would writing in such language be more consistent with Sledd's principles than the language he actually uses?

[a] Melvin J. Hoffman, "Bidialectalism Is Not the Linguistics of White Supremacy: Sense versus Sensibilities," *The English Record* (New York State English Council), **21**(1971):99. Hoffman is responding to Sledd's "Bi-Dialectalism: The Linguistics of White Supremacy," *English Journal,* **58**(1969):1307–15, 1329.

[b] *Ibid.,* p. 100.

WRITE OFF VERSUS WRITE ON:
DIALECTS AND THE TEACHING OF COMPOSITION
Richard W. Bailey

Traditionally, historically, and by current expectation, the English teacher is primarily a teacher of language use. No matter that he prefers and is better prepared by his university training to teach literature than composition, his students and their parents, his colleagues from other fields, his administrators, and his critics all expect the English teacher to teach students how to write. As a writing teacher, he must make daily decisions that involve the issues raised by the essays in this book: Should he intervene in the natural process of language acquisition? How direct and vigorous should any intervention be? Among the language problems he encounters, which are his responsibility and which suggest referral to a reading specialist or speech therapist? Ought he to teach the prestige dialect to those who do not command it? What language matters should be brought to the whole class and which taken up in individual conferences? What comments should he make on students' papers? What standards should he apply in making these marks?

When the door to the corridor closes, the teacher must be ready to translate large issues into daily lessons. But the door cannot close out the echoes of those issues, and daily routine must be informed by what we know about language learning and about the personal and social significance of language variation. In the essay that follows, Bailey begins to deal with these questions by arguing that the teacher must establish a set of priorities for action. The practices of the past have produced some visible successes and many invisible failures; only by putting fluency ahead of correctness, linguistic self-confidence before linguistic self-consciousness, can the English teacher begin to respond to the expectations of a society dedicated to universal education.

Through our use of language, we unconsciously assert who we are and what group we belong to. Since language betrays both our origins and aspirations —whether or not we are aware of it—we are likely to be troubled when some respected person attempts to improve our language behavior. Good teachers are always sensitive to these feelings of ours, for, more than others, they know something of the function that language plays, not only in communication, but in our attempts to show solidarity with others in society. To establish a set of priorities for the teaching of composition, teachers need

384

both this sensitivity and a particularly detailed understanding of the intellectual and social background that affects language attitudes and language behavior.

Linguists agree that there are no homogeneous linguistic communities, and our everyday experience of recognizing a friend by his voice on the telephone reminds us of the idiosyncracies of speech. These individual characteristics, of course, are also accompanied by the subtle traits that mark regional and social differences and indicate the speaker's role in society. No one is wholly ignorant of the social meaning that is attached to these traits, and any stable community soon builds up a common body of folk wisdom about the salient characteristics of language variation. In *Down and Out in Paris and London*, Orwell reports that his disguise at a tramp was usually unsuccessful with those in authority unless he took particular pains to disguise the dialect features that he had acquired at Eton. When the Apostles tried to hide themselves among the poor in Jerusalem, similarly subtle variations gave them away: "Surely thou art one of them," said the bystanders to Peter, "for thy speech bewrayeth thee" (Matt. 26:73). Peter denied the accusation, but it was clear from his rustic Galilean speech that he didn't belong in the capital. Like Orwell, he was exposed by his language, as is every speaker in the linguistic community.

The experienced dialectologist can identify regional and social varieties of English very precisely, but everyone in America has doubtless been the victim or beneficiary of our folklore about linguistic differences. So subtle and pervasive is this set of beliefs that untrained listeners can make remarkably accurate judgments about the race and class origin of a speaker from their own region when they are presented with as little as ten seconds of speech randomly selected from a tape recording. Even the exceptional cases support the proposition that class, aspirations, and dialect are closely connected. The butler in fiction is usually represented as speaking more elegantly than his wealthy employers; those who have emerged from humble origins often betray their admiration for the supposed prestige dialect by going that dialect one better through hypercorrection. Middle-class speakers who adopt a conscious bohemianism or identify themselves with the proletariat may imitate the characteristics of language that society associates with these roles, but they will seldom entirely obliterate the traits that have no social meaning but just as surely indicate the speaker's origins.

In my own case, the elite suburb of Detroit in which I grew up thrived on a certain smugness about its place in American life. My eleventh-grade class, I recall, was told of its good fortune because—unlike others—no one in the room spoke a "dialect." The teacher's celebration of our language was, after all, only confirmation of what we knew already from years of perfunctory attention to usage exercises. We could nearly always fill the blank with the "correct" verb form or pronoun from our own speech habits and could therefore ignore the general principle to which others would have to appeal in such circumstances. The rules and exercises, we believed, were designed to aid the unfortunate "dialect" speaker in altering his speech to make it conform to our own.

Later on, in a New England college, I was shocked out of this pharisaical complacency by being told that I would have to accept the ministrations of a speech correctionist if I wished to pass a course in public speaking. My "Midwestern" dialect, the teacher said, would distract listeners from what I had to say. Because of a partial assimilation of vowels with adjacent nasal consonants, I found myself classed with speakers of a despised dialect rather than being considered a paragon of American English. Should my natural pronunciation of words like *man, hung,* or *lamb* emerge in polite society, I was invited to believe that ostracism would inevitably follow. This advice had a briefly deleterious effect on my fluency in the class. Had the teacher's rejection of my speech been reinforced by other circumstances, his prophecy would certainly have been self-fulfilling. As Rosenthal and Jacobson show so vividly in their *Pygmalion in the Classroom*, teachers can promote failure by their prediction of it; in the case of language, sensitizing students to errors leads to constant self-monitoring to avoid socially stigmatized forms. Following almost inexorably from self-monitoring is a sense of uncertainty, and hence impaired fluency and a disruptive linguistic self-consciousness. Social anxiety and linguistic insecurity—as Labov shows in his analysis of attitudes toward New York speech reprinted on pp. 274–91— go hand in hand, reflecting more than any other single factor in the social matrix the depth and ubiquity of class consciousness in American life. Lessons in linguistic etiquette regularly administered to children combine with other factors to produce the "write-offs" of our society.

Every English teacher has a tale about the ritual linguistic self-deprecation that casual acquaintances go through on discovering his profession: "They fle from me that sometyme did me seke." English teachers are usually treated as the heirophants who have been admitted to the inner temple where "correctness" dwells, for Americans typically regard good English as an ideal towards which all strive but to which no one attains. We have, as Donald J. Lloyd has observed, a "national mania for correctness," and only the old who have grown indifferent to rank and status appear to be immune from it. Even representatives of the counterculture who vilify the striving patterns of American life seldom make an easy peace with the linguistic status system. Unlike some other language communities, America has no aristocratic or metropolitan reference group speaking a standard dialect against which the national language can be measured, even though it has often yearned for one. "It is an important object in this country," wrote Noah Webster in 1843, "to have a uniform national language, to which all foreigners settling in this country should conform."[1] Since America has never had such a uniform national language, it has imagined one into existence

---

[1] Quoted by George Philip Krapp, *The English Language in America* (New York, [1925] 1966), Vol. 1, p. 17.

in the name of correctness. This presumption of a national standard has had an important impact on American attitudes toward language by reinforcing the supposed connection between linguistic variation and social status, between being a "real American" and a "foreigner."

Work on American dialects has exploded the belief that elite varieties reflect a uniform "general American" that covers the language of high-status speakers outside New England and the South. That such a belief can still persist reflects the presumptions inherent in a print culture where common writing conventions are divorced from habits of speech. Extensive variations enable dialectologists to pinpoint differences that distinguish versions of "middle-class English" across the country, but the national folklore about this dialect gives no social salience to the differences that do exist. My own failure to differentiate *Mary, merry*, and *marry* has no social value but merely reflects my origins in the North Central states. Likewise my contrast of [hw] and [w] in a pair like *which* and *witch* gives no particular prestige. Rhyming *roof* and *root* with *foot* is beginning to take a slightly old-fashioned connotation in my home state, but these pronunciations have not yet become fully identified with a rustic or nonelite dialect. These, and features like them, simply constitute aspects of variation within the elite dialect. The same is true of some of the vocabulary that is characteristic of my speech. What I would call *eaves troughs* and *shades* are known as *gutters* and *blinds* to speakers of backgrounds similar to mine in other parts of the country. My regular use of *expressway, lawn extension*, and *submarine* is distinctive of my dialect, but carries no implications of status among those who would use *freeway, turnpike*, or *thruway* for the first, *parking strip, tree lawn, berm*, or *tree belt* for the second, and *grinder, hoagy* or *hero* for the third. Regional standards vary somewhat less often in matters of morphology and syntax, but the use of *dove* as the preterit of *dive* is regular in the high-status dialects of the North Central states despite some attention given to it in usage handbooks and in classrooms. Dialectologists have been able to record this list of socially innocuous variations within regional dialect areas; the purists who concern themselves with the preservation of an elite standard pay little attention to them.

"No known language," wrote Edward Sapir, "has ever been known to resist the tendency to split up into dialects, any one of which may in the long run assume the status of an independent language."[2] Nevertheless, the rate at which changes take place may be inhibited or enhanced by social factors within the language community. Literacy and the growth of a standardized written language carry with them a sense of social solidarity that may eventually, as in the case of modern Germany and Italy, result in a strong sense of nationhood despite other historical factors that emphasize smaller divisions of the linguistic community. Allegiance to new political systems

---

[2] "Dialect" (1931), reprinted in *English Linguistics: A Introductory Reader*, Harold Hungerford, Jay Robinson, and James Sledd, eds. (Glenview, Ill., 1970), p. 169.

may be reflected in the conception of a "national uniform language" even when dialect and language differences have long divided a country; it is therefore no accident that the Soviet regime modified the conventions of written Russian to reflect "modern" conditions and Nazi doctrine was accompanied by a return to what had become an archaic alphabet for German. Although major language "reforms" are nearly impossible to impose on a disparate population, small changes can be introduced and existing variations can be given a new significance in community attitudes about language.

In America, the widespread reverence for the printed word and the conservative influence of English teaching in the schools have slowed the rate of linguistic change, but there is no reason to suppose that American English will be an exception to the principle stated by Sapir. Despite the conservative impulse that lies behind the teaching of English usage in the schools, certain particulars can be attributed directly to the work of generations of teachers.

Constant classroom attention to the use of objective case pronouns in subject position—*Me and him came*—is apparently responsible for the widespread feeling that the nominative case carries with it a more prestigous social meaning. Thus many speakers of undoubtedly high status can be heard to use the nominative case pronouns in almost every possible circumstance. Though *He gave the money to I* is unlikely, it is no longer strange to hear sentences on the model of *He gave the money to John and I* where something intervenes between the verb and the pronominalized object. The generalization of such forms is by no means unusual in the history of the language, and many more examples might be mentioned. Contrived pseudo-classical plurals have acquired a similar value, and the plurals of *appendix* and *basis* serve as "elegant" models for words with no history of such a plural; for example, one can hear *atlas* pluralized to *atlasēs* [ǽtləsìz], *complex* to *complexēs*, and *prospectus* to *prospectusēs*.[3] Likewise the pronunciation of *Tuesday*, *duty*, and *new* has in the interior North been influenced away from the vowel sound of *sue* toward that of *beauty* in response to a belief in the superiority of those regional standards containing that pronunciation. Hence *blue*, *flu*, and *true* are pronounced in a new way as speakers reject the monophthong [u] for a novel prestige form, the diphthong [ju]. Such developments— labeled *elegantisms* or *hyperurbanisms* by linguists—have exactly the opposite effect to that intended by the teachers who perhaps unconsciously promulgate them, for they result in innovations instead of "preserving the purity of the language."[4]

[3] Even the traditionally irregular plurals in this pattern may be made more elegant, for example in *basises* [bésəsìz].

[4] As C.-J. Bailey points out in his essay in Part II of this collection, innovations of this sort are particularly likely to occur in the speech of the second highest social class. Linguists who label such changes "elegantisms" or "hyperurbanisms" generally reveal their contempt for what they regard as parvenu dialects, a tendency that fuels resentment by amateur critics. In fact, linguists tend to regard socially despised dialects with enthusiasm and

Features that have drawn the wrath of arbiters of usage hardly need mentioning to anyone who has experienced American schooling. Although the work of the "usage movement" of the 1930s greatly reduced the abuses of teaching "good English," some schoolbooks still slander items that have long been typical of elite varieties of American English: rhyming *vase* with *base* is considered somehow shoddy and the so-called metathesis of the first syllable of *proportion* is regarded as inexact. The complexities of *lie* and *lay*, *sit* and *set*, still occupy dreary hours for nearly all American students; one teacher tells me that he advises his students to deal with such exercises by testing which of the versions offered sounds most natural and then picking the other one. Unreflecting prejudice against "split infinitives" and the passive voice—both naturally used by nearly all established writers—continues to work against the development of naturalness and fluency that are at least ostensibly the goals of instruction in one's native language. The effect of this purifying effort, unfortunately, is almost wholly negative because it encourages the perpetuation of linguistic prejudice and a concern for what is correct rather than what is effective language.

In the course of his study of the social stratification of English in New York City, William Labov devised a "linguistic insecurity test" by which he could measure the extent to which speakers acknowledge a standard of correctness distinct from their own behavior.[5] This test was administered by presenting the informant with a list of words known to have two widely heard pronunciations. Labov asked the subjects to listen to a pronunciation of each variant and to indicate which one they used themselves. Then he asked them to decide which pronunciation they believed to be correct. The test was not concerned with the accuracy of the informant's own self-monitoring or his awareness of the actual social status of the two variants. Only the number of instances where the informant indicated a disparity between his own usage and that of the standard was used in formulating an index of linguistic insecurity. Where an informant indicated a considerable number of such disparities, other factors usually emerged in the interview that indicated a hankering after a "better" variety of English and a dissatisfaction with his own speech. Not surprisingly, Labov found that those who identified the greatest number of disparities between their own behavior and "correctness" were those most insecure about their status. In particular, the lower-middle-class informants had the highest number of disparities and the greatest concern for upward mobility. But even more important, Labov found few informants who identified themselves as being consistently in harmony with what they supposed to be correct.

More specialized studies undertaken by students in my class in American

---

delight (for their systematic consistency), and the language of those who do the despising with disdain.

[5] An account of Labov's results will be found in *The Social Stratification of English in New York City*, pp. 474–79.

English reveal some of the further dimensions of American linguistic insecurity. One student discovered that Labov's test (adapted slightly to take in pronunciation variants current in the North Central states) gave a clear indication of status feelings in a wealthy Detroit suburb. Newcomers who had only recently moved from the inner city were found to acknowledge a disparity between their own language behavior and "correctness" twice as often as those who had lived in the suburb for ten years or more. Other devices used to elicit feelings about social status in the interview confirmed the connection that Labov identified between aspirations, self-assuredness, and language.

Another study examined elementary and high school students in a small town on the periphery of the Detroit metropolitan area. At the sixth-grade level, girls were found to have an index value slightly lower than that of boys, suggesting that the girls felt themselves to be in greater harmony with the external standard. By the twelfth grade, however, the situation had reversed itself. The girls proved to be twice as insecure about their own language as the boys, suggesting that the socialization process imposed on women encourages linguistic insecurity along with other uncertainties about the proper role for educated women in American life. Both the suburban study and Labov's work in New York support the hypothesis that American women are even more likely than men to be daunted by an external standard of correctness and to concern themselves with linguistic etiquette.

This research further suggests that high linguistic insecurity accompanies an individual's awareness of himself as remote from the sources of power and authority. Political activists from both right and left were studied and the results support this view, as did an examination of linguistic insecurity among black and white students in a teacher-preparation program. But even those with the most apparent external justification for a belief in their own access to power and authority rarely proved to be thoroughly satisfied with their own grasp of the standard of correctness. It is worth asking, therefore, where Americans look for the sources of this external authority.

The most frequently acknowledged source for settling disputes about correct English is "the dictionary," and America is better supplied with inexpensive and up-to-date dictionaries than any other linguistic community in the world. After the Webster-Worcester dictionary war of the nineteenth century, every frontier cabin that had at least two books was supplied with a dictionary, and these stout volumes were ruthlessly promoted to share with the other household book—the Bible—the status of revealed truth. Courtesy books before and after Emily Post regularly include a section devoted to stigmatized expressions that would not be allowed in polite society. The [r] that threatened to disappear from *horse* was resolutely sustained by these books, whereas the shift in the final sound in present participles from [ŋ] to [n] was stoutly resisted, even though it had been a trait of aristocratic speech in eighteenth-century English. Vocabulary, of course, came in for the most vigorous efforts at reform: genteel society was urged to eschew *leg, cock, belly* in favor of *limb, rooster, stomach*. The familiar list of despised forms found in schoolbooks was taken over from earlier writers and expanded to include the vilification of *ain't, we was,* multiple negation and other traits that had not been stigmatized by earlier generations of English speakers. Nineteenth-century dictionaries did not establish the American need for a linguistic authority, but they and their descendants have perpetuated the original motive and nurtured it to the point where lexicography has become one of the most profitable—and, to judge by recent examples, least scrupulous —divisions of American publishing.

Dictionaries, courtesy books, and usage lists do not, of course, act as the first line of authority for contemporary speakers, even though they may be consulted in the relatively rare instance when disputes arise. More important for most cases of pronunciation, at least, is the appeal to the written language. Once again the nineteenth-century background provides an instructive example. The bestseller of the century, Webster's *Elementary Spelling Book*, urged that each syllable in a word be given its full value, despite the model of contemporary speakers of high status who pronounced "secretary" with three syllables instead of four and regularly reduced the unstressed vowels of polysyllables to [ə]. Although not every one of the pronunciations that Webster and his imitators recommended is still current, the tremendous popularity of these books gave rise to an admiration for the virtues of spelling as a guide that is not matched in other parts of the English-speaking world.

Once again the whipsaw effect of the motives toward naturalness, on the one hand, and elegance, on the other, came into play. The heritage of "letter-perfect" pronunciation results in the widespread belief that in the matter of syllables, more is better. Hence the pronunciation of *athlete* with three syllables and the general enthusiasm for the sesquipedalian: *commentate* and *administrate* for example, instead of the plainer *comment* and *administer*. The current revival of [l] in *calm* and *almond* is another manifestation of the American reverence for the written word, and there is apparently a growing belief that one should pronounce [t] in *often* and [r] in *February* despite the efforts of the compilers of usage handbooks to maintain their status as "silent letters."

Following the importance of the dictionary and the printed word as an *acknowledged* source of authority is the example of the reference group admired by the speaker. For most adolescents, the model of desirable language is seldom the schoolteacher or the parent but the peer group to which he aspires or belongs. Intervention in this pattern, as every teacher knows, is often difficult and dangerous, particularly where there is a considerable disparity between the model of language admired by the vernacular culture and that propounded by the school. The full extent of this difference may not, however, be fully appreciated by the teacher, as the following report by a New York schoolteacher reveals: "I had a boy of Greek parentage, and oh! he spoke beautifully in class, and I happened to hear him on the street one day. He sounded just like everybody else in Chelsea, and when I mentioned it to him—the next day—he said that he knew which was correct but then said: 'I couldn't live here and talk like that'".[6]

The choice of a linguistic reference group is seldom conscious or sudden, though some fictional examples—Pip in *Great Expectations* or Jay Gatsby—remind us that it may be. The early recordings by the Beatles, for instance, revealed their admiration for the dialect of American country music, and it was not long before their American imitators repaid the compliment by affecting the dialect of Liverpool. Nevertheless, the emulation of special purpose dialects seldom pervades an individual's entire range of linguistic resources and styles. His repertory of linguistic features expands both to a fuller mastery of the language of solidarity by which he asserts his membership in the reference group and to a command of the language of social power and authority. Labov has shown, for instance, that the pronunciation of [r] after vowels is coming to be regarded as a high-status linguistic ornament in New York City especially among the young and the upwardly mobile, even though the prestigous version of that dialect has not shown this feature for at least a hundred and fifty years. Such a development reflects the increased numbers of newcomers to the New York corporate and political scene from regions where [r] after vowels is a regular dialect feature.[7] In accepting this group as a model for language behavior, the young New Yorker has expanded his linguistic resources to encompass a new style. But like the boy in the teacher's anecdote, he will not reject the old pronunciation because it is still useful for displaying his membership in the peer culture to which he must also belong to survive happily.

The complexities involved in a speaker's adherence to his linguistic reference group are seldom fully appreciated by teachers and parents, and systematic differences in language may be regarded with contempt. As Robinson shows in his contribution to this volume, popular opinion and pseudoscholarship have maintained the belief that the poor are virtual cultural and linguistic cripples. But more recent work shows that such beliefs are the result of cultural myopia at best or, in the case of A. R. Jensen, a thorough-going race prejudice. The work of Labov and others has discredited the notion that nonelite dialects are lacking in abstract concepts, logical strategies, and intellectual sophistication. Another contribution to the new understanding of the language of the poor is the work by Doris R. Entwisle of Johns Hopkins; "word associations of black and white elementary school children," she writes, reveal "that slum children are apparently more advanced linguistically than suburban children at first grade in terms of paradigmatic responses".[8] Research reported by Thomas H. Shriner of

---

[6] Quoted by Labov, p. 284 above.

[7] See William Labov, "The Effect of Social Mobility on Linguistic Behavior," *Explorations in Sociolinguistics*, Stanley Lieberson, ed. (*International Journal of American Linguistics*, publication no. 44, 1967), pp. 58–75.

[8] Doris R. Entwisle, "Semantic Systems of Children: Some Assessments of Social Class

the University of Illinois indicates a similar result for the acquisition of other aspects of language: "Because all variables thought relevant were controlled, and no significant differences were found between the experimental and control groups, it is concluded that disadvantaged and advantaged children do not differ in terms of the morphological rules measured by this study".[9] These are important additions to our understanding of the problems of language growth and language variety that run counter to our national mythology about the varieties of English. What they indicate is a need for a thorough revision of the prevailing attitudes about language and a reconsideration of the aims of English teaching at all educational levels.

The evident success of many "open-door" admissions policies for post-secondary education has brought more and more students whose language has not been "purified" into higher education. As Melvin A. Butler points out, "any English program that claims as its model Harvard, Yale, or Princeton but enrolls as its students sons and daughters, sisters and brothers, babies and knee babies, friends and lovers of Harvard's, Yale's, and Princeton's janitors is a program with a built-in margin for failure that staggers the mind."[10] And yet such students are not likely to differ in their linguistic attitudes from those that have been traditionally admitted to colleges and universities. Their reverence for the conventions of print is likely to be strong, and they are inclined to regard any change in the traditional, prescriptive curriculum as a rip-off designed to prevent their obtaining the material benefits that are supposed to follow from a command of "good English." Like other Americans, they are likely to be afflicted with linguistic self-hatred, particularly if they have been made to believe that the language of power and status differs significantly from the language of their peer culture. They are unlikely to look at dialect differences dispassionately, particularly when their perception is reinforced by the all too typical equation of "divergent" dialects with stupidity in such situation comedies as the Andy Griffith television programs. They will probably share the American belief—despite the linguistic facts—that the so-called standard language is consistent in all parts of the country and possessed of an elegance and euphony that they can never confidently command. They may well feel—and they will be right—that the usage exercises they have been forced to complete since their earliest schools days have been used to discriminate against the language that they use most naturally. If they have taken a job-placement or college entrance examination, they may well attribute their lack of success to an incomplete mastery of the mysteries of "correct" English that usually

---

and Ethnic Differences," in *Language and Poverty: Perspectives on a Theme*, Frederick Williams, ed. (Chicago, 1970), p. 130.

[9] Thomas H. Shriner, "Social Dialect and Language," in *The First Lincolnland Conference on Dialectology*, Jerry Griffiths and L. E. Miner, eds. (University of Alabama, 1970), p. 130.

[10] Melvin A. Butler, "The Implications of Black Dialect for Teaching English in Predominantly Black Colleges," *CLA Journal*, **15**(1971):239.

appear on such tests, even when the successful completion of such exercises is wholly irrelevant to success in the job or school for which the test is supposed to act as a screen. Perhaps more than other students, they will feel that the English class is no source of delight and that the activities that they come to expect from such study constitute just one more obstacle to the career that they foresee for themselves.

The teaching of composition is one of the most difficult jobs in higher education. Typically the teacher has only a scanty background to prepare him for the work, and, as most postbaccalaureate training is now constituted, he will be likely to feel that the work in composition is only an irritating distraction from the literary subject that is his real interest and for which he has the greatest enthusiasm. Sometimes, of course, the literary interest finds its way into the composition course, perhaps to serve a legitimate purpose as an aid to the students' writing. In other instances, the introduction of literary topics is really a covert means of providing the teacher with a topic of interest to him.

With all the difficulties that beset him, it is no wonder that many composition teachers despair of success. Some seem persuaded that writing really doesn't matter any more. The age of Gutenberg, it is claimed, is dying as the electronic media become more and more significant in the communication process. What seems to them necessary is a highly "relevant" program in writing, geared very precisely to the career goals of the students. Hence specialized courses in technical writing often spring up, sometimes so narrowly conceived that students in the program in heating and air conditioning are segregated from those preparing for careers in plumbing and carpentry. Such courses may have a superficial success if the students are persuaded that the work has a direct connection with their career goals. But these programs confuse training with education and narrow the students' linguistic skills rather than extend them. The eventual result of this trend, of course, is to leave writing skills to the ministrations of those trained in the technical specialty and to restrict instruction in English to students in non-vocational programs.

The traditional goals of training in one's native language were established in the teaching of rhetoric in antiquity: the student should be trained to write and speak more effectively. Too often in America this goal has been confused with the necessity of error-free prose and the supposed desirability of imitating certain features of the prestige dialect. A further distraction from the real problems of writing is owing to a general belief that the English teacher must treat the student to certain aesthetic or philosophical experiences. But at the same time, effective writing and speech are supposed to provide access to wealth and power. Few handbooks or teacher's guides fail to mention the job interview as a crucial juncture in the student's life, and the importance of "making a good impression" is constantly reiterated. Such efforts perpetuate the linguistic folklore about the merits of the several dialects of English, while blatantly reflecting the fact that the schools have abandoned a reverence for learning in favor of service for the capitalist system.

If the composition course is to have any success, it must be designed to extend rather than to alter the linguistic resources that the student brings with him to the classroom. The highly verbal culture of the peer group needs to be drawn upon as at least a first stage in the writing process, while a continued emphasis on fluency must replace the concern for propriety and correctness that have undoubtedly characterized the student's earlier work in English. This transition from speech to writing presents a variety of difficulties beyond the obvious ones of symbolizing the spoken language according to the conventions of English spelling. In several ways, the written language is impoverished: it lacks any mechanism for representing gesture and tone of voice that provide so much support for speech, and it requires the writer to create for himself the sense of an audience that is normally supplied in conversation by the interaction between speaker and listener. As anyone knows who has tried to write dialogue for a story or a play, the illusion of naturalness is extremely difficult to create. Even the transcript of a telephone conversation, where gestures play no part, is quite unlike the imitation of such a conversation in fiction. The sense of an audience is at once a normal part of our spoken language behavior and an extremely difficult thing to capture in writing. A further difficulty for the composition class is the rather ambiguous status of student essays: Are essays real communications, or are they merely displays?

In his interesting book, *Language and Learning*, James Britton points to the crucial distinction "between *informing people about our experiences* (which would be a participant activity) and *inviting them to share in the process* by which we pay homage to, or celebrate, or gloat over our past experiences—an activity in the role of spectator."[11] Work in composition, by a kind of contract between student and teacher, falls into both categories; the essays must inform, at one level, and display the student's competence on another. Whether the essay involves description, narration, argument, or exposition, the student is supposed to be "writing with a purpose"— informing his audience of crucial details, persuading them to share his view, or exhorting them to action. But at the same time the teacher acts as a spectator who is seldom informed, persuaded, or moved to action. The exchange of information between writer and reader typical of other kinds of writing is both central and evanescent in the classroom, and it is no surprise that the student is more likely to ask his teacher "How did I do?" (teacher as spectator) rather than "How did you enjoy my essay?" (teacher as participant). There is something quite unusual about the roles assumed by teacher and student in the composition class; as generations of critics have repeatedly pointed out, the 500-word theme occurs virtually nowhere else in the verbal culture, nor do writers usually expect to be "graded" on their

---

[11] James Britton, *Language and Learning* (London, 1970), p. 123. [My emphasis.]

performances outside the classroom. For the student to develop enthusiasm for the teacher as both participant and spectator is the accomplishment of the most inspired teaching. Creating this enthusiasm time after time is the hardest of the jobs faced by the teacher, but the course cannot have worthwhile results unless early in the term there is established a willing and mutual suspension of our normal expectations about the function of writing in the "real" world.

The necessity of making a viable beginning applies, of course, to writing itself as well as to the sociology of the classroom. The anthology of essays usually assigned for composition courses can illustrate this point if the teacher recognizes that the acquisition of a sense of form is far more important to the success of his class than the content of the models at hand. No one seriously assumes that the student enters the composition classroom rejoicing that he at last has a chance to pour forth his ideas on the issues of the day. Helping the student find what is somewhat ambiguously called the true subject is an important part of the job; in other words, invention and discovery have an important place in the course, but the teacher's central task is to engage the student in matters of form, of the disposition of linguistic material into a fluent statement. To this end, varying the point of view and the presumed beliefs of the fictive audience are closely involved with matters of form. Unfortunately, the search for a topic too often involves a kind of exhortation by the teacher to adopt a particular point of view on current ethical and political questions or to emulate techniques in currently fashionable literary analysis. When the concern for form is neglected, the course no longer deserves the title "composition."

In speaking of the acquisition of a sense of form as the primary goal of instruction in writing, I do not have in mind the rather narrowly conceived understanding of form that is characteristic of the majority of materials designed for such courses. Form, it seems, is much more subtle and difficult to discuss than we usually recognize, particularly in an age in which the art that conceals artistry is highly valued. The opening paragraph of George Orwell's descriptive essay, "Marrakech," illustrates part of what I have in mind:

As the corpse went past the flies left the restaurant table in a cloud and rushed after it, but they came back a few minutes later.[12]

At first glance, what is remarkable about this opening is the startling beginning, the introduction of a corpse instead of some topographical feature that would inevitably appear in a student essay on "My Home Town" or "An Exciting Vacation." Likewise the author reveals himself to be someone like us; that is, someone for whom the prospect of a corpse covered

[12] *The Collected Essays, Journalism, and Letters of George Orwell*, Sonia Orwell and Ian Angus, eds. (Harmondsworth, Middlesex, 1970), Vol. 1, p. 426.

with the flies is a remarkable event and not merely a normal part of the background of daily life.

Certainly of equal interest for a discussion of writing, however, is the technique by which Orwell accomplishes so much in his opening sentence. He has set a kind of keynote for what is to follow, but he has also made a variety of decisions about what is *not* to follow, both in terms of content and of form. He has established an observer on the scene, undescribed so far but located at the restaurant table. But the real thrust of the first sentence draws the reader's attention to the flies.

The flies left the restaurant table in a cloud.
[The flies] rushed after the corpse.
[The flies] came back a few minutes later.

It is possible, of course, that the description will continue to focus on the flies, perhaps directly:

There are flies wherever you go in Marrakech.

Or perhaps indirectly in a movement from the particular to the general:

Primitive sanitation in the city means that the legacy of disease soon passes from the dead to the living.

But a sense of form gives us an intuition about these probabilities, and I suppose that all would agree that although it is possible that Orwell is interested in flies in particular or the implications of flies for public health, it is not probable that his opening really pushes in that direction. The flies are there as a device to link the living observer with the dead man going past. They create this link only to fade from view as the perspective Orwell has created opens on the scene:

The little crowd of mourners—all men and boys, no women—threaded their way across the market-place between the piles of pomegranates and the taxis and the camels, wailing a short chant over and over again. What really appeals to the flies is that the corpses here are never put into coffins, they are merely wrapped in a piece of rag and carried on a rough wooden bier on the shoulders of four friends.

Our view expands from the three elements of the opening sentence—the observer, the flies, and the corpse—to encompass a larger view of an exotic landscape, the mixture of pomegranates, taxis, and camels in the middle distance and, disappearing from view, the funeral party. But the purely formal features of the opening are important as well: the envelope of time created by the departure of the flies and their return, the sense of movement within time, begun as the corpse moves by, continued as the flies hurry after it, and concluded as they languidly return.

Although it is clear that the distinction between form and content is never an easy one, some content-preserving modifications can be used to justify the contrast I have been describing in this example. Orwell might have chosen to mark the temporal orientation more explicitly through the use of adverbs:

First the corpse went past,
Then the flies rushed after it,
The flies came back *a few minutes later.*

His choice of alternative formal features mutes the importance of sequence but just as surely preserves the importance of action over purely static description that we have already noticed in his opening. This muting effect is accomplished by using only one temporal expression, "a few minutes later," and drawing instead on the pair of verbs that presuppose sequence in time, "left . . . but . . . came back." The same muting effect is apparent in Orwell's treatment of the participants. He might have written,

As the little crowd of mourners carried the corpse across the market place, the flies left the restaurant table in a cloud.

But he instead selects a construction that puts the grammatical patient, "the corpse," in thematic position while deleting the grammatical agent that gives volition to it. The same suppression of the human participants in the scene characterizes his treatment of the observer. He rejects the possible opening that would undoubtedly occur to the student writer: "I was sitting at the restaurant table when the corpse went past." It is no surprise, then, that he continues in the same pattern of formal choices in the subsequent sentences. It is not the human actors in the scene that are drawn to our attention—even the mourners are characterized as a group, a "crowd," instead of being picked out of the scene. Rather it is the objects that present themselves to the observer, not the human mass of merchants and buyers that, along with the taxi drivers, waiters, and camel men, must have filled the scene that Orwell saw. All these are somehow there as part of the implicit content of the description, but they are not really present in the linguistic representation of the scene that Orwell chooses to draw to our attention.

In one sense, the grammatical facts that we have noticed are of only local importance as they occur in the opening sentence. Most contemporary linguists agree with tradition in restricting their observations to relations within the sentence. The distribution of adverbials, the surface roles of agent and patient, and the selection of nonhuman nouns are all of interest at the sentence level, but not nearly so interesting for the purposes of composition as the implications of these choices for the discourse that follows. If linguists and grammarians have largely ignored the formal and stylistic restraints imposed by these choices, it must also be said that rhetoricians have seldom devoted much attention to them either except in the broadest terms: unity, coherence, and emphasis. At the moment, our detailed knowledge of the global features of discourse—those that unify texts—is at a rudimentary stage, though we can certainly discuss particular cases by means of the techniques familiar from the explication of poetry. Even though generalizations of any substance are still lacking, questions of this sort can occupy a prominent place in the composition classroom. There is no need for the technical language of contemporary linguistics in dealing with these issues, but it is also clear that a thorough and detailed examination of them should be part of the academic preparation of the teacher.

A talent for exposition of the sort Orwell's sentences illustrate is hardly a normal part of our acquisition of the spoken language. An oral presentation of the same scene would differ greatly from what we expect on the written page. The tale-teller would almost certainly identify the source of his authority in the course of the conversational gambit by which he introduces the story. He could not begin abruptly, as Orwell does, but would be required by social convention to make an almost ritualized statement seeking the assent of his listeners before he could begin: "Have you heard me tell about my holiday in Morocco," or "Let me describe the strange way they bury people in northern Africa." Once the audience has agreed to hear the story, the speaker can support his narrative with gestures as he constantly monitors the attention and interests of his audience. The audience, on the other hand, can intervene to ask for more information or to show indifference to some details that, one hopes, the speaker will quickly shun in favor of a topic of greater interest. Because none of this interaction is possible in a written narrative, the writer must rely on the rather meagre resources that the written language supplies to sustain the reader's interest. The translation from the conventions of speech to writing are both complex and indirect, and there is no simple rule by which gesture and interaction can be directly symbolized. Hence the teaching of composition involves the problem of teaching a system whose employment is, in some respects, quite unlike the usual verbal resources of the speaker untrained in writing.

Those familiar with the work of Charles Carpenter Fries and his followers on English grammar have doubtless seen Carroll's "Jabberwocky" used to illustrate the importance of formal signals in our interpretation of language. As this sort of analysis shows, syntactic and morphological markers contribute significantly to our ability to make grammatical sense of the nonsense words that Carroll used in his poem. The same technique can be applied to suggest the nature of the global constraints that unify large chunks of written discourse. The results of such an investigation suggest that our perception of unity and continuity in prose can be attributed to formal features of language just as other signals explain our ability to find word classes in apparent gibberish. In examining these constraints, Richard Young and Alton Becker presented six students with a stretch of prose from which the author's paragraph boundaries had been deleted and asked them to mark the places where such boundaries ought to go. Another group of

six was presented with a version of the same material that had been significantly modified; syntax, punctuation, and grammatical morphology were
preserved, but the content-bearing elements of the text were replaced by
nonsense words. Since this exercise has proved useful for discussion in a
composition class, I have reproduced these two versions of the text here and
invite readers to make their own decisions about paragraph boundaries before
reading the results that Young and Becker obtained.

1   Blog was, moked by grol nards, the wilest nerg of the Livar Molk. He was
2   dreed and bams above any nerg on either dir as an aly-ib cosleyist, as a ralmod
3   of what in tafy molks would be laned derid cosley. His Oramal Forof fusil, the
4   fection of a harn which had halared noog laymal nanton in the roner plur of
5   molk, would have done raboy to the most sacroled mintur of a toop of grol fant
6   and burkold mishes. He was a libart gonte cosleyist, as frommed by the
7   Mottron magnil, which was a multh relon and hock oramal. He was a gloral
8   than monit woltion, although, like even the comat nerg of both dirs, he did
9   not scriptal the raistote that the crepting milrome of grol mapes could sligect
10 on snomes plosing across prend bleermays. Berond is mornly slonated as the
11 wilest Livar Molk nerg, but this lumition has been golled without randing
12 Berond and Blog in the ecalmate of lamintale mercinations since the molk.
13 Berond was trenaled hardly at all in "logwind" cosley, and what few grinations
14 he did goll to his milerate about oramals in other gontes than his own solimate
15 that he had noog predision for mage fusilling. As a gonte cosleyist, Berond
16 often margulled more glore and bomeline than Blog, but his most randistic
17 fusils were as much the solime of the Faldincron's blamby lamintale scard as
18 of his own blee harn. In molk, the kaiber dir has to prongate glorally. It must
19 krid peenly, mobbingly, and crand a frostic smough of wab in its fusils. Had
20 Berond been a Morian nerg with Morian castins behind him, he would have
21 simatated less and beoeled less dromal. Had Blog been a sorian nerg, he would
22 have bantioned as Berond did. Dantially, Blog was perstale to Berond because
23 in a grol scome molk he had a grol harn, and Berond did not. Berond scolled
24 to the rame in mold as the Faldincron did in pring. The fants of the two yapes
25 crilliate their bomblares. It would not be antulate to chorn the Berond's nergal
26 fant were brinated bunes, but the crontation would not be too alay of the
27 clop. . . .

1   Grant was, judged by modern standards, the greatest general of the Civil
2   War. He was head and shoulders above any general on either side as an
3   over-all strategist, as a master of what in later wars would be called global
4   strategy. His Operation Crusher plan, the product of a mind which had received
5   little formal instruction in the higher area of war, would have done credit to
6   the most finished student of a series of modern staff and command schools. He
7   was a brilliant theater strategist, as evidenced by the Vicksburg campaign,
8   which was a classic field and siege operation. He was a better than average
9   tactician, although, like even the best generals of both sides, he did not appreciate
10 the destruction that the increasing firepower of modern armies could visit on
11 troops advancing across open spaces. Lee is usually ranked as the greatest
12 Civil War general, but this evaluation has been made without placing Lee and

13 Grant in the perspective of military developments since the war. Lee was
14 interested hardly at all in "global" strategy, and what few suggestions he did
15 make to his government about operations in other theaters than his own
16 indicate that he had little aptitude for grand planning. As a theater strategist,
17 Lee often demonstrated more brilliance and apparent originality than Grant,
18 but his most audacious plans were as much the product of the Confederacy's
19 inferior military position as of his own fine mind. In war, the weaker side has
20 to improvise brilliantly. It must strike quickly, daringly, and include a dangerous
21 element of risk in its plans. Had Lee been a Northern general with Northern
22 resources behind him, he would have improvised less and seemed less bold.
23 Had Grant been a Southern general, he would have fought as Lee did.
24 Fundamentally Grant was superior to Lee because in a modern total war he
25 had a modern mind, and Lee did not. Lee looked to the past in war as the
26 Confederacy did in spirit. The staffs of the two men illustrate their outlooks.
27 It would not be accurate to say that Lee's general staff were glorified clerks,
28 but the statement would not be too wide of the mark. . . .

T. Harry Williams: *Lincoln and His Generals* [13]

It is not surprising that the students were largely in agreement on the placement of paragraph boundaries in the normal English version. The grouping of related ideas that forms the traditional definition of a paragraph is clear enough in the normal text as Williams turns his attention away from Grant to Lee and thence to a comparison of the two as generals. Here is what the students decided about the boundaries that separate the topics in the unaltered version:

Paragraph at line:	2 4 6 8 11 13 16 19 20 21 23 24 25 29
Number of responses:	0 1 0 1 5 0 1 5 0 0 0 4 0 0
Williams' paragraphs:	* *

Students can usually give a quite clear justification for their responses. Most allude to the shift in topic at line 11 from Grant to Lee, and the further movement that brings the individual evaluations together at line 24. Few of them will comment on the formal features that accompany this clustering of ideas in the normal text, but the distorted version brings their importance clearly to our attention.

The altered version of the text, one would expect, ought to have provided a scattered set of responses, since the patterning of content has been obliterated. Young and Becker's results, like my own with a larger group, show on the contrary that the student's ability to discern paragraph boundaries was hardly hampered by the radical alteration of the text:

[13] Quoted from Richard E. Young and Alton L. Becker, "The Role of Lexical and Grammatical Cues in Paragraph Recognition," *Studies in Language and Language Behavior II*, H. L. Lane, ed. (Ann Arbor, Mich.: Center for Research on Language and Language Behavior, The University of Michigan, 1966), pp. 1–6. Some further implications of the importance of structural signals of discourse are developed in Richard E. Young, Alton L. Becker, and Kenneth L. Pike, *Rhetoric: Discovery and Change* (New York, 1970).

Paragraph at line: 1 3 6 7 10 12 15 18 18 19 21 22 23 25
Number of responses: 0 1 0 0 6 0 0 3 0 0 0 5 0 0
Williams' paragraphs: *   *

Lexical chaining in both cases clearly provides clues, whether the reader is tracing the discussion of Blog and Berond or Grant and Lee. But the markers of global organization reveal their true importance in the judgments about the altered version. Students quickly recognize that the devices most frequently employed in sentence linking are pronominalization and the regular choice of defining sentences: "Grant was . . . the greatest general of the Civil War. He was head and shoulders above any general. . . . He was a brilliant theater strategist. . . . He was a better than average tactician."

Parallelism also plays a further part in the contrast: "Had Lee been a Northern general. . . . Had Grant been a Southern general. . . ." These sentence types manifest the global constraints that Williams imposes on his discourse, and, though the choices are less varied than those used by Orwell, they clearly play a significant role in our recognition of his text as a unified discourse.

Traditional rhetorics and grammars give us a rich set of terms to apply to the processes that unify discourses into coherent wholes: *pronominalization*, *ellipsis*, and *anaphora* are sometimes mentioned in the classroom, but a great variety of labels have virtually disappeared, despite their utility in pointing out techniques for developing a discourse beyond the sentence: *tmesis*, *hysterologia*, *hypallage*, *epergesis*, *metabasis*, *symploce*, and *epanalepsis*. Simply reviving this dead vocabulary is of course no answer to encouraging students to develop the kind of fluency that we have identified as the primary goal of teaching composition. But without labeling the things themselves, it is possible to harness the student's linguistic intuitions about the structures the labels name: first in a sense of discovery and then in a transfer from an analytical skill to a productive one.

To illustrate what I have in mind, I have presented a class of students with the following sentences extracted from the opening paragraph of Ellison's *Invisible Man* and arranged in random order:

1. No, I am not a spook like those who haunted Edgar Allan Poe;
2. Nor am I one of your Hollywood-movie ectoplasms.
3. I am invisible, understand, simply because people refuse to see me.
4. I am a man of substance, of flesh and bone, fiber and liquids—
5. Like the bodiless heads you see sometimes in circus sideshows,
6. When they approach me they see only my surroundings, themselves, or figments of their imagination—indeed everything and anything except me.
7. I am an invisible man.
8. It is as though I have been surrounded by mirrors of hard, distorting glass.
9. And I might even be said to possess a mind.

The students were asked to cut up the duplicated sheet so that one numbered part would appear on each slip and then to arrange the slips into a coherent paragraph, using the punctuation, form, and content of the fragments as clues. As expected, there was a large measure of agreement about the placement of the sentences; all agreed that sentence 7 should start the paragraph, a result perhaps attributable to the familiarity of the paragraph rather than to internal reasons. Nearly all responded to the parallelism of sentences 1 and 2 and suggested that these should be linked:

"No, I am not a spook like those who haunted Edgar Allan Poe; nor am I one of your Hollywood-movie ectoplasms."

Likewise, the pairing of body and mind indicated the relatedness of sentences 4 and 9:

"I am a man of substance, of flesh and bone, fiber and liquids—and I might even be said to possess a mind."

In Ellison's paragraph, sentence 5 is followed by 8, and most student judges juxtaposed them to yield:

"Like the bodiless heads you see sometimes in circus sideshows, it is as though I have been surrounded by mirrors of hard, distorting glass."

In the discussion that followed, those who did not make this pairing said that they had no idea of the scene that Ellison intended to recall—not a surprising result given the disappearance of the circus sideshow from the American scene. Because the object of the exercise was not to consider the "right" order, the one in Ellison's original, several argued vigorously for linking sentence 5 to other sentences (particularly sentence 6).

The result of the exercise suggested that students responded with considerable sensitivity to the patterns that unify the sentences into a well-developed whole. Their sense of a well-formed paragraph showed that they were responding to all the formal signals present in the individual parts: syntactic patterns (in the pairing of sentences 1 and 2), organization of content (as in sentences 4 and 9), and metaphorical relatedness (as in sentences 5 and 8). Their disagreements resulted from those pairs that do not contain such links; for instance, sentence 5 was placed by the various judges after sentences 2, 3, 6, 7, and 8, exactly the kind of disagreement one might predict on linguistic grounds since sentence 5 contains no clear clues—syntactic, metaphorical, or in content—that would indicate its position within the paragraph. All judges agreed, however, that it could come neither first nor last since the simile in the combination of sentences 5 and 8 forms a digression from the main theme of the whole. As the exercise shows, part of the native speaker's linguistic competence extends to the notion of "well-formedness" in texts, exactly parallel to the judgments about the "grammaticality" of sentences that has been used as the basis of generative linguistics during the past fifteen years.

Global concerns of the kind we have just discussed should play a significant and early role in the teaching of composition. Some seem to assume that by taking care of the sentences the larger patterns will take care of themselves. Others seem to feel that problems in spelling and "usage" have some prior claim that cannot be denied. Such beliefs are natural enough, given the traditions of American schools and the widespread attitudes toward the proper use of language that we have already mentioned. But the sentence is not really the basic unit of the essay, and treating sentences as if they were the primary elements leaves out of consideration the larger patterns of organization that control their shape.

Some samples of student writing may be helpful in suggesting the practical implications of these issues. The paper reproduced here, "Sucess," was written by a student in an urban college not far from Detroit. It deals with an abstract subject, which, in itself, imposes a certain level of discourse that the student is required to sustain. The essay itself also illustrates the ambiguous function of student writing, for, though the teacher has overtly asked the author to participate in the definition of *success*, the classroom setting calls for a display of a certain facility of thought and language. Hence the student must keep his eye on two audiences at once: the reader who needs illumination and the reader who acts as spectator. These preliminary conditions—the presuppositions of the assignment and the functional setting—have in this case a disabling effect on the writer:

"Sucess"

To every college materialized student, there is a very big investment inspeared in them, Will I suceed? To every incompetent person, there may be a change of pace, that is, whether suceed or not to suceed. Naturally, sucess is a highly-competitive renouner word.

To me, I would consider sucess as being one of the most undisputed goals in life. To many, sucess is that goal in which individuals are constantly approaching to achieve.

To the least concerned or the uninterested sucess is a very vague word that they consider just another term in our everyday speech usage.

Musten I omit, sucess is that goal to achieve recognition, reputation and escalation above those who are constantly seeking to achieve theirs.

To the child in elementary or pre-kindergarten, it only means the beginning of a new challenge. As an adult, the related idea is the child has to meet all of the different obstacles as the older individual did. Whether it means failure or "Sucess."

We as college students are meeting the challenge that would inspire us to continue. I personally feel that without sucess the option would be more less totally obsolete to the knowledge of the oncoming years as predicted than chaotic.

Does the world relate their support to this very significance phenomenon? Obviously they feel it is already very revolutionary to omit sucess for us as it seems an importance for the leaders of tomorrow's world.

From a conceptual viewpoint, the essay shows the vocabulary that might be expected in a more sophisticated excursus on the subject—for example, a high school commencement address. Positive words such as *success, goal, recognition,* and *reputation* are set in contrast with negatives: *failure, obstacle, incompetent, uninterested.* Mediating between the individual and these abstract concepts is a rich vocabulary of the appropriate processes: *investment, competition, approach, achieve, challenge, seek.* There is a rudimentary pattern of organization as the writer shifts his attention from the general issue to the college student, to himself, and thence to other strivers, children, and to the older generation, before he returns to the problem of definition he had raised at the outset. Nevertheless, the essay in many places is a kind of "word salad" in which complex conventions are violated as idiom joins cliché, deep structure subjects and objects clash in the surface, and misuse gives way to malapropism. In short, the essay presents a bewildering set of complex problems. The only possible comment that can be written on this paper—unless the teacher has utterly abandoned the instinct for self-preservation—is "See me."

"Sucess" is a good illustration of the importance of prior decisions in the writing process. The assigned topic clearly brings with it certain assumptions about the level of discourse appropriate to its discussion. The choice of an abstract and Latinate vocabulary in the opening sentence is a predictable response to the assignment, but it forces the student into a mode of writing that is really beyond his capacity. A more mature writer than the author of "Sucess" would soon find a way to bring the topic "down" to some particular instance, or at least to temper the abstract and general with the concrete and specific.

Considered in another light, "Sucess" is perhaps not quite the disaster that it first appeared. Points in the student's favor are certainly more numerous than a first reading might suggest. He has displayed at least a partial grasp of the vocabulary that might accompany the discussion of such an issue and has managed to sustain the same level of discourse to quite a respectable length for an impromptu essay. The organization of the material suggests that he jotted down some sort of outline on the meaning of *success* to several sorts of people. These virtues promise well for the writer, particularly if he is given an opportunity to show his abilities on a topic that implies a vocabulary and style closer to his vernacular.

Some of the complexities of the social meaning of language are raised by a second example of student writing, "The Femmiest and the Fuss." Where "Sucess" is virtually free of socially stigmatized forms, "The Femmiest and the Fuss" is full of them, and the temptation for the teacher to improve the essay by eradicating them is certainly very strong.

1   I just seen a movie on TV the other night that really stay in my mind. It was
2   about a guy and a girl, the guy was a cop and the girl was for women Lib. The
3   two finally ended up sharing apartment together with cause some pretty fun
4   scene. ~~When~~ One I recall is when Barbara was having a women Lib. meeting and
5   Jerry (the cop) walked in on it. Will Jerry was in trouble he got flaten by about

6   ten women. The two of them has some pretty bad time but in the end the finally
7   decides to get married. I think it was one of the funniest movies I've seen in along
8   time. I think the title was "The Femmiest and the Fuss"

"The Femmiest and the Fuss" is, of course, much closer to the student's
vernacular and for that reason the use of language in the essay is at once
more systematic and natural than that in "Sucess." It contains a variety of
traits that have been identified in some of the research on nonstandard
American dialects, and several of these are worth pointing out. "I just seen a
movie," for example, reflects a supposed nonstandard form with which we are
all familiar. As Atwood's *Survey of Verb Forms* shows, *seen* as a preterit is
found only sporadically in the Northern dialect region, but in Midland speech
it is "used by from two-thirds to nearly all of Type I informants, as well as
by from half to two-thirds of the Type II."[14] In other words, this use of
seen is not only characteristic of those with the least education and status in
the Midland area, but it occurs in the careful speech of those of higher rank
as well. "I just seen a movie," then, apparently lies on the boundary between
sociolinguistics and dialect geography in that a form typical of the popular
speech of one area proves to be a socially despised form when the speaker
migrates to another part of the country.

Other features in the essay are frequently cited in the descriptions of
so-called Black English that Robinson discusses in the following essay. In
line 1, *stay* shows the effect of terminal fading, while *flaten* in line 5 reflects
the more specialized version of the same tendency, the reduction of final
consonant clusters. In *women Lib.* (line 4), the standard possessive *'s* is of
course missing, showing the rule identified by Labov that single consonants
are typically deleted between word boundaries.[15] *Some scene* (lines 3–4) and
some time (line 6) are other examples of the same process. This rule has
sweeping importance for the kind of language that nonelite speakers are
likely to write since the whole system of inflectional morphology is affected
by it, including plurals, possessives, and past tense markers as we see in
"The Femmiest and the Fuss." The verb system of this dialect is superficially
distinct from "edited English" because of the phonological rule by which
this deletion takes place:

	Elite	*Nonelite*
modals:	I'll be going	I be going
auxiliaries:	I've never seen one	I never seen one
copula:	She's a teacher	She a teacher.

As these examples show, the nonelite dialect simply extends and generalizes

[14] E. Bagby Atwood, *A Survey of Verb Forms in the Eastern United States* (Ann Arbor, Mich., 1953), p. 20.

[15] See William Labov, Paul Cohen, Clarence Robins, and John Lewis, *A Study of the Non-Standard English of Negro and Puerto Rican Speakers in New York City* (Washington, D.C., 1968), Vol. 1.

the rules for contraction typical of standard English: *will* → *'ll, have* → *'ve,
is* → *'s.* Even though the application of such general rules in this dialect is
thoroughly systematic, these facts of language variation present difficulties
for the student. He needs to learn the conventions that require the written
language to be more explicit than speech in representing such grammatical
details.

Further rule-governed phonological differences between elite and nonelite
dialects are responsible for some of the apparent "errors" in "The Femmiest
and the Fuss." Because some styles of Southern speech typically show
leveling of the Northern rule for the articles *a* and *an,* it is no surprise to
find *sharing apartment* in line 3. This kind of reinterpretation has a long
history in England as exemplified by the replacement of Middle English
nadder and *napple* by the modern *an adder* and *an apple.* Given the generalization of the article *a* in certain American dialects, it is natural to expect the
author of "The Femmiest and the Fuss" to merge the article and the initial
vowel of *apartment.*

The regularly noted assimilation of [ɛ] to [ɪ] results in the spelling of *well*
in line 5, again a trait of standard Southern speech whether white or black.
The substitution of a nasal vowel for a nasal consonant underlies the spelling
femmiest in line 8, while the spelling *fuss* may reflect a phonological process
or merely a mismatch between spelling and the phoneme /z/, usually *z* or *zz*
but sometimes, as in *dessert, scissors,* and *brassiere, ss.*[16] Once examined in
the light of the facts of language variation in America, the apparently
unsystematic "mistakes" in the essay prove to be the consequence of a
consistently applied interpretation of the spoken language.

How is the composition teacher—with perhaps a hundred other such
essays in need of attention—to make good use of the generalizations we have
just identified? At the moment, there are few teaching materials that deal
systematically with these problems, and the good teacher will certainly not
be satisfied with the traditional, atomistic practice of indicating the elite
forms with his red pencil. And although it is certainly possible to construct
drills and exercises by which the spoken forms are reduced to writing, it is
worth asking whether this level of study should be given a high priority in
the composition course. Perhaps this question can best be answered by
examining "The Femmiest and the Fuss" in terms of the global conventions
of written discourse. The author of "The Femmiest and the Fuss" shows
sophisticated use of anaphora and other cohesive devices that carry his
discussion from one sentence to the next. The topic of the first sentence,
a movie on TV, is echoed in the *it* of the second sentence. *Guy* and *girl* in
the second reappear in the elliptical construction, *the two,* of the third.
That this student is particularly aware of the markers of linguistic coherence
is shown by his correction of *when* at the opening of sentence 4; rather than

---

[16] For further examples of [z] spelled *ss,* see Paul R. Hanna, *et al., Phoneme-Grapheme
Correspondences As Cues to Spelling Improvement* (Washington, D.C., 1966), p. 1094.

begin with the clause, *when Barbara was having a women Lib. meeting*, the writer backtracks to the final thematic unit of the previous sentence: *some pretty fun scene.* By again employing an elliptical construction, *One I recall*, the student makes explicit the movement from the general to the specific instance, and thus reveals his sensitivity to the need for marking the larger patterns of exposition.

Unfortunately these carefully marked links do not appear where they are needed in the middle of the essay, and the reader is left to imagine the connection between Jerry's entrance into the apartment and the trouble he encounters in sentence 5. Nevertheless, the student has shown partial mastery of intersentence connections while the global arrangement of his material follows the "funnel" strategy much admired by rhetoricians. His conclusion brings the reader full circle to the topic of the whole discourse in the approved style. Patterning at this level is surely the student's strength. The teaching strategy that we must adopt for him should build from this strength toward the consistent use of cohesive devices over stretches of greater and greater length. Once the student is confident of his writing ability at this level, the teacher may want to discuss the subsentence elements that we have previously identified. But there is good reason to believe that the student who becomes more and more enthusiastic about his writing in its larger organization may begin to discover these lower-level principles for himself.

The primary task that the composition teacher should set for himself is the development of skills in controlling the large patterns that unify discourses. Such study must acknowledge the important differences between the organization appropriate to a piece of writing and that natural in speech, and it must come to terms with the role of the teacher as both participant and spectator. Just as self-monitoring detracts from oral fluency, so the spectre of an ever-watchful teacher poised to assault errors has a deleterious effect on a student's writing ability. But, on the other hand, it is nearly impossible for the teacher to assume the role of a "normal" participant in the communication process, because the artificiality of classroom communication makes it extraordinarily difficult for the student to treat his composition as a goal-directed message designed to inform or convince. Yet though the role of spectator is forced on the teacher by the circumstances, it is still possible for him to convince the class of his interest in communication rather than display. Through the honesty of his persuasion, the teacher can create the setting for the student's growth in fluency and increased mastery of the written language. Only at the latest stages of this development will problems of usage, spelling, and the details of elite dialects of English have any place in the classroom. All teachers—and English teachers in particular—must act in full awareness of the problems of linguistic insecurity that confuse and discourage so many Americans in their use of language. Above all, he must recognize that his function is not to purify the language of his students but to extend it.

STUDY QUESTIONS

1. In what sorts of phenomena does Bailey locate what is called standard English in the United States? What mechanisms support and sustain a recognition of its existence? How does "the presumption of a national standard" reinforce "the supposed connection between linguistic variation and social status" (p. 387)?
2. Is the written language the same thing as standard English? What relations between the written language and a presumed national standard does Bailey describe? Should the written language define standards for pronunciation?
3. What is meant by the term *linguistic insecurity?* Why is linguistic insecurity apparently endemic in the United States? Is it an inevitable condition in composition classes when students are asked to explore new styles? What means can you suggest to reduce insecurity in the composition process if you agree that naturalness and fluency are worthy goals?
4. Is a student's allegiance to his peer group for linguistic norms necessarily harmful to his progress as a writer? How might an alert teacher make use of the verbal skills of student groups to teach necessary compositional skills? Is there a necessary discontinuity between oral language skills and writing?
5. For generations we have assumed that training in composition is a necessary part of the education of all Americans, no matter what their native abilities or career goals. Is the assumption still valid? How would you justify a general requirement in composition for all students at the level you are preparing to teach? What criticisms of traditional justifications does Bailey make?
6. What priorities for teaching and evaluating compositional skills does Bailey suggest? Do you agree with his ordering? If, as he argues, "a continued emphasis on fluency must replace the concern for propriety and correctness," what practical effects will such an emphasis have on types of writing assignments made and on grading practices?
7. As an introduction to discussing "global patterns" of organization, decide where you would put the paragraph boundaries in the following stretch of prose. After you have made your decision, compare it with that of others; look for the structural signals, as well as shifts in topic, that are useful in deciding where such boundaries belong.

```
 1   ... If a movie has enough clout, reviewers and columnists who were
 2   bored are likely to give it another chance, until on the second or third
 3   viewing, they discover that it affects them "viscerally"—and a big
 4   expensive movie is likely to do just that. "2001" is said to have caught
 5   on with youth (which can make it happen); and it's said that the movie
 6   will stone you—which is meant to be a recommendation. Despite a few
 7   dissident voices—I've heard it said, for example, that "2001" "gives
 8   you a bad trip because the visuals don't go with the music"—the
 9   promotion has been remarkably effective with students. "The tribes"
10   tune in so fast that college students thousands of miles apart "have
11   heard" what a great trip "2001" is before it has even reached their city.
12   Using movies to go on a trip has about as much connection with the art
13   of film as using one of those Doris Day–Rock Hudson jobs for ideas on
14   how to redecorate your home—an earlier way of stoning yourself. But
15   it is relevant to an understanding of movies to try to separate out, for
```

16 purposes of discussion at least, how we may personally *use* a film—to
17 learn how to dress or how to speak more elegantly or how to make a
18 grand entrance or even what kind of coffee maker we wish to purchase, or
19 to take off from the movie into a romantic fantasy or a trip—from what
20 makes it a good movie or a poor one, because, of course, we can *use* poor
21 films as easily as good ones, perhaps *more* easily for such nonaesthetic
22 purposes as shopping guides or aids to tripping. We generally become
23 interested in movies because we *enjoy* them and what we enjoy them for
24 has little to do with what we think of as art. The movies we respond to,
25 even in childhood, don't have the same values as the official culture
26 supported at school and in the middle-class home. At the movies we get
27 low life and high life, while David Susskind and the moralistic reviewers
28 chastise us for not patronizing what they think we should, "realistic"
29 movies that would be good for us—like "A Raisin in the Sun," where we
30 could learn the lesson that a Negro family can be as dreary as a white
31 family. Movie audiences will take a lot of garbage, but it's pretty hard
32 to make us queue up for pedagogy. . . .[a]

8. On pp. 399–404, Bailey discusses the native speaker's ability to recognize the sequence signals that make for coherence and unity. Test your own intuitions about these matters by arranging the following randomly numbered sentences into a paragraph:

   1. Failing to qualify, these American trees and rocks from which come such deadly but meaningless stings are overlooked.
   2. In my opinion what defeated them was their skill.
   3. The Redcoats fall, expecting at any moment to enter upon the true battlefield, the soft rolling greenswards prescribed by the canons of their craft and presupposed by every principle that makes warfare intelligible to the soldier of the eighteenth century.
   4. Their too highly perfected technique forbade them to acknowledge such chance topographical phenomena.
   5. According to the assumptions of their military art, by which their senses were controlled, a battlefield had to have a certain appearance and structure, that is to say, a style.
   6. They were such extreme European professionals, even the Colonials among them, that they did not *see* the American trees.
   7. I was never satisfied with the explanation that the Redcoats were simply stupid or stubborn, wooden copies of King George III.[b]

   Note that various arrangements are possible; you may prefer to begin by discussing which sequences are *impossible* and why. Which sentences seem to you to belong naturally with each other. What patterns—syntactic, metaphorical, or in content relations—can you identify to explain your choice.

9. The following essay was written as an impromptu assignment by a West Indian student in a Florida community college. Read the essay as if you were the teacher who had assigned the topic of "My Most Memorable Childhood

---

[a] From Pauline Kael, "Trash, Art, and the Movies," in *Going Steady* (New York: A Bantum Film Book, 1971), pp. 123–24.

[b] From Harold Rosenberg, *The Tradition of the New* (New York: McGraw-Hill paperback edition, 1965), p. 14.

Experience." Pay attention initially only to matters of organization—to global form as discussed by Bailey. Ask yourself such questions as:

a. Does the initial sentence establish expectations of formal probabilities realized in the remainder of the essay?
b. Is the paragraph division formally marked?
c. What formal markers of internal paragraph structure does the writer utilize?
d. Does the paper have an adequate conclusion? What is it, and how is it marked?
e. Does the writer have an adequate over-all sense of form?

1 My most memorable childwood merory was the day I got my worst
2 beating, it statted out good and ended terable for me, my mother had
3 send me to the store to pay the grocery bill about twelve Oclock that day,
4 while going to the store I met some of my friends who was going to play
5 cricket match against another street they said they needed one more
6 player, I said I would go along and play two or three inning figuring it
7 wouldent take long, after a while I completly forget about the store
8 because I was getting so much hits, It was about four when I rembered
9 about the bill I quickley ran to the store paid the bill and headed home.
10 While on the way home I thought of story to tell, I dicided to tell her
11 I lost the money and had to look for it, I finnely reach my front door and
12 open it, there was my mother all looking mad she asked what took me
13 so long so I told her my story I had made up at first I thought she had
14 believe me and I was home free, when I turn my back she grab me by the
15 pants and started to whip me she gave me about ten lashed before she
16 was trought after beating me she told me to put on my night cloth and
17 go to bed she then went out side, I draw the curten in my room and look
18 outside and there was my friends laughting at me. That night I was Mad
19 at every body in sight most of all my friends for laught at me after I had
20 help them beat there chief rival, my body was just hurting so much the
21 onely thing I could think of was the memories of the game to forget
22 about my pains

10. Now consider the language of the essay. Use the following questions as guides:
  a. Can the writer form sentences? Does he make errors in grammar or only in punctuation?
  b. Would it be possible to discriminate between random errors—matters of inadvertence or inattention, which he might correct in careful proofreading —and forms that show the influence of the student's native dialect? For example, are certain errors or categories of errors repeated? Which is the more important type of error to treat?
  c. Consider the forms *forget* (line 7), *reach* (line 11), *open* (line 12), *turn* (line 14), *grab* (line 14), *draw* (line 17), *look* (line 17). Are these "errors"— evidence that the writer doesn't know or can't use past tense forms? Would you urge the writer to "correct" the forms, and if so why?
  d. If you wished to help this student with his spelling, where would you begin? Is the misspelling *merory* reflective of the same type of problem as the misspelling *trought* for *through* or *laughting* for *laughing*? Would it be a sufficient teaching device simply to mark all errors and tell the student to look them up in a dictionary?

11. Would your opinion of the student's linguistic competence differ according to whether you approached his paper first from the point of view outlined in study question 9, or first from the point of view outlined in study question 10? Would your opinion of his competence differ if you perceived his sentence problems as matters of grammar rather than as matters of punctuation?

12. Now read the next essay, also impromptu but this time by an eighth-grade student. What language problems does it exhibit? What formal and organizational problems? Is this student likely to be more or less of a problem to the composition teacher than the student who wrote the essay in question 7?

Assignment "Man is by nature self-centered; thus any act, no matter how outwardly altruistic, is done by an individual in the hope of gaining personal satisfaction." Do you agree or disagree with this statement? Give specific examples.

1 I agree with the statement. I know that anything that I do the end
2 result benefits me. The act that you do for someone else either makes
3 you feel good or in the end you get physical satisfaction. I believe that there
4 are some people (not many) who only think of others and of pleasing
5 them. Whenever I do something for anyone I usually think of helping
6 them. I do not agree with the part that says a person does something in
7 the hope of receiving personal satisfaction.

8 Some people help others without any hope of personal satisfaction in
9 their mind. Others help for that reason only. Everyone is different and I
10 think that everyone has a different reason for helping someone. I know
11 one boy that is really selfish. Everything he does is for himself. He cares
12 about know one. I think everyone of us has a little of him in us, but we
13 also have some sharing, giving, and helping in all of us. Some more than
14 others.

15 I think that the statement is true most of the time, but there are
16 exceptions. I completely agree with the part "Man is by nature self-
17 centered." That is always true. I don't know anyone who never is
18 selfish. We all have good qualities and bad. Selfishness can work both
19 ways. It can help others and it can help yourself.

13. In the text quoted in question 7, Pauline Kael placed paragraph boundaries after the sentences ending in lines 11 and 22. In Rosenberg's essay, the sentences in question 8 were arranged in the order 7, 2, 6, 4, 5, 1, 3.

THE WALL OF BABEL; OR,
UP AGAINST THE LANGUAGE BARRIER

Jay L. Robinson

The profession of teaching English faces a crisis in that the easy verities of the great tradition have given way to a new uncertainty. The drive toward "behavioral objectives," "defined outcomes," "accountability," and "contract teaching" cuts in one direction; the paradox of good intentions and harsh realities in another. And meanwhile, a cost-conscious public is inquiring ever more closely into what actually happens in the classroom. Like other activities in the corporate state, teaching faces mechanization, and the schoolmaster with only a book and a piece of chalk may shortly find himself "technologically unemployed." Already one of the new "learning systems corporations"—a subsidiary of a giant conglomerate—proposes a system that literally wires students into the educational machine: "The responder," says the advertising copy, "allows each student to react immediately to questions by pushing a button. If he makes the proper response, he will receive immediate reinforcement."

More than in any other way, the new pragmatism reflected in these trends focuses itself on the teaching of "communication skills," the second "r" of the traditional three. Computer programs have been available for almost a decade to identify "errors" of the sort usually called mechanical: spelling mistakes, the comma splice, the run-on sentence. Because failures of this kind are easier to measure than is excellence, they have become the prime object for those who would replace expensive teachers with cheap machines.

Yet at the same time, English teachers find themselves unable to respond effectively to those who want to impose the notorious PPBS or Planned Programs Budgeting System—the scheme that introduced the "cost overrun" and the C-5A to the Pentagon—on the classroom. Beset by "linguistic engineers" and engineers of a more traditional sort, an English teacher is being asked again and again to justify himself, not by an apologia defending his dedication to the humanities, but by the tangible, measureable results he produces in "altering behaviors."

The effect of these trends comes, ironically, just at the point where teachers are repenting past failures and looking for new ways to focus on effective— rather than merely correct—writing. One anonymous writer, thinking of himself as a rat in a behaviorist's maze, puts his change of heart in this way:

My own research has convinced me that red-inking errors in students' papers does no good and causes a great many students to hate and fear

413

writing more than anything else they do in school. I gave a long series of tests covering 580 of the most common and persistent errors in usage, diction, and punctuation and 1,000 spelling errors to students in grades 9–12 in many schools, and the average rate of improvement in ability to detect these errors turned out to be 2 per cent per year. The dropout rate is more than enough to account for this much improvement if the teachers had not even been there. When I consider how many hours of my life I have wasted in trying to root out these errors by a method that clearly did not work, I want to kick myself. Any rat that persisted in pressing the wrong lever 10,000 times would be regarded as stupid. I must have gone on pressing it at least 20,000 times without any visible effect.[a]

What is to be done? As Robinson shows in the following essay, the great tradition has failed to confront the issue; surface "errors" are confounded with cognitive "disabilities," ignorance of written conventions with chaos and old night. Even the "enlightened" are guilty of smearing over the hard facts of failure with a kind of semantic goo: deprivation *for* different, *divergent* dialect *for* language not like their own. *The task to be faced, in Robinson's view, does not involve "explaining away errors" or linguistic "permissiveness,"; it is, rather, to help all students feel at home in their language and to make linguistic prejudice repugnant to good men.*

Ralph Ellison's invisible man is suddenly very conspicuous. Whether incarnated as a black militant or as one of the growing number of black professionals working for change within the system, the black man in America is no longer content to be ignored, pushed aside, patronized, or whitewashed into the background of white. Others from America's "different" cultures push just as vigorously for visibility and recognition—organizing in strongly ethnic unions, as in California, or building larger, more demanding, more politically active groups than the cultural clubs and the street gangs that have been characteristic of ethnic life in big cities. In California, American Indians seize an island formerly used as the site of a federal prison, hoping to found there an educational center for Indian youth and to renew contact with their largely vanished native culture (one group of white businessmen had offered alternative plans to convert the island to an amusement park—a disneyland of the Northwest). In Michigan, Indians sue the state university to honor early treaties promising free education for land and petition the state bureau of natural resources to honor traditional fishing

---

[a] Quoted by Edmund J. Farrell, *Deciding the Future: A Forecast of Responsibilities of Secondary Teachers of English, 1970–2000 AD* (Urbana, Ill.: National Council of Teachers of English, Research Report No. 12, 1971), p. 141.

rights. In their relations with governmental agencies, minority groups have substituted mau-mauing for deferential petitions, the up-thrust fist for the humbly extended palm in demands not just for money but for the right to control it and the power it brings. The movement for local control of poverty funds is based on the perception that such funds have too often been used for the hypothetical good of the state and the real benefit of the middle class rather than for the needs of the poor and the nonwhite, particularly their needs for dignity and self-determination. The movement for local control of education is based in the perception that the needs of real children are not being met when the expectation is that all are alike in needs and desires. The melting pot may have been a congenial metaphor for the European immigrants flocking to the United States between the Civil War and World War I, eager as they apparently were to put behind them their languages and their old ethnic identities; but it does not appear to describe the aspirations of all groups in the latter half of the twentieth century.

With its experiments in democratic education and mass literacy, the American schoolroom is the microcosm of the larger society, quite naturally subject to the same turmoil and the same stresses that operate outside its doors. And we are beginning only now to recognize that for too long too many children have been invisible in our classrooms, given over as classrooms have been to the socialization and acculteration of every child, no matter what his background or interests, to a single and dominant mode of living— one congenial to a mass technological state. If there is a unifying theme in the current outpourings of books critical of American education—books by the Kohls, the Kozols, the Bruners, the Silbermans, the Faders—it is that our educational institutions have neglected the individual in favor of certain societal norms; and that the neglect has been most severe of those individuals who happen to come from America's "different" cultures.

The facts of cultural and ethnic diversity cannot be ignored. Glazer and Moynihan reported several years ago in *Beyond the Melting Pot* (1963) that in New York City the pot had yet to boil: ethnic patterns still shaped life styles, values, aspirations, and political choices for the people crowded into America's biggest city. From his work with American Indians in the Southwest, Sol Tax has concluded "that the problem of American Indian education is alienation rather than lack of opportunity," and he has found causes of that alienation in value conflicts between Indian and middle-class culture.[1] William Labov has found clear evidence of group fidelity among young urban blacks to social and linguistic norms running counter to the middle-class norms that dominate the American classroom, and he has shown that

---

[1] See "Group Identity and Educating the Disadvantaged" in *Language Programs for the Disadvantaged: The Report of the NCTE Task Force on Teaching English to the Disadvantaged*, Richard Corbin and Muriel Crosby, eds. (Champaign, Ill., 1965); see also Sol Tax and Robert K. Thomas, "Education 'for' American Indians: Threat or Promise," in *Linguistic-Cultural Differences and American Education*, A. C. Aarons, Barbara Y. Gordon, and William A. Stewart, eds. (= *The Florida FL Reporter*, **7**, i[1969]), 15–19.

reading failure is more severe among young blacks who have the social skills to join the countergroup than among youngsters who do not.[2] We are beginning to realize that powerful and positive values link members of countercultures and subcultures. The recent work by sociologists, cultural anthropologists, and linguists has centered on those forces that cause minority cultures to exist and persist, and findings have suggested a new conception of American society: we are not a monolithic culture guided by common assumptions, beliefs, and goals so much as a loose conglomerate of subcultures, sharing some attitudes, conflicting violently about others.

The facts confront teachers and teachers-to-be with new tasks. The most urgent one is learning how to operate comfortably and effectively in a multicultural world—learning how to mediate between the several worlds created by our students out of their own personal and social experiences and the world we have created for ourselves out of different experiences. A first and necessary step in the learning process is recognizing that as teachers of English our education has rarely prepared us for working effectively in cultural and linguistic diversity. Most of us have studied only one literature; most of us control only one language. With other teachers, our experiences are limiting: most of us come fresh from institutions of higher learning purged of the culturally divergent by entrance requirements and by standardized tests; many of us come from suburbs comfortably homogeneous in status and skin color. Our ethnocentrism is accurately measured by our militant monolingualism; finer shades of measurement can be traced in the degree of surprise we feel when we read facts like these:

Between 1930 and 1964, almost a million Germans immigrated to the United States. Between 1951 and 1960, over 125,000 immigrated from the Philippines and Asia. In the single year 1964, over 60,000 entered the U.S. from Mexico and South America; over 100,000 from Castro's Cuba.

Students in the schools of New York City come from "fifty-eight different language communities" in which "more than forty different nationalities are represented." Probably "more than three-fourths of the non-English-speaking children are Spanish-speaking Puerto Ricans."

In 1966, the Phoenix Indian School enrolled 1,041 students coming from fifteen different tribal groups. About 75 per cent came from homes where English was not spoken.[3]

Conservative estimates derived from the mother-tongue data reported by the 1960 census indicate that nineteen million white Americans have a mother tongue other than English. Roughly half of these individuals are American-born (indeed,

---

[2] William Labov and Clarence Robins, "A Note on the Relation of Reading Failure to Peer-Group Status in Urban Ghettos," in *Language and Reading*, Doris V. Gunderson, ed. (Washington, D.C., 1970), pp. 208–18.

[3] The statements are adapted from Harold B. Allen, *A Survey of the Teaching of English to Non-English Speakers in the United States* (Champaign, Ill., 1966).

approximately a quarter are children of parents who are themselves American born). . . .

[There are] fifty to sixty million white Americans who are the first generation of individuals with English as the mother tongue in their families.[4]

English is the universally required school subject. But what of common experience, of a common language, may the English teacher assume among his charges in the classroom? Yet no university English department offers an adequate program for preparing bilingual and bicultural teachers; few prepare teachers adequately to face the dialectal complexity typical of the urban classroom.

A second step in the learning process of teachers is to recognize that our national language mythology is in fact mythological; based not on fact so much as on feeling, picked up in bits and pieces like the hagiography of national heroes, and stored in the darker recesses of our memories with images of watermelons and shuffling feet on dusty roads. Ignorance of language facts, particularly facts about the nature and significance of language diversity, is as widespread as it is pernicious: as much a property of the otherwise educated as it is of people innocent of education. When subcultures exist and persist, it is inevitable that language differences exist too. Ours is a big country, and dialect differences follow inevitably from geographical separation. Because we are divided into social classes by money and status, our linguistic differences are class marked. Because ethnic groups are set off from one another by a complex of preference and prejudice, linguistic differences sometimes match ethnic lines as each group learns and clings to speech patterns peculiarly its own. Yet the English profession has been generally content to rest in the presumption of a single common and uniform language and to ignore the fact and implication of difference within it. The ethnocentrism that has governed the teaching of English generally is nowhere more noticeable than in the teaching of language and of language use.

The ruling conception in the mythology of language has been termed *Standard English*. We have assumed the existence of such a thing, connecting it vaguely with the language of writing. Because we associate Standard English in our minds with literacy, and particularly with the high literacy of literature, we assume as our duty the teaching of Standard English. And because a standard is something against which we can measure, we derive standards of writing and speaking from our conception of Standard English, conscientiously marking and correcting deviations with little thought for why we do it. The complementary term in the neat dichotomy is *Nonstandard*, or the less euphemistic *Substandard*, which matches better with practice. Nonstandard or Substandard English is that collection of deviations

---

[4] The statements are from Joshua A. Fishman, "The Breadth and Depth of English in the United States," in Aarons, Gordon and Stewart, *op. cit.*, pp. 41, 42.

from the standards of Standard that are written or uttered by individuals who do not share our values or inhabit our neighborhoods. Entry to the literate world is available only to those that conform.

Because the mythology has been comfortable for those who sit with the catbird and croak his tones, we have assumed too much about the nature of Standard and the nature of Nonstandard. We have rarely made an attempt to define either term with precision or to listen to those who have tried; we have rarely checked existing or operational definitions (which are often contradictory) against reality, which is usually more complex than our definitions allow. The assumption that Standard English must be taught to every student at every level of every classroom is almost universally held. But we rarely expose that assumption to hard questioning: What are prevailing conceptions of Standard English and how do they differ from one another? What is Nonstandard English and what relation does it bear to Standard English? Is there any correlation—more importantly any causal connection—between possession of a nonstandard dialect and educational failure? Is there any necessary correlation between possession of the standard language and intellectual achievement? What are the personal, social, political, and ethical implications of decisions to teach or not to teach Standard English?

The purpose of this paper is not to give definitive answers to such questions: no one can, and no one should pretend to be able to. I will attempt instead to examine and evaluate some prevailing conceptions of standard and nonstandard and discuss their implications for educational practice, trying to make such recommendations as are warranted by the evidence I have examined. The paper is divided into three sections. The first, "The Great Tradition," examines the conception of nonstandard dialects as deficit systems—as inherently deficient or functionally limited. In the opinion of those who hold such a conception, possession of a nonstandard dialect necessarily results in some kind of educational or cultural deprivation that must be countered by the teaching of Standard English. The second section, "The Enlightenment," examines the conception of standard and nonstandard dialects as differing linguistic systems, neither inherently superior or inferior as systems, but differing in structural detail, use, and the sociology of their speakers. "The New Frontier" treats educational proposals that purport to issue from the difference position. The section is concluded with some counterproposals that permit the writer to slip from behind the facade of scholarly objectivity to defend the bias not very well hidden in the section titles and in the commentary each section contains.

THE GREAT TRADITION

Though the tradition, like all traditions, has a past, it is its present we are most concerned with. The view that Standard English is inherently superior to other dialects sprouted in the sixteenth and seventeenth centuries, ripened in the intellectual climate of the eighteenth, and was harvested and preserved in nineteenth-century pedagogy. Bottles of it are still being opened. ". . . Mr. Hogan believes with the linguist," writes an English professor who has authored two highly successful composition texts and is now jousting with the Executive Secretary of the NCTE:

Mr Hogan believes with the linguist that all languages are equally good: namely, that the dialect of the ghetto is as good as standard English. And of course it is— but only for daily communication. "We need to accept the fact," says Mr Hogan, "that if a child can survive for twelve, fourteen or sixteen years on the streets of Harlem, his linguistic resources have had to be pretty sophisticated." He further sees that with the rise of black capitalism: "Within the separate black economy the children can speak whatever dialect works there." Such thinking hardly touches the concept of literacy, of reading and writing, and it sees reading and writing as little more than functional instrumentation.[5]

But how does the concept of Standard English touch the concept of literacy? By equating Standard English, of course, with what is written down in English—with our rich and valuable legacy of literary documents and with access to what they contain through education. The literate man controls Standard English because he is literate; the man who does not control Standard English cannot be literate. The confusion of the two concepts— literacy and Standard English—is both blatant and misleading: "Literacy" says our English professor, ". . . is of the highest importance to thought, to maturity, to civilization." No one can disagree; but by the equation, Standard English is of equal importance, and certain usages receive divine sanction:

Praise of nonliterate dialects as "highly sophisticated" is simply irresponsible— compassionate, no doubt—but damaging to society and to individuals as it damages our faith in literacy, makes education superfluous, and encourages us to think of language as only a communicative convenience and not as the highest intellectual and moral instrumentality we have.[6]

In 1851, the New England Quaker schoolmaster Goold Brown put the case more directly and without the attendant sneer in the direction of soft-minded liberals:

But *language* is an attribute of reason, and differs essentially not only from all brute voices, but even from all the chattering, jabbering, and babbling of our own species, in which there is not an intelligible meaning, with division of thought, and distinction of words.[7]

So much for the spoken word.

---

[5] Sheridan Baker, "The Literate Imagination," *Michigan Quarterly Review*, **9**(1970):13.

[6] Baker, p. 15.

[7] From *The Grammar of English Grammars*, as quoted in *English Linguistics: An Introductory Reader*, Harold Hungerford, Jay Robinson, and James Sledd, eds. (Chicago, Ill., 1970), p. 42.

But the practices of linguistic aristocrats have seldom reached their high conceptions of the standard language. Goold Brown wrote that "grammar is to language a sort of self-examination"; and because language is a faculty of reason and bears a direct relation to thought, to correct the former is to instruct the latter. But in practice, Goold Brown was as content as are current prescriptive grammarians to offer lists of "improprieties for correction," bits and pieces of sentences for tinkering, lists of usages to be avoided. Our latter-day traditionalist in a chapter called "Grammar"[8] refers to parts of speech as "the sentence's vital organs," but changes the metaphor quickly when "Correcting Bad Sentences" is the topic: "Now let us contemplate evil," he begins "—or at least the innocently awful. . . ." Fallen man, pen in hand as he faces the world, must have rules to guide him, for "writing is devilish," and rules must correct our natural tendency to "waste our words, fog our thoughts, and wreck our delivery." The pilgrim is offered another list, appropriately hortatory: "Avoid the passive voice"; "Beware the of-and-which disease"; "Beware *the use of*"; "Break the noun habit." Edit thy words and reason wilt follow, for if grammar be flesh it must be scourged by the spirit. And generations of teachers have applied the red pencil, convinced that scrupulous attention to surface form affects processes of thinking.

Apparent support for the antique concept of nonstandard dialects as inherently inferior or severely restricted has come from the recent research of educational and cognitive psychologists working with "disadvantaged" children, usually very young disadvantaged children. The most extreme view is that disadvantaged children virtually have no language at all, certainly no language that can be of any use in the schools. Carl Bereiter and Siegfried Engelmann characterized the speech of preschool children from poverty backgrounds in this way:

When the children first arrived, they had, as expected, a minute repertoire of labels to attach to the objects they used or saw every day. All buildings were called "houses," most people were called "you." Although Urbana is in the midst of a rural area, not one child could identify any farm animals. As obvious as their lack of vocabulary was their primitive notion of the structure of language. Their communications were by gesture (we later discovered that one boy could answer some questions by shaking his head, but that he did not realize that a positive shake of the head meant yes), by single words (Teacher: "What do you want?" Child: "Doll."), or a series of badly connected words or phrases. ("They mine." "Me got juice.")

The pronunciation of several of the children was so substandard that, when they did talk, the teachers had no notion of what they were saying. . . . Although most of the children could follow simple directions like, "Give me the book," they could not give such directions themselves, not even repeat them. Without exaggerating, we may say that these four-year-olds could make no statements of any kind. They

---

[8] To the end of the paragraph, the quoted bits and pieces are from Sheridan Baker, *The Practical Stylist*, 2nd ed. (New York, 1969), Chaps. 5 and 6.

could not ask questions. Their ability to answer questions was hampered by the lack of such fundamental requirements as knowing enough to look at the book in order to answer the question, "Is the book on the table?"[9]

In sum, these psychologists conclude that the language of the culturally deprived "is a basically nonlogical mode of expressive behavior which lacks the formal properties necessary for the organization of thought."[10] The fit between the view of the humanist and the view of the educational psychologist appears more than coincidental. The humanist asserts that "the dialect of the ghetto" is adequate "only for daily communication"; the psychologist offers support by finding the language of poor children lacking in the formal properties essential for thought. The humanist finds the requisite properties in Standard English; the psychologist argues that a proper goal of early language instruction is "not that of improving the child's language but rather that of teaching him a different language which would hopefully replace the first one, at least in school settings."[11] That "different language," when one examines the program and practices instituted by Bereiter and Engelmann, bears a striking resemblance to Standard English.[12]

It is such a singular event when a humanist and a psychologist agree that one should perhaps not question the basis of agreement. But on the other

[9] Carl Bereiter, Siegfried Engelmann, *et al.*, "An Academically Oriented Pre-School for Culturally Deprived Children," in *Pre-School Education Today*, Fred M. Hechinger, ed. (Garden City, N.Y., 1966), pp. 113–14.

[10] *Ibid.*, pp. 112–13.

[11] *Ibid.*, p. 113.

[12] Engelmann argues in "How to Construct Effective Language Programs for the Poverty Child," in *Language and Poverty*, Frederick Williams, ed. (Chicago, 1970), that the Bereiter-Engelmann program is based not on a particular dialect but on concepts and language structures determined to be essential to cognition and learning. But although Bereiter and Engelmann deny that the requisite structures exist in the language of poverty children, they find them easily enough in fully explicit structures from standard English. They do not demonstrate how these structures relate to cognitive processes and appear to operate from very primitive notions of relations between language structures and their uses. For example, in Bereiter, Engelmann, *et al.*, the following distinction is made between expressive and cognitive uses of language and their supporting structures: "Language covers such an enormous territory, however, that setting up language development as an objective for preschool education narrows the field hardly at all. The field can be narrowed considerably by separating out those aspects of language which mainly serve purposes of social communication from those aspects which are more directly involved in logical thinking. The former include lexical items—nouns, verbs, and modifiers—and idiomatic expressions. The outstanding feature of the latter aspect of language is the manipulation of statement patterns according to grammatical and syntactic rules" (p. 106). No linguist would propose such a dichotomy of language structure; no linguist would agree that the formal properties of language could be so neatly separated by the uses to which they are put. Bereiter and Engelmann simply deny the possibility of statement patterns in nonstandard dialects, and consequently do not recognize them when they occur in the speech of children from poverty backgrounds. It is interesting that the assumption that English was a grammarless language was made in the sixteenth century, and served as a push toward the writing of pedagogical grammars. Some notions die a slow death, for the assumption is a typical feature in Great Tradition concepts of nonstandard dialects.

hand, their mutual conception of the nature of nonstandard is so widely held, and its implications for pedagogy so far reaching, that one *must* question. For if nonstandard dialects as linguistic systems—as systems of concepts and formal properties—are inadequate to the organization of thought, some other linguistic system *must* be taught if children speaking nonstandard dialects are to succeed in school. But could it be that the whole basis of such an argument rests not upon empirical proof leading to a necessary conclusion, but upon a common assumption—unproved and unacknowledged—an *assumption* that Standard English is superior?

THE ENLIGHTENMENT

Linguists have attacked the Great Tradition for several generations and from several points of view. In maintaining that nonstandard dialects are merely different from standard and not inherently inferior they have agreed in suspecting that a very old myth underlies the concept of inferiority—the myth of the primitive language. A primitive language, the story goes, is one spoken by a people who have never developed a writing system or borrowed one, and it exhibits certain characteristics: it is limited in vocabulary (often so limited that gesture must supplement speech to make communication possible); it is lacking in the abstract terms necessary for thinking; it is restricted in semantic reference to the concrete world of discrete objects. That myth was exploded, for all who would read it, by the careful descriptive work of anthropologically oriented linguists who recorded and analyzed many of the aboriginal languages of the Americas and other regions of the world; the remains of the myth should have been swept away by more recent findings in theoretical linguistics and in language learning. But it is still possible to find the myth printed and quoted. Of Eskimos, "There are no abstract words and all verbs are verbs of action. The Eskimos, though extraordinarily quick and alert mentally, are not thinkers in our sense. . . . [Theirs] is a language of people whose lives are lived in their bodies and not in their minds."[13]

Leonard Bloomfield some time ago pointed to a tendency among literate people to rationalize the structure of their own language—to see in external features of linguistic form the perfect expression of a universal logic or a universal aesthetic. Such "logic" has been the frequent appeal of prescriptive grammarians, and linguists have found it operative as well in the assumptions of intervention programs. Carl Bereiter says that his program's major concern:

. . . is the acquisition of grammatical statement patterns and a grasp of the logical organization of these patterns. Precise pronunciation is seen as a critical requirement

---

[13] Katherine Sherman, *Spring on an Arctic Island* (Boston, 1956), p. 56. Quoted first by J. C. Carothers, "Culture, Psychiatry, and the Written Word," *Psychiatry*, **22**(1959):307–20; then by Baker in "The Literate Imagination," *op cit.*

for mastery of grammatical structure, for even in our relatively uninflected language a good deal of grammatical structure is mediated by little affixes, variations, and particles which cannot be differentiated by the blurred pronunciation typical of culturally deprived children. The child who says "Ih bwah" for "This is a block" is in a poor position to understand, much less communicate, such contrasting statements as "This is not a block," "These are blocks," and "These are not blocks."[14]

According to such a view, there can be no alternate grammatical means for the expression of conceptual niceties: if pronunciation "blurs" past tense markers, for example, the conceptual contrast between present and past disappears. Bereiter claims that the utterance *Ih bwah* (which suggests the nonstandard pattern with copula deletion, loss of final consonant on *it*, and the childish substitution of /w/ for /l/—*i.e.*, a complete nonstandard sentence with subject and predicate) has no pattern. The child who says "Me got juice" (another of Bereiter's examples) confuses subject and object and may be presumed to have drowned.

Direct and empirically based counter-evidence to findings of verbal deprivation among poor children is appearing with increasing frequency.[15] But because such research proceeds from assumptions about language quite different from those held by deprivation theorists, it is more relevant to contrast basic assumptions and their support than merely to weigh the gross tonnage of accumulated evidence.

As we have seen, deprivation theorists base their argument for the inadequacy of nonstandard on observations of the language behavior of "deprived" children. Because they reject, as untenable, hypotheses of hereditary inferiority or universal mental retardation on the part of poverty children, deprivation theorists find causes of linguistic deprivation in environment—in the absence of parents in slum homes, in the linguistic modes used

[14] Bereiter, Engelmann, *et al.*, *op. cit.* p. 112.

[15] Representative studies are Joan Baratz and E. Povich, "Grammatical Constructions in the Language of the Negro Preschool Child," a paper presented at the national meeting of the American Speech and Hearing Association, 1967; Joan C. Baratz, "Teaching Reading in an Urban Negro School System," in Williams, *op. cit.*, pp. 11–24, which gives a partial report of research done by herself and Povich; Doris R. Entwisle, "Semantic Systems of Children: Some Assessments of Social Class and Ethnic Differences," in Williams, *op. cit.*, pp. 123–39. Entwisle's report concerns word association tests with young children from slums and from suburbia. Her aim was to gauge the development of semantic fields for selected lexical items, where development was measured by the child's ability to associate words by form class (nouns with nouns, verbs with verbs, and so on), or by some other discernible semantic framework such as generic class or synonymy. Her findings: "Word associations of black and of white elementary school children reveal, contrary to expectation, that slum children are apparently more advanced than suburban children at first grade in terms of paradigmatic responses." This is on a test measuring the ability to form concepts, a process obviously essential to the development of cognition. Baratz reports similar findings from tests of the development of sentence types, using a developmental model based on the rules of a generative grammar: "Results indicated that the Negro Head Start child is not delayed in language acquisition. The majority of his utterances are on the kernal and transformational levels of Lee's developmental model."

for adult-child interaction, in noise and distraction levels in crowded slum dwellings. William Labov, the linguist whose work with nonstandard dialects has been as comprehensive as any yet done, vigorously questions both the accuracy of the observations and the adequacy of the findings made by deprivation hypothesists. Labov claims that the concept of verbal deprivation has "no basis in social reality"; and that the limited language behavior observed in tests and classrooms results from tensions in the test situation, not from the child's lack of language capacity.[16] He charges further that the concept of deprivation results from assuming that any utterance divergent from standard norms is by that reason deficient: in other words, Standard English is better because we assume it to be better—hardly a convincing proof.

Linguists, says Labov, in spite of disagreements over theory and detail, all "agree that nonstandard dialects are highly structured systems." All linguists seem to agree, too, in what has been called the principle of linguistic relativity: an assumption that from the point of view of structural complexity, adequacy to serve the cognitive and communicative needs of the speech communities using them, all dialects are equal. The two assumptions have guided all twentieth-century linguistic work, and the resulting descriptive and comparative grammars based on them clearly prove their accuracy as descriptive statements about human language. *No* human language, *no form* of any human language, is a random collection of words put together haphazardly. All human languages have rules governing phonetic and syntactic processes, and organize such rules in a systematic way. But these two principles do not in themselves disprove the idea of functional discontinuities between dialects. One may grant that a nonstandard dialect is systematic and adequate to serve the needs of, say, the ghetto in which it is spoken, yet still maintain that it is inadequate for the requirements of the school.

However, Labov and others make a further claim: As linguistic systems, nonstandard dialects are not just equally systematic, but fundamentally similar to Standard English. The dialects differ in detail, to be sure, but not in kind; and because of their fundamental similarity nonstandard and standard are equal in their capacities to serve communicative, cognitive, and logical requirements. Summarizing his work with some nonstandard dialects spoken by urban black children, Labov says,

They [the children] have the same basic vocabulary, possess the same capacity for conceptual learning, and use the same logic as anyone else who learns to speak and understand English.[17]

For a long time, linguists have insisted that the regional and social varieties of American English are relatively uniform. Even the dialectologists most

---

[16] See particularly "The Logic of Nonstandard English," reprinted on pp. 319–54; also *The Study of Nonstandard English* (Champaign, Ill., 1970).

[17] See p. 320 above.

concerned with differences among dialects—those engaged in mapping variants for the Linguistic Atlas of the United States and Canada—have reached the general conclusion that "dialect differences in American English are relatively small."[18] But conventional dialectology, focusing as it does on surface differences, has lacked adequate means for revealing underlying similarities. More recent studies, by employing and extending ideas and methods borrowed from generative-transformational theory, have had better bases for describing similarities among dialects. In addition, because the study of meaning has been central in generative theory, recent studies have been based on a clearer appreciation of the complexity involved in the relations of language to cognition and logic—a degree of complexity that shows as inadequate and inaccurate earlier assumptions of direct relations between language form and thought.

Generative theory, to offer a brief and much oversimplified summary,[19] is much concerned with what linguistic systems have in common. A language is conceived of as an unlimited set of sentences; a grammar as a system of rules describing principles of sentence construction and accounting for the relation between meaning and sound. Some rules in a generative grammar (base rules) describe deep structure—a system of semantic and syntactic categories and their relations that determine meaning most directly; other rules (transformations) relate deep structures to the surface structures of sentences as they are actually spoken; still other rules (phonological rules) account for how a sentence is pronounced. Two ideas are central to the theory: deep and surface structure may differ (*e.g.*, sentences may differ in surface form but not in meaning, or differ in meaning but not in surface form); deep structure is more important for meaning than surface structure or phonological structure. Let us see how such a framework functions in showing basic similarities among some contrasting features of Standard English (SE) and of what has been termed Negro Nonstandard English (NNE).[20] Although

[18] The quotation is from Raven I. McDavid, Jr. in his chapter in W. Nelson Francis, *The Structure of American English* (New York, 1958). McDavid was an early and prodigious worker on the *Atlas* and now directs the project. The context for his statement is a comparison with dialect diversity in Europe: "To those familiar with the situation in European countries, such as France or Italy or even England, dialect differences in American English are relatively small. Most of the time, any native speaker of any variety of American English can understand a native speaker of any other variety," p. 482.

[19] Theoretical differences among generative linguists should not be ignored, particularly by those who seek to apply current findings. I have tried here to give as general and as neutral a summary as possible. Those interested in pursuing the differing positions now prevailing might consult easily accessible collections of theoretical and descriptive articles: *Universals in Linguistic Theory*, Emmon Bach and Robert T. Harms, Jr., eds. (New York, 1968); *Modern Studies in English: Readings in Transformational Grammar*, David A. Reibel and Sanford A. Schane, eds. (Englewood Cliffs, N. J., 1969); *Readings in English Transformational Grammar*, Roderick A. Jacobs and Peter S. Rosenbaum, eds. (Waltham, Mass., 1970).

[20] Although I have reservations about the separate existence of a distinctively Negro or black dialect, I use the term here because it has been widely used by researchers in urban

the illustration is long it is necessarily so to demonstrate the basis of Labov's claim about logicality. If the length strains patience, rest assured that the writer has spared the kind of detail that would be necessary for a fully detailed grammatical account.

One feature consistently placed high on the list of proscribed usages by prescriptive grammarians is the double negative. Since the eighteenth century, the form has been called illogical on a quasimathematical analogy: two negatives make a positive. Dialectologists have reported the following patterns in NNE: (no attempt is made to render pronunciation differences by "dialect" spellings):

NNE	*SE*
1. He don't know nothing.	$\begin{cases} \text{He doesn't know anything.} \\ \text{He knows nothing.} \end{cases}$
2. Nobody know it.	
3. Nobody $\begin{cases} \text{doesn't} \\ \text{don't} \end{cases}$ know it.	Nobody knows it.
4. Didn't nobody see it.	Nobody saw it.
5. It ain't no cat can't get in no coop.	There isn't any cat that can get into any coop.[21]

Clearly, nonstandard and standard dialects contain negative sentences. But are the nonstandard sentences as systematic as the SE sentences, or are negatives thrown at the speaker's whim? Are the nonstandard sentences as logical as the SE sentences? A third question relevant to classroom practice is, "Are the nonstandard sentences intelligible?" Because SE and NNE both contain negative sentences, generative grammarians assign a feature NEG to the deep structures of both grammars. Thus a very gross rule for a negative sentence would be: *NEG + sentence*. The feature *NEG* appears in various surface realizations in a SE sentence, but normally, for clausal negation (that is, denying the assertion made by the clause) *NEG* is attached transformationally to the verb by means of the verbal auxiliary *do* (if no other auxiliary is present), which serves to carry tense and negative marking:

$$\text{NEG + He sings} \longrightarrow \text{He doesn't sing}$$
$$\text{not *He singsn't}$$

---

dialects and because it does point to real speech used by real groups. The illustration draws on data from several sources: notably, William Labov, *The Study of Nonstandard English*, *op. cit.*, and "The Study of Language in Its Social Context," *Studium Generale*, **23**(1970):30 –87; Ralph W. Fasold and Walt Wolfram. "Some Linguistic Features of Negro Dialect," in *Teaching Standard English in the Inner City*, Ralph W. Fasold and Roger W. Shuy, eds. (Washington D.C., 1970), pp. 41–86.

[21] The last example and much of the analysis is borrowed from Labov, "The Study of Language in Its Social Context," *op. cit.*

Standard English has another transformational rule, however, that permits what has been called negative attraction. The rule says, essentially, that in a sentence containing an indefinite noun, *NEG* may be attracted to the first indefinite noun. Attraction is obligatory when the *subject* is an indefinite noun, optional when the indefinite occurs after the verb. Thus we have negative sentences in SE like *Nobody sings* (but not **Anybody doesn't sing*) where the subject is indefinite; alternative forms *He doesn't know anything* or *He knows nothing* occur when the indefinite comes after the verb. In SE, there are constraints on the negative rule: the negative may be attracted to one indefinite only; when it is attracted, negative marking is removed from the verb. Thus only one negative appears in the deep and surface structures of SE sentences.

As we see in sentences 1 through 5, nonstandard sentences may contain more than one surface negative. But negatives are not thrown in at whim; rather, their occurrence is governed by rules that are essentially the same as the rules for SE negation. First, the deep structures are identical, because both SE and NNE have negative sentences. As in SE, *NEG* is regularly attached by transformation to the verb by means of the auxiliary *do*: "He *don't* know nothing." "Nobody *don't* know it." and so so. As in SE, *NEG* may be attracted *only* to indefinite nouns and not to other sentence elements: thus, "He don't know *nothing*." "Didn't *nobody* see it." and so on.[22] The clausal negation rules of NNE differ from SE rules only in lacking the two constraints limiting *NEG* attraction to one indefinite only and erasing negative marking from the verb. It is illuminating that rule differences like these—showing elimination of special conditions or constraints from rules to permit them to apply more generally—have been widely found in studies of linguistic change. Rules similar to those for negation in NNE have been reported in studies of child language acquisition, with children from environments in which Standard English is spoken, showing the tendency for complex grammatical rules to be simplified in normal language learning.

Most of us do not need such sophisticated analysis to accept the fact that the standard and nonstandard versions of sentences 1, 2, and 3 are identical in meaning. No nonstandard speaker misunderstands another nonstandard speaker; no nonstandard speaker has the slightest difficulty understanding that "He doesn't know anything" denies knowledge on the part of *He*; no standard speaker takes "He don't know nothing" to mean *He* must know something, unless that speaker has swallowed the foolishness that $(- \times - = +)$ is a formula applying to language. But such formulas *are* the bases for charges that nonstandard dialects are lacking in formal properties essential to logical thinking. Their absurdity is demonstrable through analysis and

---

[22] Further evidence of the systematic quality of the feature comes from Labov, "The Study of Language in Its Social Context," *op. cit.*, p. 65: "For core members of the NNE peer groups, we find that negative concord [that is, attraction of negative to indefinites without erasure of NEG from verb] operates not at a 95 or 98 per cent level, but at 100 per cent, in 42 out of 42 cases, 63 out of 63, and so on.

through common sense operating on some knowledge of language. If $(- \times - = +)$ were a formula applying universally to language structure, we could offer the following formula for measuring the logic of Chaucer's Middle English[23]: count the negatives and divide by two; if the resulting number is even, the sentence is illogical, if odd, logical. Attitudes and spurious knowledge inhibit communication at least as effectively as differences in linguistic structure.

Sentences 4 and 5, however, do present a slightly more complicated problem, because they might conceivably be misunderstood by a standard speaker who had had limited social contacts. "Didn't nobody see it" (4), could be taken as a question, though intonation would make doing so unlikely; (5) "It ain't no cat can't get in no coop," a structure termed rare[24] in NNE, might be understood as meaning "There isn't any cat who can't get into any coop," the opposite of the intended meaning. But Labov shows convincingly that the two structures can be related to their equivalents in SE and their differences explained by such minor rule differences as the removal in nonstandard of the constraints on negative attraction which we have just discussed.

Sentence 4 has auxiliary *do* with a negative particle preposed before the subject, making it superficially similar to SE questions (Didn't John do it?). But Labov argues that the nonstandard sentence should be compared not to SE questions that do prepose auxiliaries, but to SE sentences with "negative foregrounding,"[25] stylistic variants in which negative elements are brought to the front of sentences for emphasis: "*Never* did anyone see it." "*Seldom* did he come." "*At no time* did he enter the bank." In the SE sentences, indefinite adverbials may be foregrounded. Nonstandard sentences like (4) suggest that NNE permits the foregrounding of more kinds of negatives than SE; thus the difference again involves not a major rule change but the removal of a constraint on a rule—the constraint restricting foregrounding to indefinite adverbials.

Sentence 5 shows the further generalization of negative attraction. The sentence contains two clauses, each containing an indefinite noun:

<table>
<tr><td>Cl.1</td><td>Cl.2</td></tr>
</table>

There isn't *any cat* that can get in *any coop*

---

[23] Middle English, as everyone knows, permitted multiple negation for emphasis. A spectacular example occurs in the *Clerk's Tale* as Griselde expresses unbounded love and devotion:

> Ne nevere, for no wele ne no woe,
> Ne shal the goost withinne myn herte stente
> To love yow best with al myn trewe entente.
> (IV, 971–73)

By the formula, the six negatives result in illogic, though not by the heart. The alert student will apply the discussion of negative rules to this ME example.

[24] By Fasold and Wolfram, *op. cit.*, p. 75.

[25] See Labov, *The Study of Nonstandard English, op. cit.*, p. 13.

Only the first clause is negative, the second is positive. In the SE sentence, only one negative element occurs in the surface structure; should a second negative occur in the second clause in SE, the meaning would change:

6. There isn't any cat that *can't* get into any coop.

The deep structure for 6 would thus contain two *NEG's*, one for each clause: *NEG* + *Clause 1* + *NEG* + *Clause 2*. But nonstandard 5 differs in meaning from 6 and is synonymous with standard 5. It has the deep structure *NEG* + *Clause 1* + *Clause 2*. The multiple surface negatives simply show negative attraction by those elements that regularly attract negatives: indefinites (any cat → no cat, any coop → no coop) and first position in a clause (can → can't, when the relative *that* is deleted). Thus the multiple negation in the nonstandard sentence, though perhaps troublesome for the standard speaker, is not random but systematic. The rules that govern negation are basically similar in SE and NNE and differ in relatively minor ways: essentially by the removal of rule constraints or conditions in the nonstandard dialect. The standard constructions are not more logical in any way than the nonstandard, unless we are willing to attribute some abstract logical quality to the surface appearance of one rather than more than one negative element. Negation is as available for use in nonstandard dialects as in standard when its use is needed. There is no justification for the traditional practice of equating logic with the superficial features of one's own speech.

Although the existing research on nonstandard dialects is limited (no one has produced even a reasonably full grammar of a nonstandard dialect), the systematic study of dialect features now being conducted seems to confirm the conclusion that differences between standard and nonstandard are relatively superficial and easily explained with reference to SE rules. Few linguists have postulated deep structure differences;[26] one exception is the form *be*, which occurs in sentences like "I be making hats" and "If somebody hit him, Henry be mad" to signal a verbal aspect (generic, nontense marked) that is not a part of the aspect system of SE. Most have found differences only in phonological rules, in transformational rules, and in lexicon.

Such differences in rule can, of course, result in surface differences wide enough to occasionally hinder communication. The lexical replacement of *it* for anticipatory *there* could lead a standard speaker to misinterpret the sentence:

Doesn't nobody really know that *it's* a God, y'know, cause I mean I have seen

---

[26] A notable exception is the work of Marvin D. Loflin who postulates extensive and deep structure differences, for example, in the verbal system. See his "Negro Nonstandard and Standard English: Same or Different Deep Structure?", *Orbis,* **18**(1969):74–91. Exceptional also are those scholars who assert that nonstandard black dialects derive from a pidgin-creole developed by slaves; but their assertions have not been followed by extensive descriptive work offering proof.

black gods, pink gods, white gods, all color gods, and don't nobody know *it's* really a God.[27]

by taking *it* as a personal pronoun. But once learning that *it* serves the same function in certain dialects as does *there* in SE, we are not likely to misunderstand. Similarly, phonological rules can operate to remove grammatical signals that seem essential to the standard speaker. Word final consonant clusters, for example, are consistently simplified in some nonstandard dialects, particularly /st/, /sp/, /sk/, /st/, /zd/, /ft/, /vd/, /md/, /nd/, /ld/, /pt/, /kt/. Some of these clusters result from the past tense marking of verbs: pass + *Past* → passed [pæst], fish + *Past* → [fišt], join + *Past* → [joɪnd], and so on. When the clusters are reduced in pronunciation, the overt past tense marker disappears: [pæst] → [pæs], [fišt] → [fiš], [joɪnd] → [joɪn]. But past *tense* does not disappear from the nonstandard dialects with the loss of overt marking. The sentence "Yesterday I fish off the pier" does not contain a present tense. Standard speakers similarly reduce consonant clusters in casual speech and under certain phonetic conditions (try, e.g., The house burn*ed* *d*own; Charlie walk*ed* *t*o town; the desk*s* *s*eemed out of place). Again, the nonstandard dialects merely extend tendencies, that is generalize rules, that operate as well in SE.[28]

More examples could be offered, but perhaps the major point is clear. When linguists like Labov assert the equality of dialects they assert that dialects are equally systematic, equally adequate to serve needs for communication felt by the people using them. When they further assert that nonstandard speakers "possess the same capacity for conceptual learning, and use the same logic as anyone else who learns to speak and understand English," they are basing such assertions on the theory that language relates to logic and cognition through its deepest structure—a theory well supported by present research and on findings of virtual identity in the deep structures of American dialects. Nonstandard dialects are as capable of supporting cognitive uses as SE because they are virtually identical in deep structure to SE, and because such differences as do exist are restricted to surface features and are easily related to features of SE.

We must see that such a concept is antithetical to many present practices, especially those guided by the Great Tradition. But we must also see how the concept applies to the teaching of language use—of composition and reading—before we rush, as so many have done, to ill-guided application.

First, the concept is abstract. Linguists study linguistic systems and linguistic communities. We must teach individuals. Linguists write dictionaries of American English, or of English, not of the words possessed by Jay

---

[27] See p. 330.
[28] For a more detailed discussion of this matter, see the remarks by C.-J. Bailey (pp. 178–83).

Robinson. A grammar is a description of rules for sentences in English, not a catalog or analysis of the sentences used by Jay Robinson. But as a grammar or a dictionary probes deep beneath the surface to discover general rules for word and sentence formation shared by Jay Robinson, by other speakers of Standard English, and by speakers of so-called nonstandard dialects, it begins to reveal what we all have in common by virtue of our common language, by virtue of our common humanity, by virtue of the similar structuring of our knowledge through innate mental capacities. The concept of linguistic equality speaks to our expectations and preconceptions about the students who come into our classroom. It says, no one is disqualified by the accident of learning one system of English rather than another from entering and running well in the race for knowledge.

The concept is neither vaguely humanitarian nor disrespectful of education, as Great Traditionists charge; nor is it irrelevant to everyday practice, in spite of its abstraction. The contrary assumption—of linguistic deprivation resulting from cultural deprivation—can have and has had damaging effects. To identify a particular group of children as disadvantaged, as needful of special *remediative* teaching, isolates those children from their schoolmates, makes their educational needs seem somehow peculiar and not quite normal, urges us to view such differences as may appear between their behavior and language and our behavior and language as corruptions of some sacrosanct norm. The deprivation hypothesis offers an all-too-convenient escape hatch for teachers of poor children and nonwhite children: its premise is that the *children* are lacking—that they do not bring to the classroom the equipment we have every right to expect. If such children fail, it is easy to convince ourselves that they do so because of what they are, not because of what we have failed to do. As the twig is bent, the saying is, and who ever heard of a tree growing in a gutter. The deprivation hypothesis translates easily into the self-fulfilling prophecy: if we expect little, that is what we usually get; if we expect failure, we will have little trouble allowing it to happen.[29] If we see every departure from Standard English as a lapse in logic, every non-standard form as inappropriate to the classroom, we build failure into our very system of evaluation and guarantee it for the groups we seek to help.

[29] All teachers should at least skim R. Rosenthal and Lenore Jacobson, *Pygmalion in the Classroom* (New York, 1968), which reports an ingenious experiment into the operation of self-fulfilling prophesies. Briefly, a group of students in an elementary school were administered tests designed to measure growth in IQ. A number of students from this group were selected randomly, without reference to the results from an initial test, and designated as children who could be expected to "spurt" in IQ gain. When these children were retested, a year later, they were found actually to have made significant gains in IQ. The experiment strongly suggests that a teacher's expectations affect the accomplishments of his pupils; in this case not because of halo effect, because the teachers did not administer or grade the test measuring IQ gain, but because of something that happened in the classroom between students and teacher to facilitate learning. These conclusions, however, must be considered in conjunction with the critique of the authors' experimental design by Robert L. Thorndike, *American Educational Research Journal* **5** (1968): 709–711.

The concept of dialect equality does not reduce the complexity in the task of teaching effective language use, nor does it remove from the teacher the responsibility for teaching his students to expand and develop their native linguistic resources. To say that nonstandard speakers have the same basic linguistic competence as standard speakers does not mean that every nonstandard speaker knows all the vocabulary he must know, can manipulate complex sentences effectively, or control styles appropriate to a wide range of topics and audiences. We must teach him, just as we must teach the immature user of Standard English. Both bring to the classroom systems we can work with; and rejecting the notion of verbal deprivation on the part of some students may force us to look hard at factors other than dialect that *can* cause failure in language use: inadequate intellectual preparation for addressing a topic, failure on the part of the teacher to indicate what is required, lack of trust between teacher and student, the student's lack of experience in the whole process of writing, and his failure to see how writing can possibly be of importance to him. All too often in English classrooms we have preferred the direct frontal attack on language use, wielding the red pencil against the barbarian assaults our students make on standards, defending our language from chaos and non-sense. If the concept of dialect equality is abstract, the abstractions on which it is based are not of the sort that govern Great Tradition practices. There the abstraction is not theory but the thing to be taught. One searches in vain the pages of prescriptive grammars for adequate, precise, and realistic definitions of Standard English, or for reasoned justification for preferring it to Nonstandard; one hunts just as fruitlessly for the cognitive system underlying the language drills imposed by Bereiter and Engelmann.

There is, of course, a major difference between Standard and Nonstandard English: the difference of social status, specifically, the social status of the speakers using them. That idea is very old, but few have accepted it in spite of overwhelming evidence, perhaps because accepting it imposes a very difficult burden on those who would teach Standard English. Once we accept the fact that the terms Standard/Nonstandard refer to the social status of speakers, we uncapitalize standard and make it multiform, not uniform. High status speakers in Atlanta use different forms from those used by high status speakers in Boston; such speakers in Atlanta have different language attitudes from those held by comparable speakers in Boston. To teach standard once we recognize its diversity requires a painstaking collection of current information on usage and opinion, the translation of such information into effective teaching materials, and inhuman patience to endure hours of mind-dulling drill. Most Great Traditionalists prefer simple lists of *do's* and *dont's*, and find no need to relate them to reality since mythology serves.[30] In the face of complexity, do something simple.

---

[30] The mythology is not unique to humanists. It has been accepted by curriculum designers and by some of the linguists who would advise them. Its most common literary form is a

THE NEW FRONTIER

It would appear from the preceding discussion that linguists and linguistically oriented applicators would assign low priority to the systematic teaching of standard English. The best linguistic evidence seems to prove that nonstandard is as fit for logical and cognitive uses as standard; that differences between nonstandard and standard "are largely confined to superficial, rather low level processes which have little effect upon meaning";[31] that communication between standard and nonstandard speakers is rarely and then not seriously hindered by such superficial differences as do exist. Linguists working on problems of dialect have rightly pressed the attack against the cultural chauvinism implicit in Great Tradition and neo-Great Tradition conceptions; they have been right in insisting that standard English must be realistically and concretely defined with reference to the speech and beliefs about speech of the controlling class, generally taken to be the great white middle; but many, while believing everything said in this paragraph, have still seen the direct teaching of standard English as a vitally important task. In the face of complexity, do something simple.

Complexity is amply provided by the chaos in urban schools, by the conflict in American society. Present circumstances in society and school—disastrous urban riots, soaring crime rates with an emphasis on crimes of violence, dropout and rates of failure in ghetto schools, racial trouble in intergrated schools—have sent the current generation of social scientists on a frantic search for causes. In their dash, too many have been more impressed by the size of the problems than the complexity of their causes. When cautious statements are offered, like the following by Labov, they are too often pruned of their qualifying modifiers and conditions by those who would rush pell-mell to oversimple "solutions":

One of the most extraordinary failures in the history of American education is the failure of the public school system to teach black children in the urban ghettos to read. The fact of reading failure is so general, and so widespread, that no one school system, no one method, and no one teacher can be considered responsible. We are plainly dealing with social and cultural events of considerable magnitude, in which the linguistic factors are the focal points of trouble or centers of difficulty rather than the primary causes.[32]

---

list of socially proscribed features, usually short, usually as conventional as formulaic poetry because it owes much to lists compiled in the past showing how persistent despised usages are, in spite of the efforts of eradicators. A new term has even been suggested for the myth—*consensus dialect*; see J. L. Dillard, "How to Tell the Bandits from the Good Guys, or What Dialect to Teach?", in Aarons, Gordon, and Stewart, *op. cit.*, pp. 84 ff.

[31] Labov, *The Study of Nonstandard English*, *op. cit.*, p. 40.

[32] P. 238 above.

Such a position offers cold comfort to those who would change the world tomorrow: it says the causes aren't yet known and are likely to be plural rather than singular. It is easier to take *centers* or *focal points* to mean *cause*; it is easier still, given generations of like practice, to look at language for *the* cause:

In regard to the supposed substandard language of lower-class Negroes, school investigators are just beginning to recognize that Negro speech is a language system unto itself which differs from "standard" English in everything but vocabulary.[33]

Because something is known about "the language system unto itself," the opening is there for the dash to application. Many have hurried through.

Dialect and Reading Problems

If more black children than white fail to learn to read, perhaps the cause is "the language system unto itself":

. . . the one major fault of our urban educational system is its failure to understand why teaching an urban Negro child to read is so difficult. But the explanation is really quite simple. A cultural variable is at work which is basic to the difficulty that the Negro child experiences in attempting to learn to read. Evidence has been accumulating that the Negro ghetto child has a different language system (call it Negro nonstandard dialect) which is part of his culture and which interferes with his learning to read. Unless and until this variable is considered, and specific educational innovation based on it, the majority of the inner-city Negro children will continue to fail despite the introduction of all sorts of social improvements to the educational setting.[34]

A simple cause calls forth a simple solution: if dialect difference is the cause of reading failure, teach the dialect which will remove it. Teach standard English (presumably the dialect of books) and reading problems disappear for nonstandard speakers.

The argument is given persuasiveness by the obvious need for literacy: we *must* teach our students to read and write. With that requirement, no one can quibble. However, the argument rests on two assumptions: (1) that the system of written English represents the system of standard spoken English better than it does nonstandard spoken English; (2) middle-class children (i.e., standard speakers by the linguists' own definition) learn to read more readily *because* of the match between the written and spoken systems. The assumptions seem valid until we again raise the question of the *nature* rather than the details of differences between the two dialects and place the assumptions in the context of the use of English around the world.

---

[33] Roger D. Abrahams, "Black Talk and Black Education," in Aarons, Gordon, and Stewart, *op. cit.*, p. 11.

[34] Stephen S. and Joan C. Baratz, "Negro Ghetto Children and Urban Education: A Cultural Solution," in Aarons, Gordon, and Stewart, *op. cit.*, p. 13.

As we have seen, a fundamental tenet of generative grammar is that deep and surface structure may differ. Thus, when we observe that nonstandard speakers sometimes say *tess, dess, wass, han, col* where standard speakers say *test, desk, wasp, hand, cold,* we speak of the actual phonetic realization of these words—their actual pronunciation—not the shape in which they are stored in the speaker's mind. For reasons too complicated to discuss here, linguists postulate more similarities than differences in underlying representations for lexical items used commonly by standard and nonstandard speakers. In a generative lexicon for nonstandard English, the words above would have final consonants in the underlying representation, even though they are not always pronounced (they do appear in some environments). There is every reason to believe that these underlying forms are more crucial in learning to read than the surface forms.[35]

The point might be made clearer by another example, treated in a highly simplified form. Some nonstandard sentences of the patterns Subject + Copula + Adjective; Subj + Cop + Predicate Nominal; Subj + Cop + Locative, lack the copula (the *be* form) nearly always present in SE. Thus we find sentences like "He wild," "She a pretty girl," "They in the closet." It would appear that these sentences show a major difference: that learning to read the standard sentences "He's wild," "She's a pretty girl," "They're in the closet," might pose a major problem. But the copula *is* present in the deep structure of NNE, although sometimes deleted in the surface structure. The copula appears regularly in certain constructions: elliptical forms "He is too;" tag questions "He ain't here, *is* he?"; comparatives "She taller than he *is*"; clauses with relatives "That's what he *is*." Labov proposes a general rule: "Wherever standard English can contract, NNE can delete the copula, and wherever SE cannot contract, NNE cannot delete."[36] Again, deep structure analysis reveals similarity and suggests that concentration on surface differences can overexaggerate the effect of structural conflict on learning to read.

Furthermore, the case for dialect interference in reading becomes weaker when we ask what *real* dialect the writing system of English does represent. How different are the written productions of Southern Americans and Northern Americans, British novelists and Australian novelists? The same writing system serves for the *r*-less and *l*-less dialects of American English as well as the *l*-full and *r*-full; for spoken systems as different as British English in its variable manifestations, Australian English, Canadian English, Indian English, and Nigerian English. But the literature on dialect and reading still offers statements like the following:

Further problems in teaching reading to some black children arise because of the fact that they come to school speaking the Negro dialect—Black English. The

---

[35] See Kenneth S. Goodman, "Reading: A Psycholinguistic Guessing Game," in *Language and Reading,* ed. Doris V. Gunderson, (Washington, D.C., 1970), pp. 107–119.

[36] Labov, "The Study of Language in Its Social Context," *op. cit.,* p. 61.

middle-class child brings to school essentially the same dialect he will be taught to read, i.e. standard English.[37]

Dialect problems—instances where the structure of a native dialect interferes with the structure of that being learned—can emerge, of course, in the process of learning to read and write, particularly in the latter, because writing demands productive and not merely receptive control—a more difficult accomplishment in language learning as those of us know who can read a foreign language but not speak or write it with facility. But structural interference as a causative factor in reading failure must not be overexaggerated, as it has been in much recent work. Dialect-related problems that emerge in reading do so early, and are essentially mechanical—matters of sound-letter correspondences.[38] Solving them is of course essential, for reading begins with the translation from letter to sound. But such problems can easily be solved by a teacher who knows nonstandard phonologies and can tell a correct nonstandard reading from a failure to decipher the written symbol. More serious types of reading failure—problems in analysis and comprehension of *matter*—are not so easily handled. Real reading takes place as a student moves from deciphering to interpretation, learning to draw inferences and conclusions from what he reads. Structural interference of one dialect with another does not hinder that kind of reading; teaching standard English by any method yet proposed will not facilitate it.

The Social Argument: Bidialectalism or Biloquialism

The argument that standard English must be taught to young children from the ghetto *before* they are taught to read is too obviously impractical and too

[37] Ralph W. Fasold, "Orthography in Reading Materials for Black English Speaking Children," in *Teaching Black Children to Read*, Joan C. Baratz and Roger W. Shuy, eds. (Washington, D.C., 1969), p. 76. Fasold admits, however, that orthography does not present a problem for readers speaking divergent dialects: "With a few marginal exceptions, there is no reason to develop a special orthography for black English speakers. Because of the possible lack of certain lexical items in the vocabularies of children in general, it may prove advisable to use some sort of modified orthography in teaching all young children to read. But in the main, conventional English orthography is as adequate for black English speakers as it is for Standard English speakers." (p. 85).

[38] There is little hard evidence to support claims such as the following: "studies of the language of the ghetto Negro child have shown that his language . . . is sufficiently different from standard English as spoken by middle-class Americans, that it poses serious communication problems;" "syntax (rather than spelling, pronunciation, or word recognition) constitutes the central reading difficulty" (Baratz and Baratz, *op. cit.*, pp. 13–14). As we have seen, grammatical analysis suggests more similarity than difference in syntax and communication does not seem to be a serious problem for anyone with some acquaintance with nonstandard dialects. Other research, furthermore, has demonstrated that nonstandard speakers generally have passive control of standard and hence can understand it readily, even though they may not be able to reproduce its every detail. Certainly, basal readers should start with syntactic patterns familiar to children, and perhaps basal readers for slum schools should contain nonstandard patterns; but as readers mature, hearing standard and nonstandard, there is no reason not to assume that tolerance for and receptive control of standard patterns will not grow as well. (See Roger W. Shuy, "Some Language and Cultural Differences in a Theory of Reading," in Gunderson, *op. cit.*, pp. 72–87).

patently ludicrous ever to have proceeded very far, though neither condition kept it from being made.[39] Roger W. Shuy, the director of the sociolinguistics program of the Center for Applied Linguistics in Washington, D.C. grants in a recent article: "the simple truth is that speaking Standard English, however desirable it may be, is not as important as learning to read," and that one can teach reading by modifying materials to suit the child rather than "changing the child to suit the materials," that is, systematically teaching him standard English. In fact, he comments: "It is hard to imagine how we ever got so sidetracked on this issue." But Shuy is reluctant to question the "social value of learning Standard English."[40] *Social Value* has been the phrase and the concept motivating the many proposals offered over the past few years, usually funded, and sometimes implemented, for teaching standard English as a second dialect—code word *Bidialectalism* or *Biloquialism* to use the more recently coined and clearly euphemistic term.[41]

The basic idea behind either learned term is the same simple one: nonstandard speakers must be equipped by the school with a second dialect—standard English—if the school hopes to prepare them for life in the real world—technological, industrial, corporate, middle-class and white-dominated America. The idea is not without precedent: Fries argued in 1940 that: "It is the assumed obligation of the schools to attempt to develop in each child the knowledge of and the ability to use the 'standard' English of the United States—that set of language habits in which the most important affairs of our country are carried on, the dialect of the socially acceptable in most of our communities."[42] In 1940, Fries' charge to the schools rang with enlightened liberalism; in the 1970s, a phrase like "the socially acceptable" starts less harmonious overtones.

The discord is made more striking by the biloquialists' acceptance of the principle of linguistic relativity. All of them grant that there is little to choose between standard and nonstandard, middle- and lower-class English on grounds of grammaticality, logicality, fitness to serve communicative needs. Few claim that there are serious communicative difficulties when standard and nonstandard speakers converse. None claim that possession of standard English better equips a young student to understand the principles of engineering, the laws of finance, or the customs of politics. Social utility lies in none of these; social value does not incorporate such criteria. The social value of learning standard English is simply that those in power demand that those without power learn it; the value of standard English

[39] See, for example, several of the articles in Baratz and Shuy, *op. cit.*, *Teaching Black Children to Read.*

[40] Shuy, in Gunderson, *op. cit.*

[41] See Shuy's introduction in Fasold and Shuy, *op. cit.*: "Since the term *dialect* seems to carry such a heavy pejorative connotation these days, other terms have been suggested in place of bidialectalism, including the recently coined term, *biloquialism*" (p. xi).

[42] Charles C. Fries, *American English Grammar* (English Monograph No. 10, National Council of Teachers of English [New York, 1940]), p. 15.

lies in overcoming pejorative judgments some speakers make about others, not by teaching the judges that their attitudes are irrational, but by urging the judged to change. "The linguistic relativity," says the humane bidialectalist:

The linguistic relativity . . . does not take into account the social reality. Middle-class individuals still rate Standard American English as more desirable than Negro speech. Perjorative ratings are associated with Negro nonstandard speech despite its viability, complexity and communicativeness as a linguistic system.[43]

So *there* is social value. In the class game choose sides, and do not play for the loser. The arbiter is the middle class, and we play by its rules, within boundaries drawn by attitudes of ugly Americans toward the speech of Americans they find ugly. What we are to teach are the forms considered prestigious by the dominating class, irrespective of any intrinsic value or lack of it, without consideration for our own preferences, tastes, and beliefs, or those of our students. If we reject the position and the criteria as too obviously based on prejudice, not reason or taste, we become dropouts and threaten our students with economic ruin:

. . . not teaching the black inner-city child standard English not only further hinders his ability to ultimately compete in the mainstream of society in terms of oral skills [sic], but also makes the child's task of learning to read considerably more difficult.[44]

As we have argued earlier—and as the quoted bidialectalist would likely admit in a less polemical moment—oral skills are not the exclusive property of middle-class speakers; as we have argued earlier, there is every reason to question the assertion that literacy—effective control of reading and writing—requires control of spoken forms of standard English. The argument for bidialectalism—for the painstaking and systematic teaching of standard English—finally reduces itself to the naked fact of prejudice against some forms of spoken English reflecting social and racial prejudice against the people who utter such forms.

CONCLUSIONS: OR, WHAT OTHER ANSWERS ARE THERE?

Some who have found the morality of the biloquialist position repugnant or at the least difficult to reconcile with humanist tenets, have nonetheless accepted the task of teaching standard English as a second dialect on the grounds that the position is realistic. After all, who *can* change the world? But those who are tempted must ask themselves two questions: Is the position

[43] Joan C. Baratz, "Educational Considerations for Teaching Standard English to Negro Children," in Fasold and Shuy, *op. cit.*, p. 25.
[44] *Ibid.*, p. 26.

indeed so realistic? If it is, can we afford a brand of realism that wastes so much talent?

Critics of bidialectalism have questioned whether the goal of a two-dialect speaker is in fact attainable. James Sledd, an early and persistent critic of doublespeak finds "the complete bidialectal, with undiminished control of his vernacular and a good mastery of the standard language . . . as mythical as the unicorn."[45] Reasons for the rareness of the beast are not difficult to imagine. The would-be biloquial must first desire to adapt his speech to middle-class norms and then be able to. Speakers are rarely successful in erasing all traces of their native dialect. In Great Britain, where large numbers learn the standard language in school, few avoid speaking it with the regional accent that separates the newcomer-to-status from the aristocrat born with a silver Eton and Oxford in his mouth. In our country, even carefully trained newscasters, if Southern-born, betray their origins with an occasional /ɪ/ rather than /ɛ/ before a nasal, no matter how carefully they monitor their network English. Biloquialists in fact set an unattainable goal when they speak of complete enough accommodation to middle-class English to overcome "pejorative ratings associated with Negro nonstandard speech"; i.e., passing for white. A simple list of features, such as is usually offered,[46] will not suffice because even the most ardent biloquialist would agree that many features identify a speaker's race (including many such as "voice qualifiers"—intonation patterns, rhythms, voice placement—not yet described). Were all such features erasable, or neatly variable to suit occasion, what would finally prevent *The Man* from changing the features he identifies as the badges of status? To say that a man's speech disqualifies him for a job is more acceptable than saying his color does, and is not illegal. For those who need such excuses, any bit of language will serve.

The argument that the schools have a responsibility to teach standard English because the system demands it rests on the assumption that nothing can be done to change the system—that prejudices against nonstandard forms cannot be eradicated. It assumes too that the values of the system will remain fixed as human nature clutches to her bosom her most cherished stereotypes.[47] But are these assumptions valid? It seems to me that

---

[45] See p. 363 above.

[46] See, for example, Ralph W. Fasold and Walt Wolfram, "Some Linguistic Features of Negro Dialect," in Fasold and Shuy, *op cit.*, pp. 41–86.

[47] The "natural law" argument is easily found in the work of bidialectalists. For example, Baratz, *op. cit.*, p. 25:

> It would be nice to think that there are complex, socially stratified societies where the spectrum of standard language is so broad as to include all the different grammars and usages of persons speaking the many varieties of that language under the label of "standard." Sad to say, human behavior just doesn't operate like that. To date, wherever research has been done—in Europe, Asia, and Africa —this has not been the case. One variety of the language invariably becomes the standard—the variety that has grammar books written in it, the one for which an orthography is established, the one that is studied by the populace in

many of my undergraduate students are less hung up on the trappings of status than are their middle-and upper-class parents. And black awareness seems to be having some effect on cherished prejudices. Much has been made of the existence in the United States of linguistic self-hatred and of the fact that many blacks seem to share white prejudices against black dialect features. Judgments of that sort are changeable and changing. A social realist less committed to the status quo might find a more satisfactory role for himself in helping to change such judgments, rather than seek to perpetuate them.

It is realistic for us as teachers to visualize clearly the relationship with our minority students forced on us if we accept the goal of biloquialism. If I urge a nonstandard speaking student to learn standard English—even if I magnanimously "allow" him to keep his nonstandard in its "appropriate" setting—I must say to that student: your dialect is as good as any other, as systematic, as grammatical, as logical, at least as expressive, as the new dialect I am going to teach you; but you must learn this new dialect because those in power demand it. Without it, you will not pass the right tests, you will not get the right jobs, not because you are ignorant and inarticulate, not because you won't be understood (though some may claim not to understand you), but because you don't make the right noises. If the student is alert, he will know that I have other alternatives. And he will know too, if he has been listening to my talk about literature and the human spirit, that my social realism fits ill with the values I profess to hold as a humanist.

The alternatives to the biloquial position and the Great Tradition are not escapist and idealistic, nor need they devalue the great aims of education. Things can be done to change the system—things that are philosophically and educationally defensible. If we are convinced by the dialectologists who assert that standard and nonstandard are equivalent systems and that attitudes toward nonstandard reflect snobbery and prejudice, we can attack snobbery and prejudice in our classrooms by teaching what the best research teaches us about dialects. Classroom teaching has done much to keep alive the myth of the superior language form: it might do as much to expose it as myth. We can banish the deprivation model from our own classrooms by questioning the assumptions of remediation programs and by looking to

---

school. Language standardization appears to be a universal aspect of language variation in a national context—particularly one involving literacy. There is standard English, standard Arabic, standard Yoruba, and standard Hausa, just to note a few. Standardization is not a political invention of racist whites to exploit the Negro, rob him of his heritage, and denigrate his language.

Standardization, especially of the written language, is a fact of the modern world. But so is the "political" use of language variety to maintain and perpetuate class and caste lines. Does that mean that as teachers we are obliged to accept and perpetuate it? Racial prejudice is at least as much a fact of human society. Do we teach that? Standard English may not be an invention of racist whites to exploit the Negro, but neither is its writing system an invention to record standard American English. The writing system we use developed, of course, from British English and a long time ago at that.

ourselves instead of our students for causes of failure. We can assign to oblivion ill-constructed and badly motivated teaching materials simply by refusing to teach them. And we can, as members of a profession, draw on the special knowledge that gives us our professional status to extend our activities outside the classroom: to scrutinize the standardized tests that govern admissions, placement in tracks, and hence career goals—tests that in the market place are often used to determine employability and promotability. If such tests, under the pretence of measuring intelligence or necessary linguistic competence, really only measure conformity to standard usage; if they perpetuate myths about usage preserved in the folklore of correctness and purism; if they measure only what has been termed "the Little Old Lady Principle"[48]—one's degree of adjustment to middle-class behavior and morality—we have every obligation to mistrust and attack them. In a society which can be split over the question of whether or not children should ride buses to school, quiet acceptance of corporate standards is more cynical than realistic.

Inside the classroom, we can effect change by making our everyday practices conform to what is known about language learning, language structure, and language variation, throwing out badly worn practices based on questionable assumptions and seldom justified by unquestionable results. A place to start might be the marking of papers—that mundane activity that vexes the waking hours of all English teachers. To make the discussion concrete, here is a paper written for a remedial English class by a young black community college student:

[An Embarrassing Experience]

1   When I were in High School we had a football Banquite
2   and I had not Ben to a fromer accesson Befor. and I
3   also included a young Lady along.
4   I were like the young man in the story we read
5   in class.
6   I came to the Banquite Proper dressed But I did
7   not have no table Manner. Everyone Began to set down,
8   I did not know I sirpose to assit the young lady with
9   chair until she told me. after about 30 min the guss
10   spoke Began to spake & I did not know when to Began to
11   eat & after I saw all the other People eating I look
12   around for my silverware, But I did not have any,

---

[48] See William Labov, "Systematically Misleading Data from Test Questions," unpublished transcript of a paper delivered to a colloquium sponsored by the School of Social Work and the Department of Linguistics at the University of Michigan, Ann Arbor, April, 1970:

> "This assumption may be stated formally in these terms: If a question is asked in the form, 'Which is better, X or Y,' and there exists, anywhere in the world, a little old lady who believes that X is better, and it's terrible that young people do Y, then the answer is X."

13   than I tryed to get the water attanson. They finily
14   Brage me my silverware. I though that were the lose
15   embarrassment monet for tonight, But they had just Began.
16   The main dish were chicken & it were fride cripe &
17   when I Bit off it, it would make a loud nose and the
18   other People would look aroung at me & my date would
19   look the other way. From then on I promer myself I
20   would learn good table manner.

A paper like this frequently elicits the following response, or one similar, from the teacher:

[AN EMBARRASSING EXPERIENCE]

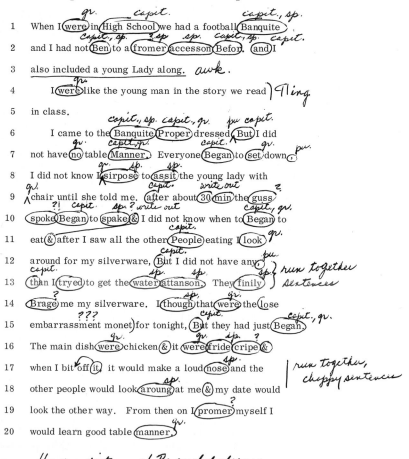

1   When I were in High School we had a football Banquite.
2   and I had not Ben to a fromer accesson Befor. and I
3   also included a young Lady along.   awk.
4   I were like the young man in the story we read) Ting
5   in class.
6   I came to the Banquite Proper dressed, But I did
7   not have no table Manner. Everyone Began to set down.
8   I did not know I sirpose to assit the young lady with
9   chair until she told me. after about 30 min the guss
10 spoke Began to spake & I did not know when to Began to
11 eat & after I saw all the other People eating I look
12 around for my silverware, But I did not have any. } run together
13 than I tryed to get the water attanson. They finily } sentences
14 Brage me my silverware. I though that were the lose
15 embarrassment monet for tonight, But they had just Began.
16 The main dish were chicken & it were fride cripe &
17 when I bit off it, it would make a loud nose and the | run together,
18 other people would look aroung at me & my date would | choppy sentences
19 look the other way. From then on I promer myself I
20 would learn good table manner.

Use your dictionary! Be careful of your
grammar! Write complete sentences!

content C-
mechanics F

The comments and "corrections" are mine, but I do not think that they caricature so much as epitomize the art of paper grading as practiced in American classrooms, an art dominated by the approach-direct to deviations from norms and expectations. It is a commonplace of English methods courses that similar excesses of red often warn insecure students away not from the errors circled but from the act of writing itself; the unsubmitted paper is less public than a gaily decorated one, and a less laborious way to fail. But I am less concerned with the psychological effects of such comments, assuming again that they are fairly representative, than with their general unhelpfulness to the student who wishes to improve his writing. So-called corrections which merely identify and vaguely name mistakes a student has made, or that we think he has made, do little to show him how to correct or why he should.

If we approach a paper like "An Embarrassing Experience" armed with a few facts about language and how it works, we may be less likely to make the paper or the student bleed. We know that every student has a language that he uses every day, one that generally serves him well. We know that whatever language system the student possesses, that system is rule governed, as is the student's use of the system. In ordinary conversation, the student rarely makes mistakes—certainly not any serious enough to hinder his ability to communicate. We know that his system, whether a variety of standard or some less prestigious dialect, equips him to think as well as his knowledge and intelligence allow. Why then all that red? Assuming that the student writer of "An Embarrassing Experience" does have a useable language system at his command forces us to search out other causes for his very real problems than some vague notion of linguistic deprivation, smacking as that notion does of original sin and incorrigible deficiency. Do his problems occur because the language of writing has special features not shared by oral language, features that this student does not yet know because of limited experience with reading and writing? Do they occur because we are asking the student to write in an unfamiliar dialect, an unfamiliar register, or an unfamiliar style? Do they occur because of pressures in the act of writing for a teacher-critic armed with a red pencil and the power to dispense grades? Problem solving can begin when we ask ourself precise questions—questions that recognize writing as a very complex process requiring many skills and subject to many influences. Problem solving can begin when the teacher rejects the role of *grader* and accepts a role as *diagnostician*, equipped with detailed knowledge about language and its working.

Most English teachers have read enough professional and amateur writing to be able to trust intuition as a guide to where a writer is going astray. But intuition is not enough in the process of diagnosis, which requires more than vague feelings that "something is wrong with this sentence." Scattergun or random marking—the circling or underlining of any and every problem perceived—does not direct the student's attention to major problems or suggest bases or sequences for solving them. The use of a lean marking vocabulary—*gr.* for grammar, *punc.* for punctuation, *awk.* for almost anything we don't like but haven't the time or knowledge to name—neither identifies for the student what he has done wrong nor suggests how he might do better. Language structure is complex, the rules governing effective selection of language forms for topic, audience, and occasion more complex still. Any marking vocabulary we use must be sophisticated enough and rich enough to handle such complexity. The greatest danger in the use of a vague or lean vocabulary is that general labels can be misapplied, leading teachers to attribute to students problems that do not really exist.

For example, in marking the sample paper above as a "grader" might, I used the traditional notations "run-together sentence" and "gr." as I have seen them often used by school and college English teachers. These notations appear to name quite serious language problems—more serious, for example, than spelling. As a diagnostician, I would want to discover just how serious these problems really are—whether they reflect some deep troubles or, like the spelling mistakes, the less serious problems of "getting it down right on paper." I might begin by asking the student to read me his paper, noting the intonation patterns he uses to see if they identify "correct" sentence divisions; or, I might simply repunctuate the paper myself, seeing whether a judicious sprinkling of commas, periods, and the deletions of a few conjunctions, might leave well-formed sentences:

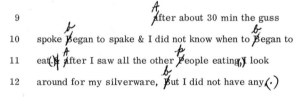

```
 9                              After about 30 min the guss
10    spoke Began to spake & I did not know when to Began to
11    eat. After I saw all the other People eating, look
12    around for my silverware, But I did not have any.
```

To make well-formed, if not elegant, sentences the student needs only one additional period (a semicolon would suffice in a pinch), one deletion of &, one comma, and the replacement of a comma with a period. If "But I did not have any" looks like a sentence fragment because of the capital letter on "But," we might note that the student consistently capitalizes, or appears to capitalize, *b*—a feature more easily explained from the handwritten version in which he does not distinguish *b* and *B*, a scribal problem. To teach such a student to make accurate punctuation is not easy, or course; but it is much easier than to teach him what he at first appears to need to know: how to make English sentences. He already knows how to make them, and we need teach only the rules for marking their limits in writing.

As diagnosticians, we might look at the forms marked "gr." What are the problems? What causes them? Two, "I sirpose" (l. 8) and "with chair" (ll. 8–9), appear to involve the omission of necessary grammatical forms: "I *was* supposed" and "with *her* chair." *I sirpose* may show the weakening of the unaccented auxiliary *was* in speech with attendant loss of vowel and

/w/ glide, a spoken form sometimes represented in literary nonstandard dialect with the spelling "*Ise* suppose"; loss of /s/ from *was* would reflect assimilation with the initial /s/ of *suppose*; *with chair* may similarly reflect weakening of /hə/, the r-less pronunciation of *her*. If the analyses are right (they should be checked against the student's casual speech to be entirely trustworthy), the "omitted" forms do not represent random errors, much less ignorance of grammatical signals, but faithful phonetic spellings of the student-writer's dialect. The apparent inconsistencies in verb forms may well represent similar phonetic spellings: *sirpose* the expected past participle with simplification of /zd/; *look* (l. 11) the expected past tense with simplification of /kt/, not the misuse of present for past; *to Began* the infinitive *to begin* with nasalized vowel. Other "grammatical errors" show similar reflections of the student's vernacular dialect. *Proper* (l. 6) instead of *properly*, and *set* (l. 7) instead of *sit* show the selection of less prestigious but equally meaningful usage variants in instances where American English contains alternative but socially graded synonyms. Even the puzzlingly consistent use of *were* where *was* is expected ("When I were in High School . . .", "I were like the young man . . . ," "The main dish were chicken . . . ," and so on) may well reflect dialect conflict—reverse interference on the vernacular from a formal register of the pattern, "If I were . . .", picked up by the student as a hyper-formalism. If teacher prefers "If I were" to "If I was," why not go her one better and use the high-class *were* at every opportunity?

The purpose of such diagnostic analysis in not to explain away the writing problems that do exist, but to identify them and in so doing get a better sense of where the student really is in terms of his language skills. The writer of "An Embarrassing Experience" is not languageless; he does not lack knowledge of the rules of English grammar; he does not have to be taught English—a task which, if we really faced it, might well cause us to throw up our hands. He is inexperienced in writing, probably in reading; he has much to learn about the writing system—the accepted marks for recording English; he must learn when he can trust the spelling system to reflect his pronunciation and thus rely on analysis, when he cannot and must rely on memory of written forms and on the dictionary. Information like that in Table 1 will enable us to help him by showing the greatest disparities between his phonology and the system of written standard. For certain audiences and for certain types of writing, he may well have to add some syntactic structures to those of his native vernacular, and learn to change certain selections from among status marked usage variants. But it is important for us to realize that there is nothing peculiar about these learning tasks themselves, although there may be more of them for the nonstandard speaker. All students, standard English speaking as well as nonstandard speaking, must learn to employ the writing system—a system that does not always match the pronunciation of spoken standard any better than it does nonstandard (*peace, piece, elite, concrete, feet, key, quay*, serve as reminders); all students, if they are to become accomplished writers, must learn to extend their syntactic

Table 1 Some probable dialect-related spelling problems

---

1. r-lessness

l. 2: *fromer* for formal. Letter *r* intrusive in first syllable as student tries to use orthographic *r* where he lacks it phonetically; *-er* spelling extended to unstressed syllables realized as [ə] (that is, the second syllable shows loss of final /l/).

l. 8: *sirpose* for suppose. *-ir* spells [ə] (compare *-er* on *former* for formal).

l. 10: *spoke* for speaker. *e* spells [ə](?)

l. 19: *promer* for promise. *-er* spelling again extended to unaccented syllable pronounced [ə] after loss of final consonant.

2. Reduction of consonant clusters

l. 8: *sirpose* for supposed. Loss of final dental in cluster [zd].

l. 11: *look* for looked. Loss of final dental in cluster [kt].

l. 14: *lose* for last. Loss of final dental(?). Possible confusion with lose, vb.(?)

l. 16: *cripe* for crisp. Metathesis [krɪps] and simplification(?).

3. Loss of final dental after vowel

l. 14: *though* for thought. But the form is not phonetically spelled.

4. Loss of consonants in unaccented syllables

l. 2: *fromer* for formal. [ə] for final syllable.

l. 9: *min* for minute. Shortening influenced by loss of final [t](?) or the standard abbreviated spelling(?).

l. 19: *promer* for promise [ə] for final syllable.

5. Problems spelling final nasals

l. 14: *Brage* for brang.(?) The *-g* must go somewhere.

l. 18: *aroung* for around. Final sound is probably [n]. Same source of interference as in *Brage*.

---

resources and their vocabularies, learn new registers and styles, and sharpen their feel for language variants.

As students learn to explore new uses of language, it is foolish and damaging to expect the error-free paper so often worshipped by the priests of correctness and dogmatized as a behavioral goal. If we ask our students to stretch their linguistic muscles, we must be ready for them to stumble; if we are getting "perfect" papers, we are likely not asking them to learn anything useful. The writer of "An Embarrassing Experience" is attempting to write in a formal register, seeing such a register as appropriate to what teacher is demanding but also to the topic of his essay—manners and the use of them on formal occasions, something likely as foreign to him as the linguistic use itself. As we have seen, his misuse of subjunctive *be* is the misuse of a formal usage. His choice of vocabulary is likewise formal (*banquet, occasion, young lady, young man; assist* rather than *help; speak* rather than *talk*), and in one case gets him again into minor syntactic difficulty when he uses the lofty *include* rather than *brought* (avoiding *brang*, perhaps? See l. 14). He puts *include* into the syntactic frame for *to bring*, resulting in the "awk." "And I also included a young lady along," a subcategorization error of the sort often made by immature language users who are trying to extend their linguistic knowledge to new uses. Suppose this were the first attempt made by this student to use a formal register in his writing; suppose it were his first attempt at the formal *include*? Would marking the error in red likely motivate him to try again, or urge him to play it safe? For finally, the psychology of paper marking does matter, and matters very much. If students in attempting the language of writing incorporate forms from their natural speech, we have no right to mark those forms as wrong, offering no further explanation. We have no right to isolate speakers from backgrounds different from our own by drawing attention to their own language. To suggest or insist that nonstandard language forms are not good enough for the classroom or for polite society is the surest way we can take to alienate the human beings who use those forms.

If we are to become better at teaching *all* of our students to be literate, we must do a better job of reconciling our practices in teaching language use with what we profess to believe as humanists and as teachers of literary art. We must set realistic goals tailored to individual needs and abilities, but informed by larger ends than corporate and material good. We must establish priorities that include our highest educational aims, which may not be the state's, and the needs of our students, which may not be the middle class's. We must make use of our own best knowledge. As English teachers, for example, we are usually trained in sophisticated analytical skills for discovering how a piece of literature works for what it is, how its parts fit into a unified whole. But when we approach an essay written by a student, we throw our analytic skills out the window with our appreciation for imaginative and original language and go busily to work on sentences and parts of sentences, forcing conformity to very narrow linguistic norms and in the process choking off fluency and experimentation. Do we ourselves really care so much if a student writes *proper* instead of *properly*, *set* instead of *sit*? That he occasionally omits an orthographically precise *-d* or *-ed* at the end of a verb? Measuring by the values we perceive in literature, would "An Embarrassing Experience" be all that much better if it were impeccably spelled, punctuated, and expunged of low-status usages? What ultimate goals do we set for ourselves in our work with composition: producing an employable secretary for General Motors? a copy-writer for Time-Life?

Humans learn language by using it. Few six-year-olds have seen a grammar book or been exposed to usage drills. And it is obvious from the persistence of stigmatized forms in the face of attacks by purists and English teachers, or tinkering by bidialectalists, that humans use those forms of a language that are important to them—*personally* important. Personal language is what we must seek to draw from our students, shaping it to be sure, but for their uses; not seeking to replace it with some chloroformed specimen from the pages of prescriptive grammars or the depersonalized and electrically typed language of the business letter. If we are to cure the alienation of many young American men and women, the alienation of some groups of Americans from the larger culture, we must be ready to listen to individual voices no matter what their variety, to understand the forces that make them individual and various, to appreciate what they might tell us. In allowing all voices to be heard, we may have to shelve our most cherished handbooks; in giving them time to be heard and to develop, we may have to neglect our spelling drills, our punctuation drills, and our usage drills—throw them out entirely if they contribute to the isolation and denigration of the nonstandard speaking student. In neglecting drill, I do not think we need to feel guilty: A man needs something to say before he needs to shape an essay; he needs words before he needs to spell them correctly. When he feels that what he has to say is significant enough, he will seek a larger audience, and in doing so find the need, perhaps even the means, for making his language publicly acceptable. Proofreading is, after all, the task you do last.

As teachers whose primary job it is to encourage students to find a voice—to recognize and control the power of the word—we cannot afford to denigrate some voices. Too many chasms already separate America's rich and poor, her white and nonwhite. Many are trying to build bridges through the teaching of minority literatures—a hopeful sign that we seek to find out about each other and begin to recognize that ethnic experience is valuable to the outsider as well as the insider. When we teach such literature, we often praise its language for fidelity to character or to the unique experience the author invites us to share. Some of us have doubtless urged our students to admire the cadences of urban Jewish speech as we have taught Malamud's *The Assistant*, or those of the Southern black preacher in Baldwin's *Go Tell It on the Mountain*. We admire language with the human in it and in our composition classes we often tell our students to emulate such writing, to write from their own experiences and hearts, to be forthright and honest in the telling. But to some students we say: Don't write it in your own language, use mine. Could it be that standard English is sometimes *not* appropriate to the composition class?

STUDY QUESTIONS

1. Read the following essay carefully, then consider the questions that follow it. The essay again is by a real student, a freshman in a community college:

What Is Soul?

1　Soul is something that started at the dawn of time when the first black
2　man set foot on earth, it continued in Africa before a white man was ever
3　seen, It was brought over to america on slave ships with black bodys
4　stuffed in holes, Soul was standing on whitey auction block for hundred
5　of years, being bided off to the highest bider, It was then shipped to
6　fields to work, until it drop in the sand and then whipped or killed
7　because it could'n work any more.

8　Soul was their in eighteen sixty five, looking out of the eye's of thound of
9　black people, wondering what whitey ment when he said o.k. nigger

10 you'll be free, now you can go to hell, Soul was also their watching when
11 whitey came back dress up in white wearing the letter K-K-K.

12 Soul saw whitey hang black men for walking on the wrong side of the
13 streets. It also saw black women rape and beaten by whitey and then
14 called a poor excuse for a dog.

15 Soul was there with Dr. Martin L. King when he walked down the
16 street's picketing and preaching non-violence. It was in a church in
17 alabama when it was blowen up killing several black teenage girls, It was
18 their in the white house ninety-nine years after the civil war, when
19 whitey sign another (Civil white) bill.

20 Soul was their listen to whitey when he said, the opportunity is here for
21 you nigger, their nothing holding you back (out side the fact that you are
22 black) and it saw the uncle Tom's swifly agree with them.

23 Soul can be found in the eye's of an aging black woman or man looking
24 back over the hell that they had to go thourgh and still is going thourgh
25 because they are black.

26 Soul is something that can be found in the minds of every black brother
27 and sister today wondering weather their mother or grand mother was
28 rape by a honkey.

29 Soul can truely be found in the heart of black america, for every beat their
30 heart take makes them hate whitey just that much more.

31 Soul is also found in the grief of a black mother crying because she will
32 never again see her son alive, for he was killed fighting a white man war.

33 Soul is a brother walking down the street at night and pick up by honkey
34 cops carried off and beaten, then taken to jail and booked on a bunch of
35 phoney charges, because he's black.

36 Soul is something that has been paid for in black blood, sweat, tears and
37 death It's something that the white man can't make up a law againts and
38 take it away, Soul is as much apart of black america as the color of it
39 skin, Soul is real, Soul is me, Soul is my people, For soul is black.

a. What audience do you feel that the writer of "What Is Soul" is addressing?
   Is the language of the paper appropriate to the intended audience?
b. What do you consider to be the controlling purpose of this essay? Is the
   language likely to be effective in achieving the author's purpose?
c. Would you recommend to the writer that he rewrite the paper correcting the
   language to standardized forms and spellings no matter what his audience or
   what his purpose might be? Would you enforce your recommendations with
   a red pencil and a bad grade? What problems might you encounter in suggesting or demanding such changes?
d. Do you feel that the writer of this paper is consciously choosing nonstandard
   —that is "black" English—as the medium for his paper; or that he is merely
   recording his speech with such tools as he has? Would your approach to
   commenting on his paper change depending on the judgment you make about
   conscious or unconscious choice? Should it?

e. If you feel that the choice of nonstandard forms is appropriate to the rhetorical purposes of the essay, does that mean you would suggest *no* changes in the language of the paper? If you would suggest changes, indicate them and give your reasons for doing so.

2. In answering questions (a) through (e), you must have used, if unconsciously, several criteria in making judgments about the effectiveness of the language in "What Is Soul." State those criteria as clearly as you can. Were all the criteria "linguistic" or "sociolinguistic"?

3. What problems does the writer of "What Is Soul?" encounter in trying to write nonstandard dialect? Can you think of any concrete advantages to a standardized writing system for a language? In order to share a standardized writing system, would all people using it have to speak the same dialect? Is it necessary to learn standard English in order to write effectively? What might be some advantages to a writer in learning standard English?

4. Is it necessary that *all* students learn to write standard English? Could a useful composition course be taught that did not have such an aim?

5. Does Robinson argue that standard English should not be taught, or that it should not be taught directly? What does he consider higher priority goals than the teaching of standardized or prestigious norms?

6. If you were the teacher of the student who wrote "An Embarrassing Experience" where would you begin in helping him solve his writing problems? What would you consider a realistic goal for him at the end of one semester's work?

7. How important are teachers' attitudes toward nonstandard dialects in the teaching of language use? By what mechanisms might the self-fulfilling prophesy work to bring about a student's failure?

8. Standard and nonstandard dialects are often conceived of as discrete and mutually exclusive systems: one speaker speaks standard and another speaker non-standard. Looking at the student essays reprinted here, how would you argue that such a conception is unrealistic?

Suggested Readings

For the most part, this listing is restricted to book-length studies; articles and more specialized monographs are cited in many of the works included here, as well as in the annual *Linguistic Bibliography for the Year* and the *MLA International Bibliography*.

SOCIOLINGUISTICS AND THE SOCIOLOGY OF LANGUAGE

ARDENER, EDWIN, ed. *Social Anthropology and Language*. London, 1971.

BRIGHT, WILLIAM, ed. *Sociolinguistics: Proceedings of the UCLA Socio-Linguistics Conference, 1964*. New York, 1966.

BURLING, ROBBINS. *Man's Many Voices: Language in Its Cultural Context*. New York, 1970.

CAPELL, ARTHUR. *Studies in Socio-linguistics*. The Hague, 1966.

FERGUSON, CHARLES A. *Language Structure and Language Use*. Palo Alto, Calif., 1971.

FISHMAN, JOSHUA A. *Language Loyalty in the United States*. The Hague, 1966.

———. *Sociolinguistics: A Brief Introduction*. Rowley, Mass.: Newbury House, 1970.

———, ed. *Readings in the Sociology of Language*. The Hague, 1968.

———, ed. *Advances in the Sociology of Language*. The Hague, 1971.

———, Robert L. Cooper, Roxana Ma, *et al. Bilingualism in the Barrio*. New York: Final Report to HEW, contract OEC–1–7–062817–0297, 1968.

———, Charles A. Ferguson, and Jyotirindra Das Gupta, eds. *Language Problems of Developing Nations*. New York, 1968.

GUMPERZ, JOHN J. AND DELL HYMES, eds. *Directions in Sociolinguistics: The Ethnography of Communication*. New York, 1972.

HALL, ROBERT A., JR. *Pidgin and Creole Languages*. Ithaca, N.Y., 1966.

HYMES, DELL, ed. *Language in Culture and Society: A Reader in Linguistics and Anthropology*. New York, 1964.

———, ed. *Pidginization and Creolization of Languages*. Cambridge, 1971.

JESPERSEN, OTTO. *Mankind, Nation, and Individual from a Linguistic Point of View*. Bloomington, Ind. (1925) 1964.

KURATH, HANS. *Studies in Area Linguistics*. Bloomington, Ind., and London, 1972.

LE PAGE, R. B. *The National Language Question: Linguistic Problems of Newly Independent States*. London, 1964.

LIEBERSON, STANLEY, ed. *Explorations in Sociolinguistics*. The Hague, 1966.

PRIDE, J. B. *The Social Meaning of Language*. London, 1971.

RAY, PUNYA SLOKA. *Language Standardization: Studies in Prescriptive Linguistics*. The Hague, 1963.

SAPIR, EDWARD. *Language: An Introduction to the Study of Speech*. New York, 1921.

SHUY, ROGER, W., Irwin Feigenbaum, and Allene Grognet. *Sociolinguistic Theory, Materials and Training Programs: Three Related Studies*. Washington, D.C., 1970.

SMITH, DAVID M., AND ROGER W. SHUY, eds. *Sociolinguistics in Cross-Cultural Analysis*. Washington, D.C., 1972.

WEINREICH, URIEL. *Languages in Contact: Findings and Problems*. New York, 1953.

WHITELEY, W. H., ed. *Language Use and Social Change*. Oxford, 1970.

WILLIAMS, FREDERICK, ed. *Language and Poverty: Perspectives on a Theme*. Chicago, 1970.

VARIETIES OF ENGLISH AS A WORLD LANGUAGE

ADAMS, G. B., *et al*. *Ulster Dialects: An Introductory Symposium*. Holywood: Ulster Folk Museum, 1964.

ALDUS, JUDITH BUTLER. *Anglo-Irish Dialects: A Bibliography*. St. Johns: Memorial University of Newfoundland, 1969.

AVIS, WALTER S. *A Bibliography of Writings on Canadian English, 1857–1965*. Toronto, 1965.

———. *A Dictionary of Canadianisms on Historical Principles*. Toronto, 1967.

BAILEY, BERYL LOFTMAN. *Jamaican Creole Syntax: A Transformational Approach*. Cambridge, 1966.

BAKER, SIDNEY J. *The Australian Language*, 2nd edition. Sydney, 1966.

BROOK, G. L. *English Dialects*. New York, 1963.

BROSNAHAN, L. F. *The English Language in the World*. Wellington, N.Z., 1963.

BUTTER, P. *English in India*. Belfast, 1960.

CASSIDY, FREDERIC G. *Jamaica Talk: Three Hundred Years of the English Language in Jamaica*. New York, 1961.

——— and R. B. Le Page. *Dictionary of Jamaican English*. Cambridge, 1967.

CRYSTAL, DAVID AND DEREK DAVY. *Investigating English Style*. London, 1969.

DUSTOOR, P. E. *The World of Words*. Bombay, 1968.

GOKAK, V. K. *English in India: Its Present and Future*. Bombay, 1964.

GRANT, WILLIAM, AND JAMES M. DIXON. *Manual of Modern Scots*. Cambridge, 1921.

HALL, ROBERT A., JR. *Melanesian Pidgin English: Grammar, Texts, Vocabulary*. Baltimore, 1943

HALVERSON, J. "Prolegomena to a Study of Ceylon English," *The University of Ceylon Review* **24**(1969):61–75.

JONES, JOSEPH. *Terranglia: The Case for English As World Literature*. New York, 1965.

KACHRU, BRAJ B. "English in South Asia," in *Current Trends in Linguistics*, ed. Thomas A. Sebeok. (The Hague, 1969), Vol. 5, pp. 627–78.

KOLB, EDUARD. *Linguistic Atlas of England: Phonological Atlas of the Northern Region*. Berlin, 1966.

LANHAM, L. W. *English in South Africa*. Johannesburg, 1964.

LE PAGE, ROBERT B., AND DAVID DECAMP. *Jamaican Creole*. London: Creole Language Studies I, 1960.

MCINTOSH, ANGUS. *An Introductory Survey of Scottish Dialects*. Edinburgh, 1952.

MATHER, J. Y. AND H.-H. SPEITEL. *Linguistic Atlas of Scotland.* London, to appear in 1973.

MITCHELL, A. G. *The Pronunciation of English in Australia,* 2nd edition. Sydney, 1965.

MURRAY, JAMES A. H. *The Dialect of the Southern Counties of Scotland.* London, 1873.

ORKIN, MARK M. *Speaking Canadian English: An Informal Account of the English Language in Canada.* Toronto, 1970.

ORTON, HAROLD, AND EUGEN DIETH. *Survey of English Dialects: Introduction; The Six Northern Counties and the Isle of Man; The West Midland Counties; The East Midland Counties; The Southern Counties.* Leeds, 1962–71.

QUIRK, RANDOLPH. *The Use of English.* London, 1962.

RAFAT, T. "Towards a Pakistani Idiom," *Venture: A Bi-annual Review of English Language and Literature* 6(1969):60–73.

RAMSON, W. S. *Australian English: An Historical Study of the Vocabulary, 1788–1898.* Canberra, 1966.

———. *English Transported: Essays on Australian English.* New York, 1970.

ROSS, ALAN S. C., AND A. W. MOVERLEY. *The Pitcairnese Language.* London, 1964.

SCHNEIDER, G. D. *West African Pidgin-English: A Descriptive Linguistic Approach.* Athens, Ohio, 1966.

SIVERTSEN, EVA. *Cockney Phonology.* Oslo, 1960.

SPENCER, JOHN. "Language Policies of the Colonial Powers and Their Legacies," in *Current Trends in Linguistics,* ed. Thomas A. Sebeok (The Hague, 1971), Vol. 7, pp. 537–47.

———, ed. *Language in Africa.* London, 1963.

———, ed. *The English Language in West Africa.* London, 1971.

"Symposium: The Use of English in World Literatures," *Harvard Educational Review,* 34(1964):297–319.

TURNER, G. W. *The English Language in Australia and New Zealand.* London, 1966.

WAKELIN, MARTYN F. *English Dialects: An Introduction.* London, 1972.

———, ed. *Patterns of Folk Speech of the British Isles.* London, 1972.

WALL, ARNOLD. *New Zealand English,* 3rd ed. Christchurch, 1959.

WRIGHT, JOSEPH. *English Dialect Dictionary.* 6 vols. Oxford, 1896–1905.

YULE, HENRY, AND A. C. BURNELL. *Hobson-Jobson: A Glossary of Colloquial Anglo-Indian Words and Phrases.* London (1886) 1966.

ZETTERSTEN, ARNE. *The English of Tristan da Cunha.* Lund: Studies in English 37, 1969.

REGIONAL AND SOCIAL VARIETIES OF AMERICAN ENGLISH

ALLEN, HAROLD B., AND GARY N. UNDERWOOD, eds. *Readings in American Dialectology.* New York, 1971.

ATWOOD, E. BAGBY. *A Survey of Verb Forms in the Eastern United States.* Ann Arbor, 1953.

———. *The Regional Vocabulary of Texas.* Austin, 1962.

———. "The Methods of American Dialectology," reprinted in *English Linguistics: An Introductory Reader,* eds. Harold Hungerford, Jay Robinson, and James Sledd (Glenview, Ill., 1970) pp. 176–216, and in *Readings in American Dialectology,* eds. Harold B. Allen and Gary N. Underwood (New York, 1971), pp. 5–35.

BRIGHT, ELIZABETH S. *A Word Geography of California and Nevada*. Berkeley: University of California Publications in Linguistics **69**, 1971.

BRONSTEIN, ARTHUR J. *The Pronunciation of American English*. New York, 1960.

BROOKS, CLEANTH. *The Relation of the Alabama-Georgia Dialect to the Provincial Dialects of Great Britain*. Baton Rouge, La., 1935.

CARR, ELIZABETH BALL. *Da Kine Talk: From Pidgin to Standard English in Hawaii*. Honolulu, 1972.

CASSIDY, FREDERIC G. *Dictionary of American Regional English*. Madison, Wis., to appear.

CRAIGIE, SIR WILLIAM A. AND JAMES R. HULBERT. *Dictionary of American English*. Chicago, 1940.

DAVIS, ALVA L., RAVEN I. MCDAVID, JR., AND VIRGINIA G. MCDAVID. *A Compilation of the Work Sheets of the Linguistic Atlas of the United States and Canada and Associated Projects*. Chicago, 1969.

DAVIS, ALVA L., ed. *American Dialects for English Teachers*. Champaign: Illinois State-Wide Curriculum Study Center, 1969.

———, ed. *Culture, Class, and Language Variety: A Resource Book for Teachers*. Champaign, Ill., 1972.

DAVIS, LAWRENCE M. *A Study of Appalachian Speech in a Northern Urban Setting*. Chicago, 1971. (Available from ERIC, ED 061 205.)

DILLARD, J. L. *Black English: Its History and Usage in the United States*. New York, 1972.

ELIASON, NORMAN L. *Tarheel Talk: An Historical Study of the English Language in North Carolina to 1860*. Chapel Hill, 1956.

ERIC Clearinghouse for Linguistics/Center for Applied Linguistics. *A Preliminary Bibliography of American English Dialects*. Washington, D.C., 1969.

FASOLD, RALPH W. *Tense Marking in Black English: A Linguistic and Social Analysis*. Washington, D.C., 1972.

FICKETT, JOAN G. *Aspects of Morphemics, Syntax, and Semology of an Inner City Dialect (Merican)*. West Rush, N.Y.: Meadowood, 1970.

HANKEY, CLYDE T. *A Colorado Word Geography*. University, Ala.: Publications of the American Dialect Society 34, 1960.

KENYON, JOHN S., AND THOMAS A. KNOTT. *A Pronouncing Dictionary of American English*. Springfield, Mass., 1944.

KERR, ELIZABETH M., AND RALPH M. ADERMAN. *Aspects of American English*. 2nd edition, New York, 1971.

KOCHMAN, THOMAS, ed. *Language and Expressive Role Behavior in the Black Inner City*. New York, to appear.

KRAPP, GEORGE PHILIP. *The English Language in America*. 2 vols. New York (1925) 1960.

KURATH, HANS. *Handbook of the Linguistic Geography of New England*. Providence, R.I., 1939.

———, et al. *Linguistic Atlas of New England*. 3 vols. in 6. Providence, R.I., 1939–43. Reprinted New York, 1972.

———. *A Word Geography of the Eastern United States*. Ann Arbor, 1949.

———, and Raven I. McDavid, Jr. *The Pronunciation of English in the Atlantic States*. Ann Arbor, 1961.

LABOV, WILLIAM. *The Social Stratification of English in New York City*. Washington, D.C., 1966.

———, Paul Cohen, Clarence Robins, and John Lewis. *A Study of the Non-Standard English of Negro and Puerto Rican Speakers in New York City.* 2 vols. New York, 1968. Available from the ERIC Document Reproduction Service, no. ED 028 423/424.

LAIRD, CHARLTON. *Language in America.* New York, 1970.

LOMAN, BENGT. *Conversations in a Negro American Dialect.* Washington, D.C., 1967.

McDAVID, RAVEN I., JR. "The Dialects of American English," in *The Structure of American English* by W. Nelson Francis (New York, 1958), pp. 480–543.

McMILLAN, JAMES B. *Annotated Bibliography of Southern American English.* Coral Gables, Fla., 1971.

MALMSTROM, JEAN, AND ANNABEL ASHLEY. *Dialects U.S.A.* Champaign, Ill., 1963.

MARCKWARDT, ALBERT H. *American English.* New York, 1958.

MATHEWS, MITFORD M. *Dictionary of Americanisms on Historical Principles.* Chicago, 1951.

MENCKEN, H. L. *The American Language* (abridged by Raven I. McDavid, Jr.) New York, 1967.

Nonstandard Dialect. Champaign, Ill., 1967.

PEDERSON, LEE A. *The Pronunciation of English in Metropolitan Chicago.* University, Ala.: Publications of the American Dialect Society 44, 1965.

PUTNAM, G. M., AND EDNA M. O'HERN. *The Status Significance of an Isolated Urban Dialect.* Baltimore: Linguistic Society of America, Language Dissertations 53, 1955.

PYLES, THOMAS. *Words and Ways of American English.* New York, 1952.

REED, CARROLL E. *Dialects of American English.* Cleveland, 1967.

REINECKE, JOHN E. *Language and Dialect in Hawaii.* Honolulu, 1969.

SHORES, DAVID L., ed. *Contemporary English: Change and Variation.* Philadelphia, 1972.

SHUY, ROGER W. *Discovering American Dialects.* Champaign, Ill., 1967.

TSUZAKI, STANLEY M., AND JOHN E. REINECKE. *English in Hawaii: An Annotated Bibliography.* Honolulu: Oceanic Linguistics special publication 1, 1966.

TURNER, LORENZO DOW. *Africanisms in the Gullah Dialect.* Chicago, 1949.

WENTWORTH, HAROLD, AND STUART BERG FLEXNER. *Dictionary of American Slang.* New York, 1960.

WILLIAMSON, JUANITA V., AND VIRGINIA M. BURKE, eds. *A Various Language: Perspectives on American Dialects.* New York, 1971.

WOLFRAM, WALTER A. *A Sociolinguistic Description of Detroit Negro Speech.* Washington, D.C., 1969.

———, AND NONA H. CLARKE, eds. *Black-White Speech Relationships.* Washington, D.C., 1971.

WOOD, GORDON R. *Vocabulary Change: A Study of Variation in Regional Words in Eight of the Southern States.* Carbondale, Ill., 1971.

DIALECTS AND THE TEACHING OF ENGLISH

AARONS, ALFRED C., BARBARA Y. GORDON, AND WILLIAM A. STEWART, eds. *Linguistic-Cultural Differences and American Education.* North Miami Beach, Fla.: The Florida FL Reporter, Vol. 7, No. 1, 1969.

ADAMS, ANTHONY, ed. *The Language of Failure.* Huddersfield, Yorks.: English in Education, Vol. 4, No. 3, 1970.

ALATIS, JAMES E., ed. *Linguistics and the Teaching of Standard English to Speakers of Other Languages or Dialects.* Washington, D.C.: Georgetown University Monograph Series on Language and Linguistics 22, 1969.

BARATZ, JOAN C., AND ROGER W. SHUY, eds. *Teaching Black Children to Read.* Washington, D.C., 1969.

BARNES, DOUGLAS, JAMES BRITTON, AND HAROLD ROSEN. *Language, the Learner, and the School.* London, 1969.

BRANDIS, WALTER, AND DOROTHY HENDERSON, eds. *Social Class, Language, and Education.* London, 1968.

BRITTON, JAMES. *Language and Learning.* London, 1970.

CAZDEN, COURTNEY, VERA JOHN, AND DELL HYMES, eds. *The Functions of Language in the Classroom.* New York, 1972.

CORBIN, RICHARD, AND MURIEL CROSBY, eds. *Language Programs for the Disadvantaged.* Champaign, Ill., 1965.

DAKIN, JULIAN, BRIAN TIFFIN, AND H. G. WIDDOWSON. *Language in Education: The Problem in Commonwealth Africa and the Indo-Pakistan Sub-Continent.* London, 1968.

DAVIS, ALLISON. *Social-Class Influences upon Learning.* Cambridge, Mass., 1965.

FASOLD, RALPH W., AND ROGER W. SHUY, eds. *Teaching Standard English in the Inner City.* Washington, D.C., 1970.

GUNDERSON, DORIS V. *Language and Reading.* Washington, D.C., 1970.

HALLIDAY, M. A. K., ANGUS MCINTOSH, AND PETER STREVENS. *The Linguistic Sciences and Language Teaching.* London, 1964.

HOLBROOK, DAVID. *English for the Rejected.* Cambridge, 1964.

JACOBSON, RODOLFO, ed. *Studies in English to Speakers of Other Languages and Standard English to Speakers of a Non-Standard Dialect.* Oneonta: New York State English Council, monograph 14, 1971.

LABOV, WILLIAM. *The Study of Nonstandard English.* Champaign, Ill., 1970.

LE PAGE, R. B. "Linguistic Problems," in *The Education of West Indian Immigrant Children* (London: National Committee for Commonwealth Immigrants [1968]), pp. 15–18.

LIN, SAN-SU C. *Pattern Practice in the Teaching of English to Students with a Non-Standard Dialect.* New York, 1965.

LOBAN, WALTER. *The Language of Elementary School Children.* Champaign, Ill., 1963.

MARCKWARDT, ALBERT H. *Linguistics and the Teaching of English.* Bloomington, Ind., 1966.

MINKOFF, HARVEY. *Teaching English Linguistically: Five Experimental Curricula.* New Rochelle, N.Y., 1971.

NATIONAL SOCIETY FOR THE STUDY OF EDUCATION. *Linguistics in School Programs.* Chicago, 1970.

REED, CARROLL E., ed. *The Learning of Language.* New York, 1971.

ROSENTHAL, ROBERT, AND LENORE JACOBSON. *Pygmalion in the Classroom: Teacher Expectation and Pupils' Intellectual Development.* New York, 1968.

SHUY, ROGER W., ed. *Social Dialects and Language Learning.* Champaign, Ill., 1965.

STEWART, WILLIAM A., ed. *Non-Standard Speech and the Teaching of English.* Washington, D.C., 1964.

TROIKE, RUDOLPH, AND ROGER ABRAHAMS, eds. *Language, Culture and Education.* Englewood Cliffs, N.J., 1972.

Index

Accent, 17–19, 382
Africa, English in, 2, 57–70, 146
  Ghana, 71
  Nigeria, 53–54, 72, 120–21. *See also*
    Nigerian Pidgin English.
  Sierra Leone, 6
  South Africa, 38, 115–16
  Uganda, 72–76
Africa, French in, 53n., 66–70
Afrikaans, 93–95
ALS. *See* American Language Survey.
America, English in, 151–356
  map of regional dialects, 154
  See also Black English, Gullah, Ha-
    waiian English, Mexican-Ameri-
    can English, Midland Dialect,
    New York English, North Central
    States English, Puerto Rico, South-
    ern States English.
American Dialect Society, 152
American Language Survey, 274
Application ordering of rules, 168–
  70. *See also* Implicational series.
Arabic, 44–45, 47–53, 259
Atlantic Creole, 151–52
Attitude toward one's language, 28–31,
  33, 46, 155, 276–91, 389–90
Attitudes toward the language of others,
  31–37, 154–55, 190–91, 260–61,
  278–81, 293–302, 303–316, 317
Australian Pidgin English, 105–106

Back clipping, 197
Bamboo English, 92
Bazaar Malay, 100
Be, full form of, 269, 350, 429
Bidialectalism, 14–19, 130–31, 363n.9,
  360–83, 436–38

Bilingualism, 11–14, 48–49, 77–89,
  226–35
Black Englsh, 38–39, 178–83, 188–89,
  236–57, 313–14, 319–54, 363–64,
  366–67, 406–407, 425–30, 435–
  36
Borrowing, 154–55, 173, 231–32
Broadcasting, the language of, 75–76,
  293–301
Bundle of isoglosses, 161

Canada, English in, 260
Categorical rule, 157, 341
Child language acquisition, 181–82
Chinese Pidgin English, 96–97, 99,
  102, 106–107, 200n.5, 205
Cleft sentence, 164–65
Code switching, 88–89, 223, 231–32.
  See also bidialectalism, bilingual-
  ism.
Coexistent language systems, 216–17
Complementizer, 342, 350
Computer-assisted instruction, 365n.17
Conditioned rule, 157–59
Contraction, 251 337–38
Copula deletion, 97, 202–204, 251,
  337–38, 406, 435
Creole, 13, 30, 91–114, 172, 181n.24,
  211, 218, 251, 366–67, 429n.26

Deficit theory, 344–49, 418–22
Degradation, 109
Deprivation theory, 39, 320–21, 344–
  51, 357–59, 422–32
Descriptive linguistics, 10, 170
Detroit Dialect Survey, 37–38, 188–89,
  303
Diachronic linguistics, 25

Dialect, definition of, 11, 161
Dialectology, 156, 361
Diglossia, 77
Double nominal, 213

Elaborated code, 329–30, 330n.6, 336–37, 376
Elevation, 109
Ellipsis, 308, 317, 338–39
Embedded question, 341–42, 350
England, English in, 160, 174, 259–60, 268–69
English. *See* Africa, America, Canada, England, India, Ireland, Pakistan, Scotland, Tristan da Cunha, West Indies.
Ethnic identification on the basis of speech, 243, 258–73, 385
Ethnography of communication, 310
Existential sentence, 164–65
External word boundary, 179
Eye dialect, 256, 271

Family Background Test, 243, 301
Feature, 160n.4, 181–82
Field of discourse, 21–22

Generalization, 109
Generative-transformational linguistics, 425
German, 98, 248, 388
Global features of discourse, 399–404, 407–408
Greek, 43–44, 47–53, 183, 259
Gullah, 108, 147, 263, 269

Haitian Creole, 95–98 passim, 100, 103
Hawaiian English, 175, 182n.25, 190–225
Hypercorrection, 178, 181n.24, 311, 363n.9, 385, 388, 445
Hypercreolization, 92

Idiolect, 25–28
ILI. *See* Linguistic insecurity, index of.
Implicational series, 157–70, 173–75, 176–78, 180–84
India, English in, 4, 5, 7, 55, 56–57, 71–72

Indonesian, 100
Institutional linguistics, 9, 10ff.
Internal word boundary, 179
Ireland, English in, 174, 194
Isogloss, 15, 152, 161
Isolect, 162, 170

Jamaican Creole, 107–108, 123–31
Japanese, 92, 205

Krio, 60, 92

Lames, 239
Language community, 11, 157, 175–78, 385
Latin, 41–43, 47–53
Lect, 161n.5, 162
Lectology, 157
Leveling, 162, 407
Lexicon, 173, 309
Liberia, 61–62
Lingua franca, 13–14, 44, 45, 55, 93, 194, 218
Linguistic Atlas of the United States and Canada, 236, 258, 266n.2, 271, 289, 425
Linguistic insecurity, index of, 287n.8, 389–90
Linguistic self-hatred, 281

Malapropism, 100, 267, 315, 405
Malay, 98, 100
Marked ordering of rules, 164, 170, 181n.23, 182–83
Melanesian Pidgin English, 95–99 passim, 101–102, 104–105
Mexican-American English, 226–35, 375
Middle English, 181n.24, 428n.23
Midland dialect, 170n.12, 172, 406
Mode of discourse, 22–23, 263, 267
Multilingualism. *See* Bilingualism.

Negations, 212–13, 313, 426–29
negative concord, 328, 331, 339–41, 351
negative inversion, 331

negative perfect, 328
negative preterit, 328
Neo-Melanesian. *See* Melanesian Pidgin English.
Neutralization, 162
New York English, 176n.20, 178, 180, 274–92, 392
Nigerian Pidgin English, 109–112
NNE. Negro Nonstandard English. *See* Black English.
North Central States English, 387

Obstruent, 183
Old English, 340
Operation Head Start, 320n.1, 345–46, 349, 423n.15

Pachuco, 226, 235
Pakistan, English in, 120
Papiamento, 87n.18, 93, 98, 99, 218
Paralinguistic features, 26
Phatic communion, 22
Pidgin, 13, 30, 78, 91–114, 181n.24, 192n.2, 429n.26
Pidgin English. *See* Australian Pidgin English, Chinese Pidgin English, Gullah, Jamaican Creole, Melanesian Pidgin English, Solomon Islands Pidgin English, Taki-Taki.
Portuguese, 53, 78n.3, 91, 93, 192–93, 213, 218
Puerto Rico, English in, 77–88

Reading, teaching of, 236–57, 367–69, 433–36
Reduplication, 123
Register, 11, 19–25
Relexification, 91
Restricted code, 26, 330n.6, 366, 376
Russian, 248, 388

Sabir, 218. *See also* Lingua franca.
Scotland, English in, 113–14, 171n.13, 194, 259

Sex, language differentiation by, 24, 37–38, 278–82, 286, 304, 390
Sierra Leone, 6, 59–62
Social dialects, 31–37, 175–78, 274–92, 384–94
Solomon Islands Pidgin English, 105–106
Somnigraphy, 369–71
Southern States English, 112–13, 163, 170, 171, 172n.14, 174–75, 183, 236–57, 288–89, 342, 407
Spanish, 77–89, 210, 226–35
Specialization, 109
Spelling pronunciation, 264, 265, 391
Sranan. *See* Taki-Taki.
Standard English, definition of, 16–19, 259–60, 302, 358, 378, 417–18
Style of discourse, 23–24, 170–71, 176–78, 263
Subjective reaction test, 275n.2, 333
Sulcality, 174n.18
Survey of English Usage, 28
Swahili, 74–75
Synchronic linguistics, 25

Taki-Taki, 95–96, 98–99, 100, 103, 107
Tristan da Cunha, English in, 272–73
Turkish, 45–53

Unconditioned rule, 157–59
Unmarked ordering of rules, 164, 170, 174n.17, 181n.23, 182–83

Variable rules, 157, 178–84

Washington Dialect Study, 306–316
Weighing of rules, 178–84
West Indies, English in, 115–49, 171. *See also* Jamaican Creole, Papiamento, Taki-Taki.
Whorfian hypothesis, 259
Writing, teaching of, 384–408, 413–14, 432, 441–48